D1547428

Aristotle and Other Platonists

ALSO BY LLOYD P. GERSON

Neoplatonic Philosophy: Introductory Readings (2004; with
John Dillon)

Knowing Persons: A Study in Plato (2003)

Aristotle: Critical Assessments (1999)

Cambridge Companion to Plotinus (1996)

Plotinus (1994)

*God and Greek Philosophy: Studies in the Early History of
Natural Theology* (1990)

Hellenistic Philosophy: Introductory Readings (1998; with
Brad Inwood)

Aristotle's Politics (1986; with Hippocrates G. Apostle)

Aristotle: Selected Works (1983; with Hippocrates G.
Apostle)

Aristotle and Other Platonists

LLOYD P. GERSON

CORNELL UNIVERSITY PRESS

Ithaca and London

Copyright © 2005 by Cornell University

All rights reserved. Except for brief quotations in a review,
this book, or parts thereof, must not be reproduced
in any form without permission in writing from the
publisher. For information, address Cornell University
Press, Sage House, 512 East State Street, Ithaca, New York
14850.

First published 2005 by Cornell University Press
First printing, Cornell Paperbacks, 2006

Library of Congress Cataloging-in-Publication Data
Gerson, Lloyd P.
  Aristotle and other Platonists / Lloyd P. Gerson
    p. cm.
  Includes bibliographical references (p.   ) and index.
  ISBN-13: 978-0-8014-4164-6 (cloth : alk. paper)
  ISBN-10: 0-8014-4164-1 (cloth : alk. paper)
  ISBN-13: 978-0-8014-7337-1 (pbk. alk. paper)
  ISBN-10: 0-8014-7337-3 (pbk. alk. paper)
1. Aristotle.   2. Platonists.   I. Title.
  B485.G36 2005
    185—dc22 2004013045

Cornell University Press strives to use environmentally
responsible suppliers and materials to the fullest extent
possible in the publishing of its books. Such materials
include vegetable-based, low-VOC inks and acid-free papers
that are recycled, totally chlorine-free, or partly
composed of nonwood fibers. For further information, visit
our website at www.cornellpress.cornell.edu.

Cloth printing   10 9 8 7 6 5 4 3 2 1
Paperback printing   10 9 8 7 6 5 4 3 2 1

To my beloved

Contents

Acknowledgments

I have been unusually fortunate in the unstinting assistance I have been given by friends and colleagues. Earlier versions of the book were read by Ian Bell, S. R. L. Clark, John Dillon, Richard Dufour, Asli Gocer, Charles Kahn, Debra Nails, Sara Rappe, John Rist, C. D. C. Reeve, and Harold Tarrant. I am deeply grateful to all of these scholars for sharing with me their learning and for their critical engagement with my ideas. An early version of the main themes in this book was presented at a conference on Plato's ancient readers at the University of Newcastle, NSW, in the summer of 2002. I benefited immensely from the very good-humored and pointed dialogue that my paper inspired. I am especially grateful to Dirk Baltzly, John Cleary, and Richard Sorabji for their helpful suggestions. Another version was presented at a colloquium at Trinity College, Dublin, where a learned and cordial audience provided me with much food for thought. Holger Thesleff offered me his warm encouragement and, from his own library, material that was not otherwise available to me. An earlier version of a portion of chapter 2 appeared in *Journal of the History of Philosophy;* material contained in chapter 4 appeared in an article in *Archiv für Geschichte der Philosophie;* parts of chapter 5 appeared in an article in *Phronesis;* and parts of chapter 8 in an article in *Oxford Studies in Philosophy.* I am grateful to the editors of these publications for their permission to reprint. The Social Sciences and Humanities Research Council of Canada endowed me with a research grant during the period 2002–4, which gave me much needed time, among other things, to complete my research.

L. P. G.

Toronto, Ontario

Aristotle and Other Platonists

Introduction

Aristotle versus Plato. For a long time that is the angle from which the tale has been told, in textbooks on the history of philosophy and to university students. Aristotle's philosophy, so the story goes, was *au fond* in opposition to Plato's.[1] But it was not always thus. The indispensable historian of philosophy Diogenes Laertius tells us, for example, that Aristotle was Plato's "most authentic disciple."[2] Beginning perhaps in the 1st century B.C.E., we observe philosophers already claiming the ultimate harmony of Academic and Peripatetic thought. Antiochus of Ascalon is frequently recognized as a principal figure in this regard.[3] A similar view is recorded by Cicero, a

1. See Zeller (1923, 475–480), whose influence in this matter as in so much else in the study of ancient philosophy is still felt today. Jaeger's role in establishing the paradigm of opposition is discussed below. See also Frank (1940, 166–185), who expresses another version of the working assumption of much Aristotelian scholarship in this century. The eminent historian of philosophy Etienne Gilson, writing about Aquinas's decision to construct his own philosophy on an Aristotelian rather than a Platonic foundation, claims in relation to the latter two that "reduced to their bare essences, these metaphysics are rigorously antinomical; one cannot be for the one without being against all those who are with the other, and that is why Saint Thomas remains with Aristotle against all those who are counted on the side of Plato." See Gilson 1926/27, 127 (I owe this reference to Francis O'Rourke). By contrast, Boas (1943, 172–193), atypically, identifies Aristotle's 'protophilosophy' as being thoroughly Platonic. See also Merlan (1953, 3–4), who argues for the Neoplatonic character of Aristotle's interpretation of Plato as well as the Neoplatonic character of "some fundamental doctrines of Aristotle."

2. See D.L. V 1, 6: γνησιώτατος τῶν Πλάτωνος μαθητῶν.

3. For Antiochus of Ascalon, see Glucker 1978; Dillon 1996b, chap. 2, and Barnes 1989, (esp. 78–81), who tries to give a sympathetic interpretation of Antiochus' 'syncretism.' As Dillon (57–58), notes, Antiochus's view of the matter undoubtedly rested in part on the availability of a great deal more of the writings of the Old Academy than is available to us. Cicero *De Fin.* V 3, 7, says, "As you have heard Antiochus say, in the Old Academy are included not only those who are called Academics . . . but even the old Peripatetics, of whom Aristotle is the first and best." See next note.

disciple of Antiochus.[4] Later, in the 2nd century C.E., we find the Platonist Alcinous in his influential *Handbook of Platonism* simply incorporating what we might call Aristotelian elements into his account of what he took to be authentic Platonism.[5] Finally, and most important, for a period of about three hundred years, roughly from the middle of the 3rd century C.E. to the middle of the 6th, Aristotelianism and Platonism were widely studied and written about on the assumption that they were harmonious philosophical systems.[6] The philosophers of this period who held this view are today usually given the faintly pejorative label 'Neoplatonists.' The label, originating in early nineteenth-century Germanic scholarship, has a dubious value as a category of historical reality. For the so-called Neoplatonists regarded themselves simply as Platonists; that is, as interpreters and followers of Plato.[7] They would have probably been more comfortable with the label 'Paleoplatonists' than with the label 'Neoplatonists.' In addition, the presumptive designation of later followers of Plato as 'neo' subtly suggests that Aristotle must have been a 'non' Platonist. This book aims to give an account of how the perception of harmony arose among these Platonists, how it was articulated and defended, and to what extent it is justified.[8] I use the accepted

4. See Cicero *Acad.* I 4, 17, who has Varro, a pupil of Antiochus, say: "But on the authority of Plato, a thinker with a variety of complex and fecund thoughts, a type of philosophy was initiated that was united and harmonious and known under two names, the Academics and the Peripatetics, and they agreed substantially while differing in their names." Also, *Acad.* II 5, 15. Antiochus was apparently reacting to the view of Philo of Larissa (158–84 B.C.E.), who claimed the harmony of the Old Academy and the so-called New Academy, which embraced a form of skepticism from the time of Arcesilaus onward.

5. See Dillon 1993, especially introd. and commentary. The fact that the Platonist Atticus (fl. 175 C.E.) wrote a treatise titled *Against Those Who Claim to Interpret the Doctrine of Plato through That of Aristotle* supports the conclusion that the harmony between Plato and Aristotle was at least a current view. Perhaps as Dillon (1996b, 247–250) suggests, Atticus was writing against the Peripatetic Aristocles, teacher of Alexander of Aphrodisias, who had argued that the philosophy of Aristotle "perfected" that of Plato. Chiesara (2001, xxi–xxiii), takes a somewhat more cautious view, claiming that Aristocles' praise of Plato did not necessarily indicate that he viewed the philosophies of Aristotle and Plato as being in harmony. Atticus held that Aristotle differed from Plato on three fundamental issues: (1) he denied that virtue was sufficient for happiness (see Baudry 1931, frag. 2); (2) he denied the providence of the divine (frags. 3, 8); (3) he denied the temporal creation of the world (frag. 4). On all three points, Atticus was assuming mainstream Middle Platonic interpretations of Plato, especially of *Timaeus*.

6. The Greek term translated here as 'harmony' and usually used by Neoplatonists to indicate agreement between Plato and Aristotle is συμφωνία. Plato *Symp.* 187B4, uses συμφωνία synonymously with ἁρμονία. The latter term tends to be reserved among the Neoplatonists for a more technical use in scientific theory. See Lloyd 1967, 275, for a sketch of the elements of harmony as seen by Neoplatonists.

7. See, e.g., Proclus *PT* I 1, who lauds Plotinus, Iamblichus, Theodore of Asine, and others as "exegetes of the Platonic revelation" (τοὺς τῆς Πλατωνικῆς ἐποπτείας ἐξηγητὰς). Two points need to be noted here. The first is Proclus's implicit assumption of the distinction between the doctrine that Plato revealed and Plato's writings and words narrowly construed, and the second is the claim that although Plotinus initiated a recovery of this doctrine (long misunderstood by inferior exegetes), he himself was no innovator.

8. See Frede 1987, intro., and particularly his remarks about doing "philosophical justice to ancient philosophy" (xiii). I believe that doing philosophical justice to both Aristotle and Plato is facilitated by a serious consideration of the harmonists' position. See also Sedley 2002,

label 'Neoplatonists' with the hope that the reader will keep in mind that 'neo' is the last thing that these Platonists wished to be.

The case for harmony is partly cumulative. The more one sees harmony in a particular area, the more one is inclined to consider it in another, perhaps hitherto unsuspected. And naturally, the more one views Aristotle's philosophy as a system, the more is one inclined to view partial harmony as suggesting, if not entailing, complete harmony. Still, from the Neoplatonists' point of view, resistance to an account of Aristotle's philosophy as a system is not all that troubling. Platonism itself provided all the systematic structure necessary.

Many scholars have noticed and argued for a Platonic influence in one or another of the texts of Aristotle. Not infrequently these interpretations are rejected for no other reason than that they "make Aristotle too much of a Platonist." But when a large number of such texts are put alongside each other, such protestations begin to seem hollow. At *some* point one might well begin to wonder whether perhaps the reason Aristotle appears to be a Platonist is that in fact he is one.

The case for harmony is also partly inferential. That is, most of the Neoplatonic material—both the commentaries and the personal writings—assumes harmony rather than presenting a brief on its behalf. Since the plausibility of the assumption is in large part what this book is about, my task is often to try to show how it helps us to illuminate some otherwise very puzzling texts. Most revealingly, we shall see time and again that a text seemingly resistant to any reasonable conclusion regarding its meaning has been rendered so by an antiharmonist assumption. When scholars repeatedly say, "This is what the text appears to mean, though it simply can't mean *that* because that would be *Platonic*," it is perhaps salutary to reexamine the assumption that leads to this cul-de-sac.

'Harmony,' when used of two philosophical positions, can of course mean many things. Most innocuously, it can mean 'not in contradiction' or, simply, 'consistency.'[9] There are countless philosophical positions that are harmonious in this sense simply because they are logically unconnected. Usually there is little point even in mentioning that A's position does not, in fact, contradict B's. Those who held Aristotelianism to be in harmony with Platonism did not mean merely that their views were not in contradiction with each other. Another relatively weak though significant sense of 'harmony' underlies the principle 'the enemy of my enemy is my friend.' With the rise of competing philosophical schools in antiquity, a member of one school might be viewed as an ally of members of another

esp. 37–39, for some additional remarks on benefiting from the interpretive stance of the Neoplatonic commentators.

9. See, e.g., Syrianus *In Met.*141, 2 for the use of συμφωνία in the sense of the 'self-consistent' doctrines of a single philosopher: namely, Aristotle.

school owing to their joint antagonisms.[10] The idea of the harmony between Platonism and Aristotelianism that drove the philosophy of our period was different from these. It was also typically not explicitly thematized. In many cases we have to infer the meaning a Neoplatonic author gives to 'harmony' from the specific claims made about putatively harmonious doctrines. Though necessarily somewhat vague, the concept of harmony contains a rich description of a nexus of relations, which emerges in the following discussion.

There are, however, some relatively clear boundaries within which all our authors were working. First, the idea of harmony rested on a perception of a sort of division of labor. Roughly, it was held that Plato was authoritative for the intelligible world and Aristotle was authoritative for the sensible world: "In every case he did not want to depart from nature but to consider the things above nature according to their relation to nature, just as the divine Plato, for his part, and in the manner of the Pythagoreans, examined even natural things according as they partake of those things above nature."[11] But this division of labor rested upon and flowed from jointly held philosophical principles. What this meant was that Aristotelian philosophical claims could be subsumed under the more capacious and ultimately true Platonic system in a way roughly analogous to the way that Newtonian mechanics can be subsumed under quantum mechanics or sentential logic can be subsumed under the predicate calculus.[12]

A slightly different way of understanding harmony would see Aristotelianism as a type or version of Platonism. I shall have much more to say about Platonism in the next chapter. Here it will perhaps suffice to indicate that many self-declared followers of Plato held philosophical positions that

10. See Sedley 1996, 97–119. Sextus Empiricus *PH* I 90, 98, points to the fact of the *disharmony* (διαφωνία) among dogmatists as the basis for one crucial skeptical argument: how can dogmatists be trusted when they disagree; which one should we trust? We should not discount as a motive among some harmonists a wish to enhance the appearance of the cogency—indeed, the inevitability—of Platonism in the face of alien attacks on it.

11. Simplicius *In Cat.* 6, 27–30. See also *In Phys.* 8, 9–15. One thinks of the great painting by Raphael, *The School of Athens*, painted in 1510, with the image of Plato and Aristotle strolling through the Academy together—Plato, holding his *Timaeus*, with finger raised upward to the heavens, and Aristotle, holding his *Ethics*, with palm facing downward to the earth. Countless generations of students have heard the misinterpretation of this painting to the effect that Raphael is contrasting the 'otherworldly' Plato with the 'down-to-earth' Aristotle. In fact, this is very likely not what Raphael had in mind. Having learned his ancient philosophy from, among others, the harmonist Pico della Mirandola (1463–1494), Raphael was probably indirectly representing the "division of labor" postulated by Simplicius. See Hall 1997, 35–37. It is worth adding that Raphael and his audience must have known that Aristotle's *Nicomachean Ethics* ends with an exhortation to 'divinization' corresponding exactly to what Plato says at the end of *Timaeus*.

12. Here, for the sake of the analogy, we should focus especially on the empirical adequacy of Newtonian mechanics within a circumscribed domain. Quantum mechanics provides a deeper and more comprehensive explanation. I thank Dirk Baltzly for his insight into this analogy.

actually contradicted each other.[13] Yet at the same time they recognized their shared commitment to the principles that expressed the essence of Platonism.[14] As we shall see, even Plato's own philosophical positions taken together could be viewed as constituting one type of Platonism, where 'Platonism' is a term practically identical with 'true philosophy.'[15] If Aristotelianism is indeed a version of Platonism, it may well be granted that it is a version propounded by a 'dissident' Platonist. Although conceding the dissidence, this book aims to concentrate on the Platonist that Aristotle was, nevertheless, held to be.

We need to make the idea of harmony a bit more precise, since not all of Aristotle's doctrines (on Neoplatonic interpretations) are harmonized with those of Plato (again, on their interpretations) in the same way. There are (1) doctrines of Aristotle that are basically identical with those of Plato; (2) doctrines of Aristotle that are superficially different owing principally to language, though they rest on principles that are identical with those held by Plato; (3) doctrines of Aristotle that are different from those of Plato because they rest on an imperfect or incomplete grasp by Aristotle of the correct Platonic principles. Examples of (1) are the superiority of the contemplative or theoretical life to any other, the immortality of intellect, and the unicity of the first principle of all; of (2), the nature of matter, the role of divine providence, the relative primacy of sensible substance, the immortality of the person, and the rejection of separate Forms;[16] of (3), the identification of the first principle of all with thinking, the completeness of the fourfold schema of causal analysis, and the identification of the first principle of all exclusively as a final cause. Depending on the context, to hold that Aristotle's philosophy is in harmony with Plato's can mean any one of those examples, though it may be doubted whether any Neoplatonic author is always so clear about the precise sense of harmony being employed.

---

13. E.g., Neoplatonists differed concerning the relationship between intellect and intelligibles, specifically how to interpret the relationship in Plato's *Timaeus* between the Demiurge and the Forms. See Syrianus *In Met.* 109, 33–110, 7, and Proclus *In Tim.* I 306, 31–307, 4; 322, 20–26; 323, 1–22, etc. See Hadot 1990, 177–182, on divergences among the Neoplatonists in their understanding of the elements of harmonization.

14. One may compare in this regard Roman Catholicism and Protestantism as types of Christianity. Despite their opposition on various points, one can reasonably insist on their underlying harmony owing to their shared principles. On this analogy, for Neoplatonists, Platonism is Christianity, Plato's philosophy is Roman Catholicism, and Aristotelianism is a type of Protestantism.

15. See O'Meara 1989, 210–211, on Iamblichus's unique and influential role in the Neoplatonic interpretation of Plato. Iamblichus was particularly concerned to harmonize Plato with Pythagoras, something that is not found at all in Plotinus, Porphyry, or to a great extent in Proclus. Iamblichus is also reported by Proclus as criticizing Porphyry for saying things that are "neither Platonic nor true" (οὔτε Πλατωνικῶς οὔτε ἀληθῶς) and for "introducing alien elements into Platonism" (ἀλλοτρίως τοῦ Πλάτωνος εἰσαγομένας). The implication of the former remark is that 'Platonic' and 'true' are least logically distinct. See Proclus *In Tim.* I 307, 4; I 152, 29; III 65, 9 (I owe these references to John Dillon).

16. See Simplicius *In Cael.* 69, 11–15; 640, 27–28; 679, 27–31.

Simplicius, one of the most prolific of the ancient commentators and perhaps our most valuable source for the entire commentary tradition, provides in his massive work on *Categories* the fundamental rationale for harmonization. Writing in his introduction about Aristotle's style of writing, he says:

> The form of Aristotelian expression both in his thought and in his writing is dense, intellectual, and vigorous. For he either straightaway brings in the solution to a problem or, collecting many problems together, he provides one concise solution that applies to all, never wishing to separate himself from the evidence. Since the evidence that leads to conviction is twofold, one kind coming from intellect and one coming from sense-perception, and since he is conversing with those who are dependent on sense-perception, he prefers the kind of evidence that is sensible. That is why his demonstrations have the force of necessity, so that even one who is not convinced owing to some unfortunate prejudice is nevertheless forced to be silent. In every case he does not wish to cut himself off from nature and so he even speculates on the things above nature according to its relation [σχέσιν] to nature, just as, conversely, the divine Plato, according to the Pythagorean practice, examines natural things according as they participate in those things above nature. Indeed, Aristotle had no recourse to myths or symbolic puzzles as did some of his predecessors, but preferred obscurity to any other masking device.[17]

After some further discussion of the reasons for the obscurity and some advice about the requirements for being a good commentator, Simplicius adds: "In my opinion it is necessary that in regard to the things that Aristotle says against Plato the commentator must not arrive at the judgment that there is disharmony between the two philosophers looking only to the words [λέξιν], but rather he must look into the meaning [νοῦν] in order to follow the trail of their harmony in most matters."[18] These texts, normative for most of the commentators from Porphyry to the end of the Neoplatonic commentary tradition, reveal several basic points about harmonization.

First, all exegesis has to be comprehensive, a point evidently at odds with the notion of a development of the thought of both Plato and Aristotle. The Neoplatonists started with the assumption that there was such a thing as Platonism more or less amenable to systemizing. Aristotle's relation to this philosophy was neither indisputable nor unambiguous. Nevertheless, on the

---

17. Simplicius *In Cat.* 6, 19–32.
18. Ibid., 7, 31–33. Elias (or David) *In Cat.* 123, 7–12, says that the exegete must not only show that Aristotle is in harmony with Plato, but that both Aristotle and Plato are in harmony with themselves: that is, they are self-consistent. Here is an implicit rejection of developmentalism in the thought of both Plato and Aristotle. The attribution of this commentary to Elias has been questioned. For my purposes, the authorship is unimportant. Olympiodorus in his *In Gorg.* 41 9, 1–4, says in passing, "Concerning Aristotle we must point out that in the first place he does not disagree at all with Plato, except in appearance. In the second place, even if he does disagree, it is on the basis of his having benefited [ὠφεληθείς] from Plato." The Neoplatonist Olympiodorus in his *In Cat.* 112, 19–113, 15, actually argues that Aristotle is right and Plato wrong in his definition of relatives (I owe this reference to Richard Sorabji).

basis of the textual evidence of the Aristotelian material extant and available to them, they held that Aristotle was in some nontrivial sense an adherent of Platonism or of its fundamental principles.

Second, Simplicius gives us one important reason for the appearance of disharmony: namely, that the starting points of Plato and Aristotle are different. Aristotle starts from nature—that is, the sensible world—and rises to speculation about the intelligible world on the basis of his account of nature. By contrast, Plato starts from what we might term a priori considerations about the intelligible world and then treats of the natural world on the basis of these. This interpretation of the approaches of Aristotle and Plato is well grounded in the texts of both authors even if it does not even begin to represent the totality of their methodologies.[19] Simplicius plainly acknowledges apparent disagreement between Plato and Aristotle, but he thinks it is only apparent—in most matters.[20] The question we need to try to face squarely is how much of this supposed harmony is fact and how much fancy.

At this point an entirely reasonable response would be; "If *that* is what Neoplatonists meant by the 'harmony' of Plato and Aristotle, then so much the worse for them!" One might be at a loss to understand how anyone reading objectively the corpus of Aristotelian texts could suppose that Aristotle did not see himself as profoundly opposed to Plato.[21] Part of my task is to show that such a perception is less well founded than one might suppose. Still, a book that aimed to do nothing more than show that a group of largely forgotten scholars and eccentric philosophers were not quite as naive as is sometimes thought would in my view be of little interest. Rather, I want to show that reading Aristotle as a Platonist, or understanding Aristotelianism as a type of Platonism, far from being an exercise in historical perversity, does actually yield significant results both exegetical and philosophical. In regard to the many problematic claims made by Aristotle, various interpretations are

19. See *Phys.* A 1, 184a16–18. Cf. *ENA* 2, 1095b3. Plato's *Timaeus* provides the most important example of his treatment of nature on the basis of principles articulated for the intelligible world. It begins with an argument for the existence of a demiurgic god and then proceeds to deduce the manner and scope of its creative activity ending in the creation of the sensible world.

20. See his *In Phys.* 1249, 12–13, where Simplicius contrasts the apparent verbal difference (in ὄνομα) between Plato and Aristotle from a putative real difference (in πρᾶγμα). The reason for the verbal difference is the different starting-points of the two philosophers.

21. See, e.g., Richard Sorabji's general introduction to the series of groundbreaking translations of the Greek Aristotle commentaries, (Wildberg 1987, 7), where he refers to the idea of harmony as a "perfectly crazy proposition," though he allows that it "proved philosophically fruitful." One might well wonder why, if harmony is a crazy idea, the attempt to show it should be other than philosophically fruitless. Sorabji in a recent as yet unpublished paper suggests as an example of the fruitful outcome of the harmonization principle the efforts by Neoplatonists to understand the Aristotelian account of sensible reality as it relates to the Platonic account of unchanging, eternal reality. See also Szlezák (1994, 215–232), who begins by asserting the huge gulf that exists between Aristotle and Plato and then goes on to show the harmony of the two "nell ambito dei motive di fondo e dei metodi" as opposed to a harmony of "dottrine" (218). This harmony includes "la concezione di filosofia" (232). One might legitimately wonder, however, if there can be a harmony in the conception of philosophy without a doctrinal harmony of some sort.

possible. I would like this book to undermine the widely held belief that any interpretation that "turns Aristotle into a Platonist" must be *ipso facto* ruled out of court.

The view that the philosophy of Aristotle was in *harmony* with the philosophy of Plato must be sharply distinguished from the view, held by no one in antiquity, that the philosophy of Aristotle was *identical* with the philosophy of Plato. For example, in Plato's dialogue *Parmenides,* Socrates suggests that Zeno's book states the "same position" as Parmenides', differing only in that it focuses on an attack on Parmenides' opponents. Zeno acknowledges this identity.[22] The harmony of Aristotle and Plato was not supposed to be like the identity of the philosophy of Zeno and Parmenides. Again, Eusebius famously tells us that Numenius asked rhetorically, "What is Plato but Moses speaking Attic Greek."[23] No Neoplatonist supposed that Aristotle was just Plato speaking a Peripatetic 'dialect.'[24]

Nor should we take harmony to indicate some sort of eclecticism or syncretism.[25] Even if these terms have some useful application to various dimly known philosophers in the period between Plato and Plotinus, they are quite useless in understanding the engagement of Neoplatonists with Aristotle. For one thing, the Neoplatonists did not believe that they were constructing some new philosophy from a supposedly neutral standpoint outside of any commitment to one philosophical school or another. For another, their universally held view that the Platonism to which they adhered was a *comprehensive* system of philosophy precluded the typical motivation of eclectic or syncretic schools. They had no inkling that the terms 'bigger,' 'better,' and 'newer' could be used honorifically in the construction of a philosophical system.

Finally, the harmony of the philosophies of Plato and Aristotle should not be thought necessarily to include the practical religious aspect of Platonism. One of the significant ways in which Neoplatonism distinguished itself from other forms of Platonism was in its religious practices, especially theurgy and prayer.[26] Iamblichus is a central figure in this regard. The idea that Aristotle's philosophy could be subsumed under Platonism left questions of religious

---

22. Plato *Parm.* 128A–E.

23. See Des Places 1973, frag. 8 who suggests, however, that Numenius's comparison was probably limited in its doctrinal ambit. Indeed, without a context it is difficult to judge its level of generality.

24. See, e.g., Ammonius *In Cat.* 3, 9–16, and the anonymous *Prolegomena to Platonic Philosophy* possibly attributable to Olympiodorus, 5, 18–30, which explains that 'Peripatetic' is a term that comes from *Plato's* habit of walking around while philosophizing. Accordingly, Aristotle (and Xenocrates), as followers of Plato, were called 'Peripatetics,' though the former taught in the Lyceum, the latter in the Academy.

25. See Donini 1988a, 15–33, esp. 27–28, for some properly critical remarks on the use of the terms 'eclectic' and 'syncretic' among historians of ancient philosophy in the 19th and 20th centuries.

26. See, e.g., Proclus *In Tim.* I 210, 27ff. Simplicius *In Cael.* 731, 25–29. See Dörrie 1976a, 514, "in der Tat war der Platonismus [i.e., Neoplatonism] im Innersten religiös fundiert." See generally on the Neoplatonic commentaries themselves as a form of prayer Erler 1987, 179–217; Van den Berg 2001, esp. 22–30, on philosophy and prayer in Proclus; Shaw 1995; Nasemann 1991 on theurgy in Iamblichus.

practice untouched. This is entirely understandable since Aristotle and Peripatetics generally had almost nothing to say about religion. Thus it should occasion no surprise that a Neoplatonist could regard Aristotle's philosophy as being in harmony with Plato's at the same time as he practiced and defended a religious life sharply different from what we could imagine that an Aristotelian might practice.[27] For example, Proclus's deeply religious way of life did not prevent him from defending harmony where he found it.

The first concrete indication we possess that Neoplatonists were prepared to argue for the harmony of Aristotle and Plato is contained in a reference in Photius's *Bibliography* to the Neoplatonist Hierocles' statement that Ammonius of Alexandria, the teacher of Plotinus, attempted to resolve the conflict between the disciples of Plato and Aristotle, showing that their understanding (γνώμην) was in fact in harmony (σύμφωνον) regarding the important and most necessary doctrines.[28] The second indication of an effort to display harmony is found in the *Suda*, where it is stated that Porphyry, Plotinus's disciple, produced a work in six books titled *On Plato and Aristotle Being Adherents of the Same School* (Περὶ τοῦ μίαν εἶναι τὴν Πλάτωνος καὶ 'Αριστοτέλους αἵρεσιν).[29] We know nothing of this work apart from the title and what we can infer from what Porphyry actually says in the extant works. It seems reasonably clear, however, that a work of such length was attempting to provide a substantial argument, one that was evidently opposed to at least some prevailing views.[30] It is also perhaps the case that

27. Hadot 1996, introd., 57–58, where she points out that Simplicius held that Aristotle's obscure style is intended to reserve his 'revelations' for the philosophical adept. But this is not, I take it, equivalent to attributing to Aristotle himself Neoplatonic religious practices. I think that this is the case even for Iamblichus, who was especially eager to emphasize the continuity of Platonism with the religion of the ancient sages of Egypt and Persia, as well as those of Greece.

28. See Photius *Bibliothoca* 214. 2, 172a2–9; Porphyry *De. Reg. An.* (frag. 302F, 6 Smith). At 214. 8, 173a18–40, Hierocles makes the bolder claim that all those from Aristotle up to Ammonius "who had a reputation for wisdom" were in agreement with Plato, and all those "born of the sacred race" from Ammonius up to Plutarch of Athens were in agreement with the "purified version of Plato's philosophy" (διακεκαθαρμένη φιλοσοφία). The qualifications are obviously intended to exclude genuine non-Platonists such as Stoics and Epicureans. More importantly, Hierocles here recognizes the need to grasp Platonism "purified." This purification must include the elimination of false interpretations, a claim that rests upon the momentous assumption that Plato must be interpreted. See Düring 1957, 332–336, for a useful compilation of the texts from the Neoplatonists relating to harmony. St. Augustine *Con. Acad.* III 19, 42, echoes Cicero's remarks on the harmony of Plato and Aristotle, noting that appreciating the harmony beneath the apparent disagreement requires discernment. See also Boethius *In de Int.* 80, 1–6, who seems to be following the Neoplatonic line.

29. See *Suda* Π 2098, 8–9 (= frag. 239T Smith). Cf. Elias *In Porph. Isag.* 39, 6–8. See Smith 1987, 754 n. 218, on the likelihood that the title of the book indicates that Porphyry argued for the harmony of Plato and Aristotle. On the meaning of the term αἵρεσις in this period, see Glucker 1978, 166–193. After discussing a large amount of evidence Glucker concludes that αἵρεσις is never used of a 'school' in an institutional or organizational sense but always of a way of thinking or set of beliefs.

30. See Schibli (2002, 27–31, with nn. 98 and 100), who mentions the prevailing view that Hierocles got from Porphyry his idea that Ammonius taught the harmony of Plato and Aristotle; see n. 96 for references and Dodds's (1960) dissent from this view. Whatever the case, Schibli

Porphyry is questioning the basis for the traditional division of the 'schools' of ancient philosophy, as found, for example, in Diogenes Laertius.[31]

That Aristotle was at least to a certain extent an independent thinker and so not simply categorized by a 'school' is hardly in doubt. But just as Plotinus's claim to be eschewing novelty may be met with some legitimate skepticism, so Aristotle's claim to be radically innovative may be met with the same skepticism. The question of whether Aristotelianism is or is not in harmony with Platonism is certainly not going to be answered decisively by anything Aristotle says suggesting that it is not. We should acknowledge that the Neoplatonists looked back at their great predecessors with some critical distance, as do we. What may have appeared to Aristotle as a great chasm between himself and his teacher may have reasonably appeared much narrower to those looking at both philosophers with the benefit of critical distance some six hundred to nine hundred years later.

The principal feature of harmony was identity of principles, as indicated above. But it was universally held by Neoplatonists that Plato had a more profound and accurate grasp of these than did Aristotle. Thus, in countless matters relating to physical nature, for example, Aristotle's preeminence was readily acknowledged. But Aristotle did not, according to the Neoplatonists, possess the correct comprehensive view of all reality.[32] In particular, most believed that he misconceived the first principle of all reality. But in part

---

goes on to suggest that Porphyry's attribution of a teaching of harmony to Ammonius is dubious. But Schibli's principal reason for saying this is that Plotinus, Ammonius's greatest pupil, must not have been a harmonist because he criticized Aristotle. Two points can be made here. First, the *Enneads* of Plotinus amply confirm Porphyry's claim (*V. Plot.* chap. 14) for the profound effect Aristotle's thinking had on Plotinus. Second, as I argue at greater length throughout this book, Plotinus's (sometimes severe) disagreements with Aristotle on various issues did not preclude his assuming a harmony between the two on a deeper level any more than, say, Porphyry's disagreements with Plotinus precluded the former's recognition of *their* harmony with each other and with Plato.

31. See D.L. I 19–20, where ten philosophical schools are listed. Diogenes also here refers to another historian, Hippobotus, who gives a similar list. See *Suda*, s.v. αἵρεσις, as well. It is possible that the division between the Peripatetic and Academic 'schools' is sharper than that between Aristotle and Plato. D.L. I, 20, gives two definitions of αἵρεσις: it refers to (1) the view of those who follow or seem to follow some principle (λόγῳ τινί) in regard to their treatment of appearances and (2) an inclination (πρόσκλισιν) to follow some consistent doctrine (δόγμασιν ἀκολουθίαν). Elias (or David) *In Cat.* 108, 21–22, offers this anodyne definition of αἵρεσις: "the opinion of educated men agreeing among themselves [συμφωνούντων] and disagreeing with others [διαφωνούντων]."

32. Numenius (in Des Places 1973, frag. 24, 57–73) attributes the disputes within the Academy after Plato (including Aristotle) to Plato's disciples having ripped his body apart "limb from limb" and thus having only a partial grasp of the entire sweep of his thought. Proclus *In Parm.* 1214, 11–12; *In Tim.* II 121, 25; 122, 28–123, 27; *PT* I 3. 12, 23–13, 5, notes the superiority of the philosophy of Plato to Aristotle because Aristotle identified the first principle with intellect which could not, owing to its complexity, be absolutely first. See also Olympiodorus *In Alcib.* 122, 12–13; 145, 6–7, and the anonymous *Prolegomena to Plato's Philosophy* 9, 28–41. On the authorship and date of the *Prolegomena*, see Westerink et al. 1990, lxxvi–lxxxix. Westerink 1987, 107, argues that according to Proclus the criterion of "true philosophy" is adherence to

because he did recognize that there *was* a unique first principle and that it was separate from and prior to the sensible world, he is legitimately counted as being fundamentally in harmony with Plato.[33]

When one philosopher or one's philosophy is held to be in harmony with a predecessor's, we naturally wonder whether the harmony is intentional or not. In the case of Aristotle in relation to Plato, the correct answer might seem to be beyond doubt. Surely, one will insist, Aristotle did not think that his philosophy was in harmony with Plato's, even if some later Platonists did. Aristotle's own view of Plato's philosophy and the philosophies of the other Academics is, however, a notoriously vexed topic.[34] There are scores of references to Plato's views in Aristotle's works: most are references to the dialogues; a few are references to Plato's 'unwritten teachings.' There are also references to what can be loosely described as Academic positions, such as a belief in separate Forms, that might well include Plato but then again might not. Insofar as Aristotle's exposition and analysis of Plato's views are based *solely* on the dialogues, they can presumably be independently evaluated for accuracy, as Harold Cherniss has done, in some cases with devastating results. Unfortunately, however, even if we imagine we can isolate the putative unwritten teachings and so refuse to let them contaminate our evaluation of Aristotle's account of Plato's views in the dialogues, we must allow that Plato's meaning is often hard to interpret.

The gap between what Plato says—or, more accurately, what Plato's characters say—and what Plato means is a potentially bottomless pit. Most students of ancient philosophy, however, suppose that there are ways to bridge the gap, reasonable assumptions that allow us to draw conclusions (modest or otherwise) about Plato's meaning on the basis of what is said in the dialogues. But to allow that there is a gap at all is to admit that there is a philosophical position or doctrine that goes beyond just what the dialogues say. For example, 'the' theory of Forms or 'a' theory of Forms may be constructed from the dialogues, but every account of Forms that I know of

---

a doctrine of a transcendent One. Since Aristotle fails to adhere to this doctrine, this criterion indicates a "rejet total de l'aristotélisme" [by Proclus]. Westerink is correct about the criterion in Proclus but mistaken, I think, in claiming that Proclus believes this to be a rejection of Aristotelianism. Nevertheless, it is important to stress that Neoplatonists generally recognized that Aristotle's account of the first principle of all was defective.

33. Ammonius *In Cat.* 6, 9–16, says the reason for studying Aristotle is that he prepares the ascent to the One: that is, the first principle of all. See Romano 1993 for some useful remarks along with texts indicating the relative comprehensiveness of Platonism to Aristotelianism according to Neoplatonism.

34. See Robin 1908, and especially Cherniss (1944 and 1945), whose magisterial works may be said to have initiated a new era in the critical analysis of Aristotle's interpretation of Plato. Robin summarized his study thus: "Aristote nous a mis sur la voie d'une interprétation néoplatonicienne de la philosophie de son maître" (600).

attempts at least to generalize from the words of the dialogues or draw out their implications.[35]

The gap between the paraphrasing of the literal and the construction of the doctrinal reflects the gap between what Plato wrote and Platonism.[36] I think we must recognize at the outset that Neoplatonists were interested in the former primarily because it was the best means of arriving at the latter—but not the only means. It hardly needs emphasizing that from the claims that 'Plato believed p' and 'p implies q,' we cannot infer that Plato believed 'q.' Still, Neoplatonists were eager to be led in their understanding of Platonism as far as possible by Plato. There were, as noted above, Aristotle's reports of the unwritten teachings. In addition, there were Aristotle's interpretations of the dialogues. These were assumed by the Neoplatonists to be informed by Aristotle's knowledge of the unwritten teachings, as well as his intimate contact with Plato over a period of many years. Since they were more concerned with Platonism than with the material contained in the published writings, it was reasonable for them to rely on Aristotle here, as it would perhaps not have been had their interest been only scholarly.[37]

Inextricably bound up with Aristotle's account or accounts of Platonism are issues regarding Aristotle's own philosophical positions. If, to put it simply, Aristotle was a Platonist, why does he appear to criticize Plato relentlessly? If, on the other hand, he was not a Platonist, why does he say so very many things that seem to be so *echt* Platonic? To begin to grasp this problem we must realize that the picture is complicated by the existence of Aristotle's dialogues or 'exoteric' writings, albeit largely available to us now only in fragmentary form. These exoteric works do appear to express views both easily identifiable as Platonic and appearing to contradict things said elsewhere in

35. The remarks by Plato at *Phdr.* 274C–277A and in the *7th Ep.* 341C–D suggesting the unreliability of the written word as a guide to Plato's inner thoughts undoubtedly added to the sense that Plato must be *interpreted.* See also *2nd Ep.* 314C, regarded by Neoplatonists as authentic. See Tarrant 2000 for a helpful study of the pitfalls and vagaries of Platonic interpretation from the Old Academy up to the Neoplatonists.

36. Shorey 1933 provides an excellent example of a scholar who attempts to sail as close to land as possible in his account of what is in the dialogues. But even Shorey again and again tries to tell us what Plato really means when he says so and so. The term 'Platonism,' of course, has a use in contemporary philosophy that is only remotely connected with its use here. See infra chap. 1. Also see Cherniss 1945, chap. 3, "The Academy: Orthodoxy, Heresy, or Philosophical Interpretation?" Cohen and Keyt 1992, 196, have a good discussion of what is involved in "supplying a missing premise" in an argument by Plato. When an interpreter does this, he is "extending an author's thought rather than expounding it." The distinction between 'expounding' and 'extending' is for the authors the distinction between Plato and Platonism. Granting this point, one wonders still what expounding Plato would be apart from trying to reconstruct to the best of one's ability the likely or most plausible premises for the arguments leading to the claims Plato makes.

37. See, e.g., Porphyry *V. Plot.* chap. 14, in which he recounts Plotinus's method of doing philosophy, in particular his absorption of the 'primary texts' followed by his unique (ἴδιος) and unusual (ἐξηλλαγμένος) approach to the theories built on these. Upon a classroom reading of Longinus's works, Porphyry notes revealingly that Plotinus remarked: "Longinus is a scholar, though not at all a philosopher" (19).

the 'esoteric' writings, though a minority of scholars have insisted that the exoteric works show no such thing.

Such apparent contradictions naturally elicit various views about a supposed development in Aristotle's thinking.[38] So, we might hypothesize, as Werner Jaeger did, that Aristotle started out as an authentic and loyal Platonist but then, as he grew intellectually, moved away from Platonism to a philosophical position that was more or less explicitly anti-Platonic. This general developmentalist hypothesis has been widely embraced and applied in the major areas of Aristotle's thought—logic, psychology, ethics, and metaphysics. The basic hypothesis is seldom questioned even when the details are disputed.[39]

Developmentalism draws much of its initial plausibility from an obvious and unquestionable fact: *of course*, Aristotle's thought developed. No one, I think, supposes that, say, Aristotle's account of sensible substance in the central books of his *Metaphysics* sprang full grown from his head. Whether his writings reflect a development is another matter. And even if they do, that is a long way from the conclusion that the development is *from* Platonism *toward* anti-Platonism as opposed to a development *within* the mind of a Platonist or an anti-Platonist, a development that is more a matter of deepening understanding than of fundamental reorientation.[40] Thus, we must not assume that Aristotle's thought developed in, say, the way that Kant's or Wittgenstein's did.

38. See Jaeger (1948), whose seminal work still dominates Aristotle exegesis today, perhaps even unconsciously in the minds of some scholars. The situation is analogous for Plato, where, however, developmentalism's hold has been slipping over the last decade.

39. See Rist (1989), who sets out to 'redo' the work of Jaeger and arrive at a more accurate chronology of Aristotle's development. But Rist retains Jaeger's Platonist/anti-Platonist hypothesis. See Wians 1996, for a good summary of Jaeger's position as well as stimulating papers showing the dominance of Jaeger despite many objections and reservations. There is also in this book an excellent bibliography that includes all the major studies in this area. Wehrle 2001, 1–29, provides an acute critique of some forms of developmentalism, but Wehrle is primarily interested in refuting developmentalism within Aristotle's metaphysics or ontology. He generally avoids dealing with the material relevant to the question of whether the 'nondeveloped' Aristotle is or is not a Platonist.

40. Owen (1960 and 1965) tries to turn Jaeger's position on its head, arguing that Aristotle started out as an anti-Platonist and moved toward Platonism. Graham (1987, 329–331) criticizes Owen's hypothesis, though he does agree that Aristotle moved towards Platonism in a specific sense, albeit contending that "Aristotle's Platonism is a mistake of major proportions" (275). Düring (1966, vii–viii) proclaims his complete rejection of Jaeger's developmentalist hypothesis. See also Düring 1956 and Düring 1964, 98–99 (where a rejection of developmentalism is coupled with a claim for the harmony of Plato and Aristotle), and Düring 1966. Düring saw that a rejection of a theory of Forms did not contradict Aristotle's commitment to the eternity of intelligible objects. Irwin (1988, 11–13) tentatively follows Owen, although he adds, "I see no good reason to believe that [Aristotle] spent most of his time deciding whether to agree or disagree with Plato, and hence I doubt if attention to debates with Plato or Platonism is likely to explain his philosophical development. I am inclined to think the comments on Plato are an incidental result of Aristotle's reflection on problems that arise for him apart from any Platonic context" (12). The extraordinary claim in the last sentence deserves further scrutiny.

Additionally, it is difficult to separate from the idea of development connotations of superiority or improvement. Development is a 'good thing,' is it not? Thus, if Aristotle's thought developed from the time he was a disciple of Plato, then he must be assumed to have become an anti-Platonist or at least to have improved on Platonism. We tend to assume that maturation, a term closely associated with development, involves betterment in thought. So, if Aristotle started out as a Platonist, it is easy to conclude that he ended up something else, something 'better.'

If one follows the Jaegerian hypothesis, then the inconvenient Platonic bits in the works that are otherwise determined to belong to the late, anti-Platonic phase of development have to be dealt with somehow. There is considerable scope for resourcefulness here. For example, we discover that a Platonic passage is a 'remnant' of Aristotle's discarded past, something like a permanent food stain on one's shirt that one must simply endure. More typically, we find that such a passage simply indicates the 'background' of the discussion, as if Aristotle were just acknowledging the air he was forced to breathe. Sometimes scholars just simply avert their embarrassed eyes. We also find suggestions of sloppy scissors-and-paste jobs or even of nefarious tampering with the texts by overzealous Platonists. All these interpretive strategies arise from a common assumption: since the 'mature' Aristotle is obviously opposed to Platonism, any Platonism in the works of his maturity must be there under false pretenses. This assumption is so widely and deeply held that it is seldom exposed to scrutiny. But it is still just an assumption for all that.[41]

Nevertheless, it will be insisted that the assumption is well grounded, even if its application is from time to time awkward. Aristotle, it is argued, *does*, in fact, truly and decisively reject Plato's theory of Forms and at least most of the ontological consequences of accepting that theory, including the diminution of the reality of the sensible world. He also rejects the immortality of the soul, arguably the central idea in Plato's ethics and psychology. In short, Aristotle is the determined opponent of what Francis Cornford aptly termed the 'twin pillars' of Platonism. Given these facts, is it not reasonable to understand Aristotle's supposed Platonism in the 'homonymous' mode? That is, some of the things he says *sound* like Platonism but they really are not; the words may be the same, but the melody is different.

The Neoplatonists generally followed an opposing assumption: Aristotle was a Platonist from first to last.[42] In order to understand and evaluate this

---

41. See Tigerstedt (1974), who shows that the impetus to developmentalism has its roots in the revolution in Platonic studies caused by Schleiermacher at the beginning of the 19th century. For it was he who spearheaded the rejection of the principal interpretive approach within Platonism: namely, that of Neoplatonism. And with a Plato viewed other than as the leading exponent of the system that is Platonism, the gap between Aristotle and Plato seemed all the greater.

42. I largely ignore what I regard as the now discredited thesis of Karl Praechter that Athenian Neoplatonists believed in harmony but Alexandrian Neoplatonists did not. See Praechter 1909, Praechter 1973, and the refutation in Hadot 1978, summarized in Hadot 1991,

assumption, we shall naturally have to have some idea of what Neoplatonists meant by the terms 'Platonist' and 'Platonism' and the range of evidence to which they appealed.

The occasions for confusion and mischief are admittedly ubiquitous when one tries to say what Plato means to express—Platonism—rather than just what Plato says. Harold Cherniss offers impressive evidence of this in his analysis of Aristotle's representations of Platonism. But Cherniss takes Aristotle to task largely because he fails to grasp Plato's meaning accurately. And this is something that one could say only if one grasped that meaning oneself. Inevitably there were disputes about Plato's meaning. Proclus and Simplicius, to take just two examples, regularly offer long lists of contrary views held by their Neoplatonic predecessors about this or that question. Therefore, one should not be overly surprised if Neoplatonists can call Aristotle a Platonist with a straight face at the same time as they note Aristotle's criticisms of Plato.

But an obvious and important objection is that disagreements among Neoplatonists are quite different from disagreements with Plato. Indeed, though Plotinus, for example, will from time to time get a bit cranky about Plato's obscurity on some matter—usually having to do with the soul—he never actually criticizes Plato in the way that he does Aristotle, the Stoics, the Epicureans, and the Skeptics.[43] So, perhaps it is a bit disingenuous of the Neoplatonists to take Aristotle's criticism of Plato as just another family squabble.

This is a serious objection, and it requires a serious answer. Here I only sketch the elements of the answer. First, Neoplatonists were keenly aware of differing views within the Old Academy, especially those of Speusippus and Xenocrates. On some matters, like Cherniss nearly fifteen hundred years later, they believed that Aristotle's criticisms were frequently aimed at Academics other than Plato. For example, it did not go unnoticed by the Neoplatonists that Plato himself evidently criticizes some theory of Forms in the first part of *Parmenides* and the views of the "friends of the Forms" in *Sophist*. Second, although they did not believe that Plato's thought developed in the sense that he held contrary positions at different times, they did believe that different dialogues revealed his thought more or less fully. If, for example, one takes Plato *au pied de la lettre* in *Phaedrus*, one will mistake his meaning regarding the immortality of the parts of the soul, more accurately expressed in *Timaeus*. This is no doubt a dangerous and contentious assumption, but if

---

176–177. See Verrycken 1990, 199–204 and 226–231, for an expansion of Hadot's argument and a tentative qualification of her conclusion. Verrycken argues that the school of Ammonius possibly instituted a simplification of the complex metaphysical system of Syrianus and Proclus. Blumenthal 1993 has proposed a revision of Praechter's view on the differences between Alexandrian and Athenian Neoplatonism. He is answered, decisively in my view, by Hadot 1996, 63–69. I shall assume but not in this book argue that whatever metaphysical simplification evolved within Alexandrian Neoplatonism, it is irrelevant to the basic harmonist orientation of Neoplatonism in general.

43. See, e.g., IV 4. 22, 10.

it is at least to some extent justified, it serves to mitigate certain criticisms of Plato by the putative Platonist Aristotle. Third, Neoplatonists took seriously Aristotle's testimony regarding Plato's unwritten doctrines.

The point I am making here is not the narrow one about the content of the doctrine of the reduction of Forms to ultimate principles but rather the one about the general relevance of oral discussion to the construction of Platonism. Neoplatonists regarded Aristotle as an extremely valuable component of the bridge across the gap between what Plato said and what Plato meant. If his criticisms of Plato stood alone without any countervailing evidence of his commitment to Platonism, then they probably would have concluded that those criticisms meant that Aristotle was not a Platonist, as, say, Pyrrho or Epicurus were not. But because there is such evidence—in fact, because there is such a *considerable* amount of evidence—they were inclined to take the criticisms of Plato as criticisms of unsuccessful versions of Platonism, not of the Platonism that Plato himself truly endorsed.[44] Finally, and most important, since Aristotle's Platonism actually was defective in certain crucial respects, he would naturally be expected to criticize Plato. That is why, after all, his philosophy was said to be in harmony with Platonism, not identical with it. Owing to the fact that the defect was a serious one, having to do primarily with the nature of an ultimate ontological principle, many other things were bound to be out of kilter. But precisely because the defect was capable of being isolated, one could say—with what justification we shall need to explore—that if one were to imagine the defect removed, Aristotelianism would just be Platonism or a creative version of it. In other words, the prodigal son was after all still an inseparable member of the family.

This is not a book directly about Neoplatonism, although I hope that an appreciation of how harmonization works among the Neoplatonists will contribute to the understanding of their sometimes desperately difficult thought. It is a book about the principle of harmony generally adhered to by Neoplatonists more or less explicitly and with greater or lesser precision. Certainly philosophers other than the ones discussed here have supported harmonization.[45] Consequently, I have felt free to draw on a wide variety of disparate sources without paying a great deal of attention to the differences among these sources in other regards. I hereby acknowledge that the differences between, say, Plotinus and Proclus are bound to be reflected in their precise understanding of harmony.[46] Yet there is in my view a baseline agreement among the Neoplatonists as to the lineaments of harmony. Disagreement about details does not change this.

---

44. See, e.g., Simplicius *In Cael.* 640, 27–32; *In Phys.* 1336, 35–36.
45. Obvious examples are Alfarabi, Pico della Mirandola, and Heidegger, although in all three cases the basis for the claim to harmony is decidedly different from that of the Neoplatonists.
46. See, e.g., Hadot 1992, 421–422, on some differences among the Neoplatonists regarding the precise nature of harmony.

In attempting to give a sense of the substance of the thesis of the harmony of Aristotle and Platonism, I have necessarily had to treat a large number of Platonic and Aristotelian (and Neoplatonic) texts in a shamelessly peremptory fashion. I am aware that I have, often in just a few paragraphs, offered interpretations of texts that have been the subject of profound and detailed investigation. My excuse such as it is—apart from the obvious one that this already long book would have had to be well nigh endless—is that the idea of harmony needs to be appreciated in extenso, as it were. And to achieve this goal I have opted to construct my case with broad strokes rather than with narrow ones. I rely on readers to remind themselves continuously that virtually every claim made in this book has been controverted. In self-defense I would add that part of the strength of the harmony thesis is that compared with various other interpretations of particular Platonic or Aristotelian texts, it aims to make sense of Aristotle's engagement with his teacher in a fairly comprehensive manner.

Chapter 1 presents an outline of what Neoplatonists generally took Platonism to be. I survey both the primary and the secondary evidence for its systematic presentation. I consider Platonism as the philosophical position arrived at by embracing the claims that contradict those claims explicitly rejected by Plato in the dialogues.

The chapter also addresses the question of whether it is possible to construct a version of Aristotelianism uncontaminated, as it were, with Platonism: that is, whether Aristotle's philosophy has a systematic profile apart from Platonic principles. To the extent that the answer to this question is in the negative, the case for harmony is strengthened.

In chapter 2 I turn to the actual texts of the Aristotelian corpus and to the Neoplatonic interpretation of these. Although there is within Neoplatonism generally an obvious distinction in genre between commentary (whether on Platonic or Aristotelian texts) and personal writings, this distinction is not of great importance for my purposes. For one thing, virtually all the commentaries on Aristotle were aimed at understanding how Aristotle's philosophy was subsumable under Platonism. In the Neoplatonic 'curriculum' the study of Aristotle preceded and prepared the way for the study of Plato. So, though the commentators are often remarkably resourceful and erudite as commentators, there is no tension between their Platonism and their reading of Aristotle. Understanding the harmony of Plato and Aristotle according to Neoplatonism is served by mining both the commentaries and the personal writings.

This chapter focuses on Aristotle's 'exoteric' writings, which both in antiquity and in modern times are widely recognized to contain many straightforwardly Platonic claims. This fact, as I have noted, is the main engine driving developmentalism. My aim here is to identify these Platonic elements and to evaluate some of the devices that have been employed to remove their Platonic sting. The Neoplatonic attitude to these writings was sophisticated and quite possibly correct. They viewed them as popular—that is, nontechnical—expressions of Platonism, not as the doomed-to-be-repudiated juvenilia of a future anti-Platonist. To the extent that developmentalism is thought, on independent grounds, to be dubious, the Neoplatonic approach to the exoteric writings gains in credibility.

If, however, the Neoplatonic reading of these works was the sole focus of their claim to harmony, it could perhaps be dismissed as fancy. In fact, the exoteric writings were of critical importance to the enterprise of harmony because what is said there of a Platonic nature is mirrored, sometimes with notable precision, in the 'esoteric' works. Naturally, the esoteric works are more nuanced and more difficult to interpret. But as we shall see, the Neoplatonic use of the admittedly Platonic-inspired *exoterica* to document the harmony of Aristotle and Plato has a magnifying effect when joined with an unbiased reading of many passages in the *esoterica*.

In chapter 3 I turn to the Neoplatonic treatment of Aristotle's *Categories*. There are more Neoplatonic commentaries on *Categories* than on any other work of Aristotle, in part because from Porphyry onward the study of *Categories* was placed at the beginning of the Aristotelian portion of the Neoplatonic curriculum. Every Platonic aspirant needed to understand this work, which was supposed to orient pupils in the right direction. And because the study of *Categories* came first, the commentaries contain a great deal of important information on how the Neoplatonists viewed the larger task of representing the harmony of Aristotle and Plato.

Since many contemporary scholars take a contrasting view and assume that *Categories* is the starting point for Aristotle's anti-Platonism or, more particularly, for his alternative ontology, it is important to see exactly how this work could have been understood as one over which Platonists could wax enthusiastic.[47] Briefly, they took the categories to apply only to the sensible world, not to the intelligible world. This is in itself a fairly obvious point. But, somewhat more contentiously, they also held that an Aristotelian account of the sensible world cohered with Platonism as they understood it. That is, Aristotelian categories were appropriate for understanding a world diminished in reality owing to its being an image of the intelligible world. So, substance and accident, species and genus were legitimate categories of the nonultimate. According to Neoplatonists, Aristotle himself was *not* committed to the view that a sensible substance such as a man or a horse was an unqualifiedly ultimate component of the world. The relative ultimacy of sensible substance or that ultimacy within a defined realm was to be fitted into a Platonic framework.

Chapter 4 discusses the Neoplatonic view of Aristotle's account of nature and of the principles of natural science. Platonism views nature, like the categories that are applied to it, as only relatively ultimate. Therefore, an account of *a* nature or of nature generally cannot be a complete account.

---

47. A recent work that starts with the assumption that *Categories* marks the beginning of Aristotle's revolt against Platonism is Mann 2000.

Accordingly, Aristotle's fourfold schema of causal analysis is a fragment of a larger Platonic schema that includes the paradigmatic cause as well as ultimate or transcendent efficient and final causes. Much of the chapter is devoted to the way the Neoplatonists harmonized Aristotle's account of nature and the principles of natural science in *Physics* with Plato's *Timaeus*.

As mentioned above, Aristotle was recognized to be authoritative in matters relating to the study of nature. One consequence of this view was that Neoplatonists were willing and eager to adopt the Aristotelian conceptual framework in the science of nature. Thus Plotinus and later Neoplatonists freely and enthusiastically used the concepts of form/matter, act/potency, and the fourfold schema of causes as part of the exposition and defense of Platonism. Adopting Aristotelian concepts even in commentaries on Platonic texts undoubtedly served the interests of the harmonists. The important question to ask, however, is whether Platonism can bear Aristotelian coloration—whether, for example, the concept of a receptacle of becoming in *Timaeus* is legitimately used by Neoplatonists to prove that a material principle belongs in the larger Platonic picture. This is one of the major questions I address.

Chapter 5 is principally concerned with Aristotle's doctrine of intellect (νοῦς), especially as it is found in *De Anima*. First, I try to show the basis for the Neoplatonic position that Aristotle is indeed committed to the immortality of intellect. The evidence for this is in fact quite substantial. But though widely acknowledged, the evidence is then frequently occluded by a concentrated on Aristotle's hylomorphism. But if we keep the account of intellect separate from the account of the hylomorphic composition of the embodied individual, it is far from obvious that either one is anti-Platonic.

From the Neoplatonic perspective, the anti-Platonic reading of *De Anima* is nothing short of bizarre. Leaving aside the need either to ignore what is said about intellect in the exoteric works or to discount that according to some developmentalist hypothesis, such a reading systematically confuses intellect with the biological conditions for embodied intellection. In short, it refuses to acknowledge that intellect is both explicitly denied by Aristotle to be the form of a hylomorphic composite and also shown by Aristotle to be immaterial, and not in the anodyne sense in which any form is immaterial. The Neoplatonists have, I try to show, a strong case for the proposition that Aristotle's account of intellect is deeply Platonic. And once this is established, questions about both personal identity and epistemology in *De Anima* can be properly seen in their true Platonic light. Thus, setting aside contemporary notions of personhood that would be anachronistically applied to antiquity, we can see the basis for the harmony of Plato and Aristotle.

Chapter 6 presents the general Neoplatonic interpretation of Aristotle's metaphysics. Not surprisingly, that interpretation rests heavily on the identification of metaphysics not only with a science of first causes and principles and a science of being *qua* being, but also with a science of theology. I do think, particularly in light of much of the foregoing, that this

Neoplatonic interpretation deserves serious attention. But in addition, the theological interpretation of metaphysics is thought by the Neoplatonists to facilitate the harmonizing of Aristotle's ontology with Plato's two-world metaphysics.

Naturally, a good part of the chapter is devoted to the relation between Book Λ of *Metaphysics* and the other essays or λόγοι that make up that work. Bearing in mind that the divine principle in Book Λ, thinking that is thinking of thinking, is not recognized to be the first principle of all, its causal role in metaphysics is still crucial. Aristotle is notoriously and frustratingly unclear about this. Is the prime unmoved mover a final cause or efficient cause or both? In trying to answer this question Neoplatonists find the similarity between Aristotle's God and the Demiurge of Plato's *Timaeus* striking and illuminating. The question about causality is the same question for Plato's Demiurge in relation to the ultimate principle of all.

I also discuss the Neoplatonists' account of the crucial defect in Aristotle's version of Platonism. There I focus primarily on Plotinus's argument that although Aristotle recognized the need for an absolutely first principle, he was mistaken in identifying that principle with thinking or a mind. The reason the first principle of all cannot be so identified is that thinking is an essentially complex activity, whereas the first principle must be absolutely simple. Aristotle, in fact, recognized the requirement of the absolute simplicity of the first principle, but he erred in holding that this could be instantiated by a mind or, even more strictly, by the activity of a mind. A mind's activity is, however, essentially intentional. Hence the basic complexity of thought.

Although thinking cannot be identified with an absolutely first principle, nevertheless thinking is, according to the Neoplatonists, an immaterial principle. Part of Aristotle's mistake was that he could not accept the possibility of a *complex* immaterial principle. He believed that immateriality entailed unqualified simplicity. So, the argument that led him to identify the prime mover with thinking also led him to conclude that the prime mover is the absolutely first principle. As I argue, the concept of immaterial complexity is an essential feature of Platonism.

I reserve chapter 7 for a discussion of Aristotle's criticisms of Forms and the Neoplatonists' reactions to these criticisms. Not surprisingly, some committed harmonists were occasionally puzzled by Aristotle's relentless criticisms of what might be aptly regarded as the centerpiece of Plato's philosophy, a theory of separate Forms. But taking a relatively large view of Platonism, Neoplatonists never understood Forms as ultimate principles. So, although the Forms were understood to be separable from (1) the sensible world, they were not separable either from (2) other Forms, (3) a divine intellect, and (4) the ultimate or first principle. Accordingly, criticisms that assumed separation in the senses (2) to (4) were regarded as misplaced, explicable either as applying to Academics other than Plato or as a function of Aristotle's defective understanding of the ultimate principle of all.

Still, if Aristotle rejects separate Forms, how can his philosophy be said to be in harmony with Plato's? The argument here depends on showing that since Aristotle shares with Plato a realist's account of sameness and difference in the sensible world—namely, a rejection of nominalism—Aristotle is committed to the ontological priority of intelligible natures to their sensible instances. The very fact that Aristotle recognizes the possibility of knowing things universally obliges him to accept some account of the grounds for the possibility of universal knowledge, an account that the universality of thought itself does not provide. Forms are not universals, and universals do not do the job that Forms must do to make universal knowledge possible. Hence, *no* theory of universals serves as a substitute for a theory of Forms.

The Neoplatonists take Aristotle's rejection of Forms to be a rejection of entities supposedly separate in senses (2) to (4). They can accept this view with equanimity because this is what Platonism holds, too. According to their understanding of Aristotle, what he has done is to reject the term 'Form' or 'Idea' as impossibly tainted and instead to substitute the term 'intelligible' (νοητόν). This is what is found present eternally to intellect, both the intellect of every person and the divine intellect. Thus is harmony restored.

In this chapter, I also briefly consider Aristotle's account of the mathematized version of the theory of Forms. I examine the question of whether or not Plato's presumed commitment to it supports or undermines the harmonists' position.

In chapter 8 I turn to Aristotle's ethics. There is not much Neoplatonic commentary material on Aristotle's ethical writings. It is, however, possible to piece together something that can legitimately be called a Neoplatonic reading of *Nicomachean Ethics* and to show how on this reading the view of happiness and virtue there is in harmony with the central idea of Neoplatonic ethics: namely, assimilation to the divine.

One of the central exegetical problems in *Nicomachean Ethics* is how the definition of happiness as virtuous activity in Book A is to be reconciled with the argument in Book K that the best life is the contemplative life. Contemporary scholars have often, somewhat ruefully, acknowledged that the latter is a deeply Platonic view, usually following this by saying that it is an aberration. Neoplatonists, by contrast, identify the contemplative life with the highest stage reachable by an embodied person in the process of assimilation to the divine. Accordingly, although the practice of ethical virtue is never dismissed as being anything other than desirable, it is recognized as inferior and belonging to a life of secondary value. Ethical value is both intrinsically good *and* instrumental to a higher stage along the path of identification with the divine in us. A careful reading of *Nicomachean Ethics* shows, I believe, that Aristotle does not think otherwise.

In the book's last chapter I step back somewhat from the Neoplatonic reading of Aristotle to ask the question of whether we should conclude that Aristotle is a Platonist in spite of himself. I mean that if we look at Aristotle entirely in Aristotelian terms, is he led to embrace principles that make him, even if reluctantly, a Platonist? I say 'reluctantly' because no Neoplatonic spin can erase the fact that Aristotle is constantly bucking against the Platonic bridle. I do not entirely discount personality differences here. But as philosophers, open to learning from the history of ancient philosophy, we would, I think, like to know whether an antinominalist, as Aristotle surely is, can consistently avoid 'succumbing' to Platonism. We would also like to know whether a realist theory of knowledge could attain a defensible basis other than with an immaterialist account of thought. And finally, we would like to know whether hylomorphism, even suitably nuanced in a way that makes it acceptable to materialism, is capable of giving an adequate account of the human person. If the answer to all these questions is no, then we should accept the harmony of Aristotle and Plato, even if, finally, we are inclined to say, "So much the worse for Aristotle."

I include in an appendix thumbnail sketches of the Neoplatonists and other writers of the period dealt with in the book, with notes about their writings, both those that still exist and those that do not. The reader is invited to consult this appendix as required or to have a glance at it before reading the rest of the book. The translations are my own except where indicated.

One of the central and overarching tasks of this book is to contribute to the recovery of what is, to borrow a felicitous phrase from Benedetto Croce, "living and dead" in both Plato and Aristotle. Of course, many others are engaged in a similar task. But I think something can be added if we look back to the 4th century B.C.E. through the prism of the Neoplatonic harmony principle. I think we can see facets of Platonism that deserve serious contemporary consideration if we look precisely at those places where Aristotle has been for so long assumed to have said "no" when in fact he was really saying yes, or yes plus a qualifying *distinguo*. If we can recover Aristotle's Platonism, we shall be better placed, or so I argue, to appropriate what is genuinely vital in what is for better or worse the dominant tradition in the entire history of philosophy. I also strongly suspect that confrontation with genuine, not *faux*, Platonism, even when it does or should result in rejection, can only be counted a plus in this regard.

With the goal of accomplishing this task in mind, I add two methodological notes. First, for the most part, in this book I assume the stance of an advocate for the harmonists' position. I do this certainly not because I believe that their interpretations of Aristotle and Plato are beyond criticism. Such criticism, however, if it is to be of any use, would have to take into account an enormously complex labyrinth of connections, including the harmonists' philosophical interactions among themselves and their readings of Aristotle based on their own principles which are themselves based upon their readings of Plato. Every step in this labyrinth increases difficulties almost exponentially. It seems to me unnecessary to add one more critical voice to this crowded array. I am aware that my advocacy will at times seem insufficiently justified. I will be content if I have clarified the interpretive positions of the harmonizing Neoplatonists to the extent that they are thereby more open to effective confirmation or disconfirmation.

Second, the nature of the ancient evidence and the specific manner in which harmony was conceived in regard to each Aristotelian doctrine seemed to oblige me to vary my approach in each chapter. In some cases, such as in chapter 5, detailed exposition of Aristotle's argument is required whereas in other cases a more general account seems sufficient for making the Neoplatonic point. And sometimes, as in chapter 8, the dearth of direct evidence from the commentators required the construction of a harmonist position that is partly hypothetical.

The contemporary philosopher Richard Rorty notes that most of what he has written over the past decade stems from his "antagonism to Platonism."[48] Rorty is quick to add that by 'Platonism' he means something more than the thoughts of the author of the *Dialogues*. He understands Platonism, broadly conceived, to embody sets of distinctions or polarities—appearance/reality; matter/mind; made/found; sensible/intellectual; 'in itself'/'for us,' etc.—that he wishes in the firmest possible way to reject. I am sympathetic at least to Rorty's broad conception of what Platonism is. So conceived, it is perhaps more easy to see why the so-called Neoplatonists viewed Aristotle's philosophy as being in harmony with the philosophy of Plato. My goal is in part to achieve a richer understanding of Platonism by showing why Neoplatonists took Aristotle to be an authentic collaborator in its development and explication.[49]

48. See Rorty 1999, intro.
49. Cf. Donini 1988b, 144: "The dialogue between the philosophies of Plato and Aristotle is something essential for all those who, at any time in the history of ancient thought, have looked back to the one or the other philosophy."

CHAPTER ONE

What Is Platonism?

In order to appreciate why some Platonists took Aristotle to be more or less one of their own, we naturally need to understand what they held Platonism to be. Among the philosophers and commentators with whom I am dealing one would be hard pressed to point to any two who are in complete agreement regarding every 'thesis' of Platonism. Although contemporary scholarship has been able to show that there was actually less disharmony among the various 'schools' of Platonism than was once thought, that areas of disagreement exist among the major figures, at least, is still an unshakable fact. I try to navigate a bit above the level of disagreement, focusing rather on the substantial points of agreement, which will, I hope enable us to see more clearly what it meant to enlist Aristotle into the ranks of Platonists.

When I say 'Platonism,' I do not mean something that might be termed 'Plato's philosophy,' where this phrase is taken to indicate the 'mind' of Plato. I happily concede at the outset that there is not now and never has been something like an entailment relationship between any version of Platonism constructed out of any evidence, textual or otherwise, and the mind of Plato. All the Platonists with whom I am dealing undoubtedly supposed that if Plato thought things that were at odds with the things he said or wrote, this fact was unknowable and irrelevant, though it is perhaps a curious fact about one person's psychology. The putative distinction between Platonism and the mind of Plato does, however, raise an important issue: whether or not 'ownership' of Platonism belongs to Plato. Let me explain.

It was fairly widely believed in antiquity that Plato was not the first Platonist, as we might tendentiously put it. Aristotle informs us that Plato

"followed the Italians (i.e., the Pythagoreans) in most things."[1] Plotinus
tells us that Plato was not the first to say the things that in fact we today
identify as Platonism, but he said them best.[2] On this view, since Plato was
not the first and therefore not the only champion of Platonism, there was
generally held to be nothing untoward in arguing that Plato *meant* what
he did not happen to say explicitly. To draw out the implications or the
true meaning of what Plato said, in other words, was part of the project
of articulating and defending Platonism.[3]

The attempt to expose the inspired meaning of Plato's words was evidently consistent with a refusal to accept Plato's authority without question.
Olympiodorus in his *Commentary on Plato's Gorgias* relates the revealing story
that his own teacher, Ammonius, rebuked a student who gave as the reason
for some doctrine or other that "Plato said it." Ammonius replied that, first
of all, that was not what Plato meant (οὐκ ἔφη μὲν οὕτως) and, second, even
if he did, it was not true *because* Plato said it.[4] Ammonius's first point is as significant as his second: Plato's words cannot always be taken at face value.
They must be interpreted. And in their interpretation they must be
defended by argument.[5]

One can usefully compare in this regard Platonism with Christianity. Both
Platonism and Christianity have founders who were regarded as themselves
belonging to a larger tradition. But both Platonism and Christianity consist

1. See *Met.* A 6, 987a30. Aristotle goes on to attribute "the peculiarities" (τὰ ἴδια) of Plato's
philosophy to his having in his youth come under the personal influence of Cratylus and
Socrates. D.L. III 5–8, confirms and expands on this account. Association of Platonism with
Pythagoreanism was a regular, albeit varied, feature of Neoplatonism. See Iamblichus *V. Pythag.*
74, 18–21 and 94, 18–22, on Plato's dependence on Pythagoras; and O'Meara 1989, 91–111.

2. Plotinus V 1. 8, 10–14: "So, these statements of ours are not recent or new, but rather
were made a long time ago though not explicitly. The things we are saying now are interpretations of those, relying on the writings of Plato himself as evidence that these are ancient
views." Plotinus is here referring to the basic principles of his own metaphysics. See V 8. 4, 51ff.
See Sedley 1997; and Boys-Stones 2001, chap. 6, for differing views of the reestablishment of
Plato as a philosophical authority for Platonists.

3. Plotinus VI 2. 1, 4–5, says that he is "trying to coordinate [ἀνάγειν] our opinions with
those of Plato." Those who assumed the harmony of Plato and Aristotle tried to do something
analogous for him. Plotinus wanted his own views to be identical with Plato's, though nobody
thought that Aristotle's were so identical. Cf. Findlay (1974, 377), describing the Platonism of
Plotinus, who says, "It is simply what one arrives at if one meditates on the major speculative
passages in Plato's written work with a willingness to carry eidetic thinking to the limit, a willingness which has not been present in many of the empiricists, pluralists, nominalists, skeptics,
formal logicians, anti-mystics and pure scholars who have ventured to interpret Plato."

4. See Olympiodorus *In Gorg.* 41 9, 10–13. In this passage he aptly cites Plato *Phd.* 91C1,
where Socrates exhorts his interlocutors to "care little for Socrates but much more for the
truth."

5. As Arius Didymus remarks *apud* Stobaeus *Ecl.* II 7, 18–19, what might appear as discrepancies in Plato were owing to his multiple 'voices' not to any contradictions in doctrine
[τὸ πολύφωνον τοῦ Πλάτωνος, οὐ πολύδοξον]. See Rist 1967, 169–187, on Plotinus's origi-
nality. Rist shows that in a number of ways Plotinus aimed to explicate and defend Platonism
more than Plato. See also Dörrie 1976a, 375–389, "Tradition und Erneuern in Plotins
Philosophieren."

of more than the accounts of what these founders said and did. Both have canonical texts, though the canon's exact composition is in some dispute. Both have proponents of sharply different interpretations of the meaning of those texts and of the relative authority of text and oral transmission. Among all these proponents of both Platonism and Christianity one may just assume a conviction that any newly articulated doctrine was in accord with the intention of the founder. But such a conviction, at least as a means of adjudicating disputes among the proponents, is really quite beside the point.

Another respect in which the comparison of Platonism and Christianity is illuminating is this: Platonism in antiquity had many features of a religion as well as of a philosophical school.[6] In this regard it was held to be open to the inclusion of truths—regarding the soul, divinity, and so on—handed down from nonphilosophical sources such as Pythagorean, Orphic, Hermetic, and Gnostic, as well as philosophical sources outside of the Platonic tradition and even non-Greek sources.[7] That is why Platonism is receptive to the idea of harmonization in general.

Once we recognize that we do not have independent access to the mind of Plato as a means of 'controlling' the expressible content of Platonism, we might be inclined to take a purely phenomenological approach: Platonism is just whatever anyone identifies as Platonism.[8] A similar approach could be taken in determining who is a Platonist. As a strictly historical method, this is not an unreasonable way to proceed.[9] But it is clearly not adequate as a means for understanding what was meant by those who recruited Aristotle into the ranks of Platonists.[10] What is needed is something like a doctrinal map of Platonism in the period under discussion. Such a map is

6. See the remarks of Dörrie and Baltes 1987, 1:11–12. The passage in Plato often used as evidence of the religious character of Platonism is *Symp.* 209E4ff., where Diotima refers to the "mystery rites" she is handing over to Socrates. That is why Plotinus believes that Platonism is not universally accessible. See V 8. 2, 45.

7. See Boys-Stones (2001, esp. 105–122), who argues that the Stoic theory of the appropriation of ancient collective wisdom through the methodology of allegorical exegesis of myth was the guiding blueprint for the construction of Platonism as a school. To this methodology the early Platonists added the claim that Plato was the supreme authority for the expression or systematization of this ancient wisdom. Boys-Stones (118, n.16) cites a revealing passage in Proclus's *PT* V 33, 21–34, 2, where Proclus speaks of his admiration for Plato's ability to clarify the same matters as expressed by (non-Greek) theologians, barbarians, and the Greek Orpheus.

8. According to Glucker 1978, 206–225, philosophers began regularly declaring themselves as Platonists in the second century C.E. Antiochus of Ascalon, e.g., was always referred to as an Academic. But see Cicero *De Nat. Deo.* I 73, where Pamphilius, the teacher of Epicurus, is referred to as "Platoncius."

9. See Dörrie and Baltes 1987, 1:4: "Platonismus wird verstanden als die Philosophie, deren Vertreter sich Πλατωνικοί—*Platonici*-nannten. Der so verstandene Platonismus gewann alsbald alle Merkmale einer philosophischen Schule—αἵρεσις—*secta*, ähnlich den Merkmalen, durch die sich die übrigen Schulen, namentlich die Stoiker, auszeichneten."

10. Aristotle in several passages uses the personal pronoun 'we' when referring to Academic positions, esp. regarding the theory of Forms. See *Met.* A 9, 990b9, 11, 16, 19, 23; 991b7. Cf. A 9, 992a11, 25, 27, 28; B 2, 997b3; B 6, 1002b14. Presumably the 'we' indicates self-identification as an Academic. Does that self-identification suggest that Aristotle's philosophy is in harmony with that of Plato? The answer to this question is the central focus of the present work.

undoubtedly going to be a bit crude and imprecise, but it will be necessary for evaluations of specific claims to harmony.

Another approach to the determination of the nature of Platonism is inspired by an idea articulated in the writings of Pierre Hadot.[11] He has argued that each of the ancient philosophical schools should be viewed primarily as devoted to a way of life and only secondarily to philosophical discourse that includes, among other things, doctrine. It was the way of life "which conditioned and determined the fundamental tendencies of [the philosopher's] philosophical discourse."[12] Hadot believes that Neoplatonists were extraordinarily perspicacious in seeing Aristotle as a Platonist because of Aristotle's fundamental commitment to a Platonic way of life: namely, to contemplation and to assimilation to the divine.[13] Hadot specifies the distinctive spiritual exercises of the Platonic way of life.[14] These include Socratic dialectic, 'practice for dying,' self-identification with the 'man within the man' or reason through virtuous living, and theoretical science itself as a sort of therapy for morbid attachment to the idiosyncratic and transitory.

Viewing Platonism in this way, one is not surprised to discover what we may term at least a disposition among Neoplatonists to see an Aristotelian way of life as being in harmony with a Platonic one. But this makes the task of defending harmony too easy and hence not very interesting. As Hadot stresses, however, commitment to a way of life and philosophical discourse are mutually supportive.[15] If Aristotle and Plato differed fundamentally in their philosophical discourse in a way that the Neoplatonists say they did not, their claim that they shared a fidelity to a particular way of life would be at best hollow. Harmonists were not of the view that a particular way of life (the Platonic one) could or did yield an Aristotelian form of philosophical discourse radically different from that of the self-proclaimed Platonists.

What Is Platonism?

I begin with the Platonic corpus as the Neoplatonists knew it. As Diogenes Laertius reports, Thrasyllus (d. 36 C.E.) divided the works of Plato into nine 'tetralogies,' or groups of four.[16] To these he appended a number of works he judged to be spurious. There is considerable controversy today over the question of whether Thrasyllus originated the division into tetralogies.[17]

11. See esp. Hadot 1995 and Hadot 2002.

12. See Hadot 2002, 273.

13. Ibid., 262.

14. See Hadot 1995, chap. 3.

15. See Hadot 2002, chap. 9.

16. See D.L. III 56; III 61 goes on to mention an earlier division into trilogies by Aristophanes the Grammarian (c. 257–180 B.C.E.), evidently based on dramatic similarities.

17. See Tarrant 1993, esp. chaps. 3–4; Mansfeld 1994, esp. chap. 2 for discussions of the controversy.

There is even greater dispute regarding his division of authentic and spurious material. From our perspective, what is most important is that the Thrasyllan scheme established the authentic corpus of Platonic writings for the Neoplatonists.[18]

The nine tetralogies include thirty-five dialogues plus thirteen *Epistles* that are counted as one work. Not all of these are today universally recognized as genuine. Of the dialogues of doubted authenticity, *Alcibiades I* was most important for Neoplatonists because that dialogue was apparently read first in the Neoplatonic 'curriculum.'[19] Among the *Epistles* of doubted authenticity, the second and the philosophical portion of the seventh were unquestionably the most significant for the Neoplatonists and used by them regularly to bolster their interpretations of the dialogues.[20]

Among the thirty-six works recognized by the Neoplatonists as genuine, some were picked out as having more doctrinal significance than others. Apparently there was by the time of Iamblichus a well-established order of study of the dialogues among Neoplatonists.[21] After lectures on Plato's life, a series of ten questions were to be answered: (1) What sort of philosophy is found in Plato? (2) Why did Plato believe it was his duty to write down his philosophy? (3) Why did he employ a literary form in his dialogues? (4) What are the elements of the dialogues? (5) What is the source of the titles of the dialogues? (6) What is the principle of division of the dialogues? (7) In what manner are the topics of the dialogues introduced? (8) What are the criteria for determining the aim of the dialogues? (9) What is the order of the dialogues? (10) What is the manner of teaching of the dialogues? Discussion of these topics was followed by introductions to the twelve dialogues contained in the syllabus of Plato's works: *Alcibiades I, Gorgias, Phaedo, Cratylus, Theaetetus, Sophist, Statesman, Phaedrus, Symposium, Philebus, Timaeus, Parmenides.*

The selection of these twelve dialogues does not in any obvious way correspond to any tetralogical order. In addition, the foregoing curriculum does not give a full picture of Neoplatonic interest in the genuine works. In fact, the most glaring omission, *Republic,* is of the utmost importance to Neoplatonists, especially its central metaphysical portion.[22] Also surprising is the

18. See Cooper 1997, which contains all of the genuine and spurious material as established by Thrasyllus. Tarrant 1993 argues that the division of the dialogues by Thrasyllus reflects a positive interpretation of Platonism rather than merely a neutral organization of the extant material. According to Tarrant, Thrasyllus is a key figure in the development of subsequent versions of Platonism. Tarrant's hypothesis seems to me to be interesting but unproven.

19. For the evidence pro and con for the authenticity of *Alcibiades*, see Pradeau 1999 and Denyer 2001. On the Neoplatonic order of studying the Platonic dialogues, see I. Hadot 1990, 44–47.

20. For an introduction to the question of the authenticity of the *Epistles* see Morrow 1962.

21. See Festugière 1969 and Westerink, Trouillard et al. 1990.

22. E.g., Henry and Schwyzer cite well over 200 direct references to *Republic* in their edition of Plotinus's *Enneads*, and Proclus wrote an extensive commentary on the work. Marinus *V. Proc.*, chap. 14, mentions a course of lectures on *Republic* and *Laws* separate from the main curriculum.

omission from the list of works to be studied of any of the so-called Socratic dialogues (with the exception of *Alcibiades I*). Their absence reflects several features of the Neoplatonic approach to Plato. First, since their approach was thoroughly 'non-developmentalist,' they did not recognize a 'Socratic' or 'early' phase of Plato's philosophy, and so the dialogues today held to represent such a phase were not relevant to revealing it. For the Neoplatonists Platonism was basically a "Platon ohne Sokrates" as Walter Bröcker once neatly put it.[23] Nor was it supposed that there was development of Plato's thought away from the constructive period of the so-called middle dialogues. So, the harmony of Aristotle with Plato was not supposed to be based on Plato's approaching in his thinking a putative Aristotelianism.[24] Second, the aporetic character of these dialogues was not directly relevant to anything like a systematic representation of Platonism. Third, their ethical preoccupation was subsumed by the more elaborate treatments in the dialogues included in the introductory twelve.

Another important feature of the curriculum is that it culminated in the two works *Timaeus* and *Parmenides,* the former being Plato's ultimate and most comprehensive statement of the structure of the sensible world and the latter containing the corresponding statement for the intelligible world.[25] Reading *Timaeus* in this way, though by no means universally accepted, is far less controversial than so reading *Parmenides*.[26]

Part of the reason for the Neoplatonic consensus that *Parmenides* contained an expression of Plato's most profound thoughts about the structure of intelligible reality was that they did not rely solely on the dialogues for their understanding of Platonism. They relied on Aristotle's and others' testimony about Plato's unwritten teachings. The view that Plato had unwritten teachings and that these differed in any way from what is said in the dialogues is a matter of intense and even bitter controversy.[27] It is rather less

23. See Bröcker 1966, which is particularly concerned with Plotinus, though the remarks hold generally, I think, for the other Neoplatonists as well. Whether this Plato is also, as Theiler 1960, 67, put it, a "Plato dimidiatus" is another question.

24. This was the view, e.g., of Stenzel 1917, 58. Ironically, Jaeger's approach to Plato, in contrast to his approach to Aristotle, was entirely nondevelopmentalist. See the interesting discussion of Kahn 1992b, 71–73.

25. See Proclus *In Tim.* I 13, 15–17, quoting Iamblichus as saying that the entirety of Plato's thought is contained in *Timaeus* and *Parmenides.*

26. Proclus *In Parm.* 630, 15–645, 8 gives a valuable history of types of interpretation of *Parmenides*—esp. its second part—within the Platonic tradition. The basic division is between a logical and a metaphysical interpretation. The logical interpretation, which takes *Parmenides* as an exercise in reasoning, was held by, e.g., Albinus *Isag.* chap. 4, Alcinous *Didask.* chap. 6, and Thrasyllus (*apud* D. L. III 58). The metaphysical interpretation, of which there are several varieties, was normative for the Neoplatonists. See Plotinus V 1. 8, 23ff. As Dodds (1928) famously argued, the positive, metaphysical interpretation may well antedate Plotinus. See Halfwassen 1992, chap. 3; Tarrant 1993, 148–177; and Bechtle 1999, 71–117 for useful summaries of the history of *Parmenides* interpretations.

27. See Krämer 1959; Krämer 1964; Krämer 1990; Gaiser 1963; Szlezák 1985 and a summary statement of it in English Szlezák 1999. The most famous and effective opponent of the idea that Plato had unwritten teachings and that Aristotle is an

a matter of contention that Aristotle does refer to unwritten teachings of the Academy that contain some sort of a theory about ultimate metaphysical principles.[28] The relation between the theory of Forms as presented in the dialogues and the alleged theory of ultimate principles presented in Aristotle's account is far from perspicuous in the Neoplatonists. But Aristotle was taken by them, not unreasonably, to be a faithful reporter of Plato's views, including views that do not for the most part make an explicit appearance in the dialogues.[29] In this regard, two well-known passages in *Phaedrus* and *7th Epistle,* along with others in *Republic* and *2nd Epistle,* bolstered the case for the existence of an unwritten teaching and its identification as a theory of first principles.[30]

The harmonization of Aristotle with Plato was based on a view of Platonism informed by the above primary evidence.[31] I shall not here argue the case for the quality of this evidence or the Neoplatonic interpretation of it.[32] I am here concerned primarily with the question of what Platonism looked like to those who accepted the evidence and allied themselves to this philosophical school. In addition to this evidence, the Neoplatonists were able to

---

accurate witness to these is Cherniss 1944 and 1945. A recent comprehensive study of the case for Plato's unwritten teachings is provided by Richard 1986. See also Miller 1995 for an illuminating study of the support provided by Plato's *Parmenides* for the doctrines testified to by Aristotle. See Vlastos 1963 for a highly influential argument critical of the thesis that Plato had unwritten teachings.

28. A convenient collection and translation of both the Aristotelian passages in which the unwritten teachings are mentioned or described and the Neoplatonic commentaries on these can be found in Krämer 1990, 203–217, and also in Findlay 1974, 413–454.

29. Aristotle's trustworthiness as an expositor of Plato has of course been strenuously disputed, especially in Cherniss 1944 and 1945.

30. See *Phdr.* 274C-277A; *7th Ep.* 341Bff. *Rep.* 509B6–10.

31. In the matter of evidence one should not underestimate the universal assumption of the genuineness of the letter by Aristotle to Alexander the Great *On the Universe* (Περὶ κόσμου) which in many respects manifests a deeply Platonic orientation. This is also plain in Alexander of Aphrodisias's treatise by the same name, which exists only in an Arabic translation; see Genequand 2001, intro. Genequand remarks that its "two outstanding characteristics . . . are thus the doctrine of imitation and that of the divine power permeating the universe. The Platonic idea of imitation fused with Aristotelian teleology becomes the driving force of the universe, ensuring its cohesion not only on the psychological, but above all on the cosmological plane" (19–20). Genequand is here speaking of Alexander's understanding of Aristotle, based in part on this (probably) spurious letter; nevertheless, no one including Alexander regarded the letter as evincing an anomalous doctrine. No doubt that is why they had no difficulty in accepting that it was genuine. See also Krämer 1972, 329–331, who discusses the insufficient evidentiary basis of some of the claims that Aristotelianism and Platonism are opposed.

32. Dörrie (1976a and 1976b), sees Middle Platonism as introducing a decisive break in the tradition going back to the Old Academy. This break is owing to the skeptical turn in the Academy beginning with Arcesilaus, and to the destruction of the Platonic library by Sulla in 86 B.C.E. Accordingly, Dörrie sees Neoplatonism, developed out of Middle Platonism, as more innovative and independent than scholars such as Merlan, De Vogel, and Krämer, have argued. One reason Dörrie gives for the novelty of Neoplatonism is that it is a "syncretism of Pythagorean, *Aristotelian,* and Academic elements" (my emphasis); see his 1976a, 284, in a review of Merlan's *From Platonism to Neoplatonism.* Also in the same volume see esp. 508–523: "Was ist Spätantiker Platonismus?"

engage with a long tradition of interpreting Plato among his self-proclaimed followers, going back to the first generation. Porphyry, for example, in his *Life of Plotinus* cites the preface to a work of the scholar Longinus, who says that Plotinus surpassed Numenius, Thrasyllus, Cronius, and Moderatus in the clarity of his exposition of "the principles of Pythagorean and Platonic philosophy" and in the "accuracy of his treatment of the same subjects they treated."[33] The later Neoplatonists, especially Proclus and Simplicius, cite Platonic interpreters freely, going back to Plato's successors in the Academy, Speusippus and Xenocrates.[34]

The Platonism of the so-called Old, Middle, and New Academies is a vast and complex subject.[35] This is not the place to offer even a sketch of its main features. Two points, however, are worth stressing. First, the soi-disants followers of Plato sometimes offered differing and conflicting interpretations of Plato without thereby feeling compelled to attribute heresy to opponents.[36] Not surprisingly, there were differences about particular doctrines, differences about the way the dialogues were to be read as a means to extracting doctrines, and differences about their import. The primary lesson we should draw from these intra-Academy disputes is that the essence of Platonism must be sought at a level of generality beyond that of specific philosophical claims. 'Platonism' was indeed a 'big tent,' though no one doubted that it was not infinitely expandable.[37] This brings me to the second point.

The feature common to virtually all versions of Platonism is a commitment to what I would term a top-down approach to the entire budget of philosophical problems extant in any particular period. What is most distinctive about Platonism, especially as it is presented by the Neoplatonists,

33. See Porphyry *V. Plot.* 20, 71–76. Dodds (1928 and 1960) argues in particular for the view that the Neoplatonic interpretation of three metaphysical levels—One, Being, Soul—is developed by Moderatus and Numenius. The invaluable *Didaskalikos* by Alcinous also indicates well-established pre-Plotinian efforts to systematize Platonism in a hierachical manner. See Dillon 1993, esp. his commentary on chaps. 9–10 of the work. See Halfwassen 1992, esp. 183–264, on Plotinus's interpretation of the Form of the Good in *Republic* as identical with the One, the first principle of all.

34. See Dillon 2003, esp. chaps. 2–3, on the support for Aristotle's testimony about the unwritten doctrines in Speusippus and the systematization of Platonism begun by Xenocrates.

35. See esp. Cherniss 1945; Dillon and Long 1988; Dillon 1990a; Dillon 1996b; Tarrant 2000; Dillon 2003. Admittedly, the extent to which the Skeptics of the New Academy can be said to have been Platonists is subject to dispute.

36. Hurling charges of heresy against those who deviated from Academic doctrine was, it seems, more a feature of Middle Platonism than of Neoplatonism. Numenius, Atticus, Antiochus, and Philo of Larissa, among others, come to mind in this regard.

37. Boys-Stones 2001, 102, asserts that "Platonism is at root . . . the belief that Plato's philosophy was dogmatic and authoritative." As Boys-Stones goes on to argue, this does not mean that Plato's words were always accepted at face value. His true meaning had to be interpreted: "Platonists were able to commit themselves to the truth of a proposition *on the grounds that* Plato had said it, and it might be, even before they themselves understood *why* it was true." "Platonist philosophy involved *imprimis* puzzling out what Plato meant as a means of advancing toward knowledge: and the real uncertainties that might be thrown up by this exegetical process (as, e.g., in Plutarch's *Platonic Questions*) show that the process was quite honest in its concept, not a disingenuous appropriation of Plato for doctrines worked out in spite of him" (103).

is that it is resolutely and irreducibly top-down rather than bottom-up. A top-down approach to philosophical problems rejects and a bottom-up approach accepts the claim that the most important and puzzling phenomena we encounter in this world can be explained by seeking the simplest elements out of which they are composed. The top-down approach appeals to first or higher or irreducible principles to account for these phenomena—among them, human personhood and the personal attributes of freedom, higher cognition, the presence of evil, and the very being of a world. The top-down approach holds that answers to questions about these phenomena are never going to be satisfactorily given in terms of elementary physical particles from which things 'evolve' or upon which the phenomena 'supervene.' According to Neoplatonism 'Platonism' is basic 'top-downism' and its only true opponent is 'bottom-upism' represented, for example, by materialists of various sorts such as the Atomists.

Here is a schematic compendium of the main elements of Platonism according to those who believed that Aristotle's writings were in harmony with Platonism:

1. *The universe has a systematic unity.* The practice of systematizing Platonism may be compared with the formulation of a theology based upon scriptures as well as other canonical evidentiary sources. The hypothesis that a true systematic philosophy is possible at all rests upon an assumption of cosmic unity. This is Platonism's most profound legacy from the Pre-Socratics. These philosophers held that the world is a unity in the sense that its constituents and the laws according to which it operates are really and intelligibly interrelated. *Because* the world is a unity, a systematic understanding of it is possible. Thus particular doctrines in metaphysics, epistemology, ethics, and so on are ultimately relatable within the system. More than this, they are inseparable because the principles that enable us to formulate doctrine in one area are identical with those that enable us to formulate doctrine in another. Many scholars have pointed out the *unsystematic* nature of Platonism understood as consisting of the raw data of the dialogues. This fact is not necessarily inconsistent with the amenability of claims made in the dialogues to systematization.[38]

2. *The systematic unity is an explanatory hierarchy.* The Platonic view of the world—the key to the system—is that the universe is to be seen in hierarchical manner. It is to be understood uncompromisingly from the top down. The hierarchy is ordered basically according to two

38. Although the so-called Tübingen school of Platonic scholarship rests upon a version of systematic Platonism supposedly drawn principally from the unwritten teachings, I am not equating the systematic aspect of Platonism with the Tübingen school's version of that; rather, given that Platonism is essentially systematic in that it is based on the relatively simple assumptions outlined here, the Tübingen school's version is only one among many possibilities.

criteria. First, the simple precedes the complex, and second, the intelligible precedes the sensible. The precedence in both cases is not temporal but ontological and conceptual. That is, understanding the complex and the sensible depends on understanding the simple and the intelligible because the latter are explanatory of the former. The ultimate explanatory principle in the universe, therefore, must be unqualifiedly simple. For this reason, Platonism is in a sense reductivist, though not in the way that a bottom-up philosophy is. It is conceptually reductivist not materially reductivist. The simplicity of the first principle is contrasted with the simplicity of elements out of which things are composed according to a bottom-up approach. Whether or to what extent the unqualifiedly simple can also be intelligible or in some sense transcends intelligibility is a deep question within Platonism.

3. *The divine constitutes an irreducible explanatory category.* An essential part of the systematic hierarchy is a divine principle adduced first and foremost to explain the order of the sensible world or the world of becoming. Platonism converges on the notion that the divine has complete explanatory 'reach': that is, there is nothing that it cannot explain. Thus ontology and theology are inseparable. The Platonic notion of divinity includes an irremovable though frequently highly attenuated personal element. This attenuation in part follows along the diverse efforts to employ both the intelligible and the simple, as well as the divine, to explain everything else. The residual personhood of the divine agent of transient order is retained in part owing to the fundamental Platonic exhortation to the person to 'become like god' (see [5] below). Additionally, benevolence and providence are viewed as essential features of the divine, equally in an attenuated sense corresponding to the 'depersonalization' of the divine.

4. *The psychological constitutes an irreducible explanatory category.* For Platonism the universe is itself alive and filled with living things. Soul is the principle of life. Life is not viewed as epiphenomenal or supervenient on what is nonliving. It is not explicable in terms of that which is nonliving. On the contrary, soul has a unique explanatory role in the systematic hierarchy. Though soul is fundamentally an explanatory principle, individual souls are fitted into the overall hierarchy in a subordinate manner. One of the central issues facing the Platonists was the relation between intellect, intellection, and the intelligibles, on the one hand, and soul on the other. Just as the psychical was thought to be irreducible to the material, so the intelligible was thought to be irreducible to the psychical. All striving by anything capable of striving is to be understood as in a way the reverse of the derivation of the complex from the simple, the sensible from the intelligible. Thus the intellectual was not an aspect of or derived from the psychical, but was prior to that.

5. *Persons belong to the systematic hierarchy and personal happiness consists in achieving a lost position within the hierarchy.* All Platonists accepted the view that in some sense the person was the soul and the soul was immortal. Since perhaps the most important feature of the divine was immortality, the goal or τέλος of embodied personal existence was viewed as 'becoming like god.' But obviously one does not have to strive to become what one already is. The task of 'becoming like god' is typically situated within the fundamental polarity in the general Greek concept of nature or φύσις between 'what is' and 'what ought to be.' Thus normativity is woven into the account of what is objectively real. We are exhorted to become what we really or truly or ideally are. One might say that the first principle of Platonic ethics is that one must 'become like god.'

6. *Moral and aesthetic valuation follows the hierarchy.* Thus things are relatively good or bad, beautiful or ugly, depending on their position within the hierarchy. The first principle of all is the standard of moral and aesthetic valuation. Absolute evil or ugliness, however this may be conceived, is identified with maximum 'distance' from the first principle. Owing to the unicity of this first principle, there is a coincidence or convergence of the principles of moral and aesthetic valuation.

7. *The epistemological order is included within the metaphysical order.* Modes of cognition are hierarchically gradable according to the hierarchical levels of objective reality. The highest mode of cognition corresponds to the first explanatory principles. All modes of cognition including sense perception and requiring sense perception as a condition for their operation are inferior to the highest mode. That persons can be the subject both of the highest mode of cognition and of the lower modes indicates an ambiguity or conflict in personhood between the desires of the embodied human being and those of the ideal disembodied cognitive agent. The conflict is reflected, for example, in the differing attractions of the contemplative and the practical.

This rather austere description is primarily intended to accommodate the existence of *varieties* of Platonism. Varieties of Platonism can actually contain contradictory positions on particular issues.[39] For example, Platonists who agree on the priority of the intelligible to the sensible or, more accurately, the imperfectly intelligible, can disagree on what the parts of the intelligible universe are and whether or not some of these are reducible to others. To take another example, Platonists who agree that

39. Indeed, Plotinus IV 8. 1, 27ff., mildly ventures the claim that there are apparent discrepancies in Plato himself: "He does not seem to be saying the same thing everywhere" [οὐ ταὐτὸν λέγων πανταχῇ φανεῖται]. Hence, Plato must be interpreted, and this interpretation must be according to criteria that are the fundamental principles of Platonism.

there is a first principle of all can hold contradictory views on its activity, its knowability, and so on. One last relatively minor example is that it is not part of the essence of Platonism to be for or against theurgical practices. But it does belong to the essence of Platonism to hold that the goal of human existence is to be somehow reunited with that from which humans are or have been separated. The view about how this is accomplished in part reflects metaphysical considerations about the relationship between persons and their intellects. It is for this reason somewhat misleading to characterize Platonism in terms of dualism(s) such as mind (soul)/body or even intelligible/sensible. The hierarchical explanatory framework of top-downism is conceptually prior to these dualisms. A type of Platonism might indeed posit such dualisms. However, more basic is the essential explanatory realism.

Here is why the dualistic characterizations of Platonism are derivative. Platonism holds that phenomena in the sensible world can be explained ultimately only by intelligible principles. But these phenomena are themselves not coherently characterizable as nonintelligible; if they were, there would be nothing to explain. So, the putative dualism of sensible/intelligible disguises rather than reveals the fundamental assumption. Again, the dualism mind (soul)/body is secondary to the Platonic position that embodied human existence has to be understood or explained in terms of intelligible ideals. Thus embodied persons are images of disembodied ideals. If anything, one insisting on dualism as a property of Platonism would be more accurate to describe it as a dualism of embodied person/disembodied person rather than a dualism of mind (soul)/body.

Understanding Platonism as what underlies the varieties of Platonism explains why some things are missing from the foregoing list.[40] First, as noted above, anything that might be termed 'Socratic ethics' is missing. The ethics of Platonism as the Neoplatonists understood it flowed from the combination of the ontology, theology, and psychology as represented largely in what have come to be known as the middle and late dialogues. The exhortation to 'become like god' is embedded in the technical metaphysical and cosmological views of *Theaetetus* and *Timaeus*.[41] Accordingly, there was for them nothing uniquely edifying in the so-called Socratic paradoxes, found principally though certainly not exclusively in the so-called early dialogues.

Second, the theory of Forms is not explicitly mentioned—partly because of the Neoplatonic assumption that the account of Forms in the dialogues needed to be supplemented with the theory of ultimate principles as it was

---

40. Compare the somewhat different schema in Merlan 1953, 1. In this book Merlan is a strong exponent of the Platonism of Aristotle. Baltes 1999, concentrating mainly on the formulations of Platonism before the Neoplatonic period, adds to his sketch of the elements of Platonism the specific doctrines of (a) the eternity of the world, (b) reincarnation, (c) personal freedom, and (d) the idea that knowledge is recollection. I doubt that (b) is an essential part of Platonism, even if no Platonist in fact rejected it.

41. See *Tht.* 176B and *Tim.* 90A–D.

described by Aristotle. In addition Aristotle's evident criticism of that theory, especially in *On the Ideas* and *Metaphysics,* did give some commentators pause about the status of Forms in Plato's own thinking. What was beyond dispute, however, is that Platonism is committed to the existence of an intelligible—that is, incorporeal realm—that is ontologically prior to the sensible realm. The precise status of the elements of the intelligible realm—τὰ νοητά—was a legitimate topic of dispute *within* the Platonic 'community.'[42] Thus a question such as "What is the range of Forms?" was widely debated.[43] What is crucial to appreciate in this regard is that all discussion about Forms was carried out on the assumption that Forms are not themselves ultimate ontological principles, given their plurality and internal complexity. The textual justification for this assumption, wholly independent of reliance on Aristotle's account of first principles, was first of all the *Republic* passage referring to the Idea of the Good.[44]

Third, there is no mention of politics, neither of the ideal state of *Republic* nor of the somewhat different views of *Statesman* and *Laws.* No doubt all sorts of extraphilosophical explanations can be adduced to explain the relative indifference of Platonists between the third and sixth centuries C.E. to political philosophy, including the increasing danger to pagans who engaged in politics. More to the point, however, is that Platonists understood political philosophy to belong to the discussion of "popular and political virtue" as described by Plato.[45] This was inferior, albeit instrumental, to the virtue that constituted assimilation to the divine. Consequently, the teaching of political philosophy, narrowly construed, was basically ignored. One entering upon the serious study of Platonism might be assumed to have already assimilated the lessons of "popular" virtue.

One can I think appreciate more fully what is included and what is excluded from the foregoing account of Platonism if one reflects on the systematic unity of its various features. As in Stoicism, in the Platonism of our period everything is connected with everything else. The difference, of course, is that whereas Stoicism is more or less consistently materialistic, Platonism maintains a nonmaterialistic and hierarchical explanatory framework. Specific problems relating to the natural world in general—that is, problems about living and nonliving physical entities, cognition, language, and morality—are all addressed within this framework. For Platonism the sensible properties of things are never the starting points for explanations,

42. See, e.g., Porphyry *V. Plot.* chap. 18, in which Porphyry recounts his own doubts about the status of the intelligible in relation to the intellect. In chap. 20 he mentions Longinus's implicit opposition to Plotinus's account of Ideas, presumably the account that makes them inseparable from a divine intellect (cf. V 5; VI 7; etc.).

43. See, e.g., Syrianus *In Met.* 107, 5ff.

44. See *Rep.* 509B and Krämer 1969a on the early interpretations of this crucial passage.

45. See *Phd.* 82A11. Cf. 69B6–7; *Rep.* 365C3–4; 500D8; 518D3–519A6. Marinus *V. Proc.* chap. 13 mentions that Syrianus included Aristotle's political works in his teaching of Proclus. O'Meara (2003) argues rightly, I think, that Neoplatonists saw political philosophy as belonging to the 'program' of 'divinization,' that is, assimilation to the divine.

though they may well be the starting points for arriving at explanations. The sensible world is always understood as explained by the intelligible world. Specifically, it is an image produced by the intelligible world. There is nothing self-explanatory about an image. Its 'real' inner workings are to be sought in that of which it is an image. Because there is an all-encompassing hierarchy ordered in terms of complexity and intelligibility, the orientation of investigation is thoroughly 'vertical' and almost never 'horizontal.' Thus there is little room for political philosophy, since political philosophy must start with irreducible political principles. But there cannot be such in Platonism. All principles for Platonism are to be located within that which is relatively simple and intelligible. The concrete and contingent nature of the distinctly political militates against the top-down approach.

The systematic unity of Platonism can be seen most clearly in its treatment of all matters of cognition. For Platonism, cognition is to be understood, again, hierarchically, with the highest form of cognition, νόησις or 'intellection,' as the paradigm for all inferior forms, including those which involve the sensible world. The representationalist aspect of all the images of this paradigm is a central focus of Neoplatonic interest. In addition, cognition is what most closely identifies souls or persons, with possession of the highest form of cognition constituting the ideal state. Since the highest form of cognition is a *non*representational state, one in which the incorporeal cognizer is in a sense identified with the objects of cognition, psychology and epistemology are inseparable from the ontological and theological principles. In short, to understand fully a matter relating to language or belief or rational desire is ultimately to relate those embodied phenomena to the simple and intelligible first principles.

Platonism by Negation

I would like now to enrich my presentation of Platonism by suggesting another approach. One might suspect a distorting effect of the anachronistic Neoplatonic 'systematization' of Platonism. It must certainly be granted that a 'system' is not so much what we find in the dialogues of Plato at any rate as what we make of what we find. I have already suggested that Platonism is inevitably and rightly taken to be something more than the sum of the conclusions of arguments in the dialogues. Nevertheless, in an effort to narrow the gap between what Plato says and the claims made about what Plato means, I suggest we consider for a bit the consequences for a philosopher who rejects the positions that are decisively rejected in the dialogues. Plato has quite a lot to say about his historical predecessors and contemporaries, and he is also often precise about what in their views he finds unacceptable. I shall try to show that if we look at Platonism as the philosophical position that results from the rejection or negation of these views, we shall be in a better position to see what it means to hold that Aristotle's philosophy is in harmony with Platonism. Although the construction of a philosophy by negation may appear obscurantist, it is at least not entirely out of keeping with the approach endemic to the competing philosophical schools beginning in the Middle Platonic period.

It will be convenient to begin with the argument in Plato's *Parmenides* whereby Socrates aims to refute Zeno's defense of Parmenidean monism. According to Plato, Zeno argued that "If things are many, then the same things must be both the same and not the same. But this is impossible: for it is not possible for things that are not the same to be the same nor for things that are the same not to be the same. So, if it is impossible for things that are not the same to be the same or for things that are the same to be not the same, it is also impossible that things should be a plurality. For if there were a plurality, they would have impossible attributes."[46] Socrates' solution to this problem is basically a theory of Forms.[47] Things *can* be both the same (ὅμοια) and not the same (ἀνόμοια) so long as we recognize the 'self-identical' (αὐτὸ καθ' αὑτό) Forms of Sameness and Not-Sameness and distinguish them from the attributes of sameness and not-sameness that things possess. In other words, a plurality is possible because any two things can be the same insofar as they are each one and not the same insofar as each is different from the other. The qualification 'insofar as' indicates that being either the same or not the same does not exclusively identify the thing, thereby producing a contradiction. The qualification is justified only because there exists in itself a Form of Sameness and Not-Sameness, and these are nonidentical.

The claim made by Socrates is perfectly generalizable and applicable to the explanation of any case of predication, whether of contraries such as same and not the same or of noncontrary attributes. Plato in effect interprets the Eleatic argument against plurality as extreme nominalism, avoidable only by a theory of Forms.[48] Part of what Platonism amounts to then is the rejection of the extreme nominalism that monism is. But this still leaves much scope for disagreement about the precise nature of the explanation

---

46. *Parm.* 127E2–8. Cf. *Phdr.* 261D. It is, I think, significant that none of the arguments against plurality quoted or paraphrased by Simplicius and Philoponus are exactly of this form. See Simplicius *In Phys.* 97, 12–16; 99, 7–16; 138, 3–6; 139, 19–140, 6; 140, 27–141, 8; Philoponus *In Phys.* 42, 9–43, 6. Plato reads Zeno such that the theory of Forms is the solution to the problem of how a plurality is possible. I leave aside here any question of whether Plato correctly understood the Eleatic position.

47. *Parm.* 128E–130A. For reasons that will emerge, it is more accurate to speak about *a* theory of Forms here than *the* theory of Forms.

48. Nominalism is the view that only individuals exist or what amounts to the same thing, the view that two things cannot be the same. Extreme nominalism is the view that there is only one individual or that "all is one." See Allen 1983, 80: "Aristotle's and Plato's diagnosis of Eleatic monism is the same: that monism rested on an implicit and unstated nominalism" As Allen notes, Aristotle *Phys.* A 3, 186a22–32, denies the fact that a thing is distinct from its attributes entails that its attributes are separate. The Neoplatonists, I think, assumed that a solution to extreme nominalism which stopped short of positing the separateness of Forms (or something doing the job that Forms do) was not sustainable. Moreover, Aristotle indirectly concedes this in his *Metaphysics* by arguing for the relative imperfection of sensible composites. See further my "Plato on Identity, Sameness, and Difference," forthcoming in *Review of Metaphysics.*

for the possibility of predication among all those who believe that an explanation is necessary. What would place Aristotle outside the Platonic camp would be an explicit denial of the claim that such an explanation is necessary or possible. As we shall see, a doctrine of universals does not constitute such a denial, since universals are not in any way the explanation for the possibility of predication.[49] Nor does Aristotle's repeated insistence on the unacceptability of certain accounts of the separation of the *explanans* constitute a blanket rejection of the possibility of explanation.

In his *Sophist*, Plato confronts Parmenides again, this time within the context of his rejection of four views of "what is real" (τὸ ὄν).[50] The first two are pluralistic and monistic: the pluralists (of various sorts) tell us what is real, such as the hot and cold or wet and dry, whereas the monists claim that reality is one. The latter two, the so-called giants and gods, actually seek to identify reality in some way. The former claim that 'reality' (οὐσία) is identical with 'body' (σῶμα).[51] The latter, whom Plato calls "friends of the Forms," claim that 'real reality' (ὄντως οὐσία) belongs only to that which is 'always in the same state.'[52] Pluralists are dismissed because though they tell us what things are real, they do not define reality. Monists fail to distinguish reality from the one thing they claim to be real.

The response to the giants or materialists is different. It is accepted by the interlocutors that they will admit that the virtues such as wisdom or justice which can come to be present in a soul are not themselves bodies.[53] Therefore, they cannot identify reality with being a body. It may be supposed that Plato is here presenting a false dichotomy: if something is not a body, it is bodiless. But this ignores the fact that though the attributes of bodies—for example, their surfaces—are not bodies, that fact does not entail that they are bodiless, in the sense of being entities that exist separate from bodies. The materialist can benignly insist that to be real is to be either a body or an attribute of a body, where all attributes are dependent on bodies for their existence.[54]

Apart from the obvious but perhaps not fatal point that this position, like that of the pluralists, tells us what is real without telling us what 'real' means, Platonism will want to insist that if 'wise' or 'just' or indeed any predicate is 'something' (τι) real, then there must be a separate entity whose name this predicate bears, even if the presence of an instance of that entity's nature is *not* separate from the subject. Materialism, unlike monism, does not purport to show the impossibility of its contradictory.

---

49. Cf. *Parm.* 132B–C, where Parmenides instructs Socrates that Forms are not 'concepts' (νοήματα) in the mind but what concepts are of: namely, the 'ones' that explain plurality. A universal 'predicable of many' is from this perspective a type of concept.

50. *Soph.* 242B–249D.

51. Ibid., 246B1. Cf. *Tht.* 155E.

52. Soph. 248A11–12.

53. Ibid., 247B7–C2.

54. Cf. *Phd.* 92E4–95A3, where Socrates shows that the soul is not immaterial in the way a 'harmony' is; it must be an incorporeal *entity*.

But if the materialists will concede that it is not possible that *only* bodies—that is, three-dimensional solids—exist, then they will eventually be forced to agree not only that incorporeal or nonbodily entities exist but that these are prior in existence.[55]

The refutation of materialism in this passage is like the refutation of monism in *Parmenides* in insisting on the reality of the complex objects of predicational judgments.[56] And it is reasonable that if Plato held that a rejection of nominalism leads to a postulation of separate Forms, then he also held that the explanation of how predication is possible entails the rejection of materialism. In other words, one who rejected materialism held a position that was at least in harmony with one that holds to the existence of separate incorporeal entities.

The famous definition of reality that the Eleatic Stranger offers the materialists at *Sophist* 247E1–4—namely, that "the things that are real are nothing else but the power [δύναμις] of acting [ποιεῖν] or being affected [παθεῖν]"—is clearly provisional, as the immediately following lines show. That it is also dialectical follows from the fact that its refutation would proceed exactly as does the refutation of the pluralists' account of reality.[57] That is, reality is clearly something other than either acting or being affected, though everything that does either is real.

The same definition is also used to defeat the friends of the Forms.[58] They hold that only Forms are real, but if so, then the activity that consists in knowing Forms has no part in the real. Indeed, asks the Stranger, are we to be persuaded that it is true that "motion, life, soul, and thought are not present in the perfectly real [παντελῶς ὄντι], that it neither lives nor thinks, but stands alone solemn and holy, having no intellect [νοῦν], being immovable?"[59] This rhetorical question is answered in the negative. Motion, life, soul, and thought belong in the perfectly real. Therefore, the perfectly real is not motionless. Hence, we cannot admit that the real is only changeless, nor can we, if we wish to include intellect in what is real, admit that the real is only what is changing. For without things that are at rest there can be no objects for intellect to attain. Therefore, that which is real or the sum of all that is real must include both what is changeless and what is changing.

---

55. At 247C, Plato allows that a diehard materialist might not agree that anything other than 'what he holds in his hands' exists.

56. This is why Antisthenes is sometimes identified either as the recalcitrant or the gentle materialist. For as Aristotle tells us, *Met.* Δ 29, 1024b32–34, Antisthenes held that a thing could be named only by its own formula, thereby making false judgments almost impossible. That is, he held that any collocations of words in a statement referring to something must all be names for the identical thing. In effect he denies the possibility of genuine predication or the possibility that two things could be the same. See Ross 1924, v. 1, 346–347.

57. See Diès 1932, 31–35.

58. *Soph.* 248A4–249D4.

59. Ibid. 248E6–249A2.

I shall return to this passage whose importance to Neoplatonism can scarcely be overemphasized. For the moment I want only to make several basic points. First, this argument does not claim that Forms change. On the contrary, it insists that there must be unchanging objects if intellect exists. But the argument does not say that these must be Forms or that they must be Forms as conceived of by their 'friends.' What Plato is rejecting is the exclusion of the activity of knowing from the realm of the really real. That is, he is rejecting the view that the only things that are real are Forms and that therefore, if Forms are known, they are known by something that is not real or less than real.

The problem then becomes discerning what the inclusion of intellect, and so on, in the really real amounts to. Why does intellect have to be so included in order for there to be knowledge of Forms? The friends of the Forms object to the claim that knowledge is an activity because this claim seems to entail that the Forms, by being known, are being affected. But why should this lead the Eleatic Stranger to insist that if knowledge, and so on, exists, then it belongs to the really real? Logically, he should only be claiming that *if* knowledge exists, and if knowledge is an activity, and if the objects of knowledge are thereby acted upon, *then* change (i.e., being acted upon) belongs to what is really real because it must belong to Forms. But in fact, as we have just seen, he goes on to insist that the objects of knowledge must be changeless.[60]

Why does that which knows Forms have to be as real as they? At least one part of the answer to this question is that intellect must be the same kind of thing as what it knows. This is exactly what Plato argued in his *Phaedo* in the so-called Affinity Argument.[61] The soul, or a part of it, must be like the Forms in order for knowledge, suitably defined, to be acquired. But we do possess knowledge, as was shown in the Recollection Argument. Therefore, our soul, or a part of it, is, like Forms, an incorporeal entity, separate from the sensible world. Thus the argument that knowledge exists is connected with the rejection of at least one version of the theory of Forms and, indirectly, with the rejection of materialism. For Plato, the falsity of materialism establishes the identity of the knowable as nonmaterial or incorporeal. Then

---

60. Cherniss (1944, 437–439) argues that what the friends are forced to admit is a Form of Motion, though he goes on to point out that the motion of intellect is not physical motion and does not imply a change in what is known. But it is difficult to see why the friends would hesitate for a moment to posit a Form of Motion, assuming that this Form is not itself in motion. Actually, the change assumed to be present in the really real—namely, 'the motion of intellect' (κίνησις νοῦ, *Lg.* 897D3)—was understood by Neoplatonists as equivalent to the 'activity of intellect' (ἡ ἐνέργεια νοῦ) attributed by Aristotle to the prime unmoved mover. Cf. *Tim.* 89A1–3. See *Met.* Λ 7, 1072b27. The term ἡ ἐνέργεια was invented by Aristotle to indicate a sort of κίνησις having no imperfection, that is, without potentiality. Aristotle identifies this activity with 'life' (ζωή), in Plato, the essential property of soul. Also, cf. Plotinus VI 2. 15, 6–8 on the identity of κίνησις and ἐνέργεια in intellect; Simplicius *In Phys.* 405, 24ff.; 822, 22–823, 4.

61. See *Phd.* 78B4–84B8, and Ross 1951, 111. I have discussed this argument in Gerson 2003, 79–88.

assuming that knowledge is at least possible, the way is open for an argument that it is possible only for a knower who is also incorporeal.[62]

There is perhaps more to it than this. For one might suggest that the incorporeal soul with its cognitive life is like changeless Forms insofar as it is incorporeal, but unlike them insofar as it is changing or in motion. And it is the latter property that should exclude it from the realm of the really real. It is for this reason that Neoplatonists generally supposed that Plato's insistence on the necessary inclusion of intellect within the realm of the really real implied the permanent connection of *some* intellect with Forms and the concomitant characterization of the really real as being other than unqualifiedly changeless or inactive.[63] In other words, the inclusion of intellect within the realm of the really real is assumed to be the inclusion of the activity of thinking within the really real.

In addition to Plato's rejection of Eleatic monism, materialism, and at least one version of a theory of Forms, there are numerous places in the dialogues where he confronts his predecessors, including Anaxagoras in *Phaedo*, Protagoras in the dialogue that bears his name as well as in *Theaetetus* along with Heraclitus, and Cratylus in his eponymous dialogue. It seems to me, however, that the core of Platonism negatively defined is the enterprise of drawing out the conclusions of the rejection of nominalism and materialism, which are in fact two faces of the same doctrine. Admittedly, this makes Platonism a very large tent, but not an infinitely large one. Anyone who agreed in rejecting nominalism and materialism but who declined to draw the same consequences from this rejection that Plato does might reasonably be thought to be in harmony with Plato despite his inadequacies. But the fact that Aristotle does not draw *all* the consequences of this rejection should not be taken to imply that he draws *none* of them. Between *all* and *none* there is the terrain upon which harmonists and antiharmonists do battle. Much of this book is concerned with showing that Neoplatonists were not fundamentally misguided in arguing that on many matters Aristotle did endorse the consequences of the rejection of nominalism and materialism, whereas many later scholars as well as defenders of Aristotle were wrong to conclude that he did not.

Is There a Non-Platonic Aristotelianism?

If the Neoplatonic harmonist assumption is correct, then the account of Platonism given above is at the same time an account of the ultimate

---

62. The claim that knowledge is impossible is not, as one might suppose, something a skeptic can maintain. Such a claim would be patently dogmatic. At best, a skeptic could claim that someone does not have the knowledge he claims to have. In *Phaedo*, Plato asserts in the Recollection Argument that we could not make the judgments about sensibles that we do—namely, that they are inferior representations of Forms—unless we had previous knowledge of Forms. The Affinity Argument then goes on to posit that we could not have the knowledge of Forms that we have just been shown to have had unless we were of the same nature as Forms—that is, incorporeal.

63. As we shall see below, there are independent reasons for supposing that Forms cannot ever be bereft of intellect.

principles of Aristotle's philosophy. This would be true even if Aristotle introduced additional special principles for nascent sciences.[64] One way to defeat the Neoplatonic assumption is to demonstrate that Aristotelians articulated and embraced distinctive Aristotelian principles in direct opposition to Platonism. In short, if the Neoplatonists are mistaken, then we should be able to discover expressions of a genuinely non-Platonic Aristotelianism.

One obvious place to look for a hypothetical Platonism-free Aristotelianism is among the Peripatetic successors to Aristotle. We can identify a plethora of self-proclaimed followers of Aristotle, from his great successor Theophrastus down to Critolaus of Phaselis at the end of the second century B.C.E. The fragments of the writings of these philosophers have been collected by Fritz Wehrli in his monumental multivolume work. It is instructive to study these fragments with a view to determining what Aristotelianism in fact meant to those who thought of themselves more or less as followers of Aristotle.

Such a study is not, I believe, a comfort to antiharmonists. Wehrli himself in his *Rückblick* on the ten volumes of fragments avers that the Peripatetics did not discover in the works of Aristotle a unified set of principles. But Wehrli also accepts the Jaegerian hypothesis of a Platonic–anti-Platonic axis of development in Aristotle. What Wehrli means by claiming that the Peripatetics did not have a distinctive Aristotelian basis for their philosophical works is that they did not have a distinctive *anti-Platonic* basis. According to him, Peripatetic philosophy crumbled into incoherence because the various empirical research projects of the Peripatetics could not find in Aristotle a clear theoretical basis.[65] Wehrli assumes that this basis would have to have been anti-Platonic. I am not now claiming that these Peripatetics were cryptoharmonists. I am only suggesting that some two hundred years of Peripatetic philosophizing without the harmonist assumption did not yield at the end something that could be called anti-Platonic Aristotelianism.

A more complex situation is found among Peripatetics from Andronicus of Rhodes in the first century B.C.E. to Alexander of Aphrodisias. This is in part owing to the syncretism I mentioned in my introduction, particularly attempts to reach common ground between Stoicism and Aristotelianism.[66] Andronicus's division of the Aristotelian corpus into logical, physical, and practical works plainly represents an attempt at acknowledging a systematic order in the *esoterica* or at least an attempt at imposing

64. See Krämer 1964, 140–149, for a detailed argument that Aristotle's first philosophy is a version of Academic Derivationssystemen: that is, 'top-down' metaphysics. One need not support all the facets of Krämer's account of Plato's unwritten doctrines to agree with the general approach of this argument.

65. See Wehrli 1967, 10:95–128.

66. See Moraux 1973, 1:273–275, who discusses the matter in reference to elements in the doxography of Arius Didymus (first century B.C.E.).

a systematic order of study on it. But the latter would make no sense unless there were a system to study.[67]

This division appears to be a commonplace in antiquity and to go back at least to the Academy. According to Sextus Empiricus, it is found in Xenocrates, Plato, Aristotle, and Posidonius.[68] In a Platonist and an incipient harmonizer such as Alcinous, it is not surprising to see such a division attributed to both Plato and Aristotle.[69] But it is far from clear that in Andronicus a systematic space for Aristotelianism is being carved out different from that for either Platonism or Stoicism. Indeed, if we can presume the influence on Andronicus by Antiochus of Ascalon through Cicero, it would not be surprising if Andronicus's division of the Aristotelian material was actually based on the conviction that Stoicism, Aristotelianism, and Platonism constituted basically one philosophical position with numerous variations.[70] Certainly there is no trace of a suggestion in any references to the division of Aristotle's works that it is a division according to a systematic unity that is distinctly non-Platonic or even non-Stoic.[71]

Aspasius the Peripatetic philosopher and commentator, whose sole surviving work is the *Commentary on Aristotle's Nicomachean Ethics*, dated by Jonathan Barnes at around 131 C.E., evinces no embarrassment whatsoever in his appeal to Platonic concepts on behalf of his interpretation of Aristotle's ethics.[72] We know far too little of Aspasius's own views to speak with confidence about any syncretism in them or of any illicit cohabiting with the Platonists. Nevertheless, there are indications in his *Commentary* that he was at least not allergic to understanding Aristotle in Platonic terms.[73]

---

67. On Andronicus's division, see ibid., 58–94. Porphyry *V. Plot.* 24 says that he followed Andronicus in dividing the works of Plotinus by subject. But Porphyry's division is more than that; it reflects a view of the Plotinian system. Also see Barnes 1997 for a deflationary view of Andronicus's role in the transmission and ordering of the corpus of Aristotle's writings.

68. See Sextus Empiricus *M.* VII 16–19. Cf. Aristotle *Top.* A 14, 105b19–25. See also D.L. VII 39, which says that Zeno of Citium was the first among the Stoics to make the division. On Plato's acceptance of the division, see Antiochus of Ascalon *apud* Cicero *Acad.* I 19.

69. See Alcinous *Didask.* chap. 3, where instead of the terms 'logical,' 'physical,' and 'ethical,' Alcinous employs the terms 'dialectical,' 'theoretical,' and 'practical.' See Dillon 1993, 57–58.

70. See Cicero *Acad.* I 17.

71. See Gottschalk 1997, 114, for some remarks on the question of whether the systematizing of the Aristotelian corpus represents a distortion of Aristotle's approach to philosophy. Gottschalk suggests that to a certain extent it does, for Aristotle was as much a *Problemdenker* as a *Systemdenker*.

72. Barnes (1999, 5–6), though he acknowledges Platonic parallels in the text of Aspasius's commentary, is skeptical of claims that Aspasius was a Platonist as well as a Peripatetic or even "a Peripaetetic whose views were strongly colored by Platonism." But I suspect that Barnes is assuming that to pledge allegiance to Aristotle is perforce to forswear Platonism. This assumption seems to me to be unjustified.

73. See Ierodiakonou 1999, 161, on the "view shared by Peripaetetics and Platonists" about the "remission and intensification of virtue"; Sedley 1999b, 165, on Aspasius's interpretation of Aristotle's account of ἀκρασία as employing a Platonic division of reason and appetite; Berti 1999, 187–190, on Aspasius's assimilation of Aristotelian πρὸς ἕν equivocity to the Platonic 'sameness' (ὁμοιότης) of the sensible world to intelligible paradigms. These examples (esp.

Alexander of Aphrodisias as perhaps the first professional Aristotelian of antiquity might have been expected to reveal a strong interest in articulating distinct Aristotelian principles, though it is admittedly not so odd that we do not find them in his commentaries on particular works. There are indeed many places in Alexander's commentaries and in his personal works as well in which he criticizes both Stoic and Platonic positions in defense of his understanding of what Aristotle taught.[74] But there are also other places in which his interpretation of Aristotle is in line with harmonization.[75]

At least two ways have been employed to construct an anti-Platonic Aristotelianism. One way occurs within the context of attempts to bring pagan Greek philosophy generally into the service of revealed theology. With Christian theological concerns in mind, John Philoponus will emphasize the superiority of Plato over Aristotle and Thomas Aquinas will do the opposite. In both cases the superiority is to be understood *au fond*, not merely in detail.[76] The other way is to refuse to connect particular Aristotelian arguments with any principles at all, apart from methodological ones, and to refuse to see Aristotle as anything other than a 'problem thinker.' Aristotle can thus be inoculated against Platonic contamination. As we shall see, part of the harmonists' strategy, in their role as commentators, is to insist that Aristotelian doctrines can and should be studied in their scientific integrity. That means that in the special sciences the specific or limited principles to be employed define the science, which is then in a sense self-contained. But this is *not* the case for the study of nature generally or for metaphysics, psychology, and ethics; in these areas fundamental and universal principles must be employed. And these are, they claim, drawn from Platonism, as outlined above. Thus if one focuses on, say, Aristotle's formal logic or his treatment of the parts of animals or rhetoric, one can plausibly suppose an Aristotelianism that is, if not anti-Platonic, at least

first) suggest philosophical commonplaces among Platonists, Peripatetics, and Stoics, too. But the existence of the supposed commonplaces should of course not be taken as evidence of philosophical disagreement. Sometimes it seems that scholars hold that appeals to such commonplaces simply must mask such disagreements.

74. See esp. Moraux 2001, 317–394, on Alexander's noetics, and 491–501, on the fragments of Alexander's commentary on Λ of Aristotle's *Metaphysics* as preserved in Averroes. See also the accompanying study of Sharples 2001, 513–592, on Alexander's attack on Stoic determinism, and 593–614, on the extant ethical material where the similarities between Alexander's interpretations of Aristotle and Platonism are at least as significant as any divergence that Alexander claims. See infra chap. 7.

75. See supra n. 31 and infra chaps. 5 and 7. Armstrong (1967, 122–123) concludes his discussion of Alexander with the observation that despite his rejection of Plato on several points, "in Alexander's noetics we see Platonism staging its comeback within the Peripatos." And in his criticism of the view of Zeller (n. 4), he argues that "Alexander . . . revived what Zeller himself considered to be the residue of Platonism in Aristotle." Here the metaphor of development gets a nice workout and embellishment, with the 'salvagable' elements of Platonism being 'refurbished.'

76. I cannot here argue the claim that, ironically, Aquinas employs Aristotelianism as he understands it in the service of what is in fact a Christianized version of Platonism.

a-Platonic. But if one turns to the study of nature generally, being, the human person, and the human good, this stance is less plausible (or so I argue in subsequent chapters). In order to construct an anti-Platonic Aristotelianism with regard to these matters, one would have to do violence to the texts or else start with an assumption about Aristotle's development that could not be supported by the texts except by the patent circularity of arranging them according to such an assumption.

CHAPTER TWO

The Exoteric Writings and the Early Aristotle

Beginning with the appearance of Werner Jaeger's seminal work, the phrase 'the Platonism of Aristotle' has usually been taken to refer to a 'phase' in Aristotle's philosophical development. In his book *Aristoteles: Grundlegung einer Geschichte seiner Entwicklung,* which appeared in 1923, Jaeger argued that a developmentalist hypothesis was needed to make sense of the Aristotelian corpus.[1] Without such a hypothesis, Jaeger argued, inconsistencies within the corpus would remain unresolved.[2] Specifically, a number of Aristotelian works appear to defend or proclaim Platonic positions, whereas a number of others appear to oppose these same positions. So, on Jaeger's hypothesis, when Aristotle entered Plato's Academy at seventeen years of age, he became a true Platonic disciple but at some later date turned away from Platonism to found his own school and to assume

1. The work was translated as *Aristotle: Fundamentals of the History of His Development* by Richard Robinson in 1948. An earlier work, Jaeger 1912, laid out the principles of Jaeger's developmentalism, concentrating on Aristotle's metaphysics. Developmentalism as a hypothesis for understanding the writings of Aristotle in fact antedates Jaeger. See Thomas Case's groundbreaking article s.v. Aristotle in the 1910 *Encyclopaedia Britannica.* The position of Case and Jaeger was endorsed and defended in Ross 1957. Wehrli (1967, 10:97), in the course of summarizing his study of the Peripatetic tradition, claims that Aristotle's followers never could resolve the contradictions between the 'exoteric' and 'esoteric' Aristotle. These followers assumed, as Neoplatonists did not, that Aristotelianism must be antithetical to Platonism. Wehrli, (95–96), also claims, however, that the failure of Peripatetics to isolate and defend distinctive Aristotelian principles "hatte seine tiefste Ursache im Werke des Meisters selbst." That is, there was no distinctive anti-Platonic Aristotelian philosophy.

2. Jaeger 1948, 34 n. 1, cites Bernays 1863 as arguing that the Platonism in the exoteric works represents 'lyrical feeling' on Aristotle's part, and Rose 1863 as arguing that this Platonism indicated the spuriousness of all the *exoterica.*

his own distinctive, anti-Platonic philosophical stance.[3] Regarding philosophical methodology, psychology, metaphysics, and ethics, Aristotle came to reject Plato's otherworldly constructions in favor of an orientation more in line with what we may call, with only a mild worry about anachronism, empirical science.[4]

Many interpretive issues are raised by Jaeger's work. Most important is the general issue of what 'development' is supposed to mean. Jaeger tended to understand development dramatically or deeply to indicate alterations in doctrine. Thus Aristotle early in his career accepted *the* theory of Forms and later on came to reject it. That is certainly a development. But there is also a less dramatic or shallow and perfectly ordinary sense of 'development' according to which a central vision or idea is worked out, adjusted, and refined over a long period of time in many individual works. According to this sense, what develops is not the central idea but the expression of it or the arguments or considerations on its behalf. The problem with Jaeger's deep developmentalism is that on almost any account of the evidence it can be trumped by shallow developmentalism. For example, on one traditional and widely held reading of Aristotle's *Metaphysics*—a reading that Neoplatonic commentators generally accepted—Aristotle's prime unmoved mover is not a Narcissus-like contemplator, but a mind thinking eternally all that is intelligible. I deal at length with this interpretation later. The point here is that on this interpretation, Aristotle's rejection of one or more theories of Forms at any point in his career is compatible with an unwavering commitment to the existence of eternal intelligibles being eternally contemplated by God. So, Aristotle's putative rejection of the theory of Forms is interpreted as a development in his understanding of eternal and immutable intelligible objects. On this interpretation, shallow developmentalism can accommodate inconsistencies within a larger constant framework.

According to Jaeger's version of Aristotle's philosophical development, Aristotle was a young Platonist who in his maturity became an anti-Platonist.

---

3. See Düring 1957, 405–406, for some critical remarks on the evidence that Aristotle 'seceded' from the Academy while Plato was alive. Aubenque 1972, 7–11, offers two basic two criticisms of Jaeger's developmentalism: (1) the multileveled nature of the composition of the Aristotelian treatises makes attempts at chronology highly problematic, and (2) what Jaeger takes to be contradictions in the texts are not so when these texts are understood with sufficient philosophical acuity. Although both criticisms admit of fairly obvious replies, underlying both is the evident circular nature of Jaeger's assumption of developmentalism. That is, the texts to which he appeals and their contradictions are interpreted in the light of the assumption that there must be contradictions, since Aristotle's thought developed away from Platonism towards anti-Platonism.

4. Witt 1996 distinguishes three versions of developmentalism: (1) psychological, exemplified by Jaeger; (2) external, exemplified by Owen 1986, and (3) internal, exemplified by Irwin 1988. Although the three versions have different starting points, they all seek to account for apparent contradictions or discrepancies in the Aristotelian corpus by distinguishing earlier and later phases of Aristotle's thought. Inevitably, these are associated in one way or another with Aristotle's engagement with Plato's Academy. Jaeger 1948, 34, claims that "it is certain that the dialogues contradict the treatises."

According to G. E. L. Owen's version, Aristotle was a young anti-Platonist who in his maturity came back to Platonism, at least in his metaphysics.[5] But on the hypothesis of shallow developmentalism we need not suppose that Aristotle developed in a deep way towards or away from Platonism; rather, we may suppose that Aristotle developed within the ambit of Platonism: that is, according to Platonic principles.

Of course, any hypothesis of deep development must focus on particular doctrines within specific areas of Aristotle's philosophy. Theoretically, it might be the case that deep development is to be found in, say, Aristotle's psychological doctrines but not in, say, his logical doctrines.[6] It might be, for example, that Aristotle changed his mind radically about metaphysics but did not change his mind at all about ethics. The same general point about shallow versus deep developmentalism applies for each segment of Aristotle's philosophy. And the more specific the deep development is supposed to be, the easier it is to redescribe that development as shallow because the specificity leaves greater room for agreement on general principles.

Neoplatonists who supposed that Aristotle's philosophy was in harmony with Plato's were not concerned with shallow, segmented developmentalism. If Aristotle's thought deeply developed in matters that did not cast doubt upon harmony, that would not be troubling or especially surprising, particularly regarding the account of sensible phenomena. In other regards, development could be accounted for as a result of Aristotle's incomplete grasp of first principles.

The Exoteric Writings

In a number of places among his extant works Aristotle refers to his "public writings."[7] In a number of others he makes specific references to works,

---

5. See Owen 1960, 164; Owen 1965, 146; Düring 1966. See Code 1996 for a good discussion of the differences between the developmentalist theses of Jaeger and Owen regarding metaphysics.

6. See, e.g., von Arnim (1924), who applies Jaeger's general developmentalist hypothesis to Aristotle's ethical theory; Mugnier (1930) and Guthrie (1933 and 1934), who apply it to Aristotle's theology; Solmsen 1929, who applies it to Aristotle's logical theory; and Nuyens (1948) (originally published in Flemish in 1939), who applies it to Aristotle's psychological theory. See also on the presumed evolution of psychological doctrine Block 1961 and Lefèvre 1972. More recently Graham (1987) has applied it to Aristotle's metaphysics. Rist (1989) has reapplied Jaeger's general developmentalist approach and arrived at somewhat different specific results; See further Rist 1996.

7. See *EN* A 13, 1102a26; Z 4, 1140a3; *Pol.* Γ 6, 1278b31; H 1, 1323a22; *Met.* M 1, 1076a28; *EE* B 1, 1218b34; *Phys.* Δ 10, 217b31. At *EE* A 8, 1217b22, he alludes to τοῖς ἐξωτερικοῖς λόγοις καὶ ἐν τοῖς κατὰ φιλοσοφίαν, suggesting a distinction between the 'exoteric works' and other works produced in a philosophical—i.e., technical—manner. The distinction *may* refer to works that are in dialogue form vs. works that are discursive. It is to be noted that Aristotle does not here suggest that the distinction between the two sorts of works is a distinction between two 'phases' of his development. Aristotle never explicitly repudiates what is said in the works to which he refers. At *EN* A 3, 1096a3 he refers to "circulated works" (ἐν τοῖς ἐγκυκλίοις), which may or may not be coextensive with the exoteric works. There is a

generally assumed in antiquity to be exoteric.[8] Unfortunately, it is not entirely clear which works Aristotle is referring to in most cases, which of his works are 'exoteric' and which 'esoteric,' or what the principle of division is between the two. Diogenes Laertius in his list of Aristotle's writings begins with a catalogue of 19 titles that were generally recognized as dialogues of Aristotle and assumed to be identical with the exoteric works.[9] The twentieth work in the list is *On the Good*, generally taken to be a report on and study of Platonic material. The important work *On the Ideas* is not listed by Diogenes but is well-attested by Alexander of Aphrodisias.[10] Its status as exoteric or esoteric is not clear.

Aristotle's so-called exoteric works were evidently well known to the Neoplatonists. Indeed, many of the fragments we have of these works come from their own references.[11] Although the Neoplatonists generally distinguished exoteric works from the so-called acroamatic works or lectures, they did not make such a distinction based upon a developmentalist thesis. For example, Simplicius writes: "Aristotle's works [συγγραμμάτων] are divided into two: (a) the exoteric works, for example, the natural studies [ἱστορικὰ] and the dialogues [διαλογικὰ] and generally all the works that are not devised with the highest degree of accuracy and (b) the lectures [ἀκροαματικὰ], in all of which there is the same careful treatment [αὕτη πραγματεία]; in these

---

reference in *Cael.* A 9, 279a30–31, ἐν τοῖς ἐγκυκλίοις φιλοσοφήμασι, which may be a reference either to the exoteric works or to public discussions in general. See also *De An.* A 3, 407b29. At *Poet.* 15, 1454b17, he refers to what he said "in the published works" (ἐν τοῖς ἐκδεδομένοις λόγοις).

8. See *Phys.* B 2, 194b35–36, and *De An.* A 2, 404b18–21, where Aristotle refers to ἐν τοῖς Περὶ φιλοσοφίας λεγομένοις.

9. See Moraux 1951 for the fundamental modern discussion of the issue along with the multitude of ancient references. Bernays 1863, 29–93, was the first scholar to identify the exoteric works with the dialogues of Aristotle. This was the view in antiquity from at least the time of Cicero. Others, such as Ross 1924, 2: 408–410, argue that 'exoteric' refers to discussion outside the Peripatetic school.

10. See Alexander of Aphrodisias *In Met.* 79, 3ff.

11. See Bernays 1863 on the predilection for and use of the exoteric works by the Neoplatonists. *On the Universe* (περὶ κόσμου), though widely considered to be spurious, should be included in the list of works regarded by Neoplatonists generally as exoteric works of Aristotle. Proclus *In Tim.* III 272, 21, does indicate a doubt in regard to its authenticity (εἴπερ ἐκείνου [Aristotle] τὸ Περὶ κόσμου βιβλίον), which has been painstakingly defended in Reale and Bos 1995. This work contains much to support the Neoplatonic reading of Aristotle as maintaining a version of Platonism. Interestingly, Barnes 1977, in a review of the Reale and Bos book, concedes that there is nothing in the content of *On the Universe* that indicates a non-Aristotelian provenance. Barnes does, however, reject its authenticity, basically on stylistic grounds. The point about content is crucial. Even if this work is not Aristotle's, Neoplatonists evidently saw in it, and in the other exoteric works, the same doctrines as expressed in the esoteric writings. The former support the reading of the latter in a way that makes them harmonious with Platonism. In addition, Alexander of Aphrodisias evidently held the work to be genuine, for he wrote a work by the same name (now preserved only in an Arabic translation), which draws also on *Physics* Θ and *Metaphysics* Λ. See Genequand 2001. Alexander's relation to Platonism is a topic for another work, but we should not, I think, be so quick to assume that the term 'Peripatetic' in the mouth of Alexander necessarily meant 'anti-Platonic.'

lectures, he cultivated obscurity, repelling in this way the less serious, so that among those he appears to have written nothing."[12]

It is particularly worth noting that in this passage Simplicius assumes that Aristotle's dialogues contain his serious thought.[13] This assumption would make it easy to maintain a similar assumption regarding Aristotle's reports of Plato's unwritten teachings. Most importantly for my purposes here, neither Simplicius nor any other Neoplatonist writing about the exoteric works believes that these works represent an early phase of Aristotle's thinking, a phase out of which he grew. We must not, however, suppose that the Neoplatonists, despite the fact that they may have had access to entire works and not fragments, have a privileged hermeneutical position. We must not suppose *a priori* that Jaeger's or Owen's views of Aristotle's development are incorrect.

In this chapter I want to examine briefly the fragments of the most important of the exoteric works in order to see whether this material can help us assess the harmonists' position. Against both Jaeger and Owen, these harmonists hold that in the exoteric works, Aristotle is expressing the same views he expresses in the esoteric works, albeit in a more popular or less technical manner.[14] We need to determine whether that is so.

Eudemus on the Soul and Forms

We do not possess any of the supposedly exoteric works in their entirety; therefore, it is impossible to make an accurate assessment of what each

12. Simplicius *In Phys.* 8, 16–20. Cf. 695, 34–696, 1. John Philoponus, in his *In Cat.* 3, 8–4, 2, gives a fuller analysis of the division of Aristotle's works, identifying the dialogues with the exoteric works and classifying them along with the extant works in the corpus as 'systematic' (συνταγματικά). These he describes as 'personal' (αὐτοπρόσωπα), implying that the former do not express Aristotle's own views. But Ammonius, in his *In Cat.* 4, 18–27 says that to separate thus the exoteric works from the personal works is a mistake. Cf. Olympiodorus *Proleg.* 7, 7–23.

13. Alexander of Aphrodisias notably and rather unsurprisingly dissents from this view. See Elias (or David) *In Cat.* 115, 3–5 (= Ross 1955, 6–7), where he cites Alexander as claiming that in the dialogues Aristotle is representing views that he (Aristotle) takes to be false.

14. See Simplicius *In Cat.* 4, 10–5, 2, for the canonical division of Aristotle's works according to the Neoplatonists. Cf. Ammonius *In Cat.* 3, 20–6, 1. The basic division is into particular, intermediary, and general works. The particular are personal writings, such as letters. The intermediary are those writings, such as the biological works, that concern species of sensible particulars, such as animals. The general works are divided into ὑπομνηματικά and συνταγματικά. The former refers to writings that are essentially notes, not completely polished or coherently focused on a single subject (such as *Physics, De Anima, Generation and Corruption,* and *De Caelo*). The latter is divided into διαλογικά and αὐτοπρόσωπα, (the latter of these including the treatises on theoretical practical science) and ὀργανικά. Simplicius *In Cat.* 4, 17–18, says that τὰ ὑπομνηματικά are "not entirely worthy of serious attention." The fact that the dialogues or *exoterica* are contrasted with works in Aristotle's "own voice" does not mean that they do not represent Aristotle's views in a popular format. See Ammonius *In Cat.* 4, 18–24. See I. Hadot 1990, 63–93, on the Neoplatonic divisions of Aristotle's writings. Bos (1987 and 1989b), argues that the *exoterica* represent a specific genre of writing, containing essentially the same doctrines as those in the *esoterica*. By contrast, Dumoulin 1981, who sees a deep Platonism in the *exoterica*, assumes therefore that they are works by an immature Aristotle.

one as a whole tells us about Aristotle's thought. Scholars have tended to focus on the attributions of particular doctrines to Aristotle that can be gleaned from the *testimonia*. Unquestionably, the doctrine that has caused the most puzzlement and has in fact generated a good deal of developmentalist speculation is that regarding the immortality of the soul. For it appears that Aristotle claims and even argues for the position that the soul is immortal. He seems in this respect to support at least one of the "twin pillars of Platonism," as Francis Cornford put it. The other of the twin pillars is the theory of Forms. The attribution of a doctrine of the soul's immorality to Aristotle is puzzling not just because he seems in the esoteric works to deny it but because for Plato the doctrine of the immortality of the soul is logically linked to the theory of Forms.[15] And Aristotle certainly seems to reject *that*, not just in the extant esoteric works but in *On the Ideas* as well.[16]

The evidence that in the dialogue *Eudemus*, Aristotle held the soul to be immortal in some way is strong, though one might question that evidence if it were the case that Aristotle clearly held the opposite in the esoteric works. I mean that if one concluded that there was an opposition between, say, *Eudemus* and *De Anima*, and if one wanted to reject developmentalism, then one might reasonably wish to question the testimony. Perhaps Aristotle was misunderstood or perhaps he was represented as having said things that he did not say because this was convenient for the purposes of the commentators. One of the reports of Aristotle's *Eudemus* is found in Elias's *Commentary on the Categories* and is particularly revealing because it also addresses the question of the relation between the exoteric and esoteric works. Elias writes:

> Establishing the immortality [ἀθανασίαν] of the soul in the acroamatic works, too, Aristotle does so with necessitative arguments, whereas in the dialogues he does so merely with persuasive arguments. For he says in the acroamatic work *On the Soul* [A 4, 408b18–29] that the soul is indestructible [ἄφθαρτος]. For if the soul were destructible, it would especially have to be destroyed by the enfeeblement that comes in old age. But it is in fact flourishing [ἀκμάζει] when the body is not [τοῦ σώματος παρακμάσαντος], just as it is the case that it is not flourishing when the body is. That which is flourishing at the time

15. See De Vogel 1965, 271–280, for a detailed argument that *Eudemus* holds to the immortality of the soul without necessarily being committed to a particular theory of Forms.

16. The provenance of *On the Ideas* is obscure. It hardly seems to be a 'popular' work or a dialogue. It is not listed as a work of Aristotle's by Diogenes Laertius. It is no different in its dense structure from many of the esoteric works; however, it also seems to have been written when Aristotle was still a member of Plato's Academy: that is, early in his career. If we assume that the exoteric works were written early as well, *On the Ideas* would seem to represent Aristotle's views about Forms at the same time as he is expressing his views about the immortality of the soul. Owen (1965, 129–135) argues for the anti-Platonism of the exoteric works in a curious way. Since *On the Ideas* rejects Forms, Aristotle must have rejected Forms in his early period. But if he rejected Forms, he must have also rejected the immortality of the soul, at least in the way that Plato in *Phaedo* links it to the theory of Forms.

when it ought to be destroyed is indestructible. The soul then is indestructible. This is the way he speaks in the acroamatic works.

In the dialogues he speaks in this way. The soul is immortal [ἀθάνατος] since all men instinctively make libations to the departed and swear by them, but no one makes libations or swears by that which is completely non-existent ... Aristotle in the dialogues especially seems to announce the immortality of the soul.[17]

We need to have before us the passage from *De Anima* to which Elias is alluding. It reads:

As for intellect [νοῦς], it seems to come to be in us as a sort of substance [οὐσία] and not to be destructible. For if it were destructible, it would be particularly so owing to the enfeeblement that comes in old age, but as it is what occurs is just as in the case of the sense organs. For if an old man were to receive an eye of a certain kind, he would see just as a young man does. So, old age is owing not to something experienced by the soul, but occurs in the body, as in the case of drunkenness and sickness. In addition, thinking [νοεῖν] and speculating [θεωρεῖν] deteriorate when something in the body is being destroyed, but it [intellect] itself is unaffected. Discursive thinking [διανοεῖσθαι] and loving and hating are not affections of that [intellect], but of the one who has that [intellect], in so far as he has that. Therefore, when he is destroyed, he does not remember or love. For it was not the intellect that [remembers and loves], but that which has [body and intellect] in common that was destroyed. Intellect is perhaps something that is more divine and is unaffected.[18]

A comparison of these two passages is instructive. Let us begin by noting that Elias assumes that immortality and indestructibility are the same thing. Although Aristotle in the passage above argues for the indestructibility of the intellect, not its immortality, later in the work it is immortality that is asserted.[19] Accordingly, Elias seems justified in his assumption. Far more portentous is his assumption that a proof of the immortality of intellect is the same thing as a proof of the immortality of the soul.

Aristotle himself makes an important distinction between 'soul' and 'intellect': "With regard to the intellect or to the speculative faculty, it is not yet clear; but this seems to be a genus different from soul and this alone is able to be separated, just as that which is eternal is separated from that which is destructible. As for the other parts of soul, it is clear from the

17. See Elias (or David) *In Cat.* 114, 25–115, 12 (= Ross 1955, frag. 3).
18. *De An.* A 4, 408b18–29.
19. See *De An.* Γ 5, 430a23. Plato in *Phaedo* first argues that the soul is immortal (102B–105E) and then argues that it is "imperishable" (ἀνώλεθρον) (106A–E). At 106E1, he moves from "immortal" to "indestructible" (ἀδιάφθορον) to imperishable. The distinction between 'immortal' and 'imperishable' seems to be that the former indicates that soul does not die when the complex body/soul dies; the latter indicates that, whether separate from the body or not, soul never ceases to be. Cf. *Cael.* A 22, 280b31–281a1 where Aristotle says that in the primary sense, "indestructible" refers to that which is incapable of destruction.

above that they are not separate, as some say."[20] The claim that Aristotle rejects the immortality of the 'whole' soul is, I think, as much beyond dispute as is the claim that he accepts the immortality of intellect. Disharmonists simply seem to assume that in this Aristotle is opposing Plato. Aristotle rejects the immortality of soul if that is taken to mean the immortality of the whole soul. Thus the allusion in the last sentence of the foregoing passage is assumed to be to Plato.[21] Nevertheless, if Plato, too, accepts only the immortality of the intellect, then the position for which Aristotle is arguing both in *Eudemus* and in *De Anima* is at least prima facie in harmony with Plato's.

The evidence regarding the question of whether Plato believed the whole soul to be immortal or only the intellect has been canvassed many times.[22] It seems fairly clear that in *Timaeus* only the intellect is held to be immortal. The argument in *Republic* can and has been taken in the same way, although some demur.[23] It is natural to take the arguments for immortality in *Phaedo* to indicate that only the intellect is immortal because in that dialogue there is no tripartition.[24] It is only *Phaedrus* that seems to hold implicitly that the tripartite soul is immortal.[25] Indeed, if it were not for the passage in *Phaedrus*

---

20. *De An.* B 2, 413b24–29. Cf. *EN* K 7, 1177a13–17, b34; *GA* B 3, 736b28–29; *Met.* Λ 3, 1070a24–26: "But if there is something that remains after [i.e., a form apart from matter], this should be considered. For in some cases there is nothing to prevent this; e.g., if the soul is like this, not all of it but only the intellect, for it is perhaps impossible for all of the soul to remain" (εἰ δὲ καὶ ὕστερόν τι ὑπομένει, σκεπτέον· ἐπ᾽ ἐνίων γὰρ οὐδὲν κωλύει, οἷον εἰ ἡ ψυχὴ τοιοῦτον, μὴ πᾶσα ἀλλ᾽ ὁ νοῦς· πᾶσαν γὰρ ἀδύνατον ἴσως). Jaeger in his edition of *Metaphysics* brackets these words as an addition from elsewhere. But though the remark is parenthetical, it does not follow that it is out of place.

21. Cf. A 5, 411b5. Hicks (1907, 327), asserts that Aristotle is here referring to Plato and then cites *Tim.* 69D as indicating that Plato not only divides the soul into three parts but actually assigns the different parts to different parts of the body. But the reference to tripartition and bodily location is just irrelevant to the question of immortality. This is particularly so since later in *Timaeus* Plato distinguishes the mortal and immortal parts, the latter being intellect: see 72D4–E1 and 90A.

22. See, e.g., Reeve 1988, 159–162; Robinson 1995. See infra chap. 5 for further discussion.

23. *Rep.* 608D–612A. See, e.g., Themistius (*In de An.* 106, 14–107, 3), who assumes that Plato holds the immortality of the soul in *Phaedrus, Phaedo, Theaetetus,* and *Timaeus* to be the immortality of intellect and not the other parts of the soul. He also mentions *Eudemus* in this regard as maintaining the same view. See also Proclus *In Remp.* I 215, 6; *In Tim.* III 234, 8–235, 9; and Damascius *In Phd.* 1, 177, who record the Neoplatonic debate over whether only the rational part of the soul is immortal or both the rational and some irrational part. The latter minority view was evidently held by Iamblichus and Plutarch of Athens. Damascius mentions that the claim that only the intellect is immortal is also the Peripatetic view. A residual dispute existed over whether or not δόξα was or was not included in the immortal intellect. See Baltes and Dörrie 2002, 6.1: 406–419, for a discussion of the various positions. Even those who argued that irrational parts of the soul were not destructible did not identify these with the authentic human being. Among contemporary scholars, see, e.g., Robinson (1995, 50–54), who argues that the entire tripartite soul is held to be immortal in *Republic,* thereby contradicting *Phaedo.*

24. See *Phd.* 78B4–84B4, although all this dialogue's arguments need to be considered in light of the claim that they all lead to the same conclusion. At 71E2, Socrates concludes his argument: Εἰσὶν ἄρα αἱ ψυχαὶ ἡμῶν ἐν Ἅιδου.

25. *Phdr.* 246A–257A.

in which the soul is likened to a charioteer with two horses, there would I think not be much reason to doubt that the view Aristotle takes is identical to that of Plato.[26]

There is, however, perhaps a deeper reason for insisting that Aristotle's view of immortality must be different from Plato's. It is supposed that even if Aristotle does acknowledge the immortality of intellect, he is not affirming personal immortality. By contrast, Plato's commitment to immortality is apparently inseparable from his commitment to disembodied punishments and rewards and at least the possibility of reincarnation.[27] In short, Plato believes in personal immortality or the immortality and continuity of the embodied person whereas Aristotle does not. Therefore, it is misleading in the extreme to say that Aristotle is in harmony with Plato on this point. Either Plato believed in the immortality of the tripartite soul, or if he did not, then his view of the intellect must be fundamentally at odds with Aristotle's such that it makes sense to assign personal properties to the former but not the latter.

I must leave aside the question of Plato's self-consistency. I do not believe that *Phaedrus* is at odds with *Timaeus* and *Republic* on the identity of that which is immortal.[28] Here I am mainly concerned with the Platonism with which, according to the Neoplatonists, Aristotle's views were in harmony. For them the identification in *Timaeus* of the highest part of the soul with the immortal part was normative. We should not be surprised if this entailed strange views about personhood, strange at least to contemporary eyes.[29] Still, I shall need to address the supposed divergences between Aristotle and Plato owing to a supposedly personal versus impersonal conception of intellect. In fact, we shall discover that a deep similarity in the Platonic and the Aristotelian conceptions of intellect produced a high degree of harmony in their views about the moral psychology of embodied persons.

There is an important reference to *Eudemus* in Themistius's *Paraphrase of Aristotle's De Anima* which has been widely dismissed as based on several misunderstandings. Themistius writes:

26. In fact, the *Phaedrus* passage evidently persuaded some Platonists, such as Alcinous, that despite what is said in *Timaeus*, the disembodied soul must in some sense be tripartite. Alcinous *Didask*. 25.7, 40–45, claims that the disembodied souls of human beings (and gods) have three parts: (a) the 'critical' (κριτικόν) or 'cognitive' (γνωστικόν), (b) the 'impulsive' (ὁρμητικόν) or 'dispositional' (παραστατικόν), and (c) the 'appropriative' (οἰκειωτικόν). Upon embodiment, (b) becomes the spirited part of the soul and (c) the appetitive.

27. Jaeger (1948, 49–53), argues that punishment for sins in the afterlife inevitably involves the survival of 'the whole soul' for Plato. Oddly, Jaeger concedes that this is not the case for *Phaedo;* hence, he wants to hold at the same time that *Eudemus* is anti-Platonic and Platonic on the matter of the immortality of the soul, disdaining the naive treatment of the work by Neoplatonists. It is not clear to me why Jaeger thinks that postmortem punishments presuppose a disembodied tripartite soul.

28. See Gerson 2003, 131–147.

29. See Van den Berg 1997 on the disputes among the later Neoplatonists concerning the interpretation of the *Phaedrus* myth in relation to the doctrine of the immortality of the soul and Shaw 1997 on the issue of the impersonality of the immortal soul.

Practically all of the arguments, including the weightiest ones, that Plato adduced on behalf of the immortality of the soul refer to [ἀνάγονται] intellect. This is the case both for the argument from self-motion (for it was shown that only intellect is self-moved if we were to substitute 'motion' for 'activity' [ἐνέργειας]), the argument that takes all learning to be recollection, and the argument from our likeness to god. And among the other arguments, someone could without difficulty apply the ones that seem more convincing to intellect, just as is the case with those also worked out by Aristotle himself in *Eudemus*. From these it is clear that Plato, too, supposes only the intellect to be immortal and that it is a part of the soul, whereas the emotions are destructible as well as the λόγος inside these, which Aristotle calls the passive intellect.[30]

Themistius is confident both that Plato assigns immortality only to the intellect and that his arguments, for the most part, lead only to this conclusion. He is apparently confident as well that Aristotle in *Eudemus* does not argue for a position different from *De Anima*.[31] We should also note in passing that Themistius does not take the argument in *Phaedrus* for immortality from self-motion to entail the immortality of anything else but intellect, despite the myth of the charioteer and the horses in that dialogue.[32] But if we presume that Themistius is reading the same work that Elias is reading, then neither does the fact that libations are made to the departed cause Themistius to qualify his claim that Aristotle consistently held only to the immortality of intellect.

A fragment from Aristotle's *Protrepticus* preserved by Iamblichus supports Themistius's reading of *Eudemus*:

> There exists nothing divine or blessed among men except that which alone is worthy of attention, whatever there is of intellect or wisdom in us. For this alone seems to be immortal and the only divine thing of ours. And in virtue of being able to share in this power, however wretched and hard life is by nature, still things have been favorably arranged so that in comparison with other things man would seem to be a god. "Our intellect is a god," says either Hermotimus or Anaxagoras, and that "the mortal always has a portion of god."

30. Themistius *In de An.* 106, 29–107, 7 (= Ross 1955, frag. 2). At 106, 15–17, Themistius is clear that he believes that the account in *Timaeus* is Plato's settled view, namely, that the two lower parts of the soul are mortal and only the highest part is immortal. Jaeger 1948, 50 n. 2, takes the words καὶ τῶν ἄλλων δὲ τοὺς ἀξιοπιστέρους δοκοῦντας οὐ χαλεπῶς ἂν τις τῷ νῷ προσβιβάσειεν ὥσπερ γε καὶ τῶν ὑπ' αὐτοῦ 'Αριστοτέλους ἐξειργασμένων ἐν τῷ Εὐδήμῳ as indicating that Themistius is implying that in fact Aristotle does not really hold that only the intellect is immortal but that his arguments can be made to yield that conclusion. So, too, Nuyens 1948, 125–127.

31. See Berti (1962, 418–421 and Berti 1975, 250–260), who argues for the consistency of *Eudemus* and *De Anima* and the harmony of the doctrine of the two works with Plato regarding immortality. Rist 1989, 166–167, discounts the evidence of Themistius, insisting that the entire soul is immortal in *Eudemus*. That is, Aristotle is still wedded to the 'Platonic' position.

32. See *Phdr.* 245C-246A. Themistius presumably reads αὐτοκίνητος instead of ἀεικίνητος at 245C5. Even if the latter is the true reading, Themistius would presumably be justified in understanding the former, given the conclusion at 245E6–7 that soul is τὸ αὐτὸ ἑαυτὸ κινοῦν. Cf. *Lg.* 896A. He is specifically taking the κίνησις of soul in *Laws* as if it were an Aristotelian ἐνέργεια.

We ought to philosophize, therefore, or say farewell to life and depart from it since everything else seems to be much foolishness and folly.[33]

Not only does this passage support Themistius's reading, but it indicates that for Themistius Aristotle no more than Plato thinks that the immortality of intellect alone diminishes *our* immortality. Far from it. The exhortation to philosophize is, as it is in Plato, an exhortation to identify oneself in some sense with intellect. This identification amounts to an appropriation or construction of selfhood. But in the Aristotelian (and Platonic) context, it is an appropriation of what one really or ideally is. The claim by Jaeger and others that the immortality of intellect alone would make a mockery of personal aspirations indicates nothing more than Jaeger's own conception of the personal.

Unfortunately, Themistius does not recount the arguments for immortality in *Eudemus*. We do, however, have the testimony of John Philoponus that in *Eudemus* Aristotle, like Plato in *Phaedo*, argued against the idea that the soul is a harmony.[34] Philoponus's testimony is hardly surprising, given that Aristotle argues at some length in *De Anima* against the same position.[35] Philoponus reports that in *Eudemus*, Aristotle argued that the soul is not a harmony because (1) the soul has no contrary, though harmony is a contrary, and (2) bodily harmony is found in health, strength, beauty, and disharmony in the opposites of these, but an ugly person has no less a soul than a beautiful one.

As Aristotle says in *Categories*, it is a characteristic of substances not to have contraries.[36] Accordingly, some have supposed that the reason Aristotle denies that soul is a harmony is that he thinks it to be a substance. That is evidently what Olympiodorus surmised from the arguments in *Eudemus*.[37] But this only need mean that it is a 'substance' (οὐσία) in the sense of 'form': that is, the form of a certain type of body.[38] This is what Aristotle says in *De Anima*.[39] And that is all that the references by Philoponus and Pseudo-Simplicius to soul as a form need mean.[40] The point here is that there is no significant difference between the reasons Aristotle gives in *Eudemus* for saying that only the intellect is immortal and whatever *De Anima* adds to Aristotle's account of soul in relation to body. The fact that soul is not a contrary does

---

33. Iamblichus *Prot.* 78, 12–79, 2 Des Places (= Ross 1955, frag. 10c, Düring 1961, frags. B108–110).

34. See *Phd.* 92A–94A. Philoponus *In de An.* 144, 21–145, 7 (= Ross 1955, frag. 7). See Dumoulin 31–40, on the comparison of the *Eudemus* passage with *Phaedo*.

35. See *De An.* A 4, 407b27–408a28.

36. *Cat.* 5, 3b25.

37. See Olympiodorus *In Phd.* 173, 20f. (= Ross 1955, frag. 7): τῇ δὲ ψυχῇ οὐδὲν ἐναντίον οὐσία γάρ·.

38. See *Met.* H 3, 1043a35–36: αὕτη [ψυχή] γὰρ οὐσία καὶ ἐνέργεια σώματός τινος.

39. *De An.* B 2, 414a13.

40. See Philoponus *In de An.* 144, 25–30 (= Ross 1955, frag. 7) and Ps.-Simplicius *In de An.* 221, 29 (= Ross 1955, frag. 8): [in the dialogue *Eudemus*] εἶδός τι ἀποφαίνεται τὴν ψυχὴν εἶναι. Dancy (1996, 258), thinks that Ps.-Simplicius is "doing his level best to read Neoplatonic doctrine into the text of Aristotle's [*De Anima*]."

not entail that soul is immortal. But if soul is not a contrary, and intellect is in some sense part of soul, then whatever reasons for holding that intellect is immortal are not negated by holding that soul is a form of a body. As we shall see, Aristotle's hylomorphic account of the soul is not fundamentally at odds with Plato's account of the embodied soul. To be sure, there are differences, but from the perspective of the harmonists, Aristotle consistently took the part of his teacher over against materialists of various stripes.

Naturally, any Neoplatonist who read *Eudemus* on the immortality of intellect would have been led to the following question: what does disembodied intellect concern itself with besides Forms or eternal intelligibles? The testimony of Proclus is interesting in this regard. Proclus is entirely aware that Aristotle repeatedly attacks the theory of Forms. According to Philoponus, Proclus says, in his work *Examination of Aristotle's Objections to Plato's Timaeus*:

> There are none of Plato's doctrines that Aristotle opposed more than the hypothesis of Ideas, not only calling the Forms 'empty sounds' in the logical works, but in the ethical works disputing against the Form of the Good, and in the physical works denying that generation can be explained by [ἀναφέρειν] Ideas. He says this in his *On Generation and Corruption* and much more in *Metaphysics* where he is concerned with principles, raising major objections in the beginning, middle, and end of that work. In the dialogues he most clearly proclaims that he is unable to sympathize with this doctrine even if he should be thought to have opposed it out of contentiousness.[41]

The reference to Aristotle's "dialogues" is generally taken to be to *On Philosophy*, where, according to Syrianus, Aristotle evidently discussed Forms.[42] Proclus certainly also knew of *On the Ideas* and its massive attack on Forms.[43] Like his teacher Syrianus, he was somewhat puzzled by Aristotle's attacks for basically two reasons. First, Aristotle's commitment to immortal intellect and especially to the existence of a prime unmoved mover who is intellect or intellection seemed to entail that there be eternal objects for intellect to contemplate. And these it would seem would look very like Forms. Second, the theory that Aristotle attacks is not the theory of Forms that Neoplatonists believed Plato held. Accordingly Aristotle's attacks must have been directed to misconceptions about Forms or, if one likes, to the characterization of eternal intelligibles as Forms.

Another fragment of *Eudemus* in a passage from Proclus at least suggests that he recognized a difference between the eternal intelligibles that Aristotle accepted and the Forms that he rejected:

---

41. Philoponus *De Aet. Mun.* 31, 17–32, 8 (= Ross 1955, frag. 10). Plutarch *Adv. Col.* 1115 B-C makes the identical claim.

42. See Syrianus *In Met.* 159, 35–160, 3. Plutarch *Adv. Col.* 1118C refers to the dialogues as Aristotle's "Platonic works." Previously (1115B), Plutarch says essentially the same thing that is found in the text from Proclus. So, apparently, we have Aristotle (on the developmentalist assumption) attacking Forms in his Platonic works.

43. See Syrianus *In Met.* 120, 33–121, 4.

The marvelous Aristotle gives the following explanation for the fact that a soul, coming from the other world, forgets here the sights there [τῶν ἐκεῖ θεαμάτων] whereas when it is leaving this world here, it remembers its experiences. And one should accept the argument. For he himself says that some people passing from health into sickness even forget the letters they have learned, but this never happens to anyone passing from sickness to health. For souls, life outside the body is natural like health and life in a body is unnatural like sickness. For there they live according to nature, but here they live contrary to nature. So, it follows in all likelihood that souls that go from there to here forget the things there, but souls that go from here to there remember the things here.[44]

Jaeger thinks that the phrase τῶν ἐκεῖ θεαμάτων is an unmistakable reference to Forms.[45] Owen is equally certain that the mythological setting of Proclus's discussion has no metaphysical implications.[46] That the phrase does not necessarily refer to Forms seems clear enough, though it must refer to *something* that is outside of or independent of the sensible world.[47] Owen is too hasty in dismissing the phrase as having no metaphysical implications, even though the discussion in which it occurred was evidently not a work of metaphysics. If the words τῶν ἐκεῖ θεαμάτων are Proclus's and not Aristotle's, what he is doing is simply noting that Aristotle recognized that some sort of νοητά must exist for disembodied νοῦς to contemplate.

But does the passage from Proclus permit us to hold that only an impersonal intellect is immortal? In particular, the last line seems to suggest that the departed souls remember things that an intellect does not. This last line could be Proclus's own inference drawn from the foregoing analogy, but in that case, one would wonder about the point of it. Assuming it to be Aristotle's own remark, one must suppose that, like Plotinus, he struggled with the notion of continuity for an embodied and disembodied person. But this should not blind us to the underlying harmony of the accounts of immortality in Aristotle and Plato—and the metaphysical implications. We shall see when we come to *De Anima* that the words "souls that go from there to here forget the things there" have a direct reference in the account of the active intellect, even if the words "souls that go from here to there remember the things here" do not.[48]

44. Proclus *In Remp.* II 349, 13–26 (= Ross 1955, frag. 5). See Berti 1962, 421–423, on the authenticity of this fragment and its implications for Aristotle's early philosophy.

45. Jaeger 1948, 51–52.

46. Owen 1965, 131.

47. Cf. *Cael.* A 9, 279a18 for Aristotle's use of a nonspatial 'there' (τἀκεῖ).

48. See infra chap. 5, on *De An.* Γ 5, 430a23–24. See Bos 1989A, 97–107, for a detailed argument to the effect that the psychological doctrine in *Eudemus* and *De Anima* is the same. The Neoplatonists' inclination to insinuate memory into the afterlife is generally in proportion to their belief that the immortal soul is more than intellect. Conversely, to the extent that they accept the narrow interpretation of *Timaeus* according to which the immortal part of the soul is *only* intellect, to that extent memory becomes irrelevant to immortal life. But it must be borne in mind that the main argumentative bases for immortality in Plato are the properties of intellect. Extraintellectual properties of the soul are adduced by Neoplatonists for religious purposes. The basis for harmony was essentially philosophical.

Protrepticus

Among the exoterica, the work of which we possess the largest portion is undoubtedly *Protrepticus*.[49] We may actually possess the work almost in its entirety, owing largely to Iamblichus, who in his own *Protrepticus* refers extensively to Aristotle's work, manifestly treating it as a product of a Platonist. Iamblichus does not suppose for one moment that it represents an early phase of Aristotle's thinking, a phase that he abandoned in his more mature writings; rather, like his own *Protrepticus*, Iamblichus treats it as a popular work expressing in a simple manner more profound Platonic ideas.[50] My purpose in this section is primarily to show that a Platonist reading Aristotle's *Protrepticus* would have no reason to conclude either that this work is not in harmony with Platonism or that it differs in any significant way from the views expressed in the esoteric works. On the contrary, according to the reports of Iamblichus and others, what one finds in *Protrepticus* are claims that are deeply in harmony with those of Plato.

Aristotle's *Protrepticus* was probably written around 350 B.C.E. and dedicated to one Themiston, evidently some sort of 'king' (βασιλέα) somewhere on Cyprus.[51] It is an exhortation to the philosophical life as that was understood in the Academy.[52] It praises the goods of the soul over the goods of the body; prefers theoretical activity to practical; and identifies the theoretical life with the happy life. Undoubtedly, the loose form of the philosophical protreptic can easily make philosophers who hold antithetic views appear harmonious just because they are both philosophers praising philosophy. After all, even the most relentlessly oppositional among the interpreters can agree that in some very large sense, Plato and Aristotle are on the same side or that the "Aristotelian spirit" corresponds to the "spirit of the Platonic Academy."[53] When, however, one examines the fragments of *Protrepticus* in detail, insofar as this is possible, one cannot help but notice something more than a generic similarity between these and doctrines

49. See Rabinowitz (1957, 52–92), who argues against the use of Iamblichus for reconstructing Aristotle's *Protrepticus* on the grounds that Iamblichus is using material from Platonic dialogues and Neopythagorean reconstructions of Speusippus rather than material from Aristotle's work. Obviously, if Rabinowitz is correct, then we are not in a position to use Iamblichus's citations from *Protrepticus* as evidence for the harmony of Plato and Aristotle. Revealingly, in my view, one of Rabinowitz's main reasons for claiming that Iamblichus's *Protrepticus* does not contain extensive citations from Aristotle's *Protrepticus* is that those citations seem to be so Platonic in content. As has been pointed out in, e.g., Düring 1961, 17, the language used by Iamblichus in those citations is unquestionably Aristotelian. There is also a remarkable similarity between the content of those citations and Aristotle's esoteric works. See Dumoulin 1981, 146–158, for a thorough response to Rabinowitz.

50. See Jaeger 1948, 60–62, for a sketch of the basis for the reconstruction of *Protrepticus* from the work of Iamblichus.

51. See Berti 1962, 463–475. I follow Düring 1961 in my understanding of the ordering of the fragments and cite Des Places's numbering in the most recent edition of Iamblichus's work. But see Des Places 1989, esp. intro. Also see De Strycker 1968, and Allan 1976.

52. See Jaeger 1948, 57.

53. The latter remark comes from Hadot 1995, 106.

rooted in the Platonic dialogues. The now familiar approach to these simi-larities is to say that Aristotle is here speaking in the name of a Platonism that he eventually repudiated. But if there is hardly a claim made among the *Protrepticus* fragments that is not repeated and elaborated upon in the eso-teric works, what then?

According to Düring, Iamblichus's first mention of Aristotle's *Protrepticus* is in the sixth chapter of his own work, where he represents Aristotle as saying:

> The things that are available to support our life—I mean the body and the bod-ily—are available as kinds of tools (ὄργανα). The use of these is always danger-ous and those who do not use them as they should produce results more bad than good. Therefore, we should desire both to possess and to use appropri-ately the knowledge by means of which we will make good use of all these. Therefore, we ought to philosophize, if we intend to take part in government in the right way and to lead our own lives beneficially. Further, some kinds of knowledge [ἐπιστῆμαι] (1) produce each of the good things in life and (2) others use these; (3) some are subservient and (4) others are commanding. It is in these more authoritative sciences that the true good (τὸ κυρίως ὂν ἀγαθὸν) resides. If, therefore, there is one science alone that has the capacity of judg-ing rightness, that is, using reason and seeing good as a whole, and this is phi-losophy, and it is naturally able to employ and direct all the other sciences, we should from every point of view philosophize. For only philosophy encom-passes in itself right judgment and unerring directive wisdom (φρόνησιν).[54]

That the body is a tool or possession of the soul and that the soul is the true person is a core Platonic belief.[55] A great deal in ethics and psychology turns upon whether we identify persons with bodies or with body-soul composites or with souls or with one part of the soul. For example, the so-called Socratic paradoxes such as "a worse man cannot harm a better man" sound like non-sense unless we suppose that bodily harm is not harm to oneself or to the soul. Indeed, Socrates' exhortation to his fellow Athenians to care for noth-ing so much as the health of their souls follows directly from the identifica-tion of a person and a soul.[56]

Aristotle, so the story goes, may have at some point early on held to the dualistic position of *Alcibiades*—identifying the person with the soul and the body as the soul's possession—but he eventually came round to the position that the person is the body-soul composite. This story seems to me to be mis-

---

54. Iamblichus *Prot.* 67, 23–68, 14, Des Places (= Ross 1955, frag. 4; Düring 1961, frags. B8–9). Cf. *MM* A 34, 1198a34-b20. This passage bears a similarity to the discussion of the hier-archy of types of knowledge in Plato's *Statesman*. See *Sts.* 287B-305D, esp. 292B-C; 300C-D; 305E. Here the 'kingly science' is endowed with the capacity for directing or commanding all the other sciences. See also *Phil.* 55-59, esp. *ad fin.*, where theoretical knowledge is held to be superior to practical knowledge.

55. See *Alc.* I 130C1-3. That the soul is identical with the person and that the body is there-fore a possession is implied at *Phd.* 76C11; 92B5; 95C6; 115C1–116A; *Tim.* 90C2-3; *Lg.* 721B7-8; 735E5ff.; 959B3-4. See also *Rep.* 443D.

56. See *Ap.* 29D7-E5.

leading on two counts. Most significantly, it misconstrues Plato's view of the embodied soul or person. But it also does no justice to Aristotle.

Although Plato undoubtedly held that in some sense the body is a possession, it is not an ordinary possession. Most possessions are distinct from their possessors. Socrates' cloak can exist without Socrates and vice versa. But this is not so for the body or for bodily states of an embodied person. For one thing, appetites and emotions belong to persons. Socrates, not his body, feels pain and joy. And though it is true that Plato can speak about some bodily states of which persons are not aware, the bodily states that include at least appetites and emotions are psychical states. And to the extent that we can say that a person is a soul, these bodily states are states of the person. Consequently, at least on one side of the question it is misleading to say that while Aristotle came to hold that the body-soul composite is the subject of appetites and emotions, Plato held that what happens to the soul is entirely separate from what happens to the body.

When Aristotle in the *Protrepticus* passage says that the body is a tool, he is not likely to be implying any sort of un-platonic dualism. But he is implying a moral and ontological superiority of the person to the body and in general a superiority of psychical goods to physical goods. This is, of course, no more a prelude to asceticism here than it is in Plato.[57] The idea of the body as a tool or possession distinct from the person does raise all sorts of difficult problems, given that bodily states are also states of the person. These are problems both for Plato and for Aristotle. It is far from clear that either one solved them. But given what has already been said about the immortality of intellect alone in both Plato and Aristotle, it should not be assumed that what Aristotle does say about embodied personhood is *not* in harmony with what Plato says, particularly when this assumption is based upon a specious contrast between hylomorphism and a form of dualism unknown to Plato.

The contrast of possessions and possessor is made again in a fragment not in Iamblichus but in a scrap of papyrus, partially duplicated in Stobaeus: "We ought to believe that happiness lies not in possessing many things but rather in how the soul is disposed." And, "If the soul is educated, then such a soul and such a man should be counted happy." And finally, "In addition, when worthless men acquire an abundance of possessions they tend to value these more than the goods of the soul, which is the most shameless thing of all. For just as a man who was inferior to his servants would be ridiculous, in the same way those for whom their possessions are of greater worth than their own nature (τῆς ἰδίας φύσεως) should be considered wretched."[58] The idea

---

57. See *Euthyd.* 280D–282D, where an argument similar to the *Protrepticus* passage is made. Jaeger (1948, 99–101), thinks that both *Protrepticus* and *Eudemus* evince a view about the "worthlessness of all earthly things" which is deeply Platonic and destined to be repudiated by the later Aristotle.

58. See Stobaeus *Ecl.* 3. 3, 25 (Oxyrrynchus Papyrus 666 = Ross 1955, frag. 3; Düring 1961, frags. B2–4). The principal contrast here is between possessions generally and the soul, though the former does explicitly include bodily excellences such as health and beauty.

that the true self is a soul and that the truest part of the self is the highest
part of the soul is the basis for Platonic ethics and psychology. It is certainly
the only reason for insisting that soul care ought to be one's highest concern, even up to death followed by nothing else.[59] If one is going to show
that this view of *Protrepticus* is superseded by a view that repudiates the identification of the true self with the soul, then one is going to have to do more
than point to those places where Aristotle treats the composite living thing
as the agent of embodied action. One is going to have to show that Aristotle's fundamental ethical and psychological doctrines could have been constructed on an alternative conception of personal identity. I believe we will
discover that this is almost impossible to do, assuming that we take account
of all the evidence.

A passage in a long citation of Iamblichus explicitly identifies the person
and the highest part of the soul:

> Further then part of us is soul and part body; and the one rules and the other is
> ruled; and the one uses and the other is used as a tool. The use of a tool and that
> which is ruled is then always arranged in relation to the ruler and the one using
> the tool. As for the soul, one part is rational (λόγος), which according to nature
> rules and judges matters with which we are concerned, and the other part both
> follows and is ruled by nature. Everything is well arranged according to its own
> proper excellence; to have attained this is good. And in fact whenever the most
> authoritative and honorable parts have their excellence, then that thing is well
> arranged. Therefore, the excellence of the better part is better according to
> nature and that which is more fit to rule according to nature is better and more
> in control, as man is in relation to the other animals. Therefore, soul is better
> than body, for it is more fit to rule, and within soul, the part that has reason and
> thought [is better than the other part]. For it is this part which commands and
> restrains us and says that something is or is not necessary to do. Whatever is the
> excellence of this part is necessarily the most choiceworthy of all things for all
> unqualifiedly and for us. For I think one would claim that this part is alone us or
> especially so [μόνον ἢ μάλιστα ἡμεῖς ἐσμεν τὸ μόριον τοῦτο].[60]

The last sentence of this passage is so strikingly similar to what Plato says
repeatedly that one would have to take it as an aberration or a rhetorical
throwaway line if one wanted to insist that it does not support the harmonists' position.[61] But this is difficult to do, especially in the light of what
Aristotle says at the end of his *Nicomachean Ethics:*

> So, since the intellect is divine relative to a man, the life according to this intel-
> lect, too, will be divine relative to human life. Thus we should not follow the

59. See, e.g., Plato's *Gorg.* 512A on the relative worth of soul and body.
60. See Iamblichus *Prot.* 71, 22–72, 14 Des Places (= Ross 1955, frag. 6; Düring 1961, frags.
B59–62). See also 78, 12–79, 2 Des Places (= Ross 1955, frag. 10c; Düring 1961, frags.
B108–110) on the divinity of reason in us.
61. See especially *Lg.* 959A4-B7. For the Neoplatonists, who assumed that *Alc.* I was genuine, the reference there, 130C1–3, is also significant.

recommendations of thinkers who say that those who are men should think
only of human things and that mortals should think only of human things, but
we should try as far as possible to partake of immortality and to make every
effort to live according to the best part of the soul in us; for even if this part
be of small measure, it surpasses all the others by far in power and worth. It
would seem, too, that each man is this part, if indeed this is the dominant part
and is better than the other parts; so it would be strange if a man did not
choose the life proper to himself but that proper to another. That which was
said previously harmonizes with that which is being said now, that which is
proper to each thing is the best and most pleasant for that thing. So, for a man,
too, the life according to intellect is best, if indeed this is especially man
(μάλιστα ἄνθρωπος). This life then is happiest.[62]

One might speculate that the implicit bipartitioning of the soul in the *Protrepticus* passage indicates a rejection of Platonic tripartitioning. But this is a
trivial point, both because Plato himself was not unreservedly wedded to tripartitioning and because a putative disagreement between Aristotle and
Plato on this point hardly undermines the basic harmonist position.[63]

On the assumption that the person is only or especially the rational part
of the soul, it is perfectly understandable that Aristotle should argue that
the activity of this part is the best human activity:

All nature, as something possessing reason, does nothing at random, but
rather everything for the sake of some end [ἕνεκα δέ τινος πάντα], and, eliminating the random, it regards an end even more than the arts, since the arts
are imitations of nature. Since man is by nature composed of body and soul
and since the soul is superior to the body and the inferior, being a servant, is
always for the sake of the superior, the body is for the sake of the soul. One
part of the soul has reason and one part does not have it; and the latter is inferior to the former so that the part without reason is for the sake of the part
having reason. Intellect belongs to the part that has reason, so the demonstration [ἀπόδειξις] forces us to conclude that everything is for the sake of
intellect. But the activities of intellect are acts of thinking, which are sights of
intelligibles, as the activity of sight consists of the seeing of visible objects.
Therefore, everything that is choiceworthy for men is so for the sake of acts of
thinking or intellect, if indeed it is the case that that everything is choiceworthy for the sake of the soul, and intellect is alone the best part of the soul, and
all other things have been constituted on account of the best.[64]

---

62. *EN* K 7, 1177b30–1178a8. See also the line here referred to, I 8, 1169a2: ὅτι μὲν οὖν
τοῦθ' [intellect] ἕκαστος ἐστιν ἢ μάλιστα, οὐκ ἄδηλον. Nuyens 1948, 93–95, suggests that the
instrumentalism of *Protrepticus* and *Nicomachean Ethics* is abandoned for a thoroughgoing hylomorphism in *De Anima*. As I mention above and shall argue, hylomorphism in action does not
contradict what is said about the identity of the person with the soul in *Protrepticus.*
63. See esp. *Tim.* 72D, where the main point is the division between the immortal part of
the soul—that is—intellect and the other mortal parts. See also *MM* 1, 1182a23ff.
64. Iamblichus *Prot.* 65, 1–18 Des Places (= Düring 1961, frags. B23–24). See *EE* H 15,
1249b16–19 for a close parallel. See Düring 1993, 92–93, for an argument that this fragment
comes from either *Protrepticus* or another lost work of Aristotle.

Aristotle continues the chain of reasoning,

> Among thoughts [διανοήσεων], the ones chosen merely for the sake of the contemplation itself are more honorable and better than the ones that are instrumental to other things. Acts of contemplation are honorable and among these the wisdom of intellect is choiceworthy, whereas acts of prudential thinking [αἱ κατὰ φρόνησιν] are honorable owing to the actions they produce. So, the good and honorable are in the acts of contemplation with regard to wisdom, certainly not in every chance act of contemplation.[65]

Noninstrumental thinking—philosophy—is identified as the most honorable and choiceworthy of activities. This is exactly what one would expect to find in a Platonic philosopher. It is the view we find repeatedly expressed in the dialogues of Plato. And it is no different from what we find elsewhere in *Protrepticus* and in Aristotle's esoteric works.[66] What is particularly important is the reason consistently given for this: a person is exclusively or primarily a contemplator; therefore, the activity of contemplation is the activity wherein our happiness is bound to reside. Since it is implausible that Aristotle changes his view on this matter between the writing of *Protrepticus* and both *Nicomachean Ethics* and *Politics*, one might wish to suggest that the way to separate Aristotle from Plato here is to lean heavily upon the words "alone or especially" and to claim that Aristotle is here saying something un-Platonic.[67] If Aristotle wishes to say that persons are especially their rational part, then perhaps this is meant to be consistent with a form of hylomorphism that is inconsistent with Platonic dualism, wherein the person is exclusively the rational part. Of course, this interpretation is of no use to those who want to maintain that *Protrepticus* is Platonic but that Aristotle abandoned the view of persons later. In any case, as we have already seen, to say that an *embodied* person is 'especially' and not exclusively the rational part is to say something that is, from the point of view of the Neoplatonic interpreters, Platonic to the core. This is so because the embodied person is the subject of bodily states. Only the disembodied person is exclusively a rational agent.

Jaeger argued that Aristotle's focus on contemplation in *Protrepticus* implies an "identification of theoretical knowledge and practical conduct" and that this identification is abandoned in *Nicomachean Ethics*.[68] According

---

65. Iamblichus *Prot.* 66, 1–5 Des Places (= Düring 1961, frag. B27). See Aristotle *Pol.* H 3, 1325b17–23; Plato *Rep.* 431A where the rational part of the soul is said to be "the best part."

66. See especially the continuous passage in Iamblichus *Prot.* 72, 14–74, 19 Des Places (= Ross 1955, frag. 7; Düring 1961, frags. B 63–73), and 86, 12–89, 25 Des Places (= Ross 1955, frags. 14–15; Düring 1961, frags. B 79–96) where the identification of the best life with the philosophical life is repeatedly made.

67. When Aristotle uses the locutions 'x ἢ μάλιστα γ' or 'x ἢ μᾶλλον γ' in referring to two possible ways of describing or categorizing something, he typically goes on to show a preference for the second alternative in the argument.

68. See Jaeger 1948, 81–84.

to Jaeger the identification is properly Platonic and the rejection properly anti-Platonic, and the alteration from the first to the second could not have occurred if there had not been a fundamental shift in Aristotle's metaphysics. Jaeger takes as proof of the shift Aristotle's use of the word φρόνησις in *Protrepticus* for theoretical knowledge and his use of this term in his *Ethics* exclusively for practical knowledge.[69]

I deal with the ethical *esoterica* in chapter 8 but I think it is worthwhile to indicate here a strange assumption that Jaeger brings to his analysis, an assumption deeply at odds with the way the Neoplatonists read both Plato and Aristotle. Jaeger assumes that for Aristotle the disruption of theoretical and practical science is equivalent to the elimination of a theoretical basis for practical reasoning. He assumes that the only possible basis for such reasoning is the theory of Forms and that Aristotle, once having rejected this theory or some version of it, must have gone on to treat ethics in an entirely un-Platonic manner. But it is simply a non sequitur to argue that without a commitment to Forms, ethics can have no theoretical basis, or even that knowledge of the theoretical basis is irrelevant to practice.

Aristotle himself in *Protrepticus* seems to suggest not that the theoretical is the practical but that the lawgiver or virtuous man is the vehicle for translating theoretical knowledge into action:

> To the philosopher alone among craftsmen belong laws that are stable and actions that are right and noble; for he alone lives by looking at nature and the divine. Like a good captain who secures his ship, he anchors the principles of his life to what is eternal and stable and lives as himself. This knowledge [ἐπιστήμη] [of the eternal and stable] is then indeed theoretical, but it provides us with the ability to arrange everything according to it. For just as sight, though it produces and arranges nothing (for its only work is to discern and to make clear each of the things seen), still provides us with the ability to act by means of it and assists us tremendously in actions (for we would be practically immobile were we to be deprived of it), so it is clear that though knowledge be contemplative, we nevertheless do countless things on the basis of it, choosing some things and avoiding others, and in general possess all good things owing to it.[70]

To say that theoretical knowledge here must be of Forms and that when Forms are rejected, the theoretical is cut off from the practical is to miss the point.[71] Aristotle argues that theoretical knowledge is superior to every other

---

69. See Xenocrates frag. 6 Heinze (1892), who says that φρόνησις has two senses: (a) the theoretical and (b) the practical. It thus appears that Aristotle is just availing himself of contemporary usage. See Düring 1961, 260.

70. Iamblichus *Prot.* 85, 19–86, 9 Des Places (= Ross 1955, frag. 13; Düring 1961, frags. B48, 50–51).

71. De Vogel (1960, 252–253), insists that Aristotle here must be referring to Platonic Forms. But this is to confuse intelligible reality, in regard to which Aristotle *never* wavered as to its relevance to knowledge and to the best life, and some theory of separate Forms or other, whose status in the Academy was *always* in contention. De Vogel, like most scholars in the grips

type of knowledge exactly because of its noninstrumentality. The relevance of the knowledge of eternal truth to action is independent of the answer to the question of whether that knowledge is necessary or sufficient for good action.[72] Aristotle seems to imply that relevance as much in his *Nicomachean Ethics* as in his *Protrepticus,* because in both works he insists on the superiority of the theoretical life. Iamblichus and others appear to be entirely justified in holding the fundamental harmony of Plato and Aristotle on this point. At the same time, it would after all not be surprising if Aristotle did dissent on the precise manner in which the theoretical is brought to bear on the practical, since he had (according to the Neoplatonists) an incomplete and thus an imperfect understanding of metaphysical principles.

The claims made in Aristotle's *Protrepticus* are not completely identical with those made in the dialogues of Plato. For one thing, the use of terms such as ἔργον, τέλος, ἐνέργεια, θεωρία, and δύναμις, which are either uniquely Aristotelian or used in a uniquely Aristotelian way, is remarkable.[73] But at its core *Protrepticus* is a deeply Platonic work, principally in its account of the embodied person and in its insistence on the absolute superiority of the contemplative life. Removing from our understanding of it a spurious Platonism, it is also in harmony with the entire corpus of esoterica. It is it seems exactly what Neoplatonists supposed it to be: a popular treatment of the basic Platonic principles by Plato's independent-minded disciple.

On Philosophy

The fragments of the dialogue *On Philosophy* provide a particularly lucid example of the presumptions scholars bring to their understanding of Aristotle.[74] Valentin Rose in the 19th century, acknowledging on the basis of the

of Jaeger's Aristotelian developmentalism, assumes that there was one and only one theory of Forms and that each text of Aristotle must be categorized according to the principle that he did or did not adhere to that theory. De Vogel (1965) reverses herself, denying that Forms are here implied. See Dumoulin 1981, 143–145, for some salutary remarks on distinguishing Platonism from the adherence to a particular theory of Forms.

72. See Monan (1968, 35–36), who argues against Jaeger that the difference between *Protrepticus* and the ethical treatises is that the former operates at a high level of generality suitable for a public work and that the latter provides fine-grained detailed analysis of how the theoretical is translated into action. Accordingly, there is "a much greater likeness between the early and late Aristotle than Jaeger's interpretation allowed."

73. See Dumoulin (1981, 133–140), who, while acknowledging the many Platonic features of the dialogue, argues that "Aristote ne se libérera que peu à peu de [l'affirmation d'une hiérarchie verticale des niveaux de réalité], et l'étude de la *Métaphysique* fait apparaître le *Protreptique* comme l'ouvrage le plus typique de la transition entre la Platonisme et l'Aristotélisme" (140). It is perhaps worth noting here that Neoplatonists embraced these and other Aristotelian terms as helpful or even essential in articulating Platonic doctrine.

74. On the authenticity of the fragments and their ordering, see esp. Untersteiner 1963. See also Berti 1962, 317–409, for a helpful analysis of the arguments contained in the fragments. Other important studies are Festugière 1944, 2: 218–259; Wilpert 1955 and 1957; Saffrey 1971; and Bignone 1973, 2: 335–538.

extant fragments the apparently Platonic character of *On Philosophy*, decided that the work must not be Aristotle's.[75] By contrast, Jaeger wants to make the dialogue conform to his developmentalist hypothesis. Since the fragments apparently contain a criticism of Forms, but since it *is* a dialogue and therefore presumably an early rather than a later work, Jaeger wants to place it somewhere midway between Aristotle's "Platonic period" and the period of his "mature philosophy."[76] But since the dialogue also apparently contains remarks about the nature of wisdom and the divine that are in line with *Metaphysics*, Jaeger variously assigns portions of that work to the middle period and eliminates as spurious fragments of the dialogue that do not conform to his thesis. Paul Wilpert, recognizing the Platonic elements in the dialogue, seeks to marginalize or eliminate the fragments that contain a criticism of Forms.[77] One could easily extend the list of scholars who have struggled to fit Aristotle into a picture where harmonization has no place. Either Aristotle is a Platonist or he is an anti-Platonist. All his works, both exoteric and esoteric, have to be arrayed along this axis.[78] And if a work seems to be both Platonic and anti-Platonic, then one proceeds to disassemble the work in order to make the elements fit the prescribed categories.

The key to understanding the flaw in such an approach is seeing the weakness of the assumption that Aristotle's attitude to Forms is the hinge upon which the door swings one way or the other. Simply stated, Aristotle's opposition to a theory of Forms does not contradict the harmony of Aristotle and Plato as the Neoplatonists understood it. The reason is that they recognized a theory of Forms as a theory about the intelligible order. A philosopher who denied the existence of such an order would indeed be anti-Platonist, and his philosophy would not be in harmony with Plato's. But there is no evidence that Aristotle denied this order and much evidence across all his works—esoteric and exoteric—that he affirmed it.

If we read *On Philosophy* from a Neoplatonic perspective, we shall see that a rejection of a theory of Forms goes along quite nicely with a commitment to Platonic principles. On this reading, we do not have to excise Aristotle's arguments that imply the existence of separate intelligibles. Nor do we have to hive off the criticism of Forms to a post-Platonic period. The principle of harmony leads us to do no violence to the text, as do the interpretations that assume the Platonist–anti-Platonist polarity.

As Berti has shown, *On Philosophy* is most plausibly taken to be a work devoted at least in part to the subject matter of wisdom or σοφία.[79] In that

75. See Rose 1863, 27–34.
76. See Jaeger 1948, 105–166, esp. 137–138. See also 13, where Jaeger avers that Aristotle's "pupils very often understood him better than he did himself; that is to say, they excised the Platonic element in him and tried to retain only what was pure Aristotle."
77. See Wilpert 1955 and 1957. De Vogel (1960, 249), arguing against Wilpert, concedes that the idea of wisdom here is, "*formally speaking*, Plato's view" (De Vogel's emphasis).
78. This is evident, e.g., in Graham 1987, 302–310, who reads the dialogues as containing a theory of substance that contains an "anti-Platonic metaphysics" (306).
79. See Berti 1962, 324–326.

case, a long fragment of the work preserved by John Philoponus is likely to be of considerable value. It says:

> Wisdom [σοφία], as it makes clear all things, was so named, being a sort of clarity [σάφειά]. Clarity was so named from the fact that it is a sort of illumination [φαές], from the words for light [φάος or φῶς], because it brings things that are concealed into the light. Since then, as Aristotle says, things that are intelligibles [νοητά] or divine [θεῖα], if they are the things most apparent [φανότατά[in their own essence [οὐσίαν], but seem to be murky and dark owing to the fact that we are enveloped in a bodily fog [ἡμῖν διὰ τὴν ἐπικειμένην τοῦ σώματος ἀχλὺν], they [ancient thinkers] reasonably enough called wisdom the science that brings these things to the light for us. . . . And finally they referred to the divine and hyper cosmic and totally unchangeable things and named the knowledge of these things the highest wisdom.[80]

The most striking thing about this passage is the identification of wisdom with a science of divine intelligibles. This is basically the way wisdom or first philosophy is identified in *Metaphysics*.[81] We have far too little of *On Philosophy* even to guess how this science is to be constructed, much less to suppose that it is constructed here in the same way that it is in *Metaphysics*. There is no hint, for example, of a science of being *qua* being or of *Metaphysics'* identification of theology or first philosophy with that. Far more important to the Neoplatonists was Aristotle's evident commitment to a science of the intelligible world distinct from a science of sensibles or physical entities. On this point alone I suspect they would have staked their claim to harmony. Questions regarding the relations between intelligibles and sensibles or those regarding the relations among intelligibles were questions debated *within* the Platonic school. Those whom everyone identified as anti-Platonists, whether materialists of various stripes or 'anti-dogmatists' such as the Skeptics, were united in denying the possibility of such a science.

The linkage of *Metaphysics* with the claims made in the passage I am assuming is from *On Philosophy* is indirectly made by Asclepius. In an extremely important passage at the beginning of his commentary, where he tries to explain the title *Metaphysics,* he states:

> The order [of study] is evident from the things that have been said previously [1, 4–3, 21]. For since nature has its origin [ἄρχεται] in things that are more perfect [τελειοτέρων] than it, and it would be incongruous for us, owing to

80. Philoponus *In Nicom. Isag. Ar.* I 1 (= Ross 1955, frag. 8). On the authenticity of the fragment, see Untersteiner 1963, 121–123. Cf. *Mun.* 6, 397b14–16. I have omitted a portion of the fragment, dealing with different senses of the terms 'wisdom' and 'wise man,' which may be not genuine and in any case is not relevant to my theme.

81. See infra chap. 6 and *Met.* A 1, 981b28; A 2, 983a4–7; E 1, 1026a15–16, 27–32; K 1, 1059a18; Λ 10, 1075b20–27. In 1026a15–16, ἡ πρώτη ἐπιστήμη or ἡ πρώτη φιλοσοφία is concerned with the 'separate' and 'immobile,' which are identified with the divine. It is clear from the opening lines of the chapter that the first science is concerned with "first principles and causes."

our weakness, to proceed straightaway to these more perfect things, we should first prefer to begin with the things that are posterior and imperfect by nature and in this way to arrive at the perfect. Since, therefore, in *Physics* Aristotle already discussed imperfect things and here [*Metaphysics*] he is discussing the perfect, it is reasonable that the present study [πραγματεία] is the ultimate one [τελευταία] for us. One has to understand that this study is titled "Wisdom" and "Philosophy" and "First Philosophy" and also "After the Physics" [i. e., *Metaphysics*], since having previously discussed natural things, in this study he is discussing divine things. Thus the study got its designation because of the order [of study]. Wisdom is a sort of clarity, for divine things are clear and most apparent. In fact, he is discussing divine things. Because of this he calls it "Wisdom." And, of course, in the work "Demonstration" he says, "as I said in the papers on wisdom," since wisdom is the science that uses demonstrative principles.[82]

The words "wisdom is a sort of clarity, for divine things are clear and most apparent" indicate that Asclepius is referring to the same work as Philoponus and connecting it with *Metaphysics*. In addition, Asclepius explains the order of study in *Metaphysics*, relying upon the fundamental Aristotelian distinction between "what is clearer by nature" and "what is clearer to us."[83] This distinction seems to underlie the colorful language of the *On Philosophy* passage. In short, it is reasonable to suppose that the Neoplatonists took the account of wisdom in *On Philosophy* as a popular expression both of what is found in the esoteric works—especially *Metaphysics*—and of a position that is in harmony with Platonism.

Given the characterization of wisdom in *On Philosophy*, it is particularly worth noting that this work also seems to contain a criticism of a theory of Forms, according to the testimony of Proclus, cited above.[84] Given this fragment alone, we cannot say that it definitely belongs to *On Philosophy*, although it does not seem to fit easily into any of the other dialogues. But we have the testimony of Alexander of Aphrodisias that in *On Philosophy* Aristotle argued against a theory of Forms that reduces them to mathematical first principles.[85] We also have a passage from Syrianus in his *Commentary on Aristotle's Metaphysics* saying the same thing, though Syrianus specifically identifies the criticism as belonging to Book α of that work.[86] We thus have good reason to suppose that in the same work in which Aristotle claims that wisdom is concerned with divine intelligibles, he also rejects one version of a theory of Forms.

---

82. Asclepius *In Met.* 3, 21–34; see also 112, 16–19. See Bignone 1973, 2: 521, and notes on this passage.

83. See *APr.* B 23, 68b35–36; *APo.* A 2, 71b33–72a6; *Top.* Z 4, 141b3ff.; *Phys.* A 1, 184a16–b14.

84. See supra n. 41.

85. See Alexander of Aphrodisias *In Met.* 117, 23–118, 1 (= Ross 1955, frag. 11).

86. See Syrianus *In Met.* 159, 29–160, 5 (= Ross 1955, frag. 11).

One might wish to argue that the refutation of a mathematized version of the theory of Forms does not by itself indicate that Aristotle would have rejected a nonmathematized version.[87] The criticism of the non-mathematized version would presumably include the mathematized version, since the latter is, according to Aristotle, a reduction of Forms to their first principles. But it might be the case that Aristotle, hospitable though he was to Forms that are not numbers, simply refused this reductive step.[88] This seems implausible mainly because no criticism of the mathematized version by Aristotle is ever accompanied by any inkling of a defense of the nonmathematized version.[89]

The theory that Forms are numbers is evidently related in some way to the reduction of Forms to the first principles, the One and the Indefinite Dyad or the Great and the Small.[90] Neoplatonists generally were well aware that Aristotle rejected the account of first principles as the Platonists understood it. That did not mean that Aristotle rejected the idea that there was a first principle or that understanding it was the goal of a science of wisdom. Nor apparently did he reject the idea that the first principle must be simple and self-sufficient. Indeed, owing to the simplicity of the first principle, Aristotle was understandably reluctant to posit a multitude of intelligible entities within it.[91] Nevertheless, he still manifestly adhered to the need to posit eternal intelligibles. That he did not accept the reductive unity of the Forms followed from his not knowing how to accept a multitude of intelligible entities. As for the identification of Forms with numbers, the Neoplatonists were themselves not very clear about how this was to be understood and integrated with the reduction of Forms to first principles.[92]

87. So Wilpert 1957, 160–162.

88. The evidence that within the Academy the hypothesis that Forms are reductively identical with numbers was at least seriously considered is very extensive. See Aristotle *De An.* A 2, 404b6–27; *Met.* Λ 8, 1073a18; M 6, 1080b11–12; N 3, 1090a16; Alexander of Aphrodisias *In Met.* 53, 9; 56, 2–3; Ps.-Alexander *In Met.* 777, 16–21; Themistius *In Phys.* 80, 3–4; 107, 14; Simplicius *In Phys.* 503, 18; 545, 22.

89. At the beginning of M of *Met.* (1, 1076a22–37), and preceding his criticism of both the unmathematized and mathematized versions, Aristotle says that he discussed these matters in his "exoteric writings." This is not strong evidence, but it does suggest that Aristotle regularly treated both versions together. That he rejected both does not imply that he did not think some versions better or more defensible than others, including versions by other members of the Academy such as Speusippus and Xenocrates.

90. For a useful collection of the evidence for this reduction, see Findlay 1974, app. I; and Krämer 1990, 203–217.

91. The principle that the divine is a first principle and as such must be simple or without parts is clearly enunciated by Alcinous *Didask.* 10.7, 34–35: "God is partless, owing to the fact that there is nothing prior to him." See Plato *Parm.* 137C5ff.; *Soph.* 245A1ff.

92. See, e.g., Plotinus VI 6, "On Numbers," where Plotinus struggles to understand the status of eternal numbers in relation to Forms. At 9, 33–34, Plotinus accepts Aristotle's testimony that Plato identified Forms with numbers, but he does not have a perspicuous view about what this means. He does allude to *Phil.* 15A, where Plato calls Forms 'monads' and thinks that somehow this is connected with the identification of Forms and numbers generally.

A passage in Cicero's *On the Nature of the Gods* indicates that book 3 of *On Philosophy* was concerned with the nature of the divine: that is, with the subject matter of wisdom.[93] Accordingly, perhaps the most famous of the fragments of *On Philosophy* is universally assigned to book 3. Simplicius, evidently relying on the commentaries of Alexander of Aphrodisias, tells us

> that [Aristotle] says that the divine is eternal (ἀίδιον), [Alexander] testifies, as do the things clearly said many times in the discussions in the works intended for the public, namely, that necessarily the first and highest divinity has to be unchanging. For if it is unchanging, then it is also eternal. By "works intended for the public" he means those advanced for the many according to an ordered elementary exposition which we are accustomed to call 'exoteric' just as we call the more serious works 'lectures' or 'doctrinal.' He deals with the above argument in his *On Philosophy*.
>
> For it is universally the case that in things in which there is something that is better in these things there is also something that is best. Since, therefore, among the things that exist one thing is better than another, there is then also something that is best, which is what the divine would be. Now that which changes does so either by another or by itself; if by another, it changes either for the better or for the worse; if by itself, either to something worse or as a result of desiring something better. But the divine has nothing better than itself by which it will be changed (for that would be more divine) and it is not allowable for the better to be affected by the worse. And, of course, if it were changed by something worse, it would have allowed something bad in it, though there is in fact nothing bad in it. But neither does it change itself owing to a desire for something better, for it has no lack of its own goods in it. Nor does it change to something worse, since not even a man willingly makes himself worse; nor does it have anything bad which it would have gotten from its change to the worse. And Aristotle got this proof from the second book of Plato's *Republic*.[94]

The passage to which Simplicius is referring in the last line makes in a somewhat more informal way exactly the same point: namely, that the divine is unchangeable.[95] The passage in Plato, however, does not contain an argument for the existence of a god, as does the present one.

---

93. Cicero *De Nat. Deo.* I 13, 33 (= Ross, frag. 26). In this passage, the Epicurean interlocutor lists four apparently different conceptions of the divine found in book 3 of *On Philosophy*. These four are: (a) all divinity belongs to a mind; (b) divinity belongs to the world itself; (c) there is *another* god (apparently apart from mind) responsible for the motion of the world; (d) the heat of the heavens is a god. According to the interlocutor, Aristotle causes confusion by differing from Plato in his account. But there is not enough evidence available to know exactly what the confusion is supposed to be or even to whom the four views of the divine among the interlocutors in Aristotle's dialogue belong. On the evidence from Cicero, see esp. Berti 1962, 375–392. Also see Reale and Bos 1975, 90–97, for the parallels to the *On Philosophy* passage in *On the Universe*.

94. Simplicius *In Cael.* 288, 28–289, 15 (= Ross 1955, frag. 16). See *Cael.* A 9, 279a30–35, a passage which seems to refer directly to the argument in *On Philosophy*. See Untersteiner 1963, 198–199, on Simplicius's probable use of Alexander here. On the argument and its context, see esp. Effe 1970.

95. *Rep.* 380D-381C. Cf. *Mun.* 6, 400b11–12, 31.

In the present argument the sense in which the divine is best is left vague, though it is natural enough to suppose that Aristotle means that the life of the divine is the best sort of life.[96] If Aristotle had not then argued that the best must be unchangeable, we might have supposed that the definite description 'best' just referred to whatever was actually best, however flawed it might be. That is, one might have supposed that Aristotle was just making the logical point that where there are two or more things one of which is somehow better than the others, then there must be one that is, among them all, the best. But this is not a possible interpretation, given the connection Aristotle makes between the best and the property of unchangeability.[97] Still, there is a gap between a notionally perfect and a really perfect god. To say that our claim that something is relatively imperfect implies a concept of perfection is a long way from saying that the existence of the imperfect implies the existence of the perfect. Aristotle must here be arguing for the latter, owing to its being somehow causally connected to the imperfect.[98]

How then is the perfect and unchangeable god supposed to be related to everything else? Luckily, a reference to *On Philosophy* in Aristotle's *Physics* provides a plausible answer. Aristotle says that "final cause (τὸ οὗ ἕνεκα) has two senses, as was said in *On Philosophy*."[99] These two senses, as is made explicit in a number of other places, refer to (1) the reason for which something is done and (2) the person or thing affected by (1).[100] For example, a medical procedure can be done (1) for the sake of health and (2) for the sake of the patient. One might characterize the distinction as one between 'aim' and 'beneficiary.' The central point of the distinction is that a final cause need not be subject to any change, as the beneficiary normally would be. So, not only is it likely that the causality of the unchangeable god in *On Philosophy* is final causality in the sense of (1) above, but we must suppose that the distinction employed in *Metaphysics* and elsewhere is already in the dialogue. Taking that work as a popular version of the more sophisticated works is then at least in this respect hardly

---

96. See, e.g., *Met.* Λ 7, 1072b28–29: φαμὲν δὴ τὸν θεὸν εἶναι ζῷον ἀίδιον ἄριστον. That the 'best' is a *life* is simply assumed by Aristotle both in *Metaphysics* and here. The point is of some importance, since it would seem to preclude the identification of god with nature.

97. See *Met.* Λ 9, 1074b26: καὶ οὐ μεταβάλλει [i.e., god]· εἰς χεῖρον γὰρ ἡ μεταβολή ("[god] does not change; for change is for the worse").

98. *Met.* α 1, 993b23–31 contains an argument that "that to which a predicate belongs in the highest degree is that in virtue of which it belongs to the others." This closely related argument is treated infra, chap. 6. De Vogel 1960, 249–251, is certainly correct that the so-called *argumentum ex gradibus* does not directly prove the existence of Platonic Forms. Wilpert (1957, 160), similarly, says of the proof that it is "Überrest aus einer schon überwindenen Stufe der eigenen Entwicklung zu sehen" meaning that it is a proof for the existence of Forms without the Forms!

99. See *Phys.* B 2, 194a36. See also *Met.* Λ 7, 1072b2; *G.A.* B 6, 742a22ff.; *EE* H 15, 1249b15; *De An.* B 4, 415b2, b20. See Simplicius *In Phys.* 303, 29–304, 6.

100. See *De An.* B 4, 415b2: τὸ δ' οὗ ἕνεκα διττόν, τὸ μὲν οὗ, τὸ δὲ ᾧ. Also, *Met.* Λ 7, 1072b2.

unreasonable. But as Simplicius suggests, Aristotle in *On Philosophy* is employing a Platonic argument.

The reason given in the *Republic* passage for the unchangeability of the divine is never retracted by Plato. Far from it. Whatever activity the Demiurge or divine intellect engages in, it does not change, for change would have to be for the worse. How the divine is supposed to be causally related to the universe is then a problem, one with which the Neoplatonists were deeply concerned.[101] Three points are crucial. First, though the final causality to which Aristotle is evidently referring in *On Philosophy* does not appear clearly in so many words anywhere in Plato's various accounts of the divine, nevertheless the fundamental Platonic doctrine of 'assimilation to the divine' (ὁμοίωσις θεῷ), coupled with the characterization of the divine as unchangeable, is not very far removed from Aristotle's characterization of god. Second, Plato's association of the divine intellect or Demiurge with Forms in *Timaeus* allows for the former to be characterized as an ideal to be emulated in exactly the same way as is the divine final cause for Aristotle. Third, the differences that nevertheless remain between Aristotle's and Plato's accounts of the divine and of its relation to the world can be explained on the basis of the former's incomplete account of first principles, just as the harmonization thesis would have it.[102]

Aristotle's exoteric works have been treated, at least since Jaeger's study, as evidence for a relatively immature phase in Aristotle's development. For most scholars that development is away from Platonism and toward a philosophical position that, however we characterize it in particular, is anti-Platonic. The fundamental criterion and mark of development is Aristotle's commitment to or abandonment of the theory of Forms. From the perspective of the Neoplatonists, this criterion is flawed principally because it rests upon an unsophisticated account of Plato's metaphysics. Armed with a better account, one can see first of all that Plato, too, is an opponent of various theories of Forms, including at least one held by certain 'friends of the Forms' and others held by members of his Academy. What Plato *is* unwaveringly committed to is the eternality and hence ontological priority of the intelligible to the sensible world. And in the intelligible world is to be found

---

101. See, e.g., Proclus *In Tim.* I 401, 18–402, 31.

102. There is a famous fragment from Aristotle's *On Prayer* preserved by Simplicius in his *In Cael.* 485, 19–22. Simplicius says that Aristotle clearly thinks that there is something higher than intellect and οὐσία because in his work *On Prayer* he says that "god is either intellect or something beyond intellect." ὁ θεὸς ἢ νοῦς ἐστιν ἢ ἐπέκεινα τι τοῦ νοῦ. This is certainly tantalizing, though highly suspicious. I tend to think that there is some mistake being made by Simplicius, though not necessarily the one hypothesized in Rist 1985: namely, that Simplicius is reporting a garbled version from a compilation of a work known as περὶ εὐτυχίας. I rather think that Simplicius is not quoting from the lost work but drawing an inference from Aristotle's characterization of god as incorporeal, unchanging, and unique. But I also think it is just possible that in this work Aristotle did consider the (Platonic) possibility that god should be identified either with intellect or the Form of the Good, which is at *Republic* 509B to be "beyond essence" (ἐπέκεινα τῆς οὐσίας).

a hierarchy and a complexity wherein a divine intellect or mind has an essential, though not absolutely primary, place.[103]

When one comes to the dialogues with Neoplatonic assumptions and not with Jaegerian assumptions, the tradition that the dialogues are popular expressions of an established philosophical position and not immature, soon-to-be discarded positions makes good sense.[104] What is especially striking about such an approach is that it lets us see that in their harmony with Platonism the dialogues differ hardly at all from that established philosophical position.

103. See De Vogel (1965, 280–291), who argues for the Neoplatonic representation of the *exoterica* as popular expressions of Aristotle's technical thought: i.e., that Aristotle's thought did not develop significantly. Further, she argues that Plato's own metaphysics, properly understood, is in harmony with this thought. Nevertheless, De Vogel is sufficiently in the grasp of the Jaegerian hypothesis to state that the Platonism in, say, *Protrepticus* is "border-line, or rather, *border-country*" (290); (De Vogel's emphasis). That is, it sits on the border between Platonism and Aristotelianism.

104. See Egermann (1959, esp. 139–142), who provides an interesting argument against the use of a presumed contrast between the *exoterica* and the *esoterica* as a basis for postulating developmentalism.

CHAPTER THREE

The Categories of Reality

The Neoplatonic treatment of Aristotle's *Categories* is especially useful for understanding how harmonization works. For one thing, there exists an abundance of Neoplatonic commentaries on Aristotle's *Categories*.[1] For another, since the study of the *Categories* was taken by the Neoplatonists as the beginning of the philosophical curriculum, a good deal of what they have to say about the harmonization of Plato and Aristotle is expressed in their commentaries on this work.[2] Finally, *Categories* itself and the *Organon* in general were assumed to be amenable to a high degree of harmonization.[3] The reasons are as follows.

1. There are eight extant Neoplatonic commentaries on Aristotle's *Categories:* those by Porphyry, Dexippus, Boethius (in Latin, but based on Greek sources), Ammonius, Philoponus, Olympiodorus, Simplicius, and Elias (or David). See Simplicius *In Cat.* 1, 3–2, 29, for the impressive and complex history of the commentary tradition.

2. To be more precise, the study of philosophy began with a general lecture on the nature and end of philosophy and then moved to a study of Porphyry's *Isagoge*, evidently taken as an introduction to Aristotle's *Categories*. Then the 'class' proceeded to *Categories* itself. See Ammonius *In Cat.* 20, 15–21; 22, 23–24; 24, 16–17, for the connection between Porphyry's work and Aristotle's *Categories*. Barnes 2003, xv, argues that Porphyry's work is an introduction to philosophy generally and only indirectly an introduction to Aristotle's *Categories*. See I. Hadot 1990, 24–25, 44–46, for a discussion of the Neoplatonic curriculum along with a convenient table of the topics treated.

3. See Hadot 1989, 21–47, for a valuable survey of the structure of the *Categories* commentary tradition and the way harmonization was reflected in a philosophical curriculum. Hadot is particularly concerned with the later Neoplatonic tradition of commentaries, that is, from the 5th century C.E. onward. Therefore, she does not treat of Porphyry and Dexippus and the *Enneads* of Plotinus, the latter containing not a commentary in the sense in which that term came to be understood from Porphyry onward but an analysis and criticism of the idea of categories that came to be reflected in the later commentary tradition. Hadot concludes that the

Plato has little directly to say about the matters discussed in the *Organon*. One can without excessive strain read *Categories* as concerned entirely with language and conceptual thinking.[4] And though Plato does have a great deal to say about these matters, it is not so clear that his remarks stand in the way of accepting the import of the far more detailed discussions of Aristotle.[5] Further, the very idea of a categorization of types of being in the world seems to reflect Plato's injunction in *Statesman* to make one's concepts correspond to natural divisions.[6] Finally, and most important, *Categories* could be considered to be intended as an introduction to the study of nature: that is, to the study of sensible composites.[7] Such a study could be assumed to be carried out under general Platonic metaphysical principles, in particular the hierarchical subordination of becoming to being.[8]

Nevertheless, what Aristotle says in *Categories* primarily about substance [οὐσία] seems to contemporary readers at least a stumbling block sufficient to deter all but the most benighted Platonist. How, it may well be asked, could anyone suppose that if Aristotle is correct about the fundamental structure of things as explained in *Categories,* one could still maintain the cogency, much less the correctness, of the Platonic position? It is the Neoplatonists' answer to this question that I want to explore in this chapter.

Aristotle asserts, "a substance spoken of in the most fundamental, primary, and highest sense of the word is that which is neither said of a subject nor present in a subject, e.g., some man or some horse."[9] From this assertion it

---

commentaries of Ammonius, Philoponus, Olympiodorus, Elias (or David), and Simplicius are in accord on harmonization (177–178). This approach originates in the commentaries of Porphyry and is evident in the extant commentary of Dexippus.

4. On different approaches to the aim or goal of *Categories*, its unity, and authenticity, see Krämer 1973, 122–123; Frede 1987, 11–48. Krämer, 125; Frede, 26–27, take *Categories* as a metaphysical work, contradicted by *Metaphysics* in its assumption of the primacy of the sensible individual. Hence on this interpretation, Aristotle's views must have developed. See Wehrle 2001, chap. 4, on the various metaphysical interpretations of *Categories* and for an argument against these. Ammonius *In Cat.* 9, 17–10, 14, assumes that *Categories* encompasses discussions of the nexus of words, concepts, and things. Wedin 2000, 67–73, takes the work as offering a 'meta-ontology' of per se or primary things. Wedin's central thesis is that in *Metaphysics* Z, Aristotle, "ever the anti-Platonist" (5), intends to explain the underlying structure of the sensible substances of *Categories.* Thus the ontologies of the two works are not in conflict.

5. Not all the commentators by any means accepted Simplicius's assertion that the duty of the commentator was to show the fundamental harmony of Plato and Aristotle. See his *In Cat.* 7, 23–32.

6. See *Sts.* 262A–263A.

7. See Porphyry *In Cat.* 56, 28–31. Ammonius (*In Cat.* 33, 25; 34, 5; 41, 10; 45, 22), is explicit in holding that the work concerns only composite substances. For a modern defense of this view, see Furth 1978. Wehrle (2001, 174–175), rightly urges that the relatively elementary nature of the work does not mean that it is elementary *metaphysics;* rather, it can be taken to be an introduction to philosophy generally and does not entail particular metaphysical views, such as that sensible substances are absolutely primary beings.

8. See esp. *Timaeus* 29A–D, where the derivative intelligibility of the world of becoming guarantees that physics is at best a "likely story" (εἰκὸς μῦθος).

9. *Cat.* 5, 2a11–14: Οὐσία δέ ἐστιν ἡ κυριώτατα τε καὶ πρώτως καὶμάλιστα λεγομένη, ἡ μήτε καθ' ὑποκειμένου τινὸς λέγεται μήτε ἐν ὑποκειμένῳ τινί ἐστιν, οἷον ὁ τὶς ἄνθρωπος ἢ ὁ τὶς ἵππος.

seems clear that (1) sensible things, like a man or horse, are fundamental substances; (2) what is said of or present in the substance is not itself a fundamental substance. On the face of it, one would suppose that by placing an individual man or horse in the focus of the account of things, Aristotle is directly contradicting Plato's view that the sensible world generally is posterior or subordinate to the intelligible world, the realm of Forms.[10] And if this is so, one naturally wonders whether "harmonization" is merely wishful thinking.

Before we accept such a conclusion, we need to realize that the Neoplatonic commentators on *Categories* did not come to their work innocent of a broad and deep knowledge of the entire Aristotelian corpus as they possessed it. Although they did not use the convention of footnotes, the references in their commentaries to other works of Aristotle are ubiquitous.[11] So, we may be certain, they knew that what is said in *Categories* hardly constitutes a definitive and unambiguous statement of Aristotle's view of substance. For example, we need to take into account what Aristotle says in *Metaphysics* about primary substance. At Z 3, 1029a30–32 we read: "Accordingly, the form of the composite would seem to be a substance to a higher degree than matter. The composite substance, that is, the composite of matter and shape, may be laid aside; for it is *posterior* and clear." What exactly this posteriority amounts to needs to be explored, but it is not obvious that if "some man" or "some horse" is a composite substance, such a thing truly is substance in the primary sense.[12]

As I mentioned in my introduction, one way of dealing with the apparent contradiction is to postulate some sort of development in Aristotle's thinking, from an 'early' phase that holds sensible composites to be primary to a 'later' phase that attributes absolute priority to something else.[13] Developmentalism as a hypothesis about Aristotle's writings is prima facie plausible though deeply unsatisfactory in its results.[14] Much the same can be said about the hypothesis of Plato's development. I am not aware that developmentalism occurred to any of the Neoplatonists as an interpretive hypothesis. No doubt part of the explanation for this is that they were interested primarily not in the history of philosophy but rather in the philosophical truths that the 'ancients' had discovered and delivered in their writings.

---

10. See further 2b6: "If primary substances then did not exist, it would be impossible for any of the others to exist" (μὴ οὐσῶν οὖν τῶν πρώτων οὐσιῶν ἀδύνατον τῶν ἄλλων τι εἶναι).

11. Simplicius *In Cat.* 7, 24–25, states that one of the requirements for a commentator is that he must be familiar with everything that Aristotle has written and not merely the work on which he is commenting. I suppose it is worth remembering that the familiarity was not impeded by translations.

12. See, e.g., Porphyry *In Cat.* 88, 13–15, who assumes that in explicating the concept (ἔννοια) of substance in *Categories* he can appropriately make use of Book Z of *Metaphysics*.

13. See, e.g., Graham 1987, esp. chap. 1. Jaeger 1948, 46 n. 3, though recognizing the basically Aristotelian content of *Categories*, questions its authenticity on developmentalist grounds.

14. See Barnes 1995, 15–22, for some characteristically acerbic and skeptical remarks about the prospects for developmentalism.

Another part of the explanation is that they took a different approach to the Aristotelian corpus, one that precluded any need for developmentalism in the first place.

One of the fundamental questions that Neoplatonic commentators generally asked about a text of Plato or Aristotle or indeed anyone else was "what is the aim or σκόπος of this work?"[15] If two works, such as *Categories* and *Metaphysics*, were supposed to have different aims, then contradictions were much less likely to be seen. In fact, it was generally supposed that these two works did have different aims, the former being 'logical' in nature and the latter being 'ontological.' The origin of the identification of *Categories* as a logical work actually seems to be Peripatetic. The very ordering of the Aristotelian corpus by Andronicus of Rhodes in the first century B.C.E. emphasizes both the introductory nature of the *Organon* and its separation from the study of ultimate principles in *Metaphysics*.[16]

Porphyry it seems follows the Peripatetic commentator Alexander of Aphrodisias in the distinction between a logical and an ontological aim.[17] In his *Commentary on Aristotle's Categories* Porphyry writes,

> The subject of this book [i.e., *Categories*] is the primary imposition of expressions, which are used for communicating about things.[18] For it concerns simple significant sounds in so far as they signify things—not however as they differ from one another in number, but as differing in genus. For things and expressions are both practically infinite in number. But his intention is not to list expressions one by one—for each one signifies one particular being—but since things that are many in number are one in species or in genus, the infinity of beings and of the expressions that signify them is found to be included under a list of ten genera. Since beings are comprehended by ten generic differentiae, the sounds that indicate them have also come to be ten in genus,

15. The canonical list of the ten questions to be answered by every Aristotelian commentator is found in Simplicius *In Cat.* 3, 18–29. Elias (or David) *In Cat.* 107, 24–26, says that the list was established by Proclus. The questions are these: (1) In how many ways are the philosophical schools named and on what bases? (2) What is the classificatory division of Aristotle's writings? (3) Where should one begin in studying Aristotle? (4) What is the goal or end of Aristotle's philosophy? (5) What are the means employed for achieving this end? (6) What is the form of expression of Aristotle's writings? (7) Why has Aristotle cultivated obscurity? (8) What are the qualities required by the exegete? (9) What are the qualities required by the reader? (10) What are the main points that have to be grasped first in the study of any particular writing of Aristotle and why are these so?. These main points are the end of the work, the use of it, the reason for its title, its place in the order of reading, its authenticity, and the division into chapters. See Mansfeld 1994 for a magisterial study of the hermeneutics of the commentators. The absence of developmentalism did not preclude the need to establish an order for the study of the works of an author.

16. See Owens 1981a, 14–22, for a contemporary view that *Categories* is "a mixture of both" logic and metaphysics. See Burnyeat (2001, chap. 5, esp. 106–108), who argues that *Categories*, since it contains no "explanatory science," is not a work of metaphysics but is intended as a work "for beginners."

17. See Strange 1992, 7–8, for a brief summary of the matter with references to the sources for the aim of *Categories*.

18. At 58, 33, Porphyry adds that *On Interpretation* discusses the "secondary imposition" of expressions: that is, the second-order characterization and classification of types of primary expressions.

and are themselves also so classified. Thus predications are said to be ten in genus, just as beings themselves are ten in genus. So, since the subject of this book is significant expressions differing in genus, in so far as they signify, and people used to call speaking of things according to a certain signification, and in general the utterance of a significant expression about something, as 'predication,' it was quite reasonable for him to give the title *Categories* to this elementary discussion of simple expressions, which considers them according to genus in so far as they primarily signify things.[19]

As Porphyry was well aware, his account of the aim of *Categories* was not universally accepted. In fact, it was apparently not accepted by his master, Plotinus, among others, who held that the work was not about the genera of expressions but about the genera of being or *things*.[20] Let us grant for the moment that the aim of *Categories* is open to question. Let us further grant that Porphyry's interpretation of that aim is not an unreasonable one. Still, one wants to insist that this interpretation does not remove the objection to harmonization. For the distinction between a logical and an ontological work does not imply that a logical work is totally innocent of any ontological commitments. Indeed, if logic is to be, as Aristotle evidently thought, an effective tool of demonstrative science, it is because that tool is shaped according to the ontological commitments of science. Chief among these commitments seems to be the absolute priority of such things as 'this man' and 'this horse.' I shall return to treat at some length the efforts to reconcile (with or without developmentalism) what is said in the passage from *Metaphysics* Z 3 (quoted above) with what is said in *Categories*. For the present I want to focus on how harmonization is understood by Porphyry to be applied to the latter.

In Porphyry's description of the aim of *Categories* he employs the phrase "simple significant sounds" [φωνῶν σημαντικῶν ἁπλῶν].[21] These are nouns such as 'man,' 'gold,' 'white,' and verbs such as 'walks.' The 'simple imposition' of these sounds (i.e., words) is their reference to particulars. So, "this man, e. g., Socrates, is white" or "this man, e. g., Socrates, walks" or "this man, e. g., Socrates, is a man" are examples of the use of simple significant words.[22] From the perspective of a Neoplatonist simple imposition here reminds one of Plato's *Sophist,* where a similar account is given of nouns and verbs together used to say something about something.[23] For example, "Theaetetus sits" says something about this man Theaetetus. Since on the

19. Porphyry *In Cat.* 58, 4–21 (trans. Strange). See 91, 11–12, where Porphyry adds that sensibles are the primary objects of signification.

20. See ibid. 59, 3–7. Plotinus VI 1. 1, assumes that *Categories* divides beings into ten genera. Cf. *Met.* Z 3, 1029a20–21. De Haas 2001 argues that Porphyry's interpretation of *Categories* is in harmony with that of Plotinus. I return to Plotinus's criticisms of this division below.

21. Porphyry *In Cat.* 58, 5.

22. At 57, 24–27, it is clear from the repeated use of τόδε that the semantic role of the words he is discussing should be understood in this way.

23. See *Soph.* 261C-263B. At 262E5, a λόγος is said always to be a λόγος "about something" (τίνος). Cf. 263A4; C9–11. I leave aside the obvious problems caused by limiting "something" to individuals. See also *Crat.* 431B.

surface Plato's account of how "Theaetetus sits" is constructed is not different from Aristotle's account of "Socrates walks," we need to ask why it should
be thought that Aristotle is not merely saying something different from Plato
in *Categories*, but something *radically different*.[24]

Typically, the belief that there is something different going on is based
on the supposition that Aristotle and Plato are offering conflicting explanations of predication. Plato thinks that in general, if 'x is f' is true where
'x' stands for some sensible thing and 'f' stands for an attribute of it, then
the explanation is that x participates in a Form of F-ness. Aristotle's explanation of 'x is f' is supposedly different and incompatible. In fact, when one
searches *Categories* for the putative alternative explanation, it becomes clear
that though Aristotle has quite a bit to say about such statements as 'x is f'
and their meaning, he does not in *Categories* regard the statement 'x is f' as
needing an explanation in the way that Plato does. So, when Aristotle claims
that 'Socrates is white' means that 'white' is present in Socrates, he is not
ipso facto contradicting the Platonic explanation for the truth of 'Socrates
is white,' namely, that Socrates participates in the Form of Whiteness.[25]

Further, when Aristotle in *On Interpretation* defines 'universal' [καθόλου]
as 'that which by its nature is predicable of more than one,' he is not obviously offering predication as an *alternative* to Platonic participation.[26] Thus
if "Socrates is a man" and "Plato is a man" mean that 'man' is predicated of
Socrates and Plato, and 'man' is taken as a universal, there is no reason I can
see for holding that *therefore* it is false that Plato and Socrates participate in
the Form of Man.[27] Nor, it must be granted, is the Aristotelian meaning any
reason to believe in the Platonic explanation.[28]

---

24. See, e.g., Mann (2000, 4), who argues that before *Categories* (and *Topics*), "there were
no things. Less starkly: things did not show up *as* things, until Aristotle wrote those two works."

25. The fact that white is 'present in' Socrates is not merely consistent with 'Socrates participates in Whiteness'; it overlaps the generalization of the claims made in *Phd.* 102E6 that
there is 'smallness in us' (τὸ σμικρὸν τὸ ἐν ἡμῖν) and in *Parm.* 132A6, where Socrates agrees
that his 'theory of Forms' begins with the assumption that, e.g., there are 'many large things'
owing to which a Form of Largeness is postulated 'over and above' these. That smallness exists
in small things does not negate the fact that this smallness is an image of the Form.

26. See *De Int.* 17a39 and *Met.* B 6, 1003a11 and Z 13, 1038b11–12: τοῦτο γὰρ λέγεται
καθόλου ὃ πλείοσιν ὑπάρχειν πέφυκεν. See also *APo.* A 11, 77a5–9, which explicitly distinguishes universals from forms in demonstration. What belongs to many and is hence the subject of demonstration cannot be a substitute for an explanation for the possibility of there being
this many. Syrianus *In Met.* 114, 9–11, clearly distinguishes the priority of the independently
existing Form from the universal: οὐκ εἴ τι οὖν ἐν ἐπὶ πολλῶν νόημα, τούτου ἐστὶν ἰδέα (οὕτω
γὰρ ἂν καὶ τῶν παρὰ φύσιν ἦσαν ἰδέαι), ἀλλ' ὧν μὲν ἰδέαι, τούτων εἰσὶ καὶ καθόλου λόγοι,
οὐ μὴν ἀντιστρέφει. See Kahn 1992a, 369, for his apt remarks on the "myth of abstraction" as
explanation. See also my "Platonism and the Invention of the Problem of Universals," forthcoming in *Archiv für Geschichte der Philosophie*.

27. Iamblichus, e.g., *apud* Simplicius *In Cat.* 53, 9–18, is reported to have treated "Socrates
is a man" as primarily referring to participation with the implication that it can also express a
predication.

28. Alcinous is a committed harmonizer in his *Didaskalikos*. At 4. 6–7, he distinguishes
knowledge of Forms from a natural conception (φυσικὴ ἔννοια), which arises from our sense

The Neoplatonists were, if nothing else, passionately interested in ultimate explanations of things. So, we need to have a closer look at the theory of Forms as providing ultimate explanations and what this means for the interpretation of Aristotle. In *Phaedo*, Plato has Socrates assert that if something is beautiful, it is 'owing to' [διότι] participation in the Form of Beauty.[29] Two lines later, this participation is assumed to be synonymous with the instrumental causality of the Form.[30] But the Forms here are adduced as a particular sort of *explanans*. In effect, they provide the explanation for the *possibility* of predication.[31] Because Forms exist, it is possible that genuine or true predication should occur.[32]

The central point to be made in this regard is that if postulating Forms explains the possibility of (nonarbitrary) predication, the actual account of predication—what it means to say that 'x is f'—is not on the face of it in danger of being in conflict with that explanation. Aristotle himself supports this interpretation in the very midst of his criticism of Plato's theory. Aristotle complains that "those who posited Ideas as causes" gratuitously introduced these Ideas "equal in number" to the things they sought to explain. For "there exists a Form having the same name as that which is predicated of the many sensibles, of substances as well as of non-substances, and of these things as well as of eternal things."[33] In a subsequent argument against Forms he claims that (according to the doctrine of Forms) Ideas are not shared as attributes, but "each Idea must be shared in this sense, namely, qua not being said of a subject."[34] Although the arguments here are difficult (they are addressed in chapter 7), what is clear is that Aristotle does not at least in this passage view the theory of Forms as being preempted by the account of predication in *Categories*, unless we choose gratuitously to understand that account as precluding the need to explain the possibility of predication.

---

perception of instances of Forms. These natural conceptions are clearly distinguished in their role from the explanatory function of the Forms themselves. Alcinous is evidently borrowing the Stoic idea of a naturally arising concept, otherwise called 'preconception' (πρόληψις). See *SVF* II 83.

29. *Phd.* 100D5–6.

30. Ibid. 100D7–8. So, I take the words ἀλλ' ὅτι τῷ καλῷ πάντα τὰ καλὰ γίγνεται καλά, eliminating Burnet's unnecessary bracketing of γίγνεται.

31. In *Parmenides* the only reason given for positing Forms is for explaining how many things can be the same. This claim may also be inferred from the account in *Tim.* 30C–31A of the Demiurge's use of the eternal paradigm of Living Thing as model for the creation of images of that paradigm. Cf. 51E. See also Plotinus VI 7. 8, where he argues that if god (i.e., the divine intellect) had the thought of making a horse, then horse had to exist already: "the horse which did not come into being must exist before that which was to be afterwards" (ll. 8–9).

32. It should be noted that Socrates' story (*Phd.* 97C–100B) about his rejection of Anaxagorean mechanical explanations and his substitution of his 'simple hypothesis' of Forms was not taken by Neoplatonists to be a *rejection* of such explanations.

33. *Met.* A 9, 990a34–b8. Aristotle uses 'Idea' and 'Form' interchangeably, but the potentiality for a distinction did not escape the notice of the Neoplatonists.

34. Ibid. 990b27–31.

For Neoplatonists generally, harmonization is made plausible by treating Plato as providing explanations for the possibility of that which Aristotle describes and categorizes.[35] Of course, from the positing of entities to account for the possibility of predication much follows, including things that are, finally perhaps, irreconcilable with Aristotelian claims. We are at this point, however, quite a distance from that stage. I here only note something to which I return later: namely, that the sort of explanation the theory of Forms was taken to be is deeply connected with the top-down approach of Neoplatonism. According to this approach, ultimate and complete explanations are not precluded by categorization or hypothesis. On the contrary, they are required for them.[36]

The distinction between participation and predication is clearly understood by the Neoplatonist Iamblichus. In his *Commentary on the Categories of Aristotle* as reported by Simplicius, he writes, "Genera are not predicated of subjects, but the predicates are different owing to these [διὰ ταῦτα, that is, because of genera]. For whenever we say Socrates is a man, we are not saying that he is the genus 'man' but that he partakes of the genus 'man.'"[37] Iamblichus does not misunderstand Aristotle to be identifying Socrates with man. He understands him to be saying something that is consistent with holding that Socrates is a man *because* he partakes of the Form of Man. This may be doubted, for Aristotle is generally interpreted to be saying that if 'man' is said of 'Socrates,' that means that 'man' does partially identify him. That is the point about essential predication.[38]

Aristotle's distinction in *Categories* between 'said of' and 'present in,' understood as a distinction between essential and accidental predication, may be thought to be the smoking gun of antiharmonization.[39] If the predicate 'man'

---

35. De Haas (2001, esp. 518–523) argues forcefully for this view. Cleary (1995, 162ff.) notices the problem in supposing that Aristotelian universals provide the foundation for science if Platonic Forms do not. Cleary's solution (174) is the distinction between synonymous and homonymous predication. He holds that Aristotle (in *Categories* at least) wants to insist that only that which is synonymously predicable of sensible particulars can serve as the basis for the scientific knowledge of them. Only universals can be identical with the predicates that denote the essence of the sensible subjects of predication. See infra chap. 7, on the difficulties Plotinus finds in such a claim.

36. See Libera 1996, 33, on the "platonisme résiduel dans l'aristotélisme," referring here to Aristotle's acknowledgment of the existence of universals. One may also compare Plato's treatment of hypothesis in his use of the divided line in *Rep.* 509D–511E. The hypothetical reasoning of mathematicians (and others) is contrasted with the aim of the philosopher to reach an unhypothetical beginning. The mathematical 'let there be a triangle' is comparable to the Aristotelian 'let there be an individual substance with such and such an accidental attribute.'

37. Simplicius *In Cat.* 53, 9–12. Porphyry *In Cat.* 72, 21–23, allows that a substance 'participates' in a universal, but it is not clear that Porphyry is not simply using 'participates' here as the obverse of 'is predicated.'

38. At *Top.* Δ 1, 121a10–19, Aristotle says that the species partakes (μετέχειν) of the genus and that 'partaking' is "defined as admitting the account of that which is partaken." See also Δ 5, 126a17–27.

39. See *Cat.* 3, 1b10–15. At 1a2 and 3b2–7 we learn that the definition is said of the substance, and at *Top.* Α 5, 101b39, we learn that a definition is of an essence. See also *Cat.* 5, 2b30–32, where species and genera are taken to be 'secondary substances.' See Anton 1968, and Mann 2000, 184–193.

is said of 'Socrates,' then this does not in fact mean that Socrates participates in the Form of Man precisely because participation is incompatible with essential predication. And though participation may not be clearly incompatible with accidental predication in the same way, it may be reasonably held that accidental predication can be properly understood (in an Aristotelian manner)only in contrast to the essential predications that belong to the first category, substance. That is, to understand what it means to say that 'white' is 'present in' Socrates, we have to understand what it means to say that 'Socrates' stands for some substance. And a substance is that which has essential predicates.

Porphyry identifies that which is 'said of' a substance as a universal [καθόλου].[40] He goes on, famously, to allow that what it means to say that a universal is said of a subject is a 'deep' matter.[41] Porphyry hereby announces the 'problem of universals' as understood by medieval philosophers: namely, the problem of the ontological status of what is said of particular substances. But later in his commentary he addresses the matter to a certain extent. He claims that we come to conceive of and apply the universal predicate as a result of perception. So, "if particular animals are eliminated, what is predicated in common of them will no longer exist either."[42]

But this leads to the objection that Aristotle himself elsewhere regards intelligible substances—namely, the mind, the gods, and Forms, if there be such— as primary substances. Therefore, how can he maintain that sensible substances are primary?[43] Porphyry's reply is most instructive:

> I shall say that since the subject of the work is significant expressions, and expressions are applied primarily to sensibles—for men first of all assign names to what they know and perceive, and only secondarily to those things that are primary by nature [τὰ τῇ φύσει] but secondary with respect to perception—it is reasonable for him to have called things that are primarily signified by expressions, that is, sensibles and individuals, primary substances. Thus with respect to significant expressions sensible individuals are primary substances, but as regards nature, intelligible substances are primary. But his intention is to distinguish the genera of being according to

40. *In Cat.* 74, 7–8. Cf. 71, 19–38.
41. See ibid., 75, 26, and especially the most influential passage in *Isag.* 1, 9–14: "For example, I shall put aside the examination of such profound questions regarding genera and species, since this requires another more detailed study: (1) whether genera and species exist in themselves or reside in mere concepts alone; (2) whether, if they exist, they are corporeal or incorporeal; and (3) whether they exist apart or in sensibles and dependent on them"(αὐτίκα περὶ τῶν γενῶν τε καὶ εἰδῶν τὸ μὲν εἴτε ὑφέστηκεν εἴτε καὶ ἐν μόναις ψιλαῖς ἐπινοίαις κεῖται εἴτε καὶ ὑφεστηκότα σώματά ἐστιν ἢ ἀσώματα καὶ πότερον χωριστὰ ἢ ἐν τοῖς αἰσθητοῖς καὶ περὶ ταῦτα ὑφεστῶτα, παραιτήσομαι λέγειν βαθυτάτης οὔσης τῆς τοιαύτης πραγματείας καὶ ἄλλης μείζονος δεομένης ἐξετάσεως). There is a certain irony in the fact that, though this passage became the *fons et origo* of the problem of universals, the word 'universal' (τὸ καθόλου) does not appear here. In fact it does not appear as a technical term at all in this work.
42. *In Cat.* 91, 2–5.
43. Ibid., 91, 14–17.

the expressions that signify them, and these primarily signify individual sensible substances.[44]

What is clear from the passage above is that the 'said of' relation is not taken to be primarily participation in Forms. What is said of a particular substance is a universal. A universal is a word or concept.[45] In no sense does a universal *replace* the explanatory role of a Form.[46]

Porphyry was in part relying on the great commentator Alexander of Aphrodisias for his understanding of universals in Aristotle. As we shall see, Alexander's account is encouraging to the harmonist, especially since it comes from perhaps the first state sponsored 'professor' of Peripatetic philosophy. Alexander was no doubt in some sense a committed Aristotelian partisan, which would presumably suggest his rejection of a theory of Forms taken as a theory of universals. Alexander's consideration of this matter, however, is far from exhausted by this peremptory characterization. His account is frequently and I believe unfairly dismissed as incoherent.[47]

Alexander in his commentary on Aristotle's *Metaphysics* endorses the Aristotelian position that everything that is separate is an individual.[48] Yet he acknowledges that a plurality of individuals may possess the same nature.[49] This nature is *neither* an individual *nor* a universal, for the universal is just this nature as conceived.[50] The universality is accidental to the nature.[51]

---

44. Ibid., 91, 19–27 (trans. Strange). Cf. Dexippus *In Cat.* 45, 5–12; Ammonius *In Cat.* 9, 17–24.

45. See Porphyry *In Cat.* 57, 6. Cf. Plotinus (VI 3. 9, 23–40), who argues against taking the universal as an explanation of the presence of an attribute.

46. See Simplicius (*In Cat.* 82, 35–83, 10), who says that that which is common (τὸ κοινόν) must be understood in three senses: (1) that which transcends the particulars and is the cause of what is common in them owing to its nature; (2) that which is common in particulars; and (3) that which exists in our concepts owing to abstraction. According to Simplicius, when Aristotle is speaking in *Categories* about (2) and (3), he is simply ignoring, not rejecting, (1). See Asclepius (*In Met.* 193, 9; 433, 9–436, 6), who cites Syrianus as making a similar distinction. See also Porphyry *In Cat.* 90, 30–91, 18; Ammonius *In Cat.* 41, 10–42, 26 and 68, 25–69, 2, and his *In Cat.* 41, 8–11, where a distinction between intelligible and sensible genera and species is assumed; Proclus *ET* Prop. 67; Elias (or David) *In Cat.* 48, 15–30; 113, 14–29.

47. See Moraux 1942, 61–62; Tweedale 1984; Sharples 1987; Moraux 2001. On the presumed incoherence of that account see, e. g., Tweedale 1993, 79–81: "I think it must be confessed that Alexander's theory borders on incoherence" (81). But see Lloyd 1981 for a defense of Alexander's account.

48. See *In Met.* 210, 13–21.

49. See *Quaest.* I 3, 12–13.

50. See *Quaest.* I 11b, 27–29: ἀλλὰ δεῖ τι εἶναι πρᾶγμα, ᾧ τὸ καθόλου συμβέβηκεν, καὶ ἔστιν ἐκεῖνο μὲν πρᾶγμα τι ᾧ τὸ καθόλου συμβέβηκεν, τὸ δὲ καθόλου οὐ πρᾶγμά τι κυρίως, ἀλλὰ συμβεβηκός τι ἄλλῳ. οἷον τὸ ζῷον πρᾶγμά τί ἐστι καὶ φύσεώς τινος δηλωτικόν, σημαίνει γὰρ οὐσίαν ἔμψυχον αἰσθητικήν, ὃ κατὰ μὲν τὴν αὑτοῦ φύσιν οὐκ ἔστι καθόλου. See Lloyd 1981, 155, on Alexander's conceptualism.

51. See Tweedale 1984, 285ff.

This nature is prior to any individual that possesses it.[52] It is also prior to the universal.[53]

If one does not keep the nature distinct from the universal, it is easy to fall into two mistakes. First, there is the mistake of supposing that Alexander means to hold that when no universal thinking or predicating is occurring, then things do not have the natures they have. But clearly Alexander wants to hold nothing of the sort. Second, there is the more subtle mistake of holding that the disappearance of the basis for universal predication—namely, the presence of a plurality with the same nature—indicates the absence or disappearance of the nature. This is not the case, however, if the nature is prior to the universal. Though Alexander believes that if there is only one individual with a given nature, there is no basis for universal prediction, he obviously does not maintain the contradictory position that the nature the individual possesses would therefore not exist.[54]

The distinction between nature and universal should be plain if we consider that if there is only one individual possessing the nature, then, though the universal does not exist, the nature does.[55] But what if there are *no* individuals possessing the nature? Does the nature no longer exist? Certainly, the genus would no longer exist, since the universal disappears. From the foregoing, it seems that Alexander wants to reject Forms only if they are taken as separate universals: that is, if universality is not understood as accidental to their natures.[56] In addition, he seems to recognize that the natures in which individuals share serve an explanatory function distinct from the role that universals fulfill. The nature animal is distinct from and prior to the universal animal which is predicated of many individual animals that share this nature. It is distinct from the genus or species.

We may, however, wonder whether the priority possessed by the nature is *ontological* priority: that is, whether Alexander is implicitly endorsing a

52. See *Quaest.* I 11b, 29–32: ὑπάρχει [the nature] δὲ αὐτῷ ὄντι τοιούτῳ ἐν πλείοσιν εἶναι καὶ κατ' εἶδος ἀλλήλων διαφέρουσιν. συμβέβηκεν οὖν αὐτῷ τοῦτο [universality].

53. See ibid., 7–8: δεῖ γὰρ εἶναι πρῶτον τὸ πρᾶγμα [the nature] τοῦ συμβεβηκότος αὐτῷ. ὅτι δ' ὕστερον [the genus or universal] τοῦ πράγματος, δῆλον. See Sharples 1987, 1202.

54. The medieval distinction between universals (a) *ante rem*; (b) *in re*; and (c) *post rem* has its origin in the Neoplatonic understanding of the dispute. See Proclus *In Euc.* 50, 16–51, 13; Ammonius *In Por. Isag.* 41, 17–22; 42, 10–21. Particularly in the latter passages, however, where Ammonius is referring to Porphyry's problem explicitly, it is evident that the question of an *ante rem* universal is bound up with the dispute, instigated by Porphyry in opposition to Plotinus, regarding the question of whether or not the Forms were in the divine intellect. The *ante rem* universal is here being conflated with the nature itself, which is none of (a) or (b) or (c) above.

55. See *Quaest.* I 11b, 19–22.

56. Alexander of Aphrodisias *In Met.* 199, 34–35, says that scientific knowledge is about the "universal that is eternal" (καθόλου ὅ ἐστιν ἀίδιον). This is apparently an allusion to *Met.* E 1, 1026a30, where Aristotle says that first philosophy is universal science. Alexander's language evidently did add to the confusion. For example, Dexippus *In Cat.* 45, 8–9, identifies universals as simple causes and as having their being in themselves (τὰ καθ' αὐτὰ παρ' αὐτῶν ἔχοντα τὸ εἶναι). See Ammonius *In Cat.* 25, 9 where he introduces the term 'universal substances' (καθόλου οὐσίαι), which Ammonius takes to be the ontological correlates of the generic and specific concepts (ἐννοηματικά, 9, 9).

version of a theory of Forms shorn of the burden of being a theory of universals. Indeed, it is difficult to see how, if ontological priority is not what the nature has, that nature would not be reduced to the universal. Fortunately, speculation on this matter is unnecessary. For Alexander in his *De Anima* distinguishes enmattered forms [ἔνυλα εἴδη] from the forms that are completely separate from matter.[57] These two types of form are objects of two different types of thought.[58] The latter are just the natures previously distinguished from universals. For example, bronze is distinct from what it is to be bronze [τὸ εἶναι χαλκῷ]. And it is the latter that is causally responsible for the former.[59]

Alexander does not offer an argument for the postulation of separate natures. Nor does he offer an argument for his subsequent claim that these separate natures are eternally thought by an eternal mind and in being thought are thought universally.[60] I cannot here enter into the complex and fascinating issue of how this latter claim is related to Platonists' treatment of Forms as thoughts in the divine mind of the Demiurge or to Alexander's identification of the eternal mind that eternally thinks the separate natures with the mind of the unmoved mover *and* the agent intellect in Aristotle's *De Anima*. I only wish to emphasize that Alexander, in offering an account of universals which he presumably takes to be in line with that of his master Aristotle, does not contradict the underlying reason for postulating Forms. In fact, he seems to rely on it. And his rejection of a theory of Forms applies *only* to a theory which incorrectly takes Forms to be universals.

How does this implicit distinction between Form and universal affect the seeming connection of 'said of' predication with essentialism? Universals—that is, secondary substances—when correctly predicated of a subject, reveal [δηλοῖ] the nature of that subject.[61] Accidents, when correctly predicated of a subject, are less informative. There are two ways of understanding what it means to reveal the nature of a subject through predication of species and genera. First, we can understand that what is revealed is the identity of the subject. We reveal, say, what Socrates is. 'Socrates is a man' is usually understood in this way. We can, alternatively, understand that what is revealed is the nature in which Socrates participates. That Socrates participates in this nature does not imply that Socrates is identified by this nature, at least not that he is identified in a way that is compatible with essentialism rigorously construed.

---

57. See *De An.* 87, 5–16. The term is evidently Platonic in origin, though not explicitly in Plato. See Alcinous *Didask.* 4. 6–7 on "enmattered forms." Dillon (1993, 69) claims that the idea is derived from Aristotle and not from Plato. It is, I think, instructive to note the various claims of filiation. Aristotelians, like Alexander, happily used terms current among Platonists such as Alcinous to express Aristotelian ideas. The Neoplatonists concluded without difficulty that Aristotle was himself building on Plato's own ideas. See infra chap. 6.

58. *De An.* 87, 24–88, 3; 89, 13–15; 90, 2–11.

59. Ibid., 87, 10–11: ὃς ἐν τῇ ὑποκειμένῃ ὕλῃ γενόμενος ἐποίησεν χαλκὸν αὐτήν.

60. Ibid., 90, 11–13.

61. Ibid., 92, 7.

Ordinary predication seems to imply that there is some criterion for the identification of the subject of the predicate independent of the predicate.[62] Normally, the identification is made according to some theory of reference. When Plato discusses ordinary predication, he presumes a simple theory of reference as in the passage from *Sophist* mentioned above.[63] The statement 'Theaetetus sits' must be about 'this man here, Theaetetus.' Clearly, Theaetetus is identified by ostensive reference independently of the predicate 'sits.' Aristotle, however, seems to want to hold that there is a fundamental difference in a statement 'x is f' where 'f' is said of 'x' and 'f' is 'present in' 'x.' If 'f' is said of 'x,' then on the usual interpretation, 'f' identifies 'x.' But if that is the case, then it is not clear straightaway how 'x' independently identifies x.

Plotinus, articulating what he takes to be the Platonic account of the 'said of' relation, writes: "For when I predicate 'man' of Socrates, I mean it not in the sense in which the wood is white, but in the sense that the white thing is white; for in saying that Socrates is a man, I am saying that a particular man is man, predicating man of the man in Socrates, but this is the same thing as calling Socrates Socrates, and again as predicating 'living being' of this rational living being."[64] These rather paradoxical sounding remarks require some background in order to be appreciated. Plotinus is a strong opponent of Aristotle's categories, *if* these be understood as unqualifiedly applicable to the intelligible world as well as to the sensible world.[65] Plotinus argues strenuously that substance as conceived of in *Categories* does not belong to the intelligible world, principally for the obvious reason that a sensible substance contains matter. Since Plotinus also holds that the sensible world is an image or εἰκών of the intelligible world, he is prepared to allow that what is said about that image—for example, what is said about sensible substance—might be applicable 'analogously' or 'homonomously' to the intelligible world.[66] What Plotinus rejects, however, is the inference to the absolute priority of sensible substance or, in other words, to the claim that the categories are *the* categories of being.[67] Such a claim to priority is precisely

62. I leave out here the unnecessary complication of a possible existential presumption in predication. One reason for thinking that one cannot say anything about a nonexistent object is that it cannot be identified independent of its predicates.

63. See *Soph.* 262E-263E.

64. VI 3. 5, 18–23. Cf. Simplicius *In Cat.* 79, 26–27.

65. See VI 1. 1, 19–22. Cf. Simplicius *In Cat.* 73, 27–28. See Evangeliou 1988, 94–181, on Plotinus's criticism of Aristotle's categories and Porphyry's attempt to defend Aristotle.

66. See VI 3. 5, 1–3. On the sensible world as an image of the intelligible world, see VI 3. 1, 21; II 3. 18, 17; II 9. 4, 25; VI 2. 22, 36. Simplicius *In Cat.* 80, 5–6, says that predication of sensible substances should be understood as made in virtue of the sameness (ὁμοιότητα) of the substance with respect to that upon which it depends, namely, the transcendent cause (τὸ ἐξῃρημένον).

67. See *De An.* B 1, 412a6, where οὐσία is given as γένος ἕν τι τῶν ὄντων. The genitive here suggests that there are *other* genera among 'the things that are.' Cf. *Cat.* 2, 1a20; *Met.* Λ 1, 1069a30–36. At *Cat.* 5, 2a35, Aristotle is sometimes taken to be referring to what is ontologically ultimate: namely, 'primary substances' (τῶν πρώτων οὐσιῶν). See, e.g., Wedin 2000,

an inversion of the ontological order of intelligible model and sensible image.[68] In the next chapter I deal with Plotinus's reasons for thinking that Aristotle himself, as opposed to Peripatetic followers, is not committed to such an inversion. Here I am concerned with how Plotinus thinks that Aristotle in *Categories* might be thought to be in harmony with Plato.[69]

With the qualification that the sensible world is an image of the intelligible world, Plotinus is open to acknowledging and employing the fundamental distinctions made in *Categories*.[70] In particular, he recognizes a fundamental difference underlying the 'said of' and 'present in' relations.[71] The difference is reflected in the foregoing quotation. There is no question in Plotinus's mind that there exists, for example, something to which the name 'man' refers primarily and something to which the name 'white' refers primarily. These things are Forms. The white man Socrates participates in both of them. But where Plotinus demurs is at the suggestion that Socrates is essentially a man, where this is interpreted to mean that the question 'is this a man?' is supposed to elicit the identical answer when asked about the Form and Socrates. Essential predication is, according to Plotinus, supposed to identify. It does not identify Socrates, for he can change while his essence does not. Simply put, Socrates is much besides what the Form of Man is. Elsewhere, Plotinus contrasts the intelligible world where the question 'what is it?' is a question about everything that a Form is and that same question

---

76–80. But cf. *Cael.* A 3, 270b11 where the phrase is used of that which is relatively primary in bodies. Wedin himself acknowledges that composite sensible substances are only primary relative to the other categories and to secondary substances.

68. See *Top.* Z 4, 141b28–34, where Aristotle argues that the genera are "prior in knowability" (γνωριμωτέρων) to the species and differentia. If the genus is removed (συναναιρεῖ), so are the species and differentia. As Aristotle claims at *Cat.* 1, 1a12–15, properties are named 'paronymously' from the nature which they exemplify, e.g., 'grammatical' from 'grammatical [knowledge]' and 'brave' from 'bravery.' See Annas 1974. Cf. *Met.* Δ 11, 1019a1–4, where Aristotle claims that A is prior in substance to B, if A can exist without B. He attributes this sense of priority to Plato.

69. At the beginning of VI 3. 1, which is the last section of the long treatise whose first two parts are VI 1 and VI 2, Plotinus summarizes those two parts by saying, "I have spoken of how it seems to me to be with regard to substance and how it might be in accord (συμφώνως) with the opinion of Plato." VI 1. 1–24 is an analysis of the Aristotelian categories in general and substance in particular.

70. De Haas 2001, 498, argues that Plotinus, especially at VI 3. 9–10, believes there are Platonic grounds for "holding that the *Categories* has a role to play in a Platonic ontological framework." Specifically, Plotinus takes Aristotle as attempting to comply with Plato's strictures about accounts of the sensible world in *Tim.* 49A1–52D1 and *Phil.* 17B-18C (516–518). Plotinus's own positive efforts to provide an Aristotelian classificatory scheme for the sensible world reflect the presumption of harmony.

71. See VI 3. 3, 1–4, where Plotinus distinguishes between the things predicated (κατηγορούμενα) and accidents (συμβεβηκότα). It is clear enough from the context and elsewhere that 'the things predicated' refers to the species and genera of an individual sensible substance. See VI 1. 25, 21–22; VI 2. 19, 14; VI 3. 5, 18, 23. Plotinus does, however, occasionally use the term κατηγορούμενον when speaking of an accidental attribute such as 'white' that is 'present in' Socrates.

asked of something in the sensible world where the answer to the question includes *less* than everything that the thing is.[72]

Plotinus accommodates Aristotelian essentialism in distinguishing 'this man is a man' from 'this man is white.' The distinction is between participation in a Form and the presence of an instance of a Form in an individual where the latter only indirectly indicates participation in a Form. So, 'this white is white' is as much an essentialistic statement, according to Plotinus, as 'this man is a man.' Nevertheless, one is inclined to respond that the *contrast* between an essential predication and an accidental predication is not thereby accounted for. When Aristotle says that "Socrates is a man," he means that Socrates would no longer be Socrates if he were no longer a man, whereas when he says that "Socrates is white" he means to imply that Socrates would still be Socrates if his color were to change. It is because Socrates has an essence that he can remain the same throughout accidental changes. Although Plotinus can reply that he, too, believes that if this man is no longer a man then this man (Socrates) would no longer be this man, that does not seem to be adequate. Why? Because it is thought that 'man' identifies this man in a way that 'white' does not. In what way?

Clearly for the Platonist the identity of the man Socrates is not the same as the identity of the Form of Man.[73] There is nothing other than the Form of Man that is identical with what 'man' names. In the Platonic universe the identity of sensibles can only be determined relative to Forms. For example, in *Republic* we can say of some x that "it is and is not at the same time."[74] I take it that the words 'at the same time' exclude the possibility that Plato is indicating contingent existence or even just 'existence.'[75] But the central point here is that some have thought Plato must mean that the only predicates that apply to things that 'are and are not at the same time' are attributes or relatives (i.e., some Aristotelian accident), and not some kind or species (i.e., some Aristotelian secondary substance), precisely because it makes no sense to say Socrates is and is not a man at the same time, whereas it makes perfect sense to say that Socrates is larger than one thing and smaller than another at the same time. That this is an interpretation unsupported by the text and counter to claims made elsewhere regarding the range of Forms I shall not here attempt to show. What I want to indicate is that it is an interpretation that Plotinus in particular and the Neoplatonists generally do not accept.

It is trivially true that this man is not both a man and not a man at the same time. But it is far from trivially true to claim that what I refer to as a man is not something other than a man at the same time. In the latter case,

---

72. See VI 5. 2, 18–28.
73. See VI 3. 4, 17: "the Form of Man and man are identical," which means that the Form of Man is identical with what it means to be a man. Consequently, *this* man Socrates is not identical with what it means to be a man.
74. *Rep.* 478D5–6: εἴ τι φανείη οἷον ἅμα ὄν τε καὶ μὴ ὄν.
75. See Vlastos 1981 on the problems with the 'existential' interpretation of this line.

I am referring to some 'perceptibles,' to use a neutral word, and claiming that *these* are a man. But as Plato himself notes in another context, the λόγος of a Form does not include any perceptibles in it. For example, the λόγος of Beauty will not include Helen's coloring, shape, and so on, beautiful though she be and, we may add, beautiful owing in some sense to that coloring, shape, and so on. But these perceptible attributes would belong to an account of the contrary of beauty as well. So, what exactly does it mean to say that '*this* is beauty' apart from 'this beauty is beauty' and, by extension, '*this* is a man' apart from 'this man is a man'?

What Aristotle has to say in reply to this question in *Metaphysics* is controversial and obscure. In chapter six I explore his response in the proper context. The Neoplatonic response is that participation in a Form does not *eo ipso* fix identity. The Neoplatonists could read Aristotle as conceding as much when he says that "the essence of man and man are not the same thing."[76] One might point out on Aristotle's behalf that the essence of man and man are not the same thing if two men are to have the same essence. But then it must be added that *this* man is an actualization of the essence of man. And in that case the Neoplatonist will reply that the essence of man, being thus made to be logically posterior to that which actualizes it, cannot explain anything.[77] The dilemma thrust upon one who takes essentialism to be a doctrine that reveals the identity of things is this: 'man' names either a universal or a Form. The former explains nothing; the latter explains only if it is ontologically prior to and therefore separate from that which it explains. If the essence is a universal, then it explains nothing. If the essence is to explain, then it must do so as the Form does, by being ontologically prior to and therefore separate from that which it explains. There is no tertium quid. So, the essence only can explain if it does not fix identity.

Should we say that the requirement that the essence fix identity is too strong? Perhaps the identity of the individual need only be functionally related to the essence. Thus the individual remains the same individual throughout its existence because of its 'controlling' essence. But composite sensible individuality is constituted by accidental attributes. If the accidental attributes determine identity, then identity can change with the gain or loss of any attribute. Since this is evidently something that Aristotle does *not* want to say, he has to show that though essence does not unqualifiedly fix identity and though accidental attributes do not fix identity either, somehow identity is functionally related to essence. And, we may add, the identity here must be diachronic. That is, it is not enough to say that the individual is a man because he has the essence of man, though he might change into another individual with the same essence.

76. See *Met.* H 3, 1043b2–3.
77. See the explicit recognition of the posteriority of the universal at *De An.* A 1, 402b7–8: τὸ δὲ ζῷον τὸ καθόλου ἤτοι οὐθέν ἐστιν ἢ ὕστερον.

The way that Aristotle expresses this position is to say that the individual's identity is qualifiedly determined by its essence. Though this is the nub of the problem, the point is that the Neoplatonists could legitimately interpret this claim such that it does not undermine the explanatory role of Forms. For the qualified identity of an individual and its essence seems to be very much like the qualified identity of an image with that of which it is an image.[78] The qualified identity of the sensible substance with its essence is like the qualified identity of a participant in a Form with that Form.[79]

Another way of identifying an individual in *Categories* is via the differentia. The strength of the Neoplatonic approach to *Categories* is nowhere more evident than in the way the Neoplatonists address the question of the status of the differentia.[80] According to *Categories*, the differentia is that which distinguishes one species from another within a genus.[81] Thus among the differentiae of the genus animal are terrestrial, two-footed, feathered, and aquatic. The differentiae themselves cannot just be species—that is, secondary substances—for they themselves would then require differentiae to differentiate them from each other and from the species whose differentiae they supposedly are. So, it would seem that they must be attributes of some kind. But *Categories* appears to countenance as attributes only the individual accidents of a substance, that which is present in the subject. In addition, the differentia cannot be present in a subject if, as it seems, it belongs to the species.[82] What then is the 'status' of the differentia?

It is easy to transform this question into an unsolvable problem *if* one supposes that *Categories* is offering up an ontology.[83] Nevertheless, there is at least on the surface a problem about the categorical status of the differentia which is neither a subject nor present in a subject, nor said of a subject in the manner of a secondary substance, nor both said of and present in a subject in the manner of the species and genera of the accidental categories. If in short the differentia is neither a substance nor an accident, what could it be? Porphyry's answer to this question is that the differentia is an essential or substantial quality (ποιότης οὐσιώδης).[84] Such qualities are complements

---

78. Cf. Syrianus *apud* Asclepius (*In Met.* 435, 22–36), who argues that the Form is a unifying power (ἐνωτικὴ δύναμις) for the particular sensible substance.

79. See *Phd.* 74C4–5: Οὐ ταὐτὸν ἄρα ἐστίν, ᾗ δ' ὅς, ταῦτά τε τὰ ἴσα καὶ αὐτὸ τὸ ἴσον. Cf. 74C10-D5. The point here is not that equal things are not identical (ταὐτόν) with the Form of Equality but that the equality of equal things is not identical with the Form of Equality. Yet the equality in equal things must be the same as (ὅμοιον) equality in the Form; otherwise, the Form's explanatory role would be eliminated. The properties of nonidentity plus sameness amount to an analysis of qualified identity. See Alexander of Aphrodisias *In Met.* 83, 10–12 on the Academic position that the λόγος of an instance of a Form is distinct from the λόγος of the Form itself.

80. See Porphyry *Isag.* 8, 8–12, 11; Porphyry *In Cat.* 94, 30ff.; Dexippus *In Cat.* 48, 20–49, 24; Ammonius *In Cat.* 45, 7–47, 13; Simplicius *In Cat.* 97, 24–102, 10.

81. See *Cat.* 3, 1b16–24. Cf. *Met.* I 7, 1057b7.

82. See *Top.* Δ 6, 128a20.

83. As does, e.g., Mann 2000, 194–195. See also Morrison 1993.

84. See Porphyry *In Cat.* 95, 19. Cf. *Isag.* 18, 16–19.

(συμπληρωτικαί) of substances. Complements are those things which, having been removed, their subjects are destroyed. These subjects might seem to be individual substances. If Socrates loses his rationality, he can no longer survive. But this is also true of the secondary substance, the species. Hence as Aristotle says, the differentia is predicated both of the species and of the individual.[85] Indeed, as Simplicius argues, the differentia is predicated synonymously of both species and individual.[86] Neither man nor Socrates the man could exist if the differentia rationality were removed.

As a logical point, this is impeccable. Just as the species and the genus are said synonymously of individuals, so is the complement of the species said synonymously of species and individual. This must be the case since (1) the species just expresses what it is that all the individuals have in common—that is, what is identical in them—and (2) the differentia is a 'part' of the species.[87] In short, synonymy is guaranteed by the logic of class inclusion. As an ontological point, however, there are difficulties. In particular, the differentia 'rationality' seems to be neither an accident of Socrates—that is, present in him—nor a species, since it is not a substance. No doubt this problem can be posed as a dilemma for Aristotle, though he seems to be quite unaware of it. The Neoplatonic commentators simply assume that the logical or semantic classifications made in *Categories* are precisely not intended as ontological principles. Since a sensible substance is not unqualifiedly basic in the world, even if it is basic in the *sensible* world, its logical priority in the schema of *Categories* does not presume its absolute or unqualified ontological priority. So, the exhaustive fourfold logical division is not an ontological division with seemingly no place to locate the differentia. The differentia 'rationality' is a part of an intelligible substance or essence and is prior to the sensible substance. Or more accurately, 'said of' and 'present in' invert the ontological order for classificatory purposes.

According to Plotinus a sensible substance is a conglomeration (συμφόρησις) of qualities (ποιοτήτων) and matter.[88] The 'real' 'this' (τόδε τι) is not Socrates but the Form of Man. Socrates is by contrast a 'such and such' (ποιόν τι) and an image of that Form.[89] The consequences of this claim for the principle of harmonization cannot be overstated. So long as we interpret Aristotle as speaking about images of what is really real, we can follow his way of categorizing these images. Thus, to say that Socrates is essentially a man is not to make a claim about what is ultimately real but to make a logical claim about a stipulated subject. Stated in a slightly different manner, to

85. *Cat.* 5, 3b1–2.
86. Simplicius *In Cat.* 101, 12–24, fleshing out the answer of Iamblichus. Cf. Ammonius *In Cat.* 48, 3.
87. See Ammonius *In Cat.* 47, 2–13.
88. See VI 3. 8, 19–20. Although this passage presents this characterization of a sensible substance dialectically, it seems from VI 3. 10, 15–16 and VI 3. 15, 24–27 (though the language is slightly different) that it is one to which Plotinus is in fact committed. Cf. Dexippus *In Cat.* 58, 27, and Simplicius *In Cat.* 96, 3.
89. See VI 3. 15, 24–39.

say that this man Socrates belongs to the category of substance is to treat him *as if* he were an ultimate item in reality with an essence that fixes his identity throughout his life. If Aristotle had written only *Categories* or if only that work had survived, the rather strict logical interpretation of that work would be difficult to gainsay. It is only because *Metaphysics* was written and survives as well that we tend to see *Categories* as having ontological implications that are contrary to Platonism.[90] But the Neoplatonists had well-thumbed copies of *Metaphysics,* too. They believed generally that there was good reason to deny that Aristotle in that work held that things like this man Socrates were ultimate items of his ontology. I explore these in chapter 6.

The way the identity of a substance is characterized in *Categories* is this:

> The property [ἴδιον] of substance appears above all [μάλιστα] to be that while it remains identical in number, it is receptive of contraries. In other words there is no other thing that someone could adduce as being one in number that is receptive of contraries. For example, a color, which is one and the same in number, will not be both light and dark nor will the same action which is one in number, be vicious and virtuous, and similarly in the other cases, for things that are not substances. But a substance, being one and the same in number is receptive of contraries. For example, some man, being one and the same, is at one time white and another time becomes dark, at one time hot and another time cold, at one time vicious and another time virtuous.[91]

As Aristotle goes on to explain, it is in virtue of a change (μεταβολήν) the substance undergoes that it is able to admit of contraries.[92] One can certainly take this passage as indicating Aristotle's primary criterion for substantiality *tout court.* But if one does that, one is necessarily committed to the view that what Aristotle says in *Metaphysics* Book Λ indicates a change or development in Aristotle's account of substance. For there he says:

> There are three kinds of substance. One genus of substance is the sensible, on which all agree, one type of which is destructible, for example, plants and animals, and the other is eternal,[93] and it is of these that it is necessary to grasp the elements, whether they are one or many. Another is immovable substance, and some say this is separate [χωριστήν], whereas some divided it into two, namely, those who divided [this class] into Forms and mathematicals, whereas

---

90. See Owens (1981a, 19–20), who argues against seeing *Categories* as being in conflict with *Metaphysics*, particularly in its focus on the sensible individual. Since the sensible individual is not the primary focus of the science of being in *Metaphysics*, there is no conflict. Connecting *Categories* to *Metaphysics* is, of course, an important step in the harmonization program. See Porphyry *In Cat.* 91, 19–27; Ammonius *In Cat.* 36, 2–9.

91. *Cat.* 5, 4a10–21. Ammonius *In Cat.* 36, 13–22, argues that Aristotle says "appears above all to be" receptive of contraries because he does not believe that a substance unqualifiedly 'is' above all receptive of contraries. The use of δοκεῖ often does have a dialectical force in Aristotle's idiom.

92. *Cat.* 5, 4a33–34; b2–4.

93. I follow Frede 2000, 78–80, in reading and translating μία μὲν αἰσθητή, ἣν πάντες ὁμολογοῦσιν, ἧς ἡ μὲν φθαρτή, οἷον τὰ φυτὰ καὶ τὰ ζῷα, ἡ δ᾽ ἀίδιος.

others posit only the mathematicals. Sensible substances are the subject of physics, for they have motion, whereas the other is the subject of another science, if there is no one principle common to them.

But sensible substances are changeable [μεταβλητή]. If change proceeds from opposites or from intermediates, but not from all kinds of opposites (for voice is nonwhite), but only from [the opposites] that are contraries, there must be something underlying that which changes into the contrary.[94]

According to the Neoplatonic commentators it is evident that Aristotle does not and never did hold that changeable substances are the only substances there are. Not only is Book Λ of *Metaphysics* taken to be relevant to Aristotle's intentions in *Categories*, but so is what he says in the exoteric works as well. If one does not simply assume that *Categories* must represent an early phase of Aristotle's development (presumably along with Books Λ and E), then it is reasonable to suppose that nothing said about substance in *Categories* is intended to contradict claims about unchangeable substances.[95] That is, *Categories* is not correctly understood as implicitly assuming the absolute priority of sensible substance. Further, if the science of unchangeables includes the study of changeables with respect to their being, the situation of *Categories* within a subordinate science—that is, the science of changeables—is nicely accounted for according to the harmonization principle. The science of the sensible world can be fitted into or under the broader science that includes the sensible world from the perspective of first principles and of being. This science is Platonic science.[96] It is not undermined by a nonabsolutist categorization of things in the sensible world with composite substances as the focus.

94. *Met.* Λ 1, 1069a30–b6. See Frede 2000, 70–77, for a discussion of this difficult passage. As Frede notes, the words "... whereas the other is the subject of another science, if there is no one principle common to them" are ambiguous, depending on whether we think the condition is fulfilled or not (73). As we shall see in chap. 6, there is good reason to believe that Aristotle thinks that, by the end of Book Λ, he has shown that changeable and unchanging substances do have one principle: namely, the prime unmoved mover. But if this is so, it does not mean that there is just one science of both changeable and unchanging substance. It means rather that there is one science that deals with changeable substance (i.e., physics) and another (i.e., theology) that deals with both changeable and unchanging substances. That science deals with them insofar as they are beings, whereas physics deals with changeable substances insofar as they are changeable. See *Met.* E 1, 1026a27–32.

95. See Porphyry (*In Cat.* 99, 2–3), who, however, is referring to eternal movable substances that are not receptive of the contrary of rest, since they are eternally in motion. Simplicius *In Cat.* 114, 29–31, says ὡς τὸ ἰδίωμα (being receptive of contraries) ἐνταῦθα πάσης τῆς ἐν μεταβολαῖς δυναμένης γίνεσθαι οὐσίας τίθεται, ἀλλ' οὐ τῆς κατὰ τὸ ἀμετάβλητον οὐσιωμένης. Cf. 115, 9–10. Simplicius *In Cat.* 116, 25–33, goes on to mention Iamblichus's interpretation, according to which 'being receptive of contraries' can apply to unchangeable substances by 'analogy.' On this, see Dillon 1997; Cardullo 1997.

96. See Ebbesen 1990, 144, on Porphyry's interpretation of *Categories* in relation to metaphysics roughly as Newtonian physics is related to Einsteinian physics. The disanalogy is that Aristotelian logic "must not extend its field of operation to ontology proper which can be investigated only in Platonic terms."

The relatively unknown Dexippus provides a valuable part of the story of harmonization in his one extant work, *On Aristotle's Categories*.[97] It appears that Dexippus was a pupil or disciple of Iamblichus. He seems to have been committed to harmonization, but, two generations after Plotinus, he sees it as requiring the integration of Aristotelianism with Platonism as interpreted by Plotinus.[98] Yet Plotinus, as we know, strongly criticizes Aristotle. Therefore, Dexippus, no doubt in many ways dependent on Porphyry and Iamblichus, feels he has to defend the harmonizing interpretation of *Categories* against Plotinus's attacks. Thus, so to say, if Plotinus had seen clearly what *Categories* was about, he would have realized that Aristotle is actually in harmony with Platonism. The general point is of some importance because it is precisely in this way that Aristotle's explicit attacks on Platonism are frequently interpreted according to the harmonization principle.

Dexippus follows the Porphyrean explanation of the aim of *Categories* in both his *Isagoge* and his *Commentary*.[99] According to Dexippus, the work is for beginners and is about words, not things. In reply to the objection that Plotinian criticisms of Aristotle's account of substance cannot be fairly answered by assuming that Aristotle is a Platonist, Dexippus appeals to Book Λ of *Metaphysics* to show that Aristotle himself was aware that in talking about sensible substance he is leaving out of account supersensible substance.[100] That this claim is implausible can be maintained, I think, only if one uncritically assumes developmentalism in Aristotle's thought. In any case, Dexippus wants to show not just that *Categories* has a limited aim but that everything said there is in harmony with Platonic principles.

> For this is what Aristotle lays down about these substances in Book Λ of *Metaphysics* and here he subsumes the multiplicity of substances under substance in general. He brought them all together into one system and traced them back to one originating principle. For it will hardly be that anything else would participate in unity, if substance itself, which has its being in the One, is to be denied that completeness which is attributable to unity. So, since intelligible reality is ineffable, he makes use of the name of 'substance' metaphorically and analogically from what is familiar to sense perception.[101]

Note first of all Dexippus's assumption that an account of the multiplicity of types of substance must be rooted in an originating principle (ἀρχή) and the further assumption that this originating principle is the Neoplatonic

97. See Dillon 1990b.

98. See the valuable article P. Hadot 1990, 125–140, for the mediating role of Porphyry in Dexippus's approach to harmonization.

99. See Dexippus *In Cat.* 40, 19–25.

100. See ibid., 41, 7ff. See *Met.* Λ 1, 1069a30ff.; 6, 1071b3. As Dillon 1990b, 75, notes, Dexippus's account of Aristotle's division of substance into (1) immovable substance (god or the gods) and (2) sensible substance, which is divided into (a) everlasting (the superlunary bodies) and (b) destructible bodies, is confused. The appositeness of the citation of this passage, however, is clear.

101. Dexippus *In Cat.* 41, 13–19 (trans. Dillon).

One.[102] It is enough for harmonization that Aristotelian principles imply Platonic principles, even if Aristotle does not himself explicitly recognize this implication.

In addition, Dexippus gives us the principle according to which the term 'substance' is applicable to intelligibles. The term is applied to intelligibles metaphorically or analogously.[103] Dexippus's understanding of the distinction between metaphor and analogy is not exactly transparent. If he is following Porphyry, then a term is applied metaphorically when it has a proper designation and is applied to something else which has its own proper designation. A term is applied analogously to two or more things when neither has its own proper designation. Since Dexippus holds that intelligible reality is ineffable, he evidently supposes that it does not have its own proper designation. Therefore, if 'substance' is used to designate it, it is done by analogy. But then it would not be applied analogously to sensible substance if 'substance' is its proper designation. In that case 'substance' would presumably be applied metaphorically to intelligibles. The central point Dexippus is making, I think, is that 'substance' in *Categories* is applied properly to sensibles and metaphorically to intelligibles, but the metaphor is of a special sort (i.e., analogical) because intelligibles are ineffable.

If the sensible world is an image of the intelligible world, as Platonists generally hold, then the metaphor should go the other way. Intelligibles should be the primary designate of whatever terms are applied both to them and to sensibles. That is what Plotinus did in designating the 'real' man as the Form of Man and Socrates as man metaphorically. But here the order of designation is reversed, and the reason seems to be epistemological. Aristotle himself maintained the principle that "the natural way to proceed is from what is more known and clearer to us to what is by nature clearer and more known."[104] This is the order of investigation. It is how knowledge of first principles is attained. By contrast, the order of scientific demonstration is from what is "more known by nature" to "what is more known to us."[105]

Dexippus actually assumes (perhaps from Porphyry or Iamblichus) a benign and favorable interpretation of Aristotle. He assumes that the epistemological order from the immediate, sensible, and particular to the intelligible is a passage from effect to cause. The ineffability of the cause is a

102. Cf. Ammonius *In Cat.* 6, 9–13. See P. Hadot 1990, 134–135, on Porphyry's possible role in effecting the connection of a putative first principle above substance in Aristotle with the Neoplatonic One. See I. Hadot, 1989, 97–103, on the Neoplatonic interpretation generally of Book Λ of Aristotle's *Metaphysics*.

103. See P. Hadot (1990, 136–137), who suggests that Porphyry (*In Cat.* 66, 34ff.), though he chastises Atticus for failing to distinguish metaphor and analogy, does not himself distinguish these. But *In Cat.* 67, 26 clearly classifies analogy as a form of homonymy, distinct from metaphor.

104. See *Phys.* A 1, 184a16–18. Cf. *EN* A 2, 1095b3.

105. See *APo.* A 2, esp. 71b29–72a5, where Aristotle argues that the things that are most universal (καθόλου μάλιστα) are unqualifiedly prior by nature and more knowable than sensibles.

separate point. Aristotle's doctrine might be interpreted by an opponent as self-defeating if in thus proceeding the result is not a cause but merely universals. As we have seen, Neoplatonists are not hostile to an Aristotelian account of universals. They are hostile to an account that mistakes universals for explanatory entities. It is not, Neoplatonists would insist, because man is a rational animal and rational animals are capable of laughter that man is capable of laughter, so long as one supposes that 'man' and other such terms designate universals. On the contrary, only the intelligible realm explains the connections here below that Aristotle characterizes in terms of species, genus, differentia, and property. But in this case, the intelligible realm is not to be construed as a tableau of universals.[106] And the differences between the true causes and their effects mean that epistemologically one proceeds from effects that can be described in perceptible terms to causes that are utterly incapable of being so described.[107] Dexippus seems exactly right to maintain that both Plato and Aristotle believe that these causes could not be substances in the sense in which the effects are substances.

Daniel Graham has argued at great length that the account of substance in *Categories* actually contradicts the account of substance in *Metaphysics*. Graham himself believes that in the latter work, by identifying form with substance, Aristotle makes "an unnecessary and damaging concession to Platonism."[108] Hence on Graham's account of Aristotle's 'two systems,' the Neoplatonists' claim that *Categories* expresses the same (i.e., Platonic) view as *Metaphysics*, albeit in a simplified form, cannot be correct—unless, that is, Aristotle is contradicting himself.[109] On the system contained in *Organon* in general, substances are atomic; on the system contained in *Metaphysics*, substances are hylomorphic: that is, composed of form and matter. Graham argues that the motivation for Aristotle's abandonment of the first system and embrace of the second is to provide the basis for a satisfactory account of change.[110] For this, a concept of matter is needed, as Aristotle explains in *Physics*. I have more to say in the next chapter about matter in Aristotle,

106. At *In Cat.* 45, 5–12, Dexippus argues for the priority in nature of universals, implicitly distinguishing two senses of 'universal.' Ultimately, this use of 'universal' goes back to Aristotle himself. See *Met.* E 1, 1026a30. Simplicius *In Cat.* 82, 10–14, notes that Iamblichus is opposed to Alexander of Aphrodisias's view of universals (cf. Dexippus *In Cat.* 45, 12–31). Wedin 2000, 111–121, argues that Aristotle's identification of species as existentially dependent on individuals is an "anti-Platonic" claim. But this is because Wedin (114) assumes that Forms are species and species are universals.

107. Porphyry *In Cat.* 91, 26, argues that intelligibles are primary substances in nature. This is not intended to contradict the point that 'substance' is applied to them metaphorically. See P. Hadot 1990, 138, with references to Porphyry's *Sent.* §§. 19, 27, 35, and 38.

108. See Graham 1987, 288. See also Mann (2000, 205–206), who, after arguing extensively that *Categories* is intended to provide a radically new alternative to Platonic metaphysics, claims that "in the central books of *Metaphysics* Aristotle largely abandons his earlier picture [that is, the picture in *Categories*]. For Aristotle comes to think that ordinary things cannot after all be fundamental items."

109. See Graham 1987, 79–81, for a table summarizing the two systems, called by Graham S_1 and S_2.

110. Ibid., 119–155.

here I focus on the contention that the hylomorphic conception of substance is incompatible with the atomic conception of substance found by Graham in *Categories* and also in the rest of *Organon*.

Graham finds in the passage quoted above from *Categories* [5, 4a10–21] "a glimmer of an insight into the nature of change."[111] But because there is no temporal dimension mentioned explicitly in the criterion of substance, that "being one and the same in number, [substance] is receptive of contraries," Aristotle cannot be said here to have the concept of matter necessary for an account of the principles of change. Graham says this despite the fact that Aristotle in the next sentence gives an example of the reception of contraries, explicitly mentioning the temporal parameter [ὁτὲ μὲν . . . ὁτὲ δὲ].[112] Still, we can concede Graham's point that an underlying principle of change is not explicitly mentioned in *Categories* and that this principle is not thematized, as it is in *Physics* and *Metaphysics*. Nevertheless, the more important point is Graham's claim that the introduction of the concept of matter as a component of substance in the latter works heralds a fundamental change in—indeed, a reversal of—doctrine. For sensible substance, latterly composed of matter and form, is no longer fundamental as it supposedly is in *Categories*.[113]

Assuming that Graham is correct in holding that sensible substance is not ontologically ultimate in *Metaphysics* just because it is composed of form *and* matter, the question then becomes, is it so in *Categories*, as Graham claims?[114] In order to maintain this position, one would first of all have to disregard the claims in the *exoterica* regarding God, intellect, and "divine intelligibles." Otherwise one would be forced, as is Graham, to assign *Eudemus*, *Protrepticus*, and *On Philosophy* to the period in which Aristotle was committed to the second of his two systems and had rejected the first.[115] Second, one would have to excise from *On Interpretation* the passage in which Aristotle says: "It is evident from what has been said that that which necessarily exists exists in actuality, so that if eternal things [τὰ ἀίδια] are prior, actuality is also prior to potentiality. And some things are actualities without potentiality, for example, the primary substances [αἱ πρῶται οὐσίαι], some things are actualities with potentiality, and these are what are prior

---

111. Ibid., 122.

112. Actually, at 5, 4a10–11, the line Graham quotes, Aristotle does not mention temporality, but at a16–17, when he repeats the criterion, he immediately adds it.

113. Nevertheless, Graham (1987, 207–210), actually insists that Aristotle never abandoned the first system. Indeed, Aristotle "asserts some key principles of S₁ in S₂," though he was evidently unaware that that he was simultaneously maintaining two inconsistent systems.

114. See ibid., 89: "The ontology of the *Categories* is an ontology in the absolute sense." See Wehrle 2001, 20–25, for what I take to be a powerful and decisive refutation of this view. Both Porphyry (*In Cat.* 99, 1–2) and Dexippus (*In Cat.* 57, 13ff.) assume that the criterion of being receptive of contraries does not apply to eternal sensibles, such as the Sun. Simplicius (*In Cat.* 114, 21–22) assumes that it does not apply to "intelligible substance" (νοητὴν οὐσίαν). Cf. Ammonius *In Cat.* 51, 14–15.

115. See Graham 1987, 302–310.

by nature, though posterior in time, and some things are never actualities, but are potentialities alone.[116]

Graham recognizes that this passage contradicts his claim that sensibles, albeit *atomic* sensibles, are the primary substances. So, he rejects the passage as "an insertion (by Aristotle no doubt) which does not belong to the original version of *On Interpretation.*"[117] This is of course possible. But the motive for claiming it is odd. It is that only in Aristotle's later period, the period of his second system, did he come to identify 'primary substance' with the supersensible. This, too, is perhaps possible. But what I find highly implausible, if not impossible, is that Aristotle at any point in his career held the view that what undergoes change—sensible substance—is absolutely fundamental in the universe.[118]

Whether or not one shares Graham's interpretation of *Categories,* that interpretation is plainly part of the legacy of developmentalism. One may reject developmentalism, or a segmented version of it, without taking the harmonists' line.[119] But from the Neoplatonists' perspective, doing so would require a reading of *Metaphysics* every bit as one-sided as the sort of reading of *Categories* offered by Graham. As a matter of fact there is far more unambiguous evidence throughout the Aristotelian corpus to support the view that sensible substances are not absolutely basic in the universe than there is evidence to the contrary. Graham's conclusion that Aristotle's path was actually a devolution downward to Platonic ignominy contradicts both Jaegerian developmentalism and any form of antidevelopmentalism. It is not unreasonable, or so it seems to me, to question the common underlying assumption that leads one scholar to argue that Aristotle traverses the path from pro- to anti-Platonist and another to argue (on the same evidence) that he does the reverse.

116. *De Int.* 13, 23a21–26. Ackrill 1979 ad loc. says this paragraph "reeks of notions central to the *Metaphysics* but is out of place in the present work and only tenuously connected with what preceded." Ackrill's first point is not inapposite, though the second point can be challenged. Dancy 1996, 261, takes the absence of the notion of matter from *Organon* as a significant indicator of Aristotle's development.

117. See Graham (1987, 99), who follows Frede (1970, 81, n. 16) in considering the passage a late insertion. Maier 1900 argues that the entire work is late. I do not understand why Graham (299) thinks that the reference to "the primary substances" is identical to a reference to "the unmoved mover." Presumably, in wishing to make this passage late, he identified what is only a general reference, paralleled in early works (e.g., *Metaphysics* α), with a doctrine, that of the unmoved mover, that is arguably later. So, Rist 1989, 84–85. Reeve (2000, 113 n. 24), without specifically mentioning Graham, argues against those who assume that because matter is missing from *Organon*, the hylomorphic analysis is not presumed.

118. Wehrle 2001, 209–214, aptly cites *Top.* E 7, 137b11–13, where Aristotle says that an animal is "composed of soul and body" (τὸ ἐκ ψυχῆς καὶ σώματος συγκεῖσθαι). He also cites *Cat.* 5, 3a28–32, where Aristotle refers to the 'parts' of the [sensible] substance. In this light of this passage, Graham's claim that the substance is an atomic individual can have only a *logical* meaning not a *metaphysical* one.

119. See, e.g., Wedin 2000, which takes this approach. Wedin finds *Metaphysics* in harmony with *Categories* by rejecting Books E and Λ as relevant to the main argument of that work. In his approach to reconciling *Categories* and *Metaphysics,* Wedin is anticipated in general by Brinkmann 1996, though Brinkmann (301–302), takes Book Λ as completing the argument of the central books.

Chapter Four

Nature and Its Principles

Aristotle was held by Neoplatonists to be an authority for the under-standing of the sensible or physical world. There are a number of areas, especially relating to the biological sciences, where Plato was mainly silent and where Aristotle's views were in our period dominant if not completely unchallenged.[1] The very fact that the Neoplatonic curriculum began with an extensive study of Aristotle before moving on to Plato indicates that the student would hardly be expected to be led astray by imbibing Aristotelian wisdom. Still, an antiharmonist might well suppose that a deep study of Aris-totle's account of the physical world would yield principles in use that were on reflection incompatible or out of tune with Platonism. From the vast amount of material that for Aristotle falls under the rubric 'physics,' this chapter concentrates on the principles of natural science.[2]

I try to show two things. First, I want to show that the Neoplatonists more or less accepted Aristotle's principles of physical science and held these to be in harmony with an overall Platonic view of the world. Thus Plato's 'two-world' metaphysics, to put it crudely, is not compromised or undermined by Aristotle's account of nature. Aristotle may be right or wrong about the cor-rect account of this or that astronomical or biological or chemical issue, but

1. E.g., Philoponus *In GA* 21, 1–10, says that Plato treats of the generation of elements (in *Timaeus*) but that this treatment is not extended to the generation of living things. That is, the principles employed in the former cannot be applied to the latter. By implication, Aristotle's account of the latter is available and is not out of harmony with Platonism.

2. In the Aristotelian corpus as received by later Greek philosophy, 'physics' includes some 800 pages of Bekker text out of a total of 1500. It includes everything from the treatise known as *Physics* up to the treatise known as *Metaphysics:* that is, all the material relating to the physi-cal world or to the study of nature.

he is not basing that account on principles that are not in harmony with Plato's own. Second, I aim to show how Neoplatonists employed Aristotelian principles and concepts in order to articulate a *Platonic* account of nature. That this could be done in an unforced manner reveals I think, some of the lineaments of harmony.[3]

Matter in Aristotle and the Platonic Tradition

It is convenient to begin with Simplicius's statement of how Aristotle's schema of causal analysis compares with Plato's. At the start of his *Commentary on Aristotle's Physics* he says that among principles (ἀρχαί), Aristotle affirms two causes (αἰτίαι), the productive (ποιητικόν) and the final (τελικόν) and two contributory causes (συναίτια), the form (εἶδος) and the matter (ὕλη).[4] The latter are generally speaking elements (στοιχεῖα). To these, says Simplicius, Plato added two more; to the causes he added the paradigmatic (παραδειγματικόν), and to the contributory causes he added the instrumental (ὀργανικόν).[5]

Several things are immediately evident from this passage. In general, we see here the Neoplatonic strategy of incorporating Aristotelian philosophy into the larger Platonic vision. Aristotle's four causes or modes of scientific explanation are fitted into the more comprehensive Platonic scheme. The fit is not entirely straightforward. Aristotle does use the term 'contributory cause' for matter, in the sense of a material condition.[6] Logically, this would make form the other 'co-contributor,' though Aristotle does not speak in this way. On the contrary, he appears to view his four causes as the framework for scientific explanatory adequacy and in no way subordinate to other more fundamental causes.

3. Proclus (*In Tim.* I 6, 21ff.; 237, 17ff.; III 323, 31ff.), takes Aristotle's physics as an inferior version of the physics of *Timaeus*, produced in a spirit of emulation (ζηλώσας). This emulation is sometimes assumed to imply antagonism. But the verb ζηλόω can have a straightforward nonpejorative connotation, implying a positive view of that which is emulated. If Aristotle wanted to 'outdo' Plato in his account of nature, that does not suggest that he rejected the general principles upon which both the Platonic and Aristotelian accounts rest.

4. Aristotle *Met.* Δ 1, 1013a16–17, says that 'cause' has as many senses (ἰσαχῶς) as 'principle' because all causes are principles. As Alexander (*In Met.* 247, 8ff.), states, however, the account (λόγος) of each is different. A principle is an ultimate cause. Cf. *GC* A 7, 324a27: ἡ γὰρ ἀρχὴ πρώτη τῶν αἰτίων. It was, accordingly, not unreasonable for Neoplatonists to suppose that the fourfold schema of causal analysis was not exhaustive in Aristotle. Nature, e.g., was a principle only in a qualified way, because nature was not, as Aristotle argues in *Physics*, unqualifiedly self-explanatory.

5. Simplicius *In Phys.* 3, 16–18. Cf. 10, 25–11, 15 where Simplicius refers the sixfold Platonic analysis to Porphyry. Also 314, 9–23; 316, 23–26. Cf. Philoponus (*In Phys.* 5, 16ff.; 241, 3–27), who gives the same two lists, adding two important points: (1) Aristotle does not use the paradigmatic cause added by Plato because he is confining himself to the science of nature, and (2) Aristotle assimilates the instrumental contributory cause to the material cause. Later, (244, 14–23), he adds that Aristotle assimilates the paradigmatic cause to the form. Thus Aristotle collapses the six Platonic causal principles into four.

6. See *Phys.* A 9, 192a13–14: ἡ μὲν γὰρ ὑπομένουσα συναιτία τῇ μορφῇ τῶν γιγνομένων ἐστίν, ὥσπερ μήτηρ. Cf. *Met.* Δ 5, 1015a21, where the examples are breathing and food which are necessary for an animal to live.

Simplicius's addition of the paradigmatic and instrumental causes is especially revealing of the Neoplatonic strategy. For reasons already discussed in the previous chapter, Neoplatonists denied on Platonic grounds the sufficiency of the enmattered form to explain sameness in difference; hence, the postulation of a paradigmatic cause was required. In addition, they denied that nature was reducible either to an unqualified productive cause or to form or to matter alone. An unqualified productive cause must be an unmoved mover—that is, a mover not needing an explanation for *its* motion; otherwise, its explanatory power is removed. So, Simplicius asserts, nature is an instrumental cause because nature is a moved mover. But nature as a moved mover is neither form nor matter, since these, as such, do not move at all. The collapse of the full panoply of Platonic causes into four is thus seen as a sort of conceptual ellipse, useful though it might be. But it guarantees that nature and the Aristotelian science of nature are not self-contained or self-sufficient.

The basic distinction between cause and contributory cause is made by Plato in *Timaeus*. It is well to have the key passage before us:

> Now all these things [mechanical explanations] are among the contributory causes [τῶν συναιτίων] which the god uses as subservient to achieving the ideal [τὴν τοῦ ἀρίστου ἰδέαν] to the extent possible. But they seem to most people to be not contributory causes but causes [αἴτια] of all things, producing their effects by cooling or heating, compacting or rarefying, and suchlike. But it is not possible for such things to have any rationality [λόγον] or intellect [νοῦν] leading to anything. For we must state that that alone among all things to which it is fitting for intellect to belong is soul and that this is invisible, whereas fire and water and earth and air are all visible bodies, and the lover of intellect and of knowledge must necessarily pursue the first causes of the intelligent nature [τῆς ἔμφρονος φύσεως] and only then the second causes, such things as are moved by others and of necessity move different things. We, too, must proceed in this way. We must speak of both kinds of cause, but distinguish causes that work with intellect to produce noble and good things from those, deprived of intelligence, that each time produce a disordered chance result.[7]

In this passage the productive and final causes, along with a sort of contributory cause that is instrumental, are evident.[8] The paradigmatic cause—namely, Forms (and perhaps the Demiurge itself)—are readily supplied from elsewhere in the text.[9] What Aristotle and Simplicius call 'form' is taken to be identical with the 'likenesses' of the paradigmatic Forms, which

---

7. *Tim.* 46C7-E6. Cf. *Phd.* 95B-99D. At *Lg.* 892C2–5, those who deny that soul is prior to nature in the order of explanation are criticized.

8. Cf. *Tim.* 29A; 76D-E; *Phil.* 53E; *Rep.* 530A5–7; *2nd Ep.* 312E.

9. See *Tim.* 30C-31A; 52A. See Proclus *In Tim.* I 419, 16–420, 19, esp. 420, 1–2, who stresses that the Form of Living Animal is not just the paradigm for all that is intelligible but also paradigmatic life.

are imposed on the universe by the Demiurge.[10] This seems to leave the material 'contributory cause' unaccounted for.

Simplicius, along with the Neoplatonists generally, has no doubt at all that Plato has accounted for material causality, for their standard way of referring to the likenesses of Forms is as enmattered forms (τὰ ἔνυλα εἴδη).[11] But it is widely if not universally believed that Plato had no concept of matter whatsoever and that Aristotle's proposed identification of matter with the 'receptacle of becoming' in *Timaeus* or with the principle of the 'Great and Small' (= Indefinite Dyad) is a mistake.[12] So, a good place to focus seems to be on whether the harmonizing of Aristotle and Plato with respect to an overlap in a doctrine of material causality has any merit.

Aristotle says that "Plato in *Timaeus* says that matter and space are the same; for the participant and space are one and the same. Although the manner in which he speaks about the receptacle in *Timaeus* is different from the way he does in his unwritten doctrines, he explicitly states that place [τόπον] and space [χώραν] are the same."[13] If it is true that space is a receptacle for becoming, it seems less clear that this is to be identified with matter.[14] Aristotle further claims that Plato identifies matter with the Great and

10. See *Tim.* 52A4–6: τὸ δὲ ὁμώνυμον ὅμοιόν τε ἐκείνῳ [the unchanging Form], and 53B5, where these are identified with shapes and numbers: εἴδεσί τε καὶ ἀριθμοῖς. Cf. 53C5; 54D4–5; 55D8. Cf. Simplicius *In Phys.* 295, 12–296, 9.

11. Cf. Plotinus I 8. 8, 13–16; VI 1. 29, 11–14; VI 7. 4, 19; Simplicius *In Phys.* 1, 16; Proclus *In Parm.* 705, 37; 839, 33; 1053, 11; *In Tim.* I 3, 2; I 10, 14; II 25, 2; II 36, 29. The usage is endorsed in Alexander of Aphrodisias *In Met.* 178, 33; 360, 4–5; 373, 23; 639, 14–15; where it is specified as applying to the 'sublunary.' See Alcinous *Didask.* 4. 6–7. Two passages from Plato were typically used to justify the terminology: *Phd.* 102E, where Plato speaks of the 'largeness in us' as opposed to 'Largeness itself,' and *Parm.* 130E, where he speaks of the 'likeness in us' as opposed to 'Likeness itself.' The use of the phrase τὰ ἔνυλα εἴδη as a general term for 'f in us' or 'f in any subject' is a good example of how Peripatetic terminology is embraced by Neoplatonism to express Platonic concepts.

12. Actually, there are two passages in Plato where the term ἡ ὕλη does appear in something other than its common meaning of 'wood.' See *Tim.* 69A6, where Plato is evidently using the term metaphorically to refer to the 'building blocks' of his cosmology: namely, the cooperating principles of reason and necessity. See also *Phil.* 54C1, where 'raw materials' in the process of becoming may be the sense, though the term is certainly not thematized here, and in any case it does not refer to matter in the sense in which Aristotle and the Neoplatonists believed that Plato was talking about matter. On the other hand, Plutarch (*On the Defect of Oracles* 414F4–415A1), says that Plato discovered the concept of matter, though the term was introduced later. Cf. Alcinous (*Didask.* chap. 8), who, too, assumes that the receptacle is another name for matter.

13. Aristotle *Phys.* Δ 2, 209b11–16. Cf. *GC* B 1, 329a23. The identification of the receptacle and space is made at *Tim.* 51A4–B1; 52A8; B4, D3. Plato does not here use the term 'participant' (τὸ μεταληπτικόν), although he does say that the "mother and receptacle" (μητέρα καὶ ὑποδοχὴν) is "receptive" (μεταλαμβανόν). Simplicius *In Phys.* 545, 23, takes the reference to the "unwritten doctrines" to be to Plato's lecture or lectures *On the Good.* On the near identification of place and space by Plato and Aristotle, see Morison 2002, 117.

14. Taylor 1928, 347, asserts flatly that "matter plays no part in Plato's cosmology at all." Taylor is followed by Cornford 1937, 180–181; Cherniss 1944, 172–173; Cherniss 1945, 22–23; Cherniss 1965, 377; and Brisson 1994, 261–266, among others. Among the scholars who take the receptacle to be matter in some way are Sachs 1917, 223–243; Claghorn 1954, 18–19; Schulz 1966, 108–111; Gloy 1986, 82–89; Morison 2002, 113–119. See Miller 2002, chap. 1, for a good summary of the various positions.

the Small, or the Indefinite Dyad.[15] Let us examine briefly the textual basis for this identification.

In *Timaeus*, having distinguished the three fundamental and universal principles of Forms, copies or likenesses of Forms (ἀφομοιώατα), and space (χώρα), Plato proceeds to describe the last mentioned.[16] It is a receptacle (ὑποδοχή), place (τόπος), seat (ἕδρα), nurse (τιθήνη), mother (μήτερα), invisible (ἀνόρατον), shapeless (ἄμορφον), all receptive (πανδεχές), and 'not permitting itself to be destroyed.'[17] It is compared to a mass of gold which can be shaped in different ways though it does not take on any of the characteristics manifested in it.[18] The receptacle is like the base of perfumes, itself without any of the qualities infused in it.[19] It has its own 'anomalous motion' and prior to the imposition on it of 'forms and numbers' by the Demiurge, the elements in it have "traces (ἴχνη) of their own natures."[20]

The interpretation of the *Timaeus* passage is for the Neoplatonists closely connected with the interpretation of a passage from *Philebus*. In *Philebus*, Plato says that "everything that exists now in the universe" belongs to one of four categories: (1) the unlimited (ἄπειρον); (2) the limit (πέρας); (3) the mixture of the two (συμμισγόμενον); (4) the cause of the mixture (τῆς συμμείξεως τὴν αἰτίαν).[21] Category (1) consists of everything that admits of "the more and the less" or of "too much and too little" (examples are hotter and colder, wetter and drier, more and less, faster and slower, greater and smaller); (2) consists of a precise quantitative determination or ratio imposed upon (1). Category (3), the mixture of (1) and (2), is illustrated by health, music, weather, beauty, strength, and so on; (4) is identified with intellect (νοῦς), that which causes (3) to come to be. This passage is full of difficulties. Fortunately, we do not have to address them all.[22] What we are primarily concerned with is Aristotle's justification for associating matter with the Great and the Small. Although 'greater and smaller' are one sort of (1), Plato does not give the entire class the name that Aristotle gives it, nor does he anywhere call it an Indefinite Dyad. For those who have no confidence whatsoever in Aristotle's testimony about the unwritten teachings of Plato, this will be enough to indicate that Aristotle is interpreting Plato in a tendentious manner rather than straightforwardly reporting his view. The Neoplatonists, however, were generally completely open to Aristotle's testimony in this regard. Both Plotinus and Porphyry, for example, accept the

---

15. *Met.* A 6, 987b19–22; 988a11–13; *Phys.* A 4, 187a17; Γ 4, 203a5–15.
16. *Tim.* 52A8ff.
17. For 'receptacle' see *Tim.* 49A6; for 'place' see 52A6; for 'seat' see 52B1; for 'nurse' see 52D5; for 'mother' see 50D3; for 'invisible,' 'shapeless,' and 'all receptive' see 51A7; for 'not permitting itself to be destroyed,' see 52A8.
18. Ibid., 50A5-C6.
19. Ibid., 50E4–51A1.
20. Ibid., 53B2.
21. *Phil.* 23C4-D8.
22. For a good summary of the problems and basic interpretations, see Gosling 1975, 185–206.

identification of matter with the receptacle of *Timaeus* and the class of the unlimited in *Philebus*.[23]

Nevertheless, the receptacle cannot be unqualifiedly identical with (1) above, for the simple reason that the former is seemingly without definite qualities whereas the latter consists precisely in unlimited qualities, or continua of contraries.[24] It is not difficult to see the basis for confusion. The *Timaeus* passage concerns the world prior to the imposition of order by the Demiurge.[25] For the moment it does not matter whether 'prior' is understood temporally or logically. The *Philebus* passage gives the components of the world 'now'—that is, presumably 'after' the work of the Demiurge is completed. Accordingly, if the receptacle is matter in some sense, it is matter in a way different from the way that the unlimited is matter. It is unqualified matter as opposed to the particular matter relative to a particular type of mixture. The receptacle is matter to the "traces of elements" in it. These, having been mathematically ordered by the Demiurge, comprise the various types of matter apt for the imposition of a further mathematical order which produces, say, health as opposed to sickness or beauty as opposed to ugliness.

Aristotle tells us that by 'matter' he means "the primary underlying subject (τὸ πρῶτον ὑποκείμενον) in a thing, from which, as something present (ἐνυπάρχοντος) but not as an attribute, something else is generated."[26] So, when Aristotle identifies the receptacle and the Great and Small or Indefinite Dyad, we may assume that he means to attribute to Plato the concept of an underlying subject of generation or, more generally, of change. That Plato is committed to the irreducibility of an underlying subject of change seems to be implied by, among other things, the refutation of extreme Heracleiteanism in *Theaetetus*.[27] That he is committed to it in a way that is in harmony with the way Aristotle is committed to it is less certain. For one thing, since, as we have seen, Plato does not accept Aristotelian essentialism, he

23. See Plotinus III 4. 1, 1–2; III 6. 13, 12–18; III 6. 14, 29–32; and Porphyry *apud* Simplicius *In Phys.* 453, 30.

24. It is striking that Plato says four times in the space of half a page that the receptacle is 'without shape or form' (*Tim.* 50D7, E4; 51A3, A7). See Gill 1989, 47: "But the matter of the physical world [i.e, proximate matter] is not, as so many have thought, the receptacle."

25. The passage in *Tim.* 48B3–52D4 comes with an explicit frame: τὴν [φύσιν] δὴ πρὸ τῆς οὐρανοῦ γενέσεως . . . οὗτος ἐν κεφαλαίῳ λόγος [of what there was] πρὶν οὐρανὸν γενέσθαι. Everything inside this frame concerns the universe prior to the operation on it by the Demiurge where 'prior' should not necessarily be temporally.

26. *Phys.* A 9, 192a32–33. Cf. *GC* A 4, 320a2–3, where the concept of an underlying subject of generation is extended to that which underlies any change at all.

27. See *Tht.* 181B–183C, esp. 182A3–B7, where Plato introduces the concept of quality (ποιότης) and distinguishes between the general qualities 'hotness' or 'whiteness,' 'an agent' (τὸ ποιοῦν), and the particular quality 'hot' or 'white' that the agent comes to possess. See also *Symp.* 207D4-E5; *Phd.* 102E3–6. In both these passages there is a clear distinction between an underlying subject or continuant and its properties. See Miller (2002, 59–61), who argues that the receptacle is intended by Plato to be the (causal) condition for the possibility of coming to be or change. As such it at least *functions* in the manner in which matter does in Aristotle's physics.

can hardly be committed to a distinction between essential and accidental change and the concomitant concepts of different kinds of underlying subject for each.[28] For another, Aristotle makes a point of emphasizing the distinction between matter and privation (στέρησις), insisting that Plato neglected to consider the latter.[29] Since the three Aristotelian principles of change—form, matter, and privation—are inseparable parts of the account of change, this apparent oversight on Plato's part in regard to privation itself makes us suspect that his understanding of matter diverges from Aristotle's.

Plotinus, despite his rejection of Aristotelian essentialism, holds that the Platonic and Aristotelian accounts of matter are the same but for Aristotle's insistence on making matter and privation different principles.[30] Plotinus tells us that matter is without magnitude (οὐ μέγεθος), bodiless (ἀσώματος), invisible (ἀόρατος), without quality (ἄποιος), impassible (ἀπαθής), unalterable (μὴ ἀλλοισῦσθαι), indestructible (ἀνώλεθρος), unlimited (ἀόριστος), indefinite (ἄπειρον), and without bulk (οὐ ὄγκος).[31] He gives two reasons for positing such a principle: (1) a receptacle or substrate for the presence of forms in the physical world is needed because these forms are images, and images need a medium in which they can be reflected; (2) an underlying principle of generation and change in general is needed.[32] The negative characteristics listed above are all deduced from the exigencies of a principle fulfilling these requirements.[33]

Because matter is impassible, or incapable of being affected, it cannot be identified with a principle that can be combined with form to produce something else. "This is Plato's thinking about it [the receptacle as matter], that is, he did not posit its participation (τὴν μετάληψιν) as being like a form coming to be in an underlying subject and giving it shape so that a single composite (ἓν σύνθετον) comes to be when the two are conjoined (συντραπέντων), in a way mixed together (συγκραθέντων) and both being affected (συμπαθόντων)."[34] Plotinus has a point. Matter conceived of as an

28. We should add the qualification that the geometrical construction of the elements by the Demiurge provides the basis for an elemental essentialism. It is not a huge speculative leap to extend this to a version of essentialism for the things composed of the elements: i.e., the mathematical 'recipe' for the construction of living things.

29. *Phys.* A 9, 192a3–12: Plato recognized that "something must underlie" but he "overlooked the other nature" (τὴν γὰρ ἑτέραν παρεῖδεν): namely, privation. Simplicius (*In Phys.* 245, 19–29; 246, 2–16), argues that Plato did indeed recognize the principle of privation (calling it ἀπουσία, in accord with Aristotle *Phys.* A 7, 191a6–7, instead of στέρησις), identifying it with the receptacle. Cf. Philoponus *In Phys.* 182, 20–25; 183, 11–184, 8.

30. See Corrigan 1996, 158–160, for a nuanced appreciation of Plotinus's critical approach to Aristotle which is at the same time in the spirit of harmonization.

31. For 'without magnitude' see Plotinus III 6. 16, 27; 'bodiless' see II 4. 8, 2; II 4. 9, 5; II 4. 12, 35; 'invisible' see II 4. 12, 23; III 6. 7, 14; 'without quality and impassible' see II 4. 2; III 6. 7, 3; III 6. 9, 36–9; III 6. 11, 45; 'unalterable' see III 6. 10, 20; 'indestructible' see II 5. 5, 34; 'unlimited' see II 4. 10, 4; 'indefinite' see II 4. 15, 11, 19; 'without bulk' see II 4. 11, 25–27.

32. Ibid., II 4. 1–2; III 6. 11; III 6. 14, 1–5.

33. See esp. ibid., III 6. 13, 27–32. This argument is similar to Aristotle's argument in Book Γ of *De Anima* that the intellect must not itself actually have any form if it is to receive all forms.

34. Ibid., III 6. 12, 1ff.

element in a composition in the sense of a mixture cannot be the same thing as matter conceived of as a substratum. The gold that is shaped is still gold, unlike the shortening and flour whose mixture is the piecrust. Matter in the sense in which Plotinus finds it in Plato cannot be combined with anything, any more than, say, distance and time can be combined to make them into something else. Aristotle, however, frequently refers to the 'composite' of matter and form.[35] Mixture is exactly what impassibility excludes.

Plotinus's rejection of matter as an element in a mixture is the reason he insists, against Aristotle and in defense of Plato, that matter and privation are identical.[36] The reason why Plotinus cannot accept a distinction between matter and privation is that this is a distinction between relative and absolute nonbeing.[37] Matter is relative nonbeing, and privation is absolute nonbeing.[38] Making matter relative nonbeing suggests that when what is missing from relative nonbeing is supplied, then unqualified being is achieved. Thus the putative composite is what the matter succeeds in becoming when informed. Such a composite, so long as it exists, continues to have relative nonbeing in relation to all the things it can become, though it would have nonrelative—that is, unqualified—being in regard to what it is. So, the composite human being is a complete, full-fledged being, though since she can acquire all sorts of attributes that she does not currently possess, she continues to have matter or relative nonbeing in relation to these. By insisting on the identity of matter and privation, Plotinus can maintain that any material thing, insofar as it is material, cannot be said to *be* unqualifiedly. This is of course what the Platonist wants to do in insisting on the diminished reality of the physical world.

How, we may well ask Plotinus, can an individual be material *without* being a composite in the way that he denies it is? The answer he gives is that matter, which is identical with the unlimited (ἄπειρον), is to be understood as the property or hallmark of images.[39] More precisely, it is the condition for the possibility of images. That is why there is unlimitedness and hence matter even in the intelligible world, since there intellect and Forms are images of the first principle of all. Things in the physical world, which are images of images, have less being that the 'higher' images. Nothing can turn an image into that of which it is an image. That is why the matter that is necessarily present in any image is not to be understood as perfectible by the imposition of form.[40]

---

35. E.g., see *Phys.* A 7, 190b10–11; *Met.* H 2, 1043a27–8 with H 3, 1043a30; *Cael.* A 9, 277b30–33. He also uses synonymously the term τὸ σύνολον. See, e.g., *Met.* Z 15, 1039b20.
36. Plotinus II 4. 14–16. Cf. I 8. 5, 20–25; I 8. 11, 1–7. By contrast, Proclus *De Mal.* 32, 14–15, explicitly denies that matter and privation are identical. Simplicius *In Phys.* 246, 2–12, says that privation is an 'accidental cause' and that is why Plato did not introduce it.
37. See Aristotle *Phys.* A 9, 192a3–6.
38. See *Met.* Δ 22, 1022b22–1023a7 on privation.
39. See Plotinus II 4. 15, esp. 21–28.
40. *Met.* Γ 5, 1009a32–36, says that in one way things can be generated from nonbeing, meaning matter, and in one way they cannot, meaning absolute nonbeing. Cf. Γ 5, 1010a20–22.

Another way Neoplatonists approach the issue is in terms of the distinction between potency and actuality in Aristotle. Aristotle does not exactly identify matter with potency, though he comes close. In *Physics* he seems to claim that matter "in the sense of potency" (κατὰ δύναμιν) is indestructible.[41] Plotinus agrees to identify matter and potency *tout court*, though he insists on the fundamental difference between matter in the sense above and, as he says, "matter in the way bronze is."[42] In other words, he seems entirely open to the employment of the Aristotelian language so long as it does not imply the mitigation of the permanently derivative status of the physical world.

We have here the key to the Neoplatonic, sometimes tacit embrace of a good part of the Aristotelian terminology. For example, there is nothing un Platonic in explaining the acquisition by bronze of a new shape in the way that Aristotle does. Within a limited context the explanation provided by saying that the bronze is potentially the statue or material for the statue is even in line with Plato's own words, as we saw above. And to add that the bronze is still the same bronze upon being shaped is no doubt correct and illuminating, especially if it gives the lie to those who deny the possibility of change. But the Neoplatonists draw the line at turning the principle of matter into a principle of relative nonbeing so that explanatory adequacy is thought to be achieved in making the statement above. That is, if matter is, as Aristotle would seem to have it, different from privation, then all there is to say about a material substance will be said within the ambit of his fourfold scheme of causal analysis. Thus, along the line of material causality, to say that the human being's body is matter to his soul is to have provided one cornerstone of a complete scientific explanation. And since the soul is the actuality of that matter, the successful account of that enmattered form will reach the end of an explanatory track.

The contrasting Neoplatonic position can be stated simply as an insistence that there is no explanatory adequacy in the account of images without adducing their paradigmatic causes: that is, without introducing the Forms, the Intellect that contains these, and the first principle of all, the One.[43] For them an Aristotelian physical explanation has an 'as if' quality,

41. *Phys.* A 9, 192a27. See also *Met.* Θ 1, 1046a23; K 2, 1060a19–21. The last passage says that "it [matter] exists not in actuality but in potency" (αὕτη γε μὴν ἐνεργείᾳ μὲν οὐκ ἔστι, δυνάμει δ᾽ ἔστιν.). This is ambiguous, though it comes close to being an identity statement of a sort. Madigan 1999, 154, says that Aristotle in this passage "correlates matter with potentiality."

42. II 5. 4–5, esp. 5, 8–9. At III 6. 7, 9, Plotinus says that matter is not δύναμις, using the term in the sense of 'power' according to which the One is δύναμις πάντων. Plotinus II 5. 1–2 tends to identify potency with what Aristotle calls "productive or active potency": that is, the potency for producing a change in another, as opposed to passive potency, which is potency for being changed by another. See *Met.* Δ 12, 1019a15–23; Θ 1, 1046a23–27. Plotinus's preferred way of speaking is to say that the bronze is in potency (δυνάμει) to the statue, indicating a passive potency, but that courage is a potency (δύναμις) for the actuality that is a courageous act.

43. One of Aristotle's fundamental principles is that knowledge is of the "first causes or principles" (τὰ πρῶτα αἴτια, αἱ πρῶται ἀρχαί) which explain why things are the way they are. See *Phys.* A 1, 184a12–14; *APo.* A 2, 71b9–12. cf. *Meno* 98A3–4 where knowledge is distinguished

a sort of strategic pretense of adequacy. If you treat flora or fauna or astronomical bodies as if they were basic, then Aristotelian explanations are acceptable. If you recognize that they are not, then those explanations will not be adequate.[44] In addition, owing to the fact that nature is a moved mover and not an unmoved mover, it is an instrumental cause. Hence, no explanation can end with the claim "nature is like that", where an ending means that further requests for explanation are pointless or unintelligible. Nature is not an *unqualified* principle of motion and rest.[45]

Aristotle himself seems to recognize the explanatory roadblock thrown up by matter when he claims that the "underlying nature is knowable by analogy" (κατ' ἀναλογίαν).[46] That is, the underlying nature as a principle of nature is analogous to an underlying subject, like the bronze. Superficially, this seems rather inconsequential if we focus, as perhaps we inevitably do, on the bronze, which both has its own nature and already has some shape before being made into a statue. But matter is only analogous to this. It has no nature or shape of its own, nothing that is knowable. So, if the science of nature is a science of things with matter, the self-sufficiency of this science is suspect.

This point is well made by Proclus at the beginning of his commentary on *Timaeus*. Proclus begins by stating that the science of nature (φυσιολογία) is traditionally divided into parts, the study of matter, the study of form, and finally the study of why matter and form are not true causes but only contributory causes, whereas the true causes are the productive (ποιητικόν), the paradigmatic (παραδειγματικόν), and the final (τελικόν). He then turns first to Plato's scientific predecessors, especially Anaxagoras, and then to a contrast between Aristotle's treatment of the causes with Plato's:

> Not all, but the more accurately minded of the leading figures of the school after Plato,[47] think that what exists by nature includes the form along with the

---

from true belief by "an account of the cause" (αἰτίας λογισμῷ). Cf. Plotinus VI 7. 2, 15–19. Proclus *In Remp.* I 263, 23ff., draws the natural comparison between what is said in *Meno* and Aristotle's doctrine of knowledge as being of the universal and unalterable. He also notes the similarity between Plato's and Aristotle's accounts of the radical distinctness of knowledge and belief.

44. Cf. Simplicius *In Phys.* 363, 8–10: "In general, if enmattered forms are participations in primary Forms, they are images fashioned in their likeness. Every image then is related to its model."

45. The definition of 'nature' at *Phys.* B 1, 192a21ff. stresses the relative priority of nature in relation to artifacts and accidental composites as a cause of motion and rest. Those who would take Aristotle to be maintaining an anti-Platonic position here must insist that the relative priority is actually absolute priority. In other words, they must hold that nature is self-explanatory. But as we shall see infra chap. 7 Aristotle explicitly denies this.

46. *Phys.* A 7, 191a7–8. This claim is typically associated by Neoplatonists with Plato's claim in *Tim.* 51A7-B1 and 52B2, that the receptacle "partakes in a puzzling way of the intelligible and is most difficult to apprehend" and is apprehended by a sort of "illegitimate reasoning" (νόθος λογισμός). See, e.g., Simplicius *In Phys.* 246, 25–28. At *Tim.* 50D7-E1, the receptacle is described as "without character" (ἄμορφον).

47. This is usually and probably correctly taken to be a direct reference to Aristotle, though it might well encompass Plato's successors Speusippus and Xenocrates.

matter, reducing the principles of bodies to matter and form. For even if they did make some sort of mention of the productive cause, as when they say that nature is a principle of motion [cf. *Phys.* B 1, 192b8–27], they nevertheless remove from it [the productive cause] the function of making and being principally productive [τὸ δραστήριον καὶ τὸ κυρίως ποιητικόν]. They do this because they do not allow that in it [nature] are the rational principles [λόγους] of the things made by it. And granting that many things come to be by chance, in addition to their not agreeing to the preexistence of a productive cause of all natural bodies unqualifiedly, but only of those that are generated, they expressly say that there is not a productive cause of eternal things. It also escapes their notice that they are either making the entire universe to be a product of chance or claiming that bodily things make themselves.

Plato alone, following the Pythagoreans, gives over to the 'all receptive' and to the enmattered form the role of contributory causes of things that exist by nature, subordinating them to the principal causes of generation. He explores the primary causes [τὰς πρωτουργοὺς αἰτίας] before these, the productive, the paradigmatic, and the final. To account for these, he established intellect as demiurgic cause of everything, and an intelligible cause, in which everything is primarily, and the Good, which is situated prior to the productive cause in the order of desire. Since that which is moved by another is dependent on the power of that which moves it, it cannot produce itself. That is, it is clearly not of a nature to perfect or produce itself, but for all these it needs the productive cause and is held together by that. And so it is appropriate that the contributory causes of things that exist by nature are dependent on the true causes, by which they have been realized [productive cause], in relation to which they have been made [paradigmatic cause] by the father of all things, and on account of which they have been generated [final cause]. It is likely, therefore, that Plato has given to us, after a most exacting examination, all these [true causes] and made the other two, the form and the underlying subject, dependent on them . . . All that which has been produced by secondary causes has as [primary cause] that which exists primarily and inexpressibly and inconceivably.[48]

Proclus's point here is principally the superiority of the Platonic approach to the science of nature over the Aristotelian approach. But he incidentally provides the rationale for the harmony between the two. So long as an Aristotelian realizes that physical science cannot be explanatorily exhaustive, its ambit is secure.[49]

48. Proclus *In Tim.* I 2, 16–3, 32. Cf. III 222, 7–27 and *ET* Prop. 56, on the instrumental character of 'secondary' causes in relation to 'primary' causes. See I 425, 4–7 for Proclus's argument that neither the Demiurge nor the Form of Living Animal can be identified with the Good itself, owing to their complexity.

49. Cf. *In Tim.* I 337, 29–338, 5; 346, 29–347, 2; 348, 23–27, where Proclus argues that the scientific character of (Platonic) physics depends upon connecting what is learned about nature with immutable and incorporeal first principles. See O'Meara 1989, 183–185, on the strategy revealed in these Proclean passages.

There is an important sense in which Aristotle himself recognizes this point when he sets down the limitation of physical science. In the last book of *Physics,* Aristotle says that nature, taken as a principle of motion, is a hypothesis.[50] To Neoplatonic ears, this sounds like the hypothetical reasoning of Plato's *Republic,* which should lead ultimately to an unhypothetical understanding of first principles.[51] Simplicius sums this up nicely in noting the direction of the entire *Physics:* "Thus the truly marvelous Aristotle brought his teaching about physical principles to the point of the theology of the supernatural and showed that the entire physical or bodily order was dependent on the nonbodily and boundless intellectual goodness above nature, in this also following Plato."[52] Simplicius goes on to identify this "intellectual goodness" with the Demiurge, an "intellectual god." He further suggests that apparent differences between Aristotle and Plato in this regard are owing to the fact that the former couched his argument in terms of an explanation of motion and movables, whereas the latter couched his explanation in terms of coming-to-be; the one arrives at a "primary unmoved mover" and the other arrives at "that which is always the same in the same way."

In addition, in a passage I consider at some length in chapter six, Aristotle in his *Metaphysics* lays it down that if supersensible substance did not exist, then physical science would be the first science.[53] But since, as Aristotle will go on to show, and has repeatedly insisted elsewhere, supersensible substance *does* exist, it follows that physical science is not the first science. Of course, we cannot say without further ado that the demotion of physical science to second place entails a rejection of its autonomy. That is what the Neoplatonists assume. We need to look at additional considerations on behalf of the view that explanatory adequacy for the subjects of physical science is not to be found within physical science and that Aristotle's own principles support this view.

Let us return to matter. The basis for the Neoplatonic view that explanations proffered in terms of matter and form cannot be adequate is the ineluctable presence of the former. If part of what a sensible composite is includes matter, then the putative definition of it cannot be unequivocally intelligible. For example, if in defining a circle one had to include in the definition something about the chalk used to draw a circle on a blackboard, one could not thus define a circle adequately. The definition of a circle should have nothing to do with chalk.[54] In his *Metaphysics,* however, Aristotle insists that "of a definition [τοῦ λόγου], one part is always matter and one part is the actuality."[55] And in his *Physics* he states that "perhaps [ἴσως] that

50. *Phys.* Θ 3, 253b5–6.
51. See Plato *Rep.* 510B–511C, and Simplicius *In Phys.* 1194, 24–30.
52. Simplicius *In Phys.* 1359, 5–8.
53. *Met.* E 1, 1026a27–29.
54. The example is from Plato *7th Ep.* 342Aff.
55. *Met.* H 6, 1045a34–35. The majority of the mss. add the words "e.g., a circle is a plane figure." These words are excluded by Jaeger. If the words belong in the text, they do not give the complete definition of a circle but only the genus, the logical matter.

which is necessary [τὸ ἀναγκαῖον: i.e., matter] is in the definition."[56] If matter is knowable only by analogy, then one might well inquire as to how explanatory adequacy is going to be attained by including it in the definition. Yet Aristotle also says, 'There is neither definition (ὁρισμός) nor demonstration of particular sensible substances because they have matter the nature of which is such that it is possible for it to be and not to be.'[57]

One standard scholarly resolution of the foregoing claims is that the definition of sensible substances includes the matter but only 'logically' or 'abstractly,' so that no particular matter is included. Thus the definition of a circle does not include the chalk; it includes only the line that is a locus of points equidistant from a point apart from that line. And the definition of a human being does not include a particular body but only that there be a body of a certain kind: that is, "an organic body."[58] Thus in the definition of sensible substances in general we include form and matter of a certain kind.[59] But in what sense is "matter of a certain kind" matter? The definition of a man as a bipedal animal, for example, is supposed to include the genus 'animal' as matter. But 'animal' does not name the underlying nature that is knowable only by analogy. The reference made to the putative matter in this definition is not a reference to anything that belongs to the science of the changeable. Either the definition of sensible substances includes matter in another way or it includes no matter at all, in which case it is not in principle different from a definition of the incorporeal paradigm. How can definitions of sensibles *as such* be self-standing?

It is useful here to compare the definitions of elements in Plato and Aristotle. Plato in *Timaeus*, defines the elements or primary bodies in terms of solid geometrical shapes.[60] For example, to water is assigned the icosahedron. The phenomenal properties of these elements seem to be the 'traces' found in the receptacle prior to the imposition of 'forms and numbers' by the Demiurge.[61] By contrast, Aristotle in *On Generation and Corruption* defines them in terms of the contrary phenomenal properties, hot and cold,

---

56. *Phys.* B 9, 200b4–5.
57. *Met.* Z 15, 1039b27–30. Cf. Z 7, 1032a20–22; *Cael.* A 12, 283b4.
58. See, e.g., Gill 1989, esp. chaps. 4–5, though Gill is somewhat critical of this account, arguing that the definition does not include a "distinct matter" (133).
59. Cf. *Phys.* B 2, 194b9: ἄλλῳ γὰρ εἴδει ἄλλη ὕλη.
60. *Tim.* 53C-55C.
61. Ibid., 53B-C. When the receptacle is said to be 'fiery' or 'watery' in its pre-cosmic state, it is implausible that this should indicate geometrical structure rather than phenomenal properties. Taylor 1928, 312, thinks that the phenomenal properties depend on the geometrical structure, but this is only subsequent to the efforts of the Demiurge, who linked them inextricably together. There are several reasons for this. If the 'traces' were traces of the Forms that are used by the Demiurge to shape the world, then they would be traces of geometrical shapes. But the pre-cosmic elements are described phenomenologically, not mathematically. If the pre-cosmic hotness were a trace of a Form, presumably it would be a Form of Hotness or of Fire. But making the pre-cosmic element a trace in this way would mean that this Form was paradigmatically hot—which seems exactly what the description of the Demiurge's work is intended to preclude. The Demiurge does not import hotness into the cosmos; it is already there.

wet and dry.[62] For example, water is cold and wet. In each definition, matter is included along with the contraries.[63]

If the Form of Water is an incorporeal entity, it is difficult to see what it would mean to insinuate phenomenal properties into it. Presumably this Form would be exceedingly cold and wet. This is nonsense, and there is no reason to suppose that Plato ever succumbed to this nonsense, especially after he began to consider the mathematical reduction of Forms. Once we see the definition of the elements separated from the hypothesis that explains the phenomenal properties of their cosmic images, we can see that it is the Demiurge who is made responsible for matching up a geometrical structure with a type of phenomenal property and for establishing their necessary connections. Thus it is not the case that Plato deduces physics from mathematics. Nothing in the nature of the geometrical structure of water entails that cosmic water feel watery to us as opposed to fiery. That is why a definition of phenomenal water is a definition of an image needing to be supplemented by a definition of the Form of Water: that is, by a mathematical definition.[64] Plato's actual explanation of why the geometrical shape and the phenomenal property go together—that the Demiurge thought that it would be better this way—may be no more satisfying, but it is a different explanation nonetheless from what is often supposed.

In *De Caelo*, Aristotle provides a battery of arguments against any mathematical account of the elements, including Plato's in *Timaeus*.[65] As Aristotle succinctly puts it, "the principles of perceptibles should be perceptible."[66] And summarizing his argument, he says, "From what has been said, it is clear that the difference of the elements does not depend on their shape. Since the most important differences of bodies are those of their works (ἔργα), states (πάθη), and powers (δυνάμεις), we should consider these first . . . ."[67] Definitions in terms of this triad are not obviously inconsistent with the mathematical definitions unless we exclude from the latter a necessary connection with the phenomenal. Aristotle is being rightly caustious in insisting that there is no necessary connection between a shape per se and a phenomenal property, whether this be expressed as a work or a state or a

---

62. *GC* B 2, 330a30–33/a6.

63. Ibid., B 1, 329a24b5.

64. Cf. Simplicius *In Phys.* 296, 32–297, 35.

65. See *Cael.* Γ 7–8.

66. Ibid., 7, 306a9–10.

67. Ibid., 8, 307b19–23.

68. Alcinous *Didask.* 12. 2, 6, says of the ἴχνη that they are only δεκτικόν τῆς τῶν στοιχείων δυνάμεως, which suggests that they are phenomenal properties. Proclus, on the other hand, in his *In Tim.* I 270, 9–26, and I 383, 24–385, 16, argues that the pre-cosmic elements do have a connection with the Forms independent of the subsequent intervention by the Demiurge. But Proclus says this because he holds that Plato believes that "God [i.e., the One] is the absolutely first and ineffable cause of the existence of matter "(384, 30–385, 3). Hence God, via the instrumentality of the Forms, is able to introduce a measure of intelligibility into the pre-cosmic world prior to the intervention of the Demiurge, who adds order and beauty to the disordered intelligibility. See also I 387, 5ff.

power. But this is not the view that Plato was understood by the Neoplatonists to have held.[68] The real dispute is whether an Aristotelian definition of the elements which includes the phenomenal contraries is self-standing or even potentially explanatorily adequate.[69]

A definition that includes one or more of the triad of works, states, and powers is on the face of it quite different from a taxionomical definition in terms of kinds. This is so principally because each of the members of the triad is, for Aristotle, functionally related to a kind; that is, a kind is always included in its definition.[70] But even if the triad can function independently of subjects within an explanatory system—for example, if we interpret Aristotle as an antirealist—still Aristotle has to import matter into the definition. And as soon as he does that, he is faced with the question, why is *this* individual necessarily *that* kind of thing? Why, for example, is this stuff water and not fire? Presumably, the answer is something like this: because it necessarily has these properties and anything with these properties is water, where "these properties" refers to a type not a token. But then we want to ask: where did the necessity come from? Aristotle's unwavering answer to such a question is that if we have the correct definition, then there is no further answer to be given. That is just the way things are.

The necessity to which Aristotle is here committed is hypothetical.[71] And he adds in the last sentence of the second book of *Physics*, "Indeed, even in the definition there are some parts [serving] as matter of the definition."[72] For the Neoplatonist, the identification here of matter as necessity is irresistibly comparable to necessity in *Timaeus*, the "kind of wandering cause" (τὸ τῆς πλανωμένης εἶδος αἰτίας).[73] By the words "by necessity" (ἐξ ἀνάγκης) Plato means, minimally, whatever contributes to the composition of cosmic sensibles other than what comes about by "the works of intellect" (τὰ διὰ νοῦ δεδημιουργημένα): namely, the works of the Demiurge.[74] As we

69. Moravcsik 1991, 42–43, argues that Aristotle, against Plato, separates the question of explanatory adequacy from the question of ontological ultimacy. Moravcsik is, I think, importantly correct in holding that explanatory adequacy can always be achieved independently of ontological considerations when that explanation is sought, as it always is, relative to a context. The harmonist's point, however, is that contextualized explanatory adequacy in the Aristotelian mode never in principle closes off the path to a search for ontological ultimacy.

70. See *Met.* Z 5, where Aristotle argues that the subject is included in the definition of a state. Cf. *Cat.* 8, which deals with states as a type of quality.

71. *Phys.* B 9, 200a30–32: "It is clear, then, that the necessary in natural things is what we call 'matter' and also the motions of matter" (φανερὸν δὴ ὅτι τὸ ἀναγκαῖον ἐν τοῖς φυσικοῖς τὸ ὡς ὕλη λεγόμενον καὶ αἱ κινήσεις).

72. Ibid., 200b6–7. Cf. *Met.* Z 11, 1036a29ff.

73. See *Tim.* 47E–48E; 68E–69A. See Simplicius *In Phys.* 388, 11ff., who specifically compares the hypothetical necessity here with the *Timaeus* passage.

74. *Tim.*, 47E4.

75. See Miller (2002, esp. chap. 5), who argues that the 'third kind' (τρίτον εἶδος) at *Tim.* 49A1–2, which is usually taken to refer to the receptacle understood as either matter or space (or place) or the confused amalgam of the two, actually refers to a metaphysical principle, distinguished from the other 'two kinds': namely, the intelligibles and their sensible images. If this is so, then it is plausible to take this metaphysical principle as being instantiated by *two different*

have seen, this includes the receptacle itself and the 'traces' of the elements.[75] Following Aristotle's identification of the receptacle with matter and treating the phenomenal properties of things as independent of the works of intellect, it is natural to infer that a definition of sensibles that includes the matter cannot be entirely perspicuous to the intellect. It cannot be understood on its own. Specifically, it must be understood as an image of a paradigmatic cause. Thus for the Neoplatonist it is not paradoxical to say that Socrates is a man but that the definition of man is not a definition of Socrates, for whatever uniquely belongs to Socrates does not belong to that definition. In other words, a definition of Socrates' humanity, the *way* Socrates instantiates humanity, is not thoroughly intelligible because it must include that which is other than a work of intellect. It includes matter and the contraries or phenomenal properties belonging to that which happens 'by necessity.'[76]

Aristotle gives three examples of hypothetical necessity: a house, health, and a human being.[77] In each case, if the thing is to exist, then certain 'material requirements,' as we might say, must be met. Whatever these might be in any particular case, they are not in principle different from the material requirements involved in the instantiation of a Platonic Form.[78] What is most interesting about Aristotle's examples, however, is the collocation of the natural and the artificial. In the case of a house, its definition includes or is perhaps identical with the purpose or final cause.[79] This is so because the entire intelligible content of a house as such is contained in the purposes of house-dwellers. There is nothing about, say, the shape of a house that reveals its purpose. It is true that certain shapes may be excluded by these purposes, as well as certain types of material, but the shape that any house does have is functionally related to the purpose. But if houses cannot be understood apart from the purposes of house-dwellers—that is, apart

---

physical principles: namely, matter and space (or place). This would mean that Plato never intended to merge these. If true, this would mean that Aristotle at least tendentiously portrayed Plato's account. If Miller is correct, complaints like those of Sayre 1983, 250, that the receptacle cannot, as Plato characterizes it, be both space and in space, are misguided. Sayre argues that owing to the incoherence of the characterization of the receptacle, Plato should be understood to be signaling the futility of trying to understand how participation works. See further Sayre 2003.

76. Simplicius *In Phys.* 295, 25–296, 2, clearly makes this point.

77. *Phys.* B 9, 200b1–4.

78. At *Tim.* 69A6, after completing the description of the two types of explanation, necessity and reason, Timaeus says that they now have at hand "the material ready for us like carpenters." It is true that the 'material' includes both explanations, but it is equally true that the 'works of necessity' are the material for the imposition of a rational order on the cosmos. Cf. esp. 69A2–5: "... Without the necessary, those other objects, about which we are serious, cannot on their own be discerned and hence cannot be comprehended or partaken of in any other way."

79. See, e.g., *Met.* Z 17, 1041a27. A few lines after the reference to the essence of a house perhaps being identical with its final cause, (1041b5–10), Aristotle makes exactly the same point about a man.

from rational purpose—then the treatment of a human being along the lines of a house is of some importance.

On the one hand, there is hardly any doubt at all that Aristotle generally elides formal and final explanations for natural substances as well as for artifacts.[80] On the other hand, there is considerable debate over whether this means that explanatory adequacy is or is not containable within the definitional framework. I mean that the comparison of a human being and a house invites the question of whether the former can be understood independently of an externally imposed purpose. There is a great deal to be said on both sides of the issue. We need to look carefully at how the hypothesis of the harmony of Aristotle's account of the physical world with Platonism helps us see our way clear to a resolution.

Paradigmatic Causes and Eternity

It may seem obvious that Aristotle explicitly rejected the 'paradigmatic cause': "It is clear, therefore, that as for the causes of forms [i.e., enmattered forms] as some are accustomed to call 'the Forms', if they are something separate from particulars, they are of no use in generations, that is, of substances. Nor would they be, at least for his reason, substances existing in themselves."[81] As Aristotle goes on to argue, it is "man that begets man," not the Form of Humanity. Some contemporary scholars have insisted that this passage constitutes Aristotle's misguided and unequivocal rejection of the sort of explanation given in *Phaedo*.[82] It is unnecessary to point out that if Forms are not intended to explain generation, then their uselessness for this task is neither here nor there. Nevertheless, it would be a rejection of paradigmatic causes to claim that the *only* sort of explanation needed to say why *this* substance came to be is its specific progenitor, that is, its parent or parents. I spoke in chapter three and I speak again in chapters six and seven of the explanatory role of Forms in predication. Here, however, I address briefly the problem of generation, as conceived by Aristotle himself. For it seems that Aristotle's naturalistic account of the generation of composite substances is in one relevant respect manifestly inadequate. It is this inadequacy—or so I argue—that the Neoplatonists took for granted in their appeal to the Platonic paradigmatic cause as a necessary supplement.

---

80. See *Phys.* B 7, 198a25–26: τὸ μὲν γὰρ τί ἐστι καὶ τὸ οὗ ἕνεκα ἕν ἐστι. Cf. B 8, 198b3–4; 199a31–32; *De An.* B 4, 415a25–b7.

81. *Met.* Z 8, 1033b26–29. Cf. 1034a2; A 9, 991a21, 27; M 5, 1079b24–26. The word παράδειγμα is specifically used in all these passages.

82. See e.g., Vlastos 1973a, 88–92 and Gallop 1975, who are rebutted by Lennox 2001, 147–153 and n.33. Lennox 183, argues that Aristotle understands perfectly well what Plato is offering in *Phaedo* as a causal explanation of the presence of form and that "this man (i.e., the father) explains the presence of that man (i.e., the son)" is the appropriate explanatory corrective to "the Form of Humanity explains the presence of this man." But the Neoplatonists as well as Plato do in fact provide arguments for the view that "being of no use for generation" does not exhaust the exigencies of the explanation of generation.

Aristotle maintains in *De Anima* that the members of plant and animal species "partake of the eternal (τοῦ ἀεί) and divine to the extent possible" by reproducing their own kinds.[83] In a famous and contentious passage in *Generation of Animals,* Aristotle amplifies these remarks:

> Now among things that exist, some are eternal [ἀΐδια][84] and divine while others can exist or not exist. But that which is noble and divine is, according to its own nature, eternally [ἀεί] the cause of what is better among things that can be better or worse, while that which is non-eternal can exist or not exist and partakes of the worse and the better. And since soul is better than body and the ensouled is better than the soulless owing to its soul and being is better than not being and living better than not living, for these reasons reproduction [γένεσις] of living things exists. Now since it is impossible for the nature of such a kind to be eternal,[85] that which comes to be is eternal in the only manner possible for it. Since it is impossible for it to be eternal as an individual (for the essence [οὐσία] of things is in the particular but if it were such, it would be eternal), it is possible for it to be eternal in species [εἴδει]. This is the reason why there exists eternally the class [γένος] of human beings, animals, and plants.[86]

I agree with those who maintain that this passage should not be taken as an argument for the eternity of the species as such. It seems clear enough that Aristotle wants to argue that the individual living thing attains immortality and eternity only via reproduction. But it is in my view a mistake to infer from this that paradigmatism is thus abandoned or even that paradigmatism has nothing to do with the explanatory framework here invoked.

The denial that the species as such is eternal might mislead one into supposing that the desire for eternity in the individual members of the species does not require an explanation. Thus, the eternity in question is thought to be a concomitant of the individual's reproductive activity.[87] But in the

---

83. *De An.* B 4, 415a22-b8. Cf. Plato *Symp.* 207C9-D3: "For with animals the explanation is the same as with us, that is, the mortal nature seeks to the extent possible to be eternal and immortal. This is possible for it only by reproduction . . ."; *Lg.* 721C2-6.

84. Assuming τὸ ἀεί and τὸ ἀΐδιον are used synonymously.

85. Lennox (2001, 136), reads the clause thus: "While if the being were a such, *it* (not the generated thing) would be eternal" and he takes it as indicating, counterfactually, the Platonic alternative claim that species are eternal because their Form is eternal.

86. *GA* B 1, 731b24-732a1.

87. Lennox 2001, 137, says that "the best *possible* state of affairs for organisms, given that each of them cannot exist eternally, is that each of them be a member of an everlasting, continuous series of organisms which are the same in form if not in number. Reproduction occurs *because* it procures the best possible state of affairs for the reproducing organism" (my emphasis). This seems to make eternity an (accidental) achievement of individuals, not an endowment. But it is not clear to me why it is supposed by Lennox to be in the interests of individual members of a species that they reproduce. In addition, if it is not necessary that they reproduce, then it is possible that they should not. See *GC* B 11, 337b7: "Someone intending to take a walk may not do so." In that case the eternity of the species is only an exaggerated expression of its longevity or perdurance. Cf. Aristotle's argument in *Phys.* Θ 1, 251b28-252a5 (that if it were possible that motion cease, then motion could never have begun) and *Cael.* A 12, 283a24-b5.

passage above, Aristotle says, "That which is noble and divine is, according to its own nature, eternally (ἀεί) the cause of what is better among things that can be better or worse, while that which is non-eternal can exist or not exist and partakes of the worse and the better."[88] Even if the cause is construed other than as a paradigm, it is a mistake to infer eternality from the bottom up rather than from the top down.[89] Such an inference can be made only if we ignore Aristotle's explicit claim that the explanation for the achievement of 'the better' among plants and animals is itself eternal.

This explanation is easily lost or ignored if one focuses on the next line alone and takes it to negate what has just been said. This would happen if Aristotle's assertion that the species as such cannot be eternal were taken to constitute a denial of paradigmatism rather than what it clearly is: namely, a denial that the individual can be eternal in any way other than by reproducing. It is impossible for a species to be eternal, because a species does not exist apart from matter. The denial of eternity of the species as such is a denial of the existence of a paradigm only if a paradigm is taken to be a species—if, say, the Form of Whale is taken to be the species whale. Since for Aristotle the species exists separately only in the individual member or abstractly in the mind of one who know it, someone who held the species to be identical with the paradigm might be thought to hold that this paradigm is an individual, too: the paradigmatic member of the species, so to speak. Aristotle does certainly reject such a view. But it is neither obvious that this is Plato's view nor that Aristotle is not otherwise committed to paradigms properly construed: that is, as being other than separate individual members of the species.

Simplicius argues for precisely this position: "I think that it is possible to use Aristotle's assumptions (ὑποθέσεσι) to show that the causes of [enmattered] forms are distinct (διωρισμένα) from them and are paradigms of them. We say that the natural things exist as a result of the participation of matter and form, with the matter participating in the form according to an internal participation (κατὰ τὴν ἐν αὐτῇ μέθεξιν)."[90]

Simplicius's strategy is to show that Aristotle himself is committed to participation by enmattered form in separate, paradigmatic Form analogous to the participation of matter in enmattered form. He is aware, however, that this needs to be shown:

---

88. See *Met.* α 1, 993b23–30, and infra chap. 6, 180–188.

89. The argument at *GC* B 11 to the effect that there are some necessary processes among the things that 'are and are not' applies to the cycle of elemental change and not to animal and plant reproduction. In opposition to this, Lennox (2001, 139), thinks that animal and plant reproduction is in fact a "continuous reproduction of the form of the kind." This is not likely to be the correct explanation of the eternity of the species, given that it is clearly possible for the individual plants and animals not to reproduce. Lennox goes on (140) to offer a probabilistic argument for eternity. Thus the "natural disposition for the most part is all that is required to ensure the future recurrence of organisms the same in form." But if it is possible that each individual does not reproduce, then it is difficult to see wherein lies the eternity of the species.

90. *In Phys.* 296, 32–297, 1.

But perhaps someone will not concede that there is participation for the forms here, [rather claiming] that these have a prior existence [προηγουμένην ὑπόστασιν]. For in the intelligible world [ἐκεῖ] [one might argue] there is no man or horse, but rather causes of these [here below] which exist in different forms, though they are productive of these; for example, man comes from god and that which is in motion comes from that which is immovable, and these are not the same in form [as their producers]. Those who makes these claims should be asked whether they suppose that beauty, goodness, essence, life, knowledge, actuality, and number exist in the intelligible world—or anything else similarly sublime. Because Aristotle concedes that these exist in the intelligible world. He makes this clear when he says that [the intelligible world] is desirable for everything and that intellect is in essence activity, thus identifying essence and life and intellect, attributing beauty and goodness to them, and saying that the immovable causes are equal in number to the heavenly bodies.

But it is also clear that Aristotle is displeased with those concepts of forms that, along with the names derived from things here, also drag with them the definitions which include the physical and material elements of things here. That is why he is unhappy with certain of the names, though he does not think it inappropriate to apply certain of the purer names from here to the things in the intelligible world, such as beauty, goodness, essence, life, intellect, and actuality.

If then someone were to say that these do exist in the intelligible world, but not in the way that the forms do here, we would agree with this, but we would require of him to say the same thing for Human Being and Horse and similar [Forms] in the intelligible world. For we do not believe that Human Being in the intelligible world is bodily, since it is not even the case that a human being is bodily in his physical definition, though we do believe that there is some likeness between the bodily human being and disembodied Human Being just as there is between bodily beauty and disembodied Beauty. In general if the forms here are generated, and if everything generated is necessarily generated by some cause that has previously acquired the definition of what is generated, in order that the generation should not be nonrational or unlimited, and if what is generated is likened [ἀφομοιοῦται] to the definition, there would in this way be a paradigm for things generated.[91]

Simplicius makes a number of important points in this passage. Principally, he wants to argue that paradigmatic causes are not perfect particulars because all particulars—in the sensible world, at any rate—contain matter.[92] The participation, and hence the paradigmatism, is of the enmattered

91. Ibid 297, 11–35. (trans. Fleet, slightly modified). Simplicius's use of the term ἀφομοιόω here follows *Tim.* 50D1; 50E3; 51A2. The term indicates the correlate of παράδειγμα. Cf. *Tim.* 28A7; 29B4; 48E5; and esp. 31A4–8. Fine 2003, 380–384; 392–396 argues that Plato's paradigmatic causes are equivalent to Aristotle's essential causes. This seems wrong, however, since for Aristotle the definition of the essence of a sensible will include the matter whereas the definition of a paradigmatic cause will not.
92. See Malcolm (1991, chaps. 5–7), who argues that Plato's Forms are paradigms and therefore perfect examples of what their names name. Malcolm claims with certain qualifications

form in the separate Form. Simplicius, however, seems to base his argument that participation or paradigmatism is required on the grounds that enmattered forms are generated and that the generation is always according to the 'definition.'

Aristotle says in a number of places in his *Metaphysics* that the forms of sensibles are *not* generated; rather, it is the composite individual that is generated (or destroyed).[93] Since the composite includes the enmattered form, that which is not generated cannot refer to *this*.[94] What cannot be generated Aristotle calls 'the definition' (ὁ λόγος), which is presumably why Simplicius says that generation is always according to this. But 'definition' is Aristotle's typical shorthand way of referring to that which is expressed in a definition. What is expressed in a definition cannot then include or refer to the enmattered form.

Those who take Aristotle to be committed to the rejection of paradigmatism absolutely insist that what is expressed in a definition is eternal only potentially, not actually. And this potential eternity is achieved via the generation of composites including their enmattered forms. It would, however, be incoherent to maintain that what the definition refers to is only what is generated as opposed to that of which each generated enmattered form is an instance.

Aristotle makes an interesting concession to this line of thinking when he states that, "It is not yet clear if the essences (αἱ οὐσίαι) of destructible things are separate (χωρισταί). But it is clear that some of these are not, in such cases where it is not possible for them to exist apart from individuals, such as in the case of a house or a utensil. Perhaps then these things are themselves not substances nor are any other things that are not composed by nature. For one might suppose that nature alone is the essence in destructible things."[95] The interesting concession is that the criterion of nonseparability is here evidently not matter. If it were, then it would be obvious that the essence of an animal or plant can no more exist separately from the individual than can the essence of a house. The criterion that is applied here is artificiality. Since Aristotle himself says that 'we' (those in the Academy) do not allow Forms of artifacts, the distinction between the artificial and the natural is here all the more significant.[96]

---

that the paradigmatic status of the Form means that its instances are approximations of that Form. It is not clear, however, how the image that Simplicius takes an instance of a Form to be could approximate that paradigm. Malcolm's approximation interpretation follows from his view that Forms are self-predicative: that is, they perfectly exemplify what their names name.

93. See *Met.* Z 8, 1033b11–19; 9, 1034b7–19; 15, 1039b20–1040a8; H 3, 1043b14–21.

94. See esp. *Met.* Z 15, 1039b24–25: "For it is not the essence (τὸ εἶναι) of house that is generated, but the essence of *this* house." If there is a distinction between the essence of house and the essence of this house, the individual cannot be identical with the former.

95. *Met.* H 3, 1043b18–23.

96. *Met.* A 9, 991b6–7. Cf. M 5, 1080a4–5, however, where, Aristotle says "they", not "we."

In a true or pure artifact the maker or her conception is the paradigm. One does not have to follow a pattern in making something—say, an abstract work of art. But if an animal or a plant generates a defective version of itself, the defective product is relative to a paradigm other than the generator. It is relative to that which is expressed in the definition of the species.[97] One could deny this by effacing the distinction between the artificial and the natural and holding that all generation is like the making of an adventitious artifact. Whatever the merits of this position, it is certainly not Aristotle's. For his entire physical science rests upon the distinction between the artificial and 'things existing by nature.'

Final Causality and Nature

In the same passage of *Physics* in which Aristotle identifies formal and final explanations, he adds the crucial claim that "nature is a final cause."[98] This seems to be about as unambiguous a statement as one would need in order to insist on the self-sufficiency of nature in an Aristotelian explanatory framework. Aristotle's general account of final causality is frequently discussed against the background of his argument against those—for example, the Atomists—who deny final causality, saying rather that nature acts by chance or necessity.[99] It is not so frequently noticed that when Aristotle finally rejects their position, he rejects both chance and necessity as substitutes for final causality. He does not, of course, reject chance and necessity altogether. But necessity in nature, as he proceeds to tell us, is hypothetical necessity. Consequently, unqualified necessity has no part in final causal explanation, and hypothetical necessity belongs there only as an explanation of the conditions for that which the final cause explains.[100] So, if the self-sufficiency of the Aristotelian explanatory framework depends on nature being a final cause, nature must be construed apart from material causality. Neoplatonic harmonists will, typically, see the separation of final causal explanation from necessity as implying its identification with the 'works of intellect.' Antiharmonists will want to insist that understanding nature itself as a final cause indicates precisely the way the harmonists have

97. To say that an animal or a plant has a natural disposition "to make a copy of itself," as does Lennox (2001, 140), is, I think, to ignore the problem; for the plant or animal is itself a copy of its progenitor. Assume, as Aristotle apparently does, that there is an endless (potentially? actually?) series of progenitors. Are they then *all* copies? Of what, precisely?

98. *Phys.* B 7, 198b4; B 8, 199b32–33. Here the term used is ἕνεκα του, literally 'on account of something.' Cf. B 2, 194a28–29: ἡ δὲ φύσις τέλος καὶ οὗ ἕνεκα.

99. The central passage is *Phys.* B 8.

100. This is most clearly stated at *Phys.* B 8, 200a13–15: "What is necessary then exists by hypothesis and not as an end; for it exists in matter, while the final cause is in the account" (ἐξ ὑποθέσεως δὴ τὸ ἀναγκαῖον, ἀλλ' οὐχ ὡς τέλος· ἐν γὰρ τῇ ὕλῃ τὸ ἀναγκαῖον, τὸ δ' οὗ ἕνεκα ἐν τῷ λόγῳ). See Cooper 1985, esp. 159–161, on the relationship between the Democritean necessity that Aristotle rejects and the hypothetical necessity that he accepts. According to Cooper, the former is subsumed under the latter: that is, the absolutely necessary effects of the natural bodies and elements become hypothetically necessary for the constitution of natural substances.

gone wrong. Indeed, they tell us that it is the burden of Aristotle's entire philosophy of nature that we do not need to go beyond nature to achieve explanatory adequacy.

Antiharmonists will appropriately point to Aristotle's pithy remark, "So, if there is a final cause in art, so also in nature. This is most clearly seen in a doctor who heals himself; nature is like that."[101] So much for final causality in the sense of purpose applied *ab extra*. But as we have already seen in the discussions of *On Philosophy* and *De Anima*, Aristotle repeatedly and consistently distinguishes two senses of final cause: (1) the result for the sake of which and (2) the person or thing for whom or for which something is done.[102] It is clear that for Aristotle, god or gods or any transcendent principle of nature is not a final cause in the sense of (2). The gods are not benefited by anything done in nature, since this would presuppose a deficiency in natural things that could somehow be remedied. It is precisely in the sense of (1), however, that nature is a final cause. Nature acts always to achieve a benefit or goal or realization of something's natural capacity.[103] So, our question becomes, how is (1) related to (2), or more pointedly, what function if any does (2) serve in natural explanations?

If the final causality in (1) were applicable only to the conscious purposes of human beings, it would be easy enough to identify it as an ideal toward which we strive. Aristotle certainly speaks in this way both in *Metaphysics* and in *Nicomachean Ethics* when extolling the life of contemplation.[104] Perhaps then we could say that (2) applies universally to everything that is natural, whereas (1) applies only to persons who can actually have ideals, which they hold before themselves as inspiration. Aristotle, however, though he limits the contemplative ideal to persons, never limits the application of (1) to persons. That is, everything in nature, and nature itself, acts to achieve a good.[105] So, perhaps then it is the case that things that are not conscious act to achieve a goal or end in the sense of (1) just because they act to achieve an end in the sense of (2). They achieve their ideal by fulfilling their nature.[106]

That this cannot be the entirety of the matter is clear if we consider why we need (1) even for agents with conscious purposes. After all, if (2) can explain the activities of plants and animals, why does it not explain the activities of humans, including their desire to possess theoretical knowledge? Putting the question otherwise, could we not make the ideal toward which all the things that exist by nature aim ex post facto? That is, could we not define the ideal as the immanent nature which is or is not fulfilled individually

---

101. *Phys.* B 8, 199b29–32.
102. See *Phys.* B 2, 194a33–36 (which refers to the *On Philosophy* text); *De An.* B 4, 415b2–3, 20–21; *GC* B 6, 742a22ff; *Met.* Λ 7, 1072b2–3; *EE* H 15, 1249b15–16.
103. See Kullmann 1985 for a good presentation of he different senses of final causality.
104. *Met.* Λ 7; *EN* K 7.
105. See *GC* B 10, 336b27–337a7; *Met.* Θ 8, 1050b22–30; *Cael.* B 12, 292a22–b25.
106. This would seem to be the meaning of "final cause" at *Phys.* B 7, 198b3–4.

or even collectively? Thus (1) would not represent an explanation at all, any more than a universal attribution inductively arrived at explains anything about that to which it applies. For example, the viviparous nature of mammals does not *explain* why mammals give birth to live young rather than lay eggs. Is anything else needed?

Evidently the answer for Aristotle is yes. In a passage in *Metaphysics* Book Λ (discussed at length in chapter six), he states, "We should examine in which of two ways the nature of the whole has the good and the best, whether as something separated (κεχωρισμένον) and by itself (αὐτὸ καθ᾽ αὐτό) or as the order (τὴν τάξιν). Or does it have it in both ways like an army? For an army's goodness is the order and is the general, but more in the latter. For he does not depend on the order, but the order depends on him."[107] The principal point of this passage relevant to our current question is that far from reducing (1) to (2), Aristotle here emphasizes the primacy of (1) over (2). If anything, he could be said to be reducing (2) to (1) in the sense that all the explanatory force is in (1). It is because things aim to achieve an ideal that they fulfill their natures. That is the way each achieves that ideal. Thus in *De Anima*, Aristotle says that "all living things desire that [the divine, τοῦ θείου] and do what they do according to nature for the sake of that."[108] In this passage it is clear that final causality in the sense of (2) is not limited to those living things with conscious purposes. But this would seem to make the irrelevancy of (1) apart from (2) all the more patent. Thus the ideal is determined by nature as fulfilled and does not determine it in any way. Why then is the divine a *separated* final cause?[109] Why is nature itself held by Aristotle to be explanatorily insufficient?

Simplicius suggests a reason: "Thus regarding the productive cause Plato assigns the role of being the principal productive cause to the demiurgic intellect, whereas Aristotle, in addition to this, assigns it to nature (which Plato places among the instrumental causes, since it is both moved by a cause and moves other things) and to accidents, like luck and chance."[110] He adds later that

> [Aristotle] wants to make the principal productive cause separated and independent of that which comes to be. For the intrinsic cause (τὸ ἐνυπάρχον αἴτιον), such as the form or the nature in the sense of the formal principle, is

107. *Met.* Λ 10, 1075a11–15.
108. *De An.* B 4, 415b1–2. Cf. Plato *Symp.* 206E.
109. See Sedley 2000, n. 12, who claims that κεχωρισμένον "does not . . . necessarily mean something transcendent or extra-cosmic, but simply something over and above the ordering itself, as the prime mover plainly is." I do not understand what "over and above" means in this context if it does not mean "transcendent or extra-cosmic." No doubt, "separated" does not always mean 'separated in reality' for Aristotle; something can, e.g., be separated merely in thought. But nothing that is so separated can have an explanatory role as the prime mover is intended to do in this passage.
110. See Simplicius *In Phys.* 223, 16–20. Cf. 295, 28–30, where Simplicius explicitly mentions the *Metaphysics* text and draws the implication that the paradigmatic cause must be separate and that a definition of a sensible substance is accordingly primarily of that.

contained in [that which comes to be]. We should remember that here
Alexander agrees that nature is not a productive cause in the principal sense,
but is rather a formal [cause] because it is not primary among the producers.
Further, instruments seem to be causes of motion, but even these are not principally productive, since they do not move principally; rather they move by
being moved.[111]

The reason nature is not self-explanatory, even though it be a principle of
motion and standstill, is that it is an instrument of motion—a moved
mover—and not an unmoved mover. Thus even if nature always acts for the
good by actualizing the potency in anything that exists by nature, nature's
so acting is not self-explanatory.[112]

Many scholars who have insisted on the irreducibility of (1) to (2) have
reflected on how an unmoved mover, as characterized by Aristotle, can serve
an explanatory role as final cause. Charles Kahn, who has provided one of
the most thoughtful and forthright expressions of this position, says, "For
Aristotle, this law [that actuality produces actuality] is *explained* by some relation of desire or assimilation to the Prime Mover as the paradigm Being
which is eternally in act because its essence is actuality as such. As with the
biological reproduction of like by like, so with the physical and metaphysical production of actuality by actuality: producing more of the same is the
best approximation to a stage of complete and permanent actuality."[113] I
think that Kahn himself would recognize that this is unsatisfactory. The very
reason why Aristotle insists on not eliding (1) and (2) and on making the
former prior to the latter is that an 'internal' final cause does not explain
anything on its own. And that is because actuality always precedes potentiality in the order of explanation. Whether the sum of the members of an
animal species or other natural kind be infinite or not, that sum is not, on
Aristotle's own terms, self-explanatory. If this were not the case, then (1)
would be adequate as a final cause. And this is so whether or not the 'external' good includes interspecific benefit. I mean that whether or not plants
exist for our sake, the fulfillment by plants of their own natures is not adequately accounted for by saying that they act to fulfill their own natures and

111. Ibid. 315, 10–16. Cf. 287, 7–30, where Simplicius compares the instrumental causality of nature with the primary causality of soul in both Plato and Aristotle.

112. See Simplicius *In Phys.* 317, 4–28, where he argues that a true principle of change
must be unchanging. Therefore, even soul, a self-mover, is not strictly speaking a principle of
change. The principle of change must be intellect. Proclus *In Parm.* 785, 19–786, 17, argues
that nature cannot be self-constituted (αὐθυπόστατος) because it cannot be self-moving and it
cannot be self-moving because it is corporeal: that is, it has parts outside of parts. E.g., nothing
can cause itself to be heated as a whole at the same time that it is caused to be heated. So, if
nature is not self-constituted—that is, roughly, self-explanatory—then there must be a cause of
it outside of nature. At *Phys* B 2, 194a12, we read that 'nature' refers both to form and to matter. At 1, 193b4, it is the shape (μορφή) or form (εἶδος) as opposed to the matter. But the nature
of changeable things could not exist without matter, since their form is the actualization of that
matter. So, the claim that nature is a *principle* of motion and standstill is not unreasonably rel-
ativized to the science of changeables.

113. See Kahn 1985b, 190.

that this is for their own good. *Why* should they act to fulfill or actualize their own natures? *Why* should nature move in this 'direction' rather than in its opposite? One could, I suppose, say that this is just the way nature is, but then one would not be following Aristotle.

How, though, does a self-absorbed unmoved mover provide an explanation? Kahn says that Aristotle "sees nature as a vast self-maintaining system of interlocking goals, corresponding to different levels of order and regularity, culminating in the most perfect order of all, the motion of the fixed stars. The Prime Mover is Aristotle's 'scientific' substitute for the mythical Demiurge, both as immediate cause of the supreme celestial rotation and as ultimate cause of the entire system—the οὗ ἕνεκα of nature as a whole."[114] One would not have thought that the prime unmoved mover is necessary even as immediate cause of the supreme celestial rotation if all it does is live its self-absorbed life. It is not at all clear why if, for example, grass grows just because it is its nature to do so, the motion of the outermost sphere is not similarly explained. On the contrary, if the primary final cause of nature is, as Aristotle insists, external to all nature, including everything that has no conscious desire, it seems clear that Aristotle could not have meant to insist on the self-sufficiency of nature, either.

How is it supposed that the good that is present in the universe comes from the supreme good? Simplicius argues that according to Aristotle, "the final cause, being established as an object of desire for the other producers, is revealed to us from the primary producer."[115] Simplicius's point addresses the obvious lacuna in interpretations such as those of Kahn. The operation of a separated and ultimate final cause is explained by a similarly separated, ultimate, and unmoved productive cause. As Simplicius argues: "As for Aristotle, no one disputes that he calls God or the Prime Mover a final cause. But that he also calls God a productive cause is sufficiently shown I think by his designating as productive cause that from which comes the origin of motion in his division of causes in the second book of his *Physics.*"[116] Simplicius proceeds to cite support for his position from *De Caelo, On Generation and Corruption,* and *Metaphysics.*[117] Next he acknowledges Peripatetics such as Alexander, who, while accepting that there is an ultimate final cause, deny that it is also a productive cause. Finally he provides two further arguments.

This fact alone would be enough, that he defines as productive cause that from which comes the origin of motion, and that he calls intellect, or the unmoved cause, that from which comes the origin of the motion that follows celestial

114. Ibid., 196.
115. Simplicius *In Phys.* 318, 2–3. Cf. Aristotle *Phys.* B 3, 195b21–22, where Aristotle says that "the highest cause" must be sought in each case; the productive cause must be correlated with the highest final cause. Cf. Simplicius *In Phys.* 326, 30–33.
116. Simplicius *In Phys.* 1361, 11–14 (trans. Sorabji, slightly modified). See Sorabji 1988, 275–276, for a translation of the entire passage.
117. See *Cael.* A 4, 271a33; *GC* A 3, 318a1; *Met.* α 4, 984b15.

motion. For it is the unmoved that is the origin, via the motion of the heavens and that of sublunary things.

> But besides in the second book of *Physics* [B 6, 198a5] he says that luck and chance are accidental causes which supervene on intellect and nature, the causes that are in themselves productive. "Both," he says, meaning luck and chance, "belong to the mode of causation called 'that from which motion arises.'" And he adds, "luck and chance are the causes of things which might have been caused by intellect or nature, but which have in fact resulted from some accidental cause arising." But nothing that is accidentally such is prior to what is in itself such. So, chance and luck are posterior to intellect and nature. In that case, however much chance might be the cause of the heavens above, intellect and nature must be prior causes of our universe and of many things in it besides.[118]

The first argument depends on Simplicius's previous arguments that that which moves by being moved cannot be a primary productive cause. Thus, when in Book H Aristotle discusses the "primary mover, not in the sense of final cause, but in the sense of that from which the motion arises," Simplicius assumes that Aristotle does not mean 'absolutely' or 'unqualifiedly' primary, because this mover is itself moved.[119] Although there is a productive cause that is not a final cause, there can still be a productive cause (an absolutely first productive cause) that is a final cause.

The second argument rests on the priority of intellect and nature to luck and chance.[120] A longer version of the argument appears in the commentary on the passage in *Physics* dealing with luck and chance.[121] Granting that things do happen by luck or chance, the argument is basically that this is intelligible only if we understand what it would mean for these things to happen by intellect or nature. The operation of either intellect or nature is always for a goal or final cause. So, one cannot consistently or rationally hold that everything in the universe happens by luck or chance and thus without final cause. Presumably, if one were to object that luck and hence intellect can be removed from the equation, and accordingly *everything* can be attributed to chance or nature, Simplicius would have two replies: first, the type of finality that embraces all nature is not the finality of nature; second, the kind of productive cause that nature is cannot be an absolutely first productive cause because nature is among things that move by being moved.

Syrianus argues: "It is clear to someone who examines with understanding what has been said that [the separate Forms] are productive of things here. For the explanation for essence and form cannot be one thing and

---

118. Simplicius *In Phys.* 1362, 16–29 (trans. Sorabji, slightly modified). See Sorabji 1988, 273–281, with notes, for references to the other Neoplatonists who held basically the same view. Simplicius (1363, 8–12) identifies it as the view of his teacher, Ammonius.

119. See *Phys.* H 1, 243a3; H 2, 243a33; and Simplicius *In Phys.* 1048, 7–18.

120. Aristotle correlates luck with intellect and chance with nature.

121. Simplicius *In Phys.* 354, 4–356, 30, which appropriately refers to Plato *Laws* 10 as providing the relevant context for Aristotle's discussion of luck and chance.

[the explanation] of finality (τελειότητος) another."[122] Syrianus's argument rests on a point already familiar from *Physics*, that in nature formal and final cause are one. The internal finality of nature is an image of external paradigmatic finality. More particularly, according to *Timaeus*, the Demiurge, wishing to make the world as good as it possibly could be, made it according to the eternal paradigm.[123] For Syrianus, as we shall see in chapter seven, the focus is on the indispensability of the paradigmatic cause in explanation. On the one hand, Aristotle is assumed by most (including Syrianus) to have rejected Platonic Forms. On the other hand, in many passages and in many ways he opens lines of investigation into paradigmatic causality. It is just that he rejects one or more theories of Forms as satisfying that investigation.

Proclus makes a similar argument, alluding to Aristotle's concession of the externality of final causality:

> If someone should say [namely, Aristotle *Met.* Λ10, 1075a11–15] that the cosmos indeed has a cause, not, however, a productive but a final cause, and that all things are thus related to that cause, he is right in making the Good preside as cause over the whole. But let him say whether the cosmos receives anything from this Good or receives nothing from it that corresponds to its desire. If it gets nothing, its striving would be in vain for a being that never enjoys at all the object of its desire. But if it receives something from it, that cause is surely and eminently the Good which it bestows upon the cosmos, particularly if it not only gives good to the cosmos but also does so in virtue of its essence. And if this is true, it will be what establishes the universe, since it will first be the cause of its being [τοῦ εἶναι] if it is to give it its good in virtue of its essence. And so we are at the same doctrine as before; that cause will be not only a final, but also a productive, cause of the All.[124]

It seems not at all unfair for Proclus to insist that the good which the universe aims to achieve is instilled in it and further that it is not nature itself that instilled it. If it were nature, then there would be no need for an external final cause.

Part of the resistance to the idea that Aristotle has left the door open to an external productive intellect is undoubtedly that he characterizes the external intellect as entirely engaged in self-contemplation. But it is not obvious that the Platonic tradition views the productive intellect or the Demiurge otherwise. For one thing, there is more or less a consensus among Neopla-

---

122. Syrianus *In Met.* 117, 30–32. Cf. Simplicius (*In Phys.* 223, 20–22), who distinguishes the paradigmatic cause and the productive cause, though the two are in reality identical. See Steel 1987.

123. *Tim.* 30C2–31A1. Proclus *In Parm.* 788, 1–29, follows Syrianus in calling the Forms productive causes. This is because the Forms are identical with the Demiurge, who is, Proclus is careful to say, more than the Forms themselves (763, 16–20).

124. Proclus *In Parm.* 788, 12–28 (trans. Dillon, slightly modified). Cf. *In Tim.* I 267, 4–11. At I 404, 7–21, however, Proclus chides Aristotle for eliminating "unparticipated intellect" (ἀμέθεκτον νοῦν) from his philosophy.

tonists that the representation of the generation of the universe by the imposition of shapes and numbers on it by the Demiurge is mythical, not literal.[125] Further, the Demiurge as intellect is not identified with soul, though this does not preclude its having life.[126] Finally, the Demiurge is emphatically not viewed by the Neoplatonists as a *personal* deity in the biblical sense.[127] In claiming that Aristotle's prime unmoved mover and Plato's Demiurge are similar or the same, they were not implicitly or explicitly doing so on the basis of anthropomorphic characteristics. It is not so far-fetched to suppose that the prime unmoved mover is Aristotle's version of the Demiurge *if* we do not think that the latter is more than a separate intellect.

An additional consideration is this. The general Neoplatonic interpretation of the Demiurge's activity as eternal naturally makes common cause with Aristotle's own view.[128] This is so precisely because Aristotle criticizes Plato for holding that the world was created in time.[129] Since, according to Proclus, Aristotle is mistaken in this interpretation, he is despite himself in agreement with Plato. More profoundly, Aristotle, in holding both to the nontemporal order of the universe and to the explanatory subordination of physics to first philosophy, would seem to be committed to the hierarchical top-down approach of Platonism.

Nevertheless, productivity is not the same thing as contemplation and should not be summarily demythologized. First, we may recall the fragments

125. It is important to distinguish two different questions: (1) is the creation of the universe in *Timaeus* a myth? and (2) is the creation temporal or nontemporal? It is usually assumed that if the creation is not a myth, then it must be temporal. See, e.g., Vlastos 1965. But the Neoplatonists do not generally believe that the creation is a myth, not that the creation was temporal. See Proclus (*In Tim.* I 276, 30–277, 32), who surveys the traditional interpretations, including the interpretations of those, such as Atticus and Plutarch, who hold to temporal generation of the cosmos. The primary study of the Neoplatonic interpretation of the generation of the world in *Timaeus* is Baltes 1976. See also the more recent article Baltes 1996, in which the author provides an abundance of evidence against the interpretation that the creation is temporal. Useful summaries of Neoplatonic views are in Phillips 1997, and Lernould 2001, 129–151. Also see Zeyl 2000, xx–xxv, for a good summary of the major points for and against a literal reading.

126. As Aristotle says (*Met.* Λ 7, 1072b27), the activity of the divine intellect is life (ζωή). Plato seems to hold that there is no intellect without life. See *Soph.* 249A-B; *Tim.* 30B2, and 46D5–6. This is basically a terminological difference. Aristotle defines "soul" more narrowly than does Plato (see infra chap. 5). Menn 1995, 10–24, argues against the thesis of Cornford and Cherniss, among others, that intellect cannot exist apart from soul. I think that all these scholars have made a terminological dispute into a matter of principle. The problem originates in Plato's argument in *Phaedo* that "soul" refers both to "life" and to "that what has or brings life to a body." Separated from the body, the distinction drops away and paradigmatic life, as it were, obtains. That life is identical with intellectual activity or thinking.

127. E.g., Plotinus's discussion at VI 7. 1–3 is almost entirely devoted to showing that the productive activity of intellect does not include planning, decision-making, etc. The providence that exists in intellect is of a different sort. See Proclus *In Tim.* I 303, 24–312, 26, for a survey of interpretations of the Demiurge within the Platonic tradition. Although there are differences within the tradition, there is agreement that the Demiurge is intellect, possessed of all and only the properties of intellect. Cf. Hackforth 1965, 445.

128. See Proclus *In Tim.* I 217, 7–219, 31, for the basic interpretation along with Proclus's criticisms of the alternatives.

129. See Aristotle *Phys.* Θ 1, 251b14–28.

of *On Philosophy* which seem to understand the divine as a productive intellect. Perhaps more to the point, especially for those taking a developmentalist view of Aristotle, the concept of productive intellect is definitely at play in Book Γ, chapter 5, of *De Anima*. As we saw in the previous chapter, some, like Alexander of Aphrodisias, took productive intellect to be identical with the prime unmoved mover. This is a weighty consideration for Neoplatonic harmonists, given that Alexander was not likely to have been trying to accommodate his interpretation of Aristotle to a Platonic point of view. But even if we reject the identification that Alexander makes, as I think we should, the evidence for a productive role for the prime unmoved mover is still significant.[130] It follows from Aristotle's apparent commitment to the position that nature is not unqualifiedly ultimate in the explanatory order. And the more this productive role is acknowledged, the more difficult it is to resist the conclusion that the prime unmoved mover in relation to intelligible reality is a version of the Demiurge in relation to the Forms.

---

130. See Giacon 1969; Broadie 1993; Berti 2000, 186–189 and 200–206, for various arguments for the view that the prime unmoved mover is either an efficient cause rather than a final cause, or an efficient cause as well as a final cause, or an efficient cause by being a final cause.

CHAPTER FIVE

Psychology: Souls and Intellects

In 1939 the Dutch scholar F. A. Nuyens published a book titled *Ontwick-kelingsmomenten in de Zielkunde van Aristoteles*, better known among scholars in the French translation published in 1948 under the title *L'Evolution de la psychologie d'Aristote*. In this work Nuyens embraces the fundamental Jaegerian position of Aristotelian developmentalism and attempts to apply it in detail to the psychological doctrines.

Nuyens distinguishes three phases in the development of Aristotle's psychological doctrines: (1) a Platonic phase (represented by *Eudemus* and to a lesser extent by *Protrepticus* and *On Philosophy*), wherein the soul is conceived of as an entity separate from the body;[1] (2) a "mechanistic instrumentalist" phase, in which the body and soul continue to be held to be separate entities, but the body is an instrument of the soul, located now in the heart (this phase of Aristotle's psychology is to be found in parts of *Parva Naturalia*, *Metaphysics*, *Eudemian* and *Nicomachean Ethics*, and *Politics*);[2] (3) a final phase (represented primarily by *De Anima*, but also by other parts of *Parva Naturalia*, *Metaphysics*, and *On the Generation of Animals*) in which the soul is conceived as the form of the body.[3]

1. See Nuyens 1948, 48.
2. Ibid., 57.
3. Ibid., 58. Jaeger 1948, 332–334, claims that "the third book of *On the Soul* [*De Anima*], which contains the doctrine of *Nous*, stands out as peculiarly Platonic and not very scientific. This doctrine is an old and permanent element of Aristotle's philosophy, one of the main roots of his metaphysics." But Jaeger thinks that this 'element' does not cohere with the empirical psychology, which "belongs to another stage of development—in fact, to another dimension of thought." Nuyens 1948, 219–220, argues against Jaeger that Book Γ's account of νοῦς can be integrated with the rest of the work so long as the agent intellect is eliminated from the functioning of intellect in the soul (296–310).

Nuyens's thesis has been subjected to extensive criticism, especially with respect to the sharp distinction he makes between phases (2) and (3).[4] Nevertheless, his fundamental idea—a development away from Platonic dualism and toward Aristotelian hylomorphism—remains virtually unquestioned. And it is on the basis of this idea that Aristotle's mature psychological doctrine is usually interpreted. The principal focus of the interpretations that assume the anti-Platonism of *De Anima* is the account in Book Γ, chapter 5, of the so-called agent or active intellect. Endless contortions are contrived in order to show that when Aristotle states that intellect is "immortal and eternal" he does not mean that it is immortal and eternal. Of course, there is much more to Aristotle's psychology than the seemingly cryptic doctrine contained in Γ 5. The anti-Platonist assumption extends beyond a denial of immortality to the entire array of epistemological considerations. Perhaps because it is assumed that for Aristotle the soul is in no way immortal—or perhaps despite this assumption—it is also assumed that Aristotle's epistemology is deeply at odds with Plato's. Aristotle the hylomorphist or, more crudely, Aristotle the 'empiricist' is diametrically opposed to Plato the 'dualist' or 'rationalist.'

From the Neoplatonic perspective, it is not too excessive to call these assumptions bizarre. For them, Aristotle plainly makes large epistemological and psychological claims in *De Anima* that are in harmony with Platonism. At the same time, however, it must be recalled that the principle of harmony recognizes Aristotle's regency in comprehending the details of the physical world. Much of what is said in *De Anima* regarding, for example, sense perception, is held simply not to be in disharmony with Platonism. What is said here supplements the basic Platonic position. One could—unjustly, from the Neoplatonists' point of view—give an account of the entire *De Anima* that is radically un-platonic even in its treatment of matters on which Plato is largely silent. But to do so would be to start from an assumption that is both unwarranted and unsupported in the text.[5]

In order to see the basis for the Neoplatonic position that the noetics of Aristotle and Plato are harmonious, we need to take a fairly lengthy and complex exegetical path. Part of their case rests upon their claim that Aristotle has a unified account of intellect and that intellect can only be seen in its correct relation to soul when this is revealed. This unified account, however, has been strenuously disputed both in antiquity and in modern scholarship. So, it will be necessary to show that there *is* a coherent story being told in *De Anima* before we can see that it is a Platonic one.

4. See esp. Block 1961; Hardie 1964; Lefèvre 1972; Charlton 1987; Wedin 1988; Frede 1992; Cohen 1992; Dancy 1996. Shields (1988, 106) attributes to Aristotle a doctrine he dubs 'supervenient dualism.' As Robinson 1991, 210–212, shows, however, 'supervenience' cannot plausibly be supposed to characterize Aristotle's account of intellect. In addition, hylomorphism understood as supervenience solves no problem posed by dualism.

5. See Blumenthal 1990 for a survey of the background to the Neoplatonic commentaries on *De Anima.* Blumenthal is highly critical of the interpretive value of these commentaries. See also Blumenthal 1981.

The Definition of the Soul

I start with Aristotle's famous definition of soul in general at the beginning of Book B of *De Anima:* [soul is] "the primary actuality [ἐντελεχέια] of a natural body with organs' [σώματος φυσικοῦ ὀργανικοῦ]."[6] Many questions need to be addressed regarding this definition. I want to concentrate first on the widespread assumption that with this definition Aristotle sets himself squarely in opposition to Plato.

There is indeed evidence in Book A to suggest that Aristotle means to reject Plato's definition of the soul.[7] In the second chapter, of that book he argues against those who say that soul is a self-mover (τὸ αὐτὸ κινοῦν), evidently a reference to Plato's definition of soul in *Phaedrus.*[8] In the next chapter Aristotle presses on with the criticism of those who say that the soul is a self-mover, linking this definition explicitly with Plato's *Timaeus.*[9] He then proceeds to a battery of arguments—eight in all—against the claim made in *Timaeus*'s account of the creation of the world-soul that soul is a

---

6. *De An.* B 1, 412b5–6.

7. Hippolytus (d. ca. 235 C.E.) *Refutation of all Heresies* I 20: "In practically all matters Aristotle is in harmony (συμφωνός) with Plato, except for his teaching regarding the soul. For Plato says that the soul is immortal, whereas Aristotle says that [. . .] remains and after this to be dissipated into the fifth element." Despite the evident lacuna in the text indicated by the brackets, it is clear that Hippolytus understands the basis for the anomalous disagreement between Aristotle and Plato to be in the matter of immortality. But Hippolytus, who is in this work generally concerned to identify various Christian heresies with different pagan philosophical schools, is not especially interested in anything like a clear or nuanced appreciation of the ancient texts. Later in the work (VII 19, 5–6) he says ruefully that it is not possible to say what Aristotle's doctrine of the soul is in *De Anima.* He adds that the definition of the soul given by Aristotle requires 'great study.' For a valuable account of Hippolytus's treatment of Aristotle see Osborne 1987, 35–67. Eusebius in his *Preparation for the Gospel* XV 9, 14, 1–5, quotes the Platonist Atticus (2nd century C.E.) as saying something similar. Atticus, however, adds that whereas Aristotle holds that intellect can exist apart from soul, Plato holds that it cannot: Ὁ μὲν γάρ φησι νοῦν ἄνευ ψυχῆς ἀδύνατον εἶναι συνίστασθαι, ὁ δὲ χωρίζει τῆς ψυχῆς τὸν νοῦν. καὶ τὸ τῆς ἀθανασίας. ὁ μὲν μετὰ τῆς ψυχῆς αὐτῷ δίδωσιν, ὡς ἄλλως οὐκ ἐνδεχόμενον, ὁ δέ φησιν αὐτῷ μόνῳ χωριζομένῳ τῆς ψυχῆς τοῦτο περιγίνεσθαι. ("For the one [Plato] says that it is impossible for intellect to exist without soul, while the other [Aristotle] separates the intellect from soul, and the one [Plato] gives immortality to intellect along with soul, while the other [Aristotle] says that mortality pertains to intellect alone separated from soul.")

8. *De An.* A 2, 404a21. See *Phdr.* 245C–E; *Lg.* 895E. But see also *Met.* Θ 2, 1046b17: "The soul has a principle of motion" (ἡ ψυχὴ κινήσεως ἔχει ἀρχήν). Cf. b21; and *PA* A 1, 641a27–28, where soul is said to be a "moving cause."

9. What Aristotle actually says is ὁ Τίμαιος φυσιολογεῖ, which is sometimes taken to be a reference to the literary character Timaeus, who is in turn taken to represent the thought of Plato. See Ross 1924, 1: xxxix–xli, for the argument that the use of the definite article in reference to a name in a Platonic dialogue indicates the character and not the historical person. But Themistius *In de An.* 19, 23–24, says that in this passage Aristotle is contradicting not Plato, but rather Timaeus. At 12, 28, Themistius seems to distinguish between "Timaeus in Plato and Plato himself." Some (e.g., Todd 1996, 159 n. 26) believe that Themistius intends to make no distinction between Plato and Timaeus. See Ballériaux 1994 for an argument against Blumenthal 1991 that Themistius is not an 'orthodox' Peripatetic. According to Ballériaux, Themistius's interpretation of Aristotle on intellect is, rather, entirely within the Neoplatonic tradition, depending especially on the interpretations of Plotinus.

magnitude.[10] It does appear as if the claim that soul is the actuality of a particular kind of body is meant at least indirectly to contradict the claims that soul is self-moving and a magnitude. For this actuality is neither a magnitude nor is it, as Aristotle goes on to argue, something that can move itself.[11]

The Neoplatonists approached the question of the harmony of Aristotle and Plato in psychological matters in part in the light of the assumption that what Aristotle says in the exoteric works is a popular version of what he says in the esoteric works. We have already seen that there are reasonable grounds for so assuming and for questioning developmentalist assumptions. The Neoplatonists generally read the dialogues as committed to the immortality of intellect alone, which is how they interpreted Plato, mainly on the basis of *Timaeus*.[12] So, for them the question is not the harmonization of two opposing views on immortality so much as the harmonization of two accounts of how immortal intellect is related to embodied soul.[13]

Aristotle is clear enough at the beginning of *De Anima* that the study of soul belongs to physical science and is distinct from a study of that which is separable from soul: namely, intellect, which belongs to first philosophy.[14] Pseudo-Simplicius in his *Commentary on Aristotle's De Anima* makes the connection between what Aristotle says here and what was said at the beginning of *Parts of Animals*: "So, it is clear that we are not to speak of all soul; for not all soul is natural, but some one or more parts of it."[15] But the commentator understands that even if there is a separable intellect, still the natural scientist will need to take account of intellectual operations of the soul. In fact, the study of soul belongs between the study of the objects of first philosophy and the non-intellectual entities in nature.[16] Aristotle does not help matters much by remarking in the second book that intellect or the "speculative faculty," that which, if anything can exist separately, seems to belong to a kind (γένος) different from soul.[17] Granted this, we are hardly in a better

10. *De An.* A 3, 406b31–407b26. Cf. *Tim.* 34Bff.

11. Ibid., A 3, 406a3–b10; A 4, 408a30–b18.

12. See Guthrie 1955 for a lucid defense of the position that Neoplatonists were not misled in thus identifying Plato's view.

13. See supra chap. 4, n. 126.

14. See *De An.* A 1, 403a27–28 with 403b15–16 and the entire argument at *PA* A 1, 641a32–b10, where Aristotle holds that natural science does not encompass the study of the entire soul. This would seem to leave the study to first philosophy.

15. *PA* A 1, 641b8–9 (= Ps.-Simplicius *In de An.* 2, 27–28). See also *Met.* E 1, 1026a16.

16. Ps.-Simplicius *In de An.* 3, 14–28.

17. *De An.* B 1, 413b26: ψυχῆς γένος ἕτερον. An alternative translation is "a different kind of soul." The Greek is ambiguous. Cf. A 4, 408b18–29. See Philoponus (*In de An.* 9, 28–11, 29), who takes Aristotle to be advancing the same doctrine as Plato. See the summary of the argument at 12, 10–12 and infra n. 107. Plato, e.g., at *Rep.* 439E1–2 uses the phrase "forms of soul"(εἴδη τῆς ψυχῆς) and at *Tim.* 70A1–6 "kind of soul" (τὸ γένος τῆς ψυχῆς), in both cases indicating what are elsewhere called 'parts', that is, functions or capacities. If νοῦς is a γένος altogether different from ψυχή, that is because the life (ζωή) that belongs to the former is different from the life that belongs to the latter. Whether this difference is to be understood (a) as a difference among species of life or (b) according to focal meaning, where primary life is attributable only to the divine way of living or (c) purely equivocally is a question evidently connected to our interpretation of the dependence relations within first philosophy.

position to know how Aristotle's treatment of the soul that is not separate differs from Plato's. As Pseudo-Simplicius aptly remarks, the definition of soul that Aristotle offers at the beginning of Book B clearly does not apply to this separable intellect.[18] Indeed, as Aristotle himself goes on to argue, a single definition of soul that covered all kinds of soul, though evidently possible, as we have seen, would be useless if we can also give a definition of each different kind of soul.[19] So, it is possible that Aristotle's criticisms of the general definitions of soul given by, among others, Plato, have at least to be considered differently from criticisms of definitions of particular kinds of soul. Part of the problem is that Plato nowhere gives anything like a definition of the human soul.

Plotinus in his treatise *On the Immortality of the Soul* directly confronts the Peripatetic definition of soul as "actuality of a natural body with organs."[20] He raises two objections to so defining soul: (1) if the soul is the actuality of a body, then dividing the body would involve dividing the soul; (2) defining the soul in this way will not allow us to explain the conflict of reason and appetite, that is, incontinence. He then adds that perhaps these objections can be overcome if the definition excludes acts of thinking or intellect and is limited to nonintellective soul. In fact, this is what Aristotle appears to have done when he suggests that immortal intellect is a different kind of soul. But this is not entirely satisfactory either, since if sense perception were an activity of an actuality of a body, it would not be possible for the form of sensibles to affect the faculty of sense perception in the way that it does.[21] That is, sensibles would affect the soul in the way that they affect things without soul. Similarly, when the soul desires things other than food and drink, the desire itself could not belong to the form of a body. The reason for this, which Plotinus discusses elsewhere, is that such desires require self-consciousness, which is not a property of bodies. That leaves soul as principle of growth. But, in the case of a plant, for example, if the soul is the form of that body, then the decay of the plant while the root lives would not be possible.

This is a mixed bag of criticism. In particular, Plotinus seems to conflate objections owing to the presence in the soul of activity that is inescapably intellectual and objections that are not so based. But more important, it is not even clear how much Plotinus actually disagrees with Aristotle. At the beginning of the same treatise, Plotinus raises the question of whether the self (ὁ αὐτός) is identical with the whole human being (ὁ ἄνθρωπος) or only

18. Ps.-Simplicius *In de An.* 102, 21–22.

19. *De An.* B 3, 414b20–415a3. Ross 1961, 223, emphasizes that this passage does not recant the definition of soul at 412b5–6. Ps.-Simplicius *In de An.* 106, 33–107, 14, argues that there is a single general account of the soul, but it is not univocal; rather it is equivocal, with a primary and derivative references. The primary here would be the simplest soul which is present in all the more complex versions. For a modern version of this interpretation, see Matthews 1992.

20. See Plotinus IV 7. 8[5].

21. Ibid., IV 7. 8[5], 19–23.

the soul. At the end of the chapter he concludes that "the soul is the self" (ἡ ψυχὴ αὐτός) and the body is not part of the self; it is either a tool (ὄργανον) of the soul or is related to it as matter to form.[22]

Plotinus explicitly rejects the latter alternative in favor of the former.[23] Yet on one interpretation of Aristotle's definition of the soul, it is not so clear that these really *are* alternatives. For as Abraham Bos has recently argued at length and with an enormous amount of evidence, the word ὀργανικόν does *not* ever mean 'organic' in Aristotle; rather, the word regularly means 'instrumental' in all its occurrences.[24] Particularly important is the passage earlier in *De Anima* where Aristotle is criticizing the Pythagoreans and Plato in their account of the soul's relation to bodies. He scorns the idea that the soul can enter different kinds of bodies; it is as if on their showing the art of carpentry could embody itself in flutes rather than in carpenter's tools. In fact, "each art should use its own tools or instruments (τοῖς ὀργάνοις), and the soul should use its own [type of] body."[25] If we take Plotinus to be using the word in the same way that Aristotle apparently does, then Plotinus seems to agree with Aristotle that the soul uses the body as a tool or an instrument. In fact, that is precisely how Plotinus elsewhere describes his preferred way of treating the relation of soul to body.[26] But how could that which uses the body as an instrument also be a form or actualization of that body?

At the end of the first chapter of the second book of *De Anima*, wherein Aristotle offers his definition of soul, he concludes: "It is not unclear then that the soul or parts of it, if by its nature it has parts, cannot be separated from the body; for the actualities of some [living things] are those of the parts themselves. But nothing prevents some actualities from being separable, because they are not actualities of any body. Further, it is not clear whether the soul as the actuality of the body is like the sailor on the ship."[27]

Plotinus claims that the comparison of the soul/body relation to the sailor/ship relation is good but not completely adequate. For though the soul can be separate from the body like the sailor from the ship, the analogy does not adequately indicate the intimate connection of soul and body. For one thing, the soul is in the whole body, whereas the sailor is not in or on the whole ship. So, it seems that Plotinus does in a way want to argue, like Aristotle, that the soul uses the body as a tool or instrument, but that it does not do so in a way suggested by the term 'actuality.' And this is clearly because Plotinus wants to deny that the soul is unqualifiedly inseparable from the body. But the part that he wants to insist *is* separable is the intellect. So, too,

22. Ibid., IV 7. 1, 22–25. Cf. Plato *Alc. I* 129E5; 130C3.

23. Plotinus IV 3. 20, 36–37: ἀλλ' οὐδὲ ὡς εἶδος [the soul] ἐν ὕλῃ . . .

24. See Bos 2003, chap. 5.

25. *De An.* A 3, 407b24–26. See *PA* A1, 642a9–13, where the body is compared to an axe as an instrument of a certain sort suitable for a certain job. Ps.-Simplicius *In de An.* 90, 29–91, 4, argues that ὀργανικόν is to be understood in this way.

26. See Plotinus IV 3. 21.

27. *De An.* B 1, 413a4–9.

does Aristotle. Based on a passage such as this, one might surmise that the dispute between Plotinus and Aristotle comes down in part to whether we should call separable intellect soul or not. But this superficial discord masks a potentially deeper difference. Leaving aside separable intellect, Plotinus, in his objections to the definition of soul as the actuality of a body, principally wants to argue that cognitive psychic functions cannot be explained if the soul is defined in that way. In addition, if soul is the actuality of a body, the very instrumentality of the body—that which Plotinus embraces and Aristotle himself accepts—is inexplicable. For instruments are subordinated to their users, whereas a potency is not subordinated to its actuality in the same way.

In the passage above, the striking last sentence cannot refer to the separable intellect which, Aristotle implies, is not the actuality of the body.[28] He is referring to that which is the actuality, and he is allowing that it is unclear whether *this* can be understood to be like the sailor on the ship. If we understand the term ὀργανικόν in the definition of the soul as 'instrument,' then the point of the proposed analogy would not be the separability of soul but its function as controller or subject that uses the body as instrument. Aristotle at least appreciates the problem Plotinus raises for the definition of soul as actuality of a body.[29]

An insightful comment made by Pseudo-Simplicius on the same text of Aristotle goes to the heart of the issue:

The words "the actuality of some [living things] are of the parts themselves" apply to the inseparable life of all bodies. The words "nothing prevents some

28. Contrary to e.g., the argument of Furth 1988, 155.

29. As apparently does Alexander of Aphrodisias (*De An.* 15, 9–16), who denies that the soul can in any sense be a captain (κυβερνήτης) in relation to the body. He suggests that it can be compared only to the art of piloting a ship (τὴν τεχνήν τὴν κυβερνητικήν). Alexander insists that the soul can only be like a form to the body's matter (23–26). Hicks 1907, 320, describes Aristotle's hesitation to insist that the soul is not at all like the sailor, "a remnant of Platonism." Robinson 1983, 128–131, makes the analogy unproblematic, which belies Aristotle's evident puzzlement. He sees the instrumentality of the body that is being indicated here, but he thinks there is no problem with the soul also being the form of the body. But how, we may ask, can a form that is an actuality of matter use its matter as an instrument? See Wedin 1988, 214–216, who, like Alexander and against Robinson, rejects the argument that the separability of the soul is at issue in this analogy. But Wedin's view that the analogy is about the efficient causality that the soul exercises is, it seems to me, at odds with his functionalist interpretation of the soul. See Heinaman 1990, 92–99, on why the soul must be the subject of psychic states or activities. Regarding 408b13–15, where Aristotle says that it is better to say that the human being is angry than that the soul is angry, Heinaman argues that it is the composite that is the subject of the anger considered as a complex of activity and bodily change, whereas it is the soul that is the subject of the psychic state of anger (see 97 n. 28, for the many references in *De Anima* and elsewhere where Aristotle says that the soul is the subject of mental states and activities). More particularly, it is the part of the soul that is intellect that is the subject of thinking. It is far from clear why the addition of a body to the subject of an activity that has no organ and is incorporeal is supposed to help. Among those who take 408b13–15 as emblematic of hylomorphism, see, e.g., Hicks 1907, 275; Barnes 1971a; Owens 1981; Modrak 1987, 115.

actualities from being separate, because they are not actualities of any body"
apply to the life that is separate in every way. By means of these [expressions]
he observes the duality [τὸ συναμφότερον] of soul. For the actuality that uses
[the body] is in a way inseparable by its completely [ὅλως] using the body and
in a way separate by its transcendently [ἐξῃρημένως] using the body as an
instrument that is serving it. If it uses the body in one way and in one way does
not use it at all, as the example of the sailor makes clear, that which does not
use it is separate in every way.[30]

The commentator carefully distinguishes the completely separate soul from
the soul that is in a way separate and in a way not. This duality of the embodied soul is indicated by the contrast "completely [ὅλως] . . . transcendently
[ἐξῃρημένως]." What is meant here is, I think, the contrast between those
psychic functions in which we are unaware of a subject or agent other than
the living body and those in which we are aware of a subject or agent that is
apparently other than the body. For example, the soul uses the body "completely" when we digest food and breathe; it uses the body transcendently
when we consciously desire something and move to obtain it: say, we desire
to cool off and move to open the window. The Neoplatonic commentator is
concisely and accurately indicating exactly the issue that leads Plotinus to
agree with Aristotle, albeit somewhat grudgingly, at the same time as he is
criticizing him.[31]

The antiharmonists among contemporary scholars are nothing if not
transparent in attempting to read Aristotle as expressing exclusively an anti-
Platonic view of the soul. One option is simply to dismiss *De Anima* 413a4–9
as not seriously intended.[32] Another option is to give a 'deflationary'
account of separable intellect, pressing hard on a functionalist interpretation of cognition in the hylomorphic composite.[33] If, however, we find reason to resist such an account, we shall see that separable intellect inevitably
draws Aristotle into the Platonic orbit in his attempt to account for embod-

30. Ps.-Simplicius *In de An.* 96, 3–10. See also 23, 24–24, 9; 90, 29–91, 4. Cf. Proclus *In Tim.*
II 285, 26–31; *In Parm.* 798, 8; *ET* Prop. 64. Bos 2003, 126–129, argues similarly that Γ 4–5
constitutes the affirmative answer to the question Aristotle raises at the end of Book B.

31. See Themistius *In de An.* 43, 28. See Kahn 1992a, 362: " . . . the lack of unity in Aristotle's account of the soul can be seen as an accurate reflection of the complex, paradoxical structure of the human condition." See Philoponus *In de An.* 48, 2–10; 16–22, where the comparison
with the sailor is taken to imply that there is a distinction between the essence of soul (= the
essence of the sailor *qua* human being) and the activity of the soul when embodied (= the activity of the sailor *qua* sailor).

32. See, e.g., Blumenthal (1996, 94–97), who thinks that this comment is "difficult to reconcile with the text of Aristotle" and most likely a "piece of residual Platonism which Aristotle
for some reason never excised" (97). Hamlyn and Shields (1993, 87), dismiss the passage as
"a lecturer's aside." Robinson 1983, 128–131, defends the analogy of the sailor on the basis of
his dualistic interpretation.

33. See Wedin 1988, esp. chaps. 5–6; Wedin 1989; Cohen 1992. Contra, see Heinaman
(1990, 100–102), who offers several cogent reasons for rejecting functionalism, all of which
amount to denying that psychic activities can be attributes of bodies. See Burnyeat 1992; Code
and Moravcsik 1992; McDonough 2000.

ied intellectualized activity.[34] If separable intellect were not somehow necessary to account for embodied cognition, then that cognition could perhaps be explained functionally: that is, in terms of the material organism's functions. But this Aristotle will not do.

Aristotle's theory of cognition will occupy us at length in the next section. Here I sketch briefly the reason for holding that the separable intellect is the hinge upon which the harmonizing of Aristotle and Plato in psychology turns. This amounts to showing (1) that there must be a separable intellect and (2) that given a separable intellect, the account of embodied human cognition will necessarily be in line with Platonism.

A hylomorphic account of cognition without the separable intellect would involve forms of cognizable things being present somehow in the nonseparable intellect. On this basis alone, a functionalist account would be plausible. But the presence of forms of cognizable things in a nonseparable intellect is for Aristotle no more a description of cognition than is the presence of information in a computer a reason for believing that the computer cognizes anything.[35] Without the separable intellect, there could be no cognition. And the reason is that cognition is essentially self-reflexive for Aristotle. That is, cognition is a state in which cognizable form is present in the intellect *and* the cognizer is aware of the presence of form in *itself*. By contrast, if the cognizer were aware of the presence of form in that with which it were not identical, then a vicious infinite regress would threaten. The presence of form in the original nonseparable intellect would be sufficient for there to be cognition. Now here is the crucial next step. Cognition, being essentially self-reflexive, could not occur in a material entity. Even if we posited a separable intellect along with a nonseparable one, if either or both were material, self-reflexivity could not occur. Cognition would be a case of one material entity related to another, not to itself.

The incorporeal separable intellect is not an appendix or add-on for Aristotle, required only for very high-level cognition, or a dispensable residue of some outmoded account. It is essential to the account of embodied human cognition. And because cognition is essentially self-reflexive, the intellect must be incorporeal. And because of *this*, Aristotle's definition of the soul as an 'actuality' is inadequate, at least as it is supposed to apply to

34. Robinson (1983) argues for this position. His account of "Aristotelian dualism" would, I think, do equally well as an account of Platonic dualism of the embodied person. For another version of Aristotelian dualism, see Heinaman 1990. Heinaman argues that Aristotle is an "emergent dualist" with respect to the soul and body (91). He leaves intellect out of this account. Heinaman recognizes that emergent dualism is not incompatible with a physical account unless the soul's distinctness from the body entails that it is an incorporeal entity. Its existence as such would be entirely problematic unless it could exist on its own.

35. Robinson (1983, 125–126), thinks that the passive or nonseparable intellect must be incorporeal because it is receptive of forms. Without the separable intellect, however, it need be incorporeal only in the anodyne sense that the forms in it are not material. In fact, the incorporeality of the passive intellect only follows in a non-question-begging way from the incorporeality of the separable intellect.

the account of the souls of cognizers. As I argue below, understanding the role of agent or active intellect in thinking leads us to deny that there are two intellects, active and passive. In fact, there is good reason to conclude that tere is only one intellect in Aristotle's account of cognition in *De Anima*. On the basis of this conclusion, and granting that this intellect is immortal, the way is open to appreciating the harmonists' position.

Plato's understanding of embodied human cognition is, according to Neoplatonism, founded on the same principles and, as we might have predicted, faced with the same problems. To begin with, Neoplatonists generally held that cognition was essentially self-reflexive and that self-reflexivity required incorporeality.[36] Revealingly, one of the problems Plotinus finds with Aristotle's definition of the soul as an actuality of a body is that, so defined, we cannot account for personal psychic conflict. A conflict in a person who desires to do something and at the same desires not to have that desire put into action is not explicable or even possible if the subject of both desires is not the same entity. This is so because the conflict requires that one be aware of the original desire in oneself and also aware of the desire in oneself not to have the original desire be put into action. If the subjects of the desires were different entities, we would not have a case of incontinence or personal psychic conflict, but a case of interpersonal conflict. When we resist the desires of those who wish to do us ill, we are not being continent. But the subjects of both desires could not be the same entity if that entity were material. The incorporeality of the soul is thought to follow from, among other things, the irremovable cognitive dimension in personal psychic conflict.

I return to the Platonic side of the harmonizing project at the end of the next section. For now, I only hope to have indicated that the Neoplatonic assumption that, appearances to the contrary notwithstanding, Aristotle is deeply imbued with Platonism in his psychology hardly deserves to be thought of as whimsical or naive wishful thinking. But the general strategy I have just sketched needs now to be supported by an examination of the texts.

Aristotle's Account of Embodied Human Cognition

The governing idea of Aristotle's account of embodied human cognition deserves to be acknowledged as one of the most elegant ideas in the history of philosophy. Roughly, the idea is that cognition is the mirror image of reality. Or, to change the metaphor, the stages of cognition unpack the packaged real world in reverse order. The object of the most elementary act of cognition, a particular case of sense perception, is a particular physical object, sensible in its particularity. What is sensed directly are the accidental attributes

---

36. See Plotinus V 3. 13. See Gerson 1997. Deuse 1983 109–112, provides a valuable survey of the Middle Platonic background to the Neoplatonic understanding of the Platonic account of the soul, esp. of the gradual proliferation of various interpretations of the implications of what is said in the dialogues.

of a particular, typically an individual, substance. These accidental attributes are the actualizations of the substance. Thus the realization of, say, Socrates, here and now, is his particular shape, color, position, and so on. Socrates, the individual substance, is himself the actualization of the species human being. He is one realization or way that that species is actualized in the world. The species is in turn the actualization of the genus animal, or one realization of animality. Finally, and perhaps somewhat more obscurely, the genus animal is one actualization of being or natural being, one way that being is realized in the sensible world. So, the directly sensible attributes of a particular substance are reality actualized, here and now.

The nesting or packaging of reality that I have described is also analyzable in terms of form and matter. The essence of cognition generally includes the presence of form without matter. The presence of form without matter is not accurately described in representationalist terms, for the form is not a representation of the composite of form and matter; rather, the form accounts for all the actuality or present reality of that composite. Therefore, since only reality is cognizable, the cognition of form is the cognition of reality.[37] Beginning with the cognition of forms in sense perception, the goal of human cognizers is typically to realize some higher cognition of the nest of actualities and their interrelationships. In a way, there is a strict causal connection between the particular accidental attributes of an individual substance and the species and genus to which it belongs. In other words, there is something about the nature of humanity that explains, say, Socrates' present height. But of course there is not a necessary connection. This is easy to see if we consider that, first, a human being does not have to have Socrates' height (even Socrates himself did not have that height) and, second, that his height was no doubt affected by considerations other than that he is a human being. But there *is* a necessary connection between the nature of humanity and a certain *range* of heights. And there is another necessary connection between that range and the disjunct consisting of all the possible heights that Socrates, as a human being, could have had.

Although there is no direct inference available from the sense perception of Socrates' height to scientific knowledge of the necessary range of heights for human beings, still there is a nexus of causal connections between that height and the necessary properties of human beings on the one hand, and that height and the necessary properties of other things in nature that provide the necessary and sufficient conditions for the result that is perceived here and now. In short, the process of cognition is a process consisting in operations performed on the forms of sensibles in order to discover their causes.

What we are primarily concerned with is Aristotle's description of the process of cognition after sense perception has occurred. We want to know

---

37. I leave aside for the moment the point that in a way we can cognize more than what is real, including what is possible but not actual, what is impossible, etc.

about these 'operations' performed on the forms of sensibles. This quest takes us into the most difficult part of Book Γ of *De Anima*. At the beginning of its chapter 3 Aristotle remarks that his predecessors have tended to define the soul by two differentiae: (1) the ability to locomote and (2) thinking, understanding, and sense perception (τὸ νοεῖν καὶ φρονεῖν καὶ αἰσθά-νεσθαι).[38] Chapters 3 to 8 focus on (2); chapters 9 to 13 on (1). Aristotle first addresses the error of those who have thought that sense-perception and thinking are the same kind of thing. They have done so because they believe that thinking, like sense perception, is corporeal (σωματικόν).[39] He then tries to show that imagination (φαντασία) is distinct from both. His main argument against those who conflate sense-perception and thinking is that sense perception (of proper sensibles) is always true, even among animals, whereas thinking discursively (διανοεῖσθαι) is subject to error or deception (ἀπάτη) or may be done falsely (ψευδῶς), and it belongs to no animal that does not also possess the power of reasoning (λόγος).[40]

The argument appears to be almost absurdly question-begging: thinking is different from sense perception because all animals have the latter, but only those possessing the power of reasoning have the former. In fact, the argument makes far better sense once we realize that Aristotle's principal point—that his opponents cannot account for falsity or error—is connected by him with their claim that thinking, like sense perception, is a corporeal process.[41] The argument is this: thinking cannot be the same thing as sense perception because if it were, then thinking would be corporeal (since sense perception is corporeal). But if thinking were corporeal, then the sort of error or falsity that belongs to one kind of thinking, discursive thinking, could not occur. Therefore, only those with the capacity for discursive thinking, that is, only those with reasoning power, can make errors. So, we need to focus on why Aristotle believes that this is so.

---

38. *De An.* Γ 3, 427a17–19.

39. Empedocles seems to be the principal target here. See A 2, 404b13–15 and 5, 410a28. But in the first passage Aristotle goes on to say that Plato in *Timaeus* constructs the soul "in the same manner" (τὸν αὐτὸν δὲ τρόπον). Interpreting Plato as a materialist regarding the soul in *Timaeus*, which means taking the text literally, certainly leaves what is said elsewhere in the dialogues problematic. But if we separate soul and intellect in Plato as we must in Aristotle, it is not so obvious that a hylomorphic account of the former differs significantly from what Plato says about soul, including the fact that it is a magnitude. One may compare in this regard Plato locating the parts of the soul in parts of the body with Aristotle's locating the operation of the unmoved mover at the circumference of the universe. See *Phys.* θ 10, 267b9, and Graham 1999, 177–178.

40. *De An.* Γ 3, 427b11–14. The shift from το νοεῖν to τὸ διανοεῖσθαι is explained by the fact that the former can also be used for the sort of thinking that has no falsity. See Γ 6, 430a26, where the initial term used for this is νόησις. Later on (e.g., 430b12), he uses the verb νοεῖν. Whether the absence of falsity in this thinking is the same as or only analogous to the absence of falsity in sense perception is another matter. Here, by 'discursive thinking' Aristotle means the sort of thinking that conclusively proves that sense perception is not the same sort of thing as thinking. See Themistius *In de An.* 88, 9–18.

41. *De An.* Γ 3, 427a26-b2.

By "possessing the power of reasoning," Aristotle means, roughly, having the ability to make and to understand universal judgments.[42] Elsewhere he defines 'falsity' (τὸ ψεῦδος) as "expressing (τὸ λέγειν) what is as not being or what is not as being."[43] So, his claim is that only those equipped with the capacity for universal cognition can make errors of the relevant sort. It is not immediately obvious why a corporeal process could not involve an error in which it 'expresses' what is as not being or vice versa, particularly if we interpret 'express' as 'represent' or 'misrepresent.' Imagine, say, an animal that responds to environmental changes by certain bodily changes like growing fur. But then imagine the animal, owing to a hormonal imbalance, misrepresenting or misreading the season by growing fur in summer. So, in this example, it seems that the animal thinks that it is winter when it is summer. No universal thinking seems to be needed for such an error.

Consider another example. A materialist such as Empedocles could say the following. Let the corporeal process be twofold, like that involved in a thermostat. One part achieves a state, and another part monitors that state. In that case, error would arise when there was incorrect monitoring. The problem is not that every error involves at least one universal, so that to subsume a particular under the wrong universal constitutes the error. If failing to subsume a particular under the right universal is understood as simply misclassification according to some rule, then any lowly animal that mistakes as food something that is not would be engaged in reasoning. This is surely not what Aristotle wants to say.

In the remainder of chapter 3 Aristotle tries to show that imagination differs from both sense perception and discursive thinking. He immediately gives the reason why imagination has to be included in his account of cognition: "It [imagination] does not occur without sense perception, but without it there is no judgment [ὑπόληψις]."[44] Sense perception is not sufficient to account for animal cognition; most animals, Aristotle says, have imagination.[45] But if imagination were the same as discursive thinking or judgment, then we would have to allow that animals possessing imagination would possess the latter. As we have seen, however, Aristotle wants to claim that discursive thinking and judgment do not belong to animals because they do not possess the capacity for reasoning.

---

42. Cf. B 5, 417b22–23. See also *APo.* A 31, 87b28–39; *De Motu An.* 1, 698a11; *Phys.* A 5, 189a7; *Met.* A 1, 981a15, 21; K 1, 1059b26; N 10, 1087a15–21. All these passages contrast cognition of particulars in sense perception with reasoning about and with universals.

43. *Met.* Γ 7, 1011b26–27. A similar definition is provided for false belief at E 4, 1027b18–27; Θ 10, 1051a34-b9; and *De Int.* 1, 16a11–16.

44. *De An.* Γ 3, 427b15–16. As Hicks (1907, 457), notes, we expect the term διάνοια here instead of ὑπόληψις. But the latter is the result of the former, that is, of the process of discursive reasoning. The term ὑπόληψις, evidently coined by Aristotle, is generic and includes ἐπιστήμη, δόξα, and φρόνησις; see 427b25. The Platonic importance of thus subsuming ἐπιστήμη and δόξα within a generic unity is discussed below.

45. *De An.* Γ 3, 428a21–22.

The argument that imagination is different from sense perception seems quite straightforward.[46] Imagination can occur when there is no sense perception. Many animals possess sense perception but apparently do not possess imagination. Sense perception, strictly speaking, is always true, whereas imagination is frequently false, presumably in the sense that what is imagined is not actually present: that is, not actually sensed.[47] But if imagination is frequently false and many animals do possess it, then what becomes of the argument that what differentiates thinking in general from the sort of thinking that requires reason is that only those with the latter can make errors? It seems that if animals possess imagination and they can make errors, there is no need to deny that discursive thinking can be corporeal, and so no need to deny that animals can possess it.[48]

The argument that imagination is not the same thing as discursive thinking is rooted in the larger claim that thinking in general is not the same thing as judgment.[49] That is, there is a type of thinking which is entirely within our power, whereas there is a type of judgment—namely, belief (δόξα)—which is not. Strictly speaking, this will not work, since imagination *might* be supposed to be a different form of judgment, the form that *is* in our power. Presumably, Aristotle is here using the species 'belief' for the genus 'judgment' as he seems to do elsewhere.[50] The idea that a belief is not up to us is initially puzzling. Aristotle does not mean that we cannot change our beliefs or even that we are not responsible for them. He means that to have the belief that 'p' is the same as to have the belief that 'p is true.' It is to be committed to the truth of 'p.'[51] Therefore, if we should come to believe that 'p is false,' we could no longer believe that 'p.' Although we can, of course, have beliefs that are false, we cannot have beliefs that we believe to be false. In other words, opining that 'p is false' is equivalent to opining that 'not-p is true.' This element of commitment seems to belong to all three species of judgment, which is, incidentally, why it is natural to take belief to be synonymous with judgment in the argument that imagination is not judgment.

46. Ibid., 428a5–18.
47. See Schofield 1992, 260–261, who, though, seems to identify the false imaginings with what he calls "non-paradigmatic sensory experiences" such as hallucinations, afterimages or dreams..
48. See Caston 1996.
49. *De An.* Γ 3, 427b16–17: ὅτι δ᾽ οὐκ ἔστιν ἡ αὐτὴ νόησις καὶ ὑπόληψις, φανερόν. There is no need to bracket νόησις (as does Ross in his edition). Lines 27–28 indicate that Aristotle is here using the term in the most general sense according to which the two species of thinking (τὸ νοεῖν) are νοῦς in the sense of intuition and ὑπόληψις. Thinking in general is generically separated from τὸ αἰσθάνεσθαι and φαντασία.
50. See *De An.* Γ 11, 434a17–20, and *EN* Z 3, 1139b17. Neither of these passages says exactly that judgment and belief are identical. They both can be taken to mean 'judgment in the specific sense of belief.' But insofar as all belief for Aristotle involves some commitment or position taken on the part of the cognizer, it seems fair enough to accept the basic contrast between imagination and belief.
51. *De An.* Γ 3, 428a19–21. The word for 'commitment' here is πίστις.

There is an important point here for the argument that discursive thinking cannot be corporeal. If having a belief that 'p' entails a simultaneous commitment to the truth of 'p,' the subject of the belief and the subject of the commitment cannot be different. They must be identical. The reason why beliefs are not in our power is that our coming to believe that 'p is false' immediately and necessarily causes us not to believe that 'p.' But if a belief is a corporeal state, it is difficult to see why it is at least not logically possible that the belief that 'p' and the belief that 'p is false' or 'not-p' should not coexist as two distinct corporeal states. But if this is logically possible, then that for which this is logically possible cannot have judgments at all. For to believe 'p' and 'p is false' is, as Aristotle says, not to have a belief at all.[52]

Aristotle next provides a separate argument for the claim that imagination is not belief.[53] It is not entirely clear at first why a separate argument is necessary. He has already shown that thinking is not the same thing as judgment by arguing that imagination is not the same thing as belief. Perhaps the reason is that an opponent might suppose that the type of thinking that has been shown not to be identical with belief is something other than imagination, even though Aristotle *seems* to be referring to it in his argument.[54] An opponent might reason that if beliefs can be true or false and imagination can be false, then imagination can also be true, in which case imagination might be the same thing as belief or judgment.[55] But the way imagination is false is not the way judgment is false. Falsity in the latter involves the simultaneous conviction (πίστις) of truth, whereas in the former it does not. Imagination cannot be belief, precisely because there is no conviction in imagination and the truth or falsity that it has is independent of the subjective state of the one imagining.[56]

Nor can imagination be belief that occurs (a) through sense perception or (b) with sense perception or (c) as a result of combination with sense perception.[57] These three possibilities are clearly derived from Plato, although it is not entirely clear that (a) in particular represents what Plato actually says.[58] Aristotle says that none of these can be the case both because of the arguments against imagination being *either* sense perception or belief, and

---

52. See *Met.* Γ 4. Even if we hypothesize that in fact the putative corporeal belief states are like a single on-off switch, so that an animal could not believe 'p' and 'not-p' simultaneously, this hypothesis does not speak to the logical possibility of simultaneous contradictory beliefs.

53. *De An.* Γ 3, 428a18–24.

54. Ibid., 427b17–20, where the activity is described as image-making (εἰδωλοποιοῦντες).

55. Ibid., 428a18. Here Aristotle contrasts imagination with ἐπιστήμη and νοῦς which are always true.

56. Ps.-Simplicius *In de An.* 205, 1–2: οὐ γὰρ ταὐτὸν ἡ τοῦ πράγματος γνῶσις καὶ ἡ τοῦ ὅτι ἀληθὴς ἡ γνῶσις ἀντίληψις.

57. *De An.* Γ 3, 428a24–b9.

58. See for (a) *Tim.* 52A7, C3, where Plato is speaking about the mode of apprehending sensibles and says we do so δόξῃ μετ' αἰσθήσεως. At C3, he refers to the sensible as a φάντασμα. For (b) see *Soph.* 264A4–6; for (c), *Soph.* 264B1–2.

because of the following additional consideration. Belief is precisely of what is perceived. So, it is possible to have true belief about a sense perception and yet at the same time have a false appearance, as when we believe truly that the sun is large though it appears—that is, we imagine it—to be small.[59] But then if imagination is in some way a belief, either one will have, counter to the hypothesis, abandoned one's belief that the sun is large when imagining it to be small, or one will have the belief that it is large and the 'belief' that it is small at the same time, which is impossible.

Pseudo-Philoponus has an incisive discussion of this passage.[60] He interprets the argument as based on the possibility of a quarrel between sense perception and belief. Nothing, says the commentator, could be the product of such a quarrel.[61] That is, even if imagination were somehow based on sense perception and belief, it would have to arise only with the resolution of the quarrel. Yet there is imagination at the moment the quarrel is occurring. The commentator then helpfully supplies a number of arguments built out of what is said earlier in *De Anima* that support the claim that imagination is not a product or result of sense perception and belief. Clearly, he wants to nail this point down. And it is immediately evident why. This passage, he says, is directed against Plato. In fact, it appears directly to contradict what is said in his *Sophist*.

Pseudo-Philoponus does not deny that Aristotle is criticizing Plato; rather, he wants to argue that Aristotle has misunderstood him and that he, Aristotle, actually holds a view similar to the one expressed in *Sophist*.[62] He argues that Plato is not talking about imagination in the sense in which Aristotle is addressing it here. Plato is talking about the "false appearances that seem to be true" (τὰ ψευδῆ φαντάσματα τὰ δοκοῦντα ἀληθῆ εἶναι). There are many kinds of falsehood. Here, what is being referred to is the sort of falsehood that arises when the oar in water seems to be bent. This is intermediate between sense perception and belief. That is, thinking that the oar appears bent is neither an unmitigated perception nor a belief with commitment, the belief that it is in fact not bent. It is said to be intermediate because "appears to be bent" is the result of the sense perception and a kind of belief *without* commitment. It is only a product of sense perception and belief in the sense in which an intermediate is the product of extremes (τῶν ἄκρων). And then, he concludes, Aristotle himself has said as much when he earlier remarks that "when we are acting on a sensible object accurately, we do not say, for example, that it appears to us to be a human being; we do so rather when we are not sensing the object distinctly, and it is only in that

59. The term used here for 'appear,' φαίνεται, part of the problem, since it is an ordinary word that can be used synonymously with 'seem' (δοκεῖ). Hence a belief or δόξα can be associated with the verb φαίνεται, thereby suggesting that imagination or φαντασία is somehow associated with belief.

60. Ps.-Philoponus *In de An.* 501, 11–504, 30.

61. Ibid., 502, 17–18. Cf. 503, 5–8.

62. Ibid., 504, 4ff.

case that [the imagination is] true or false."[63] The commentator interprets these lines as indicating a 'false appearance' that seems to be true, which is exactly what Plato says. But then Aristotle should allow that imagination in the sense of 'appears to' has a kind of intermediate status between sense perception and belief. And if he does this, there is no real conflict.

Aristotle proceeds to define imagination as a "motion produced by the actuality of sense perception."[64] In his treatise *De Somno* he gives the same definition but adds the important additional claim that imagination is the same faculty as sense perception, though they differ in being (εἶναι).[65] Aristotle typically uses this locution to indicate that there is one reality that can be variously defined, such as the road that can be defined according to opposite directions. Earlier in *De Anima* he says that the organ of sense perception and the power or faculty are the same, though they differ 'in being' and, even more clearly, that the actualization of a sensible object and the actualization of sense perception are the same, though they differ 'in being.'[66] So, there is one faculty or state, which is having the form of the sensible without the matter but essentially two different descriptions of this. In the case of sense perception, the sensible object is present; in the case of imagination, it is not. That is, the latter may operate when the sensible object is gone. There is one faculty operating under two different circumstances.

The falsity that is the natural and frequent accompaniment of imagination is evidently not the falsity that makes the assimilation of discursive thinking to sense perception impossible. When the dog imagines falsely that his master is approaching, he is not in error in the way that someone with the capacity for discursive thinking may be in error. Why not? Pseudo-Simplicius supplies a clear answer:

> Conviction [πίστις], which accompanies every rational and intellectual cognition, is not present in any wild beast since irrational cognition cannot grasp something as being true, but is only cognition of the thing which it is able to cognize, being true but not judging the very fact that it is true. For the cognition which grasps that it is cognizing the thing itself in general, or that it is doing so truly or falsely, turns towards itself [ἐπιστρεπτικῆς εἰς ἑαυτὴν], for it will itself cognize itself. But all irrational life is focused only on what is external, since it strives only for things outside and cognizes those only.[67]

---

63. *De An.* Γ 3, 428a12–15. The words τότε ἀληθὴς ἢ ψευδής are held by Ross not to make sense. He substitutes πότερον for τότε. Hicks 1907, 463, brackets the entire phrase.

64. *De An.* Γ 3, 429a1–2.

65. *De Som.* 459a15–22. Nussbaum 1985, 234–236 and 255–261, argues that this means that imagination and sense perception are different aspects of the same faculty, the same thing viewed in different ways. This would perhaps require us to discount those passages in which Aristotle seems to accept that there are creatures with sense perception but without imagination. See Γ 3, 428a10ff.; B 2, 413b21ff., and 415a10–13.

66. See *Phys.* Γ 3, 202a18–21; *Met.* K 10, 1066a23; *De An.* B 12, 424a25; Γ 2, 425b26–27.

67. Ps.-Simplicius *In de An.* 211, 1–8 (trans. Blumenthal).

The basic distinction being made here is between a cognitional state which in some way succeeds in representing what is external to it and another cognitional state which recognizes or is aware of the representation. That the latter is required for someone to be deceived or in error or to maintain falsehoods seems exactly right. 'Turning towards oneself' or self-reflexivity is necessary for the conviction that makes possible the sort of error or falsity that rational animals can have. But that does not quite settle the matter. For it is not clear why self-reflexivity cannot occur in that which is corporeal, and so it is still not clear why thinking is different from sense perception.

In order finally to address the question of the distinctiveness of thinking from sense perception, Aristotle turns in chapter 4 to an account of intellect (νοῦς). By 'intellect,' Aristotle says he means that by which the soul thinks discursively and judges.[68] We recall that judgment is the result of the process of discursive thinking and that judgment is the genus whose species are belief, knowledge, and prudence. Aristotle has assumed that cognition in general is divided into sense perception and thinking. Imagination is produced by sense perception. Its presence does not entail the presence of thinking.[69] He has already shown that imagination is not judgment. It remains to discuss intellect and to show that discursive thinking and judgment are not to be assimilated to sense perception. That is, thinking is necessarily incorporeal.

Chapter 4 begins by conceding the fact that thinking is analogous to sense perception. Just as the form of sensibles must be somehow in the senses, so the form of 'thinkables' or intelligibles must be in that which thinks, the intellect.[70] But since the intellect can potentially think anything, it must be unmixed (ἀμιγῆ) altogether. Aristotle here implies that this is the case for each sense; the faculty of hearing, for example, must be unmixed with sounds if it is to hear. Intellect is not limited to one type of intelligible, so it must be completely unmixed. Hence its entire nature is to be potential (δυνατός).[71] It cannot be actually any of the things it thinks, that is, it cannot be mixed with any of these. "Therefore, it is not even reasonable that it [intellect] should be mixed with body, for it might then acquire some quality, for example, coldness or heat, or there might even

---

68. *De An.* Γ 4, 429a23: λέγω δὲ νοῦν ᾧ διανοεῖται καὶ ὑπολαμβάνει ἡ ψυχή.

69. Cf. Γ 3, 427b27–28 with 428a24, where Aristotle says that animals can have imagination even though they do not have λόγος. If thinking requires the possession of λόγος, as seems reasonable, then imagination is not a species of thinking. The lines 427b27–28—"As for thinking, since it differs from sensing, and since one [species] of it is thought to be imagination and the other to be judgment" (περὶ δὲ τοῦ νοεῖν, ἐπεὶ ἕτερον τοῦ αἰσθάνεσθαι, τούτου δὲ τὸ μὲν φαντασία δοκεῖ εἶναι τὸ δὲ ὑπόληψις)—should therefore not be read as indicating that φαντασία and ὑπόληψις are two species of τὸ νοεῖν (viz., τούτου). He means that φαντασία and ὑπόληψις are two phases in the process of coming to think. The first phase is not thinking itself. See Γ 7, 431a14–17; Γ 8, 432a7–14; *De Mem.* 1, 449b31–450a1. See Schofield 1992, 273.

70. *De An.* Γ 4, 429a17–18: ὥσπερ τὸ αἰσθητικὸν πρὸς τὰ αἰσθητά, οὕτω τὸν νοῦν πρὸς τὰ νοητά.

71. Ibid., Γ 4, 429a21–22.

be an organ for it, just as there is for the faculty of sense perception. But as it is, this is not the case. And those who say that the soul is the 'place of forms' speak well, except that it is not the whole [soul that is the place of forms] but only the thinking part, and this part is not actually the forms, but is them in potency."[72]

The reason why the intellect must be unmixed with that which it thinks is clear. But the reason why it must be unmixed with body is not so clear. Since the intellect cognizes intelligible forms without their matter, why is it "not even reasonable" to suppose that it is itself mixed with some matter: namely, bodily matter? As Aristotle emphasizes, he is speaking here not about a form or property of a body, which is in a way unmixed with matter by definition, but of an entity, the intellect, which is not a property and obviously, since it is pure potency, not a form either. The fact that it is to be receptive of all possible intelligible forms does not seem to disqualify it from being corporeal.[73] Evidently, there is something about the 'information' of the intellect by intelligible forms that makes it impossible for it to be like a body similarly informed.

Aristotle immediately gives us the explanation: "And whenever it [the intellect] becomes each [intelligible] in the way that someone who knows is said to actually know (this happens when he is able to actualize his knowledge by himself [δι' αὑτοῦ], even then it [the intellect] is somehow still in potency, but not in the way it is in potency before it learned or discovered. And it is then that it is able to think itself."[74] The basic distinction here is between (1) the intellect becoming an intelligible form and (2) a further actualization of the intellect. It is this actualization that enables the intellect to 'think itself.'[75] It is presumably this latter actualization that constitutes thinking in the primary sense.[76] The distinction between (1) and (2) is sometimes loosely characterized as the distinction between having and using knowledge. But using knowledge is not the point here. Aristotle has already anticipated the distinction earlier when he distinguishes two sorts of actualization of knowledge: (1) acquiring the knowledge and (2) "bringing it to mind at will" (βουληθεὶς δυνατὸς θεωρεῖν).[77] We might characterize this as awareness of the presence of the form in the intellect in contrast to its simple presence. If this is basically correct, then the question we face is

72. Ibid., Γ 4, 429a24–29.

73. As Hicks 1907, 476, notes, Aristotle is following Plato's reasoning at *Tim.* 50A-51A about the receptacle which has no form (μορφὴν οὐδεμίαν) itself in order that it can receive all forms (50E). But it is not clear whether the receptacle is incorporeal.

74. *De An.* Γ 4, 429b5–9.

75. Ross 1961, ad loc., following Bywater, prints δι' αὑτοῦ instead of δὲ αὐτὸν, presumably repeating the point in the line above. But it is hard to see why the point would be simply repeated or why, if it is a mere repetition, αὐτός is used. See Owens 1981b for an argument in defense of the mss. reading (with references to the Neoplatonic commentators who all followed the mss.), and Wedin 1988, 166–167.

76. Cf. *Met.* Θ 8, 1049b12–17, on the priority of actuality to potency in 'definition.'

77. *De An.* B 5, 417a27–28. Cf. 417b24: νοῆσαι μὲν ἐπ' αὐτῷ, ὁπόταν βούληται.

why full-fledged, actual thinking consists in intellect thinking itself and why this requires that the intellect be unmixed with body.

Even if we were to decide that in chapter 5 Aristotle is introducing a second intellect, the argument about the requirements for intellection would remain. Further, if one were to concede the unity of intellect over against claims for its disruption into two, its capacity for intellection could not be maintained if intellect were thereby assimilated to soul or to a genuine part of it. Since soul is the actuality of a body, the presence of form in the intellect could then only be the presence of form (i.e., first actualization) in a body or part thereof. That is, it could only be the actualization of a part of the body. But then the actuality of intellection (i.e., second actualization) could only be some further psychic activity consisting of a psychic actualization of a body performed on the first psychic actualization. In that case, the identity of intellect *qua* informed and intellect *qua* aware could not be maintained. The putative intellect or cognizer could never know (second actualization) what it knows (first actualization).

This is precisely the crux of the dispute between a functionalist and a dualist interpretation of soul and body in Aristotle. To take the functionalist line, which implicitly or explicitly treats intellection as one of soul's functions, is to make thinking, as Aristotle understands it, impossible.[78] But to take the dualist line seems to fly in the face of Aristotle's insistence that soul is the actuality of body.[79] It would be more accurate to insist on the dualism of separable intellect and soul, which still leaves us with the problem of how soul or the composite can access the operation of intellect in its discursive thinking and other forms of cognition.

The Neoplatonic commentators have clearly in focus the point that is being made. Both Philoponus and Pseudo-Philoponus signal it in a number of different places. The point is that cognition generally requires self-reflexivity (τὸ πρὸς ἑαυτὸ ἐπιστρέφειν), and no body is capable of this.[80] As the latter commentator states it, "self-reflexivity is nothing but the grasp of one's own actual states" (τὸ τῶν οἰκείων ἐνεργειῶν ἀντιλαμβάνεσθαι). The reason why no body is capable of self-reflexivity is straightforward. If the putative bodily cognizer is in a state of information, then the grasp of that state will, *ex hypothesi*, be a bodily state. One bodily state grasping the state of another body will not be a case of the cognizer 'thinking itself.' It will be a case of one cognizer grasping the state of another cognizer.

It may be objected that construing the identity of the cognizer in this way begs the question. If we assume that the cognizer is a body, then one part of that body can be related to another part of the same body and the body can be 'thinking itself' in a nonproblematic fashion. This objection is neither

---

78. See supra n. 33.

79. Substantial dualism is not at issue. What is in apparent conflict with hylomorphism is the implication that the subject of intellection should be distinct from the composite.

80. See Philoponus *In de An.* 14, 29–38; 161, 31–162, 27; 292, 5–13; Ps.-Philoponus *In de An.* 466, 12–467, 12.

coherent nor, more important, true to what Aristotle says. Six times in the remainder of this section of *De Anima* Aristotle asserts that "actual knowledge is the same as that which is known."[81] By this he cannot mean (1) above—that is, that actual knowledge is the same thing as the presence of the form in the intellect, because the presence of the form in the intellect is then still 'somehow in potency' (δυνάμει πως) to actual knowledge.[82] He must mean (2), the unqualified actuality of thinking. But because the intellect in (1) is identical with the form that informs it, the intellect in (2), when it knows, must be the same as the intellect in (1).[83] If it were not, then the form that is in the intellect in (1) would have to inform the intellect in (2), and another intellect would have to be posited to be aware of the presence of form in (2). That is why it is incoherent to suggest that the intellects could be different, as they would have to be if cognition were a bodily state or activity. According to this objection, cognition would be a relation—perhaps a representational one—between a cognizer and that which is external to it. But that is precisely the view that Aristotle is opposing.[84]

Pseudo-Philoponus has an interesting criticism of Aristotle which indirectly supports the foregoing interpretation.[85] He raises the problem of how an intellect can know itself if the object of intellect is other than it. He claims that Aristotle's solution is to make the object of intellect an intellect, so that knowledge of the object of intellect is self-reflexive knowledge. But that would mean that if God is an object of intellect, then God is an intellect.[86] According to the commentator's Christian Neoplatonic position, God is greater than intellect. This, as he confidently believed, is where Aristotle went wrong. So, he argues, the correct solution is that "everything that thinks itself

---

81. *De An.* Γ 7, 431a1. See Γ 4, 430a4–5; Γ 5, 430a19–20; Γ 6, 430b25–26; Γ 7, 431b17; Γ 8, 431b22–23. I leave out Γ 4, 429b9 as perhaps problematic. See also *Met.* Λ 9, 1074b38–1075a5.

82. Cf. *De An.* Γ 4, 429b30–31.

83. Cf. Reeve 2000, 181: "Understanding [the activity of intellect] is a reflexive process that always involves self-understanding, then, for the same reason that seeing always involves light."

84. Victor Caston suggests to me in private correspondence that *De An.* Γ 2, 425b12–17 provides a counterexample to the claim that Aristotle holds that the self-reflexivity of intellection guarantees the nonbodily status of the intellect. For in this passage, Aristotle argues that sense perception is self-reflexive. So, self-reflexivity would seem to be possible for material entities, such as animals. This is a weighty objection, but one that, I believe, Aristotle can answer. First, the word αἰσθανόμεθα is used here to mean awareness or consciousness, not sense perception strictly speaking. See *EN* I 9, 1170a25–b5 where it is similarly used to indicate the awareness of activities, such as walking and thinking, that are not sense perceptions. This awareness is cognitive and not perceptual and so evidently a type of thinking, and as such it does not belong to animals who are incapable of thinking. So, one reason for supposing that self-reflexivity does not entail nonbodily status—namely, that self-reflexivity can belong to animals who are not, in Aristotle's view, nonbodily—is eliminated. Second, though sense perception is bodily, and the awareness that sense perception is occurring is a type of thinking and could occur only in that which is capable of thinking, this does not mean that thinking is bodily (or that sense perception is not).

85. See Ps.-Philoponus *In de An.* 527, 5–528, 4.

86. Cf. 528, 13. Cf. Plotinus V 1. 8, 5: δημιουργὸς γὰρ ὁ νοῦς αὐτῷ [i.e., Plato]. Plotinus then argues that there must be a principle beyond Intellect.

is intellect" (πᾶν τὸ νοοῦν ἑαυτὸ νοῦς), not that "every object of intellect is intellect" (πᾶν τὸ νοητὸν νοῦς).[87] In fact, this is what Aristotle does say. The commentator is right in believing that Aristotle makes the first principle of all an intellect because of the nature of intellect and the exigencies of a first principle. But he is mistaken in believing that Aristotle holds that the first principle of all is an intellect *because* it is an object of intellect.[88]

The incorporeality of intellect does not sit well with hylomorphism. The first actuality of intellect, (1) above, or the acquisition of intelligible forms, is distinct from the first actuality that the soul is. In addition, the separability of intellect and the inseparability of other 'parts' of soul make a general hylomorphic account of the soul problematic if not impossible.[89] That intellect stands outside of or is separable from a hylomorphic composite is the key concession that the Neoplatonist would seek from the Aristotelian; it is, after all, the core Platonic view.[90] Thus far, there seem to be good grounds for the conclusion that the concession is in fact made in *De Anima*.

De Anima, Gamma 5

The discussion of intellect in *De Anima* is enormously complicated by the notorious fifth chapter of Book Γ. As is evident from a perusal of the Neoplatonic commentators, there were widely divergent views regarding its meaning and its implications for harmonization.[91] I aim to show in this section that what is said about intellect in chapter five is a continuation, indeed, a crucial continuation, of what has hitherto been said about it. No second intellect is here being introduced. In fact, there is a fairly straightforward interpretation of the so-called agent intellect and passive intellect which has little to do with the divine intellect and which has everything to do with Aristotle's analysis of human thinking.

I provide a translation of the text for reference, along with divisions of the main points discussed below:

---

87. Ps.-Philoponus *In de An.*, 527, 37–38.

88. See infra chap. 6 for a discussion of Aristotle's argument that the first principle of all must be an intellect.

89. See B 1, 413a2–5. On separability see Γ4, 429b5.

90. See Proclus *In Tim.* II 285, 27–31, where the soul that animates the body is distinguished sharply from the partless separate soul or principle—namely, the intellect. Proclus is ultimately relying on the proofs for the immortality of soul in *Phaedo*. What is proven to be immortal is intellect. See also *In Tim.* III 335, 14–17. Cf. Plotinus IV 4. 29, 14–15, where he distinguishes the "life in the body which is proper to it" from the life that can be separate from the body.

91. E.g., see Ps.-Philoponus (*In de An.* 535, 1–19), who mentions four interpretations—by Alexander of Aphrodisias, Plotinus, Marinus, and Plutarch of Athens—in addition to his own. In the main he agrees with Plutarch. Ps.-Simplicius *In de An.* 240, 2ff., offers his own distinctive interpretation. We can infer that Iamblichus evidently had his own view from what Pseudo-Philoponus says in his commentary, 533, 25–35. Proclus *In Tim.* III 334, 3ff., is at least seized with the common problem of the relation of intellect to soul in Platonism and in Aristotle.

[A] Since just as in everything in nature there is something which serves as the matter in each genus (this is that which is all of those things in potency), as well as something else which is the cause and is productive [ποιητικόν] by making all things, as in the case of art in relation to matter, so necessarily there exists these differences in the soul. [B] And intellect is this sort of thing in one sense by becoming all things, and in another by making all things, like a sort of disposition [ἕξις], in the way that light does. For in a certain way light makes potential colors actual colors. [C] And this intellect is separable [χωριστὸς] and unaffected [ἀπαθὴς], and unmixed (ἀμιγής), being in its essence [τῇ οὐσίᾳ] in actuality [ἐνέργεια]. For that which acts is always more honorable than that which is acted upon, and the principle is more honorable than the matter. [D] Actual knowledge is identical with that which is known; potential knowledge is, however, prior in time in the individual, but as a whole it is not prior in time. [E] But [intellect] is not at one time thinking and another time not thinking. [F] Having been separated [χωρισθείς], it is just what it is, and this alone is immortal and eternal. [G] But we do not remember because while this is unaffected, the passive intellect is destructible. [H] And without this, it [i.e., the individual] thinks nothing.[92]

The general point of the chapter is frequently represented as the introduction of two intellects: the passive (παθητικός) intellect and the productive or active or agent (ποιητικός) intellect.[93] But as has been often noted, Aristotle does not use the latter term and the former is used only here, predicatively.[94] Outside this chapter he speaks simply and solely of intellect. But the duality of principles or aspects of intellect that this chapter is indisputably concerned with is prepared for in the previous chapter. As we have seen, Aristotle's general account of intellect leads him to distinguish the actuality of cognition that is the presence of an intelligible form in the intellect and the further actuality that is the awareness of the

---

92. Γ 5, 430a10–25: [A] Ἐπεὶ δ' ὥσπερ ἐν ἁπάσῃ τῇ φύσει ἐστὶ τι τὸ μὲν ὕλη ἑκάστῳ γένει (τοῦτο δὲ ὃ πάντα δυνάμει ἐκεῖνα), ἕτερον δὲ τὸ αἴτιον καὶ ποιητικόν, τῷ ποιεῖν πάντα, οἷον ἡ τέχνη πρὸς τὴν ὕλην πέπονθεν, ἀνάγκη καὶ ἐν τῇ ψυχῇ ὑπάρχειν ταύτας τὰς διαφοράς· [B] καὶ ἔστιν ὁ μὲν τοιοῦτος νοῦς τῷ πάντα γίνεσθαι, ὁ δὲ τῷ πάντα ποιεῖν, ὡς ἕξις τις, οἷον τὸ φῶς· τρόπον γάρ τινα καὶ τὸ φῶς ποιεῖ τὰ δυνάμει ὄντα χρώματα ἐνεργείᾳ χρώματα. [C] καὶ οὗτος ὁ νοῦς χωριστὸς καὶ ἀπαθὴς καὶ ἀμιγής, τῇ οὐσίᾳ ὢν ἐνεργείᾳ· ἀεὶ γὰρ τιμιώτερον τὸ ποιοῦν τοῦ πάσχοντος καὶ ἡ ἀρχὴ τῆς ὕλης. [D] τὸ δ' αὐτό ἐστιν ἡ κατ' ἐνέργειαν ἐπιστήμη τῷ πράγματι· ἡ δὲ κατὰ δύναμιν χρόνῳ προτέρα ἐν τῷ ἑνί, ὅλως δὲ οὐδὲ χρόνῳ, [E] ἀλλ' οὐχ ὁτὲ μὲν νοεῖ ὁτὲ δ' οὐ νοεῖ. [F] χωρισθεὶς δ' ἐστὶ μόνον τοῦθ' ὅπερ ἐστί, καὶ τοῦτο μόνον ἀθάνατον καὶ ἀΐδιον [G] (οὐ μνημονεύομεν δέ, ὅτι τοῦτο μὲν ἀπαθές, ὁ δὲ παθητικὸς νοῦς φθαρτός)· [H] καὶ ἄνευ τούτου οὐθὲν νοεῖ.

93. See Alexander of Aphrodisias *De An.* 88, 17ff.; *Mantissa* 106, 19ff. Alexander distinguishes two intellects, one of which is the active intellect, which Alexander identifies with the prime unmoved mover. The other intellect is divided into two parts: (1) that which is matter for reception of forms (ὁ νοῦς ὑλικός) and (2) that which can receive these forms and so think (ὁ νοῦς νοῶν, ὁ νοῦς ἐν ἕξει) (*De An.* 84, 14–85, 5). Themistius (*In de An.* 108, 28–34), apparently relying on Theophrastus, also thinks there are two intellects: one is a part of the soul and is perishable; one is a mixture of passive and active principles and is imperishable. See Hicks 1907, 498ff., for a two-intellect assumption. More recently, Caston (1999) has defended a version of Alexander's position.

94. See Blumenthal 1991, 191.

presence of that form. And as we have also seen, this twofold actuality belongs to a unified intellect.[95]

In [A], the general principle is enunciated.[96] In everything in nature there is that which serves as matter and that which serves as productive cause, as, for example, in art working on matter.[97] The principle is then applied to the soul. How it is to be applied is not obvious. But just to anticipate a bit, in [F] we get a hint that intellect's role in instantiating the general principle requires intellect to operate in a way other than the way it does when it is separated, presumably, from soul.[98] The general principle is going to be instantiated by intellect operating within the soul. It is going to be instantiated by an account of how thinking works.

The crux of the problem is [B], for it has frequently been understood to indicate that there are two intellects.[99] But the contrast ὁ μὲν . . . ὁ δὲ in lines 14–15 is evidently meant to reflect the τὸ μέν . . . ἕτερον δὲ contrast in lines 10–11, and though the general principle *may* be instantiated by two separate entities, it need not be. Indeed, since Aristotle is talking about how

95. Wedin 1988, chap. 5, rejecting the idea that there are two intellects in *De Anima*, argues in detail for a deflationist account of productive intellect, that is, for its nontranscendental meaning and what he calls a "cognitivist account of individual noetic activity." What this means is that there are two aspects of mind, the receptive and the productive, and fully actual thinking occurs if the intellect not only produces the object of thinking but also produces itself by producing that object (see 168, 175).

96. Note that the beginning of the passage, ἐπεὶ δ' . . . suggests a continuation of the train of thinking of chap. 4 and not the introduction of an entirely new subject. In fact, chap. 5 aims to explain how thinking is possible for an individual.

97. Cf. *Met.*, Z 7, 1032a17–20; Z 8, 1033a24–31; H 6, 1045a30–33. Ross, followed by Hamlyn, among others, is wrong to bracket ὥσπερ, as Caston (1999, 205) rightly notes. Wedin 1985 thinks that the ὥσπερ needs to be eliminated if, as he goes on to argue, God is not alluded to by the phrase 'agent intellect.' I do not see this need, since, against Wedin, I think that the references to intellect, though not references to God, are references to that which in some sense transcends nature because it is separable.

98. See Berti (1975, 256), who makes the obvious point that if the intellect is what it is when separated, then, when not separated, it is other than or not only what it is. Berti (257) draws the obvious conclusion: "l'intelletto "passivo" non è un altro intelletto, che esiste accanto all'intelletto "prodottivo," ma solo una delle funzioni possedute in potenza da questo." See for a similar view De Corte 1934, 45–48; 73–81. Against this, Caston 1999, 207–211, argues that χωρισθείς should be translated "when it occurs separately," which seems to me to strain against the ordinary grammar. Caston's recourse to this translation is forced on him by his assumption that there are two intellects being discussed in this chapter. Wedin (1988, 190–195), argues that separability here indicates only conceptual separateness, as in the case of the objects of mathematics. He claims that this separateness pertains only to productive mind because it alone is incorporeal. But this is not the case. Wedin himself concedes that it is the whole intellect that must be considered apart from matter. So, he maintains that only the productive (i.e., agent) intellect can be *adequately* considered without matter (192–193). Aristotle, however, does not call the objects of mathematics 'immortal.'

99. See Hicks 1907, 500. The key words καὶ ἔστιν ὁ μὲν τοιοῦτος νοῦς τῷ πάντα γίνεσθαι, ὁ δὲ τῷ πάντα ποιεῖν have been typically understood as referring to two intellects, one of which becomes all things, while the other makes all things. It seems, however, that the use of τοιοῦτος here refers to the just employed analogy, in which everything in nature contains the two principles, active and passive. It would not make sense to say that in everything in nature there are two *things* as opposed to principles. I do not think the ἔστιν has to be taken as existential in order to justify this interpretation, as does Hicks. We can simply take τοιοῦτος as predicative.

the general principle operates in the soul, it seems highly likely that the material and active elements of the instantiation of the principle are not, in their operation, separate from each other.[100] The words τοιοῦτος νοῦς indicate that intellect is such as are the things that fall under the general principle. If it only indicated the material principle, then that would suggest that the reference to the active principle was a reference to another intellect. But this would make the first five lines pointless and the motive for the introduction of the second intellect unintelligible.

Even if we construe the line so as to indicate two intellects, the whole point of the analogy is that these intellects in concert produce intellection. And given that Aristotle has said, and will say five more times by the end of chapter 8, that that thinker must be identical with what is thought, postulating two intellects does not solve anything. No doubt that is why some scholars want to excise chapter 5 altogether. But we have already seen that a continuation of the answer to the questions raised in 4 is needed. It is the duality of a single intellect that is at issue.[101]

The material principle in the analogy "becomes all things", where 'becomes' is a gloss on 'in potency.' Matter as such does not become substance except in the atemporal sense. The sense in which intellect becomes all things—that is, is in potency to all things—does not, therefore, indicate that intellect undergoes a change, a change that consists in its 'acquisition' of form.[102] After all, intellect has already been claimed to be 'unaffected.' It is in potency analogous to the way that the body is in potency to the soul.[103] That is why the active principle is compared with a "disposition." The primary meaning of ἕξις, Aristotle tells us, is "a sort of actuality of that which has and that which is had, as if it were an action of a sort or a motion."[104]

100. Caston 1999, 206–207, denies that the principle is meant to be applied here to the individual soul. Though Caston is correct that 'in' (ἐν) has many different senses in Aristotle, chap. 5 is right in the middle of the section of *De Anima* that discusses thinking in the human soul and it would be extremely odd if Aristotle were here introducing divine thinking. But more to the point, Aristotle needs to do what he does in chap. 5, as I shall show. It is not a superfluous aside. Thus, ὥσπερ need not be bracketed, even though what is discussed in the following is in nature, since intellect is also separate from nature.

101. See De Corte (1934, 54), who states the position as clearly as possible: "L'intellect agent et l'intellect possible forment deux entités réellement distinctes en tant qu'ils sont agent et patient, c'est-à-dire en tant que facultés, mais ils sont intelligence. L'intellect agent n'est pas l'intellect, l'intellect possible n'est pas l'intellect, mais intellect agent et intellect possible sont l'intellect."

102. See B 5, 417b5–9: "For that which possesses knowledge becomes that which exercises that knowledge, and this becoming either is not an alteration (for the progress is toward itself and in its actuality) or is an alteration of a different kind. For this reason, it is not right to say that a thinking human being, whenever he thinks, is changed." (θεωροῦν γὰρ γίνεται τὸ ἔχον τὴν ἐπιστήμην, ὅπερ ἢ οὐκ ἔστιν ἀλλοιοῦσθαι (εἰς αὐτὸ γὰρ ἡ ἐπίδοσις καὶ εἰς ἐντελέχειαν) ἢ ἕτερον γένος ἀλλοιώσεως. διὸ οὐ καλῶς ἔχει λέγειν τὸ φρονοῦν, ὅταν φρονῇ, ἀλλοιοῦσθαι . . .)

103. Cf. B 1, 412a27–28: "For this reason, the soul is the first actuality of a natural body having life potentially within it" (διὸ ἡ ψυχή ἐστιν ἐντελέχεια ἡ πρώτη σώματος φυσικοῦ δυνάμει ζωὴν ἔχοντος).

104. See *Met.* Δ 20, 1022b4ff. Cf. *Met.* Λ 3, 1070a11–12 where the nature or form of a composite is said to be a ἕξις. Cf. *Phys.* Γ 3, 202a13–21 where Aristotle explains the unity of the agent and patient in motion or change: μία ἡ ἀμφοῖν ἐνέργεια (18).

But we may well ask, "In potency to what?" Not to another intellect, surely, but in potency to thinking, that is, actual thinking. As Caston and others have noticed, the word νοῦς is used in *De Anima* both for the substance and for the activity. Thus Aristotle can without any apparent strain speak about "practical intellect" (πρακτικὸς νοῦς) and "theoretical intellect" (θεωρητικὸς νοῦς).[105] Similarly, he can speak about soul as 'nutritive' (θρεπτική), "generative" (γεννητική), "thinking" (νοητική), and "discursive thinking" (διανοητική).[106] The distinction of the two principles no more indicates two intellects than does the distinction between practical and theoretical intellect, and no more than the distinction among psychic functions indicates multiple souls.

The analogy proposed in [B] is that as agent intellect is to passive intellect, so is light to colors in potency. Light actualizes the colors, and the agent intellect actualizes the forms in the passive intellect. This is a continuation of the same general point that was made in Γ 4, 429b5–9. First, the intellect acquires a form, and then the form is actualized—in the earlier passage presumably by the intellect that actually thinks, and in the present passage by the intellect that actually "illuminates." What is here new is that the step from first to second actuality is made. The light metaphor neatly indicates this. But those who want to insist on two intellects, in fact, do not merely make chapter 5 irrelevant; they make it contradict what is said in chapter four. For the implicit step from first to second actuality in chapter four is *within* one intellect. To make this a step from what happens in one intellect to what happens in another is not just irrelevant but incoherent as well.

If we resist the dubious benefits of postulating two intellects, then we shall not be impelled to deny that the intellect characterized in [C] in exactly the same way that it is characterized in chapter 4 is so characterized because it is the same intellect.[107] What [C], taken along with [F], tells us is that when separated from the soul, intellect is essentially in actuality.[108] That is, it does

105. Cf. B 3, 415a11–12, where Aristotle speaks of θεωρητικὸς νοῦς, and Γ 10, 433a16, where he speaks of πρακτικὸς νοῦς—both of which indicate ways in which intellect functions. Practical intellect is equivalent to the type of ὑπόληψις that is φρόνησις and theoretical intellect is equivalent to the type of ὑπόληψις that is ἐπιστήμη. In both cases, 'intellect' refers to that 'owing to which' the soul engages in a type of thinking. Cf. Γ 4, 429a23. Though Caston 1999, 203, recognizes these manners of describing intellect, he insists that the "perishability" of "passive intellect" entails its distinction from imperishable agent intellect. But if the qualification 'passive' is only an attribute of intellect when, as I am arguing, it is in the embodied soul, then the fact that intellect is imperishable does not yield any contradiction at all.

106. See B 4, 416b25; Γ 4, 429a28; Γ 7, 431a14; Γ 12, 434a22. Cf. B 4, 416a19, where it is the δύναμις in the soul that is qualified as 'generative' or 'nutritive.'

107. See Nuyens 1948, 304. Hicks (1907, 502) thinks these characteristics apply differently to agent and passive intellect. Wedin (1988 182–95), owing to his deflationary view of what he calls 'productive' (i. e., agent) intellect, dismisses the separability and immortality of the individual intellect.

108. Caston 1999, 207–211, translates "when it occurs separately," arguing that Aristotle is here making a "taxoniomical point." That is, he is referring to a type of intellect,—namely, God's: "The occurrence of this type in the world is just the occurrence of that which alone is immortal and eternal." I doubt that the aorist passive participle χωρισθείς can be translated in

not ever cease from its activity of thinking. Its activity is analogous to the first actuality of a composite living thing. This seems to indicate the separation of the "more honorable" active principle from matter. But if there is one intellect, then how can this more honorable active principle be separated from itself: namely, from the "passive" principle?

The answer I believe is this. Intellect is always intellect: that is, it is always engaged in self-reflexive activity. This is the case both when intellect is "in the soul" and when intellect is separate. But when it is in the soul—when it is accessed by that which operates in nature—that access is always via images.[109] The passive intellect (i.e., intellect operating passively) is the locus of the actualization of forms in the images available originally through sense perception. Intellect itself operates without images. That is, its self-identical activity has nothing in it that is alien. "It is what it is" and nothing more. By contrast, when intellect is in the soul, it is employed in cognition via images that are other than it.[110] That is why in this case it is not only what it is. The obverse of cognitive identity for embodied cognizers is qualified identity of knower and known. Unqualified identity is available only for that which is cognitively identical with that which is not other than it.

There is no question that thinking, for Aristotle, does not essentially require images. God is the paradigmatic example of such thinking. But God's thinking is not, as Aristotle insists, merely imageless; it is also like the thinking that is knowledge, that is, thinking in which the knower and the known are identical.[111] This is exactly what is said in [D].[112] So, though "the soul does not think without images", thinking without images evidently does occur in a way in us. This is intellect's thinking. It is different from soul's thinking, which is discursive.[113] The thinking that is episodic, the thinking that is implicitly referred to in [E], is not intellect's thinking. It is the thinking that accesses form, that is, what is intelligible, through images. By contrast, intellect is *always*

---

this way. More important, χωρισθείς picks up καὶ οὗτος ὁ νοῦς χωριστός in line 17, which itself refers to intellect in lines 14–15, which is said to be "in the soul" in line 13. In addition, Caston (211), argues that the words "is what it is" when said of the separable intellect, refer to the activity of thinking. That is, the separable intellect "is *nothing but activity*" (Caston's emphasis). But the majority of mss. have ἐνεργείᾳ not ἐνέργεια. Taken thus, the words indicate that intellect, an incorporeal entity, engages in its activity essentially. They do not indicate that there is no distinction between the substance and its activity. By implicit contrast, the way its activity is employed or accessed by the soul is not essential to it. See Themistius *In de An.* 97, 29; Ps.-Simplicius *In de An.* 533, 8–9.

109. See Γ 7, 431a16–17: διὸ οὐδέποτε νοεῖ ἄνευ φαντάσματος ἡ ψυχή. Cf. Γ 8, 432a7–10.

110. See Kosman (1992, 355–356), who in my view rightly argues that "Νοῦς ποιητικός, therefore, does not, strictly speaking, make consciousness, by action for example upon a pathetic mind incapable of thinking by itself. It is simply νοῦς understood in its role of self-actualization in θεωρία."

111. See *Met.* Λ 9, 1074b36–1075a3.

112. Ross 1961 brackets the entire line. His only reason for doing this is that it is repeated at the beginning of Γ 7, 431a1–3.

113. Cf. Γ 7, 431a14–15: τῇ δὲ διανοητικῇ ψυχῇ τὰ φαντάσματα οἷον αἰσθήματα ὑπάρχει.

thinking.[114] To fail to distinguish the thinking of intellect from the thinking of soul is an error analogous to failing to distinguish the subjecthood of soul from the subjecthood of the composite human being. Just as the soul can be thought of as an instrument of the composite, so intellect can be thought of as an instrument of soul.[115] But just as the instrumentality of soul does not preclude its being the subject of mental states, so the instrumentality of intellect does not preclude *its* being a subject.

Perhaps the best name for the thinking that consists of successful access of forms is 'understanding.'[116] For example, one imagines or draws a triangle in a circle and then a square in another circle, and then comes to understand (or does not: Aristotle has no perspicuous answer to the 'how' question here) that a *plane figure as such* is inscribable in a circle.[117] What one understands is a truth about what is not an image but what is imaged in the drawn triangle and the circle. What is understood is not itself an image or even how an image represents something else. What is understood is that of which the image is an image. It is, roughly, a type of mental 'seeing' which, in potency, is equivalent to the presence of the form in the intellect and, in actuality, is the awareness or accessing of that presence. Without intellect, the soul could retain images but could not access the forms whose actualizations the images represent. Without soul's imagistic activity, intellect would be just what it is and unusable by the composite.

That is what [F] implies.[118] The main reason for holding that separated intellect is not identical with the thinking that is the prime unmoved mover is that for the latter there is no distinction between substance and activity, no distinction between intellect and thinking, whereas a separated intellect would still be in potency to its thinking.[119] Another subsidiary reason as

114. Wedin 1988, 189–190, argues that [E] does not imply that intellect is always thinking. He claims that it means only that either intellect is active or it is not. But this seems to make the subject of νοεῖ not intellect but soul. This is not grammatically impossible, though it makes the statement false. The soul does think episodically. Wedin seems committed to the view that in no way can intellect be the legitimate subject of νοεῖ independently of soul. This in turn rests upon Wedin's assumption that intellect cannot be an immortal entity.

115. Cf. Γ 8, 432a1–3: "The soul, then, is like someone's arm; for just as the arm is an instrument of instruments, so the intellect is a form of forms and the faculty of sense perception is a form of sensibles" (ὥστε ἡ ψυχὴ ὥσπερ ἡ χείρ ἐστιν· καὶ γὰρ ἡ χεὶρ ὄργανόν ἐστιν ὀργάνων, καὶ ὁ νοῦς εἶδος εἰδῶν καὶ ἡ αἴσθησις εἶδος αἰσθητῶν).

116. See Burnyeat 1981.

117. See the remarks of Kahn (1992, 361), who finds in Aristotle no resolution of the tension between the accounts of separable intellect and soul as the actualization of a body. Yet as Kahn goes on to argue, Aristotle accepts the tension in his desire to do justice to the "split nature of human beings."

118. The word χωρισθείς is unintelligible if taken to refer to what is already unqualifiedly separate: namely, an active intellect. E.g., Modrak (1987, 225), supposes it must in effect refer to a condition contrary to fact. On the other hand, if it is intellect there is being referred to here, that is nothing at all puzzling about the word.

119. *Met.* Λ 9, 1074a33–35, which is the culmination of several arguments to the effect that God cannot be in potency to his thinking. But an intellect is in potency to its thinking. In general, any substance is in potency to its activities. So, God cannot be an intellect. God must be the activity that is thinking thinking about thinking.

Aristotle argues earlier in *Metaphysics,* is that the perfect actuality that turns out to be 'thinking thinking about thinking' must be unique.[120] The immortality of the intellect without which any particular human being cannot think at all is not in question. What is supremely questionable is whether that separate intellect is continuous with me.[121]

What we do not remember probably cannot be identified with what we did not experience. That is, what we do not remember cannot be embodied experiences, requiring sense perception, imagination, and so on. Indeed, insofar as memory depends on these, we could not remember disembodied experience. But if we could not remember, would it be because of the impossibility that memory should operate across the passage from disembodiment to embodiment, or because we in no sense existed, in which case we obviously could not remember? If the former, what we do not remember must be what we as disembodied intellects experienced. If the latter, then what is the point of introducing the denial of memory?

What exactly is the position that is supposed to make the former alternative impossible? Presumably, it is that human beings have a beginning in time as well as an ending, and that before that beginning they did not exist. Therefore, there would be a note of irony in the claim that "we do not remember." It is undoubtedly true that Aristotle holds that human beings do not preexist their biological beginning. But the claim that a person or self or agent of intellection—a thinker—is extensionally equivalent to a human being is much more problematic.

First, as we saw in chapter 2, Neoplatonists report the doctrine of the dialogue *Eudemus* as affirming the preexistence of intellect and offering an explanation for our present inability to remember. It should be emphasized that if intellect is separate from the human being, then its preexistence is no less plausible than its postexistence. This is evidently why Iamblichus, as reported by Pseudo-Philoponus, identifies the account of intellect here with the Platonic doctrine that learning is recollection.[122] Iamblichus adds, reasonably enough, that intelligibles must therefore be in the intellect.

There is, however, a weightier consideration that should give us pause before we dismiss out of hand the obvious implication of the claim that we do not remember intellect's operation. Leaving aside the question of separation,

120. See *Met.* Λ 8, 1074a31–38. This passage is actually an argument for the uniqueness of heaven. But this is shown by showing that the prime unmoved mover must be one in number as well as in formula: ἐν ἄρα καὶ λόγῳ καὶ ἀριθμῷ τὸ πρῶτον κινοῦν ἀκίνητον ὄν.

121. Wedin 1988, chap. 6, maintains the difference between divine and human intellect by arguing that the immortality of chap. 5 is "something like an "as-if" immortality" (210) and only "an analogue to the unmoved mover" (217). I suspect that Wedin's reluctance to take Aristotle at his word in regard to the immortality of intellect is that he assumes this means personal immortality. Perhaps it does, but not likely in a sense of 'personal' that Aristotle would share with Wedin.

122. See Pseudo-Philoponus *In de An.* 535, 25–35; 537, 1; 541, 6. See Nuyens 1948, 307–308, on the evidence that in Aristotle the word ἀίδιος always indicates existence without beginning or end.

Aristotle would seem to be committed to the claim that the human being, not the intellect, is the subject of thinking.[123] But it is precisely *not* the so-called hylomorphic composite that is the subject of self-reflexive thinking. It must not be supposed that by embracing hylomorphism, Aristotle has immunized himself from the considerations that lead to Platonic dualism, principally the incorporeality of thought. If Aristotle's position is incoherent, that incoherence is in harmony with Plato's.[124]

Point [G] implies that if there is continuity, it is not memorial. Generally, if memory is a function of the image-making power, there is no memorial continuity between intellect when it is 'just what it is' and the embodied person, whether this be the intellect prior to or posterior to its association with the embodied person.[125]

The mistake usually made at this point in the exegesis is to identify the 'passive intellect' that is said to be 'destructible' with a supposed intellect in chapter 4 which is different from the intellect oddly now introduced in chapter 5.[126] But Aristotle consistently says that intellect *simpliciter* is 'unaffected' and 'immortal' whereas 'passive intellect' is 'destructible.' There is, however, no reason to suppose that this 'passive intellect' refers to anything but the manner in which intellect is accessed by the soul: that is, the νοητικὴ ψυχή. The point of entrée to intellect is via its reception of images. As I argued above, the phrase 'passive intellect' does not indicate a type of intellect, but an attribute of intellect possessed by it when it is 'in the soul.' That

---

123. See supra n. 29.

124. Granger 1996 contrasts what he calls 'attributivism' and 'substantialism' as the two fundamental interpretations of the nature of soul in *De Anima*. According to the former, soul is considered to be a property; according to the latter, soul is a 'thing.' Granger argues that there is evidence for both interpretations in the text and that in fact Aristotle has a confused notion of soul, which should be understood as a 'property-thing.' Revealingly, Granger assimilates substantialism to Cartesian dualism. (57, 80–81, 111). That is, he assumes that if the soul is a 'thing,' then it must be a thing in the way that Descartes held the soul to be a thing in relation to another thing: namely, the body.

125. Caston 1999, 213–215, argues that we translate "We do not remember that while this cannot be affected, the intellect that can be is perishable," which he characterizes as Aristotle's "philosophical and urbane" use of "we do not remember" invoking "our vulnerability and mortality." Such a use seems entirely out of place here and in this translation the first δὲ is pointless. Wedin (1988 179–181), holds that we do not remember the thinking that occurred in past experiences, as opposed to the things then thought. Thus, we do not remember the activity of productive (agent) mind alone, because without content there is no memory. But on this view, remembering would be impossible, not just something that we do not do. See Proclus *In Remp.* II 349, 13–26, for the fragment of Aristotle's dialogue *Eudemus* in which Aristotle offers an explanation for why we do not remember our life prior to embodiment; see Berti 1962, 421–423, on the authenticity of this fragment and its implications for Aristotle's early philosophy. We do not need to deny that the account of soul in *De Anima* represents a development in Aristotle's thinking in order to assert the relevance of the *Eudemus* passage. Even if soul is the actuality of a body, (1) the career of intellect is another story, and (2) our identity with intellect is puzzling, though there is no question that we are in some sense identical with it if we are able to think.

126. Caston 1999, 203, draws the conclusion that there are two intellects in chap. 5 because "[the passive intellect] is perishable, while [the agent intellect] is immortal and eternal."

attribute is not essential to intellect. That is why, when separate, intellect is 'just what it is.'[127]

The primary contrast in [G] is between intellect—first mentioned in line 14 (τοιοῦτος νοῦς), then picked up again in line 17 (καὶ οὗτος ὁ νοῦς), then again mentioned in line 24 (τοῦτο μὲν ἀπαθές)—and 'the passive intellect' (ὁ δὲ παθητικὸς νοῦς) in lines 24–25. One thing is certain from this contrast is that the property of intellect mentioned in lines [B] 14–15— namely, 'becoming all things' (τῷ πάντα γίνεσθαι) belongs to intellect in contrast with 'passive intellect.'[128] It is therefore not plausible that 'becoming all things' be glossed as 'being passive.' On the contrary, intellect, that in one aspect 'becomes all things', is 'unaffected.'

The line contained in [H] is radically ambiguous, as all the commentators have noted.[129] Grammatically, the most plausible referent of τούτου is the 'passive intellect.' Assuming this, we might suppose that the subject of νοεῖ is just intellect. But it is simply false that intellect does not think without passive intellect. When separated, that is, when there is no passive intellect, intellect is 'just what it is': that is, it is thinking unmediated by images. So, it is unlikely that intellect is the subject. The two circumstances in which it would be correct to say that thinking does not occur are either when the individual is not actually thinking or when the individual is bereft of images for one reason or another. The first possibility is implicit in lines 21–22, where the continuous activity of intellect is contrasted with the episodic thinking of the individual. I believe that the second possibility is what is being alluded to in the last line of the chapter and that the grammatical subject of νοεῖ is "the individual" in line 21. This grammatical subject is extensionally equivalent to 'the composite' or, more accurately, 'the soul' as subject of embodied discursive thinking and believing.[130] It is also equivalent to the passive intellect if we understand that as νοητικὴ ψυχή.

In further defense of this interpretation, recall that the entire theme of this chapter is how the principles of matter and agency operate *in the soul*. The soul does not think without images, and it does not think without intellect. Having images alone is not enough for thinking; otherwise, animals, which have images, would think.[131] What 'having intellect' amounts to for soul is being able to access the activity of intellect. This activity is accessed every time the soul is actually thinking, that is, every time the soul is self-reflexively aware of the presence of intelligible form in intellect via the

127. On any interpretation of intellect that takes its 'separation' to indicate that its status within soul is different from its status outside of soul, the change from not being separate to being separate is bound to be some sort of 'Cambridge change.' That is, after all, what 'unaffected' must imply.

128. Cf. A 4, 409b29.

129 See esp. Hicks 1907, 509.

130. Cf. 429a22–24, where the subject is the same.

131. Cf. *APo.* B 19, 1999b37–100a3, where animals without λόγοι are said to have no type of cognition or γνῶσις apart from sense perception.

soul's images.[132] The activity to which the soul has access is the awareness of being cognitively identical with all that is intelligible. The images that soul acquires and manipulates are like a partial template held up to intellect by soul. By these images, the soul is able to understand episodically and therefore be in a way self-reflexively aware of what it is that intellect is eternally identical with. It is also, again episodically, able to identify itself with the activity of intellect.

The idea that when soul thinks (always with images), it identifies itself with intellect (which is essentially imageless thinking) is most famously alluded to by Aristotle at the end of *Nicomachean Ethics,* where he extols the contemplative life.[133] Among other things, Aristotle there says that the activity of intellect is the divine part of the soul.[134] In engaging in this activity, we immortalize (ἀθανατίζειν) ourselves.[135] And each human being is this part especially (μάλιστα).[136] In thinking, we access a divine activity but we do not become God. Those who think that the agent intellect in Aristotle's chapter 5 is God must suppose that we access this activity when we think without doing what it is that the putative divine intellect that 'makes all things' does. That is, we must think without engaging in the activity that is actual thinking. Presumably, we would do this by accessing what intellect is thinking about 'through the back door': that is, by using or gazing upon the passive intellect in a way different from the way that the agent intellect acts upon the passive intellect. I cannot imagine what this is. But more important, this view falsely supposes that there is some way actually to think about intelligible form without being cognitively identical with that form: that is, without engaging in intellect's activity. But Aristotle repeatedly insists that thinking is cognitive identity.

Intellect is available as an instrument for soul because we are able to identify ourselves with intellect's activity. The ideal identity of a person is as an intellect. This identification is what the exhortation by Aristotle to "live according to the best part of the soul in us" amounts to.[137] It is not an exhortation to live according to the passive intellect, whatever that might mean. It is straightforwardly an exhortation to theoretical thinking, to identification with the activity of intellect, an activity that is unmixed with matter, and unaffected by anything that happens in imagination or sense perception, and separable from the composite. But even when soul is not engaged in the best kind of thinking—theoretical thinking—soul accesses intellect when it is engaged in any type of thinking. When, for example, soul has an occurrent belief, it must be self-reflexively aware of having this belief, that is, self-reflexively aware of

132. It is important to emphasize that the awareness of intelligible form is necessary for thinking. Otherwise, a parrot would be thinking when it accesses its own images.

133. *EN* K 7.

134. Ibid., 1177b26–31.

135. Ibid., 1177b33.

136. Ibid., 1178a2, 7; see also I 5, 1166a22, and I 8, 1169a2, which make the identical claim.

137. Ibid., 1177b34.

the mental state it is in, which includes the presence of representational images. Intellect's activity is the activity of what we are 'especially.'

An explicit statement of this particular facet of harmony is made by Pseudo-Simplicius at the end of his commentary on *De Anima*, Book Γ. The commentator—who holds not merely that Aristotle's doctrine is in harmony with Plato, but that Aristotle is the "best exegete of Plato"[138]—reflects on the meaning of the last three lines of our text:

> It is worth commenting on the whole argument by which he is encouraged to declare that the soul's substantial intellect [τὸν οὐσιώδη τῆς ψυχῆς νοῦν] is immortal and everlasting, so that thereby we may admire his harmony with Plato, and also his greater working of details, which Plato handed down in a more general and synoptic way appropriate to his earlier time. . .
>
> So Aristotle starts from here [what Plato calls the self-moving nature of the soul] and shows that the productive element [ποιητικόν] in the soul, which Plato himself had said was separable and impassible and unmixed, is a principle and a kind of being that is causal and of a higher status than matter and everything that comes into being . . .
>
> From there he takes its being non-material [ἄυλον] (for everything that is in matter is divisible) and active with respect to itself, and shows that everything non-material thinks itself. And when he has shown that it is simultaneously thinking and object of thought and simple, in so far as it does not think with a part of itself and is not being thought with another part, but that the whole of it does both, he shows that it is immortal and everlasting. For what is separate and simple and its own and gives itself life and perfects itself, in such a way that in its inclination to the outside secondary lives and beings gush forth, is shown to be not only capable of receiving death and destruction, but also to be predominantly the bearer of life and being [οὐσίας], and thereby immortal too.
>
> So the whole argument, to put it together concisely, is something like this: it is clear that the question is only about our soul. In our soul there is not only what is acted on but also what acts, the principle and the cause of the things that happen. Further what acts in the soul is able to think itself and unites its activity indivisibly with its substance . . .
>
> This, as we have said, is discussed by Aristotle entirely in harmony with Plato's exposition starting from the soul's being self-moved. . . . This then is, I think, clearly and necessarily concluded, that what only acts in the soul is immortal and everlasting. He has done well to add 'everlasting,' as Plato added 'indestructible' in the *Phaedo*. . . . But why "and this alone is everlasting"? It is because, as he indicates clearly, the possible intellect is perishable.

138. See Ps.-Simplicius *In de An.* 245, 12, for the remark on Aristotle's exegetical prowess. That most scholars today react derisively to this remark is, I think, only an indication of a difference in meaning of the term 'exegesis.' Ps.-Simplicius thinks that Aristotle is a great exegete of Plato in the same way that Proclus thinks that Plotinus is a great exegete of Plato—that is, of the truths revealed by Plato.

Someone might raise the question how that too, being intellect, is destroyed, if it, too, is non-material. For every kind of intellect is held to be non-material, and for this reason every kind of intellect is intelligible, but it is not also the case that a non-material form is also an intellect. The passible intellect is material and potential and precisely this, passible and imperfect intellect as a whole, so long as it is passible. And for this reason it is perishable and passible. It becomes non-material and intellect in act and intelligible in contact with what acts, perfectly non-material and perfect intellect in its ascent to the one that is active. . . .

And, as it were, objecting to the soul having been shown to be everlasting, he asks how we do not remember things before birth if it had previously existed everlastingly? By this it is clear again that his discussion is about the soul, and not about the higher intellect. For what sort of problem would he have had about why we do not remember, if it is the things superior to us that are everlasting? And the solution to the objection is appropriate to soul, namely, that the intellect that acts is impassible and for this reason immortal, while the passible intellect is perishable *qua* passible, as I said, as also when it is being brought together with what is at rest, and without the passible intellect, *qua* passible and proceeding as far as corporeal lives, the impassible intellect clearly thinks none of the things that can be remembered, which is what Aristotle is talking about.

Those things, as he himself teaches us elsewhere [*On Memory* 450a23–5], are things that can be imagined. Therefore in thinking about things that can be remembered we do certainly need the reason that proceeds as far as the imagination, and without this not even the impassible intellect will think any of the things that can be remembered. The 'nothing' must not be understood simply as meaning that the impassible intellect thinks nothing without the passible one. For how will it still be separate, how unmixed, how activity in its substance? For even while it is still giving life to this body, the soul sometimes lives and thinks separately. "What god is always," he says in the *Metaphysics* book Lambda, "that we are sometimes," clearly as far as our power allows.[139]

I have quoted the commentator at such unusual length for several reasons. First, this passage is a stellar piece of Neoplatonic commentary. It also provides an excellent example of how the harmony between Plato and Aristotle was understood. Finally, I quote it because I think that for the most part the commentator, whoever he might be, is essentially right in his interpretation. He is not like some contemporary commentators who, grudgingly admitting that chapter 5 is thoroughly dualistic and hence incompatible with hylomorphism, then go on simply to dismiss it because it does not fit in with their theory about the doctrine in the rest of the work.[140]

139. Ps.-Simplicius *In de An.* 246, 17–248, 16 excerpted (trans. Blumenthal). See Blumenthal 1991, 200–202, on this passage.
140. See, e.g., Wilkes 1992, esp. 125–127. Caston 1999, 224, suggests that if this chapter were to have dropped out of the text, we would not have "missed anything significant as regards the psychological *mechanisms* of thought." Instead, what these few lines are supposed to do is explain "how mind fits into the world and where it tends, and above all, how we, like the heavenly spheres, are moved in all we do through our imperfect imitation of God."

Among the salient features of this passage are (1) the claim that Aristotle's account of the immortality of intellect is substantially the same as Plato's account of the immortality of the soul, which in turn is assumed to be the same in *Phaedo* and *Phaedrus;* (2) the association of the incorporeality of intellect with self-reflexivity; (3) the insistence that the intellect under discussion is the individual intellect; (4) the explanation that memory depends on imagination and therefore that in the absence of that which makes imagination possible, memory is not possible, which is why we do not remember (but the commentator adds that "without this not even the impassible intellect will think any of the things that can be remembered"); (5) the clear inference that, since it is separate, intellect cannot engage in the sort of thinking that requires images, though it can nevertheless engage in some kind of thinking, similar to the thinking of the divine intellect.

Regarding (1), though Neoplatonists beginning with Plotinus were openly puzzled by many of the things Plato says about the soul, they were generally in agreement that *Timaeus* represents the correct and basic Platonic view: namely, that only intellect is immortal.[141] But intellect is evidently a part of the soul and cannot arise apart from soul.[142] So, the obscurity of the relation between intellect and soul is rooted in Plato's own account. This would not, however, be so much of a puzzle if we could locate the person or self or subject of mental and bodily states unambiguously in either the soul or the intellect. To put the matter in a slightly different way, is the immortality of my intellect the immortality of me, and if it is, in what sense am I identical with an embodied subject? Clearly, Plato does want to say that in some sense, the immortality of my soul—that is, the immortality of the part of my soul that is my intellect—is the immortality of me. But he is far from forthcoming about how the identical subject can be both nothing but a thinker and also the subject of embodied states. Plato's lack of clarity about these matters is undoubtedly to a certain extent responsible for the commentator's confidence that Aristotle is indeed in harmony with Plato. But it is also far from foolish to read Aristotle's words in a way that does make his position harmonious with Plato's.

In (2), the commentator demonstrates how Aristotle can be said without irony to be Plato's greatest exegete. The argument that self-reflexivity is a mark of the incorporeal intellect is a large and central theme among Neoplatonists, especially the later Neoplatonists.[143] It is not thematized in Aristotle, nor is there a technical term for it, but as we have seen, there are good

---

141. See *Tim.* 41C-D, 61C7, 65A5, 69C8-D1, 72D4-E1, 73D3. In none of these passages is the term 'intellect' used for the 'immortal part' of the soul, though that is the clear implication. See *Phd.* 78B4-84B4; *Rep.* 608D-612A. Themistius *In de An.* 106, 14-107, 29 explicitly identifies the intellect in *Timaeus* with the agent intellect in chap. 5 of *De Anima.* See Proclus *In Tim.* III 234, 8-235, 9, and Damascius *In Phd.* 1, 177, who record the Neoplatonic debate over whether only the rational part of the soul was immortal or both the rational and some irrational part. The latter minority view was evidently held by Iamblichus and Plutarch of Athens.

142. See *Tim.* 30B, 46D5-6; *Phil.* 30C; *Soph.* 249A.

143. See Gerson 1997.

grounds for interpreting his argument in chapters 4 and 5 of Book Γ as using self-reflexivity to show that intellect is incorporeal. What is striking about the commentary quoted above is the assumption that Aristotle is revealing what is implicit in Plato's argument for the incorporeality and hence immortality of the soul.[144]

The basic distinction that Aristotle employs between the presence of the intelligible form in the intellect and its actualization is taken directly from Plato. In *Theaetetus* Socrates makes the distinction between possessing (κεκτῆσθαι) knowledge and having (ἔχειν) it.[145] This is apparently the distinction between the presence of what is known and the actual awareness of the presence, though Plato has no word for 'actualization.' This distinction is made on behalf of the attempt to give a general account of false belief, an attempt that finally fails. But if mere possessing of what is known were knowledge in the proper sense, then false belief would be logically impossible or at least no different from ignorance. Still, even if we grant that the basic distinction between possessing and having knowledge in *Theaetetus* contains the core of the idea of self-reflexivity, this dialogue says nothing about the connection between self-reflexivity and incorporeality. We need to turn to *Phaedo* for that.

The so-called recollection argument for the immortality of the soul in *Phaedo* notoriously claims that we had knowledge of Forms prior to our embodiment.[146] The so-called affinity argument claims that knowers such as ourselves must be like the incorporeal and hence immutable entities that they know.[147] I have elsewhere undertaken a detailed analysis of these two arguments, so I shall not do so here.[148] Two points about these arguments are relevant here. First, whether or not it is possible, according to Plato, to obtain knowledge of Forms while embodied, the knowledge we possess in the embodied state prior to recollection is not occurrent and is not knowledge in the primary sense; it is like possessing but not having the knowledge or, as Aristotle puts it, possessing it but not using it. Second, it is only something that is separate and incorporeal, as Forms are supposed to be, that can know them. Despite the fairly widespread view that the affinity argument is embarrassingly weak, Plato can be seen to be making a shrewd intuitive leap in supposing that knowledge is possible only for

144. Cf. the famous passage at *GA* B 3, 736b27–29: "It remains, then, for intellect alone to enter from outside and alone to be divine. For no corporeal activity has any connection with its activity" (λείπεται δὴ τὸν νοῦν μόνον θύραθεν ἐπεισιέναι καὶ θεῖον εἶναι μόνον· οὐθὲν γὰρ αὐτοῦ τῇ ἐνεργείᾳ κοινωνεῖ ἡ σωματικὴ ἐνέργεια). See Moraux 1942, 94–108 and Moraux 1955 on this passage, esp. as it is understood by Alexander of Aphrodisias. Moraux claims that in Alexander's acceptance of the divinity of intellect, despite his odd interpretation, "il se montre partisan d'un illuminisme étranger à la philosophie d'Aristote et fortement apparenté au platonisme" (95). Also see Sharples 1987, 1204–1214.

145. See *Tht.* 197B–C.
146. The entire argument occurs at 72E3–78B3.
147. The affinity argument occurs at 78B4–84B4.
148. See Gerson 2003, chap. 2.

incorporeal entities. The basis for the intuition is the idea that knowledge is essentially a self-reflexive state.[149] This is the state of the disembodied knower prior to embodiment. The supposition that knowledge is only possible for incorporeal entities is of a piece with Plato's argument in *Republic* that knowledge is only *of* incorporeal entities.[150] The Neoplatonic observation of Aristotle's exegetical prowess grows in weight in my view in the light of these considerations.

Regarding (3), much of the discussion of chapter 5 founders on explaining the disquieting duplication of intellects that the text seems to endorse. It is difficult enough one might have supposed, to identify or at least correlate me as the subject of bodily states with *one* intellect. If the 'passive' intellect is assumed to be me or mine, then the 'active' intellect is a very good candidate for an 'I-know-not-what.' It would seem that the Peripatetic view, beginning with Alexander of Aphrodisias, that the agent intellect is identical with the divine intellect is based precisely on a inability to see what else it could be identified with.[151] Pseudo-Simplicius, by contrast, has no difficulty following the plain sense of the text, which is that the two principles 'in the soul' (ἐν τῇ ψυχῇ) are in the individual human soul, which is, after all, the subject of the entire section of the third book.[152]

Assuming that it is one individual soul that is being discussed, the commentator gives an unforced reading to the words "we do not remember" (4). To take these words as referring to our inability to remember *embodied* experiences is implausible in the extreme, though this fact has not prevented scholars from opting for this interpretation at the same time as they

149. This idea makes its way into contemporary epistemology as the claim that 's knows p' entails and is entailed by 's knows that s knows p.' Though this claim is not universally endorsed, even those who do endorse it typically do not infer from the claim the conclusion that if knowledge is to be possible for s, then 's' must stand for an incorporeal entity. But if s is *not* an incorporeal entity, then in what sense does 's' stand for the same entity in both occurrences in 'sKsKp'?

150. See *Rep.* 476A9–480B12 and Gerson 2003, chap. 4. If knowledge (ἐπιστήμη) is only of incorporeal entities, then we should not suppose the objects of knowledge to be propositions. Thus, non-propositional knowledge amounts to the presence of the knowable in the intellect plus the awareness of the presence. Presumably, for a disembodied intellect there is no presence without awareness of presence and vice versa.

151. See Alexander of Aphrodisias *De An.* 89, 16–18, and Moraux 1942, 97–99. Cf. Themistius (*In de An.* 102, 30–103, 19), who caustically criticizes Alexander's view. Themistius goes on to argue (103, 21–105, 12) for the unity of the agent intellect in separation from the individual human being. His argument is that there is no way to individuate a multiplicity of incorporeal intellects. But the putative multiplicity is not a multiplicity of perfect actualities. If the perfect actuality that is the prime unmoved mover is unique, then there must be some potentiality in each of the multiplicity. It seems to beg the question to assume that this potentiality must be corporeal. Among the modern scholars who have followed Alexander are Clark 1975, 174ff.; Guthrie 1981, 309–327; Rist 1989, 181–182; Caston 1999, esp. 211–212.

152. Plotinus IV 8. 8, 1–3, notoriously held that a part of intellect does not 'descend' but remains in the intelligible world. Later Neoplatonists generally rejected this view. See, e.g., Proclus *In Parm.* 948, 13ff. Ps.-Philoponus *In de An.* 535, 5–539, 10 attacks Plotinus as well and allies himself with the view of Plutarch of Athens that the individual intellect is in focus here.

recognize its implausibility.[153] Pseudo-Simplicius takes the words to indicate the fundamental difference between us in the disembodied and
embodied states and to be giving the reason—though there is a sort of identity between the two states—that identity is not memorial.[154] On the
assumption that Plato maintained that genuine knowledge is only occurrently available to us in the disembodied state, the claim in *Phaedo* that we
can recollect is not a contradiction of this. It is the claim that if we had not
had knowledge of Forms in the disembodied state, we would not be able to
make the judgments about the sensible world that we do, however we characterize these judgments cognitively.

That brings us to (5) and the subject of the verb 'thinks' in the two claims
"but it is not the case that [?] thinks sometimes and does not think sometimes" and "without this [?] thinks nothing." In the first, Pseudo-Simplicius
apparently has a text without the negative so that it says "it sometimes thinks
and sometimes does not," in which case the subject must be the one intellect that is ours. This line then would be addressing the question (raised just
above at 4, 430a5–6) of why thinking is not everlasting (ἀεί). But the textual problem is not an insuperable impediment to understanding the meaning of the passage. If we read "but it is not the case that [?] thinks sometimes
and does not think sometimes," Aristotle is still referring to our intellect and
indicating that although our intellect is always active, we do not remember
the activity in which it engages independently of our imagination.[155] That
is, we do not remember how we think when we are disembodied. Indeed, *we*
do not think continuously. On this reading, the final words "without this [?]
thinks nothing" refer, as the commentator believes, to the fact that we do
not think without the passive principle, anticipating what is said in chapter
7, that the soul does not think without images.[156] But the operation of intellect apart from the embodied soul is different. That we do not remember
what it is like to be a disembodied thinker is a fairly safe claim. That the Platonic tradition could be said to be almost obsessed with trying to understand
what disembodied thinking is like, in a way that Aristotle plainly is not,
should not be taken to imply that what Aristotle does say is not in harmony
with that tradition.

153. See Hicks 1907, 507–508; Hamlyn and Shields 1993, 141. It is very hard to see how
this text can be plausibly interpreted as a parenthetical explanation of why we forget things,
since of course we also do remember things. The text, however, is unqualified: 'we do not
remember.'

154. Cf. Themistius *In de An.* 100, 37: ἡμεῖς οὖν ὁ ποιητικὸς νοῦς.

155. De Corte (1934, 65–73), understands the subject as τὸ νοοῦν κατ᾽ ἐνέργειαν. That
is, while the intellect passes from potency to actuality (and back), the intellect as active does
not. De Corte argues that the phrase ἀλλ᾽ οὐχ ὁτὲ μὲν νοεῖ ὁτὲ δ᾽ οὐ νοεῖ does not imply that
some intellect νοεῖ ἀεί.

156. See Blumenthal 1991, 197–199, 202–203, on the tendency of some Neoplatonists,
such as Proclus and Philoponus, to identify the passive intellect with imagination on the ground
that genuine intellect must not be passive at all because it is immortal. This is the view taken
up by Brentano 1867.

The next chapter of Book Γ is usually taken as a miscellany of remarks about thinking. It has never been noticed, so far as I know, that if one ends chapter 5 with the question "what is thinking like without images?" then the first sentence of chapter 6 is naturally taken to be an answer to that question: "the thinking (ἡ νόησις) of indivisibles (τῶν ἀδιαρέτων) is among things concerning which there can be no falsity."[157] We have already seen that discursive thinking (τὸ διανοεῖσθαι) can be true or false.[158] This would suggest that 'thinking' here refers to an activity other than discursive thinking, which leads to judgment. But knowledge (ἐπιστήμη) is also a form of judgment, and there can be no false knowledge. Nevertheless, knowledge does have a contrary, Aristotle says, and that is ignorance.[159] One reason judgment can be true or false is that it always involves some sort of combination or complexity of concepts (ἡ σύνθεσις τῶν νοημάτων).[160] So, it is supposed that the thinking of indivisibles is of indivisible concepts. Among these indivisibles are length, a species, a point, privations, and realities that have no contraries. At the end of this chapter Aristotle characterizes this thinking as about "the what is with respect to essence" (τοῦ τί ἐστι κατὰ τὸ τί ἦν εἶναι).[161] It is hard to see how an essence can be a simple concept, for Aristotle says that there is an "essence only of those things whose formula is a definition."[162] So, in thinking of an essence one would be thinking about the combination that is the formula.

Already in chapter 4, Aristotle had addressed the question of the cognition of essence:

Since there is a difference between magnitude and the essence of a magnitude, between water and the essence of water, and so too in many other cases, but not in all (for in some cases, a thing and its essence are the same), [intellect] discriminates between flesh and the essence of flesh either by different [faculties] or by the same [faculty] differently disposed towards them. For flesh exists not without matter but as this snubness in this [nose]. Accordingly, it is by the sentient faculty that [intellect] discriminates the hot and the cold and the things whose flesh is a certain ratio; but it is by a different faculty, one which is either separate or related to it as a bent line when straightened is to the bent line itself, that [intellect] discriminates the essence of flesh. Again, of things which exist by abstraction, the straight is like the snub, for it exists with that which is continuous; but its essence, if it is different from the straight, is discriminated by a [faculty] different from [that which discriminates the straight]. For let [the essence] of the straight be duality. Then [intellect] discriminates duality by a different [faculty] or else by the same [faculty that discriminates the straight]

157. *De An.* Γ 6, 430a26–27.
158. Ibid., Γ 3, 428a13: διανοεῖσθαι δ' ἐνδέχεται καὶ ψευδῶς.
159. See *APo.* A 16, 79b23–29, where Aristotle says that one may be ignorant by 'negation,' meaning that there is an absence of knowledge, or by 'disposition,' as when one has false belief about that of which one might have had true belief.
160. *De An.* Γ 6, 430a27–28. The combination refers to the activity of joining concepts, not to a logical joining. Cf. Γ 8, 432a11–12.
161. *De An.* Γ 6, 430b28.
162. Cf. *Met.* Z 4, 1030a6–7.

but when this faculty is differently disposed. In general, then, to the extent that things are separable from matter, so are those concerning the intellect.[163]

It is apparently intellect that operates either separately or in conjunction with sense perception. When it operates in conjunction with sense perception, it does so on the basis of images. When it does so separately, apparently it does so without images.[164]

We can get some assistance in the understanding of this passage from *Metaphysics*, Book Θ where Aristotle speaks about cognition of 'incomposites.'[165] One sort of incomposite about which there is no falsity is 'white' or 'wood' in contrast to 'white wood,' or 'incommensurable' and 'diagonal' in contrast to 'incommensurable diagonal.' It is clear enough here that incompositeness is relative, since wood, for example, is a certain kind of organic form in matter and so necessarily composite. The general point is that whereas a judgment that 'this wood is white' or 'the diagonal is incommensurable' are complex affirmations and are true (or possibly false in the case of the former), cognitions of 'wood,' 'diagonal,' and so on, are true in "another sense" for "truth about each of these is to have contact with it or to assert it" (τὸ μὲν θιγεῖν καὶ φάναι). Similar remarks may be made about incomposite substances (τὰς μὴ συνθετὰς οὐσίας).[166]

Returning to chapter 6 of *De Anima*, whatever exactly the indivisibles are, the thinking of them is not the thinking that is true or false: namely, judgment. Therefore, there are no good grounds for supposing that when in the next two chapters Aristotle says twice that there is no thinking without images, he means that to refer to the thinking of chapter 6.[167] There is no

163. *De An.* Γ 4, 429b10–22. At b13, 15, 17, and 21, modern commentators usually take the subject of κρίνει to be the human being, but b3 and b9 make it fairly clear that the subject must be νοῦς.

164. See Ps.-Simplicius *In de An.* 230, 34ff., and Themistius *In de An.* 96, 8–97, 7, esp. 19–21 where Themistius distinguishes intellection requiring images and intellection that does not. See also Lowe 1983, 115–119 (in reprint), though Lowe believes that the two sorts of thinking both require images, and Kahn 1992a, 370–372. Wedin 1988, 245–254, argues that all human thought require images. Since the productive mind is for Wedin an aspect of the human mind, he is led to deny that there is any (human) thinking at all without images. This is supposed by Wedin to be an anti-Platonic point. But Plato does not maintain that embodied persons think without images either. Aristotle seems to agree with Plato's view that what is true about our intellects is not identical with what is true about human beings. We are, when disembodied, identified with our intellects.

165. Cf. *Met.* Θ 10, 1051b17–1052a11, where the term is τὰ ἀσύνθετα rather than τὰ ἀδιαίρετα. These seem to be synonymous.

166. Jaeger 1948, 204–205, identifies the cognition of incomposites here as a "sort of intellectual vision" and claims that it "is the only remnant of Plato's contemplation of the Ideas that has survived in Aristotle's *Metaphysics*."

167. *De An.* Γ 7, 431a16–17, where we note that it is the soul that is said to need images, not intellect; Γ 8, 432a8–9. Berti 1978, 142ff., argues that since the soul never thinks without images, the cognition of indivisibles cannot be anything like an intuition of incorporeal entities. In fact, according to Berti (146), cognition of indivisibles is for Aristotle knowledge of universals—in particular, the essence of universals. But if this is so, it must be stipulated that universals are not νοητά, but νοήματα. or 'concepts.'

doubt a close connection between the two but little reason to suppose an identity. That a combination of νοήματα is required for true or false beliefs and that this combination is composed of πρῶτα νοήματα does not entail that the latter are the indivisibles that intellect thinks.[168] Rather, these indivisibles are the νοητά that intellect directly contacts.[169] Further, that it is intellect that combines νοήματα does not mean this is exclusively what intellect does.[170] The intellect by means of which we know and judge rightly is a "part of the soul" insofar as it is embodied, whereas the intellect that can exist separately belongs to a "γένος different from soul."[171]

One of the very striking features of this entire section is that Aristotle seems implicitly to correct Plato by making belief and knowledge species of the same genus, namely, judgment. The term 'judgment' (ὑπόληψις) is Aristotle's invention, and the generic unity of belief and knowledge seems to deny Plato's argument in *Republic* that knowledge and belief are mutually exclusive: that is, that there is no knowledge of the objects of belief and no belief of the objects of knowledge. But in addition to the present passage, there are a number of texts in Aristotle where he explicitly says that in some sense there can be belief about the proper objects of knowledge, though he never says that there can be knowledge of the proper objects of belief.[172]

Plato in *Republic* makes a clear distinction between knowledge and belief and their objects and sets these up on his famous divided line, but later he

168. See Ps.-Simplicius *In de An.* 248, 18–261, 32, where this interpretation is developed at some length. He distinguishes 'thinking' from 'psychic thinking.' See also Ps.-Philoponus *In de An.* 553, 19–554, 7, where the commentator distinguishes between intellect that is occupied with 'simples' or 'incomposites', and intellect—in the sense of discursive reasoning leading up to belief—that is occupied with 'composites.'

169. When Aristotle describes the functioning of intellect in *Met.* Λ, νοήματα have no part to play. See Λ 7, 1072b18–24.

170. *De An.* Γ 6, 430b5–6. Cf. Γ 4, 429a23. Themistius *In de An.* 114, 31–115, 9 argues that if the unmoved mover can think without images, then our intellect is capable of doing so as well. For the inferiority of our intellects in relation to that of the unmoved mover is not that the former cannot think incorporeal forms but that it cannot do so 'continuously and everlastingly' (συνεχῶς καὶ ἀεί).

171. See *De An.* Γ 4, 429a10–11, and n. 15 supra. Kahn 1992a, while rejecting the claim that Aristotle is a 'Cartesian dualist,' agrees that the definition of soul does not apply to intellect, which is incorporeal and separate. This seems to me to concede the only dualism that is relevant here, namely, Platonic dualism. Kahn further argues (362–363) that the need for images is a need only for thinking in the sense of discursive thinking and belief. It is not needed by separate intellect. At *Met.* Λ 9, 1074a6–10, in a very difficult passage, Aristotle seems at least to envisage intellection of 'indivisibles' (ἀδιαίρετα) by human beings as well as by God, whose intellection is unqualifiedly without images. Brunschwig 2000, 298–301, argues that although the passage focuses on the difference between human and divine intellection, it presupposes that there is much in common between them. Wedin 1988, 220–245, argues at length against the 'isomorphism' of human and divine intellects.

172. See *Post. An.* A 33; *Met.* Z 15; *Met.* Θ 10, 1051b13–17. At *EN* Z 2, 1039a6–17, Aristotle distinguishes two different parts of the soul, the scientific (τὸ ἐπιστημονικόν) and the calculative (τὸ λογιστικόν), the first of which reasons about things which cannot be otherwise and the second of which reasons about contingent matters. It is the latter that is related to belief. Aristotle adds that these two parts are distinguished by a certain similarity and affinity (καθ' ὁμοιότητά τινα καὶ οἰκειότητα) for their objects.

claims that knowledge, strictly speaking, belongs only to the top segment of the top section of the divided line. That is, knowledge is, strictly speaking, only 'thinking' (νόησις) as opposed to discursive thinking.[173] And that is achieved without images.

What Aristotle has done is to take the term 'knowledge' as one achievement of discursive thinking and reserve the term 'thinking' for something else, that which he discusses in chapters 5 and 6. What Aristotle would call knowledge, Neoplatonists understand Plato to call 'discursive thinking' (διάνοια) because it involves propositions and hence images of ultimate reality. One must not suppose that for Plato, cognizing a proposition such as "sugar is soluble in water" or "the diagonal is incommensurable with the side of the square" could possibly represent the highest form of cognition for the simple reason that cognizing these involves images, specifically the words or thoughts out of which the propositions are made. When Aristotle says that images are essential for thinking, he appears to be saying exactly what Plato says when he insists that discursive thinking requires images. Aristotle is referring to the kind of thinking that is discursive thinking and that, for him, includes knowledge as one form of judgment. The thinking that involves no images is exactly like the thinking that is found at the top of the divided line.

Whether or not such thinking is available to embodied human beings, the paradigmatic thinker, the Demiurge, is a disembodied intellect. Disembodied intellection is according to Aristotle not just what the prime unmoved mover does but also what *we* do insofar as we are identifiable with the activity of our own intellects. This identification (discussed further in my chapter eight) is not merely an ideal but is the condition for the possibility of thinking with images: that is, for the possibility of higher cognition altogether. The Neoplatonists who saw Aristotle in harmony with Plato in regard to the intellect were not, it seems, far off the mark.

---

173. See *Rep.* 533D-E. On imageless thought in Plato, see 510B, 511C, and 532A.

CHAPTER SIX

Aristotle's Metaphysics

If one were to undertake even a casual investigation of the reception of Aristotle's *Metaphysics* in the ancient philosophical world, one would perhaps be surprised at how little influence that work appears to have had. Indeed, one would be hard pressed to point to anyone over a period of some five hundred years who could be said to have had a passable understanding of it.[1] It is only beginning with the great commentator Alexander of Aphrodisias that serious study of *Metaphysics* can be dated. After Alexander, the study of that work or, more accurately, of that collection of λόγοι or treatises that came to be known as τὰ μετὰ τὰ φυσικά, was largely in the hands of Neoplatonists. Porphyry tells us in his *Life of Plotinus* that his *Enneads* are "full of concealed (λανθάνοντα) Stoic and Peripatetic doctrines" and that, "in particular, Aristotle's *Metaphysics* is concentrated (καταπεπύκνωται) in them."[2] A measure of that concentration may be found in the some 150 direct references in *Enneads* to that work as listed in the *index fontium* of the edition of Henry and Schwyzer. That there are in addition countless indirect references is beyond doubt. After Plotinus, and up until the Middle Ages, virtually all treatment of *Metaphysics*, whether through commentary or in doctrinal studies, belongs within the Neoplatonic tradition.

---

1. See Wehrli 1974, where one will find among those identified as 'Peripatetics' few and mostly unedifying references to *Metaphysics*.

2. See *Life of Plotinus* 14, 4ff. Since Plotinus is a resolute opponent of both the Stoics and the Peripatetics, 'concealed' should not be taken to mean that he was surreptitiously advancing the opinions of these schools. The point is more subtle. Plotinus incorporates Stoic and Peripatetic doctrines where and when he thinks they are in harmony with Plato. For Plotinus, unlike many of his successors, harmonization is implicit and is accompanied by criticism, even severe criticism in many places.

Unlike *Categories*, where, given a few reasonable assumptions, harmonization is not exceptionally difficult to maintain, matters seem to be quite different with *Metaphysics*. For there Aristotle argues strenuously against what he takes to be Plato's version of the science that he, Aristotle, is trying to construct. He rejects various theories of Forms and theories of the reduction of Forms to first principles. He offers an argument for the existence and nature of an unmoved mover that seems deeply un-Platonic. In short, he seems to reject the fundamentals of Plato's account of the intelligible world. It is hard to see how attempts at harmonization could possibly succeed. In fact, the apparent implausibility of the harmonization principle is behind many interpretations of the science proposed in *Metaphysics*. These interpretations seek to understand Aristotelian metaphysics as essentially anti-Platonic. Part of what I aim to show in this chapter is that such anti-Platonic interpretations of *Metaphysics* are incoherent and unsustainable.

The Shape and Theme of *Metaphysics*

The relative disunity of the fourteen books that have come down to us under the title *Metaphysics* has been studied for a long time.[3] Leaving aside the vexed issue of the chronology of the λόγοι that make up *Metaphysics*, the "methodological sequence of the treatise," as Joseph Owens put it, is not impossibly obscure.[4] Book A contains the first treatment of the entire work's subject. Books B, Γ, and E 1 follow the first book. Together A, B, Γ, and E 1 provide a sort of introductory treatment to the science that in A is termed "wisdom regarding first principles and causes"[5] and in E 1 is termed variously "first philosophy," "theology," and a science of "being *qua* being."[6] The little treatise E 2–4 and the central Books Z, H, and Θ 1–9 seem to follow upon Book Δ, thereby introducing a new thread of investigation of the same science described in A–E 1. The short treatise Θ 10 contains a relatively independent treatment of being in one sense. Book I and M 1–9 seem to presuppose both B and Z, thereby uniting the two streams A–E 1 and E 2–Θ 10. The treatise M 9 (1086a21ff) -10 seems to refer both to A and to Z. Book K seems to be a summary of material in B, Γ, and E. Book α seems to be an independent introduction to theoretical philosophy in general and the science of separate substance in particular. Its designation as α indicates its late insertion into the main grouping. The first five chapters of Book Λ parallel the treatment of substance in ZHΘ. The remainder of the book is a treatise on separate substance. It seems quite unconnected with the central threads of argument. Book N seems to be an independent treatise dealing mainly with Plato's theory of principles.

3. See Brandis 1834; Bonitz 1848, 3–35; Jaeger 1912, chaps. 7–8; Owens 1951, 69–106.
4. See Owens 1951, 83–92.
.5. See *Met.* A 1, 982a1–3: ὅτι μὲν οὖν ἡ σοφία περί τινας ἀρχὰς καὶ αἰτίας ἐστὶν ἐπιστήμη δῆλον.
6. See Ibid., E 1, 1026a10–32.

Historically, the most contentious issue arising with regard to the methodological sequence is the status of Book Λ. As mentioned above, one of the names for the science Aristotle is developing is 'theology,' and so *prima facie* it is not at all surprising that Λ 6–10, a treatise on theology, should be a part of the main argument, even if it is inserted obliquely, so to speak. But the contention arises because it is difficult to see precisely how this treatise carries forward the argument of A–E 1 and E 2–Θ. Indeed, because it is so difficult to see this, it is tempting to separate the theology of Λ and make it the basis for a science different from the one described in the main sequence. In effect, it is assumed that causes and principles or being *qua* being can be studied apart from theology. But this leaves entirely opaque the sense in which the science of causes and principles and being *qua* being is identified by Aristotle with theology. The point is simply that there is no positive reason for supposing that the science of causes and principles and being *qua* being is anything but theology. There is only the negative reason that the only coherent treatment of theology by Aristotle does not obviously 'fit in' with the science described in these other ways.

One passage, sometimes ignored and sometimes very oddly understood, is crucial to the construction of Aristotle's scientific program. At the end of E 1, we read,

> One might raise the question whether first philosophy is universal or whether it concerns some one genus or nature. For mathematical science does not treat all its objects in the same manner; geometry and astronomy are each concerned with a particular nature, while universal mathematics is common to all. So, if there is no other substance (οὐσία) besides those that exist by nature, natural science would be first science. If there is some immovable substance, this would be prior, and the science of it would be first philosophy, and first philosophy would be universal in this way because it is first. And it would be the concern of this science to study being *qua* being, both what it is and what belongs to it *qua* being.[7]

On the face of it, this passage seems to say something quite unbelievable. It seems to say that if God or the gods—immovable substances—do not exist, then physics would be first philosophy. Physics, for Aristotle, is the study of the movable *qua* movable.[8] Why, we may well ask, could there not be a science

---

7. Ibid., E 1, 1026a23–32. Cf. the doublet at K 7, 1064b6–14. See Owens (1951, 295–298), who stresses the 'Platonic background' of the conception of being here. "Being and Entity are apparently conceived—somewhat as in Plato—in terms of permanence and unchangeableness" (298). The word 'background' seems to be the most popular one among scholars for indicating that Aristotle is saying Platonic things but that he is not really committed to the things he says.

8. *Met.* E 1, 1026a12. At *Phys.* B 7, 198a29–31, Aristotle distinguishes on the one hand a science of immovables and *two* sciences of movables, one for indestructible movables (i.e., astronomy) and one for destructible movables. This would suggest that Aristotle has in mind 'universal physics' corresponding to 'universal mathematics' and that the hypothetical point that without the existence of immovable substances physics would be first philosophy refers to universal physics.

of being *qua* being independent of the science of movables *qua* movables even if immovables do not exist? Just as mathematics studies movables *qua* immovable, that is, in abstraction from their movability, so the putative science would study movables *qua* their being in abstraction from their movability. In fact, it is very widely supposed that Books ZHΘ do precisely that.[9]

For example, Terence Irwin argues that if first philosophy is theology and studies being *qua* being, then in addition to studying being *qua* being, it will have special objects of its own to study. But from this "it does not follow that (1) being *qua* being is eternal and separable or (2) that the content of the science of being *qua* being depends on whether there are special objects for theology or (3) that the proper study of beings *qua* beings requires study of them *qua* eternal and incorporeal beings. If there were no beings higher than natural beings, then physics would be the primary science. There would still be a universal science; but since there would be no special beings with only the properties of being *qua* being, the universal science of being could not completely describe any actual beings, but would be a part of physics."[10]

The proper interpretation of this very contentious and much-discussed passage turns upon an ambiguity in the sentence, "If there is no other substance (οὐσία) besides those that exist by nature, natural science would be first science." Irwin and others take the sentence to imply that if immovable substances did not exist, then not only would natural science be the first science, but it would therefore be a *different* science: that is, it would include the science of being *qua* being as a part of it. This is by no means the only possibility. For the sentence might be taken to assert simply that if immovable substances did not exist, then natural science as presently constituted—that is, as the science of movables *qua* movable and *not* the science of being *qua* being—would be the first science. What leads scholars to reject this straightforward reading is that it would seem to leave entirely unclear where the science of being *qua* being would in that case be found. Would not such a science have to be part of physics, since it would not be the science of immovable substances?

The answer to this objection to the second reading is that since Aristotle holds that the existence of immovable substance or substances can be shown to be a necessary truth, only impossibilities follow from its denial. That is,

---

9. Jaeger 1948, 217–219, attempts to solve the problem by suggesting that 1026a26–32 belongs to an earlier—that is, theological—phase of the ultimate science, *before* it became identified with the science of being *qua* being. Jaeger's reasoning is circular: the science of being *qua* being must be a nontheological science; therefore, the identification of the two cannot be true. See Patzig 1961, 35–37, for a related refutation of Jaeger's view. Wedin 2000, e.g., takes the science of being *qua* being to be exclusively identifiable with the study of sensible substance in ZHΘ. This science is, according to Wedin, an alternative to Plato's theory of Forms. Reeve 2000, 279, assuming that the science of being *qua* being cannot be theology, suggests that 1026a29 ("if there is an immovable substance, it would be prior and [the science] of it would be prior and first philosophy") is a 'slip' not intended by Aristotle.

10. See Irwin 1988, 544 n. 42. Kirwan (1993, 188–189), holds much the same view.

one does not have to find a notional or hypothetical subject for the science of being *qua* being on the assumption that the necessarily existing subject of this science does not exist. We should, I believe, understand the ambiguous sentence as claiming that if immovable substance does not exist, then *per impossibile* the first science would be the science of movables (of course), and there would be no separate science of being *qua* being. One does not have to show how physics could be that science, since this is an impossibility. That is, showing that physics is or contains the science of being *qua* being involves showing something that would follow from the opposite of a necessary truth—namely, a necessary falsehood. Nothing can or needs to be shown in this way. The intuitive plausibility of supposing that if the only things that exist are movables, there could naturally be a science of their being as opposed to a science of their movability is illusory.[11]

If what I have called the straightforward reading of this passage is correct, then when Aristotle says at the beginning of Book Z that the question "what is being is just the question what is substance," he is presuming that this question must be answered 'theologically', so to speak.[12] Accordingly, all the discussion to follow throughout ZHΘ about sensible substance is undertaken with a view to understanding the absolutely primary focus of the science of being *qua* being, immovable substance. This is what Aristotle says a bit later, indicating that he is studying sensible substance because it is the natural starting point for reaching immovable and, therefore, nonsensible substance.[13]

It should be clear that this reading of the disputed passage in Book E is in general congenial to Neoplatonists.[14] It is a reading that supports Simplicius's observation that Aristotle understands intelligible reality on the basis of the principles of sensible reality. That he so proceeds does not gainsay the priority in reality of the intelligible to the sensible. Still, it will be urged that harmony is here maintained at the cost of triviality, for the manner in which Aristotle holds the intelligible to be prior to the sensible is significantly different from the way Plato does that. We need to complete the picture of the basic structure of *Metaphysics* to see that the harmony principle is anything but trivial.

The methodological unity of the main sequence of *Metaphysics* includes the claim that by studying immovable substance, we understand being *qua* being. Immovable substance is the explanatory focus of the fledgling science. In Book Γ Aristotle famously suggests that 'being' is a term that must

11. This conclusion is basically shared by Owens 1951, 298–300; Kahn 1985a; Frede 1987; Reeve 2000, 287, though Reeve implicitly denies this, when he argues (299) that "Aristotle has provided us with a recipe for constructing a naturalistic and Godless primary science on his behalf."

12. See *Met.* Z 1, 1028b1–3.

13. See ibid., Z 3, 1029a33, b3–12; Z 11, 1037a13–17; Z 17, 1041a6–9.

14. See, e.g., Asclepius *In Met.* 358, 23–25; 364, 21ff. Also see Merlan 1953, esp. 140–177, on the essential unity of the theological orientation of Aristotle's metaphysics with the science of being *qua* being.

be understood neither synonymously nor homonymously in all its uses, but rather, like 'health,' it needs to be understood πρὸς ἕν.[15] In addition, "in every case a science is concerned mainly (κυρίως) with what is first, both in the sense of that on which everything else depends (ἤρτηται) and that owing to which everything else is named. Accordingly, if this is substance, it is of substances that the philosopher should possess the principles and causes.[16]

If one were to read the passage from Γ in isolation, one might suppose that the substance on which "everything else depends" is the individual sensible substance that is the focus of investigation in *Categories*. In fact, reading the passage in the light of *Categories* alone seems a good deal less reasonable than reading it in the light of other programmatic parts of *Metaphysics*, including Book E. That is precisely what the Neoplatonists did. They inferred that "that upon which everything else depends" is the object of the science that is called 'theology.' In Book Λ that is what Aristotle says: "Such then, is the principle upon which depends (ἤρτηται) the heaven and nature."[17] That the dependence is causal is also not in question. The primary focus of the science is the primary cause.

A puzzle, however, remains. The passage from Book Γ focuses on substance that has "principles and causes," whereas in Book Λ the unqualifiedly primary substance, "that upon which everything depends," does not *have* principles and causes; rather, it is itself a principle and cause. Even if Book Γ is, for this reason, thought to look forward to Book ZHΘ, and not Book Λ, nevertheless the substances that have principles and causes will be dependent on that which is a principle and cause.[18]

Alexander of Aphrodisias, the Peripatetic commentator most assiduously studied by Plotinus, seems to have simply assumed that the dependence of the focus of the science of being is causal:

> And there will, then, be one science of all being, since being is of the same nature, but this science will be in the highest degree involved with the primary being, that which is being in the most proper sense, on account of which other things are beings. People say that substance is such a thing, for the being of other things depends on substance, and it is on account of substance that they too are beings. So the philosopher, whose treatise is concerned with

15. See *Met.* Γ 2, 1003a33–b22. Alexander of Aphrodisias (*In Met.*, 246, 10–13) explicitly connects this passage with ει, 1026a 23–32.

16. Ibid., 1003b16–19.

17. Ibid., Λ 7, 1072b14.

18. Cf. Ibid., Γ 3, 1005a33–b1: "But since there is a scientist who is yet above the physicist (for nature is only one genus of being), the inquiry into these axioms, too, should belong to him who investigates universally and about first substances" (ἐπεὶ δ᾽ ἔστιν ἔτι τοῦ φυσικοῦ τις ἀνωτέρω (ἓν γάρ τι γένος τοῦ ὄντος ἡ φύσις), τοῦ καθόλου καὶ τοῦ περὶ τὴν πρώτην οὐσίαν θεωρητικοῦ καὶ ἡ περὶ τούτων ἂν εἴη σκέψις). See Syrianus (*In Met.* 57, 22ff.), who connects the study of substances with principles and causes and the study of substances that are principles and causes via the unity of theoretical science. Cf. Asclepius *In Met.* 231, 22–232, 11. See Patzig 1961, 43–46, for a succinct modern statement of this interpretation.

being insofar as it is being, has to inquire after the principles and causes of substances. For the principles of substance would be the principles of all beings, given that substance is the principle and cause of the being of the other things.[19]

We should not suppose that the dependence of all things on substance for their 'being' (εἶναι) means primarily or exclusively existential dependence. The claim is perfectly general: substance is the principle (ἀρχή) and cause (αἰτία) of the being of other things. That is, regarding anything about whose being one can intelligibly ask for its principle or cause, substance will be the answer.

Although the claim about types of dependence is general, one might suppose that the ambit of items covered by the claim is limited. Again, drawing on *Categories,* one might suppose that since substances themselves are "neither said of nor present in" and are therefore ontologically basic, they cannot be included in the scope of the claim. That is, what Aristotle means to assert is that the dependence of everything that is not a substance is to be explained causally by a substance, but substances themselves do not similarly require such explanation. In that case, dependence is entirely within a type of substance: sensible attributes are explained by sensible substances, and, supposing that supersensible substances exist, they are the principles and causes of their own attributes.

In Book Γ, Aristotle continues his discussion of the science of being: "For each genus of things there is both one power of sense perception and one science; grammar, for example, which is one science, investigates all kinds of speech. Accordingly, it belongs to one generic science to investigate all kinds of being,[20] and for each specific kind of being, it belongs to one specific science to investigate it."[21] This passage may seem to make matters worse. If we take theology as the science of being *qua* being and therefore as the science that studies "all kinds of being," then this passage seems to count 'theology' twice. That is, theology would be both the science that studies being *qua* being and the science that studies one kind of being: namely, supersensible or immovable being. But in fact, the passage in Book E resolves the difficulty. First philosophy is universal precisely because it studies one kind of substance, that which is absolutely prior: namely, the immovable. Upon what is this universality based? Not commonality, if the Γ passage is right that being is πρὸς ἕν. It is only the dependence of everything on what is first as cause and principle that preserves universality at all.

19. *In Met.* 244, 17–24 (trans. Madigan). Cf. 250, 26; 266, 10–13; 696, 31.

20. Aristotle goes on in Γ to give examples of the 'kinds of being': same/different; like/unlike; equal/unequal; motion/rest; genus/species; part/whole; prior/posterior, and so on. The later Neoplatonists did not fail to notice that these correspond, albeit roughly, to the list of contrarieties that are investigated in the second part of Plato's *Parmenides.*

21. *Met.* Γ 2, 1003b19–22 (trans. Madigan). The words τά τε εἴδη τῶν εἰδῶν are difficult. See Ross 1924, 1:257; Owens 1951, 275 and n. 55.

Alexander understands the passage in a slightly different way, wanting to maintain a residual conceptual distinction between first philosophy and theology:

> The things said have shown that the division of being into genera, which he carried out in the *Categories*, belongs to first philosophy. At the same time, he has also indicated to us, through these considerations, how philosophy is one science: by being universal. Its species match the species of being. For its species are: first philosophy, which is called wisdom in the proper sense, being the science of things eternal, unmoved, and divine (while wisdom is universal and primary, given that it is concerned with being insofar as it is being, not with a kind of being; there are, under this, a kind of first philosophy concerned with the primary substances, and a natural philosophy concerned with natural things, in which there is motion and change, and there is a kind of philosophy which considers matters of action, for some beings are of this sort).[22]

As Alexander reads the words τὰ τε εἴδη τῶν εἰδῶν, Aristotle is distinguishing a kind of philosophy—namely, the study of immovable substances—from 'generic' philosophy, which studies being *qua* being. If, however, we advert to the claim that first philosophy is universal because it studies the immovable, there can *only* be a conceptual distinction between theology and the science of being *qua* being.

The mere apparent programmatic identification of theology with a science of being *qua* being might have been enough for the Neoplatonists, as it evidently is not for contemporary scholars. But in fact, there is considerably more textual support for that identification in *Metaphysics* as that collection of treatises has come down to them and us.

The Case of Alpha Elatton

As already mentioned, the relative independence of Book α of *Metaphysics* from the main methodological sequence has long been recognized. Its awkward fit, indicated alone by its label, and its disjointedness have even prompted some to doubt its authenticity.[23] But these doubts are largely based on circular reasoning: the work is not Aristotle's because it does not fit into our conception of Aristotle's philosophy as determined by a consideration of works other than the disputed one.[24] The typical strategy for accepting the likely authenticity of the treatise while isolating the 'true' doc-

22. *In Met.* 245, 33–246, 6 (trans. Madigan).
23. See, e.g., Jaeger (1948, 169), who rejects Aristotle's authorship of Book α, attributing it instead to Pasicles of Rhodes. Part of Jaeger's reason for rejecting the book's authenticity is that though it bears a strong resemblance to Aristotle's dialogue *Protrepticus*, Jaeger did not think it could be an early work of Aristotle. And since, owing to its Platonic orientation, it could not of course be a later work, it must be the work of another.
24. See Szlezák 1983, 221, and Berti 1983, 260–265 on the question of the authenticity of the treatise.

trinal content of *Metaphysics* against contamination by it is developmental-ist.[25] The Neoplatonists apparently considered the possibility of its inau-thenticity but thought on balance that it was a genuine work of Aristotle.[26] They eschewed developmentalist hypotheses, as we have seen. So, it fell to them to make Book α an integral part of the Aristotelianism that is in har-mony with Platonism.

Alpha Elatton begins with some generous and irenic remarks about "the investigation of truth" (ἡ περὶ τῆς ἀληθείας θεωρία). Aristotle sermonizes on the collaborative aspect of such investigation. No individual can grasp all truth, but in consort, philosophers can make substantial progress. Such a remark is entirely congenial to the Neoplatonic perception of Platonism. Even Plato himself could not grasp all truth, though he stood head and shoulders above anyone else. The commentators would see nothing here inconsistent with the assumption that Aristotle regarded himself as a part of that tradition.[27]

The next main point Aristotle makes is that philosophy is correctly called "knowledge of truth" (ἐπιστήμην τῆς ἀληθείας).[28] Specifically, it is theoretical knowledge of truth, as opposed to practical knowledge that aims at action. Aristotle now continues to explain what knowledge of truth consists in:

> But we cannot know what is true without knowing its cause. Of things to which the same predicate belongs (τὸ συνώνυμον), the one to which it belongs in the highest degree is that in virtue of which it belongs to the others. For exam-ple, fire is the hottest [of things called 'hot'], for fire is the cause of the hot-ness in the others. So, that is most true that is the cause of truth to whatever is posterior to it. Therefore, the principles of eternal things (τὰς τῶν ἀεὶ ὄντων ἀρχὰς) are necessarily eternally the truest, for they are not true merely at one time, nor is anything the cause of their being (αἴτιον τοῦ εἶναι); rather, they are the cause of the being of the other things. Accordingly, as each thing stands in respect to its being, so it stands in respect to its truth.[29]

If one reads this passage with the operating assumption that the mature Aristotle is an anti-Platonist, then one is going to be very tempted to assign the entire book to something like a Platonic phase of Aristotle's early

25. See, e.g., Berti 1983, 265ff. Developmentalist explanations for α include my own; see Gerson 1991.

26 See Asclepius (*In Met.* 4, 17–22; 113, 5–8), who is perhaps relying on the Peripatetic acceptance of authenticity. See Alexander of Aphrodisias *In Met.* 137, 2–3. Alexander goes on to stress the continuity with Book A.

27. When in *EN* A 6, 1096a16, as a preface to his criticism of Plato, Aristotle makes the famous remark "We love Plato and those in the Academy, but we love the truth even more," he says something that Neoplatonists would heartily endorse. Aristotle is here probably echoing Socrates' remark in *Phd* 91C: "Care little for Socrates, but greatly for the truth." Cf. *Rep.* 595C; *Phdr.* 275B-C.

28. *Met. α* 1, 993b20. See A 3, 983b2–4.

29. *Met., α* 1, 993b23–31.

development.[30] If, on the other hand, one does not make this rather gratuitous assumption, then the situation is different.

The claim that we do not know a truth without knowing its cause is thoroughly Aristotelian and is anticipated in *Metaphysics* itself in Book A.[31] It is, however, not entirely perspicuous. For in Book A, Aristotle also makes a distinction, familiar from *Posterior Analytics*, between knowing 'the fact' (τὸ ὅτι) and knowing 'the reason for the fact' (τὸ διότι).[32] This distinction suggests that it is possible to know *some* truths without knowing their cause: that is, without knowing their διότι. If this is so, then what does it mean to claim that "we cannot know what is true without knowing its cause"? One way of reconciling the claim with the distinction is to say something like the following. There are different types of knowing and different types of truth. One can know a truth in one sense of 'know' and one sense of 'truth' without, in another sense, knowing its cause. Knowing causes involves knowing truths in another sense; it involves knowing things that themselves do not have causes. These things or truths are somehow more ultimate. This way of interpreting the claim is in fact supported by the remainder of our passage and the remainder of the book. The interpretation assumes both epistemological and ontological gradings and the correlation of these. So, our passage goes on to claim that that which is most true (ἀληθέστατον) is the cause of 'posterior truths.'[33] The knowledge we may obtain of that which is most true is superior to what we may obtain of the posterior, caused truths.[34] One would, I think, have to find very strong reasons for rejecting the apparently deep Platonic orientation of these claims. Gradable cognition and gradable objects of cognition play a central role in Plato's philosophy.[35] But a number of other claims made in our passage actually go further.

First, Aristotle tells us that when predicates are applied synonymously to different things, that to which the predicate belongs in the highest degree is that in virtue of which it belongs to the others. That to which the predicate belongs in the highest degree is the cause of the being of the others. As Aristotle explains in *Organon*, τὸ συνώνυμον refers to predication where

---

30. See, e.g., Aubenque 1972, 60, "le témoin d'une phase encore platonicienne"; Ferrari 2002, 303: "L'impianto teorico generale del ragionamento aristotelico risulta dunque di matrice platonica, e in particolare esso sembra derivare dall metafisica contenuta nei libri centrali della *Repubblica*."

31. See *Met.* A 1, 982a2–3; A 2, 982a28–29, b1–3; A 3, 983a25–26. See also Alexander of Aphrodisias *In Met.* 147, 3–148, 12.

32. See *Met.* A 1, 981a27–30 and *APo.* A 13, 78a22. Also, *EE* A 6, 1216b39.

33. Jaeger in his edition of *Metaphysics* (1957), reads ἀληθέστερον instead of ἀληθέστατον with Alexander of Aphrodisias (*In Met.* 146, 22; 148, 23) and against all the manuscripts.

34. See *APo.* A 24, 85a21–24, where Aristotle states that we know each thing to a higher degree when we understand it in virtue of itself rather than in virtue of some other thing. That which is without a cause would be most knowable because there is nothing else in virtue of which it needs to be understood.

35. See esp. *Rep.* 476Aff. on the grading of cognition and being. Graded cognition follows graded being.

things have a name and definition in common.[36] By contrast, homonymy occurs when two things have only a name in common. Synonymy implies univocal predication. So, a genus is univocally predicable of all its species and a species is univocally predicable of all its individual members. But in our passage the univocity is *gradable*. Both fire and whatever is made hot by fire are correctly called 'hot' univocally or synonymously, but fire is 'hottest' because it is the cause of hotness in other things.[37]

The term 'gradable univocity' nicely glosses the term 'participation' as used by Plato. Thus in *Phaedo* we read, "It seems to me that if anything else is beautiful besides the beautiful itself, it is beautiful for no other reason at all other than it participates in that beautiful; and the same goes for all of them."[38] As Socrates goes on to assert in this passage, something other than the Form of Beauty is called 'beautiful' owing to the instrumentality of that Form.[39] It is difficult to fault the commentator Asclepius, who simply assumes that when Aristotle uses the term τὸ αὐτό to refer to that which is the cause of gradable univocity, he must be referring to Platonic Forms, or at least to that which is an 'intelligible' (τὸ νοητόν) or paradigmatic cause.[40]

Plato does not himself use the term 'synonymous' (τὸ συνώνυμον) to indicate predication of Form and participant. Part of the problem with which we and Neoplatonic commentators both have to struggle is that Aristotle typically casts his discussions of Plato and his other predecessors in his own technical language. Though it would be a mistake to suppose that this fact always guarantees distortion of representation, exegetical care and philosophical imagination are nevertheless indispensable tools for seeing clearly what is going on.

In Plato's *Parmenides*, Parmenides offers the young Socrates a principle for positing Forms: "Whenever many things seem to you to be large, it probably seems to you that there is, looking over all of them, one and the same Idea. Hence you think that Largeness is one thing."[41] This is a passage to which I return in the next chapter. Here I only want to stress that a three-fold distinction is being made: (1) that which is large; (2) that in the large

---

36. See *Cat.* 1a6; 3b7; *Top.* Δ 3, 123a28–29; Z 10, 148a24–25; H 4, 154a16–18.

37. The gradability of hotness must be distinguished from the degrees of hotness possessed by things made hot by fire. Degrees of hotness in this sense are discussed in *GC* B 7, 334b8ff. Fire is said to be hottest not because there is nothing hotter but because it is uniquely the cause of hotness in everything else.

38. *Phd.* 100C4–7 (trans. Gallop). Gradable univocity reflects the fact that Form and image are the same (ὅμοιον), though only the Form is 'itself in itself' (αὐτὸ καθ᾽ αὐτό) what its name names.

39. See 100D7–8. That a Form and a participant should be univocally called 'f' does not preclude the Form from being uniquely that which its name names. See on this point Nehemas 1979, 98–99.

40. See *In Met.* 119, 8–16.

41. *Parm.* 132A1–4. I am assuming, like most scholars, that Socrates' ready assent to this principle signals Plato's recognition that this is indeed the principle on the basis of which he argues for Forms. One can go on to argue either that the recognition of the principle dooms the theory of Forms or that it does not.

thing in virtue of which the predicate 'large' is correctly used of it; (3) the Idea of Largeness. In the next lines Parmenides uses the principle for generating what has become known as the Third Man Argument: "But if you consider in your intellect's eye Largeness itself and the other large things in the same way (ὡσαύτως), will not some other large appear, owing to which all of these will appear large."[42] This is not the place for a discussion of the third-man argument or the Neoplatonic analysis of it. What should draw our attention in the present context is that Plato himself seems to offer the basis for holding that predicates are applied synonymously—that is, univocally— to Form and participant. For just as it is univocity that leads Socrates to posit a Form in the first place, so it is an implied univocity of Form and participant that generates the putative vicious infinite regress.

Still, something does not seem quite right here. A building does *not* seem to be large in the same way that the Form of Largeness is large. True. But can we say the same thing about the largeness in the building and the largeness in the Form of Largeness?[43] Curiously, Aristotle himself is apparently puzzled about how to characterize predication of Form and participant. Alexander of Aphrodisias, in his commentary on *Metaphysics,* cites a great deal of Aristotle's work *On the Ideas.* In considering the argument that tries to establish Forms from relatives, Alexander reports Aristotle as making the distinction between synonymous and homonymous predication.[44] He then reports Aristotle arguing that a predicate such as 'equal' is homonymously predicated of the Form of Equality and of an equal thing.[45] This is so because the account or λόγος of the equality of equal things 'here below' is never received 'accurately' (ἀκριβῶς). What this means, roughly, is that if you were to give an account of the equality of two equal sticks or stones—to use the famous *Phaedo* example— you would necessarily include in that account elements that have nothing to do with equality: for example, that one stick is a foot long and the other stick is a foot long. That is how, after all, they got to be equal.

Immediately after this, however, Alexander adds: "Even if someone were to accept that the likeness is not homonymous with its pattern,[46] it still follows that these equal things are equal as likenesses of that which is strictly and truly equal. And if this is so, there is some equality itself in the principal sense (κυρίως), relative to which things here, as likenesses, are both produced and called equal, and this is an Idea, a pattern for those things which are produced relative to it."[47] It is not entirely clear whether the first sentence

---

42. 132A6–9.

43. See, e.g., *Phd.* 102D6–7 where it is asserted that neither the Form of Largeness nor the largeness in Simmias will ever permit the small.

44. *In Met.* 82, 1ff.

45. Ibid., 83, 6–10. Alexander actually says we predicate "the Equal itself" (τὸ ἴσον αὐτό) of things here, but he probably means the absolute nature of equality; otherwise, the argument from relatives would not be an argument that establishes Forms; it would be an argument that assumes Forms.

46. That is, it is synonymous.

47. *In Met.* 83, 12–17 (trans. Madigan).

is Alexander's addition or a quotation from Aristotle's *On the Ideas.* We can certainly understand that, on the basis of the *Parmenides* passage, both Aristotle and Alexander would hesitate to reject synonymy as applicable to Form and participant. The crucial point is that when we read Aristotle in *Metaphysics α* using synonymy to characterize eternal causes and that which they cause, we quite naturally take him to be *Platonizing.* But there is a deeper issue beyond a gentlemanly accord in language.

The reason Plato would hesitate to say that a building and the Form of Largeness are synonymously large is, as I have suggested, that they are not large in the same way. More precisely, if the Form of Largeness just is Largeness, then it is a kind of category mistake to call it 'large.' If the Form of Largeness is more than just Largeness, then perhaps it can properly be called 'large' but surely not in the way that anything else is large: that is, by having some specific quantity. Plato seems to face a dilemma in accounting for the manner in which the Form's name is predicated of it and its participants.[48]

It seems reasonable to ask, though, why Plato cannot have recourse to the very same distinction Aristotle employs in Book α. If something can be hot (synonymously) without being fire, why cannot something be large (synonymously) without being the Form of Largeness? It is clear that Aristotle doubts that the situations are parallel. In his *Topics* he averts on several occasions to a putative distinction between a Form and the nature that the Form's name names.[49] A Form of Human Being is immortal because it is a Form, but if the Form of Human Being is a human, then, since humans are mortal, it too will be mortal. So, the Form of Human Being would have to be immortal and mortal, which is impossible. What Aristotle seems to be assuming is that Plato cannot avail himself of a distinction between the Form and its nature such that one can say that it is possible that contradictory predicates such as 'immortal' and 'mortal' can apply alternately to the Form *qua* Form and the Form *qua* its nature. It is precisely such a distinction that would enable us to maintain synonymous application of predicates to the Form's nature and its participants, even as we maintain homonymous application of the same predicates to the Form itself and those participants.

Aristotle, however, has no difficulty in maintaining the distinction between fire and hotness that he disallows for the Form of Human Being and immortality. Something can be hot synonymously with fire without being fire (or on fire) because there is a real distinction between fire and its property hotness. What is the difference? Presumably, the difference is that

---

48. The modern discussion of the so-called self-predication of Forms begins with the seminal article of Vlastos in 1954 and proceeds apace to the present. Some useful discussions of the many versions of self-predication can be found in Patterson 1985, 65–81; Rickless 1998; Malcolm 1991; Nehemas 1998, 176–195; Silverman 2002, 110–114. The sense in which Form and image or instance can be the same yet ontologically different is well brought out in by Peterson 1973, 470. Thus, the Form is the nature that its name names, though there may be participants in it.

49. See *Top.* E 7, 137b3–13; Z 10, 148a15–22; H 4, 154a15–20.

fire is a natural element, composed of matter and form, whereas a Form is a putative intelligible entity. Real internal distinctions of the sort that Aristotle must maintain in order to carry out any complex analysis of sensibles are not held by him to be available within the intelligible or supersensible world. Even if Forms *did* exist, they would have to be nothing but what their names name. There could not be, for example, a Form of Human Being really distinct from its nature or from any other property that one might wish to posit for it in virtue of being a Form.

Aristotle nowhere argues for the rejection of real distinctions within intelligible entities. As we shall see later in this chapter, the Neoplatonic argument that Aristotle's incorporeal prime unmoved mover is irreducibly complex goes a long way toward blunting arguments against Forms based on a denial of real distinctions within intelligible entities.

The next major claim in our passage is that the principles of eternal things and things 'most true' are causes of the being of other things. The 'eternal things' are evidently eternal sensibles—that is, the heavenly bodies—which are in Book Λ contrasted with transitory sensibles, and their 'principles' are the unmoved movers.[50] The phrase 'cause of being' is fairly common in the Aristotelian *corpus*. It usually designates the formal cause or essence of a sensible composite. In Book H, Aristotle argues that "the substance is the cause of the being of each thing" (ἡ οὐσία αἰτία τοῦ εἶναι ἕκαστον).[51] Occasionally, the phrase is used of an efficient cause, as when Aristotle says that a father is the "cause of the being" of his children.[52] Once, it is used of the matter in a composite.[53] In his criticism of the doctrine of mathematical first principles, Aristotle says that for one who posits Ideas and claims that numbers are Ideas, these numbers are a kind of cause of being of other things.[54]

In our passage it is simply unclear how the principles of eternal things are supposed to be the causes of the being of noneternal things. That Aristotle's language and broad claims here are in general congenial to Platonism is hardly in doubt. According to Plato, the Form of the Good is the cause of the "being and knowability" of the other Forms, and the Demiurge is the cause of intelligibility in the sensible world.[55] The combined causality of the Good and the Demiurge is explicit.

But it will perhaps be said that in fact the manner according to which Aristotle later in *Metaphysics* understands the priority and causality of the

50. See *Met.* Λ 1, 1069a31, and Alexander of Aphrodisias *In Met.* 148, 22–149, 13.
51. *Met.* H 2, 1043a2–3. We find both αἰτία and αἴτιον τοῦ εἶναι used indifferently. See also Δ 8, 1017b15; Z 17, 1041b26–29; H 3, 1043b13–14 with 1043a2–3; H 6, 1045a8-b20; *APo.* B 1, 90a9–11; *De An.* B 4, 415b12–13.
52. See *EN* Θ 11, 1161a16; Θ 12, 1162a7; H 2, 1165a23.
53. See *Cael.* A 12, 283b5, and perhaps *Met.* B 4, 1000a16.
54. See *Met.* N 2, 1090a3–7.
55. See *Rep.* 509 A-B; *Tim.* 28C, 46E4, 47E4, 53B5. See also *Rep.* 511C3-E4 and 585B-D on ontological truth. See Routila 1969, 18–23; Aubenque 1972, 60–61; Szlezák 1994, esp. 225–227, for arguments for the Platonic character of Book α.

eternal to the noneternal is specifically anti-Platonic.[56] So, Aristotle's putative Platonism does not bear hardheaded scrutiny. Specifically, Aristotle will later argue against Plato that separating the οὐσία of a thing from it leads to absurdity. And so the phrase ἡ οὐσία αἰτία τοῦ εἶναι ἕκαστον cannot be understood in Book α to indicate anything that is in harmony with the view that separate Forms are the eternal causes of the being of other things.

The core of the reply to this objection is that Neoplatonists did not suppose that Forms understood or misunderstood as ultimate, isolated, nonliving first principles *could* be the causes of the being of anything. First, they did not believe that Forms were ultimate principles and they did not believe that Plato believed it either. Second, because they believed in intelligible complexity, they did not believe that Forms were isolated islands of intelligibility. Third, they did not believe that Forms existed independently of an eternal intellect.[57] And we shall see that they at least had some grounds for thinking that Plato did not believe this either. In short, the view that the general account in Book α, chapter 1 should not be taken as being in harmony with Platonism is based on a view of what Platonism is which the Neoplatonists rejected. In addition, what Aristotle rejects are misconceptions about Platonism. Forestalling the rejoinder that this is just wishful thinking on their part, the Neoplatonists would say that what Aristotle positively asserts about the intelligible world and its causality can be accommodated within Platonism. Nothing that is true in what he says contradicts Plato in this regard.

The remainder of Book α begins with the Platonic assertion "Moreover, it is clear that there is some [first] principle (ἀρχή τις) and that the causes of things are infinite neither in series nor in kind."[58] After having identified the science of truth with the science of causes, Aristotle proceeds to demonstrate that first causes exist. He shows that in the lines of material, formal, efficient, and final causality there must always be a first uncaused cause, both in kind and in number. The arguments that follow are based on the principles that (1) an actual infinity is impossible; (2) without a first, that is, uncaused cause, there is no cause; and (3) without a first cause, scientific knowledge is impossible.[59] It is no doubt tendentious to take 'first principle' in the Neoplatonic sense of 'first principle of all,' that upon which every-

56. See, e.g., Berti (1975, 241–250), who argues that while the prime unmoved mover is a cause of the being of everything, Aristotle's conception of being is different from Plato's or, more precisely, from the position that Aristotle attributes to Plato. Berti cites *Met.* B 4, 1001a9–12, where Aristotle says that Plato held that being is a distinct nature, something that Aristotle denies in claiming that being is "said in many ways." According to Berti (249), the prime unmoved mover, which is a final moving cause, is the cause in virtue of which everything has its matter: that is, it is the form conceived of in its achievement (ἐντελέχεια) (249).

57. See, e.g., Asclepius *In Met.* 165, 35–37: πρὸς τούτοις δέ φαμεν ὅτι καὶ νοηταὶ οὐσίαι ὑπάρχουσιν οἱ λόγοι οἱ παρὰ τῷ δημιουργῷ, καθ' οὓς λόγους ποιεῖ τε πάντα καὶ προάγει; and 166, 29–31.

58. *Met.* α 2, 994a1–3.

59. See *Met.* Λ 6, 1072a15–16, for the argument that if B causes C, and A causes B, then A is more truly the cause of C than is B.

thing else depends. It is tendentious, that is, only if one simply ignores *Metaphysics* Λ and Aristotle's description of the prime unmoved mover as the ἀρχή upon which the heavens and nature depend.[60] Aristotle was correct, so the Neoplatonists believed, to posit a single primary causal principle. He was mistaken in identifying it with an unmoved mover that is an eternal intellect. But this misidentification does not invalidate the basic principles or many of the conclusions Aristotle arrives at concerning the nature of this unmoved mover.

Book Λ, 6–10. Theology and Metaphysics

If one takes seriously the identification of a science of being *qua* being with theology, then one is at least bound to pay attention to the only reasonable facsimile of a treatise on theology in the Aristotelian corpus: Book Λ of *Metaphysics*. It is not my intention here to offer a full-fledged treatment of this marvelous and infuriating work. I propose rather to focus on the issue raised in the book which is undeniably crucial to the Neoplatonists' harmonization project: namely, Aristotle's account of the nature of God or the prime unmoved mover. Two features of this account are especially important. First, Aristotle argues that an unmoved mover is the first principle of all. Neoplatonists deny that the first principle of all can be the sort of thing Aristotle argues that the prime unmoved mover must be. Second, Aristotle famously characterizes the prime unmoved mover as "thinking thinking of thinking" (ἡ νόησις νοήσεως νόησις). Neoplatonists reject the interpretation of this phrase as implying that God thinks about nothing but the subject of thinking; rather, they argue, as do many after them, that in thinking about thinking, God thereby thinks all that is thinkable or intelligible. If this is so, then Aristotle's apparent rejection of various theories of Forms has to be seen in a new light. Specifically, what God thinks about may be justifiably understood to be nothing else but Plato's Forms correctly construed. If God's activity is understood in this way, Aristotle's failure to see clearly the necessity that the absolutely first principle of all must be absolutely simple does not prevent his mischaracterization of the first principle from being accepted as a true—that is, Platonic—characterization of the *second* principle. Not only is harmonization thereby confirmed, but the central impediment to harmonization—the apparent rejection of Forms—is appropriately dislodged.

These two features of Aristotle's account are closely connected. This is so because the reason Aristotle's God is unacceptable as a first principle of all is its complexity. This complexity is the complexity of thinking. For Neoplatonists, thinking is an essentially complex activity. So, if the prime unmoved mover is thinking at all, it cannot be the absolutely simple first principle. To show that God's thinking includes all that is intelligible is

---

60. *Met.* Λ 7, 1072b13–14. The word ἀρχή in 994a1 could perhaps be taken simply to mean 'beginning' or 'first' if read in isolation from the rest of *Metaphysics*, esp. Book Λ.

tantamount to establishing the basis for the complexity. For God cannot be unqualifiedly identical with all intelligible objects and be thinking about them at the same time. But even if it is true that all intelligibles are thought together as one simple object, the duality of subject and object of thinking is unavoidably complex.

Book Λ, chapters 1 to 5 constitute a summary treatment of sensible substances and their principles and causes. The connection between chapters 1–5 and the rest of Book Λ seems smooth enough. Chapter 1 proposes a study of three types of substance; chapters 1–5 discuss the first two types, and chapters 6–10 discuss the third. This suggests that Book Λ represents an independent and unified treatise on substance separate in composition but thematically in tune with Books ZHΘ and a continuation of the program set forth in Books A-E.[61]

At the beginning of chapter 6, Aristotle refers to chapter 1, where he had distinguished three types of substance: (1) sensible and perishable; (2) sensible and eternal (ἀΐδιος); and (3) unchangeable (ἀκίνητος). Some, says Aristotle, claim that the third class exists separately (χωριστήν). Among these, some distinguish Forms and mathematicals (e.g., Plato), some identify these (e.g., Xenocrates) some recognize only mathematicals (e.g., Speusippus).[62] The division is odd because Aristotle is going to argue in chapter 6 that there must exist some eternal and unchangeable substance.[63] Furthermore, such a substance must be incorporeal (ἄνευ ὕλης) *because* it is unchangeable: that is, perfectly actual.[64] And finally, Aristotle will conclude that the eternal and unchangeable substance is separate.[65] It is therefore strange for Aristotle to identify implicitly as opponents of his those who think that class (3) is not null. Aristotle, as much as Plato, Xenocrates, and Speusippus, believes that unchangeable, incorporeal, eternal, and separate substance exists. All we can say prudently at this point is that Aristotle's rejection of his predecessors' theories about the existence of separate substance is in need of qualification.

The proof for the existence of eternal and unchangeable substance is borrowed from Book Θ of *Physics*.[66] That proof tried to show the existence of an

61. See *Met.* E 1, 1026a10–12, which fixes theology as the speculative science that studies separate substance. Λ 1 and 6 taken together implicitly identify the subject of Λ 6–10 as that science.

62. See *Met.* Z 2, 1028b19–24; M 1, 1076a20–21 with Ross's notes. But see Dillon 2003, 48ff., for an argument that Speusippus did not abandon Forms but, rather, "restructured and rationalized them" maintaining, like Aristotle, that the possibility of knowledge requires eternal and unchanging objects.

63. *Met.*, Λ 6, 1071b4–5.

64. Ibid., 1071b20–21. Cf. Λ 2, 1069b3. At Λ 7, 1073a5–6, Aristotle says that the prime unmoved mover is without magnitude (μέγεθος) and that this has been shown (δέδεικται). Laks (2000, 239) thinks that the reference must be to *Physics*. But it is more likely that "without magnitude" is understood as equivalent to "without matter" and that Aristotle is here referring to Λ 6, 1071b20–21. See Berti 2000, 192.

65. *Met.* Λ 7, 1073a4.

66. For a useful outline of the argument in *Phys.* Θ, see Graham 1999, 183–190.

unmoved mover, given that motion cannot have a beginning or an end. Aristotle adds in passing that it will not do simply to posit eternal substances to explain necessary motion, as do those who posit Forms and mathematicals. For unless there is in them some principle of change, their eternal existence will explain nothing. But even such a principle would not be enough, unless that principle were eternally in actuality. So, it is not enough, says Aristotle, merely to show that there exists something that is capable of causing motion without moving itself. It must actually and eternally do so; otherwise, it would be possible, counter to what has already been shown, that there might not be motion. The necessary existence of motion requires an unmoved mover that is eternally in actuality. This would be the case only if the substance (οὐ-σία) of the first principle were actuality (ἐνέργεια). That is, there can be no possibility that the unmoved mover ever does not cause motion.[67]

In Book Λ, Aristotle has claimed that Forms are posited by Plato as the essential natures of things, not as principles of motion.[68] So, it is not quite correct to read Aristotle's rejection of Forms as suitable for the role of prime unmoved mover as if that is what Plato took them to be. In fact, the textual grounds for holding that Plato never took Forms as such to be 'kinetic' or 'productive' (κινητικὸν ἢ ποιητικόν) of motion is quite overwhelming. In *Timaeus* we read that this role is assigned explicitly to the Demiurge, at least insofar as cosmic motion is concerned.[69] Thus, a Neoplatonist would be justified in supposing that the rejection of Forms as putative unmoved movers amounts not to a rejection of Forms *simpliciter* but to a rejection of a misconception about their explanatory role.[70]

The central claim in the passage above is that the substance of an unmoved mover must be actuality. Almost as an afterthought, Aristotle adds that *these* substances must be incorporeal, which follows from their eternity. Mention of a plurality of actual, incorporeal substances anticipates his discussion in chapter 8.[71] But the postulation of a plurality of actual incorporeal substances conflicts with another argument in chapter 8 for the uniqueness of a perfectly actual incorporeal unmoved mover.[72] The putative plurality of actual unmoved movers is contradicted by the need for matter or potency to make them numerically distinct. What is perfectly actual

67. *Met.* Λ 6, 1071b12–22.

68. *Met.* Λ 7, 988b2–4. Cf. Λ 6, 1071b14–16.

69. See *Tim.* 30B, 53B.

70. Berti 2000, 188–190, observes that the rejection of Forms as movers is in fact taken by Aristotle as a reason for positing instead an unmoved efficient cause. That is, Forms are rejected because they do not fulfill the role of a first principle as efficient cause, not because they do not fulfill the role of first principle as final cause. This interpretation would be in line with the Neoplatonic interpretation of Plato according to which the efficient causality is attributable to the Demiurge or to the Demiurge plus the One.

71. See *Met.* Λ 8, 1074a15.

72. Ibid., 1074a31–38. Cf. *GC* B 10, 337a20–22, where Aristotle assumes that even if there is a multitude of eternal circular motions requiring a multitude of eternal movers, they must all be "under one principle" (ὑπὸ μίαν ἀρχήν). Plotinus makes the same point at V 1.9 about the necessary uniqueness of a perfectly actual first principle.

can have no potency or matter. Aristotle's problem is really the problem discussed above: namely, his commitment to the incompositeness of the incorporeal. Two or more absolutely simple and therefore actual incorporeal substances would seem to be for Aristotle an impossibility.[73]

That the perfectly actual substance should be incomposite, and uniquely so, might not seem to be a problem. Of course, its incompositeness cannot be that of a Platonic Form, *if* a Platonic Form is taken to be a universal or if it is identified as a potency.[74] So, what Aristotle needs to postulate for the actual substance that is the prime unmoved mover is incomposite activity. That activity is thinking (νόησις), the activity of an intellect (νοῦς).[75] Here in full is the passage in which the nature of this substance is described:

On this principle then depends heaven and nature. Its way of life [διαγωγή] is the best, a way of life that we enjoy for a little time. It must always be in that state, something which is impossible for us, since its actuality is pleasure. For this reason, waking, sense perception, and thinking are most pleasurable, and hopes and memories are pleasurable because of them. Thinking in itself is concerned with that which is in itself best, and thinking in the highest sense is concerned with that which is best in the highest sense. And the intellect thinks itself according to participation in the intelligible [νοητοῦ]. For it becomes intelligible by touching and thinking, so that intellect and that which is intelligible are the same. For that which is receptive of that which is intelligible, that is, substance [οὐσία], is intellect. And it is active when it is in this state. So, it is actuality rather than potency which seems to be the divine state of intellect and its contemplation [θεωρία] is the most pleasurable and best. If this is so, then God has always what we have sometimes, and this is marvelous. And if it is greater, this is even more marvelous. But this is the way it is. Further, life [ζωή] belongs to God. For the activity of intellect is a life, and God is that activity. And the activity of God in itself is the best life and eternal. We say then that God is a living, eternal being and best, so that life and continuous eternal existence belongs to God. God is this.[76]

73. Lloyd 2000, 266–267, following Owens 1950 and against Jaeger 1948 and Ross 1924, suggests that the plurality of perfectly actual unmoved movers can be explained if each is a different species. If this is what Aristotle intends, then it is difficult to see how he avoids the compositeness for each species within the putative genus. Thus, suppose that the genus is divinity and each species of this genus is differentiated from the others by constituting a different way of actualizing divinity. Whether or not the differentia is just the relation of the species to the different spheres it supposedly moves, still there would seem to be necessarily some composition in species such that we can account for its thinking *and* for its being the mover of a different sphere.

74. See *Met.* Θ 8, 1051a1–2. One of Aristotle's main arguments against Forms is that nothing can be both a substance and a universal at the same time, but that is what Forms must be. See *Met.* B 6, 1003a7–13; Γ 2, 1005a5–13; Z 13, 1038b39–1039a3; Z 16, 1040b28–30; K 2, 1060b21; M 9, 1086a34. The argument can be found also in *Soph. El.* 22, 178b37–39, 179a8–10.

75. Interestingly, Aristotle appeals first to Anaxagoras for the claim that mind is actuality. See *Met.* Λ 6, 1072a5.

76. *Met.* Λ 7, 1072b13–30.

This passage, so familiar to students of Aristotle and so laden with scholarly analyses, ought still to astonish us. Without any preparation, Aristotle moves from the painfully achieved conclusion that an actual prime unmoved mover exists to the further conclusion that its actuality consists in thinking and in the final conclusion that therefore God is a life or is living.[77] We shall return in different contexts to the praise Aristotle lavishes on this life and to the telling comparison he makes with our lives. For the moment, however, we need to focus on the many extraordinary implications of his identification of the first principle of all with thinking.

First, Aristotle here asserts that the principle upon which heaven and nature depends is an intellect or, more precisely, as he will later argue, the activity of intellect: that is, thinking.[78] Undoubtedly, the reason many have sought to sever the science of being *qua* being from theology is the supposed absurd consequences of taking Aristotle here at his word. The principal absurdity is that being cannot be understood without understanding its primary referent, and this as it turns out is the activity of thinking. This of course does not mean that Aristotle is a subjective idealist, because the thinking that is the primary referent of being is uniquely that of the prime unmoved mover. Nor does it mean that in thinking, the prime unmoved mover produces the world as if the world were its thoughts.[79]

What Aristotle's claim could well mean is that just as sensible substance is prior to everything else in the sensible world, so the intelligible substance

77. What Aristotle says here coheres nicely with what he says in *Protrep.*, frags. B 87, 89, 91, Düring. De Filippo 1994, 394–400, argues that since the prime unmoved mover must be intelligible *and* perfectly actual, it must be both absolutely separate and intelligent as well as intelligible. Hence, that it is a life is ultimately inferred from its intelligibility and from the fact that what is primarily intelligible is primarily desirable (1072a26–27). This argument, as interpreted by De Filippo, would seem to be another consideration on behalf of the Neoplatonic claim that the prime unmoved mover is substantially the same as the Demiurge and that the Forms are no more external to it than are perfect intelligibles external to the prime unmoved mover. In addition, if this mover is desirable because it is intelligible, one may wonder whether its intelligibility can consist in anything other than its being the locus of all that is intelligible: that is, of eternal essences or natures. There is nothing intelligible about pure self-reflexive thinking. See also Volpi 1991 on the characterization in this passage of God as life.

78. See Giacon (1969, 88, 94), who argues basically that the final causality of the prime unmoved mover does not exclude its efficient causality, which operates on the dependent universe in a way analogous to the way that the efficient causality of the intellect operates on a thinking individual. Giacon makes the important point that the unmoved mover is not an efficient cause only in the sense that it is a final cause or vice versa. Its efficient causal activity is logically distinct from its unquestioned final causal status. Lear 1988, 307–308, suggests that Aristotle is properly described as an objective idealist because for him the physical world is dependent on mind.

79. At 1072b25–26 the words εἰ δὲ μᾶλλον, ἔτι θαυμασιώτερον ("And if it is greater, this is even more marvelous.") are tantalizingly vague. What does it mean to suggest that God's life is better than ours sometimes is? Is it better just because it is permanent? This does not seem to be the case, owing to the ποτέ in the sentence above, which in effect acknowledges the superiority of permanence. Simplicius *In Cael.* 485, 19–22, suggests that the text means that ὁ θεὸς ἢ νοῦς ἐστιν ἢ ἐπέκεινα τι τοῦ νοῦ. Cf. *EE* H 14, 1248a27. Simplicius's observation that God is supposed by Aristotle to be a first principle suggests to him as a Neoplatonist that Aristotle perhaps recognizes after all that the first principle must be prior to intellect.

that is the prime unmoved mover is prior to sensible substance. Exactly what sort of priority is this? Aristotle has already many times in *Metaphysics* argued both for the priority in substance of actuality to potency and even for the priority in substance of the eternal to the transitory.[80] The priority in substance of the eternal to the transitory looks very much like the sort of priority that Aristotle says Plato was interested in.[81] Plato held that if X can exist without Y, but Y cannot exist without X, then X is prior to Y in nature and in substance. This is a perfectly reasonable way to understand the Platonic notion of the intelligible world in relation to the sensible world.[82] And though there is no text where Plato says what Aristotle tells us Plato believed about priority, even those who rail against Aristotle's report of Plato's unwritten teaching would find it hard to reject Aristotle's report here.

If the prime unmoved mover is the absolutely primary substance, and therefore the focal point of the science of being *qua* being, everything else is or has being in a secondary way. That includes, of course, sensible substance. That sensible substance is being in a secondary, not primary, way is at least suggested by a frustratingly ambiguous statement in Book Z: "If we theorize in this way [identifying the substrate with substance], it follows that matter is substance. But this is impossible. For to be separate and a 'this' seems to belong above all to substance. For this reason [διὸ], it would seem that the form and the composite of form and matter would be substance more than the matter. The substance then composed of both, that is, of the matter and the form, ought to be set aside [ἀφετέον], for it is posterior and evident. Matter, too, is in a way clear. We must consider the third [i.e., the form], for it is most perplexing."[83] It is not easy to say what Aristotle means when he says that the composite ought to be 'set aside' and that it is 'posterior.' The train of thought perhaps provides a clue. Matter is not substance because matter is not 'separate' and a 'this.' For this reason, it seems that the form and the composite would be substance more than matter. That is, the form and the composite seem to be more substance than matter because 'separate' and 'this' apply to them. The composite then is 'set aside' because it is posterior and evident. Is it 'set aside' for later discussion or 'set aside' as the failed candidate for the prize of 'unqualifiedly primary' substance?[84]

80. See *Met.* Θ 8, 1049b11–12; 1050a5; 1050b3–4; 1050b7ff.

81. *Met.* Δ 11, 1019a1–4. See Cleary 1988, 33–52. Cf. Θ 8, 1050a4–11, b7; M 2, 1077b1–9.

82. Though it has of course been denied, e.g., in Fine (1984 and 1993, esp. 46–65); and Silverman 2002, 121–136.

83. *Met.* Z 3, 1029a26–33. See Frede and Patzig 1988, 52.

84. See *Met.* Z 1, 1028a30–31. Gill 1989, 16–19, denies that when the composite is 'set aside,' that is because its candidacy as primary substance has been invalidated by the inclusion of matter in it. Gill argues that the reason matter is disqualified—its lack of separateness and thisness—does not disqualify the composite, which is separate and a this. This, however, does not account for the composite's posteriority. *Because* the composite includes that which is neither separate nor a this in it, the composite is posterior. Wedin 2000, 172–176 argues that the priority of form to composite of form and matter does not entail the 'demotion' of the composite. But this interpretation seems to require that we take the priority of form to composite as nothing but the priority of form to matter.

It is not unreasonable to take 'set aside' as referring forward to the discussion in Book Λ, chapters 1–5. But this does not remove the reason given for its being 'set aside,' namely, that it is 'posterior and evident.' Aristotle has already argued in the same chapter that "if form is prior to matter and has more being [μᾶλλον ὄν], by the same reasoning it will be prior to the composite."[85] So, it does appear that the composite is posterior to the form, and whatever is posterior to *anything* cannot be unqualifiedly primary. Why is it posterior? The only difference between the form and the composite is that the latter contains matter. The presence of matter in the composite makes it posterior. That the presence of matter in the composite makes it posterior fits precisely the conclusion of Book Λ, chapter 6, that the essence of the prime unmoved mover must be actuality, as well as the earlier conclusions about the priority of actuality to potency and of the eternal to the transitory. That is, it fits precisely the conclusion that the prime unmoved mover is the absolutely primary substance.[86]

The posteriority of the composite to the form may be taken in two radically different ways. In one way, it could mean that the form of *this* composite is prior to it. In another way, it could mean that a substance that was nothing but form is ontologically prior to a substance that is a composite of form and matter. In favor of the latter interpretation is that if the form of the composite is prior to the composite, then we would seem to have on our hands *two* actualities, the form and the composite. But this will not do, for Socrates and Socrates' form are not two actualities. If we agree that the one actuality is the composite, and this is posterior owing to its matter, we might still want to hold that the form that is prior is only the form of the composite, but in that case the priority could only be conceptual, not ontological.[87] But this seems rather implausible, given that Aristotle has already said and will say again that the investigation of sensible substance has been undertaken in order to discover the substance that is separate from sensible substance: that is, the substance that is ontologically prior.[88]

What is especially significant here to the eye of the Neoplatonist is that the posteriority of the composite—that is, sensible substance—harmonizes nicely with the Platonic argument that the sensible world in general has less

---

85. *Met.* Z 3, 1029a5–7, reading τοῦ ἐξ ἀμφοῖν with Ross rather than τὸ ἐξ ἀμφοῖν, which would make the composite as well as the form prior to matter rather than the form prior to the composite as well as to the matter. But the conclusion that the composite is prior to the matter (though true) is not based on the same argument that makes the form prior to the matter. Cf. Z 11, 1037a29–30: "For the substance is the inhering [ἐνόν] form from which, along with the matter, the composite [σύνολος] is said to be substance."

86. See *Met.* Γ 3, 1005a35, and Λ 8, 1073a30, where the eternal and the object of theology is referred to as πρώτη οὐσία.

87. See Wedin 2000, 377, n. 54: "I agree that *Metaphysics* Z does not count Socrates as a primary substance because its primary substances are forms of such things. But, to be abundantly clear, this does not mean that they are rejected as *Categories* primary substances, for 'primary' itself is deployed differently in the late ontology, where it is a kind of explanatory primacy. Socrates never was primary in this sense."

88. See *Met.* Z 3, 1029b3–12; Z 11, 1037a13–20; Z 17, 1041a6–9.

being than the intelligible world. Aristotle has already in Book Z, chapter two alluded to the fact that though Plato believed in sensible substances, he also believed in eternal substances that have 'more being' (μᾶλλον ὄντα) than sensible substances.[89] It would seem that only someone with a deep prior commitment to *disharmony* would want to insist that Aristotle does not commit himself to the view that eternal substance has more being than sensible substance just as the form of sensible composites has more being than the matter or the composite itself. With such a commitment, however, goes one pillar of support for the view that Aristotle rejected the Platonic account of the intelligible world as the really real world and the sensible world as less than really real.

In the passage immediately following the description of the life of the prime unmoved mover, Aristotle explicitly criticizes Pythagoreans and Speusippus (but not Plato) for holding that that which is most beautiful and best is found not 'in the principle' (ἐν ἀρχῇ) but rather in the products of the principles. According to Aristotle, they argued incorrectly from the fact that whereas in plants and animals the principles are causes, it is in the products that beauty and perfection are to be found. On the contrary, says Aristotle, the imperfect comes from the perfect, as the seed comes from the man. [90] This passage is typically taken as adding little or nothing to the foregoing argument or to the following lines at the end of the chapter in which Aristotle summarizes the attributes of the prime unmoved mover. But Aristotle is not here making a point about priority within nature, a point that would be irrelevant to the aim of the entire chapter. He is making a general point about the priority of the eternal and actual and perfect to everything else and adducing Pythagoreans and Speusippus as among those who do not understand this. Aristotle's remark that the man is prior to the seed is given as an analogy or metaphor (οἷον) of the general point. The top-down approach that Aristotle here endorses in the middle of an argument for the priority of the eternal to the transitory is in fact as deeply Platonic a claim as Aristotle anywhere makes.

Divine Thinking

What we can glean about Aristotle's view on the second major issue in the passage from Λ 7—namely, the object or objects of the divine intellect's thinking—is based principally on Λ 7 and 9 and on *De Anima* Book Γ. I have already dealt with the last mentioned in a previous chapter. The central question for our purposes is whether God thinks only about his own thinking or whether he thinks about something else. The centrality of the question hardly needs emphasizing. For if God thinks about all that is intelligible—whatever precisely that might be—the eternity of what is intelligible and its

89. Ibid., Z 2, 1028b19–21.
90. Ibid., Λ 7, 1072b30–1073a3.

separability from matter and sensibles generally are as well established as the eternity and separability of God himself. The relation between God and these intelligibles would then not look very different from the relation between the Demiurge and intelligibles, as Platonists conceive of them.[91]

An enormous scholarly literature exists on this question, with the opinion fairly divided.[92] Charles Kahn provides a concise summary of the basis for the interpretation that God is thinking of all that is intelligible.[93] He lists four points against what he terms "the prevailing view" that when God knows himself he knows nothing else. (1) At Λ 7, 1072b25, Aristotle says that "God has always what we have sometimes," which picks up b14–15, "[God's] way of life is the best, a way of life that we enjoy for a little time." If what we sometimes enjoy is contemplation of intelligibles, then God's superior life can hardly be less than cognition of these intelligibles; it must be cognition of all that is intelligible. (2) At Λ 7, 1072b19–21, it is said that "intellect thinks itself according to participation in the intelligible." This is a strong indication of the meaning of the famous phrase in Λ 9, 1074b33–35 that God is "thinking thinking of thinking." It is by thinking of all that is intelligible that God thinks himself, just as we think ourselves when we think what is intelligible.[94] The difference between God and us is that (a) we are more than the activity of thinking because we are not pure actualities; (b) our thinking is intermittent; and (c) we do not think all that is intelligible at once. But none of these differences contradict the point that God's perfect self-reflexive cognition includes *content*. (3) Hence, as suggested by Λ 7, 1072b22, intellect is determined by the essences that are its objects. (4) The claim that if God knew anything other than himself he would be less perfect is spurious, because thinking is identical with its object. As Kahn puts it, "the Prime Mover is simply the formal-noetic structure of the cosmos *as conscious of itself*" (Kahn's emphasis).[95] One could dispute all these points. I only wish to stress the fact that Kahn's concluding remark, not made on behalf of a

---

91. See Plotinus (V 6; VI 7. 1–2), who argues for a characterization of Intellect, the second principle below the One, as similar to Aristotle's prime unmoved mover. Plotinus also argues that the apparent discursive reasoning and providence practiced by the Demiurge in ordering the universe (see *Tim.* 30A5, 30B4–5, 32C8, 33A6, 33B7, 33D1, 33D4, 34A8-B1, 37C8, 37D5, 39E9) is to be accounted for allegorically just as the apparent temporal origin of the universe. There is a good discussion of Plotinus's argument in D'Ancona 2003, 211–217. See Pépin 1956 on the Platonic basis for the Neoplatonic identification of Demiurge and intelligibles.

92. See, e.g., De Koninck 1991 and 1994 for many of the references.

93. See Kahn 1985, 327, n. 24. See also Giacon 1969, 97–105; George 1989, which defends a similar position based on the argument of Franz Brentano; Lear 1988, 295–309, 316–317; De Filippo 1994.

94. Cf. *De An.* Γ 4, 429b26–28; 430a2–5.

95. A fifth point should be added arising from the argument of Brentano 1977, 127, developed in George 1989. This is that in Λ 10, 1075b8–10, Aristotle rejects Anaxagoras's account of divine mind as the good, in favor of his own account. In that account Aristotle compares God as good with the way that medical science is health. The line is puzzling if it is not connected with Λ 4, 1070b30–35 which reads: "And since among natural things the mover may be, e.g., a human being in the case of a human being, while in things which come to be from thinking the mover is the form or the contrary of the form, the causes are in one sense three

Neoplatonic reading of Aristotle, is actually exactly what the Neoplatonists held Aristotle to be saying.[96]

The aversion to understanding Aristotle's God as thinking about all intelligibles is based largely on Λ 9, not on Λ 7. For it is in Λ 9, and only there, that Aristotle claims that God is "thinking thinking of thinking."[97] Many scholars infer from this phrase alone that if God is thinking of thinking, that is, thinking about himself, then God cannot be thinking of anything else.[98] Such an inference is of course invalid *unless* we suppose that that something else could not also be identical with thinking, the explicit object of thinking in Aristotle's conclusion. The justification for holding that this is so is supposedly found in the argument for the conclusion of which the claim that God is thinking thinking of thinking is a part. The central argument is this:

(1)   God is thinking what is best.
(2)   God is best.
(3)   Therefore, God is thinking himself.[99]

The first premise is directly inferable from the claim in Λ 7 that "thinking is in itself concerned with what is in itself best."[100] The problem addressed in Λ 9 is really with the second premise. This premise was also a claim or,

---

but in another sense four. For the medical art is in some sense health, the art of building is in some sense the form of the house, and it is a human being that begets a human being. Further, besides these there is that which, as first of all things, moves all things" (ἐπεὶ δὲ τὸ κινοῦν ἐν μὲν τοῖς φυσικοῖς ἀνθρώπῳ ἄνθρωπος, ἐν δὲ τοῖς ἀπὸ διανοίας τὸ εἶδος ἢ τὸ ἐναντίον, τρόπον τινὰ τρία αἴτια ἂν εἴη, ὡδὶ δὲ τέτταρα. ὑγίεια γάρ πως ἡ ἰατρική, καὶ οἰκίας εἶδος ἡ οἰκοδομική, καὶ ἄνθρωπος ἄνθρωπον γεννᾷ· ἔτι παρὰ ταῦτα ὡς τὸ πρῶτον πάντων κινοῦν πάντα). Bonitz, (1848), followed by Jaeger and Ross, changed the words ὡς τὸ in the last line to τὸ ὡς for no textual reason at all; they made and accepted the change for no other reason than that without the change, the text would naturally be read to say that God is to everything else as medical science is to health, the form of a building in the maker is to the building, and a human parent is to its child. But if this is so, then Aristotle would seem to be maintaining that God possesses the forms of all things: that is, God knows all these. George points out that in *Met.* Z 7–9, three types of production are discussed: by nature, by art, and by spontaneity (that is, when neither nature nor art is responsible). So, it would seem that in the Λ 4 passage, Aristotle is introducing a *fourth* type of production where the form is in the producer.

96. See Pines (1987, 177–191), who translates from the Arabic and Hebrew relevant texts of Themistius on the content of God's thinking. Pines argues that the Peripatetic Themistius is influenced by Plotinus and Neoplatonists generally in his contention that God thinks all intelligibles in thinking himself. He thinks that Themistius deviates from the text of Aristotle in his interpretation. On Neoplatonic or Platonic sympathies in Themistius, see Hamelin and Barbotin 1953, 38–43, and esp. Ballériaux 1994. See, however, Düring (1957, 333), who says that Themistius "is on the whole remarkably free from Neoplatonic influence," though it is clear from the passages from Themistius quoted by Düring that Themistius believed that Aristotle was in harmony with Plato.

97. *Met.* Λ 9, 1074b34–35. The genitive νοήσεως is evidently objective here.

98. See Ross 1924, 2:398–399.

99. *Met.* Λ 9, 1074b15–34.

100. *Met.* Λ 7, 1072b18–19.

perhaps better, a hypothesis, boldly made in Λ 7.[101] The problem with it is that if God is in essence an intellect that thinks, and not the activity of thinking itself, then God's essence would be a potency in relation to the activity of thinking. In that case, God would not be the best; he would be a potency in relation to the best: that is, to thinking. So, if God is best and thinking of what is best, God must be thinking, not an intellect that thinks.

The words that follow the conclusion "therefore, God is thinking of himself"—namely, "[God is] thinking thinking of thinking"—are an explication of the words "therefore he is thinking [νοεῖ] himself." They do not add a further conclusion.[102] That is, because God's essence or οὐσία is identical with his thinking and not in potency to it, when he thinks, he thinks himself. By contrast, another thinker, such as a human being, has an essence that is not identical with thinking. So, when human beings think, they are in essence not identical with what they think. Although they are not in essence identical with what they think, their thinking *is* in a way identical with what they think, as Aristotle will carefully add at the end of the chapter.[103] So, the crucial difference between God and human beings is not that God thinks of nothing but we think of something; rather, it is that God is not in potency to his thinking, while we are.[104] Therefore, God (who is just thinking) is thinking of what he himself is: that is, thinking. The point of saying that God is "thinking thinking of thinking" is not to drain all content out of God's thinking but to contrast that thinking with the thinking of things that are not essentially identical with the essence of the thinker. The exalted position of the prime unmoved mover is owing to the fact that he is nothing but thinking, not to the alleged fact that there is no content to his thinking.[105]

---

101. Ibid., 1072b14–15.

102. The sentence reads: αὐτὸν ἄρα νοεῖ, εἴπερ ἐστὶ τὸ κράτιστον, καὶ ἔστιν ἡ νόησις νοήσεως νόησις. See Brunschwig (2000, 288–290), who notices the question of the relation between the two clauses. He argues that "thinking thinking about thinking" is a necessary and sufficient condition for "God is thinking himself." I am unclear why he thinks that this adds a fresh point to the conclusion of the argument, not an explication of its meaning. I take the καί as epexegetic. The phrase '[God] thinks himself' should be closely compared with *De An.* Γ 4, 429b9: καὶ αὐτὸς δὲ αὐτὸν τότε δύναται νοεῖν. See Oehler 1962 for an argument for the view of God's thinking as purely formal and exiguous. See Krämer 1969b, esp. 363–382, for a compelling criticism of Oehler's interpretation.

103. *Met.* Λ 9, 1075a4–5: ἡ νόησις τῷ νοουμένῳ μία.

104. Wedin (1988, 220–229) argues against what he calls the isomorphic view of divine and human thought, that is, the view that human and divine thought are the same in kind. In particular, he argues against Kahn 1981, who holds this view. Wedin's principal reason for denying isomorphism is that human thought involves images, whereas divine thought does not (244–245).

105. See Norman 1969. Wedin (1988, 229–245), argues that the human mind and the divine mind are profoundly different and that therefore, since the human mind has content, the divine mind does not. But the difference between God and humans is not a different kind of mind but the fact that we have an essence that is not identical with thinking, whereas while God's essence is identical with thinking. From this difference it does not follow that God's thinking has no content.

Of course, it is possible that independently of the point Aristotle is apparently making here, he might also believe that the identity of the activity of thinking with the object of thinking eliminates content from that thinking. But there is no reason to believe that this is so on the grounds that God is thinking thinking of thinking. And in fact there are no other grounds in Λ 9 for believing this.

The chapter ends with the consideration of three problems.[106] First, in knowledge, sense perception, belief, and discursive reasoning, cognition seems to be of itself only incidentally (παρέργῳ). If thinking is like these other types of cognition, then this would conflict with the conclusion that God is identical with what he thinks. Second, if thinking is not the same thing as being thought, in virtue of which of these is God the best. That is, is he the best because of his thinking or because of his being thought? Third, is what is thought a composite (σύνθετον) or simple? If it is composite, then in thinking, God would change in passing from one part of the object thought to another.

A single solution is provided for the first two problems.[107] In contrast to other sciences, in the theoretical sciences "the formula or the thinking is the thing [i.e., the object thought]" (ὁ λόγος τὸ πρᾶγμα καὶ ἡ νόησις). In these sciences, whose objects contain no matter, thinking and what is thought will be the same. So, the thinking is not of itself only incidentally. This solution is presumably supposed to be applied to the second problem as well. Since God is identical with his thinking and his thinking is identical with the object of thinking, God's goodness is owing to his thinking. The conceptual distinction or distinction in λόγος between thinking and being thought is not grounded in a real distinction. The phrase "the formula or the thinking is the thing" supports the foregoing interpretation of "thinking thinking of thinking." Whether for humans or for God, in theoretical science, thinking is both intentional object and activity. Therefore, we need not suppose that just because the intentional object of God's thinking is thinking, that God's thinking has no content. In the case of these sciences, human thinking is thinking of thinking as well.[108] We differ from God not because we alone have content but because we are not identical in essence with our thinking.

The third problem is answered by the assertion that everything without matter is indivisible (ἀδιαίρετον). So, God is not required to change (for which potency would be necessary) in order to think. He thinks whatever he thinks indivisibly and simultaneously.[109] There is, Aristotle holds, no complexity either in the object of thinking itself or in the activity of thinking.

---

106. *Met.* Λ 9, 1074b35–1075a10.

107. See Brunschwig 2000, 293–294, on this untidy text.

108. Cf. Alexander of Aphrodisias's remark in the Arabic fragment of his *On the Universe* (Genequand 2001, §111, p. 105): "As for the fact that the intellect which is in actuality is the same thing as the intelligible <thing> and that therefore it thinks itself, this is something common to all intellects free from matter and particularly the divine intellect: being truly intelligible, it is truly thinking."

It does not seem that the characterization of God as "thinking thinking of thinking" should lead us to qualify the plausibility of the interpretation of Λ 7 above. That God is essentially thinking and that he is the object of his own thinking does not mean that God's thinking is contentless.[110] On the contrary, God's thinking of thinking is just the self-reflexive thinking of theoretical science. God differs from us in at least two ways: (1) God does not have an essence different from his activity, whereas we do, and (2) God thinks all that he thinks undividedly, whereas we embodied human beings think the contents of the different theoretical sciences in succession and via images.

On this interpretation, God is the 'locus' of all that is per se intelligible, exactly as is, on the Neoplatonic interpretation, the Demiurge of Plato's *Timaeus*.[111] The paradigmatic causality of Forms that we saw in chapter 4 explicitly adduced by Platonists as a supplement to Aristotle's four causes is hereby implicitly acknowledged by Aristotle. For what the prime unmoved mover thinks is ontologically prior to forms in matter. Next, we need to explore how Aristotle insinuates paradigmatic causality into his metaphysics.

Divine Causality

The prime unmoved mover is an entity postulated to explain everlasting motion, though we might have been led from Book α to expect that it is also in some sense a cause of being. How does it cause motion? "And this is the way in which the desirable and the intelligible (τὸ νοητόν) move, that is, it moves without being moved."[112] Aristotle goes on to explain this type of causality more precisely: "That there is final causality among immovables, division makes clear.[113] For final causality is both for something (τινί) and of something (τινός), and of these, [the prime unmoved mover] is a final

---

110. Brunschwig (2000, 301–306) argues, following Dumoulin 1986, that Λ 9 is an early 'thought experiment' wherein God is held to be 'Narcissus-like.' Brunschwig accepts the view that in Λ 7, God has simultaneous intellection of all intelligibles; that is, all essences. But he claims that in holding that God is "thinking thinking about thinking," Aristotle takes a different view. The difference is accounted for developmentally. Brunschwig's arguments, stemming from a presumed developmentalism, as expressed by Jaeger and Ross, are, I think, weak. His main arguments are (1) that Λ 7 often uses the term ἐνέργεια, whereas Λ 9 never does; (2) that the epistemology of Λ 9 is earlier than that of Λ 7; (3) that the notion of πάρεργον appears in Λ 9 but not in Λ 7, although Brunschwig concedes that the use of πάρεργον is "implicitly present in Λ 7"; (4) that divine thinking, freed from the necessity that it is of itself 'incidentally,' can be nothing but 'Narcissus-like.' If, as I contend, the only difference between Λ 7 and Λ 9 is that in the latter chapter Aristotle argues that God is essentially thinking and not essentially a mind that is thinking, then both the different emphases of the chapters and the underlying commonality can be faithfully preserved.

111. See Lear (1988, 305), who characterizes the essence that God is thinking as constituting a "higher level actuality" and then argues (307) for the unqualified ontological priority of actuality to potentiality. The actuality of the prime unmoved mover thinking all that is intelligible 'indivisibly' is, thus characterized, very much like the Demiurge eternally contemplating Forms. Cf. Asclepius *In Met.* 69, 17–21; 71, 28; Proclus *In Tim.* I 299, 13ff.

112. *Met.* Λ 7, 1072a26–27.

113. This is probably the division of contraries alluded to in Γ 2, 1004a2; I 3, 1054a30.

cause in one sense, but not in the other. It [the final cause] causes motion by being loved, and by means of what is moved (κινουμένῳ), it moves other things . . . This mover then moves of necessity, and if so, then nobly, and in this way it is a principle."[114] The identification of the prime unmoved mover both as object of desire and as object of intellection should be seen, as André Laks delicately notes, against "the Platonic horizon of Aristotle's approach here."[115] The focus of much of the contemporary discussion of the causality of the prime unmoved mover, however, is on how a final cause is able to perform the function assigned to it by Aristotle. For one thing, it would seem that that which is directly caused by the prime unmoved mover must be capable of having a desire for it; if this is the outermost sphere of the heavens, we must suppose that it has a soul or at least an intellect.[116] For another, it is far from clear why a final cause should inspire circular motion, the type of motion that ultimately requires a perfectly actual first cause.[117]

There have been numerous efforts to show that God is both an efficient cause and a final cause, or an efficient cause by being a final cause, although it is difficult to see how the perfectly actual unmoved mover can produce motion outside itself.[118] If God is an efficient cause, he evidently causes

114. *Met.* Λ 7, 1072b1–4, 10–11. On the distinction between the two types of final causality, see *Phys.* B 2, 194a33–36; *De An.* B 4, 415b2–23, 20–21; *GA* B 6, 742a22ff.; *EE* H 15, 1249b15–16; and the analysis in Gaiser 1969, 97–113, and Kullmann 1985. It is clear that the prime unmoved mover is not a final cause in the sense that it seeks to achieve a goal it does not already possess; rather, it is a final cause in the sense of a goal the achievement of which benefits something else. Nevertheless, since the prime unmoved mover possesses the best life, it *does* achieve a goal; in fact, it never fails to achieve it. Natali 1997, 112ff., argues that neither sense of 'final cause' in the cited texts applies to the prime unmoved mover: the first for the given reason above and the second because it would make the prime unmoved mover a paradigmatic cause apt for imitation. But that cannot be so, says Natali, because this is a position of "Medioplatonismo" (114). For Natali, the prime unmoved mover is a final cause not as a paradigm but strictly as an object of love (122).

115. See Laks 2000, 225. At least part of what this 'Platonic horizon' consists in is that insofar as the prime unmoved mover is a final cause, it is not so in the sense of the 'practicable good' that is a final cause in *De An.* Γ 10, 433b16. It is a final cause more like the Demiurge, who desires that all things should be good and 'be like' (ὁμοιῶσαι) the intelligible world. Cf. *Tim.* 29E1–3; 30D1–31A1. See Natali 1997, 110. The final causality of the prime unmoved mover also of course resembles that of the Form of the Good—'good' standing for that which all things desire. Thus, the prime unmoved mover collapses into one the functions Plato variously assigns to the Demiurge and to the Form of the Good.

116. As Broadie 1993 points out, the argument does not say that the outermost sphere is animated.

117. The circular motion of the outermost sphere is easier to explain if the prime unmoved mover is an efficient cause than if it is merely a final cause. See Berti 2000, 201; Plato *Tim.* 34B, 37A–C, 40A–B, 42C–D, 47D, 77B. Plato *Lg.* 897D–898C, connects the circular motion of the heavens with thought when he argues that thought *is* circular motion and that the heavens move in a circular manner in order to imitate the Demiurge. Although Aristotle criticized this view of thought (*De An.* A 3, 407a16, 32–33, b5–9), the Neoplatonists do not seem entirely unjustified in assuming that Aristotle himself basically came around to Plato's own view. See Plotinus II 2. 1; Proclus *In Tim.* II 267, 5–13. But this also seems to be the view of Alexander of Aphrodisias *Quaest.* XVII 62, 23–30; XIX 63, 20; and Themistius *In Met.* 20, 31–35. See Berti 1997, 67.

118. See Ross 1924, 1:cxxxiii–cxxxiv; Giacon 1969, esp. 87–97; and Berti 1997. Berti 2000, 202–204, argues that the words "and this is the way the desirable and the intelligible move" as applied to God do not necessarily indicate that here God is being said to be a final cause. That

motion outside himself in addition to engaging in the activity of thinking. For the activity of thinking—theoretical thinking, at any rate—is self-contained. Nevertheless, the reasons for thinking that there must be an unmoved efficient cause remain.[119]

These exegetical questions are not of paramount interest to the Neoplatonists, since they reject the claim that a substance described as thinking thinking of thinking could be the first principle of all and hence that it could be the primary or sole ultimate efficient cause. On the other hand, they agree with Aristotle that the first principle of all is the object of desire and that it is, in some sense, intelligible. This is precisely what the Idea of the Good or the One is held to be.[120] Because there is a One beyond what Aristotle calls 'God,' the final causality of the latter does not exclude a further determination of causality by the eternal. And because Aristotle's God is 'second' and not 'first,' its causality can be understood instrumentally, too. Just as the prime unmoved mover that is thinking indirectly produces motion by moving that which desires it, so this unmoved mover may be understood as an instrument of the genuine first principle of all.[121]

---

is, God's causality can be analogous to the final causality of the object of desire and intellection, by its being an unmoved or unmovable efficient cause. The analogy does not need to be read as indicating that God is a final cause analogous to another type of final cause. But then Berti must say that the words at 1072b3–4, which hold that God moves as an object of love—that is, as a final cause—must mean that God is here said to be a final cause in *another* sense: that he is the final cause of his own activity—namely, his own thinking. This is a shift from Berti's earlier view (1977, 431–432) that God operates solely as a final cause. Judson 1994, 155–171, argues that a final cause can be a "non-energetic efficient cause": that is, an efficient cause that moves while being unmoved. This is the sort of efficient cause that produces a desire. But Judson also thinks that there is evidence for the view that the prime unmoved mover is an "energetic efficient cause"— that is, an efficient cause that operates by moving itself—but that this interpretation of God's efficient causality "is simply incompatible with being an unmoved mover of any sort" (171). The claim that the prime unmoved mover's activity is that of an energetic efficient cause is argued for in Broadie 1993. But Broadie wishes to distinguish the activity of the prime unmoved mover from the contemplative activity of God, and this seems unfounded in the text. See Natali 1997 for a critique of the various modern views that God operates as an efficient cause as well as a final cause.

119. As Berti (1997, 60–61) notes, the rejection of Forms as unmoved movers in Λ 6, 1071b14–17 (cf. A 7, 988b2–4; 9, 991a11; 9, 991b3–4) would make little sense if Forms were being merely rejected as final causes: that is, if Aristotle were not claiming that Forms cannot fulfill a role that the divine mind fulfills, a role that requires activity. If all that was required was a final cause, Forms would seem to be able to fulfill this role as well as a divine mind. See, e.g., *EN* A 4, 1096b8–11 where it is conceded that the Form of the Good is loved.

120. See Plotinus V 6. 2, 7–9. He here argues that the One is 'intelligible' but not in the proper sense of that term (κυρίως). The One is also the object of desire because it is the Good. See V 6. 5, 8–9.

121. See Aristotle *Phys.* B 6, 198a10–13: "So, however true it may be that chance is the cause of the heavens, it is necessary that intellect and nature will be prior causes of many other things and of this universe" (ὥστ' εἰ ὅτι μάλιστα τοῦ οὐρανοῦ αἴτιον τὸ αὐτόματον, ἀνάγκη πρότερον νοῦν αἴτιον καὶ φύσιν εἶναι καὶ ἄλλων πολλῶν καὶ τοῦδε τοῦ παντός). As we saw in chapter four, Neoplatonists argued that nature itself was insufficient as a first efficient causal principle; hence, the coupling of nature and intellect here does not preclude the need for a first productive principle. Cf. *Mund.* 6, 397b9, where God is said to be "the cause that holds all things together" (τῆς τῶν ὅλων συνεκτικῆς αἰτίας), echoed in *Pol.* H 4, 1326a32–33: θείας γὰρ δὴ

Aristotle says that the prime unmoved mover is a principle, though the translators usually render the Greek ἀρχή tendentiously as 'first principle.' The famous passage that begins chapter 10 of Book Λ suggested to Neoplatonists that Aristotle was at the very least not closed to the possibility that the true first principle of all was not thinking thinking of thinking:

> We must also consider in which way the nature of the universe [ἡ τοῦ ὅλου φύσις] contains the good or the best, whether it has it as something separated by itself [αὐτὸ καθ᾽ αὐτό] or in the manner of an order [τὴν τάξιν]. Or is it in both ways, like an army? For goodness in an army is both in its order and in its general, but more in the general. For the order is owing to [διὰ] the general and not the general to the order. All things are somehow ordered together, but not all in the same way, even fishes, birds, and plants. And the universe is not such that there is no relation of one thing to another; rather, there is such a relation. For there is some one thing in relation to which all things are ordered together [πρὸς μὲν γὰρ ἓν ἅπαντα συντέτακται]. It is as in a household, where the free persons are least able to do what they like, but all or most of what they do is ordered, while the slaves and animals contribute little to what is common and mostly do what they like. For this is the sort of principle that nature is of each of them.[122] I mean, for example, that it is necessary at least for everything to come to be dissolved, and there are other ways in which all things share in the universe.[123]

Two analogies govern this remarkable passage, an army and a household.[124] The passage shifts from the discussion in chapter 9 of the nature of thinking to the way that the universe is related to its ultimate mover. This mover is like a general in relation to his army. The goodness in an army is in part in its order and in part in the general, though primarily in the latter. Just so, the goodness in the universe is in part in its order and in part in the separated mover. But the goodness is more in the general than in the army because the order is owing to the general.[125]

τοῦτο δυνάμεως ἔργον, ἥτις καὶ τόδε συνέχει τὸ πᾶν. Cf. also 2, 391b11 where the 'arrangement' (διακόσμησις) of the universe is owing to God. This is the term used by Plato for the Demiurge's operation on the receptacle. At 5, 396b31, the term δημιουργήσασα in reference to God is actually used.

122. See Sedley 2000, 329, on this translation.

123. *Met.* Λ 10, 1075a11–25.

124. Cf. *Mund.* 6, 400b6–11, where to the metaphors of an army and a house are added those of a captain of a ship, a charioteer, the leader of a chorus, and the law (or the lawgiver) of a city, depending on whether the text is νόμος or νομο<θέτη>ς, as Lorimer in his edition (1933) takes it to be.

125. As George 1989 points out, the metaphor of a general makes no sense if the general knows nothing. See Giacon (1969, 92), who notes, apropos of the metaphor of a general, that his causality is indicated by διά and not οὗ ἕνεκα. This would be awkward if only final causality were meant. Indeed, it is only because of efficient causality that it makes sense to say "all things are ordered together." See Irwin (1988, 105), who claims that final causality is involved in efficient causal production, and Furley (1996, 77), who identifies final causality with top-down causation, though he seems to mean 'internal' not 'external' final causality. Furley denies that the prime unmoved mover functions in any way like the Demiurge in Plato's *Timaeus*.

Let us suppose then that a disordered army is inspired by the qualities of its general and is set in order by a field officer according to those qualities. The problem with so understanding the analogy is that in the case of the universe, order is not produced out of disorder. The dynamic nature of the universe and everything in it is enough on its own to explain the order. On the assumption that here the first principle of all is a final cause and only a final cause, it is difficult to see how the order of the universe is owing to that final cause. It seems rather to be the case that the final cause, as extrinsic object of desire, is a function of that order, not its cause.

The Neoplatonic understanding of this passage is neither to reduce it to an explication of Platonism nor to dismiss it to a consequence of anti-Platonic principles. The former is implausible, and the latter makes little sense of what is being said here. If God is thinking thinking of nothing but thinking, then God is a poor candidate for the cause of order in the universe. If, however, God's thinking is the locus of eternal intelligible being, then, although God is still a poor candidate as ultimate cause of order, at least God *is* that order, paradigmatically. But given the complexity of thinking, there is every reason to suppose that the first principle of all is not Aristotle's unmoved mover. And the way that first principle is a cause of order and of being is different from and superior to the way that thinking participates in that causality.

The correct understanding of Λ 10, according to Neoplatonists, is that what Aristotle is claiming is in harmony with Platonism.[126] When Aristotle comes to investigate the order of the entire universe in relation to the prime unmoved mover, he needs to have this mover do more than it can do as mere thinking activity. He opens the door, perhaps inadvertently, to a Platonic first principle which in turn embraces the unmoved mover in the ultimate causal framework. How else can we honestly construe the last line of *Metaphysics* Λ 10, "things do not want to be governed badly", followed by the quotation from Homer. "It is not good that there be many leaders; let there be one"?[127]

---

126. See Elias (or David) *In Cat.* 120, 19–30, where he raises the question: why does Aristotle say that the first principle of all is νοῦς, if in fact he agrees with Plato that it really is the Good? Elias gives two answers. The first is that *Metaphysics* was written after *Physics* and therefore contains a principle that is "closer to nature" (φυσικωτέραν) than is the Good. The second is that Aristotle himself in his *Nicomachean Ethics* recognizes the primacy of the Good when he says at the beginning of the work, "the good is that at which all things aim." The first answer carries little force. The force of the second answer has to be understood in the light of the Neoplatonic argument that a mind or thinking could not be identified with the Good, because thinking implies desire, and desire is for the Good, which is therefore other than the thinker or thinking itself. See Hadot (1991, 182–184), who, in discussing this passage, adds that Elias shares with Simplicius *In Cat.* 6, 27–30, the interpretive principle that Aristotle consistently deals with metaphysical matters from a physical perspective, whereas Plato consistently deals with physical matters from a metaphysical perspective.

127. See, e.g., Ammonius *In Cat.* 6, 9–16; Olympiodorus [?] *Proleg.* 9, 14–30. Simplicius *In Phys.* 1361, 11–1363, 24 argues that the prime unmoved mover is an efficient as well as a final cause. But it is the efficient cause directly only of the movement of the outermost sphere (1362, 15–20). Simplicius (1360, 28–31) attributes this interpretation to Ammonius. See Asclepius *In Met.* 103, 3–4; 108, 23–25; 151, 5–32. He also cites *Cael.* A 4, 271a33, 9; 279a27; *GCA* 3, 318a1;

Plotinus's Critique of Aristotle's God as First
Principle of All

Plotinus's criticisms of Aristotle's account of the prime unmoved mover constitute one of the most far-reaching and profound lines of argument in Neoplatonism.[128] The hypothesis of an unmoved mover that is thinking thinking of thinking poses a major challenge to the Neoplatonic understanding of the Platonic first principle of all. Showing that Aristotle is wrong about how the first principle is to be characterized, however, does not mean abandoning the unmoved mover altogether. It can be accommodated or fit into the Platonic framework. Moreover, having shown that the unmoved mover is not absolutely simple, at least one reason for denying the existence of eternal intelligible entities is removed.[129]

Plotinus is not, as we have seen, an uncritical harmonizer. His approach is more subtle. While criticizing Aristotle, at the same time he freely and extensively incorporates Aristotelian language into his account and defense of Platonism. So, we might say that his harmonization efforts are implicit. These efforts bear fruit in his successors who, in part because they find it so natural to use Aristotelian language, more aggressively promulgate harmonization.

In *Ennead* V 6, traditionally titled *On the Fact That That Which Is Beyond Being Does Not Think, and on What Is the Primary and What the Secondary Thinking Principle*, Plotinus gives forceful expression to his reasons for holding that the first principle of all cannot be thinking:

> There is a difference between something thinking [νοεῖν] another thing and something thinking itself; the latter thereby goes further in escaping duality [τὰ δύο εἶναι]. The former would like to escape the aforementioned duality and think itself, but it is less able to do so, for it has what it sees in itself [παρ' αὐτῷ], but it is still different from that. The latter, by contrast, is not separated in being [τῇ οὐσίᾳ] from its object, but being with itself, it sees itself. It therefore becomes dual [ἄμφω] while being one. And it therefore thinks more fully that which it has, and thinks primarily, because that which thinks must be both one and two.

---

and *Met.* A 4, 984b15 in support of this interpretation. Philoponus (*In Phys.* 298, 6–10; 304, 5–10; *In GC* 136, 33–137, 2; 152, 23–153, 2; 297, 15–24) takes the same position.

128. Cf. Proclus *PT* I 3.12, 23–13, 5; *In Parm.* 1214, 11–12; *In Tim.* II 121, 25ff.; 122, 28–123, 27. The author of the anonymous *Prolegomena to Plato's Philosophy* (9, 28ff.) argues in addition that intellect cannot be first because everything depends on the first, but not everything has intellect. See Hager 1970, 307–364; Rist 1973/4.

129. See Des Places 1973, frags. 11, 12, 16, 17, where Numenius identifies the first principle with Noῦς and the Good (frag. 16, 1–4) and claims that it is simple' (ἁπλοῦς) because it "remains in itself," unattached to the intelligibles of which it is the cause (frag. 11, 12–17). But Plotinus's central point is that the activity of intellect is essentially complex. So, placing the intelligibles 'beneath' the first principle does not solve the problem so long as the first principle is an intellect. Proclus (*In Tim.* I 266, 28–267, 12; *In Parm.* 842, 26–35) says that Aristotle's doctrine of God is only half true. This is because an intellect eternally contemplating intelligibles is insufficient to account for the creative activity that a first principle of all must possess.

For if it is not one, that which thinks and that which is thought will be different. It would then not be primary thinking; receiving its thinking from something else, it would not be primarily thinking because what it thinks it would not be from itself, so that it would not think itself. Or else, if it has what it thinks from itself, so that it would think in the principal sense [κυρίως], it will be a duality. It must therefore be a dual-one. But if it is just one, it will not be dual, and it will not have something to think, so that it will not even be thinking. Therefore, it is necessary for it to be both simple and not simple.[130]

Despite the somewhat tortured syntax, the argument is here in fact quite straightforward. Thinking requires duality consisting of thinking and an object of thinking; hence, thinking requires relative complexity. But in primary thinking, or thinking considered paradigmatically, the complexity is not that of a thinker and something that is other than the thinker. The complexity must be *within* the thinker. The latter point is authentically Aristotelian and harks specifically to *Metaphysics* Λ 9, where Aristotle distinguishes the incidental self-thinking of thinkers other than God from the unqualified self-thinking of God.[131]

The dispute between Aristotle and Plotinus, then, is over two points: (1) whether or not thinking thinking of thinking involves complexity, and (2) if it does, whether this invalidates it as a first principle.

The first point would presumably be settled in Plotinus's favor if it could be shown that Aristotle's God must be thinking about one or another intelligible. But this is precisely why one might want to insist that God does not think of anything other than thinking.[132] In fact, Plotinus's central argument against the perfect simplicity of thinking is more profound and is independent of how we finally characterize the objects of thinking. Plotinus argues that thinking paradigmatically entails thinking about thinking because thinking is essentially self-reflexive: "So, in thinking primarily, [the thinker] would also have thinking that it is thinking, as a being that is one [ἓν ὄν], and it is not double there, even in thought [ἐπινοίᾳ]."[133] The claim that the thinker is not double indicates that there is no major real distinction between subject and object: that is, no distinction between them as entities. When thinking, the thinker is identical with what is thought, as Aristotle insists.[134] The complexity of thinking is owing to its self-reflexivity: "For

130. V 6. 1, 1–14. Cf. 1, 22–25; III 8. 9, 8–13; V 1. 9; V 3. 11, esp. the last four lines; V 3. 11, 25–30; 13, 34–36; VI 7. 35–37, esp. 37, 24–31; 39, 20–29.
131. See V 4. 2, 47–51; V 9. 8, 6; V 9. 5, 30, on the identity of thinking with its object. Seidl 1987, 165–176, argues that Plotinus misunderstands Aristotle's argument for a self-thinking intellect, by insisting that it must be complex. Seidl seems correct to insist that God's thinking is different from human thinking. Nevertheless, it *is* thinking, and that, Plotinus argues, requires a distinction between thinker, an activity, and an object thought, even if the first two are identical.
132. Plotinus does in fact also use this argument, (V 1. 9, 9–12) when, referring to Λ 8 and 9 both, he says that God is intelligible and the other unmoved movers are intelligible. Therefore, if God knows what is intelligible, he knows more than himself.
133. II 9. 1, 50–52.
134. See V 9. 5, 7: αὐτός [Intellect] ἐστιν ἃ νοεῖ.

generally it seems to be the case that thinking is a consciousness [συναίσθησις] of the whole when many things are gathered together into it [the thinker]; this occurs whenever something thinks itself, which is thinking in the primary sense. Each one is something and seeks nothing, whereas if the activity of thinking will be of that which is outside, it will be deficient and will not be thinking in the primary sense."[135]

If the prime unmoved mover were, *per impossibile*, thinking without thinking that it is thinking, it would be in a cognitive state without being aware of being in that state. It would be like someone asleep.[136] But there would seem to be an inevitable complexity of some sort involved in the thinker's being in a state of cognitive identity with that which it cognizes *and* being aware that it is in this state. Thinking is, according to Plotinus, essentially self-reflexive and therefore complex.

Why, then, should we suppose that this sort of complexity is incompatible with ultimate ontological primacy? The answer supplied by Plato and Platonism is that the Idea of the Good, the first principle of all, is beyond being or essence (οὐσία).[137] So, if, as Aristotle seems to hold, the prime unmoved mover is absolutely primary οὐσία, then it cannot be the first principle of all. The philosophical answer is that οὐσία implies definiteness or limitedness and the first principle of all cannot be limited in any way. For as first, there could be no principle outside it to provide a limit.[138] Aristotle's problem is that if the prime unmoved mover is the ultimate οὐσία, it is the ultimate 'this' (τόδε τι). A 'this,' as indicated by the Aristotelian neologism, has a definite nature even if, as Aristotle also holds, the prime unmoved mover has this nature uniquely. The principle 'beyond' definiteness is what explains definiteness, in exactly the same way that the unit explains a particular and definite plurality, whereas the unit itself, as principle, is not limited. If primary οὐσία is the activity of thinking, and thinking is self-reflexive, there must be sufficient definiteness in order to make the self-reflexivity of thinking possible.

Plotinus endorses the ultimacy of the relative unmoved mover—as οὐσία.[139] His criticism is aimed at the claim that οὐσία can be an unqualifiedly ultimate first principle of all. Accordingly, although nothing in his criticism counts against the absolute primacy of Aristotle's God in the ordering of οὐσία, he cannot be the focus of the science of being. Stated otherwise, Aristotle's hypothesis that the eternal question about being is just the question about οὐσία is disconfirmed. Primary *limited* being is not primary being *tout court*. The question 'what is being' is not answered by discovering primary

135. V 3. 13, 13–17. Cf. V 3. 8, 23.
136. See *Met.* Λ 9, 1074b18, where Aristotle reasons that if the prime unmoved mover were not thinking—that is, occurrently thinking—he would be like a man asleep.
137. See *Rep.* 509B9.
138. See V 5. 6, 5 and 14–15; V 5. 1, 2–3; VI 7. 32, 9.
139. See V 9. 3, 2, where he calls the prime unmoved mover "true being" (τὴν ἀληθῆ οὐσίαν).

οὐσία; it is answered by discovering the first principle of all that is, including οὐσία. To the extent that we are persuaded that the correct interpretation of Book Λ is that the prime unmoved mover's thinking contains content, to the same extent we should be open to the hypothesis that Aristotle's conclusion is in harmony with that of the Platonists.[140] The science of οὐσία has its foundation in the *second* principle of all, not the first. The science of being, which has its foundation in the *first* principle of all, encompasses the science of οὐσία; it is not identical with it.[141]

---

140. Asclepius *In Met.* 28, 31–32; 148, 10–11; 225, 15–17, argues for the identity of Aristotle's God and the Neoplatonic first principle of all. But owing to the plurality of intelligibles in the prime unmoved mover, it must be subordinated to God or the One. See Verrycken 1990, 218–220.

141. See Berti (1975, 181–208, esp. 206–207), who argues that what sets Aristotle apart from Platonism is the fact that, though Aristotle agrees that all reality is dependent on a single first principle, he rejects the possibility of deducing reality from that first principle. I think Plotinus shows in what sense Berti is correct. Conceiving of the first principle in a way that is, according to Platonism, mistaken, Aristotle misconceives the relation between that principle and everything else. But I believe Berti is mistaken in supposing that the difference is between a rejection and an acceptance of the deduction of everything from the first principle. I do not understand what it would mean to deduce everything from the Form of the Good or from the One. Neither Plato nor Plotinus holds that this is possible; rather, the multiplicity of Forms or the complexity of intelligible reality is a starting point for both in an inference to a first principle. The causal dependence of everything on a first principle, which Berti concedes that Aristotle accepts, is enough to warrant such inferences.

CHAPTER SEVEN

Aristotle and the Forms

The largest and seemingly most intractable impediment for the harmonist is Aristotle's criticism of Plato's theory of Forms and the alleged implications of that criticism. We have already seen that two of those alleged implications are the reddest of red herrings: namely, the idea that universals replace Forms in their explanatory role, and the idea that sensible substances are the focus of Aristotle's 'alternative' metaphysics. The Neoplatonists, too, were generally aware of the oddness in the claim that the philosopher who rejected the Forms could also be understood to hold views that were in harmony with those of Plato. There are, however, several good reasons why they did not take the rejection of Forms by Aristotle at face value.[1]

First, as we have seen, a reasonable argument could be made to the effect that Aristotle believed that the prime unmoved mover's eternal thinking is of eternal intelligible objects. These eternal intelligible objects appear to be not all that different from Forms, especially when Forms are properly understood.[2] This leads to the second point. The Neoplatonists' view about Forms was built on a reading of all the dialogues, the letters, and Aristotle's testimony. What Aristotle manifestly rejects was to these philosophers something quite different from the picture of Forms that a close reading of all the evidence would show. So, Aristotle, like Plato himself in several places, rejects an inadequate or false theory of Forms, not the true—Platonic—theory.[3]

---

1. See, e.g., Frank (1940, 35ff.), who finds "the fundamental opposition of Aristotle to Plato" to reside in the former's rejection of separate Forms.

2. See *De An.* Γ 4, 429a15, 28, 29, for the use of the terms τὸ νοητόν and τὸ εἶδος as synonymous.

3. See Krämer 1973 for a useful discussion of the various 'Academic Forms theories' against which Aristotle is reacting.

In this chapter I begin by gathering together the elements of the Neoplatonic interpretation of Plato's theory of Forms; then, I turn to Aristotle's criticisms, largely in *Metaphysics,* and try to show in what ways those criticisms do and in what ways they do not touch the theory of Forms so interpreted. Finally, I consider briefly the mathematical version of the theory of Forms and Aristotle's reaction to it.

The Neoplatonic Interpretation of Plato's Theory of Forms

We should start by recognizing that there is no straightforwardly canonical Neoplatonic theory of Forms. All our evidence leads to the conclusion that many issues regarding Forms were disputed throughout our period. For example, there were differences of opinion regarding the range of Forms, how the Forms were cognized or related to intellect, and how to describe participation in Forms. Proclus in his *Commentary on Plato's Parmenides* offers an apparently well-established list of the questionable Forms: intellect, irrational life, natures, body, matter, animals (genus or species), plants, individuals, parts of animals, attributes, artifacts and the arts, and evil things.[4] The questions originate in Plato's *Parmenides* where Parmenides queries the young Socrates on the range of Forms.[5] He seems to suggest a capacious criterion which, if identical with that contained in *Republic*, should be as large as the class of things with a common name.[6] But Plato's *Statesman* also suggests that common names in language, such as 'barbarian,' are not an infallible guide to the real divisions in the world.[7] So, the problematic nature of the range of Forms is in part rooted in Plato's dialogues and in part, as we shall see, in Aristotle's testimony. Clearly, the question of the range of Forms cannot be answered in a nonarbitrary manner until we have something like an operational definition of a Form. That is, we have to know what a Form is supposed to do before we can establish whether we must posit one or more Forms of whatever sort.

Proclus also offers a definition that he says goes back to Xenocrates, the second successor to Plato, after Speusippus, as head of the Academy: "The Idea is the paradigmatic cause [παραδειγματικὴν] of the things that are eternally [ἀεί] constituted according to nature."[8] The definition is evi-

---

4. See Proclus *In Parm.* 815, 15ff. Alcinous (*Didask.* 9.2, 24–31), writing perhaps some 300 years before Proclus, gives a similar list. See also Syrianus *In Met.* 107, 5, on the question of the range of Forms.

5. See *Parm.* 130A-E.

6. See *Rep.* 596A.

7. *Sts.* 262D-263A.

8. Proclus *In Parm.* 888, 18–19. Alcinous in the above-mentioned passage gives the same definition, adding the word 'eternal' to paradigm. See Krämer 1964, 127–191, and Krämer 1973 for an argument that Aristotle's rejection of Plato's theory of Forms occurs within the ambit of the general Academic theory of principles. Thus Aristotle was a Platonist in the same sense that both Speusippus and Xenocrates were.

dently based on Plato's *Parmenides,* where Forms are said to be "paradigms in nature," and on *Timaeus,* where Forms are repeatedly described as paradigms of the generated world.[9] Leaving aside for the moment all other pertinent questions, we need to ask first, as Aristotle himself asked, why posit paradigms?

Plato in *Parmenides* has Parmenides offer Socrates the closest thing we have in the dialogues to a *reason* for positing Forms: "I suppose that your reason for thinking each Form to be one is this: whenever it appears to you that there are some many large things, perhaps there seems to be some one character (ἰδέα) which is the same when you look at all of them, on the basis of which you think that Largeness is one."[10]

The fact that many things are the same in being large, can be explained only if there exists something whose correct name is 'Largeness.' This does not seem entirely perspicuous. For one thing, although the appearance of many large things seems sufficient to generate the need for a Form, it does not seem necessary. For, as we shall see presently, if Forms explain at all, they explain the mere possibility of a many as well as a real many. That is, if there is one large thing or no large things, but the possibility that there can be one and therefore many, then Forms will be needed to explain this, if Forms are needed at all. More important, why is an explanation for many large things needed at all, and how is a Form supposed to provide it?

The underlying argument seems to be this. If something is large, then 'large' stands for a real feature in this world. But if something else can be large, too—that is, if 'large' is not part of the identity of just one thing—then there must be *another* real part of the world that the word 'Largeness' stands for. Why? Because Largeness is what these two things share in. If 'Largeness' referred to the same thing to which 'large' referred, then the two large things could not also be the same or possess the identical nature. From here it is but a step to the conclusion that things like Largeness are the entities that provide eternally the condition for the possibility of things having words like 'large' correctly used of them.[11]

The obvious rejoinder here is that 'Largeness' does not refer to anything or, more narrowly, to any *separate* thing. Those who take this tack are divided between those who think that 'Largeness' does not refer because no two things could have the same property while remaining two things, and those

9. See *Parm.* 132D2; *Tim.* 28A7, 28C6, 31A4, 37C8, 38B8, 38C1, 39E7, 48E5. Aristotle in *On the Ideas,* according to Alexander of Aphrodisias in his *In Met.* 83, 21–22, says that being a παράδειγμα is "especially characteristic of Ideas." Cf. 86, 15: "the Idea's being an Idea consists in its being a παράδειγμα."

10. *Parm.* 132A1–3. Cf. *Euth.* 6D9-E1; *Men.* 72C6-D1; *Rep.* 597B-E. Alexander of Aphrodisias *In Met.* 80, 8–81, 22, gives the full one-over-many argument.

11. At *Parm.* 135C2, Parmenides says that without Forms "the possibility of discourse" (τὴν τοῦ διαλέγεσθαι δύναμιν) will be destroyed. Forms ensure the possibility of discourse because they ensure the intelligibility of its objects. This intelligibility consists in the samenesses and differences in the sensible world which are ultimately explained by Forms. See G. Damschen 2002, esp. 59–64.

who think that although two things can have the same property, it is not necessary to hypothesize an entity named 'Largeness' to explain the possibility of numerically distinct things having the same property. As we have already seen, Aristotle's acceptance of a universal 'largeness' does not touch the question of whether such an explanation is necessary.[12]

Proclus seems to have understood the argument as concerned with explanatory entities. Commenting on *Parmenides* 127D, Proclus argues that "it is impossible for the many to exist without the one."[13] As he goes on to explain, this is because every member of the many is complex or 'not-one.' To be a member of a many is to be complex. For example, consider a many each of which is called 'large.' If each member of the many were not complex, it would be nothing but large. In that case, there would not be many 'larges.' So, we need to distinguish that which is large (what 'participates' in large) and the largeness in it. But the largeness in the large thing is not what makes the many *this* many. That is, the largeness in each of the large things must be distinguished from the Largeness in virtue of which the many can be said to be many large things. The distinction of Largeness from the largeness of each large thing is the common currency of any non-nominalistic metaphysics. The claim that Largeness must be ontologically prior to the largeness in each large thing in order to explain the possibility of there being many large things is what distinctively characterizes Platonic metaphysics.[14]

The argument employed by Proclus concludes in a distinction—which Proclus at one point attributes to Iamblichus—between (1) that which participates (τὸ μετέχον), (2) that which is participated in (τὸ μετεχόμενον), and (3) that which is unparticipated (τὸ ἀμέθεκτον).[15] Stated otherwise, this is a distinction between, say, (1) a large thing, (2) the largeness in the large thing, and (3) the entity, whatever it might be, that possesses largeness paradigmatically. It is a distinction that is in fact well founded on claims

12. See Ferber (2001, 74–75; 2002, esp. 330–333), who argues similarly that Aristotle's claims about universality and universal knowledge do not address the problem that Forms are meant to solve. Strang (1963), thinks that if the Form is a paradigm, it must exemplify a universal. This seems to reverse the ontological and logical orders, at least if the Form is taken to be an explanatory entity.

13. *In Parm.* 696, 32–697, 21; cf. 1078, 13; 1197, 19; *In Tim.* II 304, 19. The argument is most fully set out in *ET* Prop. 2.

14. Proclus also relies on two other passages in Plato. At *Soph.* 245A it is argued that if a sum or whole is a unity, then that sum or whole cannot be just unity because it is many, that is, complex. At *Parm.* 157E-158A it is argued that what has unity cannot be just unity. In both passages Proclus takes the argument to be generally applicable to anything that can be said to be 'one f' where 'f' names a distinct property or attribute. At *Phil.* 15B1 Plato refers to Forms as 'monads' (μονάδες), alluding it seems to the 'one' that is 'over and above' any 'many.' Cf. also *Parm.* 142B5-C2 on the essential complexity of whatever can be the same as or different from something else.

15. See *ET* Props. 23 and 24; *In Tim.* II 105, 15ff.; 240, 4–7; 313, 15–24, where the reference to Iamblichus is to be found; *In Parm.* 1069, 23ff.; *In Remp.* I 259, 2–17; Asclepius *In Met.* 115, 34–36. Iamblichus also apparently believed that Plato and Aristotle were not in fundamental disagreement regarding Forms. See Iamblichus *apud* Elias (or David) *In Cat.* 123, 2.

made in the dialogues.[16] The question of whether Forms are transcendent or immanent is thus answered by a distinction between the paradigmatic version of the nature which is transcendent or unparticipated and its image or inferior version which is immanent or participated. This latter is called 'an enmattered form' (ἔνυλον εἶδος).[17]

It will be at once evident that 'enmattered form' is an accurate and reasonable way to refer to the forms in matter that Aristotle discusses in the central books of *Metaphysics*.[18] So, given the foregoing distinctions, we should not find it odd that Aristotle's discussions of sensible substance are taken to be at least covering the same territory as does Plato when he refers to sensibles and their properties. What is of course problematic is any further inference to the effect that the forms of sensible composites are to be related to nonsensible paradigms, as they are in Plato.

In *Metaphysics* Book B, Aristotle raises two aporiai he calls "most difficult." The first poses the problems of whether there is some cause besides matter, whether it is separate, whether it is one or many, whether such causes exist besides all composites or none or some, and what kinds of beings such causes are.[19] The second closely related aporia raises the problems of whether there exists something besides individuals—that is, individual composites—and how it is possible to acquire knowledge if something does *not* exist apart from the individual composites. In addition, if something eternal and immovable does not exist, generation would seem to be impossible, assuming generation out of nonbeing is impossible. Further, if matter is ungenerable, so, it seems, is form. And it seems necessary that there exist

16. The distinction is implicit in the combination of claims made in five passages: (1) *Phd.* 100D4–8, where the question of how Forms are present is left aside, though it is insisted that the Forms are the instrumental cause of things having the properties they have; (2) *Phd.* 102D6–8, where Plato distinguishes between Largeness and largeness in us; (3) *Parm.* 129A3–4, where it is said that things that are like are so because they partake in likeness, which is distinguished from a Form of Likeness (129A1); (4) *Parm.* 130B3–4, where Parmenides offers Socrates the distinction between separate (χωρίς) Likeness and the likeness we possess; and (5) *Tim.* 52A1–3, where the Forms are said never to enter into anything. See Barford (1976, esp. 203–206 and 212 n. 17), who discusses the 'argument from relatives' at *Met.* A 9, 990b15–17, which summarizes the full version in *On the Ideas* (= Alexander of Aphrodisias *In Met.* 82, 11–83, 17). Barford argues—correctly, in my view—that Plato wants to distinguish a nature as it exists in a Form from the nature as it exists in its instances or copies. I believe that this distinction implies the Neoplatonic distinction between Form and nature. Malcolm 1991, 159–166, believes that Plato failed to distinguish the Form as paradigm from the Form as universal. Accordingly, he rejects the implication drawn by Neoplatonists from the five texts above. The distinction between Form and nature is not, however, the distinction between paradigm and universal. The universal is posterior to both.

17. See *In Parm.* 839, 33–34; 863, 3. The term is also used by Iamblichus *De Myst.* VII 2. 251, 1. Syrianus *In Met.* 105, 30–35, criticizes Aristotle for thinking that Socrates [i.e., Plato] confuses the enmattered form with the transcendent Form.

18. The term is used frequently by Alexander of Aphrodisias in reference to the forms in the sensible composite substances in Aristotle's metaphysics. In his *In Met.* 133, 33, he seems to suggest that the term is Stoic in origin, even though the idea is obviously older. Cf. Asclepius *In Met.* 146, 15; 148, 26; 375, 20–21; 381, 16; 382, 20; 413, 35.

19. See *Met.* B 1, 995b31–36.

something over and above the composite individual: namely, something intelligible (νοητόν). But this raises the problem of what eternal intelligibles we should posit. Clearly, Aristotle says, we should not posit it for all, since we should not posit it for a house apart from an individual house.[20]

Aristotle offers perfunctory praise to Plato for limiting Forms to the things that exist by nature.[21] As we have seen, the definition of a Form that Neoplatonists arrived at assumes the reductionism implicit in this limitation. The question then becomes whether these Forms are necessary. Before we can answer this question as the Neoplatonists would answer it, we have to complete their sketch of the theory of Forms.

Having distinguished the Form's nature in its unparticipated and participated ontological status, questions naturally arise regarding both. According to the Neoplatonic understanding of Plato's account, the answers lie in the role of the Demiurge. The gulf between modern and ancient interpretations of Plato is nowhere more evident than it is with respect to the relation between Forms and a divine intellect. Part of the reason for this gulf is that the interpretation widely if not universally rejected by modern scholars—that the Forms are thoughts in the Demiurge's intellect—is in fact an interpretation that the Neoplatonic commentators themselves also rejected. Plato in *Parmenides* emphatically discards the view that Forms are thoughts (νοήματα) in any intellect.[22] If a Form is to fulfill its explanatory role, it must be an object of thought (τὸ νοούμενον, τὸ νοητόν) as 'one-over-many,' not a thought.

The confusion of 'thought' with 'object of thought' is evident in Alcinous, who in his *Didaskalion* uses the terms acts of thinking (νοήσεις), 'thoughts' (νοήματα), 'intelligibles' (νοητά), and 'objects of thinking' (νοούμενα) interchangeably for Forms in relation to the Demiurge.[23] By contrast, Plotinus is particularly insistent that Forms are not thoughts but, as Plato says, that which thoughts are of.[24] Proclus, in his commentary on the

---

20. Ibid., B 4, 999a24-b24. See K 2, 1060a3-7, b23-28, which expands somewhat on the two *aporiai*. The passage in K adds that if eternal separate substance does not exist, then the order of the universe will be destroyed. H 3, 1043b18-23, rejects a separate οὐσία for artifacts but leaves open the question for destructibles: that is, for substances that exist by nature. Cf. *On the Ideas* 79, 13-15, where Aristotle agrees that the 'one-over-many' argument shows that there exists something besides particulars but that this is not an 'Idea.' What this is, says Aristotle, is something common (τὸ κοινόν), but it could not be a universal, which is not required to exist by any argument.

21. See *Met.* Λ 3, 1070a13-19.

22. See *Parm.* 132B-C.

23. Alcinous *Didask.* chaps. 9-10, with Dillon 1993, 93-111.

24. See VI 6, 5-10: "First, then, we should grasp the essence of the Forms generally, that is, that they do not exist because the one thinking thinks each one, and so by that thinking provides each of them with its existence. For it is not because the one thinking thought of what Justice is that Justice came to be nor because he thought of what Motion is that Motion came to exist' (πρῶτον τοίνυν δεῖ λαβεῖν τὴν οὐσίαν καθόλου τῶν εἰδῶν, ὅτι ἐστὶν οὐχὶ νοήσαντος ἕκαστον τοῦ νενοηκότος, εἶτ᾽ αὐτῇ τῇ νοήσει τὴν ὑπόστασιν αὐτῶν παρασχομένου. οὐ γάρ, ὅτι ἐνόησε τί ποτ᾽ ἐστὶ δικαιοσύνη, δικαιοσύνη ἐγένετο, οὐδ᾽ ὅτι ἐνόησε τί ποτ᾽ ἐστὶ κίνησις, κίνησις ὑπέστη). At V 3, 5, Plotinus argues that a thought is a representation or image

Parmenides passage, makes essentially the same point.[25] So, though the Neo-platonists are generally firm in understanding that Forms are not thoughts in the intellect of the Demiurge, nevertheless they want to insist that Plato believes that Forms are inseparable from the Demiurge or divine intellect. What is the evidence for this interpretation?

Plato in *Timaeus* hypothesizes an intellect (νοῦς) as the cause of order in the universe.[26] Why is an intellect needed to explain order? Plato does not explicitly answer this question. He does, however, seem to assume that the intelligibility of the sensible world—that is, essentially, the samenesses and differences among things—rests upon a relation between or among intellects. For something to be understandable to us, it must be the product of an intellect.[27] That something *is* understandable to us indicates that an intellect has made it so. The preexistent chaos in the universe prior to the imposition of order by the Demiurge is equivalent to the existence of what is unintelligible.[28] If this is indeed Plato's view, how does he conceive of the relation between the Demiurge, the producer of order in this universe, and the Forms, the principles of order?

There are two passages in *Timaeus* which, taken together, seem to imply that the Demiurge and the Forms are extensionally equivalent. First, it is said that "the world has been produced according to that which is graspable by reason or understanding and is always in the same state." Shortly afterward, it is said that "he [the Demiurge] desired that all things should come as near as possible to being like him."[29] The natural implication is that the Demiurge produces order out of chaos according to a model that is the Demiurge himself.[30]

(τύπος) and that knowing the truth cannot amount to having an image; rather, the Forms as truth must be directly cognized. See also V 5. 1–2 and V 9. 5–8 for additional arguments for the eternal identity of intellect and intelligibles. Cf. Syrianus *In Met.* 105, 27–28.

25. See Proclus *In Parm.* 892, 9–35. Simplicius *In Cat.* 95, 10–20, adds that the Ideas are not in the Demiurge as accidents of it either.

26. See *Tim.* 47E4–48A2.

27. See *Phil.* 26E-27C, 28C-29A, esp. 28E3: "The view that everything is ordered by intellect, on the other hand, does justice to the visible order of the sun, moon, and stars and all their revolutions."

28. See *Tim.* 49A-50A, 52D-53C. That before the imposition of shapes and numbers (εἴδεσι τε καὶ ἀριθμοῖς) by the Demiurge one could have discerned traces (ἴχνη) of the elements' natures does not indicate that there is intelligibility without intellect, but rather that these traces, most likely phenomenal properties, are not 'intelligible' in Plato's use of that term. They are traces of their cosmic versions, not traces of Forms. See Perl 1998.

29. See *Tim.* 29A6-B1, 29E3. Cf. 30D1–3. Syrianus *In Met.* 106, 14–16, concludes a discussion of misconceptions about Forms with the unequivocal statement that Forms belong as a totality in the Form of Living Animal which in turn is contained in the νοῦς of the Demiurge. Syrianus adds that in the Form of Living Animal, the Forms exist intelligibly (νοητῶς) and in the Demiurge they exist intellectually (νοερῶς). Cf. 109, 31ff; Proclus *PT* V 17. This appears to be a distinction between nature nature and universal, the latter being the former for an intellect.

30. Proclus *In Tim.* I 323, 20–324, 14 follows Syrianus in distinguishing the Form in the Form of Living Animal as intelligible and the Form in the Demiurge as intellectual, basing his interpretation on the two *Timaeus* passages taken together. See also Asclepius's *In Met.* 165, 36–37; 166, 29–31.

One could perhaps without a great deal of strain make a case for a different implication. The Demiurge wants the universe to be as close as possible to him. But he is not identical with the Forms. So, to be as close as possible to the Demiurge is to be as close as possible to the Forms, but not to be identical with them.[31] The latter interpretation requires that if the Forms are external to the Demiurge, then what is internal to him are presumably the thoughts that are representations of Forms but not identical with Forms. This would make the intelligibility of the sensible world two removes from Forms, not one.

There are, I suspect, two reasons for taking the latter interpretation despite its implication that the Demiurge is no better placed in relation to Forms than are we: First, that this is necessary in order to preserve the independence of Forms; second, that it is necessary because intellect cannot be identical with Forms. Both assumptions are dubious. Forms are dependent on the Idea of the Good in *Republic* and the identity of intellect and Forms is cognitive identity: that is, the self-reflexive awareness of one's cognitive state. As we have seen, this is precisely how Aristotle understands cognition paradigmatically.[32] Cognitive identity with an object of intellect—an intelligible—is not equivalent to 'having a concept,' which certainly for Aristotle and probably for Plato involves images. Cognitive identity with the intelligible and not conceptualization is the manner in which the prime unmoved mover is characterized. It is ironic in the present context that some have thought that Plato could not have meant to 'internalize' the Forms in the Demiurge because that is an *Aristotelian* doctrine.[33]

There is another piece of evidence, overwhelmingly important to the Neoplatonists for understanding the relation of the Demiurge to Forms. In *Sophist*, Plato is arguing against supporters of incorporeal reality, whom he calls "friends of the Forms."[34] These 'friends' hold that the really real is always in the same state. As such, Forms cannot be acted upon because to be acted upon is to be moved: that is, to be in an altered state. But that would seem to make knowing Forms impossible, since knowing is a kind of acting, and being known is a kind of being acted upon. The latter implication is preposterous; therefore, motion, life, soul, and thought are present in the really real.

The relevance of this passage to the Neoplatonic interpretation of *Timaeus* is clear. According to that interpretation, what is said here undercuts nothing said elsewhere about Forms and their function. The Demiurge,

31. E.g., this is the interpretation of Taylor 1928, 81–82, and Brisson 1994, 85.

32. Cf. Aristotle *Met.* Λ 7, 1072b21, in reference to the prime unmoved mover: "intellect and intelligible are identical" (ταὐτὸν νοῦς καὶ νοητόν).

33. See Perl (1998, 84 and n. 5), who has a good discussion and criticism of this view. See Hager 1970, 29–30; 53–59, for a detailed argument for the interpretation that Plato means to 'internalize' Forms in the Demiurge.

34. See *Soph.* 248A–249B and supra chap. 1, n. 58. Aristotle himself (*Top.* Z 10, 148a14–22), argues that "those who say that there are Ideas" hold that these Ideas are "impassive" and "immobile." In other words, Aristotle is arguing against a view that Plato himself appears to reject in *Sophist.* Cf. B 7, 113a24–32.

cognitively identical with Forms, imports a sort of motion into the really real world. That motion is what in *Laws* is called the "motion of intellect" (κίνησις νοῦ).[35] It is exactly equivalent to what Aristotle calls 'the activity of intellect' in *Metaphysics* in reference to the prime unmoved mover.[36]

The principal interpretive ambiguity is in the phrase τὸ παντελῶς ὄν. The Neoplatonists as well as many modern scholars take it as equivalent to ἡ οὐσία and ἡ ὄντως οὐσία, which the friends of the Forms contrast with γένεσις and claim is 'always in the same state.'[37] If they are not equivalent, then the Stranger does not seem to be replying to their argument. In addition, if they are not equivalent, then the admission sought from the friends is that the motion of intellect, life, and soul are real things, something that they would hardly deny.[38] So, if we take τὸ παντελῶς ὄν as equivalent to 'the really real,' then we must, as the Stranger explicitly says, give up the idea that the really real world is without motion altogether. This does not, however, mean that we must also give up the idea that the Forms—that is, the objects of ὁ νοῦς or τὰ νοητά—are changeless, as the Stranger also implies.[39]

If we then allow that 'psychic' or 'spiritual' motion, life, and soul belong to τὸ παντελῶς ὄν, the following question arises: are we to understand this conclusion as indicating that Plato's conception of what is really real includes, as it were, the 'sum' of psychic motion, and so on, and motionless Forms, or is it that the essence of the really real is to be conceived as other than as the 'friends' would have it?[40] The problem with the former alternative is that there is then in the text no argument, implicit or otherwise, for including psychic motion in the really real. There is just the bald assertion or rhetorical hyperbole that it would be preposterous to exclude it.

35. *Lg.* 897D3 and *Tim.* 89A1–3: "Of motions, again, the best is that motion which is produced in oneself by oneself, since it is most akin to the motion of thinking and of the universe. Motion produced by another is inferior" (τῶν δ' αὖ κινήσεων ἡ ἐν ἑαυτῷ ὑφ' αὑτοῦ ἀρίστη κίνησις—μάλιστα γὰρ τῇ διανοητικῇ καὶ τῇ τοῦ παντὸς κινήσει συγγενής—ἡ δὲ ὑπ' ἄλλου χείρων).

36. *Met.* Λ 7, 1072b27: ἡ γὰρ νοῦ ἐνέργεια ζωή. The term ἡ ἐνέργεια was invented by Aristotle to indicate a sort of κίνησις that is without imperfection, that is, potency. See Simplicius *In Phys.* 405, 24ff.; 822, 22–823, 4 who assumes the equivalence of ἡ κίνησις νοῦ and ἡ ἐνέργεια νοῦ.

37. *Soph.* 248A7, 11–12. *Rep.* 477A3 uses the phrase τὸ παντελῶς ὄν as equivalent to τὸ παντελῶς γνωστόν. At 477A7 we have the equivalent phrase τὸ εἰλικρινῶς ὄν.

38. See Pester 1971, 103. If psychic motion belongs to the really real such that the *sum* of the really real is Forms plus this motion, then we have no explanation for the distinction between the really real and what is not really real: namely, what is becoming. If, on the other hand, the attribution of 'really real' to psychic motion does not entail that other motions are really real, this is presumably because it is a unique kind of motion. Its uniqueness is to be found in the fact that it does not involve change. It is equivalent to 'actuality' in Aristotle. If this is so, then it would seem to be impossible to separate divine intellect from Forms without making the acquisition of knowledge of Forms by divine intellect a change.

39. *Soph.* 249B12-C4.

40. Among those who hold to the view that the really real is the sum of psychic motion and immovable Forms are Diès 1932, 67–73; Cornford 1934, 246; and Ross 1951, 110–111. Cherniss (1944, 437–442; 1965, 352–354) thinks that the argument proves only that a Form of Motion must be admitted by the 'friends.' See De Vogel 1969.

Neoplatonists, however, would argue that immovable Forms and think-ing—at least the thinking of a divine intellect—are inseparable. Given that this thinking does not cause the Forms to change—for example, Oddness becoming Evenness when thought—there hardly seems to be a difference between these two interpretations. This is clear if we realize that the Neo-platonists are also assuming that οὐσία cannot be the locus of the first prin-ciple of all. Making thinking inseparable from Forms does not insinuate motion—even the attenuated motion that is equivalent to intellectual activity—into the first principle. Those who resist the idea that Plato holds that divine thinking is cognitively identical with Forms suppose that if this were true, there would then be no absolutely immobile first principle. But this supposition never seemed remotely plausible to those who saw the Forms and the Demiurge as subordinate to a first principle. The central point is the inseparability of one type of psychic motion and life from intel-ligible reality.[41]

The remaining central feature of the Neoplatonic interpretation of Plato's theory of Forms is the reduction (ἀναγωγή) of Forms to first principles. Aris-totle in the course of his discussion of Forms says: "But since the Forms are the causes of the other things, he [Plato] thought that their elements are the elements of all things that are. So, he identified the material principle as the Great and the Small and the formal principle as the One. For from the Great and the Small by participation in the One came the Forms."[42]

We already know from *Republic* that the Forms depend for their being upon the Idea of the Good. What we have here is an implicit identification of that principle with the One and the introduction of a second principle, the Great and the Small, elsewhere called the Indefinite Dyad.[43] There is no question that Plato recognized in *Philebus* two principles, the Indefinite (τὸ ἄπειρον) and the Definite (τὸ πέρας), as well as the combination of the two, and the 'cause' of the combination.[44] What is in dispute is whether these principles are to be applied solely to the composition of sensibles or whether

41. Perl 1998, 83–84, argues that since the Demiurge is not an entity that has an intellect but is intellect itself, he must be identical with 'thinking' (νόησις) and so always cognitively identical with his objects of thought. His thinking consists of the Forms. It hardly seems rea-sonable to object, as does Brisson 1994, 159 [1974 edition], that this interpretation makes Plato "too Aristotelian."

42. *Met.* A 6, 987b18–22. I follow Jaeger's text, which includes τὰ εἴδη instead of τοὺς ἀριθ-μούς, as confirmed at 988a8–14, esp. a11. At A 9, 990b17–22, Aristotle says that the arguments for Forms destroy (ἀναιροῦσιν) the first principles: namely, the One and the Indefinite Dyad. Presumably, they do so because they are arguments for the ultimacy of Forms rather than the first principles. Since Aristotle himself does not seem to recognize explicitly a principle higher than divine thinking, the harmonists will insist that the Aristotelian rejection of Forms as ulti-mate does not fatally affect their being posited altogether. See also Theophrastus *Met.* 6b11–14 on the reduction of Forms to first principles.

43. Aristotle explicitly identifies the One with the Good at *Met.* N 4, 1091b13–14, though he does not here refer specifically to Plato. Cf. *EE* A 8, 1218a24–28. See Hager 1970, 102–156, for a thorough consideration of the evidence for this identification.

44. See *Phil.* 23C–27C. Simplicius *In Phys.* 453, 30–454, 16, identifies Porphyry in his *Phile-bus* commentary as the first to support Aristotle's testimony with the *Philebus* passage.

the general approach can be translated into the intelligible world and applied to Forms. Aristotle, at any rate, has no doubt that this is what Plato did or at least that this is where Platonic speculation was leading. Closely related to the hypothesis of the ultimate principles of the One and the Indefinite Dyad is the identification of Forms with Numbers in some sense.[45]

It is true, as Cherniss and others have urged, that not all of Aristotle's references either to the reduction of Forms to first principles or their identification with Numbers clearly specify Plato as the proponent of these views, as opposed to other members of the Academy.[46] In fact, I do not think we have any way of independently assessing Plato's level of commitment to a reductionist program. Nevertheless, that Aristotle's testimony reflects intra-Academic discussions seems evident. More to the point, reductionism of some sort is strongly suggested both by the dependence of Forms on an ultimate principle and by their multiplicity within an intellect. That the reductionism had a mathematical cast is not intrinsically improbable, given Plato's strong mathematical interests.[47]

According to Aristotle's testimony, the derivation of Forms from ultimate principles—whether or not Forms are identical with Numbers—is a causal derivation. But the causality is obviously nontemporal. It is safe to say that one could write a fairly comprehensive history of Neoplatonism around the various theories offered to explain this causality and to deduce what A. H. Armstrong felicitously termed "the architecture of the intelligible universe." Here we need only to stress that the fact of reducibility means that Forms never were for the interpreters of Plato truly ultimate entities. They belonged within a larger framework. How we divide up the products of the first principle of all, including Forms, is less important than the fact that they *are* products. Forms are part of an explanatory framework that conditionally, qualifiedly explain. It is in this light that the Neoplatonic reactions to Aristotle's criticisms must be understood.

45. See *Met.* A 9, 991b9, 992b15–18; Λ 8, 1073a18–21; M 7, 1081a5–8, 12–13; M 8, 1083a18–19, 1084a7–9; N 2, 1090a4–6; N 5, 1092b8–18. See infra 232–241.

46. See Cherniss 1945, 26–28, 47–48, 58–59, for the case that Aristotle misattributes to Plato the doctrine of the reduction of Forms to Numbers. Cherniss's argument remains an indispensable prophylactic against the attribution of a settled and well-established doctrine of Form-Numbers to Plato. This argument, is impotent, however, against (1) the claim that discussions of reductionism were carried out within the Academy as an ongoing live subject and (2) the claim that the doctrine of separate Forms entails some sort of reductionism, regardless of Plato's view of how this might work exactly.

47. At *Tim.* 53B5, the shapes and numbers (εἴδεσι τε καὶ ἀριθμοῖς) that the Demiurge uses to make the pre-cosmic forces into cosmic elements are the basic intelligible features of the world. Everything else is built up from these elements. On the use of εἶδος for geometrical shape, see Taylor 1928, 358. Aristotle *De An.* A 2, 404b18, says that the Form of Living Animal (τὸ ζῷον) of *Tim.* 30C2–31A1 was derived by Plato "from the Idea of the One itself and the primary Length, Breadth, and Depth." See Findlay 1974, 54–80, for an exposition of one attempt to explain how the reductionism works. Findlay concedes (79) that the program was evidently incomplete and speculative. We might note in passing that Plato's connection of intelligibility with order suggests mathematical reductionism as a hypothesis, owing to the fact that order is essentially a mathematical notion.

It will no doubt have occurred to the reader, as it certainly occurred to Neo-platonists, that there is an apparent conflict in holding that (1) everything is derived from the Good or the One *and* (2) that there are *two* ultimate principles, the One and the Indefinite Dyad. Plotinus offers one standard solution to the problem by interpreting the Indefinite Dyad as the thinking of the divine intellect apart from or logically prior to its information by intelligibles. Thinking is like sight considered apart from actual seeing.[48] Accordingly, Plotinus wants to retain the derivation of absolutely everything from a single principle and interprets Plato as concurring in this.[49] For this reason, too, the burden of causal ultimacy is lessened for Forms.

The foregoing sketch of the Neoplatonic interpretation of Plato's theory of Forms should provide the basis for an assessment of the general claim that Aristotle's account of reality is in harmony with the philosophy of Plato despite the criticism leveled by Aristotle against Forms.

Aristotle's Criticism of Plato's Theory of Forms

In Book A, chapters 6 and 9 of *Metaphysics,* Aristotle discusses the philosophy of Plato, grouping it with the 'Italian' (i.e., Pythagorean) philosophies but distinguishing it according to its own peculiarities. In chapter 9 in particular he mentions a number of arguments for the existence of Forms and briefly adds some criticisms of these.[50] Alexander of Aphrodisias's *Commentary on Aristotle's Metaphysics* expands upon these arguments and criticisms, drawing large amounts of material from the lost work *On the Ideas*.[51] There are also criticisms of Forms in the central books of *Metaphysics* as well as in Books M and N. On the basis of these texts—to say nothing of things said in other works—there is little doubt that in some sense Aristotle is the enemy of Forms.

Matters are never quite so simple, however. First, it is clear enough that Aristotle discusses various theories of Forms, including those held by Plato's successors in the Academy. What is not always so clear is when Aristotle is discussing Plato's theory of Forms as opposed to that of someone else, perhaps one or another 'friend of the Forms.' Second, and of paramount importance, from the Neoplatonic point of view, Aristotle himself was thought to have held or, if one likes, conceded that the prime unmoved mover is eternally thinking all intelligibles (τὰ νοητά) which, as we have seen, are not implausibly identified as Forms in some sense. So, from the

48. See V 3. 1, 11–12; V 4. 2, 4–10; VI 7. 16–17.

49 See II 4. 5, 25–26; III 8. 10, 1–2; IV 8. 6, 1–6; V 3. 15, 27–29; V 3. 17, 10–14; V 5. 5, 5–7; VI 7. 42, 11; VI 9. 1, 1–2. See Hager 1970; Halfwassen 1992, chap. 3, for discussions of the Neoplatonic focus on the derivation of a 'many' from the One.

50. Chaps. 7 and 8 of Book A also include material relating to Plato but are more broadly focused.

51. See esp. Leszl 1975 and Fine 1993 for extensive discussions of the arguments in *On the Ideas* as we know them from Alexander's *Commentary*. Asclepius *In Met.* 44, 12–13, insists that Plato is similar to Pythagoras not merely in some of his views but in all.

Neoplatonic perspective, our understanding of Aristotle's rejection of the theory of Forms should not be such that it entails a rejection of eternal intelligibles. Aristotle, in short, must be understood to be arguing against an inadequate or incorrect version of the theory of Forms. Third, if Aristotle did detect one or more errors or imprecisions in Plato's thinking about Forms, then the Neoplatonists believed that they had the resources to correct or refine the Platonic account. Platonism before Plato—a good Aristotelian point, after all.

Aristotle's criticisms of Forms and their reduction to ultimate principles are of various kinds. There are arguments that seek to show that the theory is based upon principles that lead not only to the postulation of Forms that Platonists accept but to the postulation of Forms that they reject. So, the theory is internally inconsistent. There are arguments that seek to show that the principles for postulating Forms in general lead to illogical conclusions, such as the 'third man' argument. There are arguments to the effect that the conclusion 'Forms exist' does not follow from true premises adduced by the Platonists—for example, that knowledge exists and knowledge is not of sensibles.[52] And there are arguments that seek to show internal contradictions in the theory according to Aristotle's own principles. The presentation of these arguments in *On the Ideas* and in *Metaphysics* follows no discernible order. I begin my discussion with what I take to be the principal argument in the last mentioned category, because it goes to the heart of the Neoplatonic position.

The argument is that a Form is postulated as a separate individual existent (τόδε τι). But a Form is predicated (κατηγορούμενον) or 'said of' the many sensibles. It is, however, the function of a universal to be 'said of' many, not an individual. So, Forms have contradictory natures, that is, to do what Plato wants them to do, they have to be individuals *and* universals.[53] A dilemma is thus presented to the Platonists. If they wish to insist that the Form is a separate individual, then they must give up the primary function of a Form which is to be a one-over-many. If, on the other hand, they wish to maintain this function, then they can no longer insist that the Form must be a separate individual. From the perspective of one who sees the opposition of Aristotle and Plato as fundamental and unbreakable, this argument is a sort of Maginot Line. But it is a puzzling argument for all that.

---

52. At *Met.* B 2, 997b34–998a6, Aristotle reports the evidently Platonic argument that sensibles cannot be the objects of geometry and astronomy. Cf. K 1, 1059b10–12. Aristotle's well-known solution to this type of problem in *Phys.* B 2 and *Met.* M 3—namely, that mathematics treats abstractly of the quantitative properties of sensibles—is far from obviously satisfactory.

53. See *Met.* B 6, 1003a7–13, where the problem of the relationship between individuality and universality is raised as needing treatment. The argument is made against the Platonic approach at Z 13, 1038b35–1039a9; Z 16, 1040b25–30; K 2, 1061b21; M 9, 1086a32–35. The Aristotelian principle that an individual is not a universal is already stated at *Soph. El.* 22, 178b37–39 and 179a8–10.

In the passage in *Parmenides* where Parmenides offers the young Socrates a principle for positing Forms, we saw that Forms explain the possibility of predication. It is easy to slide from "Forms explain the possibility of predication" to "Forms are predicates," since it is difficult to see how else they could provide explanations. There is, however, a significant difference between "Largeness is a Form" and "there is a Form for Largeness." This difference is reflected in the Neoplatonic distinction between 'participant,' 'participated,' and 'unparticipated.' Largeness is participated or shared in by a large thing. But the Form of Largeness is unparticipated. Why is it that this distinction, developed at some length by the Neoplatonists and based upon a number of central Platonic texts, is ignored by Aristotle in this argument?

In order to make the distinction between largeness and the Form whose name is 'Largeness,' the latter has to be sufficiently complex so that we distinguish between the Form and its nature. We need such a distinction in order to be able to maintain that a large thing can participate in largeness without compromising the transcendence of the Form.

Aristotle in *Topics* makes mention of the relevant distinction. In the matter of testing whether a property does or does not belong to a subject, he asks us to consider, for destructive dialectical purposes (ἀνασκευάζοντα) to be sure, whether a predicate belongs to a Form as subject in virtue of being a Form or in virtue of its nature.[54] For example, "since being motionless does not belong to Human Being itself (αὐτοανθρώπῳ) insofar as it is a human being but insofar as it is an Idea, being motionless is not a property of human being." But then Aristotle adds that for constructive dialectical purposes (κατασκευάζοντα) one can do the opposite: namely, show that a property belongs to a Form because it belongs to its nature. The dialectical context of this passage suggests that Aristotle is here talking about conceptual distinctions that one can avail oneself of in arguing a case.[55]

That more than conceptual distinctions are at issue, however, is plain from the fact that Aristotle in *Metaphysics* uses the assumption that there is no *real* distinction between a Form and its nature to argue that if something participates in the properties that belong to Form's nature, it must by that very fact participate in the properties that belong to the Form.[56] For example, if something participates in Doubleness, it must participate in eternity, since eternity is an attribute of the Form. Something could not participate

---

54. See *Top.* E 8, 137b3–13; Z 10, 148a14–22. Owen (1968, 108ff.), distinguishing what he calls 'A predicates' and 'B predicates,' argues in effect that Aristotle is correct to hold that the distinction is purely conceptual and that it does not help Plato avoid such conclusions as that the Form of Man is both immortal (as Form) and mortal (as man). Vlastos 1973b, 323–325, responding to Owen, does not think that Aristotle ever allows the distinction to Plato.

55. This is similar to the sophistical use of conceptual distinctions mentioned by Socrates at *Parm.* 129C-E: e.g., showing that the same thing is both many and one.

56. See *Met.* A 9, 990b27–34. See Ross 1924, 1:197, on the interpretation of this obscure argument. See also Owen 1968, 123–124.

in Doubleness without participating in the properties of the Form unless there were a real distinction between the Form and that nature.[57]

The basis for the Neoplatonic response to Aristotle's argument is set forth in Asclepius's *Commentary on Aristotle's Metaphysics*:

> Aristotle here seems to be opposing Plato on Ideas. We have already seen the aim [τὸν σκοπὸν] of Aristotle regarding this matter. For it is he himself who says [1] in the work *De Anima* that "those have spoken well who have said that the soul is the place of forms," and [2] [in *Metaphysics*] that intellect in actuality is its objects, and further [3] [in *De Anima*] that intellect in potency acts and intellect in actuality makes. So, Aristotle himself straightforwardly places Ideas in the intellect. Why, then, someone might say, if he is elevating Ideas, does he seem to be quarreling with Plato? We reply that in reality he is quarreling not with Plato, although elsewhere he in fact does quarrel with Plato, but with those who have posited these Ideas as existing by themselves and as having been separated from intellect. Thus, the whole conception of Aristotle regarding Ideas has become clear to us.[58]

The passages in *De Anima* to which Asclepius is referring are (1) Γ 4, 429a27–29; (2) Γ 5, 430a19–22; and (3) *De Anima* Γ 5, 430a10–17.[59] The first passage is a quotation that omits the following important words: "except that it is not the whole soul but the thinking part of it, and that [part] is not actually but potentially the forms." The qualification, however, is mitigated by the passage in (3) where the agent intellect seems to be actually identical with forms.[60] Asclepius takes Aristotle to be railing against a view of Forms

---

57. I find it helpful to employ the technical term 'real distinction' here. There are two types of real distinction: major and minor. A major real distinction is between or among separate entities; a minor real distinction is within a single entity. E.g., Socrates is really distinct from Plato according to a major real distinction. Socrates' color is distinct from Socrates (or his height) by a minor real distinction. By contrast, Socrates, insofar as he is an Athenian, is only conceptually distinct from Socrates insofar as he is a Greek. That the idea of real minor distinctions is found in Aristotle and Plato, though the technical term is not, is, I believe, clear. A substance is really distinct from its accidents, and large things are really distinct from the largeness in them. The crucial dispute between Plato and Aristotle is whether there are real minor or major distinctions within incorporeal reality.

58. *In Met.* 69, 17–27. Cf. 71, 27–29; 90, 19. See also 433, 9–436, 6 where Asclepius cites Syrianus as countering Aristotle in the same way. See esp. 433, 30–434, 5, where Asclepius refers to Syrianus as using the term 'universal' in two senses: (a) that which is posterior and in the mind and (b) that which is substance (οὐσία), even if it be predicated of [a subject] (εἴ γε κατηγορεῖται αὐτῶν). The two senses of 'universal' are paralleled by two senses of 'predication.' In the first sense, that which is predicated does not have an independent existence; in the second sense, that which is predicated is the independent existent in whose nature individuals participate. Cf. Syrianus *In Met.* 114, 9–11. See also Elias *In Por. Isag.* 115, 4–26; Philoponus *In APo.* 242, 10–243, 25 for a similar analysis. See Romano 1993 and Libera 1996, 84–92, for a summary of Syrianus's response to ten arguments of Aristotle for the claim that a separate Form cannot perform the function of a universal.

59. See also *Met.* Λ 9, 1075a1–5. Ross in his edition of *De Anima* excludes 430a19–22 as a repetition of 431a1–3. So, there is no doubt that this is Aristotle's view.

60. Another passage earlier in *De Anima*, though not directly mentioned here by Asclepius is relevant. Aristotle says in B 5, 417b22–24, "Knowledge is of things taken universally, and these are in a certain sense in the soul." Cf. *APo.* A 31, 87b37–39.

which the Neoplatonists have themselves rejected as not Platonic.[61] It is the view that each Form is a self-contained eternal and immutable island of intelligibility. This view is in no way entailed by the fact that each Form is a 'one' over many. Nor is it entailed by the characterization of a Form as 'itself by itself,' since this locution indicates the separation of Forms from the sensible world, not their separation from each other or, indeed, from an intellect.[62]

A Form isolated in the way that Asclepius thinks both Plato and Aristotle reject would indeed be unable to function as the explanation of identity in difference. How, we may well ask, does refusing to isolate them from an intellect make any difference? The answer is that the intellect—that is, the divine intellect or Demiurge—makes it unnecessary to insist that the separate Form is predicated of those things that participate in the Form's nature. The Demiurge puts intelligibility into the things in the sensible world as images of the divine paradigm. The universality of the Form is not its function; rather, it exists universally in the intellect of a knower.[63] Thus, as we have seen earlier, Syrianus distinguishes between the Form existing as an intelligible and the Form existing intellectually—that is, in the Demiurge. When the Demiurge thinks a Form, he is thinking it universally.[64] Presumably, therefore, all thinking of Forms is done universally; this fact does not entail that the Form is itself a universal. In addition, the identity of Forms with the divine intellect guarantees the incorporeal complexity sufficient to be able to make a real distinction between a Form and its nature. To be able to be thought universally, the Form must be really distinct from the object of universal thinking.[65]

61. See Chen 1940, 10ff., for another argument that Aristotle's criticism of separation is directed at Academics other than Plato.

62. At *Parm.* 133C3-D5 Parmenides characterizes Socrates' version of the theory of Forms as holding that if Forms are separate from the sensible world, then they "are what they are in relation to each other" and not to the "likenesses in us" or whatever we call them. Proclus *In Parm.* 930, 6–931, 9 points out that if the Forms are unqualifiedly separate from us, then they will be unknowable. We need to understand Forms such that we can maintain that they are transcendent (ἐξήρηνται) and not in us and, at the same time, are present everywhere and are participated in, while not being in their participants (930, 33–37). The nature of the Form, not the Form, is present in the participant, in a diminished way. So, even the separation of Forms from the sensible world has to be qualified by the Platonist.

63. See Malcolm (1991, 54–62; 167), who supposes that the Form is intended by Plato to function as a universal. By this, Malcolm means that the Form is the "ontological basis for the application of the predicate term" (54). I think the latter claim is exactly right. But it is a mistake to think that such an "ontological basis" is incompatible with paradigmatism.

64. See Libera 1996, 105–108 on Syrianus on 'psychic Forms' as intermediary between Aristotelian concepts meditated by images, and separate Forms. Syrianus *apud* Hermias *Scholia on Plato's Phaedrus* Couvreur, 171, 4–30.

65. Plotinus, e.g., at V 9. 7, 7–14, insists that Forms exist prior to their being thought. See also VI 6. 6, 8–10. Malcolm 1991, chap. 4, and Fine 1993, 25, argue that Forms are universals; see Fine 248–249 nn. 21–22 for clarification. See Lear (1987, esp. 160–168), who argues apropos of *Met.* M 10, 1087a10–25, that Aristotle distinguishes two senses of ἐπιστήμη, the latter, active ἐπιστήμη, is of form and of a τόδε τι but *not* of the universal. This is because form itself is neither universal nor particular. On this point, see esp. Owens 1951, 389: "The form cannot be a singular. . . . It cannot be a universal."

The reason why the Demiurge's thinking the Forms universally is not reducible to conceptualization is that the Demiurge *is* the entity that each and every nature is really distinct from.[66] So, the eternal cognitive identity it has with each nature while contemplating it is not merely a representation of the Form—a representation, that is, of that which is external to intellect. Given this analysis, we can at least see the basis for the Neoplatonic view that when Aristotle says, in reference to the prime unmoved mover, that when "intellect thinks itself it does so by partaking of the intelligible" and "by thinking, intellect and intelligible are the same," he is not saying something in principle different from what Plato holds.[67]

Still, it might be supposed to strain credulity to hold that Aristotle's words "the soul is the place of forms" should be given an unqualifiedly Platonic reading. Indeed. That is why it is important to distinguish sharply between harmonization and identity. In holding that Aristotle is arguing against an unsustainable account of Forms, Asclepius does not, I think, mean to suggest that Aristotle is just defending Plato in the way that Socrates in *Parmenides* suggests that Zeno is defending Parmenides, by attacking Parmenides' opponents. That is, Asclepius is not arguing for the identity of the views of Aristotle and Plato. It is, rather, Aristotle's adherence to general Platonic principles that places his philosophy in harmony with Plato's despite their differences.

Related to the central objection that a Form cannot serve its explanatory function if it is a separate individual are the objections that Forms do not fit anywhere into Aristotle's framework for scientific explanation. Aristotle says it is evident that if Forms were to be any part of that framework, it would be as causes of the 'whatness' of things, that is, as formal causes.[68] But then Aristotle argues in Book Z that to separate the formal causes of things from those things leads to disaster.[69] As we have already seen, the Neoplatonists define a Form as a 'paradigmatic cause,' and a paradigmatic cause is distinct from the 'enmattered form.' Aristotle does address in passing the suggestion that a Form is a 'paradigm' and that other things 'participate' in Forms, dismissing the suggestion as "empty words and poetic metaphors."[70]

One reaction to Aristotle's objection is to say that he willfully misrepresents Plato.[71] Another reaction, that of the harmonists, requires that we

---

66. See Plotinus V 5: "That the Intelligibles are not Outside the Intellect and on the Good," esp. 2. 8, 9; v5.3, 1: "There is, then, one nature, for us, Intellect, which is all things [i.e., Forms], and the truth" (Μία τοίνυν φύσις αὕτη ἡμῖν, νοῦς, τὰ ὄντα πάντα, ἡ ἀλήθεια.)

67. See *Met.* Λ 7, 1072b19–21.

68. See *Met.* A 6, 988a7–11.

69. See *Met.* Z 6, where, however, it is not clear how the conclusion that "each thing and its essence are one and the same" applies to sensibles. See Code 1985, 114–119, for an argument that the conclusion applies not to the composite sensible but to the form of the composite. This, for Code, is the primary substance, that which is καθ' αὑτὸ λεγόμενον. See the detailed argument in Wedin 2000, esp. chaps. 5–7, for a variation on this view, according to which it is a form of a genus that is identical with the essence.

70. See *Met.* A 9, 991a20–22; M 5, 1079b24–26.

71. So Cherniss 1944.

consider the context of the objection. Aristotle explicitly argues against Forms in Book A of *Metaphysics* as part of a theory of causality.[72] It is clear enough that a paradigmatic cause does not fit into the fourfold schema of causality to which Aristotle is committed. No Neoplatonist supposed that in fact it did. Still, a Form as a paradigmatic cause *is* rejected. Where is the harmony in that?

Asclepius confronts the criticism that calling Forms 'paradigms' is "empty words and poetic metaphors."[73] He replies that Forms are paradigms for the Demiurge just as the physician looks to the rules of medicine within him as paradigms for treatment. What are paradigms in the intelligible world are 'images' (εἰκόνες) here below. Asclepius goes on to point out that it is a horse that produces a horse and a human being that produces a human being, not the Forms of Horseness and Humanity.[74] In other words, paradigms are not part of the explanatory framework of particular events or things. That, says Asclepius, is why we hold that Ideas of particulars do not exist; there are only Ideas of things considered universally.[75]

The point that is being made here is a shrewd one. The explanatory role that Forms are postulated to fulfill is not part of the Aristotelian explanatory framework. A Form is the explanation for the eternal possibility of intelligible real predication among sensibles. The explanation for an actual predicate is addressed exhaustively within the Aristotelian framework and acknowledged by the Platonist. The 'enmattered form' is part of that framework. Asclepius takes Aristotle to be objecting to someone who would adduce the unparticipated paradigm as part of an Aristotelian explanation.

One might interpret Aristotle's objection as aimed precisely against those who think that eternal possibilities *need* an explanation. If the explanation of the acquisition of this particular attribute by this particular substance is given, what else needs explaining? In reply to this question, the Platonist must insist that in explaining how something has acquired an attribute, one has failed to offer an explanation of how it can be true that the identity of the thing both does and does not include that attribute. To be sure, Aristotle has a great deal to say about the sense in which a substance and its attributes are and are not identical.[76] But the Neoplatonic harmonist is not, it seems, so far off the mark in holding that what Aristotle says, far from being an alternative to Platonism, presupposes Platonism.[77] Aristotle, like Plato, believes in attributes, and so the nominalist response that no explanation

72. See *Met.* A 9, 990a33-b2: "Those who posited the Ideas as causes, first, in seeking to find the causes of the things around us."
73. See Asclepius *In Met.* 87, 34–88, 18.
74. Ibid., 88, 37–89, 4. See supra n.24.
75. Ibid., 89, 6–7.
76. See esp. *Met.* Z 4.
77. See Proclus (*In Parm.* 883, 37–884, 3), who argues that identifying that which is common in things still leaves the question of the explanation of the origin of that which is common. In other words, identifying the fact that many things are large does not explain how many self-identical things can have the same attribute. Cf. 885, 1–2.

for the possibility of real predication is required because there is no possibility of predication is not available to him. Aristotle the realist is better served by the embrace of Platonism than if he is construed as basing his criticism of Platonism on nominalist premises.[78]

There is a passage later in *Metaphysics* where Aristotle seems to suggest the strategy of denying that the identity among particulars requires no explanation: "Now, if, as in the case of the elements of speech, nothing prevents the existence of many A's and B's even if there is no 'A Itself' and 'B Itself' over and above the many A's and B's, then for this reason, there will be an indefinite number of syllables that are like (ὅμοιαι)."[79]

This sort of argument may be a perfectly reasonable one for a nominalist to make. It is hard to see how it is available to someone, such as Aristotle, who wants to insist that, to employ his own example, the many A's are so called *because* they share the same form. That form is a 'this' (τόδε τι) and prior to sensible composites.[80] If there were no form, there could be no fact that consisted in something having a particular property. If there were no *eternal* Form, then there could be no eternal possibility of something having one sort of property rather than another. Nor will it do to say that the possibility is real only with the initial instantiation of the form. For that initial instantiation only demonstrates an eternal possibility. To maintain otherwise would be to confuse the conditions for the initial instantiation ("it is only now possible that x is f because such and such conditions exist") with the possibility of instantiation of one form rather than another ("given such and such conditions, it is now possible that Fness be instantiated").

Asclepius's understanding of the criticism of a Form as a useless 'paradigmatic cause' is also indirectly supported by Aristotle's account in Book M of *Metaphysics* where he says that Forms were adduced in order to provide explanations for individuals (τὰ καθ' ἕκαστα).[81] Asclepius seems justified in insisting that Forms were never intended to provide such explanations. That is precisely why there are no Forms of individuals. Even more important from the harmonists' perspective is that the explanations for individuals that Aristotle *does* provide do not preclude or contradict the role of Forms. Indeed, the enmattered form provides the link between the Aristotelian explanations and the Platonic. The enmattered form does what the

78. See Frede and Patzig (1988, 48–57) and Irwin (1988, chap. 12), who, among others, argue that in *Met.* Z 13, Aristotle's rejection of the substantiality of the universal entails his acceptance of a nominalist position: that is, the position that form is particular. Against this, see Lear 1988, 273–93, as well as the references to scholarship on both sides of the debate in Bostock 1994, 186–187.

79. *Met.* M 10, 1087a7–10. Annas 1976, 190, interprets Aristotle thus: "It is wrong to assume that things cannot share a common form without there being another thing to explain this."

80. See *Met.* Δ 8, 1017b25; H 1, 1042a29; Θ 7, 1049a35; Λ 3, 1070a11 for form as a 'this.' The form is prior because it is that by which the composite is known. See Owens 1951, 386–395, on the 'thisness' and separability of forms.

81. See *Met.* M 4, 1078b36–1079a2.

separate unparticipated Form was never supposed to do. But the enmattered form could not exist if its eternal perfect paradigm did not exist.[82]

The same basic approach employed by Asclepius is to be found in his
analysis of the so-called third-man argument in *Parmenides* against Forms.
The argument is that the principle for positing one Form 'over and above'
or separate from sensibles is the identification of a 'many,' that is, many
things with the same attribute. But it seems that that principle can be
applied to the 'many' consisting of the original 'many' plus the Form
itself. If that is the case, another Form 'over and above' the original Form
and the original many is required. And so on. Indefinitely.[83] The threat-
ened regress is presumably vicious both because it undercuts the claim
that the Form is a 'one' and because it seems to make knowledge of a
Form impossible.[84]

A general hermeneutical point to be made about this argument is important for the harmonists' approach. Plato raises one or perhaps two versions
of the argument himself.[85] Neoplatonists universally supposed that Plato did
not regard these arguments as fatal to Forms as he conceived of them. Aristotle himself mentions a version of the argument in several places, and in
all those places it appears that the argument is supposed by Aristotle to be
fatal to Forms.[86] There is one passage, however, in which Aristotle says that
it is 'they' (i.e., Platonists) who introduce the third man.[87] Aristotle cannot
but have been aware that third-man arguments were used in the Academy
to separate inadequate from adequate understandings of Forms. It was natural for Neoplatonists to assume that Aristotle's own views were in harmony
with the latter and not the former.

Asclepius makes two points against the third-man argument.[88] First, the
argument works only if Forms are conceived as existing separately from the
divine intellect. Second, since Forms are *not* absolutely separate existents,
they are not to be taken as the same as sensibles. So, a Form plus the original 'many' does not constitute a legitimate many requiring another Form
over and above it. Syrianus makes basically the same point, saying that the
Form is not 'synonymous' with the many, and adding, "The Idea should not

82. De Strycker 1955, argues that Aristotle in both *Metaphysics* and *On the Ideas* presents the
separation of Forms as part of an exclusive dilemma: either Forms are separate from sensibles,
or they are present in sensibles. But this dichotomy the Platonist need not accept: "ne croyons-
nous pas que la notion de séparation, telle qu'elle figure dans le Περὶ Ἰδεῶν et la *Métaphysique*,
soit empruntée à Plato lui-même"(138–139).

83. See Rickless 1998, esp. 518–525 and 529–533, for a good analysis of the two arguments
in *Parmenides* known as third-man arguments. Rickless includes references to the major modern discussions of them.

84. See Fine 1993, 203–204.

85. *Parm.* 131E-132B; 132C-133A. It is not clear that the second argument is identical with
the first, though it, too, purports to lead to a vicious infinite regress.

86. See *Met.* A 9, 990b17; Z 13, 1039a2; *Soph. El.* 22, 178b36–179a10. Alexander records
a fuller version from *On the Ideas* in *In Met.* 84, 23–85, 3 (cf. 93, 1–7).

87. See *Met.* M 4, 1079a13.

88. See Asclepius *In Met.* 75, 19–35.

in any way be thought to partake of anything."[89] Proclus mentions the inappropriateness of synonymy to describe the relation between the Form and its instances explaining, "The common element in the many instances is that of being derived from and having reference to one (ἀφ' ἑνὸς καὶ πρὸς ἕν). For what the one Form is primarily, the many under it are derivatively."[90]

The use of the Aristotelian phrase "derived from and in reference to one" for the relationship between a Form and an instance of a Form (that is, an enmattered form) is striking. Anyone, including Plato, who did not think that the third-man argument was fatal to Forms would have to deny that the Form and its instance are 'synonymous.' And that means that Forms are not self-predicative.[91] Anyone, including Aristotle, who took the third-man argument as having force against the postulation of Forms would have to think that Forms *are* synonymous with their instances. Aristotle's notion of one thing being derived from and in reference to another, or "πρὸς ἕν equivocity," as it is more usually known, gives the Platonist the exact language in which Forms and their instances can be indicated.[92]

Some scholars regard it as a problem that if Aristotle recognized the applicability of πρὸς ἕν equivocity to Forms and their instances, then his argument against Forms—particularly the third-man argument—is sophistical or captious.[93] On the other hand, if he did not recognize it as applicable, then what right have the Neoplatonists in holding not just that it *is* applicable but that it is a tool of harmony? That is, without the applicability of πρὸς ἕν equivocity to Forms and their instances, one would have either to concede the defeat of Platonism or to recognize Aristotle as its enemy.

One of the arguments in Alexander's report of *On the Ideas* in his *Commentary on Aristotle's Metaphysics* is the so-called argument from relatives.[94] This argument, as reported by Alexander, is an argument *for* the existence of at least some Forms, namely, Forms of Relatives. The argument purports to show that, for example, a Form of Equality must exist because things said to be equal are said to be so only as imperfect likenesses of Equality. But if this is so, then there must exist that which is Equality primarily (κυρίως) and

89. See Syrianus *In Met.* 111, 33–112, 6. See Barford 1976, 211–214.

90. See Proclus *In Parm.* 880, 8–13. Cf. Asclepius *In Met.* 46, 22; 71, 10–12; 82, 32–83,1. That Form and instance are not 'synonymous' does not preclude the identity of the nature of the Form and its instances.

91. Contra Owen 1957, 177. Plotinus II 4. 9, argues that a Form of Quantity is not quantitative and a Form of Whiteness is not white. See Fine (1993, 61–64), who thinks that Plato is committed to 'broad' self-predication. It is not clear to me whether broad self-predication is different from the Form's identity being just what its name names. Fine (230–231), takes one implication of broad self-predication to be that the Form and instance are 'synonymous,' although this synonymy is not sufficient to generate the third man argument.

92. See *EN* A 6, 1096b26–31, and *Met.* Γ 2, 1003a34-b5. See Syrianus *apud* Asclepius *In Met.* 435, 12–22, for the rejoinder to Aristotle based on a distinction between types of sameness.

93. See Owen 1960, esp. 181–190.

94. See Alexander of Aphrodisias *In Met.* 82, 11–83, 17. See on this argument Owen 1957, and Fine 1993, 142–170 (including her argument against Owen's interpretation). See also Annas 1974; Barford 1976.

truly (ἀληθῶς). This argument seems to originate in Plato's *Phaedo*, where it is directly aimed at showing that the soul preexists incarnation. This is shown by arguing that, when embodied, we are able to recognize sensibles as being equal but deficiently so, and we could not do this if we had not had previous knowledge of the Form of Equality.[95] Here, Aristotle is reported by Alexander as saying that the argument establishes Forms of Relatives such as Equality, but that the Platonists do not want to admit such Forms. The reason is that the Platonists hold that Forms "exist on their own" and so are substances, whereas relatives "have their being in relation to others."

The first point is that these Platonists who do not want to recognize Forms of Relatives must be other than Plato himself, given what is said in *Phaedo*. So, we might suppose that Plato wanted Forms of Relatives but that he also wanted to make Forms independent existents, in which case he would be making contradictory claims. But we have seen that the independence of Form from the sensible world does not entail the unqualified independence of Forms. Indeed, as we have seen above, Asclepius claims that Aristotle's arguments against Forms generally work only against those who think of Forms as existing on their own. If Asclepius is right in holding that Plato does not think that Forms exist in this way, then it is not clear that Aristotle, finally, rejects this argument from the imperfect instances to the perfect Form.[96]

Alexander reports that Aristotle provides two further objections to positing Forms of Relatives on the basis of the foregoing argument. First, if the [Idea of] Equality is equal to another Equal, there will be more than one Idea of Equality. Further, if there is an Idea of Equality, then there will be Ideas of Inequalities. For if there is an Idea of one of a pair of opposites, then there will be an Idea of the other. In addition, they agree that inequality is in more than one thing. The second argument is insignificant since it is not at all obvious why the Platonists should fear a Form of Inequality. The first argument, however, seems to threaten the uniqueness of Forms, at least Forms of Relatives.[97] But it does so only if Forms are self-predicative, or at least have the predicate that their names name

95. See the argument from recollection at *Phd.* 72E3–78B3 with Gerson 2003, 65–79, for an analysis.

96. I agree with Owen (1960, 183–84), that *Protrepticus* does not provide clear evidence of the distinction Owen believes Aristotle could have used on Plato's behalf. But the fragment from *On Philosophy* quoted supra chap. 2, n. 95, does: καθόλου γάρ, ἐν οἷς ἐστί τι βέλτιον, ἐν τούτοις ἐστί τι καὶ ἄριστον· ἐπεὶ οὖν ἐστιν ἐν τοῖς οὖσιν ἄλλο ἄλλου βέλτιον, ἔστιν ἄρα τι καὶ ἄριστον, ὅπερ εἴη ἂν τὸ θεῖον. This argument will recall *Met.* α 1, 993b24–31: "Of things that are synonymous, the one to which a predicate belongs in the highest degree is that in virtue of which it belongs also to the others." Notice that in this passage Aristotle stipulates cases where there is synonymy. In the former passage he does not draw a conclusion about synonymy.

97. The argument from relatives focuses on such Forms, leaving open the question of whether there are Forms of nonrelatives, or substantives, such as 'human being.' I am assuming that this openness reflects Academic discussions and the possibility of a reduction of Forms.

synonymously with their instances.[98] This is something the Neoplatonic commentators believe follows *only* if Forms are incorrectly understood as absolutely independent entities.[99]

Alexander also reports what appears to be a fourth objection to the argument from relatives.[100] The objection appears in fact to regard all Forms and to claim that they are all in a sense relatives. If the Form is a paradigm and paradigms are relative to what they are paradigms of, then Forms are relatives. But Form instances are images (εἰκόνες), and images are relative as well. Therefore, all things that exist by nature will be relative. The argument is offered in a passage criticizing the reduction of Forms to ultimate principles. The implication of the argument, that everything including Forms is relative to—that is, dependent upon—first principles is hardly one that Platonists would flinch from embracing. Even if Aristotle is reluctant to embrace it, his own argument in *Metaphysics*, especially Book Λ, seems to be not incompatible with it.

Once again, I am not claiming that Aristotle's arguments against Forms are frivolous or arguments for Forms in disguise. Everyone, ancient and modern, believes that Aristotle rejects *some* theories of Forms. What makes matters slightly more complicated is that the Neoplatonists also believed that Plato rejects some theories of Forms, including those held by certain unnamed 'friends.' So, the issue is whether Aristotle rejects the theory that Plato, according to the Neoplatonists, actually held. Even this is something of an oversimplification, because in some matters, such as the range of Forms and the structure of reduction, there was no canonical position. Alternative, contrary views on these matters, and others, were available to Platonists. Accordingly, some Platonists must have disagreed with Plato, assuming that Plato had definite views on all these questions.

It would not be very plausible, however, to say merely that Aristotle's refutation of some theories of Forms indicates that he himself is hospitable to another version, which just happens to be the one to which Plato adhered. There must be positive indications of harmony—not of identity, as I have repeatedly argued. These include Aristotle's support for (1) the priority of the intelligible to the sensible; (2) the eternality of form; and (3) the non-identity of form and universal.[101] If the explanatory focus of the science of being is separate substance and separate substance is identified with separate form, it is not, I would suggest, captious for Neoplatonists to conclude that Aristotle's sketch of that science—identified, we must recall, with a science

---

98. Fine 1993, 189–190, argues that Plato accepts self-predication of Forms but that this does not force us to accept that the Form of Equality is equal to something and that therefore there are two Forms.

99. See ibid., 144–149 and 228–231 with n. 27; Fine argues that Forms are synonymous with their instances. But that this does not in itself generate a vicious infinite regress argument for Plato.

100. See Alexander of Aphrodisias *In Met.* 86, 13–23.

101. See ibid., 199, 35–39 and supra chap. 3.

of theology—is harmonious with Platonism. Nevertheless, no Neoplatonists supposed that the prime unmoved mover, eternally contemplating intelligible reality, was anything more than a simulacrum of the authentic first principle of all. Although Aristotle recognized that such a principle must be absolutely simple and unique, he mistakenly identified it with thinking.

Mathematics and the Forms

One of the more vexing parts of Aristotle's criticism of Platonic metaphysics generally regards mathematics. That criticism is found principally in Books M and N of *Metaphysics*. Among the problems facing anyone trying to sort through this material is that Aristotle is evidently criticizing a number of Academic views, including no doubt Plato's but those of Speusippus, Xenocrates, and unnamed others as well. It is not always evident whose view he has particularly in mind in any one passage. Notoriously, with respect to Plato, it is difficult to correlate Aristotle's apparent interpretation of Plato's views with anything in the dialogues. Therefore, we are hardly in a good position to say that Aristotle has represented anything like a settled view of Plato as opposed to a theory up for discussion in the Academy at some time.

The problems for seeing Plato's views on mathematics through the lens of M and N of *Metaphysics* evidently infected the work of the commentators. Alexander of Aphrodisias was deeply puzzled by the books.[102] Plotinus, typically, assumes that Aristotle has an authoritative grasp of Plato's views and that his criticisms oblige Plotinus to defend Plato as expounded by Aristotle. Syrianus is certain that Aristotle seriously misunderstands Plato, though he himself is not always able to provide a perspicuous and persuasive alternative interpretation.[103] Proclus, heir to an immense treasury of speculative exegesis, offers his own original interpretation of Platonic mathematics, implicitly reading Plato in a way that enables him to respond to Aristotelian criticism.

The tentacles of developmentalism, too, are waiting for anyone entering these murky waters. Jaeger held that M 9, 1086a21, through chapter 10 and book N represent an earlier version of Aristotle's attack on Academic mathematics, whereas M 1 up to 9, 1086a21, represents Aristotle's mature treatment of these issues.[104] Jaeger gives three main reasons: (1) the text beginning at 1086a21 seems to represent a jarring break in the line of argument, suggesting the beginning of a different discussion; (2) at two places, M 10, 1086b19, and N 4, 1091a32, Aristotle uses the first person plural in referring to ostensibly Academic positions; (3) the latter parts of Book Λ, a work otherwise judged by Jaeger to be early, depend on Book N, which contains a fuller account of the criticism of Speusippus's version of Platonism.

---

102. See, e. g., Alexander of Aphrodisias *In Met.* 55, 20–56, 35.
103. See e.g., Syrianus *In Met.* 159, 33–160, 5.
104. See Jaeger 1948, 176–193, 205–208, 223–227. See Annas 1976, 81–88, for a trenchant criticism of Jaeger's view.

If, as I have already argued, the general developmentalist position of Jaeger and others has a plausibility that is more apparent than real, its application here can hardly be thought to stand on its own. For in the case of the supposed earlier mathematical works, Jaeger is not arguing that they are Platonic; rather, he is arguing that they belong to the period when Aristotle was still an Academic, albeit one of a contrarian stripe. "A Platonist without Ideas" is perhaps a way in which one version of the harmonists' position might characterize Aristotle. But if this is the way to characterize the relatively immature Aristotle, it is equally a good way of characterizing the Aristotle who wrote the works that Jaeger himself recognizes as belonging to Aristotle's most mature period.[105]

No one, including the Neoplatonists, doubts that in Books M and N Aristotle is articulating his opposition to what he understands to be Plato's mathematical metaphysics, specifically the view that mathematics deals with eternal and immutable entities that are separate from the sensible world. The manner in which the harmonists deal with this opposition is, as we shall see, familiar. That is, they will argue that Aristotle's view of mathematics is compatible with Plato's because it deals with a separate subject matter. But unlike the case of *Categories*, where we saw that one could plausibly argue that everything said about sensible substance leaves untouched matters relating to the supersensible, here the same eirenic division of labor does not work so smoothly. For Aristotle's opposition to Plato in the matter of mathematics seems to go to the heart of the dispute over what it means for reality to be intelligible. On one view, Aristotle's rejection of Platonic mathematics amounts to a rejection of the position that to understand reality is to understand it mathematically, that at the foundation of the intelligible is the mathematical. If this is so, then perhaps his rejection of Plato's mathematics has negative implications for the harmonists' position. Perhaps one cannot be a Platonist after all if one rejects Plato's mathematical metaphysics.

A sketch of the simple harmonist strategy regarding mathematics begins by recognizing that for Aristotle, mathematics is a demonstrative science of quantity (τὸ ποσόν).[106] Quantity is that which is divisible (διαιρετόν) into

---

105. At M 10, 1086b16–19, the words "If anyone does not posit the substances to be separate, and in the manner in which individual things are said to be separate, he will be eliminating substances in the sense which we mean by the term 'substance'" (εἰ μὲν γάρ τις μὴ θήσει τὰς οὐσίας εἶναι κεχωρισμένας, καὶ τὸν τρόπον τοῦτον ὡς λέγεται τὰ καθ' ἕκαστα τῶν ὄντων, ἀναιρήσει τὴν οὐσίαν ὡς βουλόμεθα λέγειν·) do not, as Annas (1976, 191–192), argues convincingly, show that this passage belongs to Aristotle's 'Academic' period. We can without difficulty understand the 'separation' of substance here in the way that both Plato and Aristotle do: that is, as independent existence. But Annas misrepresents the argument of Jaeger, who wants to insist that it is the meaning of the word οὐσία that Aristotle here seems to share with Plato, not the meaning of the word κεχωρισμένας. This is an important point if, as Annas and I both hold, Books M and N presuppose the general line of argument of *Metaphysics*. For it is precisely Aristotle's recognition that οὐσία as form is unqualifiedly separate which supports the harmonists' position. Jaeger sees this as 'early' Aristotle; Annas's argument against Jaeger implies that it is 'late' Aristotle.

106. See *Cat.* 4b20–25; *Met.* Δ 13, 1020a8–10; K 4, 1061a28–35, 1061b17–25.

parts, each of which is 'some one thing' (ἕν τι) and a 'this' (τόδε τι).[107] The two types of quantities are discrete and continuous. The science of the former generally is arithmetic; of the latter, geometry. Arithmetic deals with numbers (ἀριθμοί); geometry deals with magnitudes (μεγέθη): that is, lines, planes, and solids. Discrete quantities are indivisible and have no common boundary and no position; continuous quantities are indefinitely divisible and have common boundaries and position.[108]

The unit is the principle of number, since a number is a plurality of units (πλῆθος τῶν μονάδων).[109] Therefore, the smallest number is 2.[110] One might suppose that the point (στιγμή) is similarly the principle of magnitude (if points make up lines, and lines make up planes, and planes make up solids).[111] But for Aristotle a line is *not* composed of points as a number is composed of units.[112] That is, whereas the units of a number are its material parts, the points on a line are not its material parts. This is so basically because the divisible magnitude that is the line cannot be composed of indivisible lines. This lack of parallelism will be of considerable importance, as we shall see presently.

A number has a form and matter. Its matter consists of its units, and its form is the precise number that it is.[113] Without the form there could be no number, just an indefinite plurality. So, a number is a plurality of units of a certain type: that is, with a certain form. Similarly, a magnitude has form and matter. A triangle has as its matter its three straight lines, and its form is 'sidedness in a plane' and the angularity of these sides. Since a line is either straight or curved, straightness and curvature would seem to be its forms, which would make line itself the matter.

Since quantity is an accidental attribute of sensible substance, the science of quantity begins and ends with these. Therefore, if there were a mathematical science of supersensibles, it would be called 'mathematics' equivocally, since there are no quantities (or at least no sensible quantities) among supersensibles.[114] Here it is evident that available to the harmonist is the

107. See *Met.* Δ 13, 1020a7–8.

108. See *Cat.* 4b25–31; *Phys.* E 3, 227a10–17; *Met.* M 9, 1085b15–22.

109. See *Phys.* Γ 7, 207b7; *Met.* I 1, 1053a30.

110. See *Phys.* Δ 12, 220a27. In the Platonic framework, assuming that the Indefinite Dyad is a principle, the smallest number is the 'definite dyad' that is, 2, C_F. Sextus Empiricus *M X* 262. The number 2 is a 'pair.' . *Parm.* 143C–D. According to Iamblichus *In Nic. Arith.* 10, 18, the definition of number, taken from Eudoxus, is 'limited plurality' (πλῆθος ὁρισμένον). This would clarify the distinction between the Indefinite Dyad and the number 2.

111. See *Top.* B 18, 108b26, 30; Z 4, 141b6–12. At *Met.* Δ 6, 1016b24–26, Aristotle defines a 'unit' (μονάς) as "that which is indivisible in every dimension and without position" and a 'point' as "that which is indivisible in every dimension and with position."

112. See *Phys.* Z 1, 231a21-b20; *Met.* M 9, 1085b31–34.

113. See *Met.* N 8, 1084b5–6.

114. Forms of Quantities cannot themselves be quantities. That is why they are 'noncomparable' (ἀσύμβλητοι). See Aristotle *Met* M6, 1080a10, 29, etc. See Plotinus VI 6. 16; V 5. 4, 16–20. Iamblichus *Theol. Arith.* 52, 1–8, makes a distinction between sensible, mathematical, and intelligible 'quantity.' On Iamblichus's account of the different types of number and on its

same strategy employed in arguing that the discussion of sensible substance does not address or exclude discussion of supersensible substance.[115] But there is more to the matter than this. The fact that there are sensible substances does not even suggest that there are not supersensible ones, whereas the claim that mathematics is a science of quantity does imply that where there are no quantities, there is no mathematics, and its use for the non-quantitative is not so much equivocal as fanciful. So, though Aristotle allows that mathematics is not *about* sensibles, sensibles are in a way the basis of mathematics.[116] It deals with sensibles *qua* immovable: that is, sensibles just in their quantitative aspects.

Plotinus raises a pertinent question about this neat schema. What do numbers and magnitudes have in common?[117] That is, what is their generic nature? There are grounds in Aristotle for holding that in fact quantity is not the genus of which numbers and magnitudes are species. The principal reason is that arithmetic is simpler and prior to geometry.[118] Number or discrete quantity is inseparable from all parts of the study of continuous quantities, but the study of number as such excludes continuous quantities. This raises the crucial question of exactly how the two parts of mathematics are in fact related. Is geometry in any way reducible to arithmetic?

According to Aristotle's position, geometry is related to arithmetic because the latter is more abstract than the former.[119] Geometry considers sensibles qua solids by abstracting from—that is, leaving out everything about—the sensible other than the fact that it is a solid. One can continue the process of abstraction and consider only the plane surfaces of the solids, then go on to consider lines abstracted from the planes, points on the line, and, finally, units alone, which leaves out *everything else* about the sensibles except their numerability. Arithmetic is thus, relative to geometry, more abstractive. And yet, for example, 'three' is included in the definition of a triangle, whereas no geometric object is included in the definition of any arithmetic object. But if the *less* abstractive is more intelligible to us (though it be less intelligible in itself), then we should not need arithmetic concepts to understand geometric ones. What this suggests is that even if arithmetic is posterior to geometry in an abstractive process, there is some sort of priority that arithmetic has to geometry in our understanding.

---

background, see O'Meara 1989, 16–22; 78–79. As O'Meara shows in the summary of his useful study of Iamblichus's work *On Pythagoreanism* (86–105), Iamblichus's efforts to mathematize philosophy thoroughly along (neo)Pythagorean lines probably goes well beyond the harmonists' basic position. See, e.g., Simplicius *In Cat.* 2, 9–25, where Simplicius reports that Iamblichus suspected that Aristotle had deviated from 'ancient' Pythagoreanism.

115. See Syrianus *In Met.* 131, 37–132, 2; 186, 30–35.
116. See *Met.* E 1, 1026a7–10; K 7, 1064a32–33.
117. See VI 1. 4, 8; 4, 50–52.
118. See *APo.* A 27, 87a31–37; *Met.* M 3, 1078a9–26; M 6, 1080a12–b36.
119. See Lear 1982, 175ff.

Another way of getting at this problem is through Proclus's arguments that mathematics in general is not abstractive. In his *Commentary on Euclid's Elements*, Proclus marshals a number of arguments to show that what the mathematician studies is not abstracted from sensibles.[120] The key argument is that if the general is prior in demonstration to the particular sensibles, then it cannot be posterior.[121] In other words, the demonstration that equals taken from equals leave equals is prior to the demonstration of this for a particular type of equals. Similarly, the demonstration that a plane figure is inscribable in a circle is prior to the demonstration that an isosceles triangle is inscribable in a circle, and demonstrations regarding magnitudes in general are prior to demonstrations regarding particular types of magnitudes. If the demonstrations in mathematics are then not about sensibles, what are they about?[122]

Aristotle himself provides a weighty amount of evidence that Plato believed that mathematics concerned 'intermediaries' situated between Forms and sensibles.[123] Leaving aside the truly vexing questions of what exactly the intermediaries were and to what extent Plato believed in objects midway between Forms and sensibles, I here aim only to make the somewhat less contentious point that the objects with which the mathematician deals are themselves understood by Plato only as 'images' of Forms and not objects of knowledge.[124] This is an important point because it prevents us from supposing that mathematical objects were ever held by Plato to be *independent* objects in that way that sensibles are not. Neoplatonists in general, and Proclus in particular, did not suppose that the Platonic response to Aristotle's mathematical criticisms was to insist on the independent reality of an infinite multitude of geometric figures and arithmetic units. What the Platonist must insist on, however, is that what is true about sensibles *qua* their geometrical and arithmetic properties is true of them derivatively.[125] It is because equal

120. See Proclus *In Euc.* 12, 9ff.; 49, 12ff.; 139, 26–140, 18. Cf. *In Parm.* 894, 24ff.; 980, 17ff.; Syrianus *In Met.* 95, 29–38; 90, 17–23. See O'Meara 1989, 159, for discussion with references.

121. See Proclus *In Euc.* 13, 27–14, 15.

122. See Madigan 1999, 59–60, for a good statement of the problem that this creates for Aristotle.

123. See *Met.* A 6, 987b14–17; A 9, 991a4, b29, 992b16; B 1, 995b17; B 2, 997b2, 12, 998a7; B 6, 1002b13, 21; Z 2, 1028b19; K 1, 1059b6; Λ 1, 1069a34; M 1, 1076a19; M 2, 1077a11; M 9, 1086a12; N 3, 1090b35. See also Adam 1963, 2: app. 1 to Book 6; Brentlinger 1963; Annas 1975; Pritchard 1995, 91–118. Cherniss (1945, 35 and 76) rejects unequivocally the attribution of intermediaries to Plato.

124. See *Rep.* 510B4–5; 510D5–511A1. See Gallop 1965, 122, for an argument that the λόγοι mathematicians employ are all images. See Wedberg 1955, 66–67, for a lucid description of the differences between the mathematical intermediaries and the Forms that are Numbers. Wedberg's entire book is, as he says, largely a defense of the Aristotelian distinction between intermediaries and Forms, including but not identical with those that are Numbers. Burnyeat (1987, 219–220 n. 19) points out that there are in fact no textual grounds for assuming that the mathematical objects, as the mathematicians conceive of them, are Forms.

125. See *Phys.* Δ 12, 220b8–12; Δ 14, 224a2–15. At *Met.* N 3, 1090a35–b1 Aristotle acknowledges that the Platonic argument for separate mathematical entities is that propositions in mathematics are true without being true of sensibles. Therefore, what they are true *of* must be nonsensible. See also B2, 997b34–998a6 and Burnyeat's comments 1987, 232.

quantities removed from equal quantities leave equal quantities as remainders that if the sum of coins in each of my two pockets is equal, the sum after removing an equal number from each will be an equal number.[126]

Aristotle wants to recognize the reality of mathematical objects without identifying them as Platonic intermediaries. He says that geometers do indeed speak about realities (ὄντων). But these realities are not what is in actuality (ἐντελεχείᾳ); rather, they exist materially (ὑλικῶς).[127] The contrast suggests that 'materially' here means 'potentially,' and the idea is, presumably, that the mathematical objects exist potentially in sensibles.[128] Hence, the mathematical aspects of sensibles are equated with intelligible matter (ὕλη νοητή) as opposed to the sensible matter out of which these are made.[129]

It is difficult to resist the suggestion that Aristotle is here offering something like a constructionist view of mathematics.[130] According to this view, mathematicians construct their objects out of some preexisting material— in this case, sensibles considered as intelligible matter. Those who take Aristotle's view of mathematical objects as constructivist do so in order to contrast that view with Plato's. And yet the manner in which Plato describes the work of mathematicians in *Republic* has itself a distinctive constructivist cast. In particular, mathematicians are said to 'hypothesize' (ὑποθέμενοι) their objects of study.[131] These hypotheses would seem to be primarily, if not exclusively, existential.[132] The mathematician says, "let there be a line" or "let there be a 'three-sided plane figure" or "let there be two odd numbers." She then proceeds to draw conclusions about these.[133] When we

126. Thus, I disagree with Lear (1982, 188), who argues that the universality of mathematics can be equated with the generality of its claims. Indeed, the truths of mathematics do apply to all sensibles. But this is owing to the fact that each sensible is an instance of a figure or a number. Even if, as Lear holds, (175ff.), sensibles really do instantiate mathematical objects and do not merely approximate them, still they are instances of these objects, not the objects themselves.

127. See *Met.* M 3, 1078a29–30; and Cleary 1995, 331–339, on this passage.

128. See *Met.* Θ 9, 1051a21–33. The refutation of the view that mathematical objects exist 'in actuality' in sensibles is found at M 2, 1076a38–b11 and of the view that they exist in actuality separate from sensibles at M 2, 1076b11 to M 3, 1078a21. At M 6, 1080a37-b4, Aristotle gives three possibilities as alternatives to his own position: (1) numbers are all separate; (2) they exist in sensibles (as constituents of them); (3) some exist in sensibles and some are separate. Aristotle rejects all three views.

129. See *Met.* Z 10, 1035a12, 1036a9–12; Z 11, 1037a2–5; K 1, 1059b16; K 3, 1061a28–35.

130. See, e.g., Annas 1976, 151. Cleary (1995, 498) thinks that constructivism is compatible with Aristotle's realist view of mathematical objects, though ". . . his view of mathematical objects is more platonistic than constructivist, although such a simple dichotomy does scant justice to his complex position." By 'platonism' Cleary means the theory that mathematical objects are "independently existing abstract objects."

131. See *Rep.* 510B4–511A8.

132. See, e.g., *Phd.* 100B3, where the hypothesizing of Forms is explicitly existential.

133. It is, I think, a mistake to suppose that in this passage the mathematicians' claim to be arriving at conclusions about the "square itself" and "the diagonal itself" is intended to indicate Platonic Forms. The locution 'the x itself' for the object of mathematics is unexceptional; it just refers to 'the square' or 'the diagonal' without any implication that these are Forms. This is typical in Euclid, for example.

consider these mathematical hypotheses with Aristotle's own 'constructivist' account and his commitment to a realist foundation for mathematics, the differences between Plato and Aristotle in this regard appear to begin to recede.[134]

Proclus, despite his conviction that Aristotle misunderstands the Platonic position, develops the constructivist approach as an accurate analysis of Plato's position. He takes mathematical objects to be projections (προβολαί) of the soul onto the imagination.[135] These projections are an unfolding (ἐξελλίτουσα) of the essential (οὐσιώδεις) Forms that are eternally present in the divine intellect. They are each precisely a sketch (τύπος) or shape (μορφή) of contents of thought, that is, they are images.[136] Proclus's complaint against Aristotle is that while he grasps the constructivist aspect of mathematics, he cannot account for the eternality and necessity of the truths of mathematics. These are not truths directly about Forms, but Forms are the basis for the truths. Thus, the facts that 2+2=4 and that the line bisecting the hypotenuse of a right triangle is perpendicular to the base are eternally true not because of the existence of separate Forms of '2', 'plus', triangle', line', etc.; rather, they are true because there are eternal Forms whose being these eternal facts express or represent imagistically.

These facts do not refer directly to Forms because Forms are not self-predicative in the way that they would have to be if the facts were about Forms. If there were such a Form of, say, Triangularity or Right Triangularity, it would have to be triangular in order for the truth about the perpendicular line bisecting its hypotenuse to be a truth about *it*. If this is so, then how are the Forms and the mathematical objects actually related?

There are many passages in which Aristotle says that Plato somehow identifies Forms with numbers.[137] What exactly this means is not entirely clear.[138]

---

134. See, e. g., *Met.* E 1, 1025b3–18, and *APo.* A 10, 76a31–36, b3–11, where Aristotle characterizes mathematical hypotheses in a remarkably Platonic fashion. At *APo.* B 7, 92b15–16, Aristotle says that a geometer assumes the meaning (τί σημαίνει) of triangle and proves its existence (ὅτι ἔστι). But this proof of existence here is a proof that a triangle can be constructed, say, from three straight lines. At B 9, 93b21–28, the arithmetician is said to hypothesize both what a unit is and that it exists.

135. See Proclus *In Euc.* 13, 6–26; 17, 22–18, 4; 52, 20–53, 5; 78, 20–79, 2; 141, 2–9. On Proclus's doctrine of projection see Breton 1969, 28–31, 111–122; Charles-Saget 1982, 191–201.

136. Cf. Proclus *In Euc.* 141, 6–7: images (εἰδώλοις) and reflections (ἐμφάσεις). See Charles-Saget 1967 on the connection by Proclus of these projections with the mathematical intermediaries.

137. See *Met.* A 6, 987b18–25; A 9, 991b9–10; 992b13–17; Λ 7, 1073a17–22; M 6, 1080b11–12; M 7, 1081a5–17; 1082b23–24; M 8, 1083a17–20; M 9, 1086a11–13; N 3, 1090a16–17; N 4, 1091b26–27.

138. See Annas 1976, 62–73, for a good discussion of the issue. Annas is skeptical of Aristotle's apparent claim that Forms are identical with numbers. She cites in this regard Cherniss (1945, 59), who shows that Aristotle in fact repeatedly argues that Forms must be identical with numbers rather than merely stating that Plato held this. Accordingly, the identification would seem to be an inference that Aristotle draws from whatever it is that Plato did say. See also Ross 1951, chap. 15, esp. 217–218. Ross argues that Plato did not identify Forms with numbers but assigned numbers to Forms. That is, he classified Forms as respectively monadic, dyadic, triadic, etc.

The most illuminating passage in which Aristotle expresses this doctrine is also the most difficult:

> Further, he [Plato] says that besides the sensibles things and the Forms, and between these, there exist the mathematical objects, differing from the sensibles things in being eternal and immovable, and from the Forms in that there are many alike, whereas the Form itself corresponding to these is only one.

> Since the Forms are the causes of all other things, he thought the elements of the Forms are the elements of all things. As matter, the Great and the Small are the principles; as substance, it is the One. For from the Great and the Small and by participation in the One come the Forms, and these are numbers.[139]

Several important points emerge from this. First, in whatever sense the Forms are numbers, this is different from the sense in which the mathematical objects are numbers.[140] Second, Aristotle here recognizes that Forms are derivative, at least according to the theory of Plato he is criticizing. How the numbers that are Forms differ from the mathematical numbers and how the Forms are derived from their elements, is unclear. On one interpretation, the basic idea is that the Form of, say, Twoness or Doubleness is the paradigm of all versions or representations of it, including the (quantitative) number 2, all ratios x/y where 'x' = 2y, and so on. All these 'versions' of Twoness would be materially identical, as indicated by the '=' sign. The possibility that this approach makes the Forms themselves otiose in mathematical reasoning coupled with the claim that understanding *is* just mathematical, reveals itself in the substitution of 'mathematicals' for Forms by Speusippus or the conflation of them by Xenocrates.

The Neoplatonists are generally in accord with Aristotle in supposing that Plato somehow derived Forms from the principles called the 'Great and Small' or 'Dyad' and the 'One.' Indeed, Aristotle's account is a principal source for their supposition. Plotinus has the most elaborate discussion of how this derivation is supposed to work. The heart of Plotinian Platonism is the integration of Plato's treatment of these principles with what he says or is reported as saying about the Good, Forms, and a divine intellect. The details of this integration would take us too far afield. The important point

---

139. *Met.* A 6, 987b14–22 (trans. Apostle). The last line is disputed. Jaeger brackets the word for numbers; Ross brackets the word for Forms: ἔτι δὲ παρὰ τὰ αἰσθητὰ καὶ τὰ εἴδη τὰ μαθηματικὰ τῶν πραγμάτων εἶναί φησι μεταξύ, διαφέροντα τῶν μὲν αἰσθητῶν τῷ ἀΐδια καὶ ἀκίνητα εἶναι, τῶν δ' εἰδῶν τῷ τὰ μὲν πόλλ' ἄττα ὅμοια εἶναι τὸ δὲ εἶδος αὐτὸ ἐν ἕκαστον μόνον. ἐπεὶ δ' αἴτια τὰ εἴδη τοῖς ἄλλοις, τἀκείνων στοιχεῖα πάντων ᾠήθη τῶν ὄντων εἶναι στοιχεῖα. ὡς μὲν οὖν ὕλην τὸ μέγα καὶ τὸ μικρὸν εἶναι ἀρχάς, ὡς δ' οὐσίαν τὸ ἕν· ἐξ ἐκείνων γὰρ κατὰ μέθεξιν τοῦ ἑνὸς τὰ εἴδη εἶναι τοὺς ἀριθμούς.

140. See *Met.* M 6, 1080b11–12, where Aristotle clearly distinguishes "both kinds of numbers." The distinction in Aristotle is between formal (εἰδητικοί) numbers and unitary (μοναδικοί) numbers. See M 6, 1080b19, 30; M 8, 1083b16–17; M 9, 1086a5; N 2, 1088b34; N 3, 1090b35; N 5, 1092b20. For Plotinus, essential (οὐσιώδης) number is the same as 'formal' number. See V 5. 4, 16–17. Also, Ps.-Alexander *In Met.* 762, 26; Syrianus *In Met.* 45, 33–35; 46, 3–4.

for my purposes is that part of the sting of the Aristotelian criticism in *Metaphysics* MN is removed once we recognize that the Neoplatonists are willing to 'give' Aristotle quantitative numbers and magnitudes, especially since Aristotle's actual employment of these is not in disaccord with Plato's mathematics. Where Aristotle goes wrong, however, from their point of view, is in misconceiving the imagistic nature of mathematics. This is something that would be forced upon Aristotle if he were more explicit about his 'constructivism.' His insistence on treating 'formal' numbers as a Platonic *substitute* for quantitative numbers is misguided, owing to his infirm grasp of first principles and his failure to recognize incorporeal complexity as a metaphysical truth.

This said, it is still the case that Plato seems to hold that all the intelligibility in the sensible world is mathematical. For in *Timaeus* he says that the Demiurge acts upon the pre-cosmic chaos by imposing on it figures (εἴδεσι) and numbers (ἀριθμοῖς).[141] As Plato goes on to say, the figures are composed of numbers.[142] And as the entire passage makes plain, Plato is in his analysis of the cosmic sensible world separating off the mathematical contribution of divinity from the pre-cosmic phenomenal chaos, consisting of traces (ἴχνη) of their nature—that is, of their cosmic natures.[143] What Plato is claiming is not that the sensible world consists of nothing but what is expressible mathematically, but that all that is intelligible in it is so expressible.[144]

Aristotle is of course committed to the view that 'form' expresses all that is intelligible in nature. Matter is as such not intelligible; it is knowable only by 'analogy.'[145] What the proponent of disharmony must show is that Aristotle holds that there are forms irreducible to expression as mathematical ratios or patterns, whether these be dynamic or static. It is not enough to say that there are forms that *can* be expressed nonmathematically. As we have already seen, within the constricted confines of the sensible world, Aristotelian essentialism can operate under the aegis of Platonism. Thus, the fact that we can in some sense understand or define species according to genera and differentia that make no mention of mathematical properties is not to the point. What is crucial is whether or not these definitions

141. *Tim.* 53B5. Cf. 54D4–5; 55D8, for the justification for understanding εἴδεσι here as figures: that is, as (regular) geometrical solids, the pyramid, octahedron, icosahedron, and cube.

142. Ibid., 54D3–5.

143. See Gerson 1996 for a defense of this interpretation. The alternative is that the pre-cosmic elements show traces of their eternal paradigms. But among other things, this would presumably entail that, say, the Form of Fire is hot, since the pre-cosmic elements manifest only phenomenal qualities.

144. Cf. *Rep.* 602D-603A. See Burnyeat 1987; Miller 1999, esp. 78, 83–87. See Brumbaugh (1954, 154 in reprint), who argues that Aristotle, despite his criticism of Plato's theory of mathematics, "seems in his practice to be carrying on the techniques of the *Timaeus* throughout his whole system." Brumbaugh, for example, lists a number of passages in the Aristotelian corpus in which Aristotle employs the concept of the 'harmonic' mean to indicate what is intelligible about some sensible phenomena.

145. See *Phys.* B 7, 191a7–8.

really express unqualified understanding or amount to something like 'nominal definitions.'[146]

Aristotle rejects Platonic mathematical objects because they do not fit into his schema of causality: "But the natures which are praised in numbers, and their contraries, and the mathematical attributes in general, in the manner they are described and are posited as causes of nature by some thinkers, seem to vanish if we examine them in this manner; for not one of them is a cause in any of the senses described in the first principles.[147] As we saw in the chapter dealing with Aristotle's account of nature, the Neoplatonic harmonists' basic response to this passage is that paradigmatic causes in general indeed do not fit into Aristotle's schema. It is the other way around. Numbers do not constitute the essence of anything that exists by nature. But what ultimately is intelligible in nature is proportion or ratio or measure— generally speaking, recurring patterns.[148] These are all quantifiable. This much Aristotle does not seem to deny—at least not in practice. But the Neoplatonist would also insist that the quantitative language in which we express this intelligibility—the language pertaining to the intermediaries or Aristotle's constructs—is itself only a representation of the primary paradigms. Thus, Aristotle is correct in insisting that substance is prior to quantity, and so quantity cannot constitute the essence of substance. But the Neoplatonists do not interpret Plato as holding this; rather, they take Plato to be holding, especially in *Timaeus,* that the quantitative contains the images by which we have access to the purely intelligible—that is, superquantitative— order.[149] Assuming that Aristotle believes he has rejected this tells us nothing about whether or not his systematic attempts to understand nature and being in general can be coherently stated without the Platonic supplement.

.

146. See Thompson (1992, 269–270 in abridged edition), who distinguishes the definition of form as descriptive and as analytic: that is, in its mathematical structure. The latter is held by Thompson to be superior to the former in the sense that it enables us to attain greater understanding. Thompson's entire project of the mathematical analysis of the growth and (physical or outward) form of organisms is viewed by him as thoroughly Aristotelian. A Neoplatonist might venture the suggestion that it is thoroughly Aristotelian because it is thoroughly Platonic.

147. *Met.* N 6, 1093b7–11 (trans. Apostle). Cf. N 5, 1092b20–25: "A number, then, whether a number in general or a number whose parts are just units, is neither a cause in the sense as that which acts, nor as matter, nor as a formula or a form of things. Nor is it a cause in the sense of final cause" (trans. Apostle).

148. See Sayre 1983, 109–110, 164, on the understanding of number as measure or proportion in Plato. See also Scolnicov 2003, 104–106.

149. This superquantitative order is identifiable with the indivisible Sameness, Difference, and Being of *Tim.* 35A, one of the elements of the soul as created by the Demiurge. As superquantitative, it is also supersubstantial, where 'substance' indicates what underlies quantity and is itself quantifiable.

CHAPTER EIGHT

Aristotle's Ethics

Neoplatonic commentaries on Aristotle's ethical treatises are few and far between.[1] In fact, there exist no commentaries on these treatises by any non-Christian, Neoplatonic authors.[2] What is extant comes from a period perhaps five hundred years after the end of pagan Neoplatonism. Perhaps one reason for the absence of commentaries is that Aristotle's ethical treatises do not appear in the Neoplatonic curriculum. Despite the dearth of material, it would be a mistake to suppose that there is nothing appropriately called 'Neoplatonic ethics' or that this does not cohere with the basic harmonist position. We shall see that Neoplatonic ethics follows what should be by now the familiar program of incorporating Aristotelian doctrine into an interpretation and defense of Plato. This appears in part in the commentaries on Plato's dialogues, especially those of Porphyry, Olympiodorus on *Phaedo* and *Alcibiades* I, and Proclus on *Republic*. It also appears, perhaps surprisingly, in Simplicius's *Commentary on the Handbook of Epictetus*.

The Central Idea of Neoplatonic Ethics

Let us begin by recalling that Neoplatonism does not recognize a distinctive Socratic philosophy, something that might be set in contrast to Platonism. Hence it is not surprising to find few references to, for example, the so-called

---

1. See Rose 1871; Mercken 1990 for useful surveys.

2. Porphyry apparently wrote some sort of commentary on Aristotle's *Nicomachean Ethics*, though the fragmentary material gives us hardly any indication of what it contained. Aspasius wrote a commentary that is extant in part. This commentary, and Alexander of Aphrodisias' s *Ethical Problems* were apparently available to Plotinus (see Porphyry V. *Plot.* chap. 14).

Socratic paradoxes and to the ethical doctrines these might be thought to reflect. Rather, the Neoplatonic view of Platonic ethics is rooted firmly in the two-world metaphysics most familiar from what most have become accustomed to call "the middle dialogues."[3]

The governing theme of Neoplatonic ethics is founded on a passage in the digression in *Theaetetus* where "the whole question of human happiness and misery" is addressed.[4] It is here that "assimilation to God" (ὁμοίωσις θεῷ) is offered as the central goal of human life. Here is the exhortation in its immediate context:

> Evils are not able to be destroyed, O Theodorus, for there is always necessarily something opposed to the good—not that these evils are situated among the gods, but just that they inhabit this mortal nature and this place necessarily. Therefore, it is necessary to try to flee from here to there are quickly as possible. And flight [φυγὴ] is assimilation to God as much as possible. And assimilation is becoming just and pious with wisdom [φρονήσεως]. But, my good man, it is not at all an easy thing to persuade people that it is not for the reasons some say that it is necessary to flee wickedness and pursue virtue. It is not in order not to appear evil to others but to appear good that wickedness should be fled and virtue pursued. This is just an old wives' tale, or so it appears to me.

> Let us state the truth in this way. God is in no way unjust; rather, he is as just as is possible, and there is nothing more like him than one who would become as just as possible. It is in this matter that someone shows his true mettle or his nothingness and weakness. For the recognition (γνῶσις) of this is true wisdom and true virtue, whereas the ignorance of this is clear folly and evil.[5]

This passage, which encapsulates Platonic ethics for Neoplatonists has not received a great deal of serious attention among contemporary scholars.[6] The reason is, no doubt, as Julia Annas notes, that a notion of flight from the world seems to be in tension with a view of ethics as requiring some sort of engagement with the world.[7] Neoplatonists perceived no such tension.

The passage above makes a number of claims. It identifies flight "from here to there" with "assimilation to God as much as possible." It then identifies assimilation to God with "becoming just and pious with wisdom," which

3. See, e.g., Simplicius (*In Epic.* 4, 52–5, 4), who makes explicit the Neoplatonic propensity for placing ethical concerns generally in a metaphysical context.

4. *Tht.* 175C5–6.

5. *Tht.* 176A5–C5. Cf. *Rep.* 500D1; 631B1; *Phdr.* 253A4; *Tim.* 69A1–2; *Lg.* 716C6–7. See Aristotle *EN* K 8, 1178b25–27: "For while the entire life of the gods is blessed, the life of human beings [is blessed] insofar as it is a sort of likeness of such [blessed] activity" (τοῖς μὲν γὰρ θεοῖς ἅπας ὁ βίος μακάριος, τοῖς δ' ἀνθρώποις, ἐφ' ὅσον ὁμοίωμά τι τῆς τοιαύτης ἐνεργείας ὑπάρχει).

6. E.g., Irwin 1995 mentions it not at all. Notable exceptions are Merki 1952; Rist 1964; Roloff 1970; Annas 1999, chap. 3; and Sedley 1999a.

7. See Annas 1999, 70–71. See *Ap.* 31D where Plato has Socrates express serious scepticism about engagement in public affairs. The goal of assimilation to the divine presumably originates in part from reflection on Socrates' bold claim at *Ap.* 38A that "the unexamined life is not worth living."

in the next line is compressed to "pursuing virtue." It seems that one becomes like God by becoming virtuous. Finally, the recognition (γνῶσις) of this is true virtue. It must be admitted, I think, that if there is a tension in Plato between this worldly and otherworldly ethics, this passage has not even a whiff of it. And yet there are puzzles. First, there is the idea that being virtuous makes us like God. Plato says not that becoming virtuous is pleasing to God or that it will be rewarded by God—two things that he clearly holds in some sense—but that becoming virtuous makes one to be like God. But in what sense does God practice virtue? Or more precisely, since the passage explicitly claims that God is just, does God practice it in the way that human beings do? Second, Plato seems to make a distinction between the practice of virtues and the recognition of the fact that virtue is assimilation to God. The latter, however, is called "true virtue." It is far from obvious what the relationship is between the practice of virtue or the virtues and the recognition of what virtue is.

Before we address these puzzles and the larger question of the reconciliation of the thisworldly and otherworldly Plato, we ought to have before us the parallel passage in *Timaeus*. At the end of the dialogue, in an address by Timaeus on the care of the soul, He speaks in particular about the care of the highest part of the soul, the divine part—namely, intellect:

> Now if a human being is engrossed in appetites and ambitions and spends all his pains upon these, all his thoughts must needs be mortal and, so far as this is possible, he cannot fall short of becoming mortal altogether, since he has nourished the growth of his mortality. But if his heart has been set on the love of learning and true wisdom and he has exercised that part of himself above all, he is surely bound to have thoughts immortal and divine, if he shall lay hold upon truth, nor can he fail to possess immortality in the fullest measure that human nature admits; and because he is always devoutly cherishing the divine part and maintaining the guardian genius that dwells with him in good estate, he must needs be happy above all. Now there is but one way of caring for anything, namely to give it the nourishment and motions proper to it. The motions akin to the divine part in us are the thoughts and revolutions of the universe; these, therefore, every human being should follow, and correcting those circuits in the head that were deranged at birth, by learning to know the harmonies and revolutions of the world, he should bring the intelligent part, according to its pristine nature, into the likeness (ἐξομοιῶσαι) of that which intelligence discerns, and thereby win the fulfillment of the best life set by the gods before mankind both for this present time and for the time to come.[8]

This passage introduces several new ideas, but it cannot be said to make things easier. First, there is the strange notion of becoming immortal or becoming mortal. One would have thought that mortality and immortality are endowments, not achievements. Second, the life of happiness, though it is evidently roughly equated with assimilation to the divine, is identified

8. *Tim.* 90B1-D7 (trans. Cornford).

not with the practice of virtue at all but with the knowledge of astronomy or contemplation of the heavens.

Leaving aside for the moment the problems associated with assimilation to the divine, the fundamental problem in both passages is the connection or lack of connection between the theoretical and the practical. It is this problem of course that seems to bedevil Plato's very notion of the philosopher. And, just to anticipate for a moment, it is the central interpretive problem in relation to Aristotle's ethics. If the best life is the theoretical life, as Aristotle says, what happens to engagement with the world?

The Neoplatonists apparently saw no problem here, but this was because they insisted on seeing the ethical teaching of Plato as inseparable from the larger context of his metaphysics.[9] More accurately, it probably never occurred to them to see it otherwise. The relation of the theoretical to the practical is to be seen as analogous to the relation of the intelligible world to the sensible world and to the relation of ideal disembodied existence to embodied human life.

The theoretical or philosophical life is understood by them as the "practice for dying" of *Phaedo*.[10] This involves the "separation of soul and body."[11] It is a kind of purification (κάθαρσις).[12] That such purification means more than simply theoretical activity is evident from Socrates' claim that "in fact, temperance and justice and courage are a sort of purification of these things [i.e., of worldly considerations] and wisdom (φρόνησις) itself a kind of purifying ritual (καθαρμός)."[13] As I have tried to show elsewhere, the process of purification is intended by Plato as a sort of self-transformation, not simply or primarily a reform of outward behavior.[14] More particularly, in the light of the *Theaetetus* passage above, the purification, which is but another metaphor for assimilation to God, is a transformation of psychological agency. Whereas most people, including those who have not yet but will put on the mantle of philosopher, are moved by their particular and idiosyncratic embodied desires; the one who has been purified can identify herself with a 'God's eye view' of the world. Just as God, the locus of perfect justice, does not accord a privileged status to one's bodily appetites in judging what is best, so one who lives the best life possible for a human being is one who is oriented away from his own appetites and toward the impersonal and intelligible.

A human being acquires immortality 'as far as possible' by identifying with the immortal or rational part of his soul—'as far as possible.' This means identifying with that in him that is oriented toward the objective

9. See the useful remarks in Lloyd 1967, 293–295.
10. *Phd.* 64A5–6. Cf. 67D7–10.
11. Ibid., 65C11–D2. Cf. 66E6–67B2. Aristotle *De An.* A 3, 407b2–5, accepts the desirability of separation of intellect from the body as a commonplace.
12. *Phd.* 67C5.
13. Ibid., 69B8–C3. See Damascius *In Phd.* 1, 147–149, and 164, on the distinction between purifying and civic virtues in this passage.
14. See Gerson 2003, chap. 2.

rather than the subjective. It means wanting only what reason dictates. If one only wanted this, one's own appetites would never be the principle or ἀρχή of one's action. But this identification is never complete so long as one is embodied. And this is to say that appetites are never extirpated, only subordinated. Reason in fact frequently dictates that appetites be satisfied. But their satisfaction is determined objectively, just as one would ideally strive to satisfy or refuse to satisfy the appetites of a child in one's care.[15]

Before we ask how the virtues constitute a sort of purification, we must recall that Plato himself contrasts these virtues with what he calls "popular or political virtue" (τὴν δημοτικὴν καὶ πολιτικὴν ἀρετὴν): 'temperance' and 'justice,' so called, developed from custom and practice without philosophy and intellect.[16] The difference between these popular or political virtues and the virtues that purify is that the former do not result in self-transformation. They are entirely behavior oriented.[17] One who practices these virtues may perform actions for all sorts of motives, including those that are *not* ignoble, but these actions are not done as one who is purified would do them.

In his treatise *On Virtues*, Plotinus expresses what became the basis for the standard Neoplatonic interpretation of the virtues.[18] Reflecting on the *Theaetetus* passage, Plotinus asks how the practice of virtue can make us like divine intellect and intelligible reality, since there is no virtue there. The divine has no need of virtue because it is perfect.[19] In particular, it has no need of the popular or political virtues, which Plotinus identifies as achievements of an embodied tripartite soul.[20] Among the Forms, a Form of Virtue is present, but as the paradigm of virtue it is not virtuous.[21] Likeness to God

15. This is essentially a metaethical point. The subordination of appetite to reason does not entail virtuous behavior; the rule of reason does not guarantee imperviousness to error.

16. *Phd.* 82A10-B3. Cf. 69B6-7, where this sort of virtue is called an illusory facade (σκιαγραφία), fit for slaves. Cf. *Rep.* 365C3-4 and esp. 500D8 with 518D3-519A6 where the 'popular' virtues are identified as the "so-called virtues of the soul," and esp. 619C7-D1 for participation in virtue by 'habit' (ἔθει) 'without philosophy.' At 430C3, courage is characterized as 'political' virtue. At 443C10-D1, characterizing justice, Plato contrasts 'external' behavior with 'internal' virtue, which is concerned with what is "truly oneself and one's own." If this characterization of justice is separated from the justice that is 'without philosophy' and identified with 'true virtue' practiced by the philosopher, then, though the distinction between the two types of virtue would remain, the latter would be already indicated in Book 4.

17. See Proclus *In Remp.* I 208, 27, on this type of virtue as relational activity (σχετικὴ ἐνέργεια), roughly, interpersonal behavior. The life of relational activity is contrasted (209, 4) with the life in itself (καθ᾽ αὑτό).

18. For Porphyry's elaboration in *Sent.* 32, see infra. On Plotinus's account of the grades of virtue see Dillon 1983, esp. 93-102.

19. Cf. Plotinus I 2. 3, 31.

20. Ibid., I 2. 1. Cf. Olympiodorus (*In Gorg.* Proem, 4, 17-20), who interprets the discussion of virtue there as pertaining to political virtue as opposed to the purified virtue of *Phaedo*. See also *In Alc.* I, 4, 15ff. See also Simplicius *In Epic.* 2, 30-3, 6. See O'Meara 2003, 8-10, 40-44, for a similar interpretation of the political virtues.

21. I 2. 2, 3-4. Plotinus understands that self-predication of Forms is based on a confusion. He says that a perceptible house is made in the likeness of the intelligible house, without the intelligible house being like the perceptible one. Cf. I 2. 1, 42-45. Thus, the infinite regress argument of *Parm.* 132D-133A does not get off the ground since the Form does not have the

consists in becoming like eternal intellect, absorbed in the contemplation of eternal reality. All true virtues are understood as advancements toward identification of the person with the activity of a disembodied intellect.

Plotinus asks if the popular or political virtues are real virtues. And his answer is an insistence that whatever serves to make us godlike is a virtue.[22] He says: "These virtues do truly organize our lives and make us better by giving limit to and giving measure [μετροῦσαι] to our appetites and in general to all our feelings [τὰ πάθη]. And they eliminate false beliefs, by what is generally better and by limiting the unmeasured and unlimited."[23] These virtues, as they are described by Plato in the fourth book of *Republic*, are aspects of an embodied life under the aegis of reason.[24] Hence, "popular or political virtue" indicates the virtue of a political animal, a human being living among others. The practice of these virtues contributes to our godlikeness because they entice us toward identification with our rational faculty.[25] They do this because acting as reason dictates means at least sometimes acting against our appetites or emotions. Since each of us acts on behalf of our own good as we perceive that, continual acting under the aegis of reason and over the blandishments of appetite and emotion contributes to a self-identification with the former. We become habituated to believing that what reason determines is good is our good. This is the principal true belief that virtue substitutes for false beliefs.

What, then, of the 'higher' virtue that is a 'purification'? In contrast to the popular and political virtues that consist essentially in behavior, these virtues constitute a disposition (διάθεσις) of the soul. According to this disposition, the soul "thinks and is in this way free of affections" [ἀπαθής]."[26] It is not entirely mistaken to see in the latter claim a Stoic element.[27] Yet the

---

property that the Form's name names in the way that what participates in the Form does. Things that participate in the Form do so as a result of the intelligent activity of the Demiurge, who makes the world according to the eternal paradigm. So, when Plotinus says that there is no virtue in the intelligible world, he is inferring the particular conclusion from the general principle.

22. I 2. 1, 23–26.

23. Ibid., I 2. 2, 13–18. These virtues are here understood according to a general account of *Phil.* 23Bff., esp. 26B-C, in which the imposition by the Demiurge of form on the sensible world is taken to be the imposition of limit on the unlimited.

24. See Plotinus, I 1. 10, 11–13; Proclus *In Remp.* I 208, 29–209, 6 and 231, 17 on the identification of political virtue (πολιτικὴ ἀρετή) as including the four virtues of the embodied soul in Book 4. See also Olympiodorus *In Gorg.* 15 5, 1–4; 24 1, 2ff.

25. Plotinus actually says, (I 2. 3, 9–10) that Plato denies that the political virtues "produce likeness." Plotinus may be making a distinction between being made like (ὁμοιοῦσθαι) and the process of becoming like (ὁμοίωσις). If this is so, he is perhaps distinguishing between virtuous behavior which is a kind of likeness of the Form of Virtue and the life of the divine, and the self-transformation that occurs with a genuine conversion to a philosophical life.

26. I 2. 3, 19–20.

27. Annas 1997 argues for the Stoic Antipater's interpretation of Plato as holding the sufficiency of virtue for happiness. This argument indirectly supports the Neoplatonic interpretation of Plato as holding that the political virtues are inferior to the purified virtue of the philosopher.

goal of Neoplatonic ethics, unlike Stoic ethics, is resolutely otherworldly, and this difference, I think, inevitably affects one's orientation to embodied life.[28] Plotinus, no more than Plato, is endorsing or even contemplating the extirpation of anything that is natural to the embodied state. It is a confusion to see in this a recommendation of a kind of mortifying asceticism. It is something else.

Plotinus goes on to argue that the person purified by virtue will have transcended incontinence or weakness of the will.[29] This means that the person has no or few desires that are unchosen (ἀπροαίρετον), meaning not that he never desires food or sleep or sex or other pleasures but that he never acts on such desires except under the aegis of reason.[30] And that is because, as a virtuous person, he has identified with his rational self and never supposes that his own good is other than a rational one. We should notice here in particular how Plotinus uses incontinence to make the conceptual distinction between the two types of virtue. The popular and political virtues in *Republic* are developed on the basis of a theoretical argument explaining how incontinence is possible. The incontinent person, like the hapless Leontius, has an appetite he knows is bad but cannot control. A continent person is one who has the bad appetite but is able to control it. Someone practicing continence would be practicing the 'lower' virtue. But the truly virtuous person has been purified of bad desires. He does not have them in the first place. Or at least ideally so. Plotinus seems to recognize degrees of purification and an ideal purified state which is, nevertheless, not unqualifiedly ideal, since it is still embodied.[31]

The distinction between the two types of virtue parallels exactly the distinction between the virtuous person envisioned at the end of Book 4 of *Republic* and the philosopher or "aristocratic human being" envisioned at the end of Book 9.[32] In the case of every virtue of the purified person, there

28. See Thiel 1999. Simplicius's *Commentary on the Handbook of Epictetus* is the stellar example of how the principle of harmony is extended to embrace Stoicism.

29. I 2. 5, 17–21.

30. Cf. *Phd.* 64D3–6. As others have noted, Plotinus's asceticism is not equivalent to that of the Stoics. The distinction here between desires that are chosen and those that are not may be compared with the passage in *EN* H 6, 1147b23ff., where Aristotle distinguishes 'necessary' pleasures (those concerned with food, sex, and other bodily appetites) from those that are chosen for themselves (τὰ αἱρετὰ καθ' αὑτά: that is, victory, honor, wealth, etc.) The truly virtuous man, according to Plotinus, will not choose the latter and will not give in to the former against the deliverances of reason.

31. I 2. 4, 1–7. One might argue that in Book 4 of *Republic*, Plato holds that the presence of ethical virtue rules out continence, not just incontinence. But this is not so clear. If the appetitive part of the soul (τὸ ἐπιθυμητικόν) does its job and obeys the rational part of the soul (τὸ λογιστικόν), this does not necessarily mean that there are present no appetites whose satisfaction (like that of Leontius) would constitute a vicious act. It just means that they are not 'strong' enough to prevail. I am inclined to believe that if we take seriously the distinction between popular or political virtue on the one hand and the true virtue of the philosopher on the other, we shall be obliged to recognize that only the latter transcends continence.

32. See *Rep.* 619C6-D1 where Plato distinguishes participating in virtue through habit (ἔθει) without philosophy from the sort of virtue that has been the subject of the discussion since Book 5.

is an "activity in the direction of intellect" (πρὸς νοῦν ἐνεργεῖν).[33] The person in each case affirms her identity with reason much as someone might be said to identify with a cause or the fate of another. Such a person is profoundly different, for example, from the wise person described in Book 4.[34] The latter's wisdom consists entirely in knowing what is beneficial (τοῦ συμ-φέροντος) for each part of the soul and for the whole soul together. This must be the *embodied* soul if it is only the rational part that is immortal. And this prudential wisdom is available to one who knows that she ought to obey the dictates of the philosopher, even though she herself has no philosophy in her.[35] It is the one who pursues philosophy in a sound manner (ὑγιῶς) who is destined for happiness.[36]

In the last chapter of the treatise Plotinus asks two questions: (1) do the virtues entail each other and (2) do the higher and lower virtues entail each other? The answer to the first question is that since in the intelligible world all the Forms are mutually implicatory, so here below, possession of one virtue entails possession of all. More convincingly, Plotinus argues that since there is a single process of purification, when that process is completed, all the virtues are present.[37] This is the "principal part of the life of the serious human being [τοῦ σπουδαίου]."[38]

The answer to the second question would seem to be equally straightforward, but though the person in possession of the higher virtues is said to have the lower 'in potency,' it is not so clear that he will practice them in the way that the one in possession only of these practices them.[39] Plotinus is here worried about how one who has been purified of attachments to embodied life can be said to possess the virtues which consist in giving "limit and measure" to desires. He seems to think that practicing the lower virtues implies an 'impure' attachment to embodied life—in other words, a political life:

> But when he [the one who is purified] attains to higher principles and different measures he will act according to these. For example, he will not locate self-control in that measure [i.e., of the lower virtues], but completely separating himself as much as possible, he will completely not live the life of the good human being as political virtue conceives of it [ἀξιοῖ], but leaving this behind, he will choose another life, the life of the gods. For assimilation is in the direction of these, not in the direction of good men. The latter type of assimilation is a case of making one image like another, both of which are

33. I 2. 6, 23–27.
34. See *Rep.* 442C5–8.
35. See *Rep.* 445C10-D1, where the philosopher is described as a lover of truth and where, by implication, her wisdom consists in attaining that truth.
36. See *Rep.* 619D8-E1.
37. Ibid., I 2. 7, 8–10.
38. See I 4. 16, where Plotinus compares ὁ σπουδαῖος with the ideal of political life, ὁ ἐπιεκὴς ἄνθρωπος.
39. Ibid., I 2. 7, 10–12. Cf. I 3. 6, 17ff. where he suggests that the lower and higher virtue can grow at the same time.

derived from another. Assimilation to the other [the life of the gods] is in the direction of the paradigm.[40]

As many scholars have pointed out, this claim implies neither world-renouncing asceticism nor Nietzschean transcendence of value, any more than Socrates' claim that philosophy is preparation for dying is an endorsement of suicide.[41] There is nothing inconsistent in choosing not to live a political life and yet practicing political virtue when this is required. That is the key. Practicing this virtue as required is opposed to fetishizing it.[42] As Plotinus elsewhere says, one does not wish for the drowning of a child in order that one can practice virtue and save him.

Porphyry offers an influential expansion or precision of the Plotinian scheme.[43] In his *Sentences Leading to the Intelligible World* 32, he writes: "It has been shown then that there are four kinds [γένη] of virtue: (1) those of intellect, which are paradigmatic and coincide with its essence; (2) those of the soul already in relation to intellect and imbued [πληρουμένης] with it; (3) those of the human soul that is being purified [καθαιρουμένης] and has been purified of the body and of arational passions; (4) those of the human soul that manage the human being, putting limits to and moderating the passions [μετριοπάθειαν] by means of imposing measures [μέτρα] on the arational."[44]

As Porphyry has already explained, at each of these levels, the four virtues of temperance, courage, wisdom, and justice can be found in a distinct form. That is, the virtues at level (2) are an image of those at (1), and so on. According to Porphyry's description of these levels, (4) is equivalent to the political and popular virtue as understood by Plotinus in *Phaedo;* (1) and (2) form a division of Plotinus's theoretical virtue into its practice by intellect and by the soul. Perhaps this is in fact a division of theoretical activity as practiced intuitively and discursively. Porphyry is here relying on the distinction Plotinus makes elsewhere between using intellect and

40. Ibid., I 2. 7, 21–30.

41. See, e.g., Bussanich 1990; Dillon 1996a; Smith 1999. Porphyry's biography of Plotinus gives a vivid and moving picture of the contemplative as he navigates through everyday life.

42. See VI 8. 6, 14–18, where Plotinus expresses the core world-renouncing idea. One may compare in this regard the point of Martin Luther's obviously exaggerated remark: "Christianity has nothing to do with virtue."

43. See Hadot 1978, 152–158; Dillon 1983; O'Meara 1994; Wildberg 2002; and Lurje 2002, 242–248, on the Porphyrean gradations of virtue and their development in later Neoplatonism.

44. Porphyry *Sent.* 32, 71–78. Olympiodorus, evidently relying on Iamblichus, *In Phd.* 8, 2–3, expands the Porphyrean list of four levels of virtue to five: (1) natural (φυσικαί), resulting from temperament; (2) moral (ἠθικαί), owing to habit; (3) civic or political (πολιτικαί), concerned with the tripartite soul and the moderation of the passions; (4) purificatory (καθαρτικαί); and (5) contemplative (θεωρητικαί). The same list appears in Damascius *In Phd.* 1, 138–144. Both give the 'paradigmatic' referring to the virtues of the gods as a sixth category, alluding to Plotinus I 2. 7, 2–6. See Westerink 1976, 1:18, on Proclus's relation to Olympiodorus and Damascius; and O'Meara 2003, 46–49, on the Iamblichean additions to the Plotinian-Porphyrean schema. See also Eustratius's Christianized version of the grades of virtues and the ascent to union with God, *In EN* 4, 25–38.

being identified with it.[45] In addition, in (3) Porphyry erects a distinct form of virtue constituted by the purification process of *Phaedo*. These are the virtues of the soul that is being elevated (ἀφισταμένης) to the intellectual realm.[46] At this level, wisdom consists in refusing to share the opinions of the body (συνδοξάζειν) and in acting according to intellect; temperance, in refusing to experience what the body feels (ὁμοπαθεῖν); courage, in having no fear of separation from the body; justice, in the unimpeded rule of reason.[47]

The virtue of refusing to share the opinions of the body should put us in mind of *Phaedo*, where Socrates, in the so-called affinity argument for the soul's immortality, warns his interlocutors of the perils of embodiment: by sharing opinions and pleasures with the body, the soul is forced to become of like character and nurture with it.[48] We should not suppose that the possibility of "sharing the body's opinions" indicates that the body is being represented by Plato as the sort of thing capable of having opinions. On the contrary, one is being exhorted to refuse to share the opinions possessed by oneself insofar as one is the subject of bodily states, namely, opinions that the satisfaction of bodily desires constitutes one's own good.[49] One is being exhorted to renounce those opinions. Similarly, refusing to feel what the body feels amounts to refusing to permit one's bodily feelings to be the ἀρχή of one's actions. Courage is the refusal to believe that one's good is eliminated by the death of the human being. The unimpeded rule of reason is just the establishment of reason as the sole ἀρχή of action.

The cathartic virtues serve to indicate the continuity of the practices of ethical and intellectual virtue. That is why, as Porphyry insists, the possession of the higher necessitates the possession of the lower.[50] After all, if, say, one is three-quarters of the way toward one's goal, then one is necessarily more than halfway toward that goal. Life is a continuum in which one is either approaching or receding from the ideal state. Possession of the higher virtues indicates progress towards the goal beyond that made by possession of the lower. Because the goal is fixed, the steps leading progressively to it are also fixed.

What Porphyry has here done is in effect to recognize that the practices of the philosopher are distinct from the achievement of the philosopher as a contemplator. He recognizes philosophy as part of a virtuous way of life, other than yet (importantly) inferior to the virtuous state consisting of the contemplation of eternal truth. A moral preparation or purification of the

45. Cf. V 3. 3, 44; V 3. 4, 1.
46. *Sent.* 32, 18–19. Cf. Iamblichus *V. Pythag.* 122, 10–123, 4. Iamblichus insisted that 'theurgic' virtues were above the philosophical and necessary for union with God. See *De Myst.* II 11; Olympiodorus *In Phd.* 114, 20–22; Marinus *V. Proc.* 26.
47. *Sent.* 32, 23–29.
48. *Phd.* 83D7–8.
49. See Gerson 2003, chaps. 2–3.
50. See *Sent.* 32, 78–79: καὶ ὁ μὲν ἔχων τὰς μείζους ἐξ ἀνάγκης ἔχει καὶ τὰς ἐλάττους, οὐ μὴν τὸ ἔμπαλιν.

soul is a necessary prelude to intellectual activity.[51] In other words, one does not prepare for attainment of the virtues of the intellect merely by practicing moderation of the passions.

A Neoplatonic Reading of Aristotle's Ethics

Near the beginning of his *Nicomachean Ethics*, Aristotle declares that the present inquiry (μέθοδος) is political (πολιτική).[52] This might appear confusing only to someone who was convinced that politics, alas, has nothing to do with ethics. In saying that ethics is politics, however, Aristotle is making only a technical point about the nature and unity of practical science. There is one practical science, generically: the science of human action. As a science, it has certain universally true definitions and axioms. Ideally, its lineaments should follow the strictures laid down in *Posterior Analytics* for all sciences. But because it is practical science, it aims at action, especially the best possible actions according to some criterion of what is best. In addition, because it is concerned with action, it is subject to the imprecisions and indeterminables entailed by what actions and agents are, substances living in a contingent world. Finally, again because it is practical science, politics will include principles relating to action that would be just irrelevant in theoretical science.[53]

Given the identification of ethics as political science, it seems reasonable that Neoplatonists should assume that most of the central claims made in both *Nicomachean Ethics* and *Politics* are concerned with the popular and political virtue discussed by Plato in *Phaedo* and *Republic*, not with the purified virtue that constitutes the assimilation to the divine.[54] But the matter, as usual, is not quite so simple. For there is an aspect of *Nicomachean Ethics*— indeed, one might argue, an essential aspect—that is undeniably redolent of the quasi-ascetic, contemplative, otherworldly focus of Neoplatonic purified virtue. And a good deal of contemporary scholarship on that work is

51. Ibid., 51–55.

52. *EN* A 1, 1094b11. Cf. Z 8, 1141b23, where Aristotle says that the political habit (ἕξις) is the same as practical wisdom (φρόνησις), though they differ in essence. The difference, roughly, is that the former is concerned with the association that is the state, and the latter is concerned with the individual belonging to that association.

53. At *EE* A 8, 1218b13, Aristotle names political science 'supreme.' But as the parallel passage in *Nicomachean Ethics* makes clear (A 1, 1094a24–b10), politics is supreme within the practical sphere. It does not preempt theoretical science or theoretical activity as otherwise supreme. It is supreme because it has as its aim the ultimate goal of all action: namely, happiness. Cf. Aspasius *In EN* 1, 2–2, 2, where the commentator takes it as given that the work is concerned with political virtue which is, however, inferior to theoretical virtue.

54. See Aspasius *In EN* 99, 4; Eustratius *In EN* I 34, 19–31; 109, 9–110, 4; Michael of Ephesus *In EN* 583, 13–15 and 601, 28–29 where political virtue is necessary for "practicing one's humanity" (τὸ ἀνθρωπεύσθαι). Sparshott (1982) provides a fifteen-point structural comparison of *Nicomachean Ethics* and *Republic* showing how the former is built on the 'armature' of the latter. In passing, Sparshott adds that "the difference between the two authors is one of intent and hence of organization, not one of doctrine. Aristotle's points are all Platonic, though derived from other dialogues than the *Republic*'" (488). See in a similar vein, Adkins 1978.

devoted either to explaining it away or to ignoring it. For if it can be shunted offstage, then that which is from the Neoplatonic perspective a discussion of relatively secondary matters can be repackaged as something else. Aristotelian ethics, shorn of its Platonism, can be endowed with its own 'voice.'[55]

Book K, chapters 6 to 8, of *Nicomachean Ethics* announces that after the discussion of the virtues, friendship, and pleasure, it will undertake a discussion of happiness, this being the goal of human activities (τέλος τῶν ἀνθρωπίνων).[56] The starting point of the entire work is the assumption that happiness is the highest good for human beings. The highest good turns out to be "an activity of the soul according to virtue, and if the virtues are many, then according to the best and most perfect virtue."[57] What now remains is a discussion of the best and most perfect virtue.[58] When that is discovered, the question about the best life—taken up in Book A, chapters 2–3 and set aside—can be answered. Here is how Aristotle begins to address the question about the best and most perfect virtue:

> Since happiness is an activity according to virtue, it is reasonable that it is [an activity] according to the highest [τὴν κρατίστην] virtue. This would be an activity of the best [τοῦ ἀρίστου] [part] of human being. So, whether this is intellect or something else, which according to nature seems to rule and to lead us and to have thought about noble and divine things, and whether it is itself that which is divine or among the most divine things in us, the activity of this according to its proper virtue would be perfect happiness. That this activity is contemplative has already been stated.[59] Also, this would seem to be in agreement with what was previously said and with the truth.[60]

Aristotle proceeds to give a number of reasons why contemplative or theoretical activity is the highest virtue: (1) intellect is the highest part in us (ὁ νοῦς [κρατίστη] τῶν ἐν ἡμῖν);[61] (2) it is concerned with the highest things cognizable;[62] (3) it is the most continuous activity: that is, the activity in which we can most continuously engage;[63] (4) it is the most self-sufficient (αὐτάρκης) activity: that is, it requires the fewest conditions for its

---

55. I take no position here on the vexed question of the chronological relation of *Nicomachean Ethics* to *Eudemian Ethics* and the location of the 'common' books. The differences between the two works do not in my view suggest some large developmental thesis. Nor do they compromise the construction of a unified Aristotelian science of ethics along Platonic lines.

56. *EN* K 6, 1176a30–32.

57. Ibid., A 6, 1098a16–18.

58. Nussbaum 1987, 377, argues that it is odd for Aristotle here to propose a 'sketch' of happiness, since that is exactly what he has done in Book A, chaps. 1–7. But though Book A does indeed tell us what happiness is in general—namely, that it is virtuous activity of the soul—it does not tell us what is the most perfect virtue. Nussbaum wrongly supposes that these are not different questions.

59. See *EN* A 3, 1095b14–1096a10; Z 7, 1141a18-b3; Z 13, 1143b33–1144a6; 1145a6–11.

60. Ibid., K 7, 1177a12–19. Cf. A 5, 1097a25-b21; K 5, 1175b36–1176a29.

61. *EN* K 7, 1177a20.

62. Ibid., 1177a20–21.

63. Ibid., 1177a21.

operation;[64] (5) it is alone loved for its own sake;[65] (6) it is the activity most exempt from toil;[66] (7) it is superior in seriousness (σπουδῇ).[67] According to all these criteria, political and military virtuous activities are judged to be inferior.[68] So, "this would be the complete [τελεία] happiness of a human being, if extended to a complete [τέλειον] lifetime, for none of the [attributes] of happiness is incomplete [ἀτελές]."[69]

Aristotle now moves to the crucial reflection on this line of reasoning:

> Such a life, of course, would be greater than that of a human being, for a human being will live in this manner not insofar as he is a human being, but insofar as he has something divine in him. And the activity of the [divine part] is as superior to the activity of the other virtue as [the divine part] is superior to the composite [συνθέτου]. Since then the intellect is divine in comparison with the human being, the life according to this is divine in comparison with human life. So, we should not follow the recommendation of those who urge that those who are men should think human thoughts and that mortals should think only of mortal things, but we should try insofar as it is possible to partake of immortality [ἀθανατίζειν] and to do everything toward living according to the best thing in us. For even if this is small in bulk, it exceeds by a great deal all others in power and honor. And each person would seem to be this part, if indeed this is the authoritative and better part. So, it would be odd, if this were so, for someone not to choose his own life but a life of another.[70]

As if the main point were not sufficiently clear, Aristotle proceeds in the next chapter to consider the life "according to the other [kind of] virtue":

> The life according to the other [kind of] virtue is secondarily happy, since the activities according to this virtue are concerned with human affairs [ἀνθρω-πικαί]. For it is according to the virtues which relate one human being to another that we perform just and brave and other actions relating to contracts and needs and all other sorts of things, observing in each case what is fitting with regard to our affections [τοῖς πάθεσι]. All these appear to be concerned with human affairs. Some of them even seem to arise from the body, and ethical virtue [ἡ τοῦ ἤθους ἀρετή] is in many ways associated with the affections.

> Practical wisdom [φρόνησις], too, is bound up with ethical virtue and ethical virtue is bound up with practical wisdom, if indeed the principles of practical wisdom are in accord with ethical virtues and the rightness of ethical virtues is in accord with practical wisdom. Since these ethical virtues are connected with the affections, too, they would be concerned with the composite. And the virtues of the composite are concerned with human affairs. So, the life and

64. Ibid., 1177a27.
65. Ibid., 1177b1-2.
66. Ibid., 1177b4.
67. Ibid., 1177b19.
68. Ibid., 1177b16-24.
69. Ibid., 1177b24-25.
70. Ibid., 1177b26-1178a4. See I 4, 1166a22-23; I 8, 1169a2.

happiness in accord with these virtues, too, would be [human]. But the [life and happiness] of the intellect is separated [κεχωρισμένη].[71]

Aristotle is careful to add that although one engaged in the contemplative life needs few externals, he will, insofar as he is a human being living with many others, choose to do the things according to [ethical] virtue. Therefore, he will be in need of externals for living a human life.[72] Nevertheless, the gods are evidently the most happy, and it is absurd to suppose that they practice ethical virtue: that is, that they engage in the activities in which ethical virtue would be desired.[73] The activity of human beings that is closest to the gods is, therefore, the most happy.[74] For "while the whole life of the gods is blessed, the life of human beings [is blessed] insofar as it is a kind of likeness [ὁμοίωμα] of this activity [i.e., contemplation]."[75]

There are so many striking similarities between the foregoing passages and what Plato says in *Timaeus* and *Theaetetus* about assimilation to the divine that one cannot help but wonder at the prejudices that have induced many either to ignore or to discount them.[76] It is not just the obvious verbal parallels that are so impressive but the eccentricities of the parallels. Both Plato and Aristotle urge us to try to achieve immortality as much as possible, as if that were something both in our power and allowing of degrees. Both urge us to emulate divine life, though the focus of ethics would seem to be our ineluctable humanity. And both proclaim that the divine life is a contemplative one, specifically removed from human affairs. Finally, both rest what they say upon an assumption that the 'we' of ethical striving is in fact different from an embodied human being.

It would seem that the principal impediment to developing these parallels and drawing together Aristotelian and Platonic ethics in the way that Neoplatonists want to do is the view that the substance of the quoted passages from *Nicomachean Ethics* is detachable from the rest of the doctrine of that work. If all the talk about immortalizing and divinizing and contemplating

71. *EN* K 8, 1178a9–22.
72. Ibid., 1178b3–7. Cooper 1975, 164–165, argues that the claim that one living the contemplative life will practice the virtues does not mean that one *is* virtuous. This seems farfetched. See, e.g., B 3, 1105a28–33, referred to by Cooper, where Aristotle argues that in contrast to the arts, where the disposition of the artist is irrelevant to the product, in "things done according to virtue" the virtuous disposition is essential. In addition, the actions must be chosen for their own sake and arise from a firm and unalterable character. Cooper 1987, 187–216, retracts this interpretation.
73. *EN* K 8, 1178b7–21.
74. *EN* E 8, 1178b22–23. Cf. *Phil.* 33B6–7, where the "most divine among lives" (τῶν βίων θειότατος) is identified as the life according to νοεῖν καὶ φρονεῖν.
75. *EN* K 8, 1178b25–27.
76. Sedley 1997a is a notable exception. At 335 he says, "It seems to have gone unnoticed by scholars how accurately *the main structure of Aristotle's ethics* reflects this passage of the *Tim.* [90A-D]" (my emphasis). Sedley's argument is expanded somewhat in Sedley 1999a. Gauthier and Jolif (1970, 875), clinging to developmentalism, say, apropos of the reference to the 'divine' in this passage, that "la divinité de la partie rationnelle est une idée chère à Aristote de la période platonicienne."

and identifying with a part of ourselves is removable like an unsightly growth on the hard head of the hard body of Aristotle's no-nonsense ethics, then it should be done. A touch of developmentalism, excising the offending portions as 'residue' is one way. Trivializing the importance of the passages to the overall doctrine is another.[77] But if the Neoplatonists are correct, this is not possible, since an Aristotelian ethics limited to the discussion of popular and political virtue would be implausibly incomplete. The situation is somewhat parallel to De Anima where a discussion of the human soul—particularly, human cognition—without consideration of the separable intellect would be strangely inconclusive.

If one takes the quoted passages seriously—that is, if one takes them as a part of the ethical doctrine of Aristotle—then the two sorts of lives, the life according to the intellect and the life according to the "other virtue" are the lives that are best for "that which is dominant and better" and for the "composite." Everything depends on how we view these two descriptions of a human being. If one takes the composite as primary, then the focus will be on the ethical virtues and practical wisdom. That the bulk of Nicomachean Ethics is concerned with these matters, and the related matters of pleasure and friendship, is beyond dispute. The real dispute is whether the life of the composite and its attendant virtues is the best sort of life, or whether these virtues are inferior to another sort of virtue and another sort of life.[78]

77. Remarkably, Jaeger 1948, chap. 9, contrives to do both. He concedes that Eudemian Ethics is Platonic in its orientation, connecting it closely with Protrepticus, but then concludes that it must therefore be an early work; the "more mature" Nicomachean Ethics, however, with its "rich and humane urbanity" (243), reduces the talk about divinization and immortality to rhetorical frill. Nowhere does Jaeger explain why substantially the same remarks mean one thing in Eudemian Ethics and another in Nicomachean Ethics apart from the assumption that the development of Aristotle's ethics follows the development of theology within his metaphysics. See Defourny 1937 for a refutation of Jaeger's position. In contrast to Jaeger, Gauthier and Jolif (1970, 2: 874–875) think that the Platonism of these passage shows that Nicomachean Ethics is closely related to Protrepticus. Cf. Nuyens (1948, 192–193), who also thinks that the doctrine of Nicomachean Ethics is associated with Protrepticus. In addition, Nuyens thinks that Nicomachean Ethics must antedate De Anima, since it does not have the sophisticated notion of the composite human being that is found in the latter. Wehrli 1967, 10:106ff., argues for the correctness of the Peripatetic view that with the abandonment of the theory of Forms and, hence, with Plato's 'otherworldliness', Aristotle's identification of the contemplative life as the best life is to be discounted, indeed, disregarded. Within Aristotle's "empirische Naturwissenschaft," the contemplative life must be reduced to an occupation, "einem ungestört ruhigen Gelehrtendasein." Nussbaum 1987, 373–377, grants the Platonism of the passage, as well as similar passages outside of Nicomachean Ethics, and suggests that though it probably contains Aristotle's own words, it might have been inserted by someone else. Nussbaum makes this claim despite the fact that "ethical Platonism of some sort exercised a hold over Aristotle's imagination in one or more periods of his career. We should then view the fragment K 6–8 as a serious working-out of elements of a position to which Aristotle is in some ways deeply attracted, though he rejects it in the bulk of his mature ethical and political writings" (377). A similar view is taken in Monan 1968, 108–111, 133–134, 151–152; and Roche 1988.

78. Kraut 1989, esp. chap. 3, argues forcefully for the integrity of the primacy of the theoretical life in Book K and the conception of happiness in Book A. Kraut argues for a hierarchy of virtues, with the ethical virtues as inferior to the theoretical, adding the important point that the former have a causal relation to the latter (178–179). Also, "the best amount of ethical

Removed from its Platonic context, it is understandable that the difficulty and obscurity in the idea of "living according to the intellect" should be swamped by our attraction to the no-nonsense concreteness of Aristotle's discussion of the trials and tribulations of the composite, the human being living in the disorderly human world. But this decontextualizing is, from an interpretive point of view, quite unsatisfactory. If the Aristotle we wish to embrace is Aristotle 'lite,' fair enough. But that is not how Aristotle presents himself to us.

The distinction between the life of the composite and the life according to the dominant and best part has deep Platonic roots, evident in the *Timaeus* and *Theaetetus* passages quoted above and elsewhere.[79] Unreflectively, embodied persons identify themselves in an incoherent manner, sometimes with the subject of appetites and sometimes with the subject of cognition, sometimes with both. Platonism views philosophy as a process of gradual or perhaps not so gradual identification with intellect. The result of this identification is that one eventually alienates oneself from the life of the composite. The alienation is never perfect for one who is embodied. Political virtue, or what Aristotle calls ethical virtue, is, of course, desirable and beneficial. But its desirability and benefit should not be thought to consist in the fact that the life of the "virtuous composite" is the best achievable for persons. Aristotle tells us in so many words that it is not. He tells us exactly what Platonism says: we are ideally intellects.[80] But how, we may ask, can we be both composites and intellects? The answer to this question is readily given in Platonic terms. The person is not the composite, although the person, when embodied, is a part of the composite. Exhortations to immortalize oneself or to assimilate to the divine are equivalent to exhortations to self-recognition and self-transformation into our own ideal selves.[81]

---

virtue to engage in, from one's own point of view, is the amount that will best promote one's theoretical interests" (156). See also Tuozzo (1996), who argues for the instrumentality of ethical virtue in leading the best—i.e., contemplative—life. As Tuozzo correctly notes, apropos of Z 13, 1144a1–3, the instrumentality of ethical virtue does not preclude its being choiceworthy in itself.

79. See *Rep.* 518D-E; 589D; 590D.

80. Cf. *EN* I 4, 1166a22–23: "And it would seem that each person is that part of himself that thinks or that part most of all" (δόξειε δ' ἂν τὸ νοοῦν ἕκαστος εἶναι ἢ μάλιστα); I 8, 1168b31–33: "And just as a state and any other systematic whole seems to be that which is the most authoritative part most of all, so is the human being" (ὥσπερ δὲ καὶ πόλις τὸ κυριώτατον μάλιστ' εἶναι δοκεῖ καὶ πᾶν ἄλλο σύστημα, οὕτω καὶ ἄνθρωπος). Cf. *Protrep.* B 62, 85–86 Düring. Cooper 1975, 168–177, gives substantially the same interpretation, noting that the identification of the self with the intellect is "inherited from Plato" (175) and the same as in *De Anima* (176). See also, Reeve 1992, 133–137.

81. At *EN* I 4, 1166a32; I 9, 1170b6–7, Aristotle calls a friend "another self" (ἄλλος αὐτός, ἕτερος αὐτός). Cf. *MM* B 15, 1213a24, where we find ἕτερος ἐγώ. I take it that in these passages Aristotle is not making the point that a friend is another human being. The distinction between human being and self (αὐτός) is authentically Platonic. See *Alc. I* 131B4–5, 133C18–19; *Lg.* 959A4-B7, esp. B4: "that which is the real self of each of us, that which we call the immortal soul" (τὸν δὲ ὄντα ἡμῶν ἕκαστον ὄντως, ἀθάνατον εἶναι ψυχὴν ἐπονομαζό-

The underlying assumption of that interpretation is illuminated by an important passage in (of all places) Simplicius's *Commentary on Aristotle's Physics*.[82] Simplicius is commenting on the passage in *Physics* in which Aristotle argues that the acquisition of the habit (ἕξις) that is a virtue or a vice is not a kind of alteration (ἀλλοίωσις) in the soul but either a perfection (τελείωσις) or, in the case of a vice, a destruction (φθορά) or deterioration (ἔκστασις).[83] The issue that puzzles Simplicius is how, if the development of a virtue or a vice is not an alteration, it is not then a substantial change of some sort such that as a result the essence of the human being has been changed. If the latter were the case, then in becoming virtuous or vicious, one would become another person. But this can hardly be true since the achievement sought in the development of virtue is the ideal achievement of the identical person striving to achieve. Simplicius's solution to this puzzle is in effect to appeal to the bipolarity of Aristotle's use of 'nature' in the sense of essence. In the sense of an endowment, one's essence is not changed by the acquisition of virtue or vice. In the sense of an achievement, that is precisely what becoming virtuous or vicious does. In other words, personal development in the direction of the ideal is the central result of the acquisition of virtue.

Viewing Aristotle's account of the best and second-best lives and their attendant virtues in a Neoplatonic manner gives, I think, a useful new perspective on what is arguably the central interpretive issue in contemporary scholarship on *Nicomachean Ethics*. That is the question of whether Aristotle's view of happiness is 'inclusive' or 'dominant.'[84] The many texts adduced to show Aristotle's preference for one view over the other, or his confusion about the two views, show that the dominant/inclusivist alternative presents a false dichotomy. For one thing, there is nothing to support the view that Aristotle ever recommends exclusive devotion to contemplative activity.

But the fact that we are endowed as souls should not blur the connative aspect of identification with a psychic activity. Eriksen (1976, 89), who rejects a Platonic orientation of those passages, says, "one may say that Aristotle in his account of νοῦς makes the highest part of the soul exclusively dominating in a way that blurs his general anthropology. It might not be correct to say that Aristotle has two doctrines of man. But if he has one, it surely falls into two parts. The part concerning man as a natural species of body and soul presents another picture than the part concerning man as a philosopher and scientist with νοῦς." I would reply that the 'two doctrines' idea is entirely Eriksen's fancy and his commitment to this interpretation conceals an assumption of the disharmony of Aristotle and Plato.

82. See Simplicius *In Phys.* 1066, 3–1067, 2. See on this passage Hadot's edition of Simplicus's *Commentary on Epictetus's Handbook* 1996, 80–83 and Steel 1978, 115.

83. See *Phys.* H 3, 246a4-b3.

84. Hardie 1967, introduces the distinction. The inclusivist thesis is that happiness includes all intrinsic or noninstrumental goods. The dominant thesis is that among all intrinsic goods, there is one alone that constitutes happiness. Hardie writes, "The confusion between an end which is final because it is inclusive and an end which is final because it is supreme or dominant accounts for much that critics have rightly found unsatisfactory in Aristotle's account of the thought which leads to practical decisions" (302). See Keyt 1978; Kraut 1989, esp. intro. and chaps. 1 and 5 for discussion of the basic views. See also, Crisp 1994.

Indeed, even in urging us to try as much as possible to live like the gods, he concedes that we are not in fact gods. So, rejecting inclusivism ought not to lead one to an absurd and unsupportable alternative. Similarly, for inclusivism, there is nothing to support the view that Aristotle recommends something like a maximizing of achievement of intrinsic goods. The question of which particular goods a human being should pursue at any one time is below the threshold of scientific inquiry.

On the Neoplatonic interpretation, a human life in which ethical virtue is practiced—a political life—is of course a virtuous life, and so a happy life. But that life is inferior to a life according to intellect, a life, as Plotinus says, that does not exclude the practice of ethical virtue. So, the best life has a dominant theme or focus but includes the practice of all virtues. The problem underlying the contemporary debate rests upon the supposition by both sides that a life according to intellect is equivalent to the practice of a virtue among others, even if it is the most complete virtue. But the life according to intellect is the life of a person who is transformed in identity. Such a person engaged in this life could look back upon his own previous political life as led by his 'old self.'

The fact that the theoretical life could not be integrated into a political life is, I think, that which most clearly confirms the inferiority of political virtue to the purificatory and intellectual virtues. What makes the inclusivist/dominant contrast seem intractable and indicative of a confusion or wobbling in Aristotle is the supposition that the same entity—inevitably, the 'composite'—could view these as alternatives. When one asks "which life shall I pick" one has probably already chosen. And the frequent suggestion that one might hedge and have it both ways by living a political life with a little theory on the side (a sort of inclusivism) misconstrues the nature of the life Aristotle is recommending.[85]

It is sometimes supposed that the description of intellect as "ruler and leader" in the passage above is unserious or incautious and in conflict with what Aristotle says earlier in *Nicomachean Ethics* about practical reason being the "ruling part" of action.[86] But Aristotle is consistent and clear on this point: "Practical wisdom [φρόνησις] does not rule [οὐδὲ κυρία] over wisdom, that is, over the best part of the soul, just as the medical art does not rule health, for practical wisdom does not use [χρῆται] wisdom but sees to it that wisdom is acquired. So practical wisdom gives orders for the sake of wisdom but does not give orders to wisdom."[87] Apart from the presupposi-

---

85. Cooper 1975, 159–160, shows that when Aristotle speaks about two lives (βίοι), he cannot mean two aspects or activities of one person in his or her life. See supra, 250–252 for Porphyry's insistence that the presence of the higher virtues necessitates the presence of the lower. One who pursues intellectual virtue is not 'opting' for it in the sense that ethical virtues are being rejected.

86. *EN* Γ 5, 1113a6. Cf. *Prot.* B 23 Düring with K 7, 1177a14–15.

87. *EN* Z 13, 1145a6–9. Cf. Z 13, 1143b34; *Met.* A 2, 982a17–19 and *EE* H 3, 1249b11–15. See Woods 1982, 193–198, on the interpretation of the latter.

tion that Aristotle is distancing himself from Plato here or that he must do so if his ethical doctrine is to be rescued, there seems little reason to take this claim in a way other than that which is suggested by the passages in Book K.[88]

There may be some confusion in supposing that the primacy of practical wisdom in action is precluded or compromised by the claim that wisdom or intellect is supreme. Recognizing that intellect is supreme according to the multiple criteria of supremacy laid down in Book K, chapter 7, does not mean that theory rules practice. Although one may wish to argue that in this regard Aristotle is opposing Plato, I think this, too, is a mistake. The philosopher in *Republic* and the ruler in *Statesman* and the lawgivers in *Laws*, though they bring theory to practice, do not mistake the one for the other. The claim that the life of the intellect is the best life is not equivalent to a commitment to intellectualism in ethics, where 'intellectualism' is understood somehow to involve ignoring or discounting the concrete circumstances of life. Nor does the claim that there is a theoretical basis for practical science mean that theory rules practice; rather, it means that there are universally true grounds why a decision or choice in a particular circumstance is good or bad.

Perhaps another reason for supposing that Book K, chapter 7, does not mean what it says or that it does not imply the inferiority of the practical to the theoretical life in any way is that Aristotle seems himself to reject a Platonic intellectualist approach to ethics by rejecting the Form of the Good. What can this rejection tell us about the presence or absence of Platonism in Aristotle's ethics?

Aristotle on the Form of the Good

Aristotle begins *Nicomachean Ethics* with the statement, "Every art and every inquiry, and similarly every action and every choice aims at some good. For this reason, those who have said that the good is that at which everything aims have spoken well."[89] It would of course be a fallacy of composition to assume that Aristotle is here endorsing a unique good, such as the superordinate Form of the Good is supposed to be.[90] In fact, we have seen repeatedly that from the Neoplatonists' perspective, it is Aristotle's misunderstanding of the first principle of all that is the principal cause of his divergence from Plato. We must be careful here to realize that in rejecting a superordinate Form of

---

88. See, e.g., Joachim (1951, 217), who, in commenting on the passage in which Aristotle says that practical wisdom is inferior to wisdom, says that practical wisdom and wisdom "are intrinsically valuable as modes in which the distinctively human self—the thinking self—finds its best expression." And "Aristotle points out . . . that [they] are intrinsically valuable and are constituents of the best life."

89. *EN* A 1, 1094a1–3.

90. At *Rhet.* A 6, 1362a21–24, Aristotle says that "good is what is chosen for its own sake and that on account of which we choose other things." Cf. *EN* A 5, 1097a18, 20; E 7, 1131b23, etc. Cf. Plato *Phil.* 54C9–10: "Then, that on account of which what comes to be for something always does so is placed in the class [ἐν μοίρᾳ] of the good."

the Good, whether or not it is identical with that which is called 'the One,' Aristotle is evidently not rejecting a unique good—namely, God—which is, as we have seen, unequivocally called 'the good' in the sense of 'the on account of which' or final cause.[91] So, it would not be unfair for Neoplatonists to claim that Aristotle recognizes a unique good at which everything aims or is oriented, though, in identifying it with intellect, he does not fully recognize its nature. His rejection of the Form (or the Idea) of the Good is, accordingly, owing in part to the mistaken belief that there could not be anything transcending intellect and so there could not be a truly 'universal good.' Indeed, his identifying the good with the thinking of God seems to make the good unacceptably limited, since strictly speaking it precludes the goods belonging to anything that does not think.[92]

Aristotle raises a number of objections to those who posit a universal (καθόλου) good.[93] It is perhaps worth noticing that he refers to his opponents—those who believe that there is a universal Form of the Good—in the plural. He does not focus on Plato. This leaves open the possibility that Plato is himself not the target. But this seems doubtful. Nevertheless, the objections do not clearly indicate that the Form of the Good is understood by Aristotle to have the superordinate status it has in *Republic*.[94] As we shall see, the objection to this Form could just as well serve as objections to other Forms, mutatis mutandis. So, insofar as the objections assume that the Form of the Good is an οὐσία, rather than that which is "not itself οὐσία," as *Republic* specifically states, they do not really touch Plato's position, as understood by Neoplatonists.

The objections themselves can be concisely summarized: (1) since good varies across categories, it cannot be universal;[95] (2) the term 'good' has as many senses as the term 'being' and so cannot be universally predicable across categories;[96] (3) there are many different sciences of different goods, but if there were a universal good there would be one science of it;[97] (4) the qualifier 'each thing itself' (αὐτοέκαστον) is obscure and so it is not clear what 'Good itself' adds to the account of a particular good;[98] (5) if a white thing is no whiter by existing forever than something that existed for a day,

91. See *Met.* Λ 10, 1075a11–15. At 1075a38–b1 Aristotle says that his predecessors were right to make the good a principle, but they did not specify whether it was a principle as goal or mover or as form.

92. In the course of his objections (*EN* A 4, 1096a24–25), Aristotle says that 'good' in one sense applies to 'whatness' (τί), as in the case of God or intellect. But a 'whatness' is limited or defined.

93. *EN* A 4, 1096a11–1097a14.

94. See *EE* A 8, 1217b22–26, where the Form of the Good is set apart from the other Forms, all of which are rejected, though it is not clear even here that it is given a superordinate status. At A 8, 1218b7–14, Aristotle is denying that the Form of the Good could fulfill the role of "the political good for human beings." That is hardly something that Neoplatonists would wish to deny.

95. *EN* A 4, 1096a17–23.

96. Ibid., 1096a23–29.

97. Ibid., 1096a29–34.

98. Ibid., 1096a34–b3.

neither will the Good itself be better than a particular good;[99] (6) the Form of the Good does not make the necessary distinction between things good in themselves and instrumental goods;[100] (7) assume that the Form of the Good only refers to the good in the former sense, yet this Form does not account for the diversity of things good in themselves, such as thinking, pleasure, and honor;[101] (8) even if there is a separate Form of the Good, it cannot be the goal of action, which is the topic of this work;[102] (9) one might argue that, despite the fact that the Form of the Good does not name the goal of action, still it would be useful for action to have knowledge of this, although in fact, people successfully pursue knowledge of the individual (productive) sciences of the individual kinds of goods without paying any attention to the putative knowledge of the Form of the Good.[103]

These objections seem to amount to three basic points: (A) 'good' is not a universal, applicable univocally to anything so called (1–3, 6–7); (B) positing a Form of Good 'itself' explains nothing that is not otherwise explicable (4–5); (C) a Form of the Good is irrelevant to ethical practice (8–9). I want to focus primarily on (C), but it should be pointed out that much of what Aristotle says in (A) loses its force if the Form of the Good is superordinate and hence not an οὐσία. For it is only an οὐσία that is a 'one-over-many' and so conceivably predicable univocally of many. As for (B), Aristotle himself in the *Metaphysics* passage referred to above agrees that a separate 'in itself' good exists and that its entire role is as an *explanans*. God's life *is* better than the life or the being of anything else, and God is the good of the universe.

The claim that the Form of the Good cannot account for the diversity of things good in themselves turns upon what sort of account it is supposed to provide. The Form of the Good or the One, as Neoplatonists understand it, is superior to that which provides this sort of explanation. It is not the paradigm of essence; the Intellect and the Forms serve in that role. But the Good does account for the being or essence of everything else. And so Aristotle's complaint that the Form of the Good does not explain what it is not supposed to explain, taking this Form in a superordinate capacity, will not strike the Neoplatonists as a significant one.

That knowing the Form of the Good should be irrelevant to ethical practice is a curious and ambiguous claim. Of course, if the Form of the Good does not exist, its irrelevance follows. But if the complaint is that theoretical knowledge is irrelevant to ethical practice, it is a complaint that applies to *Nicomachean Ethics* itself, for that work is largely theoretical.[104] If, however,

---

99. Ibid., 1096b3–5.
100. Ibid., 1096b8–14.
101. Ibid., 1096b14–29.
102. Ibid., 1096b32–35.
103. Ibid., 1096b35–1097a14.
104. At A 1, 1094b10–11, Aristotle says that the study (μέθοδος) aims at (ἐφίεται) the acquisition and preservation (λαβεῖν καὶ σῴζειν, b9) of the end of the state, which is the human good (τἀνθρώπινον ἀγαθόν, b7). But what this study pursues mainly is a theoretical understanding of the human good. At B 2, 1103b26–30, Aristotle also says that the present

the complaint is that those immersed in theory are not thereby able to direct ethical and political practices, it is a complaint that has little to do with Plato. In *Republic*, for example, Plato insists that the philosophers who return to the cave be assigned fifteen years of practical administration and military training in order to acquire experience (ἐμπειρία).[105] This practical training is prior to the vision of the Good. Having had this vision, the philosophers are then allowed to rule, evidently employing a combination of theoretical and practical wisdom. So, it does not appear that Plato envisions theory as a substitute for experience or that a vision of the Form of the Good would suffice for success in practical matters.

But, granting that knowledge of the Form of the Good is not held by Plato to be sufficient for ethical success, is it even necessary? Objection (9) suggests that it is not. In this objection, Aristotle offers as counterexamples weavers, carpenters, and physicians who are able to do their jobs quite well without knowledge of this Form. One cannot see, Aristotle adds, how they would benefit from such knowledge. Indeed, one cannot. It is hard to believe that Plato thought otherwise, particularly given his apparent separation and relative devaluation of popular and political virtue. That sort of virtue is the best that weavers, carpenters, and physicians are likely to achieve.[106]

An appeal made to Aristotle's criticism of the Form of the Good in order to show his rejection of intellectualism or otherworldliness seems quite ineffective.[107] On the contrary, rejection of the Form of the Good, whether this be taken as superordinate or not, does not produce in Aristotle a view of the value of experience to ethical practice different from Plato's own. In the final section of this chapter I want to strengthen the case for harmony by showing that Aristotle's treatment of the ethical virtues is in fact remarkably similar to Plato's own.

The Doctrine of Virtue as a Mean and the Platonic Art of Measurement

Many scholars have noticed that the roots of Aristotle's doctrine that virtue is a mean are to be found in Plato.[108] I want to show that this doctrine

---

is not for the sake of contemplation but for the sake of becoming good. This does not contradict but rather supports the claim that the present study is engaged in theory.

105. *Rep.* 539E. Cf. *Phdr.* 271D-E, where the rhetorician is said to need practical knowledge in addition to theory in order to achieve his goals. Experience is necessary in order for theory to be effective in action.

106. At *EN* A 1, 1094a26-b7, Aristotle says that the architectonic political science ordains what sciences are to be studied by members of the state and to what extent.

107. See Annas 1999, chap. 5, for an argument that Middle Platonists understood that the Form of the Good was not intended to provide practical guidance. Taken as a final cause, however, it is the basis for assimilation to the divine (108).

108. See Hardie 1965; Tracy 1969; and Sparshott (1982, 499), who compares the doctrine of the mean with the view of justice as the 'harmony' of the personality at the end of *Republic* Book 4; Bosley 1996, 43–46.

supports the subordination of ethical virtue to theoretical virtue and the political life to the philosophical life.

At the beginning of Book B, Aristotle takes up the discussion of ethical virtue. This discussion proceeds from general analytic considerations, including an important discussion of volition, to the discussion of particular ethical virtues up to the end of Book E. Book Z turns to a parallel discussion of the intellectual virtues. Aristotle concludes his analysis of the elements of the definition of ethical virtue: "[Ethical][109] virtue is, then, a habit of being able to make a choice [ἕξις προαιρετική], existing in a mean [μεσότητι] relative to us, defined by reason [λόγῳ], that is, as the practically wise person [φρόνιμος] would define it."[110] As Aristotle has already explained, "Since virtues are concerned with actions and feelings [πάθη], and with every feeling and every action pleasure and pain follow, then for this reason virtue is concerned with pleasures and pains."[111] And, "we regulate our actions, some more and some less, by pleasure and pain. For this reason, then, it is necessary for the whole inquiry to be about these [pleasure and pain]. For being pleased or pained well or badly is not a small thing in regard to actions."[112] In fact, "the whole inquiry with respect to virtue and political science is about pleasures and pains."[113]

This fundamental orientation of the discussion of ethical virtue should be compared with what Socrates says in *Protagoras* at the conclusion of his refutation of the claim that it is possible to be overcome by pleasure in despite of what one believes to be good for oneself: "Well, then, people, since it has seemed to us that our own salvation depends on the correct choice of pleasures and pains, of the more or fewer, lesser or greater, farther or nearer, then does it not seem that saving our life is primarily an art of measurement [μετρητική], which is the study of relative excess and deficiency and equality?" "It must be.' 'Since it is measurement, it must necessarily be an art [τέχνη] or science [ἐπιστήμη]."[114] This art of measurement is in the first instance taken to be arithmetic.[115] It is the supposedly straightforward comparison of quantities of pleasures. But it is immediately suggested that this art is something more complicated and needs to be discussed at length.[116]

---

109. See *EN* B 5, 1106b16, for the reference.

110. *EN* B 6, 1106b36–1107a2. In the last clause, καὶ ὡς ἂν ὁ φρόνιμος ὁρίσειεν, I read ὡς with all the manuscripts instead of ᾧ with Bywater, taking the καὶ as epexegetic.

111. *EN* B 2, 1104b13–16. The connection between pleasure and pain and feelings is well explained by Leighton 1982, 217–220, as a conceptual one. That is, part of what is meant by a feeling is its accompaniment by pleasure or pain.

112. *EN* B 2, 1105a4–7.

113. Ibid., 1105a10–12.

114. *Protag.* 357A5–B4.

115. Ibid., 357A2–3. Geometrical or proportional measurement is alluded to at *Gorg.* 508A5–6; *Rep.* 558C; 561B–C; *Lg.* 757B–C. In these passages, proportionality is applied to the distribution of goods. Cf. *EN* E 4, 1131b10–1132a30; Θ 7, 1158b30–33, on the distinction applied to distributive justice.

116. *Protag.* 357B5–6. Presumably, what needs to be discussed is how to make quantitative comparisons among pleasures. See Taylor 1976, 194–199, for a good discussion of the complex issues that arise in attempting to do so.

The putative phenomenon of being overcome by pleasure, contrary to what one believes is in one's interests, turns out to be in fact a cognitive error.[117] If one actually knew what was good for oneself, one could not but act in order to achieve it. If one knew that enjoying the enticing pleasure would, in fact, all things considered, be less *pleasurable* than refraining from its enjoyment, then one could not, psychologically, opt for it.

This notoriously difficult argument against the possibility of incontinence or weakness of the will has received the most minute attention of scholars. One of the numerous interpretive questions is whether in this argument Socrates commits himself to hedonism of any sort or whether hedonism in the argument is just the material example of a putative object of desire used to illustrate a formal point about the psychology of action.[118] Although I have argued elsewhere for the latter alternative,[119] what is here more important is that virtue is being taken by Plato to be the knowledge of how to measure pleasures and pains.[120] Specifically, political or ethical virtues are meant.[121] These are the virtues concerned with the regulation of passions, wherein pleasure and pain occur, as Aristotle says.

In *Republic* Plato refers to these pleasures as "the so-called pleasures of the body."[122] They are the pleasures that belong in the appetitive part of the soul. They are "so-called," we later learn, because they are false.[123] As Plato goes on to argue both in *Republic* and in *Philebus,* it is not the case that false pleasures are not really pleasures at all. They are false because there is an ineluctable element of falsity in them. More precisely, there is a false belief embedded in the inseparable cognitive element in them.[124] What this means basically is that we cannot have pleasures and pains without cognizing them, not just 'feeling' them. And in cognizing them we necessarily involve a propositional element that is subject to objective evaluation. Although no one could gainsay my honestly expressed claim that I feel I am now experiencing pleasure, one could conceivably argue me out of the pleasure by showing me that the belief upon which it is based is false. Since for Plato no one can possibly maintain a belief believing it to be false, as soon as the false belief is discarded, the pleasure (or the awareness of the pleasure) disappears.[125]

117. Cf. *Protag.* 357D7–E2.

118. Ibid., 358C–D.

119. See Gerson 2003, 40–49, with references to the literature.

120. *Protag.* 352A–E, the beginning of the argument, where Socrates claims that knowledge of "things good and bad to do" is in fact invincible. The conclusion of the argument at 358C–D is that such knowledge—i.e., the art of measurement—is, in fact, invincible. So, it seems fairly clear that Plato is arguing that knowledge is virtue. This is the virtue the teachability of which is in question throughout the dialogue. See 361B–C.

121. Ibid., 323A7, B2; 324A1.

122. *Rep.* 442A8.

123. Ibid., 583B1–7: "the pleasures other [than those of the intellect] are neither entirely true [παναληθής] nor pure [καθαρά] but are like some shadow-painting [ἐσκιαγραφημένη]" Cf. *Phd.* 69B6; *Lg.* 663C2.

124. See Damascius *In Phil.* 167, 9–10; 172 (citing Proclus).

125. See Gerson 2003, 251–265. Pleasures are 'belief involving,' as I call them, because our ideal identity as rational agents is inseparable from our experience of them. A related point can be made for sense perception.

In *Republic, Statesman,* and *Philebus,* the art of measurement becomes the art of discovering the mean between extremes. In the Myth of Er, souls are advised on the choice of lives:

> Now, it seems that it is here, Glaucon, that a human being faces the greatest danger of all. And because of this, each of us must neglect all other subjects and be most concerned to seek out and learn those that will enable him to distinguish the good life from the bad and always to *make the best choice possible in every situation.* He should think over all the things we have mentioned and how they jointly and severally determine what the virtuous life is like. That way he will know what the good and bad effects of beauty are when it is mixed with wealth, poverty, and a particular state of the soul. He will know the effects of high or low birth, private life or ruling office, physical strength or weakness, ease or difficulty in learning, and all things that are either naturally part of the soul or are acquired, and he will know what they achieve when mixed with one another. And from all this he will be able, by considering the nature of the soul, to reason out which life is better and which worse and to choose accordingly, calling a life worse if it leads the soul to become more unjust, better if it leads the soul to become more just, and ignoring everything else: we have seen that this is the best way to choose, whether in life or death. Hence, we must go down to Hades holding with adamantine determination to the belief that it is so, lest we be dazzled there by wealth and other such evils, rush into a tyranny or some other similar course of action, do irreparable evils, and suffer even worse ones. And we must always know how to choose the mean in such lives and how to avoid either of the extremes, as far as possible, both in this life and in all those beyond it. This is the way that a human being becomes happiest.[126]

In *Statesman* the art of measurement is said to have two parts: "We divide the art of measurement in a part concerned with the relative greatness or smallness of objects and another part concerned with their size in relation to the essence necessary for becoming (τὴν τῆς γενέσεως ἀναγκαίαν οὐσίαν)."[127] The first is clearly the arithmetic comparison first mentioned in *Protagoras.* The second is rather more obscure, but as the Stranger goes on to explain, it involves measurement against the essence *as a mean.*[128] And the mean is explicated as the fitting (τὸ πρέπον), the timely (τὸ καιρόν), and the needed (τὸ δέον), and "all such [standards] that migrated from the extremes to the mean."[129] All of these specifications are context-sensitive.[130]

126. *Rep.* 618B6–619B1 (trans. Reeve).
127. *Sts.* 283D7–9. See Krämer 1959, esp. the abundant evidence adduced, 146–241, on the Platonic art of measurement—expressed in the accounts of virtue, pleasure and pain, art, and nature—as the basis for the Aristotelian doctrine of the mean. It should be added, however, that Krämer regards the art of measurement as flowing from an ontology that Aristotle rejects.
128. *Sts.* 284D5–6: "at the same time, the greater and lesser are measured not only against each other but also in relation to the generation of what is measured" (μεῖζόν τε ἅμα καὶ ἔλαττον μετρεῖσθαι μὴ πρὸς ἄλληλα μόνον ἀλλὰ καὶ πρὸς τὴν τοῦ μετρίου γένεσιν).
129. Ibid., 284E6–8.
130. See Miller 1980, 66: "As the fullest possible realization of the form, given the limits of context, the mean serves as the norm for *praxis,* the standard by which essential measure can judge speeches and action."

In the crucial passage in *Philebus*, which speaks generally about the four categories of "all that exists now in the universe," Socrates distinguishes the indeterminate class (τὸ ἄπειρον), the determinant class (τὸ πέρας), the mixture of the two (τὸ συμμισγόμενον), and the cause of the mixture, intellect (νοῦς).[131] The mixed class includes good climate, health, and "excellent things in the soul."[132] It is the class of that which is simultaneously measured and commensurate (τὸ ἔμμετρον καὶ ἅμα σύμμετρον).[133] It is highly likely that the mean in the good mixture is geometrical as well.[134]

In addition, there are a number of passages in Plato's *Laws* wherein the regulation of pleasures and pains is stated to be the essence of virtue. At the beginning of Book 2, the Athenian Stranger claims:

> By 'education' [παιδείαν] I mean the primary acquisition of virtue in children, and that is when pleasure and love and pain and hate arise in the right way in their souls, even though they are not yet able to grasp this with reason [λόγῳ]. But when they do grasp the reason, these [i.e., pleasure, love, pain, and hate] agree with [συμφωνήσωσι] with reason that they have been rightly habituated by appropriate habits. This agreement in its entirety is what virtue is. But there is a part of it which consists in being raised rightly in regard to pleasures and pains so that one hates what one ought to hate straight from the start and love what one ought to love. If you distinguish this and call it 'education,' you would, at least in my view, be naming it rightly.[135]

The virtue here that consists entirely in agreement is ethical virtue. It is concerned with the regulation or habituation of feelings according to *right* reason.[136] That is, feelings come to obey right reason in the sense of being informed by reason.[137]

A number of striking comparisons can be made between all the foregoing texts from Plato and Aristotle's definition of virtue as a mean. The

131. *Phil.* 23C9-10, D1, D7-8 with 30C7 on the identification of the cause as νοῦς.
132. Ibid., 26B5-7.
133. Ibid., 26A6-7. Cf. 64D-E.
134. See Gosling 1975, 189, 196–198, on the argument for the geometrical mean here.
135. *Lg.* 653B1-C4. See also 633C-E, 647D, 696C, 689A-D; Aristotle's definition of ethical virtue in *EN* B 6, 1106b36–1107a2, and B 5, 1106b16–17.
136. See *Lg.* 696C9-10.
137. See Plotinus's commentary on this passage, VI 4. 15, 32–40: "But this is also the vice of a human being, having in himself a populace of pleasures and appetites and fears which gain control when a human being of this sort surrenders himself to a populace of this sort. But whoever enslaves this mob and returns to that which he once was, lives according to that person, and is that person, giving to the body the things that he would give to something other than himself. But some other person lives now this way and now that way, has become a sort of mixture of a good self and a different bad self" (Τοῦτο δὲ καὶ ἀνθρώπου κακία αὖ ἔχοντος δῆμον ἐν αὑτῷ ἡδονῶν καὶ ἐπιθυμιῶν καὶ φόβων κρατησάντων συνδόντος ἑαυτὸν τοῦ τοιούτου ἀνθρώπου δήμῳ τῷ τοιούτῳ· ὃς δ' ἂν τοῦτον τὸν ὄχλον δουλώσηται καὶ ἀναδράμῃ εἰς ἐκεῖνον, ὅς ποτε ἦν, κατ' ἐκεῖνόν τε ζῇ καὶ ἔστιν ἐκεῖνος διδοὺς τῷ σώματι, ὅσα δίδωσιν ὡς ἑτέρῳ ὄντι ἑαυτοῦ· ἄλλος δέ τις ὁτὲ μὲν οὕτως, ὁτὲ δὲ ἄλλως ζῇ, μικτός τις ἐξ ἀγαθοῦ ἑαυτοῦ καὶ κακοῦ ἑτέρου γεγενημένος). The 'good self' here in comparison with the 'alien self' (ἑτέρῳ ὄντι ἑαυτου) is the 'true self' referred to at *Lg.* 959A4-B7.

geometrical—hence, relative—nature of the mean is evident in both in regard to the production of virtue. The mean is defined by reason, as this is grasped by the practically wise person. The practically wise person, like Plato's statesman, is a mediator between what is objectively virtuous and what constitutes virtue for this person in this situation.[138] And finally, habituation or imposition of the mean results in corrections to our pleasure and pain responses.

I focus now on Aristotle to show that his treatment of habituation in ethical virtue presumes a Platonic notion of personhood. For him, accordingly, ethical virtue could not be, as it is not for Plato, anything but inferior to philosophical virtue.

Aristotle distinguishes two rational parts of the soul: the part of the soul that obeys reason (ἐπιπειθὲς λόγῳ) is distinct from the part of the soul that has reason: that is, the part that is thinking (διανοούμενον).[139] The relation between these two parts and the location of ethical virtue is explained in the following crucial passage from *Nichomachean Ethics*:

> There appears to be another nature of the soul that is nonrational [ἄλογος] but which shares in reason in some way. For we praise reason or that part of the soul which has reason in the continent and the incontinent human being, since it urges them rightly to do what is best; but it appears that these men have another part which by its nature violates reason, and this part fights against or resists reason. For just as the paralyzed parts of the body when directed to move to the right [often] move contrawise to the left, so it is with the soul; for incontinent men have an impulse to move in the contrary direction. But while in the body we observe this motion in the contrary direction, in the soul we do not. Perhaps in the soul, too, we should grant no less the existence of something which violates reason: that is, a part that goes contrary to it or resists it. How this part is distinct from the part with reason does not concern us here. Now this part, too, seems to share in reason, as we said; for at least in the continent man it obeys reason, while in the temperate or brave man, perhaps it is even more disposed to listen to reason, for it agrees with reason on all matters. So, the term 'nonrational,' too, appears to have two meanings. For the vegetative part in no way communicates with reason, while the appetitive part and, in general, the part which desires shares [in reason] in some way, namely, insofar as it listens to or obeys it; and this is the manner in which a human being has reason when we speak of him as listening to or obeying his father or his friends, and not in the manner in which he has reason in mathematics. That the nonrational part is in some way persuaded by reason is indicated also by advice or by any censure or urging. And if one should say that this part, too, has reason, then also the expression 'that which has reason' would have two senses: (a) that which has reason in itself, this being the principal sense, and (b) that which listens to reason, like a child listening to a father.

138. See *Sts.* 290E-299E. Cf. *EN* B 6, 1107a1–2; Z 5 on the practically wise person (φρόνιμος). Although the practically wise person does not have 'scientific knowledge' (cf. 1140a35), she does apply the standard of right reason (ὀρθὸς λόγος). This standard, as Aristotle says (*EE* B 5, 1222b4–14), is concerned with the (geometrical) mean.

139. *EN* A 6, 1098a4–5.

Virtues, too, are distinguished according to this difference, for we call some of them 'intellectual' (e.g., wisdom and intelligence and practical wisdom) but others 'ethical' (e.g., generosity and temperance). Thus, when we speak of the character of a man, we say that he is good-tempered or temperate, not wise or intelligent, but we praise also the wise man in virtue of his disposition, and we call 'virtues' those dispositions which are praiseworthy.[140]

Ethical virtue belongs to the part of the soul that obeys (or disobeys) reason.[141] In general, this part is the locus of the affections or feelings (πάθη). As Aristotle defines the term, it includes appetite (ἐπιθυμία), anger, fear, envy, courage, gladness, love, hatred, longing, emulation, pity, and, in general, whatever is accompanied by pleasure or pain.[142] Ethical virtue, then, consists in a habit or disposition with regard to these feelings, though they are distinct from the feelings themselves. When our feelings are 'in a mean,' we are ethically virtuous; when they are not, we are not.[143] This being in a mean is what right reason ordains.[144]

A number of scholars have wondered how the foregoing description of feelings corresponds to the modern conception of emotion.[145] The particular problem is appetite, which does not seem to be entirely 'persuadable'

---

140. *EN* A 13, 1102b13–1103a10.

141. See Arius Didymus *apud* Stobaeus *Ecl.* II 51, 1–8, where a *threefold* distinction of virtues is found: (a) perfect or complete virtue, including the theoretical, the practical, and the ethical; (b) natural virtue, which is the capacity for perfect virtue; and (c) the virtue that results from the "harmony of the rational and arational parts of the soul." It is (c) that Neoplatonists will identify with "popular or political virtue." For (b), see *EN* Z 13, 1144b1–9. Aspasius *In EN* 40, 10–15, distinguishes between (a) and (d) an imperfect form of virtue according to which "people act as right reason would direct, having only a belief in what this is without having demonstrative knowledge of it." The latter is not exactly (c), though they might amount to the same thing. The basis for (d) in Aristotle is perhaps *EN* H 9, 1151a17–20, where Aristotle identifies someone with either natural or habituated (ἐθιστή) virtue who acts as right reason would dictate, It is clear from this passage that Aristotle is distinguishing a person with habituated virtue from a continent person. Simplicius *In Cat.* 237, 9–16; 287, 19–24, distinguishes three types of imperfect virtue: (e) by nature; (f) by habit; (g) by reason, meaning that the presence of virtue in only one or another of these three respects would signal imperfection. Simplicius gives as an example of (g) someone who knows what the right thing to do is, but is not inclined to do so either by nature or habit. So, (f) would seem to indicate the opposite. It is not clear if (f) is identical with or overlaps (c) and (d). Elias *Proleg.* 19, 30–20, 15, on the basis of a distinction between activity based on external reason (μετὰ λόγου του θύραθεν) and internal reason (μετὰ λόγου του οἴκοθεν), would seem to be recognizing the cases of (f) that are, in fact, identical with cases of (c) and (d). See Ierodiakonou 1999, 147–151, who provides some discussion of these passages.

142. *EN* B 4, 1105b21–23. At *Rhet.* B 1, 1378a20–23, Aristotle adds that the πάθη are "such things owing to which those who are changed [by their πάθη being changed] differ with respect to their judgments." At *EE* B 2, 1220b14, Aristotle adds the qualification 'sensory' (αἰσθητική) to pleasure and pain.

143. Here I leave out of account the important point that without 'practical wisdom' (φρόνησις) there is not real virtue, only its simulacrum.

144. See *EN* Z 2, 1139a35ff. Being in a mean and acting with right reason are distinguished from merely acting "according to right reason" at Z 13, 1144b26–27. As Gottlieb (1994) argues, the distinction is between an integrated soul and mere rule following. I take this integration under the authority of reason as profoundly Platonic.

145. See, e.g., Leighton 1982; Nussbaum 1994, chap. 3; Cooper 1996.

by reason. Indeed, in *Eudemian Ethics,* Aristotle specifically says that appetite "acts not by persuading, for it does not share in reason."[146] The problem is not with appetite acting not by persuading, for that is exactly what incontinence is, but with the claim that appetite does not share in reason, which seems to contradict the passage from *Nicomachean Ethics* if appetite is included in feelings.

The solution to this puzzle is perhaps to be found in the distinction made by Plato in *Republic* between appetite and appetite qualified in some way.[147] There Plato is arguing for a tripartitioning of the soul. He claims that appetite consists of a not entirely precise class of wants or desires such as hunger, thirst, and sex. These wants are discovered in oneself, though they cannot evidently exist without the body. An appetite is to be distinguished from an appetite qualified in some way—for example, sex with a particular person or drink of a certain sort. It is these qualified appetites, not appetites as such, that have intentional objects.[148] And these are precisely the appetites that are susceptible to persuasion. A continent person, for example, persuades himself not that he is not hungry but rather that his hunger here and now (which is perhaps inevitably particularized) is to be resisted.[149] I suggest that when Aristotle is talking about appetites as feelings, persuadable by reason because they share in reason, he is applying Plato's distinction and referring to the qualified appetites, not the appetites as such.[150]

The distinction Plato is making is not so clear. The examples of a qualified appetite he gives are for hot or cold, for much or little drink as opposed to drink, and for 'good' drink as opposed to drink. The qualifications it

146. *EE* B 8, 1224b1–2. Cf. *EN* H 7, 1149b1–4, which distinguishes cases of incontinence in which one is conquered by either appetite or anger. One is not conquered by reason in the former, whereas in the latter one is, because presumably there is a cognitive element in the anger. The fact that an appetite is not conquered by reason does not imply that it could not be so. The point of the comparison is that an angry person is conquered by a kind of reason that is not opposed by any rational calculation—i.e., he thinks he ought to be angry—whereas the one conquered by appetite is so conquered in despite of what he rationally thinks is best.

147. See *Rep.* 437D2–438A5; 505D11–E1. See also *Men.* 78B5; *Gorg.* 468B7–8. Aristotle *EN* Γ 4, 1113a15–b2, shares the principle that we unqualifiedly seek our own good.

148. Nussbaum 1994, 81, says that for Aristotle even "the bodily appetites—hunger, thirst, sexual desire—are seen . . . as forms of intentional awareness, containing a view of their object." I think this is true for appetites qualified in the foregoing manner, not for appetites as such. Unqualified appetites do not have intentional objects, though they do have objects. It is a separate but ultimately important point that even though unqualified appetites do not have intentional objects, there is intentionality in having an unqualified appetite. The primary intentional object of *any* appetite is oneself in the appetitive state. When I am aware that I am hungry, my being in a state of hunger is the object of my intentional awareness. Secondarily, I might, say, fix my appetite on a wedge of Gorgonzola cheese, in which case there is an additional intentional object. It is the secondary intentionality, infused with a cognitive dimension, that is the locus of the persuadable.

149. There are two different sorts of cases: (1) resisting hunger *now* and (2) resisting hunger for, say, an illicit food.

150. At *EN* Γ 7, 1113b27–30 Aristotle says that "no one exhorts us to do whatever is neither in our power nor voluntary, as it would be useless for one to try to persuade us, e.g., not to be feverish or pained or hungry or affected in any other such manner, for we will be affected by these none the less." He seems here to be referring to the unqualified appetites.

seems are 'adjectival,' so to speak. But this leaves unclear whether an appetite for, say, lemonade, is an appetite *simpliciter* or a qualified one, since lemonade is a species of drink, not an attribute of drink. I am not sure we can decide about such cases, though I suspect that insofar as an appetite can be altered, what is at issue is the qualification, not the appetite.[151] Central here is the possibility of theoretically isolating appetites from cognitive—that is, propositional—content.

This distinction is made precisely in *Rhetoric,*

> Now, of appetites, some are nonrational [ἄλογοι] and some are with reason (μετὰ λόγου). I mean by 'nonrational' all those that are appetites for something not on the basis of believing [τοῦ ὑπολαμβάνειν]. Such are all those that are called 'natural,' as are those that arise owing to the body, like the appetite for nourishment, drink and hunger [for food] and the appetite for a particular kind of nourishment, and the appetites connected with taste, sex, and in general, with touch, smell, hearing, and sight. I mean by 'with reason' those appetites that are appetites that arise from our being convinced [τοῦ πεισθῆναι]. For there are many things which we have an appetite to see or to possess when we hear about them and are convinced [that they are pleasant].[152]

Here Aristotle is evidently making the distinction on the basis of whether propositional content is present or not. 'Belief,' as we saw in chapter five, is always present with conviction; that is what separates it from imagination. But Aristotle locates the qualification 'kind of nourishment' on the side of the nonrational, nonpropositional. I do not think this is importantly different from what Plato says, if it is, indeed, different at all, because of the additional qualification that these are appetites that arise owing to the body. No doubt, in some sense, no appetite for any particular kind of object is natural, arising owing solely to the body. No one desires lemonade as such before knowing what lemonade is. On the other hand, one could, say, develop a craving for nicotine, which could properly be said to be bodily and immune to cognitive assault.[153]

The main problem we face is what it means for feelings to obey or be persuaded by reason. Examples of such a phenomenon are not hard to come by. My anger abates when I am persuaded that it is based on a mistake. My fear dissipates when I am made to realize that the danger is not as great as I thought. And so on. But strictly speaking, we can hardly suppose that it is the feeling or embodied psychic state that is a party to a rational conversation.

---

151. There is a similar ambiguity with regard to pleasures and whether they can be removed by persuasion, in which case they might be false.

152. *Rhet.* A 11, 1370a19–25.

153. I tend to disagree with Leighton (1982, 224–231), who argues that the exclusion of appetites from the list of feelings in *Rhet.* B 1, 1378a20–23, indicates that Aristotle has developed a sophisticated account of feelings which makes them like our concept of emotions. I think the basic distinction is between what is and what is not amenable to reason. What is so amenable includes for Aristotle more than what we would typically include in the class of emotions, i.e., appetites with a cognitive dimension.

Anger does not listen to reason in the way that one rational being listens to another. In fact, it is not difficult to see that when my feelings obey reason, this does not presume that my feelings are rational. The obedience, if there be such, is a consequence of the rational self responding to another rational self or to itself.

I take it that the former is unproblematic. When I accede to the argument of another that my anger is misplaced, and my anger abates, there is not even a suggestion that it is my anger that has understood anything or has any cognitive properties. The supposition that this is not so is, I suspect, based upon the latter case. For if I am doing the arguing aimed at persuading, with whom am I arguing other than my feeling? Is not the idea of arguing with yourself, which is something quite different from deliberation or supposal, something suspiciously like a logical impossibility? If, for example, I believe p, and that belief is a constituent or cause of my anger, then how could I also be the one arguing for not-p, the putative remedy to the mistaken belief?

In order for something like this to be possible, we might appeal to a distinction between first- and second-order desires, as, for example, Harry Frankfurt has done in a series of justly celebrated articles.[154] On such a view, I can somehow have second-order desires in relation to first-order desires. Since at least the second-order desires have a propositional component, this can contradict implicitly a hypothetical belief component of the first-order desire. Thus, I can desire to use drugs and desire that I not have this desire because, presumably, I believe that satisfying this desire is bad for me. But this belief implicitly contradicts the belief that satisfying the desire is good for me, a belief that is not unreasonably assigned to someone who has the relevant first-order desire. Frankfurt's analysis, or something like it, operates entirely in the formal mode. It has nothing to say about how it is possible for a creature to have both first- and second-order beliefs. Frankfurt himself only avers that this is a necessary property of a person, where I take him to be speaking about the conceptual content of 'person.'

Aristotle, however, in the passage quoted from *Nicomachean Ethics,* Book K, chapter 7, has already given us the basis for the distinction in the material mode. He refers to "the life according to the intellect" as "especially the human being." As we have seen, our identity as agents of thought is an ideal, distinct from our embodied identities as agents of, among other things, feelings. Biologically, so to speak, it is indeed the same human being that is the subject who feels angry and the subject who thinks or comes to think "I ought not to feel angry." But experience tells us that persons are such that they can reflect on their own subjective states. As Aristotle states in his discussion of friendship:

> Each of the definitions [of a friend] above is attributed to a good man in relation to himself, and it is attributed to others in relation to themselves insofar

154. See esp. Frankfurt 1971.

as they regard themselves as being such [i.e., good]. For, as stated earlier, virtue or a virtuous man seems to be like a measure of each man since it is a virtuous man who is in agreement with himself [ὁμογωμονεῖ], who desires the same things with respect to every part of the soul, who wishes and does for himself what is both good and appears so (for a good man makes a serious effort to do what is good) and does so for his own sake, all these being for the sake of the thinking part of the soul, which is thought to be the very man himself.[155]

It is, I suggest, the ability to be in agreement (or disagreement or *to come to an agreement*) with oneself that characterizes embodied persons. And when one does come to an agreement, it is not by reasoning with one's feelings, but by reasoning with one's own rational self, the self that is both the subject of the feeling and the subject of thought.

I believe that the so-called function argument in Book A of *Nicomachean Ethics* should be understood in the light of the foregoing.[156] The function (ἔργον) of a human being is the life of action (πρακτική) of one having reason. Of that which has reason, one part has reason in the sense that it may obey reason, and the other part has it in the sense that it possesses reason or in the sense that it is thinking.[157] It has often been noticed that the function argument corresponds very closely to the argument in Book 1 of *Republic* that Socrates gives to Thrasymachus on behalf of the conclusion that the just life is the happy life.[158] The function that Aristotle describes as 'having reason' Plato describes inductively, giving as examples taking care of things (ἐπιμελεῖσθαι), ruling (ἄρχειν), deliberating (βουλεύσθαι), and "all such things."[159] As Plato makes clear later in *Republic*, the rational function includes exacting obedience from the other parts of the soul, especially the appetitive.[160] But, as in the passages from Aristotle above, the virtue of the part that 'obeys' is the virtue of the person or subject, though not the ideal one.

The crucial point is that ethical virtue consists in the habituation of the part that "obeys reason." To hold that this part or a life lived according to it is *not* inferior to the part that 'rules' or the theoretical life is a mistake arising from a false inference drawn from the correct observation that virtuous activity is always done 'for its own sake.' Being an ethically virtuous person

---

155. *EN* I 4, 1166a10–23.

156. On the structure of the argument, see most recently Lawrence 2001 with references to the literature.

157. *EN* A 6, 1098a3–5. The use of the term πρακτική here does not limit the function to practical as opposed to theoretical activity, as *Pol.* H 3, 1325b16–22, clearly shows. In fact, Aristotle in both passages seems to be using the term πρακτική as an adjectival form of ἐνέργεια.

158. See *Rep.* 352D1–354A11. As Lawrence 2001, 449 n. 10, shows, Aristotle's version of the argument is, typically, more rigorous than Plato's. This frequent relative rigor is perhaps sometimes supposed to indicate a doctrinal difference where it in fact does not.

159. *Rep.* 353D5. Cf. *Alc. I* 130A; *Phd.* 80A, 94B; *Phdr.* 246B; *Crat.* 400A; *Phil.* 30A; and *Lg.* 896A, where Plato identifies the function of soul as ruling. In all these passages it is clear that the rational soul, or νοῦς, is meant.

160. See Gerson 2003, 99–131.

consists in developing appropriate responses to the situations in which we humans find ourselves. These appropriate responses begin with the appropriate feelings and are completed with the appropriate actions mediated by the appropriate desires.

The reason why ethical virtue is inferior to theoretical virtue is the same as the reason why the practice of ethical virtue can contribute to the achievement of theoretical virtue.[161] Ethical virtue belongs to an inferior version of the person, namely, the subject of feelings. If one were to ask oneself the Platonic question "Why be virtuous?" the only answer, finally, that is not instrumentalist or utilitarian is that everyone wants his or her own good, and being virtuous constitutes one's own good. What amounts to virtue in a particular situation is determined by reason applied by the practically wise person calculating the mean. But this claim can be stated in a purely vacuous manner such that even a Thrasymachus could endorse it. Why is ethical virtue one's own good? Or in other words, why is acting as reason determines it in one's own interest? The Aristotelian answer to this question is exactly the same as the Platonic: because one is ideally a subject of reason. One may come to realize this as one reflects on one's own appetites on behalf of their appropriate habituation. One cannot think about one's appetites or in general one's feelings without distancing oneself from them in some way. That is, as one seeks to 'persuade' one's own feelings, one at least implicitly distinguishes oneself from those feelings which are in a sense possessions. If I command my feelings, I am not those feelings, though they be mine. If one comes to identify oneself as a rational subject in this way, then one is on the threshold of appreciating that nonpractical theoretical virtue is the virtue of that ideal subject.[162]

It goes without saying that there is no guarantee that this will happen. Aristotle does not believe for one moment (any more than did Plato) that everyone is capable of coming to identify himself in a strong way as a subject of theoretical rationality. That in fact few are so capable is why the second best life, the political life, is far more common than is the theoretical life. The *political* question for both Plato and Aristotle is how to maximize the possibilities for persons to achieve the best that persons are capable of. As for what that is, Aristotle's view does indeed appear to be in harmony with Plato's.

---

161. Aspasius *In EN* 99, 4, remarks that all virtue seems to be a kind of ὁμοίωσις θεῷ.
162. See Lear 1988, 309–321; Reeve 1992, 145–159, for a similar interpretation.

Chapter Nine

Aristotle: Platonist malgré lui?

It is time to take stock and address some obvious questions. How can Aristotle's philosophy be in harmony with Plato's if Aristotle himself never acknowledges this harmony? Even if it is granted that some or most of Aristotle's criticisms are not directed at something that might deserve to be called 'mature' or 'refined' Platonism, why should we opt for the Neoplatonic interpretation of Aristotelian texts which makes them harmonious with that? Given the criticisms and the absence of an explicit commitment to harmony, is not the reasonable default interpretation of these texts anti-Platonic? This concluding chapter explores one possible way of answering this question: namely, by suggesting that perhaps Aristotle is a Platonist *malgré lui*. I mean the possibility that Aristotle could not adhere to the doctrines that he *incontestably* adheres to were he not thereby committed to principles that are in harmony with Platonism. In short, I explore the claim that an authentic Aristotelian, if he be consistent, is inevitably embracing a philosophical position that is in harmony with Platonism. That is, there cannot be an authentic form of Aristotelianism that is not in harmony with Platonism as I have been using that term throughout this study. Undoubtedly, such a claim, if it is thought to have any merit at all, will be received with displeasure by some anti-Platonic Aristotelians and with pleasure by some anti-Platonic anti-Aristotelians. I hope that pushing the application of the concept of harmony to this extent will serve to illuminate some central philosophical problems and also to enable us to understand better the contribution that both Aristotle and Plato make to their solution.

Are Anti-Nominalists All Platonists?

By 'nominalism' I mean basically what Nelson Goodman meant when he argued for a world consisting only of individuals.[1] The Platonic position, as understood by Neoplatonists, is that Platonism pretty much begins with a rejection of extreme nominalism. More particularly, it begins with the claim that a consistent nominalist could not allow a plurality (a 'many') at all in the world. That any plurality is impossible is the position that Zeno is understood to be taking on behalf of Parmenides in *Parmenides*.[2] Proclus in his *Commentary on Plato's Parmenides* implies that the recognition of the possibility of a many, that is, of a number of individuals having an identical attribute, is the ultimate reason for positing Forms.[3]

If a many is possible—that is, if it is possible that there should be many individuals that are identical in some way—then we are forced to make a distinction between the individual and the attribute or property or Form-instance or whatever we choose to call it in virtue of which that individual belongs to the many. And at this point we can note that Aristotle is without question in concert with this analysis.[4] For the distinction between substance and attribute or accident is the implicit conclusion of the identical analysis of what it means to be a many.[5] If this is so, the question we need to ask is why Platonists think that if one goes just this far, one must then go all the way and posit separate Forms? Why is it not sufficient simply to recognize a distinction between substance and attribute and reject *both* nominalism and Platonism? Or, again, why is the categorical theory of substance and attributes not an adequate response to the problem identified by Plato?

1. See Goodman 1956. Unfortunately, Goodman thereby meant to reject a commitment to classes or the extensions of properties or concepts, which he took to be identical with 'platonism.' Although Goodman was using the term primarily technically or systematically and not historically, there is obviously some connection between Platonism and platonism. Specifically, though Platonism is not accurately construed as committed to classes (since Forms are not concepts or properties), it is committed to the existence of nonindividuals: specifically, the natures that Forms' names name. Goodman, though he is not in principle opposed to the existence of 'abstract' or incorporeal individuals, was no doubt opposed to *this* brand of Platonism, too.

2. See Allen 1983, 79, "Zeno's paradox [in *Parmenides*] follows from a primitive nominalism that identifies meaning and naming in such a way that the *meaning* of a term is identified with the subject *it is true of*. Plurality implies that the same things must be both like and unlike; if the same things are both like and unlike, the opposites likeness and unlikeness are identical; this is impossible; therefore, there is no plurality."

3. See Proclus *In Parm.* 708, 1–7; 731, 8–23. In the latter passage, Proclus distinguishes the separate Form from the instance of it in the individual member of the many.

4. See *On Ideas* 79, 15–17 and 81, 8–10, where Aristotle says that the arguments for Forms show that there must exist something besides 'individuals' (τὰ καθ' ἕκαστα) and something that is predicated of a many: that is, of a many as such. This seems sufficient to establish Aristotle's antinominalistic credentials.

5. I take it that Aristotle's rejection of the analysis of predication in a nominalistic fashion— that is, as deconstruction into a sum of individuals—arises from his unquestioned assumption that 'manys' do exist. There really are things that share identical attributes. Stated otherwise, the identity of a subject is not exhausted if we exclude its attributes. Cf. *Parm.* 130B4, where Socrates accepts the description of his view as holding that there is a distinction between 'Likeness itself,' 'the likeness we possess,' and 'the possessor of likeness.'

As I argued in chapters three and seven, universals do not explain identity in difference, nor is there any reason to think that Aristotle thought that they do. Forms are hypothesized to explain the very possibility that a many should be the same or identical in some way.[6] Naturally, if the *explanans* is thought to be itself an individual, its explanatory role is completely compromised, as the regress arguments in *Parmenides* suggest. For example, if the possibility of something's being white where 'white' does not uniquely identify that something, or, what amounts to the same thing, the possibility of two things being identically white is to be explained by a Form, then a Form cannot be another white thing. I do not know if Plato always appreciated this, but there is good reason to believe that in writing *Parmenides* he did, and that Neoplatonists grasped this point quite adequately.

Aristotle concurs with Plato that, to continue with the example, whiteness is not a white thing and whiteness is to be distinguished from what is predicable of a thing that is in fact white.[7] Things said to be white are named 'paronymously' from whiteness. But Aristotle does not appear to allow that there is any explanatory connection in the paronymy relation between whiteness and white. If this is so, it is easy to understand why whiteness should be identified with a universal. Things are named white from the whiteness that is perceived to be identically present in many. So, one might be tempted to say that paronymy does not explain anything other than a semantic fact, because there is nothing to explain. The problem with Forms is that they seek to explain that which is simply a brute fact: namely, that many things can share what happens to be the identical attribute or nature.[8]

It is abundantly clear, however, that this is not Aristotle's view at all. If there were nothing to explain, then there would be nothing to know. For particulars are unknowable. At this point, it will of course be said that what is knowable for Aristotle is the universal.[9] But what is known universally cannot be a universal, because 'universal' refers to the way what is known is known, not to the 'content' of what is known. It is because the form that is known is *neither* a particular nor a universal that it can both be known and serve to explain the identity of whatever possesses it.[10] Indeed, it is the form that is the 'substance' of each thing and the cause of its being.[11] Form in this sense is identical with the 'enmattered form' of Platonism. But no substance, including the substance that is the cause of the being of an individual, is a

---

6. Cf. Aristotle *Met.* I 3, 1054a20–1055a3, where 'same' (ὅμοιον) is said to come under 'plurality' (τὸ πλῆθος). That is, a plurality can be the same in some respect. Cf. *Cat.* 8, 11a18–19. Translators who render ὅμοιον here and elsewhere as 'like' obscure the Aristotelian implication of two things being ὅμοιον that there is *univocal* predication of them as such.

7. See *Cat.* 8, 10a27ff.

8. This is the case with the so-called resemblance theory of universals.

9. See *Met.* Z 10, 1035b34–1036a1; Z 11, 1036a28–29.

10. See Owens 1951, 381–95, for a particularly cogent defense of this claim. More recently, Lear (1987) has argued for the position.

11. See *Met.* Z 17, 1041b7–9, with b27–28 and H 2, 1043a2–3. Cf. A 10, 993a19–21; Λ 3, 1070a22–23.

universal.[12] So, Aristotle is in fact committed to the view that form does in some way explain identity in difference because it is neither particular nor universal in itself. There has to be *something* like humanity and whiteness for there to be particular human beings and particular white things.[13]

As we have seen, what Aristotle apparently objects to is separation of these forms, making them Platonic Forms. But we have also seen that Neoplatonists understood the putative separation of Forms in four senses: (1) from sensibles, (2) from each other, (3) from eternal intellect, and (4) from a first principle of all. It is only in the first sense that Plato and Platonism are committed to separation. But even here, as we have seen, the separation is not unqualified. For we need to distinguish the separate Form from its nature—that which its name names—which is not separate from its participant. So, the question now becomes, why separate Forms in this way? Why cannot the enmattered form and the form that is neither particular nor universal do all the explanatory work? That is, Socrates' humanity explains his being a human, and humanity—which is neither particular nor universal but can be both—explains the knowability of Socrates' humanity. What is left out by this analysis?

Proclus gives an acute answer to this question. He is commenting on the passage in *Parmenides* where Parmenides says that if Forms do not exist, then no one will have anything to think about, and the possibility of discourse (τὴν τοῦ διαλέγεσθαι δύναμιν) will be completely destroyed.[14] Proclus explains: "Necessarily what is actualized must precede what is potential in the sphere both of cognition and of existence [νοούντων καὶ ὄντων]. So, then, the Forms exist somewhere else, prior to us, in the realm of the divine and transcendent entities [χωρισταῖς οὐσίαις], and it is from these that the forms in us are brought to completion; for if these did not exist, neither would the forms in us, nor can what is complete come from what is incomplete."[15] According to Proclus's interpretation of Plato's theory, the separate Forms are the eternal condition for the possibility of identity and difference or significant predication in the sensible world.

Does Aristotle's account of form allow for or even require separate Forms as eternal conditions for that possibility? The answer is clearly 'no' if the separate Form is conceived of such that separating the Form entails separating the nature of the Form. The answer is not so clearly 'no' if the Form and its nature are distinguishable such that the nature of that separate Form is also present in the enmattered form. In this case, everything that Aristotle wants to say about whiteness or humanity and its distinction

12. See *Met.* Z 13, 1038b8–15.
13. See Porphyry *In Cat.* 75, 24–29; 81, 11–22, for the claim that the nature is prior to individuality and universality. Graham (1987, 288), argues, "When Aristotle identifies form with substance . . . he makes an unnecessary and damaging concession to Platonism."
14. *Parm.* 135B5-C3. Cf. *Soph.* 259E4–6, where the συμπλοκή τῶν εἰδῶν is the condition for (διά) the possibility of λόγος.
15. Proclus *In Parm.* 979, 2–8 (trans. Dillon).

from Socrates' whiteness or humanity is sayable. The separation of the Form preserves the distinction between the Form's nature and the instance or image of it, *and* it does not preclude the presence of the nature in the enmattered form.

The distinction between Form and nature turns out then to be a distinction between ontological ground and content, between the eternal guarantor of the possibility of identity and difference in the sensible world and the essence or οὐσία of each such possibility. Neoplatonists recognize this eternal guarantor as the Demiurge or eternal intellect. On the interpretation of *Metaphysics* Book Λ advanced in chapter six, we can see Aristotle's surprising identification of the prime unmoved mover as an eternally active intellect in a new light. That is, owing to his recognition of the need to provide an account of the eternal possibility of a sensible world that is intelligible, he is led to posit a life, an intellect, eternally cognizing all that explains that possibility.

Aristotle evidently has no reservation about forms that are separate in the sense of (1) above in the case of intellect and the divine mind. What he evidently objects to is not the separation of forms as such but the separation that entails turning them into particulars, thereby compromising their nature as neither particular nor universal: "It is evident then that the causes of forms [that is, of enmattered forms], if we take these to be what some thinkers are in the habit of calling 'Forms,' if such exist over and above particulars, are of no use for generations or for substances. Nor would they be, at least for this reason, substances existing on their own."[16] If the putative causes of enmattered forms that Aristotle says are called Forms are the natures of Forms, then the Neoplatonists will insist that these are *not* separate in senses (2), (3), and (4) above. But they are not even separate in sense (1) from anything that participates in that nature.[17] That which grounds the existence of the natures, namely, the Demiurge, is separate in sense (1); the natures are not.[18] Yet Aristotle seems to think that separating a Form in the sense of (1) entails separating the nature of the Form in the same way, thereby making the nature a particular and triggering the flood of objections against separation. The natures are not substances any more than they are universals; the only separate substance here (in the Aristotelian sense) is the Demiurge or, equivalently, the prime unmoved mover, a divine intellect eternally active.

16. *Met.* Z 8, 1033b26–29.
17. *Parm.* 133C-D.
18. See *Tim.* 51E6–52A4: "These things being so, we should agree that there is, first, the self-identical Form, ungenerated and indestructible, which neither receives anything into itself from elsewhere nor itself enters into anything else anywhere, invisible and otherwise imperceptible. This is what thinking has for its object' (τούτων δὲ οὕτως ἐχόντων ὁμολογητέον ἐν μὲν εἶναι τὸ κατὰ ταὐτὰ εἶδος ἔχον, ἀγέννητον καὶ ἀνώλεθρον, οὔτε εἰς ἑαυτὸ εἰσδεχόμενον ἄλλο ἄλλοθεν οὔτε αὐτὸ εἰς ἄλλο ποι ἰόν, ἀόρατον δὲ καὶ ἄλλως ἀναίσθητον, τοῦτο ὃ δὴ νόησις εἴληχεν ἐπισκοπεῖν·).

The source of the difficulties raised by Aristotle is that he will not allow that in the intelligible world there is any possibility of complexity. Without such a possibility, we cannot claim that there is a real distinction between a Form and its nature, which, if true, means that the separation of the Form entails the separation of the nature, paradigmatically. Aristotle never actually provides an argument for the claim that real distinctions within an intelligible entity— analogous, say, to the real distinction between a sensible substance and its accidents—are impossible. But Aristotle evidently *does* countenance real distinctions *among* intelligibles, at least if my agent intellect is different from God's and from anyone's else's and if, as in *Metaphysics* Book Λ, chapter 8, there is a multitude of unmoved movers. In addition, if the Neoplatonists are correct that Forms are not separate in senses (2), (3), and (4), then the real distinction between a Form and its nature is just the real distinction between the divine intellect and the natures it eternally contemplates.

As we have seen, Aristotle agrees with the Platonists that the first principle of all is absolutely simple and therefore no real distinction in it is possible. He is also in agreement that a divine intellect is separate and exists necessarily. His mistake is to identify the divine intellect with the first principle. Should he recognize that the first principle transcends intellect, at least one reason for refusing to allow real distinctions in the intelligible world would disappear. And should he also recognize that intellection is essentially complex, owing to its intentionality, there would be *no* reason to deny such a real distinction.

Aristotle is committed to the view that the primary cause of motion, the prime unmoved mover, is perfect actuality. The only perfect actuality Aristotle will countenance is thinking. But if thinking is essentially complex because it is essentially intentional, then Aristotle is, like it or not, committed to incorporeal complexity and, hence, to incorporeal real distinctions. It is not clear whether his claim with regard to the divine intellect, that in it "intellect and intelligible are the same [ταὐτὸν]" is intended to preclude this complexity.[19] If it is not, then Forms (according to one interpretation) are rejected by him only to be reborn as eternal intelligibles, eternally (numerically) identical with God.

Another indication that when Aristotle is thinking of the nature of the Form he is not distancing himself from Plato is his claim that forms are not generated.[20]

> It is evident, then, that the form (or whatever we ought to call the shape in the
> sensible thing) is not being generated, nor is there a generation of it, nor is

19. *Met.* Λ 7, 1072b21. Aristotle does argue (Z 6, 1032a4–6), that "of things which are primary and are stated by themselves, then, it is clear that each of them and its essence are one and the same" (ὅτι μὲν οὖν ἐπὶ τῶν πρώτων καὶ καθ' αὑτὰ λεγομένων τὸ ἑκάστῳ εἶναι καὶ ἕκαστον τὸ αὐτὸ καὶ ἕν ἐστι, δῆλον·) Cf. Z 11, 1037b3; H 3, 1043b2. But this identity does not, strictly speaking, preclude the type of complexity to which Platonism is committed.

20. Met. Z 8, 1033a24–1034a8.

an essence (for this is that which is generated in something else by art or nature or a power). What one makes is an existing bronze sphere; he produces the form in the matter, and the result is a bronze sphere. . . .[21]

So it is evident from what has been said that what is called 'a form' or 'a substance' is not generated, but what is generated is the composite which is named according to that form, and that there is matter in everything that is generated, and in the latter one part is this and another that.

Does a sphere, then, exist apart from the individual material spheres, or a house apart from those made of bricks? Or, would generation never occur if the form existed in this way as a this? But 'form' signifies a such, and this is not a this and a definite thing; and what the artist makes or the man begets is a such from a this, and what is generated is a such this.[22]

The ungenerability of form is usually understood as the accidental generation of a form in matter when the composite is generated. That is, when a bronze sphere is generated or produced, the roundness of the sphere is indirectly produced. One cannot just produce its roundness without producing a round *something.* This is no doubt correct, but not exactly relevant to the Platonic claim of the priority of Forms. What this passage claims is that if roundness is not directly generated, this does not imply that there is an eternal sphere: that is, an eternal substance spherical in shape. Roundness is a 'such' not a this. But as we have seen, the Neoplatonists generally understood Plato to be saying the same thing: the Form of Sphere is not round. No eternal nature is an eternal substance.

What does Aristotle mean by the words "generation would never occur if the form existed in this way, as a this"? These words can hardly be said to constitute an argument to the effect that if the form existed as a this, generation of a composite particular would be impossible unless this was the *only* way that the form existed.[23] That is, if roundness existed only apart from round things, then one could not generate a thing that was round. But once we distinguish Form and its nature, and recognize that the nature is neither one nor many, neither particular nor universal, the generation of composites with enmattered forms is not precluded by the separate existence of Forms. More to the point, the ungenerability of form as such actually explains the fact that what is generated is always a 'this such.'

One fairly obvious objection to this line of argument is that even if God is eternally thinking all that is intelligible, this should for Aristotle preclude all the forms whose definitions include matter.[24] And this means that the intelligibles that God thinks do not correspond one-to-one to Forms. I think this is correct, but it hardly constitutes a problem for harmonists. Plato's *Timaeus* suggests that the intelligible paradigms have been reduced in order

21. Ibid., 1033b5–10.
22. Ibid., 1033b16–24.
23. See Ross 1924, 2:189.
24. See *Met.* Z 6, 1032a5–11; Z 11, 1037a33.

to exclude phenomenal properties. Other sorts of reduction, mathematical in nature, are possible. Platonism's Forms are intended only to account for such intelligibility as there is in the sensible world; they are not intended to explain the unintelligible. Platonists can even defer to Aristotle's authority in biological investigation, for example, in order to determine just what are the intelligible structures 'here below' that need eternal explanation. The way the reductionism goes is an intra-Academic issue, with various hypotheses being offered at different times. The question of what God or the Demiurge knows is posterior to the claim that he knows all that is knowable.

A more serious objection is that even if the intelligibles contemplated by the prime unmoved mover are the same as the Forms contemplated by the Demiurge, the *effective* role of these Forms contradicts the *ineffective* role of these intelligibles.[25] True. But this is just to say that without the true Platonic first principle, a distorted picture of the intelligible world and its relation to the sensible world is inevitable. Though Forms be supposed to be the conditions for the possibility of intelligibility in the sensible world, if that is *all* they are, it is perhaps finally not very plausible that they should be taken to be ontologically as well as logically separate. But Forms were not supposed by Plato's interpreters to be independent either of an ultimate first principle or of a separate intellect. It is to these—not to Forms themselves or their natures—that we must look to see the connection between the eternal conditions for the possibility of intelligibility in the sensible world and the realizations of that possibility.

It should be evident by now that all this does not undermine the truth of an explanation offered in the form 'man begets man.'[26] The truth of *this* claim, in turn, does not preempt the truth of the more comprehensive Platonic claim that a top-down approach to the intelligibility of 'man' is required. It is indeed difficult to make sense of many things Aristotle says without assuming that he, too, is wedded to this latter claim. But insofar as he is not, that is owing to the fact that he erred in how to conceive of a first principle of all.

Persons and Human Beings

Aristotle's so-called hylomorphic view of human beings is frequently and facilely contrasted with Plato's 'dualistic' view. It is therefore not surprising that when Aristotle says things that would be otherwise taken to be dualistic in import, these are immediately dismissed as unimportant or vestiges of Platonism or exaggerations or metaphorical or simply incomprehensible. I believe this unhappy state of affairs arises as much from a misunderstanding of Plato as it does from a misunderstanding of Aristotle.

As I have argued elsewhere, Plato's dualism is most aptly characterized as making a sharp separation between a disembodied person and an embodied

25. Ibid., A 7, 988b2–4; A 9, 991a11; Λ 6, 1071b14–17.
26. Ibid., Z 7, 1032a25; Z 8, 1033b29–1034a5.

person.[27] An embodied person viewed objectively, or from the 'outside' is identical with the natural kind, human being (ἄνθρωπος). But because there is more to the embodied person than what is available from the outside—namely, subjectivity and self-reflexive intellection—an embodied person is not exactly identical with a human being. I have already given reasons for thinking that Neoplatonists were correct to suppose that Aristotle's view was not substantially different from this. I would like now to explore a bit further, from an Aristotelian perspective, the reasons for insisting that persons are not human beings.

The key to Aristotle's efforts to accommodate Platonic dualism within an otherwise hylomorphic view of physical reality is his epistemological antirepresentationalism. By 'representationalism' I mean the whole family of theories according to which (1) knowing, or cognition generally is a mental state in which reality or the cognizable is represented by a content, and (2) the cognizer has some relation to the content: for example, she knows, believes, imagines, desires it. According to representationalism, (1) and (2) are *independently* assessable by someone other than the cognizer. Thus, for example, one can assess the truth value of the proposition that I believe and can independently assess in some way how I stand to that proposition. Generally, the latter sort of assessment is functional. That is, someone else can make an assessment of how my claim to believe a proposition functions in the economy of my psychological, social, intellectual life, and so on. Independent assessability implies transparency in principle. If I am the best judge of what content is present to me and how I stand to that content, that is a relatively insignificant empirical limitation. In principle, and depending of course on the particular theory of representation, anyone ought to be able to make as good a judgment as I of what content is present to me and of how I stand in relation to it.

Aristotle shows that he is an antirepresentationalist in these two beliefs: (1) mental content consists of forms, and these are not representations; (2) the relation of the cognizer to the mental content is in principle unique.[28] A perceptual or intelligible form is the knowable—that is, the real extra mental thing—in another state. Naturally, since anything can be stipulated to represent anything else, one *could* say that forms in the mind represent the hylomorphic composites or even the incorporeal substances that are outside the mind. But this is not to say that having the form in the mind *is* just having the representation, for the latter is posterior to the former. In fact, λόγος generally is representational and representational of cognitive states, but a λόγος is never identical with these.[29]

---

27. See Gerson 2003.

28. I use the word 'mental' here in what I hope is a nonanachronistic manner, referring simply to the cognitive aspect of psychic functioning. See Kahn (2003) for some salutary cautions about the use of the term 'mental' in regard to Aristotelian accounts of cognition.

29. In Plato the ability to give a λόγος is functionally related to knowledge, but it is not equivalent to knowledge, basically because the ability to give a λόγος could not exist without the state that the knowledge is, whereas the knowledge could exist without the ability to give a λόγος.

As we saw in chapter five, cognition is not for Aristotle equivalent to the presence of the form of the knowable in the cognizer although that presence is a necessary condition for cognition. The presence of the form is in potency to actual cognition. What is required in addition is a further relation between the cognizer and the state which consists of the form being present to the cognizer. But that relation is uniquely and nontrivially available to the cognizer. Of course, in a trivial sense only I can be related to my own mental states, indexically, as it were, just as only my cat can lick her own paws. But another cat could lick those paws, and it would be the same kind of activity. By contrast, my actual cognition requires that I be uniquely related to the mental state that I am in where 'I' refers to the identical cognizer in both cases.

The proof that the 'I' must refer to the identical cognizer is essentially a *reductio*. Assume that they are not identical. Then I am not identical with the subject of the mental state that is a necessary, though not sufficient, condition for my cognizing. But then for the 'I' that is different from the 'I' that is the subject of that mental state, there must be another mental state that I am in whose subject *is* identical with the subject who cognizes. The incorporeality or separability of the subject of cognition seems to follow for Aristotle from the above analysis of the requirements for cognition. If that subject were material, then the identity of the subject of potential cognition and the subject of actual cognition would fall apart, which is to say that there would be no difference between potential and actual cognition.[30] They would fall apart, because there would be no difference between my cognizing something potentially and then cognizing it actually, on the one hand, and my cognizing something potentially and *you* cognizing it actually, on the other. If, for example, my potential cognition were identical with a particular brain state, then if the physical connection to it by another brain state were identical to actual cognition, nothing in principle would prevent that other brain state from being yours.

The claim that the faculty of intellect is a part of the soul is on its own unremarkable and not particularly Platonic. But the matter becomes far more portentous when we consider the subject of that faculty, that which 'thinks itself.' This is so because it is difficult to identify this subject with the hylomorphic subject or the subject of other psychic states. I can feel cold

---

30. Shields (1988), thinks that Aristotle has four arguments for the incorporeality of the soul. (1) The soul cannot be moved in itself (*De An.* A 3). But every magnitude can be moved (*Cael.* A 2, 268b15–16). Therefore, the soul cannot be a magnitude. (2) The soul, as form of the body, is not generable (*Met.* Z 8; Λ 3). This is so because whatever comes to be has form as well as matter (Z 7, 1032a20), but form is not a compound (Z 8). Therefore, the soul does not have matter. (3) The soul is not divisible (*De An.* A 5, 411b27). But whatever is not divisible is not a magnitude. (*Phys.* Δ 11, 219a11; Z 6, 237a11). Therefore, the soul is not a magnitude. (4) The soul is neither one of the elements nor from the elements (*GC* B 6, 334a10–11). But all material entities either are elements or are from elements. Therefore, the soul is not a material entity. Shields recognizes that arguments for the incorporeality of the soul are to be distinguished from arguments for the incorporeality of one part of the soul—namely, intellect—with which I am now concerned. But I suggest that if the arguments for the incorporeality of the soul have any merit, they draw it from the argument for the incorporeality of intellect.

while I am actually cognizing. But the subject cognizing, if it is incorporeal, does not appear to be for Aristotle the sort of thing that *can* feel cold.

Faced with the puzzles that arise from beginning to think about personal identity from the perspective of a nonrepresentationalist theory of cognition, we can perhaps better understand the otherwise odd things Aristotle asserts about the true identity of the self. To say that "each human being is this part if indeed this is the dominant and better part," referring to "the activity of intellect" clearly reveals the tension.[31] A human being is of course *not* this part if we are referring to the hylomorphic composite. Nor is the soul this part either. But the subject of hylomorphic activities and psychic activities other than cognition does seem to be nevertheless both identical and nonidentical with the subject of 'this part' in some sense.

Aristotle is here relying on the bipolarity in the concept of φύσις. As for Plato, 'nature' for Aristotle can refer both to what is and to what ought to be, or endowment and achievement. This bipolarity is reflected most explicitly in the account of the relation between formal and final causality. The final cause of an organic individual is to achieve what it already is, as expressed in its formal cause. Yet one cannot or need not strive to achieve what one already is. But if what one is includes what one can be, then some conceptual space between endowment and achievement is attained. The phrase 'what one can be' is, however, value neutral in a way that final causality is not. It is in itself a deep feature of Aristotle's Platonism that he unhesitatingly evaluates possibilities hierarchically. Thus, his exhortation to strive to live according to the 'better part' is an exhortation to live according to the part that is more like the divine than any other. And this would be to achieve one's nature ideally.

The claim that Aristotle is anti-Platonic in matters relating to the soul typically focuses on the question of the soul's immortality: Plato accepts it, and Aristotle rejects it, and there's an end to the matter. Posing the opposition in this way is far too crude to be accurate or illuminating. For one thing, the issue for both Plato and Aristotle is personal immortality, not simply the immortality of the soul. Plato is indeed a defender of the view that the immortality of a person's soul is the immortality of the person. So much is, I think, clear. But Plato seems to identify that which is immortal with the intellect, not with the entire soul. At least this is the view of *Timaeus*, the dialogue taken by Neoplatonists as the authoritative source for Plato's views. Given this, it is certainly worth asking how a disembodied intellect is to retain any identity with the person 'here below,' who is destined for immortality and, we may disconcertingly add, for reincarnation or reembodiment.[32]

---

31. See *EN* K 7, 1178a2–3: δόξειε δ' ἂν καὶ εἶναι ἕκαστος τοῦτο, εἴπερ τὸ κύριον καὶ ἄμεινον, referring back to line 1177b30 (ὁ κατὰ τοῦτον βίος) which in turns refers back to line 19 (ἡ τοῦ νοῦ ἐνέργεια).

32. See the stimulating remarks of Clark (1975, 164–173), who argues that the identification of the person with the 'impersonal' rational faculty involves a discounting of the reality of the sensible world. Clark, however, thinks that this is true for Plato but not for Aristotle.

If the only question here regards the immortality of intellect, the evidence, viewed without prejudice, is overwhelming that Aristotle, like Plato, affirms it. That this amounts to an affirmation of personal immortality is more problematic, but only according to a conception of 'personal' that may well be anachronistic or inaccurate as applied both to Aristotle and to Plato. The activity of intellect in both Plato and Aristotle is impersonal only in the sense of being nonidiosyncratic. The contents of intellect's thinking when it is thinking that which is intelligible is the same for everyone. If I am nothing but an intellect, then, ideally, I differ from you *solo numero*. Emotions, appetites, memories, and sensations are not just numerically distinct for different embodied persons; they are idiosyncratic as well, insofar as they depend on a unique body.

The identity between a subject of intellection and a subject of the idiosyncratic states of embodiment is deeply obscure. I do not want to suggest that either Plato or Aristotle has anything like a satisfactory explanation for this. But I do wish to insist they share a conviction in general about how to bridge the gap between the embodied person and the disembodied person. By 'gap' I mean the natural disinclination most embodied persons have to embrace the destiny of a disembodied person so described. The shared conviction is that philosophical activity has a transformative effect on embodied persons. As one becomes habituated to the philosophical life, one comes to identify oneself with 'the better part.' I do not suppose that Plato or even Neoplatonists of the strictest observance believed that such identification could be perfectly achieved while embodied. But as Plato urges in *Republic*, quite reasonably enough, it is better to be closer to the ideal than to be further away. In any case, for Plato, and, as I have argued, for Aristotle as well, that is the ideal, like it or not.

It is useful to draw a parallel between a transcendental argument for the identity of a person ideally with an intellect and the transcendental argument for Forms. Just as Forms are the condition for the possibility of intelligibility in the sensible world, so the identity of the person as an incorporeal subject is a condition for the possibility of knowledge. The intellect in *De Anima*, especially Book Γ, could be understood in this way. And the words "'this alone is immortal and eternal" could be understood as applicable to 'personal' immortality taken nonidiosyncratically.

Aristotle agrees with Plato that without an incorporeal intellect, human cognition would not be possible. For actual human cognition requires self-reflexive thinking, awareness or consciousness of the presence of the form in the identical subject's intellect. The cognition of animals might seem to raise a puzzle here. Aristotle certainly recognizes types of cognition in animals, especially sense perception and imagination.[33] But he does not attribute intellect to any animals, and so he is not, on his own principles, obliged to attribute personhood to them. This fact provides an important clue. For

33. See *De An.* B 2, 413b1–10; Γ 3, 427b6–8.

intellect is the condition for the possibility not just of intellection but of all human cognition.

If in actual thinking that which thinks and that which is being thought are the same,[34] and if thinking is somehow being in relation to an intelligible form taken universally,[35] we need to ask for the connection between these two properties. Why is it that only that which thinks itself is capable of thinking universally? The connection between the two properties seems to be indicated by the claim in *De Anima* Book Γ, chapter 5, that only when separated from the body is intellect 'what it is': that is, operating uncontaminated by a body or bodily activity. It is easy enough to see why only an incorporeal intellect is capable of self-reflexivity, but it is not so easy to see why only an incorporeal intellect is capable of being identical with intelligible forms universally.

The solution to this problem depends on realizing that 'universal' (καθόλου) does not indicate the intentional object of cognition. For one thing, if it did, then when in actual thinking one became identical with what is thought, one would be identical with a universal. But this would make one identical with anyone else thinking the same universal. More important, since cognition is of intelligible form, and form is neither individual nor universal, if cognition were of a universal, cognition would not be of form. It is more accurate, both philosophically and even grammatically, to insist that cognition is of form, in a certain manner, namely—universally—rather than to allow that cognition is of a 'thing' called a 'universal.'

To think the form universally is to think it as separated absolutely from any particularity. Even for an Aristotle, who thinks himself immune to the slightest tinge of metaphysical Platonism, this means thinking the form separate from any matter. But if the form were in a material intellect, thinking that form would mean separating it from the material intellect. And then there would still be the requirement that what has been separated must inform the intellect in order to have the first actuality of knowing and then be actualized by the intellect identifying itself with that form. In other words, thinking of a form universally requires incorporeality of the thinker, just as self-reflexivity does.

If the thinker is identical with the form when thinking it universally, then how does this incorporeal subject of cognition stand in relation to the subject of, say, bodily states? We could say that when the person is not thinking, the same person reverts to or becomes a hylomorphic subject. If we say this, what shall we say when confronted with the phenomenon of a subject who thinks that resisting her own occurrent bodily appetites is desirable? Such a person is presumably both the subject of the thought that resistance is desirable and the subject of the appetite. But this seems impossible, as Aristotle himself notes: "Is it then practical wisdom that is resisting

---

34. Ibid., Γ 4, 430a3–4.
35. Ibid., B 5, 417b22–23; *APo.* A 31, 87b38–39.

[appetite]? For this is the strongest of virtues. But it is absurd [to think that practical wisdom resists appetite], for the same [person] would then [when acting against practical wisdom] be at the same time practically wise and incontinent, and no one would maintain that a practically wise man would willingly perform the worst of actions."[36]

Aristotle is here faced with the same problem Plato confronts in *Republic:* namely, the problem of how a person can act against his own interests as he conceives these. On the one hand, if he is not acting against his own interests—that is, if someone else is acting against them—then he is surely not thereby properly called 'incontinent.' But if he is acting against his own interests, is he not a sort of divided person, at least to the extent that a person is specified by his own interests as he conceives of them?

Aristotle makes the important claim that animals are not incontinent because they do not have "universal beliefs, only imagination and memory of particulars."[37] Incontinence requires that one have universal cognition, but *not* that it be actual.[38] For at the moment when one actually knows what is in one's interests, that knowledge cannot be 'dragged about,' and in that case, 'Socrates was right': that is, incontinence is impossible.'[39]

The incontinent person who acts against her (potential or latent) knowledge that what she desires is bad for her, has, in acting, a belief that the thing she is 'going for' is an instance of something that is desirable to her.[40] In short, cognition is required even in acting against right reason, in contrast to animals, which have "only imagination and memory of particulars." Plato believes that one can act against an occurent belief that what one is doing is bad for oneself. But in denying this, Aristotle is only confirming the Platonic position that the person is the rational agent or subject.[41] For someone to act against his occurent belief that satisfying his desire is not in his interests would be for him to believe simultaneously that satisfying the desire is both good and bad for him. And this means that his desire is rationally based: that is, based on the belief that what is before him is an example of a kind of thing that is satisfying.

The reason Aristotle is disinclined to accept the Platonic position, that acting against occurent beliefs is possible, is that doing so entails acceptance of a divided soul or, more correctly, a divided self. A Leontius, to use Plato's example in *Republic,* simultaneously believes that gazing on the corpses is desirable and not desirable for him. A united or single agent could not have contradictory occurent beliefs. So, Leontius must be a divided self or agent. Although Aristotle rejects the tripartitioning of the soul in favor of biparti-

---

36. *EN* H 3, 1146a4–7.
37. Ibid., H 5, 1147a4–5.
38. Ibid., H 5, 1146b31–35.
39. Ibid., H 5, 1147b15–17. Aristotle is referring to the argument in *Protag.* 351B–358D, that incontinence is impossible.
40. *EN* H 5, 1147b9–12.
41. The early Stoics denied the possibility of incontinence precisely because they identified the person with a rational subject.

tioning, more important is his unwillingness to accept the consequences of admitting the phenomenon of someone acting against his occurent belief.[42] He does this apparently to retain the unity of the person. Nevertheless, Aristotle identifies the person ideally as a subject of self-reflexive cognition, as does Plato. The subject that is able to think, and therefore to be aware of its own cognitive states, is also able to have beliefs about its own beliefs.

Aristotle's first-order beliefs are those accompanied by affective states. When he speaks of the soul that can obey reasoning, he is, I believe, speaking about these first-order beliefs. Reason is obeyed when a second-order belief overrides a first-order belief or eliminates it. Thus, when I realize my anger is unjustified, I suppress it. But my anger originally sprang from a belief that, say, I was slighted. The belief that I was in fact not slighted—the belief that overrides the original belief—does, objectively speaking, contradict the original belief. But the overriding is the elimination of the contradiction. If, against all evidence to the contrary, I retain the original belief, I am, according to Aristotle, giving in to the inferior part of the soul. But since the original belief is the belief that I have, I am giving in to the inferior part of *me*.

The identification of the true person first with the subject of thinking and then more specifically with the subject of second-order thinking is not only not anti-Platonic; rather, it differs from Plato's own psychology hardly at all. Second-order thinking is locatable in the interstice between pure theory and practical reasoning. It is the daily fare of an embodied person. Aristotle's resolve to maintain the unity of the person really amounts to a claim for the unity of the hylomorphic composite. But this is distinct from the subject of cognition, the part with which 'we are really identical.' The disunity of the person, variously identified as the subject of cognition and of embodied states, survives intact in Aristotle over against the unity of the hylomorphic composite. It is difficult to see the grounds for supposing that Plato is in disaccord with this view.

The Twin Pillars of Aristotle's Platonism

Francis Cornford famously wrote about the theory of Forms and of the immortality of the soul as the "twin pillars of Platonism." I think Cornford's observation is essentially correct and important, though we have seen reason neither to speak of 'the' theory of Forms nor to identify Plato's views about Forms simply with what is said in the so-called middle dialogues. In addition, we have also seen reason to deny that the immortality of the soul is personal immortality in the sense that that is typically and uncritically conceived of within many religions. With the appropriate qualifications made, I think it is fair to conclude that the "twin pillars" also support Aristotle's Platonism.

---

42. See Fortenbaugh 1975, chap. 2, on Aristotle's rejection of the tripartite psychology. Fortenbaugh also argues that Plato himself moved towards bipartitioning in *Laws*.

Is Aristotle *just* a Platonist? Certainly not. In this regard, I would not wish to underestimate the importance of the dispositional differences between Aristotle and Plato. This dispositional difference is in part reflected in Aristotle's penchant for introducing terminological innovations to express old (i.e., Platonic) thoughts. In working through the Aristotelian corpus with a mind open to the Neoplatonic assumption of harmony, I have found time and again that Aristotle was, it turns out, actually *analyzing* the Platonic position or making it more precise, not refuting it. In addition, I do not discount in this regard the fundamental thesis, advanced by Harold Cherniss, that Aristotle is often criticizing philosophers other than Plato or deviant versions of Platonism. It is not a trivial fact that most of Aristotle's writings came after Plato's death and after Plato's mantle as head of the Academy had passed to Speusippus and then to Xenocrates.

In my view, however, it would be a mistake to conclude from Aristotle's unrelenting criticisms of Plato and other Academics, and from the orientation of most of the corpus to categorizing and explaining sensible reality, that Aristotle is not *au fond* a Platonist. Even when Aristotle is criticizing Plato, as in, for example, *De Anima*, he is led, perhaps *malgré lui*, to draw conclusions based on Platonic assumptions. These assumptions are not so general and benign that just anyone can accept them; Platonism is not, after all, an infinitely large tent. The main conclusion I draw from this long and involved study is that if one rigorously and honestly sought to remove these assumptions, the 'Aristotelianism' that would remain would be indefensible and incoherent. A comprehensive and scientifically grounded anti-Platonic Aristotelianism is, I suspect, a chimera.

Two final points. The Neoplatonists' devotion to the study of Aristotle should not be confused with an illicit dalliance. They knew or intuited that Aristotelian analysis served Platonic ends. Neoplatonists readily adopted, apparently ungrudgingly and without mental reservation, many of the concepts by which Aristotle articulated the structure and functioning of the sensible world. They would not have done so had they thought they were introducing contaminants. If Aristotle is a kind of Platonist, then Neoplatonists were perhaps not wrong to suppose that Platonism needs Aristotle, too. My final point arises from what I hope is a pertinent anecdote told to me by one of my undergraduate professors. When he himself was an undergraduate, he took a class on John Milton by a world-renowned scholar of English literature. This scholar spent class after class lecturing on prosody in Milton's works. Finally, one student screwed up his courage sufficiently in order to ask the professor if he thought that that was all there was to Milton. The reply was, "No, of course not, there is much else besides, but that is the part that has been missed in the study of Milton for some time." I hope I have in this book provided some reason for thinking that, likewise, in the study of Aristotle, the harmonists' hypothesis is the part that has been missing for too long.

Platonists and Other Aristotelians

This list, by no means complete, is intended to give the reader a cursory sketch of the extent of writings of the Neoplatonists and others of the period, along with some indication of their doctrinal filiation.

Neoplatonists

PLOTINUS (204/5–270 C.E.). Regarded as the founder of Neoplatonism. To the best of our knowledge, his entire body of work is extant, comprising the collection of writings known as *Enneads*, Porphyry divided these into six groups of nine treatises.

PORPHYRY (234–CA. 305 C.E.). Plotinus's most prominent pupil and the editor of *Enneads*. Porphyry wrote an impressive number of works; only a few survive either as a whole or in fragments. There is evidence that he wrote numerous commentaries on Plato's dialogues—including *Cratylus, Sophist, Parmenides, Timaeus, Philebus, Phaedo, Symposium, Republic*—though it is not clear what sort of philosophical or literary works these were. He also wrote a commentary on *Enneads*. His most famous work is his (extant) *Isagoge*, an introduction to Aristotle's *Categories*, and he wrote commentaries on Aristotle's *Categories, De Interpretatione, Physics*, and perhaps *Metaphysics* and *Nicomachean Ethics*. He wrote a large number of technical, philosophical, scientific, and literary works, developing and in some ways systematizing the Platonism of his master Plotinus. His work *On the Unity of the Doctrine of Plato and Aristotle* (not extant) was evidently the first systematic attempt to defend the position supposedly held by Plotinus's teacher Ammonius Saccas.

IAMBLICHUS (CA. 245–CA. 325 C.E.). Perhaps a pupil of Porphyry but by no means an uncritical follower. His influence on later Neoplatonism was considerable, beginning with the foundation of his own school in his native Syria. There is evidence that Iamblichus wrote commentaries on Aristotle's *Categories, De Interpretatione, Prior Analytics, De Caelo, Metaphysics*, and *De Anima*, and we possess fragments of commentaries on Plato's *Alcibiades I, Phaedo, Sophist, Phaedrus, Philebus, Parmenides, and Timaeus*. Among his most famous works were the *De Mysteriis*—a reply and rebuttal to Porphyry's *Letter to Anebo*, defending the ancient oracular tradition and the practice of theurgy—and *On Pythagoreanism*, a ten-volume work, of which four volumes have survived, including his *Protrepticus*, which contains the fragments of Aristotle's work by that name.

DEXIPPUS (EARLY FOURTH CENTURY C.E.) Probably a pupil of Iamblichus. The author of a partially extant commentary on Aristotle's *Categories*, he was an explicit proponent of the harmony of Aristotle and Plato.

PROCLUS (412–485 C.E.) Pupil of Plutarch of Athens and then of Syrianus. His works constituted the most extensive systematic expression of Neoplatonism to that time. His commentaries on Aristotle are all lost, but references to them indicate that he commented on the following works: *Categories, De Interpretatione, Prior* and *Posterior Analytics*, and *Topics*. Extant in whole or in part are his commentaries on Plato's *Timaeus, Parmenides, Republic, Cratylus,* and *Alcibiades I*; the commentaries he wrote on *Gorgias, Phaedrus, Theaetetus, Symposium,* and *Sophist* are lost. Proclus's major personal works are his *Elements of Theology, Platonic Theology,* and treatises on providence and evil. He also wrote a commentary on Euclid's *Elements*.

PLUTARCH OF ATHENS (D. 432 C.E.). Head of the Platonic school in Athens and the teacher of Syrianus, Proclus, and Hierocles. He wrote a now lost commentary on at least Book Γ of Aristotle's *De Anima* and commentaries on Plato's *Gorgias, Phaedo,* and *Parmenides*.

SYRIANUS (D. CA. 437 C.E.). Teacher of Proclus and successor to Plutarch as head of the Platonic school in Athens. His partial commentary on Aristotle's *Metaphysics* is extant. Not extant are his commentaries on *Alcibiades I, Republic,* and *Laws*.

HIEROCLES (EARLY FIFTH CENTURY C.E.) Pupil of Plutarch of Athens and the most prominent Neoplatonic philosopher in Alexandria in the first half of the fifth century C.E. He wrote of Ammonius Saccas, the teacher of Plotinus, Origen, and Longinus, as the proponent of the view of the harmony of Plato and Aristotle. He is known to have written two works, the extant *Commentary on the Golden Verses of Pythagoras,* and *On Providence,* a sort of history of philosophy from a Neoplatonic perspective which is known through quotations and extensive extracts by Photius.

AMMONIUS (CA. 440–517/26 C.E.). Head of the philosophical school in Alexandria and pupil of Proclus, was the teacher of Asclepius, Philoponus, Olympiodorus, Simplicius, and Damascius. The only work of his that survives is a commentary on Aristotle's *De Interpretatione,* though there are commentaries on Porphyry's Isagoge, and Aristotle's *Categories* and *Prior Analytics* which probably originated in his lectures on these works. He also apparently wrote some small essays on metaphysical questions in Plato and Aristotle and lectured extensively on Plato, perhaps writing commentaries on *Gorgias* and *Theaetetus*.

ASCLEPIUS (LATE FIFTH–EARLY SIXTH CENTURY C.E.). Author of a commentary on Aristotle's *Metaphysics* which he tells us is "from the voice" of Ammonius, presumably indicating that it was at least based on the latter's lectures.

DAMASCIUS (CA. 462–AFTER 538 C.E.). Last head of the Platonic school at Athens. His extant works include lectures on Plato's *Phaedo* and *Philebus,* and he apparently wrote commentaries on *Alcibiades I, Republic, Sophist, Timaeus,* and *Laws.* His lost commentaries on Aristotle include those on *De Caelo* and *Meteorologica.* His main extant personal work is the treatise *On Principles,* based on Neoplatonic interpretations of Plato's *Parmenides*.

SIMPLICIUS (CA. 490–560 C.E.). Pupil of Ammonius in Alexandria and of Damascius in Athens. His commentaries on Aristotle's *Categories, De Caelo,* and *Physics* are extant; those on Aristotle's *Meteorologica* and *Metaphysics* and on Plato's *Phaedo,* Euclid's *Elements,* and Iamblichus's writings are not. The authenticity of a commentary on Aristotle's

De Anima that has come down to us under his name has been questioned. If that work is indeed his, then so too, presumably, is a commentary on Aristotle's *Metaphysics* referred to therein. Simplicius also wrote a commentary on Epictetus's *Handbook*.

JOHN PHILOPONUS (CA. 490–570 C.E.). Pupil of Ammomus, was the first major Greek Christian Neoplatonist. In scientific matters he attacked Aristotle as holding views antithetical to Christianity, eliciting from Simplicius a defense of Aristotle and of his harmony with Plato. His commentaries on Aristotle's works, largely taken from Ammonius's lectures, include those on *Categories, Prior and Posterior Analytics, Meteorologica, On Generation and Corruption, Generation of Animals, De Anima, Physics, and Metaphysics* (probably spurious), His only known Platonic commentary is on *Phaedo*. He also wrote a long work attacking Proclus, titled *De Aeternitate Mundi Contra Proclum*, plus medical, astronomical, and grammatical works, as well as a large number of works on Christian theology.

OLYMPIODORUS (BEFORE 505–AFTER 565 C.E.). Pupil of Ammonius. He wrote a *Prolegomena to Platonic Philosophy* and commentaries on Plato's *Alcibiades I, Gorgias,* and *Phaedo* and on Aristotle's *Categories* and *Meteorologica*. He may also have written commentaries on Plato's *Theaetezus* and *Sophist*.

ELIAS (SECOND HALF OF SIXTH CENTURY C.E.). Christian Neoplatonist and possibly pupil of Olympiodorus, was the author of a commentary on Aristotle's *Categories* and on Porphyry's *Isagoge*. Bits of a commentary on Aristotle's *Prior Analytics* survive as well. Elias is perhaps also the author of the anonymous *Prologue to Plato's Philosophy*.

DAVID (SECOND HALF SIXTH CENTURY–EARLY SEVENTH CENTURY C.E.). Author of a commentary on Porphyry's *Isagoge*. He may be the author of the commentary on Aristotle's *Caegories* attributed to Elias.

Aristotelians and Others

ANTIOCHUS OF ASEALON (CA. 130–CA. 68 B.C.E.). Perhaps the first harmonist. He is generally held to have argued for a return to the doctrines of the Old Academy in opposition to what he viewed as the deviations introduced by Philo of Larissa (158–84 B.C.E.). His pupil, Cicero, represents him as a Peripatetic, at least in ethical matters. He upheld the essential harmony of Stoicism both with the Academy and with Peripatetic philosophy, based on Zeno's connection with Plato's successor Polemo.

NUMENIUS (SECOND CENTURY C.E.). Apparently an influence on Plotinus, Iamblichus, and Proclus in their understanding of Platonism. He wrote works on metaphysical questions in Plato, most of which are lost, but there are fragments of his *On the Good* and *On the Divergence of the Academy from Plato*. He was among those Platonists who sought to link Plato's philosophy with Pythagoreanism and with 'Oriental' wisdom.

ALCINOUS (SECOND CENTURY C.E.). Once identified as a contemporary Platonist, Albinus, Alcinous was the author of a handbook called *Didaskalikos*, which is a presentation of Platonism in systematic form. It follows the division logic, physics, ethics, which goes back to Plato's immediate successors in the Old Academy. Alcinous reveals his harmonist assumption in incorporating numerous Peripatetic elements into his exposition of Platonism.

ASPASIUS (CA. 125 C.E.). Peripatetic who produced some of the earliest commentaries on Aristotle's works: on *Categories, De Interpretatione, Physics, De Caelo,* and *Metaphysics*. Only his commentary on *Nicomachean Ethics* survives (in part). Plotinus is said by Porphyry to have used these commentaries in his seminars.

DIOGENES LAERTIUS (CA. 200 C.E.). Diogenes' *Compendium of the Lives and Opinions of Philosophers* is the only extant history of philosophy from antiquity, and an indispensable source for the philosophy of the Hellenistic period. The fact that Diogenes mentions nothing about Neoplatonists indicates the approximate date of the work, much of which consists of a compilation of previous histories.

ALEXANDER OF APHRODISIAS (SECOND CENTURY–EARLY THIRD CENTURY C.E.). The greatest among the Peripatetic commentators on Aristotle. He was also probably the first 'professional' Aristotelian, although his opposition to Stoicism is far more explicit than any opposition to Platonism. His extant commentaries are on *Prior Analytics, Topics, Metaphysics* A–Δ, *Meteorologica,* and *De Sensu.* The commentary on *Metaphysics* E-N is not by Alexander. Its author is unknown and is usually know as "Pseudo-Alexander." A commentary on *Physics* is lost, though fragments may be found in Simplicus's *Physics* commentary. Among Alexander's personal writings are *De Anima, Problems and Solutions, Ethical Problems, On Fate, On Mixture and Increase.*

THEMISTIUS (CA. 317–388 C.E.). Generally held to be a Peripatetic commentator on Aristotle, though his supposed antipathy to Platonism has been questioned. He is the author of extant paraphrases on Aristotle's *Posterior Analytics, Physics, De Anima,* and (in Hebrew versions of Arabic translations) *De Caelo* and *Metaphysics* 12. He also appears to have written commentaries on *Categories, Prior Analytics, On Generation and Corruption* and *Nicomachean Ethics.*

Bibliography

Ancient Authors

Alcinous. 1990. *Alcinoos. Enseigment des doctrines de Platon.* Edited by J. Whittaker. Paris: Les Belles Lettres.

Alexander of Aphrodisias. 1883. *In aristotelis analyticorum priorum librum i commentarium.* Edited by M. Wallies. *CAG* 2.1 Berlin: Reimer.

———. 1887. *De anima liber cum mantissa.* Edited by I. Bruns. *CAG,* supp. 2.1. Berlin: Reimer.

———. 1891. *In aristotelis topicorum libros octo commentaria.* Edited by M. Wallies. Berlin: Reimer.

———. 1891. *In aristotelis metaphysica commentaria.* Edited by M. Hayduck. *CAG* 1 Berlin: Reimer.

———. 1892. *Praeter commentaria scripta minora : Quaestiones de fato, de mixtione.* Edited by I. Bruns *CAG* 2.2. Berlin: Reimer.

———. 1898. *In aristotelis sophisticos elenchos commentarium.* Edited by M. Wallies. Berlin: Reimer.

———. 1901. *In librum de sensu commentarium.* Edited by P. Wendland. *CAG* 3.1. Berlin: Reimer.

Aristotle. 1866. *Aristotelis qui ferebantur librorum fragmenta.* Edited by V. Rose. Leipzig: Teubner.

———. 1884. *Aristotelis ethica Eudemia.* Edited by F. Susemihl. Leipzig: Teubner.

———. 1894. *Aritotelis ethica Nicomachea.* Edited by I. Bywater. Oxford: Clarendon Press.

———. 1924. *Aristotle's Metaphysics.* 2 vols. Edited by W. D. Ross. Oxford: Clarendon Press.

———. 1933. *Aristotelis qui fertur libellus De mundo.* Edited by W. L. Lorimer. Paris: Les Belles Lettres.

———. 1949. *Aristotelis categoriae et liber de interpretatione.* Edited by L. Minio-Paluello. Oxford: Clarendon Press.

———. 1950. *Aristotelis. Physica.* Edited by W. D. Ross. Oxford: Clarendon Press.

———. 1955. *Aristotelis. Fragmenta Selecta.* Edited by W. D. Ross. Oxford: Clarendon Press.

———. 1957. *Aristotelis. Metaphysica.* Edited by W. Jaeger. Oxford: Clarendon Press.

———. 1957. *Aristotelis. Politica.* Edited by W. D. Ross. Oxford: Clarendon Press.

——. 1958. *Aristotelis topica et sophistici elenchi*. Edited by W. D. Ross. Oxford: Clarendon Press.

——. 1961. *Aristotle. De Anima*. Edited by W. D. Ross. Oxford: Clarendon Press.

——. 1961. *Aristotle's Protrepticus*. Edited by I. Düring. Stockholm: Almqvist & Wiksell.

——. 1964. *Aristotelis analytica priora et posteriora*. Edited by W. D. Ross. Oxford: Clarendon Press.

——. 1965. *Aristote. Du ciel*. Edited by P. Moraux. Paris: Les Belles Lettres.

——. 1965. *Aristotelis de generatione animalium*. Edited by H. J. Drossart-Lulofs. Oxford: Clarendon Press.

——. 1966. *Aristote. De la génération et de la corruption*. Edited by C. Mugler. Paris: Les Belles Lettres.

Asclepius. 1888. *In aristotelis metaphysicorum libros a-z commentaria*. Edited by M. Hayduck. *CAG* 6.2. Berlin: Reimer.

Aspasius. 1889. *In ethica nicomachea quae supersunt commentaria*. Edited by G. Heylbut. *CAG* 19.1. Berlin: Reimer.

Dexippus. 1888. *Dexippi in aristotelis categorias commentarium*. Edited by A. Busse. *CAG* 4.2. Berlin: Reimer.

Diogenes Laertius. 1980. *Lives of Eminent Philosophers*. Edited by R. D. Hicks. Cambridge: Harvard University Press.

Elias. 1900. *In Porphyrii Isagogen et Aristotelis Categorias Commentaria*. Edited by A. Busse. CAG 18.1. Berlin: Reimer.

Eustratius. 1962. *Eustratii et michaelis et anonyma in ethica nichomachea commentaria*. Edited by G. Heylbut. *CAG* 20. Berlin: Reimer.

Hierocles. 1974. *In aureum pythagoreorum carmen commentarius*. Edited by F. W. Koehler. Stuttgart: Teubner.

Iamblichus. 1960. *Iamblichi babyloniacorum reliquiae*. Edited by E. Habrich. Leipzig: Teubner.

——. 1922. *Theologumena arithmeticae*. Edited by V. de Falco. Stuttgart: Teubner.

——. 1975 (reprint of 1891 edition). *Iamblichi protrepticus*. Edited by H. Pistelli. Leipzig: Teubner.

——. 1975. *Iamblichi de communi mathematica scientia liber*. Edited by U. Klein (post N. Festa). Stuttgart: Teubner.

——. 1966. *De mysteriis*. Edited by E. Des Places. Paris: Les Belles Lettres.

——. 1972. *Jamblique de Chalcis. Exégète et philosophe. Appendice: testimonia et fragmenta exegetica*. Edited by B.D. Larsen. Aarhus: Universitetsforlaget.

——. 1973. *In Platonis dialogos commentariorum fragmenta*. Edited by J. Dillon. Leiden: Brill.

——. 1989. *Jamblique. Protreptique*. Edited by E. Des Places. Paris: Budé.

Numenius. 1973. *Numénius. Fragments*. Edited by E. Des Places. Paris: Budé.

Olympiodorus. 1900. *In aristotelis meteora commentaria*. Edited by G. Stüve. *CAG* 12.2. Berlin: Reimer.

——. 1902. *Prolegomena et in categories commentarium*. Edited by A. Busse. *CAG* 12.1. Berlin: Reimer.

——. 1956. *Olympiodorus. Commentary on the First Alcibiades of Plato*. Edited by L.G. Westerink. Amsterdam: Hakkert.

——. 1970. *Olympiodori in Platonis Gorgiam commentaria*. Edited L. G. Westerink. Leipzig: Teubner.

——. 1976. *The Greek Commentaries on Plato's Phaedo*. Edited by L. G. Westerink. Amsterdam: North-Holland.

Philoponus, John. 1887, 1888. *In aristotelis physicorum libros commentaria*. Edited by H. Vitelli. *CAG* 16 and 17. Berlin: Reimer.

——. 1897. *In aristotelis libros de generatione et corruptione commentaria*. Edited by M. Hayduck. *CAG* 14.3. Berlin: Reimer.

——. 1897. *In aristotelis de anima libros commentaria*. Edited by M. Hayduck. *CAG* 15. Berlin: Reimer.

——. 1898. *In aristotelis categoriae commentarium.* Edited by A. Busse. *CAG* 13.1. Berlin: Reimer.

——. 1899. *Ioannes philoponus de aeternitate mundi contra proclum.* Edited by H. Rabe. Leipzig: Teubner.

——. 1901. *In aristotelis meteorologicorum librum primum commentarium.* Edited by M. Hayduck. *CAG* 14.1. Berlin: Reimer.

——. 1903. *In libros de generatione animalium commentaria.* Edited by M. Hayduck. *CAG* 14.3. Berlin: Reimer.

——. 1905. *In aristotelis analytica priora commentaria.* Edited by M. Wallies. *CAG* 13.2 Berlin: Reimer.

——. 1909. *In aristotelis analytica posteriora commentaria.* Edited by M. Wallies. *CAG* 13.3. Berlin: Reimer.

Plato. 1900–1902. *Platonis. Opera.* 5 vols. Edited by J. Burnet. Oxford: Clarendon Press.

Plotinus. 1964, 1977, 1983. *Opera.* 3 vols. Edited by P. Henry and H-R Schwyzer (*editio minor*). Oxford: Clarendon Press.

Porphyry. 1993. *Porphyrii philosophi fragmenta.* Edited by A. Smith. Stuttgart: Teubner.

——. 1995. *Isagoge.* Edited by G. Girgenti. Milan: Rusconi.

——. 1997. *Storia della filosofia.* Edited by A. Sodano and G. Girgenti. Milan: Rusconi

——. 1996. *Sentenze sugli intellegibili.* Edited by G. Girgenti. Milan: Rusconi.

Proclus. 1864. *Procli philosophi Platonici opera inedita* (Commentary on Plato's *Republic*). Edited by V. Cousin. Paris: Durand (reprinted 1961, Hildesheim: Olms).

——. 1873. *Procli Diadochi in primum euclidis elementorum librum commentarii.* Edited by G. Friedlein. Leipzig: Teubner.

——. 1899, 1901. *Procli Diadochi in Platonis rem publicam commentarii.* 2 vols. Edited by W. Kroll. Leipzig: Teubner.

——. 1908. *Procli Diadochi in Platonis Cratylum commentaria.* Edited by G. Pasquali. Leipzig: Teubner.

——. 1933. *Proclus. The Elements of Theology.* Edited by E. R. Dodds. Oxford: Clarendon Press.

——. 1954. *Commentary on the First Alcibiades of Plato.* Edited by L. G. Westerink. Amsterdam: North-Holland Publishing Co.

——. 1960. *Tria opuscula: De providentia, libertate, malo.* Edited by H. Boese. Berlin: Walter de Gruyter.

——. 1965. *Procli Diadochi in Platonis Timaeum commentaria.* 3. vols. Edited by E. Diehl. Amsterdam: Hakkert.

——. 1965. *In Platonis rem publicam commentarii.* 2 vols. Edited by W. Kroll. Amsterdam: Hakkert.

——. 1968. *Proclus. Théologie platonicienne.* 5 vols. Edited by D. Saffrey and L. G. Westerink. Paris: Les Belles Lettres.

Sextus Empiricus. 1914–1958. *Opera.* 3 vols. Edited by H. Mutschmann and J. Mau. Vol. 4 *Indices.* Edited by K. Janaceck, 1962. Leipzig: Teubner.

Simplicius. 1882. *Simplicii in libros aristotelis de anima commentaria.* Edited by M. Hayduck. *CAG* 11. Berlin: Teubner.

——. 1882, 1895. *Simplicii in aristotelis physicorum libros commentaria.* 2 vols. Edited by H. Diels. *CAG* 9 and 10. Berlin: Reimer.

——. 1894. *In aristotelis quattuor libros de caelo commentaria.* Edited by J. L. Leiberg. *CAG* 7. Berlin: Reimer.

——. 1907. *In aristotelis categorias commentarium.* Edited by K. Kalbfleisch. *CAG* 8. Berlin: Reimer.

——. 1996. *Simplicius. Commentaire sur le Manuel d'Épictète: Introduction et édition critque du texte grec.* Edited by I. Hadot. Leiden: E. J. Brill.

Stobaeus. 1884. *Anthologii libri due priores qui inscribi solent Eclogue physicae et ethicae.* 2 vols. Edited by K. Wachsmuth. Berlin: Reimer.

Syrianus. 1892. *Syriani in metaphysica commentaria.* Edited by H. Rabe. *CAG* 6.1. Berlin: Reimer.

Themistius. 1899. *In libros aristotelis de anima paraphrasis.* Edited by R. Heinze. *CAG* 5.3. Berlin: Reimer.
——. 1900. *In aristotelis physica paraphrasis.* Edited by H. Schenkl. *CAG* 5.2. Berlin: Reimer.
——. 1900. *Analyticorum posteriorum paraphrasis.* Edited by M. Wallies. *CAG* 5.1. Berlin: Reimer.
——. 1903. *In aristotelis metaphysicorum librum a paraphrasis hebraice et latine.* Edited by S. Landauer. *CAG* 5.5. Berlin: Reimer.
Xenocrates. 1892. *Xenocrates. Darstellung der Lehre und Sammlung der Fragmente.* Edited by R. Heinze. Leipzig: Teubner.
——. 1982. *Senocrate-Ermodoro. Frammenti.* Edited by M. Isnardi Parenti. Napoli: Biblopolis.

Modern Authors, Editors, and Translators

Ackrill, J. L. 1979. *Aristotle's Categories and De Interpretatione.* Oxford: Clarendon Press.
Adam, J. 1963. *The Republic.* 2 vols. Edited with critical notes, commentary, and appendixes. Cambridge: Cambridge University Press.
Adkins, A. W. H. 1978. "Theory and Praxis in the *Nicomachean Ethics* and the *Republic.*" *Classical Philology* 73: 297–313.
Alberti, A. M., and R. Sharples. 1999. *Aspasius: The Earliest Extant Commentary on Aristotle's Ethics.* Berlin: Walter De Gruyter.
Allan, D. J. 1976. "Critical and Explanatory Notes on Some Passages Assigned to Aristotle's *Protrepticus.*" *Phronesis* 21: 219–240.
Allen, R. E. 1983. *Plato's Parmenides.* Minneapolis: University of Minnesota Press.
Annas, J. 1974. "Forms and First Principles." *Phronesis* 19: 257–283.
——. 1975. "On the Intermediates." *Archiv für Geschichte der Philosophie* 57: 146–166.
——. 1976. *Aristotle's Metaphysics: Books M and N.* Oxford: Clarendon Press.
——. 1997. "Is Plato a Stoic?" *Méthexis* 10: 23–38.
——. 1999. *Platonic Ethics, Old and New.* Ithaca: Cornell University Press.
Anton, J. 1968. "The Meaning of ὁ λόγος τῆς οὐσίας in Aristotle's *Categories.*" *Monist* 52: 252–267.
Apostle, H. G. 1966. *Aristotle's Metaphysics.* Bloomington: Indiana University Press.
Armstrong, H. 1967. "Greek Philosophy from Plato to Plotinus." In *The Cambridge History of Late Greek and Early Medieval Philosophy,* edited by H. Armstrong, 1–132. Cambridge: Cambridge University Press.
Arnim, H. von. 1924. "Die drei Aristotelischen Ethiken." *Sitzungsberichte der Wiener Akademie der Wissenschaften, Phil.-hist. Klasse* 202.
Aubenque, P. 1972. *Le problème de l'être chez Aristote.* Paris: Presses Universitaires de France.
Balleriaux, O. 1994. "Thémistius et le Néoplatonisme: Le nous pathetikos et l'immortalité de l'ame." *Revue de la philosophie ancienne* 12: 171–200.
Baltes, M. 1976. *Die Weltentstehung des Platonischen Timaios nach den antiken Interpreten.* Leiden: Brill.
——. 1996. "Gegonen (Platon, Tim. 28B7). Ist die Welt real entanden oder nicht?" In *Polyhistor. Studies in the History and Historiography of Ancient Philosophy, Presented to J. Mansfeld on his Sixtieth Birthday,* edited by K. A. Algra, P. A. van den Horst and D. T. Runia, 76–96. Leiden: Brill.
——. 1999. "Was ist antiker Platonismus?" In *Dianohmata. Kleine Schriften zum Platonismus.* 223–47. Stuttgart, Leipzig: Teubner.
Baltes, M. and H. Dörrie. 2002. *Der Platonismus in der Antike.* Bd. 6 Stuttgart-Bad Cannstatt: Frommann-Holzboog.
Barford, R. 1976. "A Proof from the Peri Ideon Revisited." *Phronesis* 21:198–218.
Barnes, J. 1971. "Aristotle's Concept of Mind." *Proceedings of the Aristotelian Society* 72:104–114.

——. 1977. Review of Reale and Bos 1975. *Classical Review* 27:40–43.
——. 1989. "Autiochus of Ascalon." In *Philosophia Togata*, edited by J. Barnes and M. Griffin, 51–96. Oxford: Oxford University Press.
——. ed. 1995 *The Cambridge Companion to Aristotle*. Cambridge: Cambridge University Press.
——. 1997. "Roman Aristotle." In *Philosophia Togata II*, edited by J. Barnes and M. Griffin, 1–69. Oxford: Oxford University Press.
——. 1999. "An Introduction to Aspasius." In *Aspasius: The Earliest Extant Commentary on Aristotle's Ethics*, edited by A. M. Alberti and R. W. Sharples, 1–50. Berlin/New York: Walter De Gruyter.
——. 2003. *Porphyry. Introduction*. Oxford: Clarendon Press.
Baudry, J. 1931. *Atticus: Fragments de son oeuvres*. Paris: Les Belles Lettres.
Bechtle, G. 1999. *The Anonymous Commentary on Plato's "Parmenides."* Bern: Haupt.
Bernays, J. 1863. *Die Dialoge des Aristoteles in ihrem Verhältnis zu seinen übrigen Werken*. 2nd ed. Berlin: Wissenschaftliche Buchgesellschaft.
Berti, E. 1962. *La filosofia del primo Aristotele*. Florence: Cedam.
——. 1975. *Studi aristotelici*. L'Aquila: L. U. Japadre.
——. 1977. *Dalla dialettica alla filosofia prima*. Padua: Cedam.
——. 1978. "The Intellection of Indivisibles According to Aristotle." In *Aristotle on Mind and the Senses*, edited by A. C. Lloyd and G. E. L. Owen, 141–63. London: Cambridge University Press.
——. 1983. "La fonction de Métaph. Alpha Elatton dans la philosophie d'Aristote." In *Zweifelhaftes im Corpus Aristotelicum. Studien zu einigen Dubia*, edited by P. Moraux and J. Wiesner, 260–94. Berlin: Walter De Gruyter.
—— 1997. "Da che è amato il motore immobile? Su Aristotele, "Metaph." XII 6–7." *Methexis* 10:59–82.
——. 1999. "Amicizia e "focal meaning." In *Aspasius: The Earliest Extant Commentary on Aristotle's Ethics*, edited by A. M. Alberti and R. W. Sharples, 176–190. Oxford: Oxford University Press.
——. 2000. "Metaphysics Lambda 6." In *Aristotle's Metaphysics Lambda*, edited by M. Frede and D. Charles, 181–206. Oxford: Clarendon Press.
Bignone, E. 1973. *L'Aristotele perduto e la formazione filosofica di Epicuro*. Florence: La nuova Italia.
Block, I. 1961. "The Order of Aristotle's Psychological Writings." *American Journal of Philology* 82:50–77.
Blumenthal, H. J. 1981. "Some Platonist Readings of Aristotle." *Proceedings of the Cambridge Philological Society* 27: 1–13.
——. 1990. "Neoplatonic Elements in the *De Anima* Commentaries." In *Aristotle Transformed: The Ancient Commentators and Their Influence*, edited by R. Sorabji, 305–324. Ithaca: Cornell University Press.
——. 1991. "Nous Pathetikos in Later Greek Philosophy." In *Aristotle and the Later Tradition*. edited by H. J. Blumenthal and H. M. Robinson, 191–205. Oxford: Clarendon Press.
——. 1993. "Alexandria as a Centre of Greek Philosophy in Later Classical Antiquity." *Illinois Classical Studies* 18:307–325.
——. 1996. *Aristotle and Neoplatonism in Late Antiquity. Interpretations of De Anima*. Ithaca: Cornell University Press.
——. 2000. *Simplicius: On Aristotle's "On the Soul"* 3. 1–5. Ithaca: Cornell University Press.
Boas, G. 1943. "A Basic Conflict in Aristotle's Philosophy." *American Journal of Philology* 64:172–193.
Bonitz, H. 1848. *Metaphysica*. Bonn: Marcus.
Bos, A. P. 1987. "The Relation between Aristotle's Lost Writings and the Surviving Aristotelian Corpus." *Philosophia Reformata* 52:24–40.
——. 1989a. *Cosmic and Meta-Cosmic Theology in Aristotle's Lost Dialogues*. Leiden: Brill.

——. 1989b. "Exoterikoi Logoi and Enkyklioi Logoi in the *Corpus Aristotelicum* and the Origin of the Idea of the Enkyklios Paideia." *Journal of the History of Ideas* 50:179–198.

——. 2003. *The Soul and Its Instrumental Body.* Leiden: Brill.

Bosley, R. 1996. "Aristotle's Use of the Theory of the Mean: How Adaptable and Flexible Is the Theory?" In *Aristotle, Virtue and the Mean,* edited by R. Bosely. Edmonton: Academic.

Bostock, D. 1994. *Aristotle: Metaphysics, Books Z and H.* Oxford: Clarendon Press.

Boys-Stones, G. R. 2001. *Post-Hellenistic Philosophy: A Study of Its Development from the Stoics to Origen.* Oxford: Oxford University Press.

Brandis, C. 1834. "Über die Aristotelische Metaphysik." *Abhandlung Berlin Akadmie,* 68–87.

Brentano, F. C. 1867. *Die Psychologie des Aristoteles, insbesondere seine Lehre vom nous poietikos. Nebst einer Beilage über das Wirken des aristotelischen Gottes.* Mainz: F. Kirchheim.

——. 1977. *The Psychology of Aristotle: In Particular His Doctrine of the Active Intellect, with an Appendix Concerning the Activity of Aristotle's God.* Translated by R. George. Berkeley: University of California Press.

Brentlinger, J. 1963. "The Divided Line and Plato's Theory of Intermediates." *Phronesis* 7:146–166.

Breton, S. 1969. *Philosophie et mathématique chez Proclus.* Paris: Beauchesne.

Brinkmann, K. 1996. "The Consistency of Aristotle's Thought on Substance." In *Aristotle's Philosophical Development,* edited by W. R. Wians, 289–302. Lanham, Md.: Rowman & Littlefield.

Brisson, L. 1994. *Le même et l'autre dans la structure ontologique du "Timée" de Platon.* 2nd ed. Sankt Augustin: Academia Verlag.

Broadie, S. 1993. "Que fait le premier moteur d'Aristote? Sur la théologie du livre Lambda de la 'Métaphysique.' *Revue philosophique de la France et de l'Etranger* 183:375–411.

Bröcker, W. 1966. *Platonismus ohne Sokrates. Ein Vortrag über Plotin.* Frankfurt: Klostermann.

Brumbaugh, R. S. 1954. "Aristotle as a Mathematician." *Review of Metaphysics* 8: 511–521.

Brunschwig, J. 2000. "Metaphysics Lambda 9: A Thought-Experiment" in *Aristotle's* Metaphysics *Lambda,* edited by M. Frede and D. Charles, 275–306. Oxford: Clarendon Press.

——. 1987. "Platonism and Mathematics: A Prelude to Discussion" in *Mathematics and Metaphysics in Aristotle,* edited by A. Graeser, 213–40. Bern: Haupt.

Burnyeat, M. F. 1981. "Aristotle on Understanding Knowledge." In *Aristotle on Science: The Posterior Analytics.* Proceedings of the Eighth Symposium Aristotlium, edited by E. Berti, 97–139. Padua: Antenore.

——. 1987. "Platonism and Mathematics: A Prelude to Discussion." In *Mathematics and Metaphysics in Aristotle,* edited by A. Graeser, 213–240. Bern: Haupt.

——. 1992. "Is an Aristotelian Philosophy of Mind Still Credible? A Draft" In *Essays on Aristotle's De Anima.* Edited by M. Nussbaum and A. Rorty, 15–26. Oxford: Clarendon Press.

——. 2001. *A Map of Metaphysics Z.* Pittsburgh: Mathesis Publications.

Bussanich, J. 1990. "The Invulnerability of Goodness: The Ethical and Psychological Theory of Plotinus." In *Proceedings of the Boston Area Colloquium in Ancient Philosophy* 6 (edited by J. J. Cleary): 151–184.

Cardullo, L. 1997. "La Noera Theoria di Giamblico, come Chiave di Lettura delle *Categorie* di Aristotele: Alcuni esempli." *Syllecta Classica* 8:79–94.

Case, T. 1910. "Aristotle." In *Encyclopedia Britannica,* 501–22.

Caston, V. 1996. "Why Aristotle Needs Imagination." *Phronesis* 41: 20–55.

——. 1999. "Aristotle's Two Intellects: A Modest Proposal." *Phronesis* 44: 199–227.

Charles-Saget, A. 1967. "Sur le caractère intermédiaire des mathématiques dans la pensée de Proclus." *Les Etudes Philosophiques* 22: 69–80.

——. 1982. *L'architecture du divin: Mathématique et philosophie chez Plotin et Proclus.* Paris: Les Belles Lettres.

Charlton, W. 1987. "Aristotle on the Place of Mind in Nature." In *Philosophical Issues in Aristotle's Biology*, edited by A. Gotthelf and J. G. Lennox, Cambridge: Cambridge University Press. 408–423.

Chen, C.-H. 1940. *Das Chorismos-Problem bei Aristoteles*. Berlin: Limbach.

Cherniss, H. F. 1944. *Aristotle's Criticism of Plato and the Academy*. Baltimore: John Hopkins University Press.

———. 1945. *The Riddle of the Early Academy*. New York: Russell & Russell.

———. 1965. "The Relation of the *Timaeus* to Plato's Later Dialogues." In *Studies in Plato's Metaphysics*, edited by R. E. Allen, 339–78. London: Routledge & Kegan Paul.

Chiesara, M. L. 2001. *Aristocles of Messene: Testimonia and Fragments*. Oxford: Oxford University Press.

Claghorn, G. S. 1954. *Aristotle's Criticism of Plato's Timaeus*. The Hague: Martinus Nijhoff.

Clark, S. R. L. 1975. *Aristotle's Man: Speculations upon Aristotelian Anthropology*. Oxford: Clarendon Press.

Cleary, J. J. 1988. *Aristotle on the Many Senses of Priority*. Carbondale: Southern Illinois University Press.

———. 1995. *Aristotle and Mathematics: Aporetic Method in Cosmology and Metaphysics*. Leiden: Brill.

Code, A. 1985. "On the Origin of Some Aristotelian Theses about Predication." In *How Things Are: Studies in Predication and the History of Philosophy and Science*, edited by J. Bogen and J. McGuire. 101–131. Dordrecht: D. Reidel.

———. 1996. "Owen on the Development of Aristotle's Metaphysics." In *Aristotle's Philosophical Development*, edited by W. R. Wians, 303–325. Lanham, Md.: Rowman & Littlefield.

Code, A., and J. Moravcsik. 1992. "Explaining Various Forms of Living." In *Essays on Aristotle's De Anima*. Edited by M. Nussbaum and A. Rorty, 129–145. Oxford: Clarendon Press.

Cohen, S. M. 1992. "Hylomorphism and Functionalism." In *Essays on Aristotle's De Anima*. Edited by M. Nussbaum and A. Rorty, 57–73. Oxford: Clarendon Press.

Cohen, S. M., and D. Keyt. 1992. "Analysing Plato's Arguments: Plato and Platonism." In *Methods of Interpreting Plato*, edited by J. Klagge and N. Smith. 173–200. Oxford: Oxford University Press.

Cooper, J. M. 1975. *Reason and Human Good in Aristotle*. Cambridge: Harvard University Press.

———. 1985. "Hypothetical Necessity." In *Aristotle on Nature and Living Things. Philosophical and Historical Studies Presented to David M. Balme on his Seventieth Birthday*. Edited by A. Gotthelf, 151–167. Pittsburgh: Mathesis Publications.

———. 1987. "Contemplation and Happiness: A Reconsideration. *Synthese* 72: 187–216.

———. 1996. "An Aristotelian Theory of the Emotions." In *Essays on Aristotle's Rhetoric*, edited by A. Rorty, 238–57. Berkeley: University of California Press.

———. 1997. *Plato: Complete Works*. Indianapolis: Hackett.

Cornford, F. M. 1934. *Plato's Theory of Knowledge*. London: Routledge Kegan Paul.

———. 1937. *Plato's Cosmology*. London: Routledge & Kegan Paul.

Corrigan, K. 1996. *Plotinus' Theory of Matter-Evil and the Question of Substance: Plato, Aristotle, and Alexander of Aphrodisias*. Leuven: Peeters.

Crisp, R. 1994. "Aristotle's Inclusivism." *Oxford Studies in Ancient Philosophy* 12:11–36.

Damschen, G.. 2002. "Grenzen des Gesprachs Uber Ideen. Die Formen des Wissens und die Notwendigkeit der Ideen in Platons *Parmenides*." In *Platon und Aristotles sub ratione veritatis*, edited by G. Damschen, R. Enskat, A. Vigo, 31–75. Göttingen: Vandenhoeck & Ruprecht.

D'Ancona, C. 2003. "The *Timaeus*' Model for Creation and Providence: An Example of Continuity and Adaptation in Early Arabic Philosophical Literature." In *Plato's Timaeus as Cultural Icon*. Edited by G. Reydams-Schils, 206–237. Notre Dame: University of Notre Dame Press.

Dancy, R. M. 1996. "Keeping Body and Soul Together: On Aristotle's Theory of Forms." In *Aristotle's Philosophical Development*, edited by W. R. Wians, 249–87. Lanham, Md.: Rowman & Littlefield.

De Corte, M. 1934. *La doctrine d'inteligence chez Aristote*. Paris: J. Vrin.

De Filippo, J. G. 1994. "Aristotle's Identification of the Prime Mover as God." *Classical Quarterly* 44:393–409.

Defourny, P. 1937. "L'activité de contemplation dans les morales d'Aristote." *Bulletin de l'Institut Historique belge de Rome* 18: 89–101.

De Haas, F. A. J. 2001. "Did Plotinus and Porphyry Disagree on Aristotle's Categories?" *Phronesis* 46:492–526.

De Koninck, T. 1991. "La Pensée de la pensé chez Aristote." In *La Question de Dieu chez Aristote et Hegel*, edited by T. De Koninck and G. Planty-Bonjour, 69–151. Paris: Presses Universitare de France.

———. 1994. "Aristotle on God as Thought Thinking Itself." *Review of Metaphysics* 47:471–515.

Denyer, N. 2001. *Alcibiades*. Cambridge: Cambridge University Press.

De Strycker, E. 1955. "La notion aristotélicienne de séparation dans son application aux Idées de Platon." In *Autour d'Aristote*, edited by A. Mansion, 119–39. Louvain: Publications Universitaires de Louvain.

———. 1968. "Prédicats Univoques et Prédicats Analogiques dans Le "Protreptique" D'Aristote." *Revue Philosophique de Louvain* 66:597–618.

Deuse, W. 1983. *Untersuchungen zur mittelplatonischen und neuplatonischen Seelenlehre*. Mainz: Akademie der Wissenschaften und der Literatur.

De Vogel, C. 1960. "The Legend of the Platonizing Aristotle." In *Aristotle and Plato in the Mid-Fourth Century*, edited by I. Düring and G. E. L. Owen, 249–51. Göteborg: Almqvist & Wiksell.

———. 1965. "Did Aristotle Ever Accept Plato's Theory of Transcendent Ideas: Problems around a New Edition of the 'Protrepticus.'" *Archiv für Geschichte der Philosophie* 47:261–298.

———. 1969. "Platon a-t-il ou n'a-t-il pas introduit le mouvement dans son monde intelligible? Critique des interpretations modernes de *Sophistes* 249A et de *Timaeus* 31B." In *Philosophy: Studies in Greek Philosophy*, I. C. J. De Vogel, 176–82. Assen: Van Gorcum.

Des Places, E. 1973. *Numénius*. Fragments. Paris: Les Belles Lettres.

———. 1989. *Protreptique*. Paris: Les Belles Lettres.

Diès, A. 1932. *La définition de l'être et la nature des idées dans le Sophiste de Platon*. Paris: J. Vrin.

Dillon, J. M. 1983. "Plotinus, Philo and Origen on the Grades of Virtue." In *Platonismus und Christentum*, edited by H.-D. Blume and F. Mann, 92–105. Munster: Aschendorff.

———. 1990a. *The Golden Chain: Studies in the Development of Platonism and Christianity*. Aldershot: Variorum.

———. 1990b. *Dexippus: On Aristotle's Categories*. Ithaca: Cornell University Press.

———. 1993. *Alcinous: The Handbook of Platonism*. Oxford: Clarendon Press.

———. 1996a. "An Ethic for the Late Antique Sage." In *The Cambridge Companion to Plotinus*, edited by L. P. Gerson, 315–35. Cambridge: Cambridge University Press.

———. 1996b. *The Middle Platonists: A Study of Platonism, 80 B.C. to A.D. 220*. 2nd ed. London: Duckworth.

———. 1997. "Iamblichus' Noera Theoria of Aristotle's *Categories*." *Syllecta Classica* 8:65–77.

———. 2003. *The Heirs of Plato. A Study of the Old Academy, 347–274 BC*. Oxford: Oxford University Press.

Dodds, E. R. 1928. "The *Parmenides* of Plato and the Origin of the Neoplatonic One." *Classical Quarterly* 22:129–42.

———. 1960. "Numenius and Ammonius." In *Les sources de Plotin*, edited by E. R. Dodds, 3–32. Geneva: Vandoeuvres.

Donini, P. 1988a. "The History of the Concept of Eclecticism." In *The Question of "Eclecticism". Studies in Later Greek Philosophy,* edited by J. M. Dillon and A. A. Long, 15–33. Berkeley: University of California Press.

——. 1988b." Science and Metaphysics: Platonism, Aristotelianism, and Stoicism in Plutarch's *On the Face in the Moon.*" In *The Question of Eclecticism,* edited by J. M. Dillon and A. A. Long, 126–44. Berkeley: University of California Press.

Dörrie, H. 1976a. *Platonica minora.* Munich: W. Fink.

——. 1976b. *Von Platon zum Platonismus.* Rheinisch-Wesfälische Akademie der Wissenschaften, Vorträge G 211. Dusseldorf: Westdeutscher Verlag.

Dörrie, H., and M. Baltes. 1987. *Der Platonismus in der Antike: Grundlagen, System, Entwicklung.* Bd. 1 Stuttgart-Bad Cannstatt: Fromann-Holzboog.

Dumoulin, B. 1981. *Recherches sur le premier Aristote: Eudème, De la philosophie, Protreptique.* Paris: J. Vrin.

——. 1986. *Analyse génétique de la Métaphysique d'Aristote.* Montréal: Bellarmin.

Düring, I. 1956. "Aristotle and Plato in the Mid-Fourth Century." *Eranos* 54:109–120.

——. 1957. *Aristotle in the Ancient Biographical Tradition.* Göteborg, Sweden: Institute of Classical Studies of the University of Göteborg.

——. 1961. *Aristotle's Protrepticus: An Attempt at Reconstruction.* Göteborg, Sweden: Universitatis Gothoburgensis.

——. 1964. "Aristotle and the Heritage from Plato." *Eranos* 62:84–99.

——. 1966a. *Aristoteles: Darstellung und Interpretation seines Denkens.* Heidelberg: Winter.

——. 1966b. "Did Aristotle Ever Accept Plato's Theory of Transcendent Ideas?" *Archiv für Geschichte der Philosophie* 48:312–316.

——. 1993. *Der Protreptikos des Aristoteles: Einleitung, Text, Übersetzung und Kommentar.* Frankfurt: V. Klostermann.

Ebbesen, S. 1990. "Porphyry's Legacy to Logic: A Reconstruction" in *Aristotle Transformed.* Edited by R. Sorabji, 141–71. Ithaca: Cornell University Press.

Effe, B. 1970. *Studien zur Kosmologie und Theologie der Aristotelischen Schrift "Über die Philosophie."* Munich: Beck.

Egermann, F. 1959. "Platonische Spätphilosophie und Platonismus bei Aristoteles." *Hermes* 87:133–142.

Eriksen, T. 1976. *Bios Theoretikos: Notes on Aristotle's Ethica Nicomachea X, 6–8.* Oslo: Universitetsforl.

Erler, M. 1987. "Interpretieren als Gottesdienst. Proklos' Hymnen vor dem Hintergrund seines Kratylos-Kommentars." In *Proclos et son influence. Actes du Colloque de Neuchâtel, Juin 1985.* Edited by G. Boss and G. Seel, 179–217. Zürich: Editions du Grand Midi.

Evangeliou, C. 1988. *Aristotle's Categories and Porphyry.* Leiden: Brill.

Ferber, R. 2001. "The Occurrence of an Essence: Dies aber is die Ousia. Einige Bemerkungen zur aristotelischen *Metaphysik* Z17, 1041b4–9." *Allgemeine Zeitschrift für Philosophie* 26: 61–75.

——. 2002. "La perla 'metafisica' nella 'paluda dei tropi.' Osservazioni intorno a *Metafisica* Z 17, 1041b4–9." In *Gigantomachia. Convergenze e divergenze tra Platone e Aristotele,* edited by M. Migliori, 317–337. Brescia: Morcelliana.

Ferrari, F. 2002. "Modelli di causalità: L'idea del Bene in Platone e Aristotele." In *Gigantomachia. Convergenze e divergenze tra Platone e Aristotele.* Edited by M. Migliori, 273–315. Brescia: Morcelliana.

Festugière, A. J. 1944. *La révélation d'Hermès Trismégiste.* Paris: Gabada.

——. 1969. "L'ordre de lecteur des dialogues de Platon aux Ve/VIe siecles." *Museum Helveticum* 26: 281–296.

Findlay, J. N. 1974. *Plato: The Written and Unwritten Doctrines.* London: Routledge & Kegan Paul.

Fine, G. 1984. "Separation." *Oxford Studies in Ancient Philosophy* 2: 31–87.

——. 1987. "Forms as Causes: Plato and Aristotle." In *Mathematics and Metaphysics in Aristotle*, edited by A. Graeser, 69–112. Bern: Haupt. Reprinted in Fine 2003, *Plato on Knowledge and Forms*, 350–396. Oxford: Clarendon Press.

——. 1993. *On Ideas: Aristotle's Criticism of Plato's Theory of Forms*. Oxford: Clarendon Press.

Fortenbaugh, W. W. 1975. *Aristotle on Emotion: A Contribution to Philosophical Psychology, Rhetoric, Poetics, Politics, and Ethics*. New York: Barnes & Noble Books.

Frank, E. 1940. "The Fundamental Opposition of Plato and Aristotle." *American Journal of Philology* 61:34–53; 166–85.

Frankfurt, H. 1971. "Freedom of the Will and the Concept of the Person." *Journal of Philosophy* 68:5–20.

Frede, D. 1970. *Aristoteles und die "Seeschlacht." Das Problem des contingentia futura in De interpretatione 9*. Göttingen: Vandenhoeck & Ruprecht.

Frede, M. 1987. *Essays in Ancient Philosophy*. Minneapolis: University of Minnesota Press.

——. 1987. "The Unity of General and Special Metaphysics: Aristotle's Conception of Metaphysics." In *Essays in Ancient Philosophy*, 81–95. Minneapolis: University of Minnesota Press.

——. 1992. "On Aristotle's Conception of the Soul." In *Essays on Aristotle's De Anima*, edited by M. C. Nussbaum and A. Rorty, 93–107. Oxford: Clarendon Press.

——. 2000. "*Metaphysics* Lambda 1." In *Aristotle's Metaphysics Lambda*, edited by M. Frede and D. Charles, 53–80. Oxford: Clarendon Press.

Frede, M., and G. Patzig. 1988. *Aristoteles, "Metaphysik Z": Text, Übersetzung und Kommentar.* Munich: Beck.

Furley, D. J. 1996. "What Kind of Cause Is Aristotle's First Cause?" In *Rationality in Greek Thought*, edited by M. Frede and G. Striker, 59–79. Oxford: Clarendon Press.

Furth, M. 1978. "Transtemporal Stability in Aristotelian Substances." *Journal of Philosophy* 75:624–646.

——. 1988. *Substance, Form, and Psyche: An Aristotelean Metaphysics*. Cambridge: Cambridge University Press.

Gaiser, K. 1963. *Platons ungeschriebene Lehre; Studien zur systematischen und geschichtlichen Begründung der Wissenschaften in der Platonischen Schule*. Stuttgart: E. Klett.

——. 1969. "Das zweifache Telos bei Aristoteles." In *Naturphilosophie bei Aristoteles und Theophrast*. Edited by I. Düring, 97–113. Heidelerg: Stiehm.

Gallop, D. 1965. "Image and Reality in Plato's *Republic*." *Archiv für Geschichte der Philosophie* 47: 113–131.

——. 1975. *Phaedo*. Oxford: Clarendon Press.

Gauthier, R. A., and J. Y. Jolif. 1970. *L'éthique à Nicomaque*. Louvain: Publications universitaires.

Genequand, C. F. 2001. *Alexander of Aphrodisias: On the Cosmos*. Leiden: Brill.

George, R. 1989. "An Argument for Divine Omniscience in Aristotle." *Apeiron* 22:61–74.

Gerson, L. 1991. "Causality, Univocity, and First Principles in *Metaphysics* ii." *Ancient Philosophy* 11: 331–49.

——. 1996. "Imagery and Demiurgic Activity in Plato's *Timaeus*." *Journal of Neoplastic Studies* 4:1–32.

——. 1997. "Epistrophe Heauton: History and Meaning." *Documenti e studi sulla tradizione filosofica medievale* 8:1–32.

——. 1999. "The Concept in Platonism." In *Traditions of Platonism. Essays in Honour of John Dillon*, edited by J. J. Cleary, 65–80. Aldershot: Ashgate.

——. 2003. *Knowing Persons: A Study in Plato*. Oxford: Oxford University Press.

——. 2004. "Platonism and the Invention of the Problem of Universals." *Archiv für Geschichte der Philosophie*. 86: 1–26.

——. Forthcoming. "Plato on Identity, Sameness, and Difference." *Review of Metaphysics*.

Giacon, C. 1969. *La causalità del motore immobile*. Padua: Antenore.

Gill, M. L. 1989. *Aristotle on Substance: The Paradox of Unity*. Princeton: Princeton University Press.

Gilson, E. 1926–27. "Pourquoi Saint Thomas a critiqué Saint Augustin." *Archives d'histoire doctrinale et littéraire du moyen age* 1:5–127.

Gloy, K. 1986. *Studien zur platonischen Naturphilosophie im Timaios.* Würzburg: Königshausen, Neumann.

Glucker, J. 1978. *Antiochus and the Late Academy.* Göttingen: Vandenhoeck & Ruprecht.

Goodman, N. 1956. "A World of Individuals." In *The Problem of Universals,* edited by I. M. Bochenski, 13–31. Notre Dame, Ind.: University of Notre Dame Press.

Gosling, J. C. B. 1975. *Philebus. Translated with Notes and Commentary.* Oxford: Clarendon Press.

Gottlieb, P. 1994. "Aristotle on Dividing the Soul and Uniting the Virtues." *Phronesis* 39:275–290.

Gottschalk, H. 1997. "Continuity and Change in Aristotelianism." In *Aristotle and After,* edited by R. Sorabji, 109–115. London: Institute of Classical Studies.

Graham, D. W. 1987. *Aristotle's Two Systems.* Oxford: Oxford University Press.

———. 1999. *Aristotle: Physics Book VIII.* Oxford: Clarendon Press.

Granger, H. 1996. *Aristotle's Idea of the Soul.* Dordrecht: Kluwer Academic.

Guthrie, W. K. C. 1933. "The Development of Aristotle's Theology, I." *Classical Quarterly* 27: 162–171.

———. 1934. "The Development of Aristotle's Theology, II." *Classical Quarterly* 28:90–99.

———. 1955. "Plato on the Nature of the Soul." In *Recherches sur la Tradition Platonicienne* vol. 3, edited by W. K. C. Guthrie, et al., 3–19. Geneva: Vandoeuvres.

———. 1981. *A History of Greek Philosophy,* vol. 6., *Aristotle: An Encounter.* Cambridge: Cambridge University Press.

Hackforth, R. 1965. "Plato's Theism." In *Studies in Plato's Metaphysics,* edited by R. E. Allen, 439–447. London: Routledge & Kegan Paul.

Hadot, I. 1978. *Le problème du néoplatonisme alexandrien: Hiéroclès et Simplicius.* Paris: Etudes Augustiniennes.

———. 1989. *Simplicius. Commentaire sur les Catégories.* Fasc. 1. Leiden: Brill.

———. 1990. *Simplicius. Commentaire sur les Catégories.* Fasc. 3. Leiden: Brill.

———. 1991. "The Role of the Commentaries on Aristotle in the Teaching of Philosophy according to the Prefaces of the Neoplatonic Commentaries on the *Categories.*" In *Aristotle and the Later Tradition,* edited by J. Annas. *Oxford Studies in Ancient Philosophy: Supplementary Volume,* 175–89. Oxford: Clarendon Press.

———. 1992. "Aristote dans l'enseignement philosophique néoplatonicien." *Revue de Théologie et de Philosophie* 124: 407–425.

———. 1996. *Commentaire sur le Marnel d'Épictète.* Leiden: Brill.

Hadot, P. 1990. "The Harmony of Plotinus and Aristotle according to Porphyry." In *Aristotle Transformed: The Ancient Commentators and Their Influence,* edited by R. Sorabji, 125–40. Ithaca: Cornell University Press.

———. 1995. *Philosophy as a Way of Life: Spiritual Exercises from Socrates to Foucault.* New York: Blackwell.

———. 2002. *What Is Ancient Philosophy?* Cambridge: Harvard University Press.

Hager, F.-P. 1970. *Der Geist und das Eine. Untersuchungen zum Problem der Wesensbestimmung des höchsten Prinzips als Geist oder als Eines in der griechischen Philosophie.* Bern: Haupt.

Halfwassen, J. 1992. *Der Aufstieg zum Einen: Untersuchungen zu Platon und Plotin.* Stuttgart: Teubner.

Hall, M., ed. 1997. *Raphael's School of Athens.* Cambridge: Cambridge University Press.

Hamelin, O., and E. Barbotin. 1953. *La théorie de l'intellect d'après Aristote et ses commentateurs.* Paris: J. Vrin.

Hamlyn, D. W., and C. J. Shields. 1993. *De Anima: Books II and III with Passages from Book 1.* Oxford: Oxford University Press.

Hardie, W. F. R. 1964. "Aristotle's Treatment of the Relation between the Soul and the Body." *Philosophical Quarterly* 14: 53–72.

——. 1965. "Aristotle's Doctrine That Virtue Is a 'Mean.'" *Proceedings of the Aristotelian Society* 65:183–204.

——. 1967. "The Final Good in Aristotle's Ethics." In *Aristotle: A Collection of Critical Essays,* edited by J. M. E. Moravcsik, 297–322. Garden City, N.Y.: Anchor Doubleday.

Hathaway, R. 1969. "The Neoplatonist Interpretation of Plato: Remarks on Its Decisive Characteristics." *Journal of the History of Philosophy* 7:19–26.

Heinaman, R. 1990. "Aristotle and the Mind-Body Problem." *Phronesis* 35:83–102.

Hicks, R. D. 1907. *Aristotle. De Anima.* Cambridge: Cambridge University Press.

Ierodiakonou, K. 1999. "Aspasius on Perfect and Imperfect Virtues." In *Aspasius: The Earliest Extant Commentary on Aristotle's Ethics,* edited by A. M. Alberti and R. W. Sharples, 142–161. Oxford: Oxford University Press.

Irwin, T. 1988. *Aristotle's First Principles.* Oxford: Oxford University Press.

——. 1995. *Plato's Ethics.* New York: Oxford University Press.

Jackson, R., K. Lycos, and H. Tarrant. 1998. *Olympiodorus. Commentary on Plato's "Gorgias."* Leiden: Brill.

Jaeger, W. 1912. *Studien zur Entstehungsgeschichte der Metaphysik des Aristoteles.* Berlin: Weidmann.

——. 1948. *Aristotle: Fundamentals of the History of His Development.* 2nd ed. Tranlsated by R. Robinson. London: Oxford University Press.

Joachim, H. H. 1951. *Aristotle: The Nicomachean Ethics.* Oxford: Clarendon Press.

Judson, L. 1994. "Heavenly Motion and the Unmoved Mover." In *Self-Motion from Aristotle to Newton,* edited by M. L. Gill and J. G. Lennox, 155–71. Princeton: Princeton University Press.

Kahn, C. H. 1981. "The Role of Nous in the Cognition of First Principles in *Posterior Analytics* II.19." In *Aristotle on Science: The Posterior Analytics,* edited by E. Berti. Padua: Antenore.

——. 1985a. "On the Intended Interpretation of Aristotle's *Metaphysics.*" In *Aristoteles Werk und Wirkung. Aristoteles und seine Schule,* edited by J. Wiesner, 1:311–38. Berlin: Walter De Gruyter.

——. 1985b. "The Place of the Prime Mover in Aristotle's Teleology." In *Aristotle on Nature and Living Things,* edited by A. Gotthelf, 183–205. Pittsburgh: Mathesis Publications.

——. 1992a. "Aristotle on Thinking." In *Essays on Aristotle's De Anima,* edited by M. C. Nussbaum and A. Rorty, 359–79. Oxford: Clarendon Press.

——. 1992b "Werner Jaeger's Portrayal of Plato." In *Werner Jaeger Reconsidered,* edited by W. M. Calder, 69–81. Atlanta, Scholars Press.

——. Forthcoming. "Aristotle and Descartes on the Concept of the Mental." In Festschrift for R. Sorabji.

Keyt, D. 1978. "Intellectualism in Aristotle." *Paideia* 7 (Special Aristotle Issue:) 138–157.

Kirwan, C. 1993. *Aristotle, Metaphysics: Books Gamma, Delta, and Epsilon.* Oxford: Clarendon Press.

Kosman, L. A. 1992. "What Does the Maker Mind Make?" In *Essays on Aristotle's De Anima,* edited by M. C. Nussbaum and A. Rorty, 343–58. Oxford: Clarendon Press.

Krämer, H. J. 1959. *Arete bei Platon und Aristoteles: Zum Wesen und zur Geschichte der platonischen Ontologie.* Heidelberg: C. Winter.

——. 1964. *Der Ursprung der Geistmetaphysik: Untersuchungen zur Geschichte des Platonismus zwischen Platon und Plotin.* Amsterdam: P. Schippers.

——. 1969a. "Epekeina tes ousias. Zu Platon, Politeia 509B." *Archiv für Geschichte der Philosophie* 51:1–30.

——. 1969b. "Grundfragen der aristotelischen Theologie." *Theologie und Philosophie* 44:363–382, 481–505.

——. 1972. "Das Verhältnis von Platon und Aristoteles in neuer Sicht." *Zeitschrift für philosophische Forschung* 26: 329–53.

——. 1973. "Aristoteles und die akademische Eidoslehre: Zur Geschichte des Universalienproblems im Platonismus." *Archiv für Geschichte der Philosophie* 55: 118–190.

——. 1990. *Plato and the Foundations of Metaphysics*. Translated by J. Catan. Buffalo, N.Y.: SUNY.

Kraut, R. 1989. *Aristotle on the Human Good*. Princeton: Princeton University Press.

Kullmann, W. 1985. "Concepts of the Final Cause in Aristotle." In *Aristotle on Nature and Living Things*, edited by A. Gotthelf, 169–75. Pittsburgh: Mathesis Publications.

Laks, A. 2000. "*Metaphysics* Lambda 7." In *Aristotle's Metaphysics Lambda*, edited by M. Frede and D. Charles, 207–43. Oxford: Clarendon Press.

Lawrence, G. 2001. "The Function of the Function Argument." *Ancient Philosophy* 21:445–475.

Lear, J. 1982. "Aristotle's Philosophy of Mathematics." *Philosophical Review* 91:161–192.

——. 1987. "Active Episteme." In *Mathematics and Metaphysics in Aristotle*, edited by A. Graeser, 149–74. Bern: Haupt.

——. 1988. *Aristotle: The Desire to Understand*. Cambridge: Cambridge University Press.

Lefèvre, C. 1972. *Sur l'évolution d'Aristote en psychologie*. Louvain: Editions de l'Institut Supérieur de Philosophie.

Leighton, S. 1982. "Aristotle and the Emotions." *Phronesis* 27:144–174.

Lennox, J. G. 2001. "Are Aristotelian Species Eternal?" In *Aristotle's Philosophy of Biology: Studies in the Origins of Life Science*. J. G. Lennox, 131–159. Cambridge: Cambridge University Press.

Lernould, A. 2001. *Physique et théologie: Lecture du Timée de Platon par Proclus*. Villeneuve d'Ascq: Presses universitaires du Septentrion.

Leszl, W. 1975. *Il De ideis di Aristotele e la teoria platonica delle idee*. Florence: L. S. Olschki.

Libera, A. d. 1996. *La querelle des universaux: De Platon à la fin du Moyen Age*. Paris: Seuil.

Lloyd, A. C. 1967. "The Later Neoplatonists." In *The Cambridge History of Late Greek and Early Medieval Philosophy*. Edited by H. Armstrong, 272–325. Cambridge: Cambridge University Press.

——. 1981. "The Signifcance of Alexander's Theory of Universals." *Proceedings of the World Congress on Aristotle* 1:155–159.

Lloyd, G. E. R. 2000. "*Metaphysics* Lambda 8." In *Aristotle's Metaphysics Lambda*, edited by M. Frede and D. Charles, 245–73. Oxford: Clarendon Press.

Lowe, M. 1983. "Aristotle on Kinds of Thinking." *Phronesis* 28:17–30.

Lurje, M. 2002. "Die Vita Pythagorica als Manifest der neuplatonischen Paideia." In *Jamblich: Peri tou Pythagoreiou biou*, edited by M. von Albrecht, J. M. Dillon, M. George, M. Lurje and D. du Toit, 221–254. Darmstadt: Wissenschaftliche Buchgesellschaft.

Madigan, A. 1999. *Aristotle's Metaphysics. Books B and K 1–2*. Oxford: Clarendon Press.

Maier, H. 1900. "Die Echtheit der aristotelischen Hermeneutik." *Archiv für Geschichte der Philosophie* 13:23–72.

Malcolm, J. 1991. *Plato on the Self-Predication of Forms*. Oxford: Clarendon Press.

Mann, W.-R. 2000. *The Discovery of Things: Aristotle's Categories and Their Context*. Princeton: Princeton University Press.

Mansfeld, J. 1994. *Prolegomena: Questions to be Settled before the Study of an Author or a Text*. Leiden: Brill.

Matthews, G. 1992. "*De Anima* 2.2–4 and the Meaning of Life." In *Essays on Aristotle's De Anima*, edited by M. C. Nussbaum and A. Rorty, 185–93. Oxford: Clarendon Press.

McDonough, R. 2000. "Aristotle's Critique of Functionalist Theories of Mind." *Idealistic Studies* 30:209–232.

Menn, S. 1995. *Plato on God as Nous*. Carbondale: Southern Illinois University Press.

——. 1998. "Aristotle's Philosophical Development." *Apeiron* 31:407–415.

Mercken, H. P. F. 1990. "The Greek Commentaries on Aristotle's Ethics." In *Aristotle Transformed: The Ancient Commentators and Their Influence*, edited by R. Sorabji, 407–443. Ithaca: Cornell University Press.

Merki, H. 1952. *Homoiosis Theoi: Von der platonischen Angleichung an Gott zur Gottähnlichkeit bei Gregor von Nyassa*. Freiburg: Paulusverlag.

Merlan, P. 1953. *From Platonism to Neoplatonism*. The Hague: Martinus Nijhoff.

——. 1970. "Nochmals: War Aristoteles je Anhänger der Ideenlehre? Jaeger's letztes Wort." *Archiv für Geschichte der Philosophie* 52:35–39.

Miller, D. 2002. *The Third Kind in Plato's Timaeus.* Göttingen: Vandenhoeck & Ruprecht.

Miller, M. 1980. *The Philosopher in Plato's Statesman.*The Hague: Martinus Nijhoff.

——. 1995. "*Unwritten Teachings in the Parmenides.*" *Review of Metaphysics* 48:591–633.

——. 1999. "Figure, Ration, Form: Plato's Five Mathematical Studies." *Apeiron* 32:73–88.

Modrak, D. K. W. 1987. "Aristotle on Thinking." In *Proceedings of the Boston Area Colloquium in Ancient Philosophy,* edited by J. J. Cleary, 2:209–36. Lanham, MD: University Press of America .

Monan, J. D. 1968. *Moral Knowledge and Its Methodology in Aristotle.* Oxford: Clarendon Press.

Moraux, P. 1942. *Alexandre d'Aphrodise, exégète de la noétique d'Aristote.* Liège: E. Droz.

——. 1951. *Les listes anciennes des ouvrages d'Aristote.* Louvain: Editions Universitaires de Louvain.

——. 1955. "A propos du nous thurathen chez Aristote." In *Autour d'Aristote,* edited by A. Mansion, 255–295. Louvain: Publications Universitaires de Louvain.

——. 1973. *Der Aristotelismus bei den Griechen; von Andronikos bis Alexander von Aphrodisias.* Berlin: Walter de Gruyter.

——. 2001. *Der Aristotelismus bei der Griechen: Alexander Von Aphrodisias.* Berlin: Walter De Gruyter.

Moravcsik, J. M. 1991. "What Makes Reality Intelligible: Reflections on Aristotle's Theory of Aitia." In *Aristotle's Physics: A Collection of Essays,* edited by L. Judson, 31–47. Oxford: Clarendon Press.

Morison, B. 2002. *On Location: Aristotle's Concept of Place.* Oxford: Clarendon Press.

Morrison, D. 1993. "Le statut catégoriel des differences dans l'Organon.'" *Revue Philosophique* 183:147–78.

Morrow, G. R. 1962. *Plato's Epistles.* Indianapolis: Bobbs-Merrill.

Morrow, G. R., and J. M. Dillon. 1987. *Proclus' Commentary on Plato's* Parmenides. Princeton: Princeton University Press.

Mugnier, R. 1930. *La théorie du premier moteur et l'évolution de la pensée aristotélicienne.* Paris: J. Vrin.

Nasemann, B. 1991. *Theurgie und Philosophie in Jamblichs De mysteriis.* Stuttgart: Teubner.

Natali, C. 1997. "Causa motrice e causa finale nel libro Lambda della Metafisica di Aristotele." *Methexis* 10: 105–123.

——. 1998. *The Virtues of Authenticity.* Princeton: Princeton University Press.

Nehemas, A. 1979. "Self-Predication and Plato's Theory of Forms." *American Philosophical Quarterly* 12: 93–103.

Norman, R. 1969. "Aristotle's Philosopher God." *Phronesis* 14:63–74.

Nussbaum, M. C. 1985. *Aristotle's De Motu Animalium: Text with Translation, Commentary, and Interpretive Essays.* Princeton: Princeton University Press.

——. 1987. *The Fragility of Goodness: Luck and Ethics in Greek Tragedy and Philosophy.* Cambridge: Cambridge University Press.

——. 1994. *The Therapy of Desire: Theory and Practice in Hellenistic Ethics.* Princeton: Princeton University Press.

Nuyens, F. 1948. *L'évolution de la psychologie d'Aristote.* Louvain: Institut supérieur de philosophie.

Oehler, K. 1962. *Die Lehre vom noetischen und dianoetischen Denken bei Platon und Aristoteles: Ein Beitrag zur Erforschung der Geschichte des Bewusstseinsproblems in der Antike.* Munich: Beck.

O'Meara, D. J. 1989. *Pythagoras Revived: Mathematics and Philosophy in Late Antiquity.* Oxford: Clarendon Press.

——. 1994. "Political Life and Divinization in Neoplatonic Philosophy." *Hermathena* 157: 155–164.

——. 2003. *Platonopolis. Platonic Political Philosophy in Late Antiquity.* Oxford: Clarendon Press.

Osborne, C. 1987. *Rethinking Early Greek Philosophy: Hippolytus of Rome and the Presocratics.* Ithaca: Cornell University Press.

Owen, G. E. L. 1957. "A Proof in the *Peri Ideon.*" *Journal of Hellenic Studies* 77:103–111.

——. 1960. "Logic and Metaphysics in Some Earlier Works of Aristotle." In *Aristotle and Plato in the Mid-Fourth Century,* edited by I. Düring and G. E. L. Owen, 163–190. Göteborg: Elanders Boktryckeri Aktiebolag.

——. 1965. "The Platonism of Aristotle." *Proceedings of the British Academy* 51: 125–150.

——, ed. 1968. *Aristotle on Dialectic: The Topics. Proceedings of the Third Symposium Aristotelicum.* Oxford: Clarendon Press.

——. 1986. *Logic, Science, and Dialectic: Collected Papers in Greek Philosophy.* London: Duckworth.

Owens, J. 1950. "The Reality of the Aristotelian Separate Movers." *Review of Metaphysics* 3:75–81.

——. 1951. *The Doctrine of Being in the Aristotelian Metaphysics: A Study in the Greek Background of Mediaeval Thought.* Toronto: Pontifical Institute of Mediaeval Studies.

——. 1981a. "Aristotle on Categories." In *Aristotle: The Collected Papers of Joseph Owens,* edited by J. R. Catan, 14–22. Albany: SUNY.

——. 1981b. "A Note on Aristotle, *De Anima* 3.4.429b9." In *Aristotle: The Collected Papers of Joseph Owens,* edited by J. R. Catan, 99–108. Albany: SUNY.

Patterson, R. 1985. *Image and Reality in Plato's Metaphysics.* Indianapolis, Ind.: Hackett.

Patzig, G. 1961. "Theology and Ontology in Aristotle's *Metaphysics.*" In *Articles on Aristotle,* vol.3: *Metaphysics,* edited by J, Barnes, M. Schofield, and R. Sorabji, 33–49. New York: St. Martin's Press.

Pépin, J. 1956. "Eléments pour une histoire de la relation entre l'intelligence et l'intelligible chez Platon et dans le néoplatonisme." *Revue Philosophique* 146:39–64.

Perl, E. D. 1998. "The Demiurge and the Forms: A Return to the Ancient Interpretation of Plato's Timaeus." *Ancient Philosophy* 18:81–92.

Pester, H. E. 1971. *Platons bewegte ousia.* Wiesbaden: Harrassowitz.

Peterson, S. 1973. "A Reasonable Self-Predication Assumption for the Third Man Argument." *Philosophical Review* 82:451–470.

Phillips, J. F. 1997. "Neoplatonic Exegeses of Plato's Cosmogony, "Timaeus" 27C-28C." *Journal of the History of Philosophy* 35:173–197.

Pines, S. 1987. "Some Distinctive Metaphysical Conceptions in Themistius' Commentary on Book Lambda and Their Place in the History of Philosophy." In *Aristotles: Werk und Wirkung,* edited by J. Wiesner. Berlin: Walter De Gruyter.

Pradeau, J.-F. 1999. *Alcibiade.* Paris: Flammarion.

Praechter, K. 1909. "Die griechischen Aristoteleskommentare." *Byzantinische Zeitschrift* 18:516–538.

——. 1973. *Kleine Schriften.* Hildesheim: Olms.

Pritchard, P. 1995. *Plato's Philosophy of Mathematics.* Sankt Augustin: Academia Verlag.

Rabinowitz, W. G. 1957. *Aristotle's Protrepticus and the Sources of Its Reconstruction.* Berkeley: University of California Press.

Reale, G., and A. Bos. *Il trattato Sul cosmo per Alessandro attribuito ad Aristotele.* 2nd ed. Naples: Vita e Pensiero.

Reeve, C. D. C. 1988. *Philosopher-Kings: The Argument of Plato's Republic.* Princeton: Princeton University Press.

——. 1992. *Practices of Reason: Aristotle's Nicomachean Ethics.* Oxford: Clarendon Press.

——. 2000. *Substantial Knowledge: Aristotle's Metaphysics.* Indianapolis, Ind.: Hackett.

Richard, M.-D. 1986. *L'enseignement oral de Platon: Une nouvelle interprétation du platonisme.* Paris: Editions du Cerf.

Rickless, S. 1998. "How Parmenides Saved the Theory of Forms." *Philosophical Review* 107:501–554.

Rist, J. M. 1964. *Eros and Psyche: Studies in Plato. Plotinus, and Origen.* Toronto: University of Toronto Press.

——. 1967. *Plotinus: The Road to Reality.* Cambridge: University Press.

——. 1973/4. "The One of Plotinus and the God of Aristotle." *Review of Metaphysics* 27:75–87.

——. 1985. "The End of Aristotle's *On Prayer.*" *American Journal of Philology* 105:110–113.

——. 1989. *The Mind of Aristotle: A Study in Philosophical Growth.* Toronto: University of Toronto Press.

——. 1996. "Taking Aristotle's Development Seriously." In *Aristotle's Philosophical Development,* edited by W. R. Wians, 359–373. Lanham, Md.: Rowman & Littlefield.

Robin, L. 1908. *La théorie platonicienne des idées et des nombres d'après Aristote; Etude historique et critique.* Paris: F. Alcan.

Robinson, H. 1983. "Aristotelian Dualism." *Oxford Studies in Ancient Philosophy* 1:123–144.

Robinson, H. M. 1991. "Form and the Immateriality of the Intellect from Aristotle to Aquinas." In *Arisotle and the Later Tradition,* edited by H. J. Blumenthal and H. M. Robinson, 207–226. Oxford: Clarendon Press.

Robinson, T. M. 1995. *Plato's Psychology.* Toronto: University of Toronto Press.

Roche, T. 1988. "'Ergon' and 'Eudaimonia' in 'Nicomachean Ethics' I: Reconsidering the Intellectualist Interpretation." *Journal of the History of Philosophy* 26: 175–194.

Roloff, D. 1970. *Gottähnlichkeit, Vergöttlichung und Erhöhung zu seligem Leben: Untersuchungen zur Herkunft der platonischen Angleichung an Gott.* Berlin: Walter De Gruyter.

Romano, F. 1993. "La défense de Platon contre Aristote par les Néoplatoniciens." In *Contre Platon. Le Platonisme Dévoilé,* edited by M. Dixsaut, 1:175–195. Paris: J. Vrin.

Rorty, R. 1999. *Philosophy and Social Hope.* London: Penguin.

Rose, V. 1863. *Aristoteles Pseudepigraphus.* Leipzig: Teubner.

——. 1871. "Uber die griechischen Commentare zur Ethik des Aristoteles." *Hermes* 5:61–113.

Ross, W. D. 1924. *Aristotle's Metaphysics: A Revised Text with Commentary and Introduction.* 2 vols. Oxford: Clarendon Press.

——. 1951. *Plato's Theory of Ideas.* Oxford: Clarendon Press.

——. 1955. *Aristotelis: Fragmenta Selecta.* Oxford: Clarendon Press.

——. 1957. "The Development of Aristotle's Thought." *Proceedings of the British Academy* 43:63–78.

——. 1961. *Aristotelis: De Anima.* Oxford: Clarendon Press.

Routilla, L. 1969. *Die aristotelische Idee der ersten Philosophie.* Amsterdam: North-Holland.

Rowe, C. J. 1971. *The Eudemian and Nicomachean Ethics: A Study in the Development of Aristotle's Thought.* Cambridge: Cambridge Philological Society.

Sachs, E. 1917. *Die fünf platonischen Körper, zur Geschichte der Mathematik und der Elementenlehre Platons und der Pythagoreer.* Berlin: Weidmann.

Saffrey, H. D. 1971. *Le peri philosophias d'Aristote et la theorie platonicienne des idées nombres.* Leiden: Brill.

Sayre, K. M. 1983. *Plato's Late Ontology: A Riddle Resolved.* Princeton: Princeton University Press.

——. 2003. "The Multilayered Inchoherence of Timaeus' Receptacle." In *Plato's Timaeus as Cultural Icon,* edited by G. Reydams-Schils, 60–79. Notre Dame: University of Notre Dame Press.

Schibli, H. 2002. *Hierocles of Alexandria.* Oxford: Oxford University Press.

Schofield, M. 1992. "Aristotle on the Imagination." In *Essays on Aristotle's De Anima,* edited by M. C. Nussbaum and A. Rorty, 249–277. Oxford: Clarendon Press.

——. 1999. "Social and Political Thought." In *The Cambridge History of Hellenistic Philosophy,* edited by K. Algra, J. Barnes, J. Mansfeld, and M. Schofield, 739–70. Cambridge: Cambridge University Press.

Schulz, D. J. 1966. *Das Problem der Materie in Platons Timaios.* Bonn: Bouvier.

Scolnicov, S. 2003. *Plato's Parmenides.* Berkeley: University of California Press.

Sedley, D. 1996. "Philosophical Allegiance in the Greco-Roman World." In *Philosophia Togata I,* edited by J. Barnes and M. Griffin, 97–119. Oxford: Clarendon Press.

———. 1997a. 'Becoming Like God' in the *Timaeus* and Aristotle." In *Interpreting the Timaeus-Critias*, edited by T. Calvo. and L. Brisson, 9:327–39. Sankt Augustin: Academia Verlag.

———. 1997b. "Plato's *Auctoritas* and the Rebirth of the Commentary Tradition." In *Philosophia Togata II*, edited by J. Barnes and M. Griffin, 110–129. Oxford: Clarendon Press.

———. 1999a. "The Idea of Godlikeness." In *Plato 2. Ethics, Politics, Religion, and the Soul*, edited by G. Fine, 309–328. Oxford: Oxford University Press.

———. 1999b. "Aspasius on Akrasia." In *Aspasius: The Earliest Extant Commentary on Aristotle's Ethics*, edited by A. M. Alberti and R. Sharples, 162–175. Berlin: Walter De Gruyter.

———. 2000. "Metaphysics Lambda 10." In *Aristotle's Metaphysics Lambda*, edited by M. Frede and D. Charles, 327–50. Oxford: Clarendon Press.

———. 2002. "Socratic Irony in the Platonist Commentators." In *New Perspectives on Plato, Modern and Ancient*, edited by J. Annas and C. Rowe, 37–57. Cambridge, Mass.": Center for Hellenic Studies.

Seidl, H. 1987. "Aristoteles' Lehre von der noesis noesews des ersten, göttlichen Vernunftwesens und ihre Darstellung bei Plotin." In *Aristoteles: Werk und Wirkung*, Edited by J. Wiesner, 2:157–76. Berlin: Walter De Gruyter.

Sharples, R. W. 1987. "Alexander of Aphrodisias: Scholasticism and Innovation." In *Augstieg und Niedergang der römischen Welt*, edited by W. Haase and H. Temporini, 36.2:1176–1243. Berlin: Walter de Gruyter.

———. 2001. "Schriften und Problemkomplexe zur Ethik." In *Der Aristotelismus bei den Griechen: Von Andronikos bis Alexander von Aphrodisias*, edited by W. Kullman, R. W. Sharples, and J. Wiesner, 3:513–616. Berlin: Walter De Gruyter.

Shaw, G. 1995. *Theurgy and the Soul: The Neoplatonism of Iamblichus*. University Park: Pennsylvania State University Press.

———. 1997. "The Mortality and Anonymnity of the Iamblichean Soul." *Syllecta Classica* 8:177–90.

Shields, C. 1988. "Soul and Body in Aristotle." *Oxford Studies in Ancient Philosophy* 6:103–137.

Shorey, P. 1933. *What Plato Said.* Chicago: University of Chicago Press.

Silverman, A. 2002. *The Dialectic of Essence: A Study of Plato's Metaphysics*. Princeton: Princeton University Press.

Smith, A. 1987. "Porphyrian Studies Since 1913." In *Aurstieg und Niedergang der Römischen Welt: Principat*, edited by W. Haase, 36.2:718–773. Berlin: Walter De Gruyter.

———. 1999. "The Significance of Practical Ethics for Plotinus." In *Traditions of Platonism. Essays in Honour of John Dillon*. Edited by J. J. Cleary. Brookfield: Aldershot: 227–36.

Solmsen, F. 1929. *Die Entwicklung der Aristotelischen Logik und Rhetorik.* Berlin: Weidmann.

Sorabji, R. 1988. *Matter, Space, and Motion: Theories in Antiquity and Their Sequel.* Ithaca: Cornell University Press.

—, ed. 1990 *Aristotle Transformed. The Ancient Commentators and Their Influence.* Ithaca: Cornell University Press.

Sparshott, F. 1982. "Aristotle's Ethics and Plato's Republic: A Structural Comparison." *Dialogue* 21:483–499.

Steel, C. G. 1978. *The Changing Self: A Study on the Soul in Later Neoplatonism: Iamblichus, Damascius and Priscianus.* Brussels: Paleis der Academiën.

———. 1987. "Proclus et Aristote sur la causalité efficiente de l'Intellect divin." in *Proclus: lecteur et interprète des Anciens.* Edited by J. Pépin and C. G. Steel. Paris: CNRS.

Stenzel, J. 1917. *Studien zur Entwicklung der platonischen Dialektik von Sokrates zu Aristoteles: Arete und Diairesis.* Breslau: Trewendt & Granier.

Strang, C. 1963. "Plato on the Third Man." In *Proceedings of the Aristotelian Society*. Supp. vol. 37:147–164.

Strange, S. K. 1992. *Porphyry: On Aristotle's Categories.* London: Duckworth.

Szlezák, T. 1983. "Alpha Elatton: Einheit und Einordnung." In *Zweifelhaftes im Corpus Aristotelicum: Akten des 9 Symposium Aristotelicum*, edited by P. Moraux and J. Wiesner. Berlin: Walter De Gruyter.

——. 1985. *Platon und die Schriftlichkeit der Philosophie: Interpretationen zu den frühen und mittleren Dialogen*. Berlin: Walter De Gruyter.

——. 1994. "La prosecuzione di spunti platonici nella *Metafisica* aristotelica." In *Aristotele. Perché la metafisica*, edited by A. Bausola and G. Reale, 215–232. Milano: Vita e Pensiero.

——. 1999. *Reading Plato*. New York: Routledge.

Tarrant, H. 1993. *Thrasyllan Platonism*. Ithaca: Cornell University Press.

——. 2000. *Plato's First Interpreters*. Ithaca: Cornell University Press.

Taylor, A. E. 1928. *A Commentary on Plato's Timaeus*. Oxford: Clarendon Press.

Taylor, C. C. W. 1976. *Protagoras*. Oxford: Clarendon Press.

Theiler, W. 1925. *Zur Geschichte der teleologischen Naturbetrachtung bis auf Aristotles*. Zürich: Füssli.

——. 1960. "Plotin zwischen Platon und Stoa." In *Les Sources de Plotin: Entretiens sur l'antiquité classique* 5, 63–103. Geneva: Vandoevres.

Thiel, R. 1999. "Stoische Ethik und Neuplatonische Tugendlehre. Zur Verortung der Stoischen Ethik im Neuplatonischen System in Simplikios' Kommentar zu Epiktets Enchiridion." In *Zur Rezeption der hellenistischen Philosophie in der Spätantike*, edited by M. Erler, T. Fuhrer, and K. Schlapbach, 93–103. Stuttgart: F. Steiner.

Thompson, D. A. W. 1992. *On Growth and Form*. Cambridge: Cambridge University Press.

Tigerstedt, E. N. 1974. *The Decline and Fall of the Neoplatonic Interpretation of Plato*. Helsinki: Societas Scientiarum Fennica.

Todd, R. B. 1996. *On Aristotle on the Soul*. London: Duckworth.

Tracy, T. J. 1969. *Physiological Theory and the Doctrine of the Mean in Plato and Aristotle*. The Hague: Mouton.

Tuozzo, T. 1996. "Contemplation, the Noble, and the Mean: The Standard of Moral Virtue in Aristotle's Ethics." In *Aristotle, Virtue and the Mean*, edited by R. Bosley, 129–155. Edmonton: Academic Publishing.

Tweedale, M. 1984. "Alexander of Aphrodisias' Views on Universals." *Phronesis* 29:279–303.

——. 1993. "Duns Scotus's Doctrine of Universals and the Aphrodisian Tradition." *American Catholic Philosophical Quarterly* 67:77–93.

Untersteiner, M. 1963. *Aristotele. Della filosofia*. Roma: Edizioni di Storia e Letteratura.

Van den Berg, R. M. 1997. "Proclus, *In Platonis Timaeum Commentarii* 3.333.28ff: The Myth of the Winged Charioteer According to Iamblichus and Proclus." *Syllecta Classica* 8:149–62.

——. 2001. *Proclus' Hymns: Essays, Translations, Commentary*. Leiden: Brill.

Verrycken, K. 1990. "The Metaphysics of Ammonius Son of Hermeias." In *Aristotle Transformed*, edited by R. Sorabji, 199–231. Ithaca: Cornell University Press.

Vlastos, G. 1954. "The Third Man Argument in Plato's Parmenides." *Philosophical Review* 63: 319–349.

——. 1963. Review of *Arete bei Platon und Aristoteles* by H. J. Krämer. *Gnomon* 41:641–655.

——. 1965. "Creation in the 'Timaeus': Is It a Fiction?" In *Studies in Plato's Metaphysics*, edited by R. E. Allen, 401–419. London: Routledge & Kegan Paul.

——. 1973a. "Reasons and Causes in the *Phaedo*." In *Platonic Studies*, 76–110. Princeton: Princeton University Press.

——. 1973b. "The 'Two-Level' Paradoxes". In *Platonic Studies*, 323–334. Princeton: University Press.

——. 1981. *Platonic Studies*. Princeton: Princeton University Press.

Volpi, F. 1991. "La détermination aristotélicienne du principe divin comme ζωή: *Met*. 7, 1072b26–30." *Études Philosophiques* 3:369–387.

Wedberg, A. 1955. *Plato's Philosophy of Mathematics*. Stockholm: Almqvist & Wiksell.

Wedin, M. V. 1985. "Tracking Aristotle's 'Nous.'" In *Human Nature and Natural Knowledge*, edited by A. Donagan, 167–197. Dordrecht: Reidel.

———. 1988. *Mind and Imagination in Aristotle*. New Haven: Yale University Press.

———. 1989. "Aristotle on the Mechanics of Thought." *Ancient Philosophy* 9:67–86.

———. 2000. *Aristotle's Theory of Substance: The Categories and Metaphysics Zeta*. Oxford: Oxford University Press.

Wehrle, W. 2001. *The Myth of Aristotle's Development and the Betrayal of Metaphysics*. Lanham, Md.: Rowman & Littlefield.

Wehrli, F. 1967. *Die Schule des Aristoteles: Texte und Kommentare*. 10 vols. Basel: Schwabe.

———. 1974. *Die Schule des Aristoteles: Texte und Kommentare*. Supp. vol. Basel: Schwabe.

Westerink, L. G. 1976. *The Greek Commentaries on Plato's Phaedo*. Amsterdam: North-Holland.

———. 1987. "Proclus et les Présocratiques." In *Proclus: Lecteur et interprète des Anciens: Actes du Colloque international du CNRS, Paris 2–4 octobre 1985*, edited by J. Pépin and H. D. Saffray, 105–112. Paris: CNRS.

Westerink, L. G., J. Trouillard et al. 1990. *Prolégomènes à la philosophie de Platon*. Paris: Les Belles Lettres.

Wians, W. R., ed. 1996. *Aristotle's Philosophical Development: Problems and Prospects*. Lanham, Md.: Rowman & Littlefield.

Wildberg, C. 1987. *Philoponus. Against Aristotle, On the Eternity of the World*. London: Duckworth.

———. 2002. "Pros to telos: Neuplatonische Ethik zwischen Religion und Metaphysik." In *Metaphysik und Religion: Zur Signatur des spätantiken Denkens*, edited by T. Kobusch and M. Erler, 261–278. Munich: K. G. Saur.

Wilkes, K. V. 1992. "Psuche versus the Mind." In *Essays on Aristotle's De Anima*, edited by M. C. Nussbaum and A. Rorty, 109–127. Oxford: Clarendon Press.

Wilpert, P. 1955. "Die aristotelische Schrift 'Uber die Philosophie.'" In *Autour d'Aristote*. edited by A. Mansion, 99–116. Louvain: Publications Universitaires de Louvain.

———. 1957. "Die Stellung der Schrift 'Uber die Philosophie' in der Gedankenentwicklung des Aristoteles." *Journal of Hellenic Studies* 77:155–162.

Witt, C. 1996. "The Evolution of Developmental Interpretations." In *Aristotle's Philsophical Development: Problems and Prospects*, edited by W. R. Wians, 67–82. Lanham, Md.: Rowman and Littlefield.

Woods, M. 1982. *Aristotle's Eudemian Ethics, Books I, II, and VIII*. Oxford: Clarendon Press.

Zeller, E. 1923. *Die Philosophie der Griechen in ihrer geschichtlichen Entwicklung*. Leipzig: O. R. Reisland.

Zeyl, D. J. 2000. *Plato. Timaeus*. Indianapolis, Ind.: Hackett.

General Index

Index Locorum

PLUTARCH

On the Defect of the Oracles

Reply to Colotes (Adv. Col.)

CPSIA information can be obtained at www.ICGtesting.com
Printed in the USA
BVOW03s2125290714

360959BV00001B/3/P